BLACK CONGRESSMEN DURING RECONSTRUCTION

A Documentary Sourcebook

Edited by Stephen Middleton

Foreword by John David Smith

Westport, Connecticut
London

Library of Congress Cataloging-in-Publication Data

Black congressmen during Reconstruction : a documentary sourcebook / edited by
Stephen Middleton ; foreward by John David Smith.
    p. cm.
    Includes bibliographical references and index.
    ISBN: 0–313–32281–3 (alk. paper)
    1. African American Legislators—History—19th century—Sources. 2. African
American legislators—Biography. 3. United States. Congress—Biography. 4.
Reconstruction—Sources. 5. African Americans—Politics and government—19th
century—Sources. 6. Southern States—Politics and government—1865–1950—
Sources. 7. Southern States—Race relations—Sources.
E185.6.B623 2002
328.73′092′396073—dc21   2002067753

British Library Cataloguing in Publication Data is available.

Library of Congress Catalog Card Number: 2002067753
ISBN: 0–313–32281–3

First published in 2002

Greenwood Press, 88 Post Road West, Westport, CT 06881
An imprint of Greenwood Publishing Group, Inc.
www.greenwood.com

Printed in the United States of America

∞

The paper used in this book complies with the
Permanent Paper Standard issued by the National
Information Standards Organization (Z39.48-1984).

10 9 8 7 6 5 4 3 2 1

In Memory of

Angela Jelks
Louis Middleton, Jr.

Friend and Brother

Contents

Foreword

During the 1870s, as Republican—controlled governments collapsed in one southern state after another, and as Republican politicians in Washington turned their backs on the interests of African Americans, blacks had every reason to fear for the future. As long as they retained the right to vote, however, blacks hoped to forestall yet more attempts by whites to segregate them into separate spaces and inferior lives.

Despite common misconceptions, in the post-Reconstruction years black southerners in fact continued to live in a world that was not yet rigidly segregated. African American life in the first New South was far less monolithic than even many historians have assumed. As David Levering Lewis notes, "[f]ormal disfranchisement, in naked violation of the Fifteenth Amendment, had not yet come about; nor had institutionalized 'Jim Crow'—banning black people from commercial establishments and public places and herding them into the last seats and rickety add-ons in trains and streetcars. This would begin in earnest a decade later." Many blacks indeed voted and were politically active and a surprisingly large number held public office well into the 1890s. According to Eric Foner, "[b]lack office-holding began in earnest in 1867, when Congress ordered the election of new Southern governments under suffrage rules that did not discriminate on the basis of race. By 1877, when the last Radical Reconstruction governments were overthrown, around 2,000 black men held federal, state, and local public offices, ranging from member of Congress to justice of the peace."[1]

In the years 1877 to 1901 eleven African Americans were elected to the U.S. Congress. In Mississippi, for example, they continued to sit in the state legislature throughout the 1880s. Six served in 1890 and one remained in 1899. "Dozens of Southern cities," Herbert Aptheker reports, "had Negroes appointed and elected officers on all levels of administrative responsibilities in the 1880's and 1890's." North Carolina's George H. White served two terms in the U.S. Congress (1897–1901) and was the last African American to sit in Congress until 1929.[2]

Black Congressmen During Reconstruction by constitutional historian Stephen Middleton of North Carolina State University provides a valuable collective biographical and documentary portrait of the twenty-two African American Republican politicians (including two senators) who, despite obstructionism by Democrats, served in the U.S. Congress, 1870 to 1901. To contextualize and underscore the importance of their political success, Middleton notes that after 1881, no African American would be elected to the U.S. Senate again until 1966, when Massachusetts voters elected Edward William Brooke III.

Overcoming all manner of racism, black congressmen of the Reconstruction era compiled an impressive record. "They were loyal to the United States in spite of its history of slavery and discrimination," Middleton writes. "They did not want to punish whites who had been slave owners, and it is clear that a few of them were willing to grant amnesty to former Confederates." Black congressmen led the way in supporting land distribution and public schools for African Americans, and they backed the Civil Rights Bill (1875) of Senator Charles Sumner that granted equal access to public facilities for members of all races.

By examining their lives, by quoting excerpts from their speeches, by rescuing their contributions from oblivion, and by capturing their importance, Middleton pays long overdue tribute to the courageous black congressmen who represented the interests of African Americans and sought to establish grassroots Republican party organizations in the South. Like Lewis and Foner, he reminds us that African Americans were active participants in the political process between the era of emancipation and the onslaught of rigid Jim Crow segregation. "Something magnificent happened between 1870 and 1901," Middleton writes, "when black Americans served in Congress. It is a phenomenon worth remembering and discussing; it is a period as dramatic as any other in American history." It is a story too important to forget.

NOTES

1. David Levering Lewis, *W.E.B. Du Bois: Biography of a Race, 1868–1919* (New York: Henry Holt and Company, 1993), 35; Eric Foner, *Freedom's Lawmakers: A Directory of Black Officeholders During Reconstruction* (New York: Oxford University Press, 1993), xi.

2. J. Morgan Kousser, "Disfranchisement," in David M. Roller and Robert W. Twyman, eds., *The Encyclopedia of Southern History* (Baton Rouge: Louisiana State University Press, 1979), 362; Herbert Aptheker, "American Imperialism and White Chauvinism," *Jewish Life 4* (July 1950): 23.

John David Smith
North Carolina State University

Preface

This is perhaps the Negroes' temporary farewell to the American Congress; but let me say, Phoenix—like, he will rise up some day and come again. These parting words are in behalf of an outraged, heart-broken, bruised, and bleeding, but God-fearing people, faithful, industrious, loyal people, and rising people, full of potential force. The only apology that I have to make for the earnestness with which I have spoken is that I am pleading for life, liberty, future happiness, and manhood suffrage for one-eighth of the entire population of the United States.   Representative George Henry White, 1901

When George Henry White of North Carolina spoke to the House of Representatives for the last time on January 29, 1901, he tolled the bell for what most of his white colleagues had hoped was the death of Reconstruction. An era of African American involvement in federal politics had abruptly come to an end. Thirty-one years earlier Mississippi had elected the first African American to Congress, a direct result of Reconstruction. By 1901, twenty-two black congressmen had served from the South during the dangerous and tumultuous years of white supremacy. Their service was not meaningless. They helped produce substantial legislation such as the Civil Rights Act of 1875. So in his farewell address George Henry White would not only look back on the record of black congressmen with pride, he forecast that a time would come when blacks would return to Congress to once again help do the nation's work.

Although the service of these early black congressmen was an astounding event, they largely remain a mystery. Many educated Americans have never heard of African American congressmen being elected in the 19th century. Moreover, only a few of the most learned individuals would recognize their portraits. Indeed, scholars have compiled various biographical collections, such as *Black Americans in Congress* (1990) by Bruce A. Ragsdale and Joel D. Treese and *Freedom's Lawmakers: A Directory of Black Officeholders During*

Reconstruction (1993) by Eric Foner. Before the publication of *George Henry White: An Even Chance in the Race of Life* (2000) by Benjamin R. Justesen, no modern study had been undertaken by scholars. Thus, these officials remain in the basement of the nation's legal history. Unlike other historic figures, they have not become national symbols, or the subjects of exhibitions. No one has compiled a current and comprehensive representation of their speeches and documents until now. This book is their exhibit—a signpost in the African American journey from slavery to active participation in the affairs of our government. It is a testament of what they said and did in Congress.

This book combines narratives and documents, including an introduction that conceptualizes the Reconstruction Period. It also consists of extensive biographies on each congressman. And it provides selections from their speeches and documents. With a copious index, as well as a primer for each set of documents it is accessible to the general reader and to researchers. Furthermore, this work covers a wide range of subjects, such as the status of American Indians, internal improvement, railroad expansion, the Spanish American War, and civil rights. It also includes some fascinating figures, such as Hiram Rhodes Revels, whom the Mississippi legislature made the first black official to ever serve in Congress. It features Robert Brown Elliot who was reputedly one of the ablest black men of his generation. And, of course, it highlights George Henry White, who claimed to be the sole representative of 9 million African Americans. They were ordinary men in extraordinary times. They demonstrated the courage that all Americans—not just African Americans—should acknowledge and admire.

When I started this project I wanted to include every word these black officials spoke or wrote. But such is neither possible nor necessary. The extracts in this book aptly portrays the content of their character. Indeed, I am awed by the task of serving as their editor. I have tried to preserve the integrity of their words while I made judicious and necessary edits. Extraneous phrases and archaic words have been eliminated, awkward sentences changed, and phrases such as *Mr. President, Mr. Speaker, Mr. Chairman, Sir,* etc. deleted. I have also shortened excessively long paragraphs and combined short ones, as well as revised a few convoluted sentences, which, I believe, would have only been troublesome for the reader. I hope that in presenting their thoughts and vision I have given them their full measure, which the bar of history has for too long denied them.

Stephen Middleton
Raleigh, NC 2002

Acknowledgments

Producing a documentary history involves a great deal of work, and requires the hands of many more people than its editor. Many dedicated individuals helped to bring this work to completion. This project began several years ago as a result of a grant from the College of Humanities at North Carolina State University. My research assistant, Charise Roberts, took on this assignment with great enthusiasm, and probably spent more time at the State Library and made more copies from the *Congressional Record* than she had initially imagined. The staff at the State Library of North Carolina was terrific. Jessie Ellis and Steve Taylor processed our requests with good cheer. This project might not have ever moved forward had Professor Eric Foner, who probably knows more about the black congressmen who are covered in this volume than any other scholar, not responded positively when I queried him about the potential value of such a project. A mere thank you to them seems inadequate to express my appreciation.

Preparation of this volume began in the History office, where Norene Miller faced the fine print of over a thousand pages. Always resourceful and efficient, Norene copied the pages again to enlarge them for better reading. Upon completion, she turned over the disks and a hard copy of the manuscript with a smile. I believe her disciplined service and the attention she automatically gives to details are partly responsible for her promotion in the department. I am also appreciative of Donna Weeks for producing the index for this book and for putting the manuscript in the form required by the publisher.

My appreciation also goes to the scholars who helped me with the narratives that appear in this volume. Professor William C. Harris, a specialist on the Civil War and Reconstruction, helped me keep the factual data straight. Professor Alexander De Grand provided valuable editorial guidance. I am privileged to call them colleagues and friends. I was pleased when Professor John David Smith agreed to write the foreword to my book. I cannot think of anyone who knows historical literature better than John David. I am also appreciative of Cynthia Harris, who was the reference editor at Greenwood Press when I submitted the proposal, for accepting this manuscript. I am also indebted to Marsha Havens, my copyeditor and to Emma Bailey the production editor assigned to this project. Their guidance undoubtedly made this a better book.

Introduction

Students of American history are usually surprised to learn that during the years 1870 to 1901, twenty-two African Americans served in Congress. Many more students are shocked when they discover that black voters elected them. An equally remarkable consideration is that Alabama, Florida, Georgia, Louisiana, Mississippi, North Carolina, South Carolina, and Virginia—former slave-owning states—sent black men to Congress. They were not placed there as a result of fraud or by federal bayonets, as the legend of Reconstruction would have it. Two of them served in the Senate; the remaining twenty were in the House of Representatives. They included lawyers, teachers, businessmen, editors, ministers, farmers, and former slaves. Some of them served in Congress into the 1890s, and one ended his term in the House of Representatives in the twentieth century. They were all Republicans, the more liberal of the two major political parties until the early days of the New Deal. Who were these black politicians? What did they do while in Congress? How did they accomplish this feat? This documentary history attempts to answer these questions. The opportunity for African Americans to vote and serve in the national legislature only five years after it abolished slavery came during Congressional Reconstruction, when the federal government finally emancipated enslaved blacks and mandated their right to vote.

During the early 1800s, the Supreme Court under Chief Justice John Marshall commonly held that federal power was superior to state power in matters of contracts and commerce, or whenever there was a clear conflict between the federal government and a state. Marshall elevated the Court, making it the final arbiter of federal law, and of state law that had a common nucleus of federal facts. By the late 1820s, proponents of states' rights began to challenge this belief. Leaders in the federal and state governments diverted a serious conflict in the early 1830s (South Carolina had threatened to secede) by reaching a compromise on lowering federal tariffs on imported goods. During this period, debate over slavery also precipitated a national crisis. However, the North and the South were not able to reach a permanent compromise over this "peculiar institution." Slavery was an important catalyst in the Civil War. When Congress adjourned in March 1865, it left Reconstruction in the hands of President Abraham Lincoln.

Lincoln believed that a state could not actually secede, and once the rebellion was over he wanted them to assume their former status with as few restraints as possible. The Lincoln Plan, dubbed the Lenient Plan, made it easy for the seceded states to return to the Union. Lincoln would grant a pardon to any rebel (Confederate civil and military officers exempted) who took an oath of future allegiance to the Union. When at least ten percent of those voting in 1860 had complied, they could organize new governments and participate fully in the affairs of their states. Lincoln was willing to forgive the South for secession, and he apparently would have allowed them to deny black male suffrage. After Lincoln's assassination on April 14, 1865, Andrew Johnson, the new president, continued many of his policies. Johnson added the grandfather clause, restricting the suffrage to white males whose grandfathers had been eligible to vote before 1860. He returned to active duty in federal and state governments formerly high-ranking ex-Confederates who had obtained a presidential pardon. The plan infuriated Radical Republicans in Congress, who believed that the seceded states would actually gain a larger representation in the federal government. (The Thirteenth Amendment abolished the Three-Fifths Clause in the Constitution, so African Americans would now be counted as whole persons.)

Congressional Reconstruction replaced the lenient policies of presidents Lincoln and Johnson. The Radical Republicans, those who wanted to punish the South for its disloyalty to the Union, developed policies that were more stringent than those enacted under Presidential Reconstruction. Congress made its decision on the basis of two key reports written following the war. Johnson had commissioned Carl Schurz in 1865 to conduct a tour of the South to make an assessment of conditions there. In 1866, Congress established the Joint Committee on Reconstruction to conduct its own investigation. Its members drew the same conclusion: true loyalty to the Union and the protection of black freedom would not likely occur unless the national government transformed the South. As Schurz wrote: "While the southern white men fought against the Union, the Negro did all he could to aid it; while the southern white sees in the national government his conqueror, the Negro sees in it his protector; while the white owes to the national debt his defeat, the Negro owes it his deliverance; the Negro, (it seems) would be led by natural impulse to forward the ends of the government."

The Joint Committee pointed out that many of the leaders in the South had not given up on secession, or on their belief that it was an appropriate response to their conflicts with the North. The Committee indicted the Reconstruction governments organized under Lincoln and Johnson, accusing them of adopting Black Codes and defining an inferior status for African Americans in an attempt to restore a form of slavery. To add insult to injury, whites had already begun to return to Congress many of the ex-Confederate officers who had once held high positions in the government and army. The Reconstruction Committee urged Congress to end southern white control of reunion and initiate its own policy of restoration—measures that would symbolize Union victory in the late war and extend civil rights to black Americans. Radical Republicans were reassured by testimony from the Reconstruction Committee that blacks had "formed an alliance, and displayed the ability" to work in concert to achieve their goals. They were ready to participate in the political process if given the chance. Congress, over Johnson's veto, adopted a series of Reconstruction Acts in the spring of 1867.

The Reconstruction Acts divided the former Confederacy into five military districts, each under the command of a general with a military force sufficient to carry out the new program. Congress authorized its military governors to supervise the registration of all qualified males, except those who had been disenfranchised for disloyalty to the Union as prescribed by Section Two of the proposed Fourteenth Amendment. They supervised elections opened to all eligible voters, convened constitutional conventions, held a state referendum on the new constitution, and protected voters in the exercise of their civic duties.

Between 1865 and 1870, Congress also produced three constitutional amendments that strengthened the authority of the federal government over civil rights. The Thirteenth Amendment abolished slavery. The Fourteenth Amendment recognized citizenship by birth in the United States, thereby making African Americans citizens of the national government and of the state where they lived. It assured its citizens of due process, and guaranteed them the equal protection of the laws. The amendment also empowered the federal government to restrain the states whenever they interfered with these rights. It would impose a penalty on any state that denied the vote to any eligible males, except those who participated in the rebellion. The Fifteenth Amendment forbade the states from using race, color, or previous condition of servitude as a basis for disenfranchising its citizens. Congress made ratification of these amendments a condition to a state returning to the Union.

The Reconstruction Acts and the Civil War Amendments gave African Americans the opportunity to participate in the political process. The majority of black Americans lived in the South, and this is where they wielded political power. They would never completely take over the political affairs of the South; yet, many southern states elected them to federal offices. Mississippi elected two senators—Hiram Rhodes Revels and Blanche Kelso Bruce. (In 1966, Edward William Brooke III of Massachusetts became the first black senator elected since 1881, and the first to be elected by popular vote. In 1992, Carol Moseley-Braun, an Illinois Democrat, was the first African-American woman to be elected to the Senate.)   South Carolina elected Joseph Hayne Rainey and Georgia elected

Jefferson Franklin Long in 1870, as the first and second African Americans to serve in the House of Representatives. For each decade from 1870 to 1901, at least one African American served in the national legislature.

Their years in politics were turbulent, primarily because Democratic lawmakers, and a few Republicans, opposed them. Unable to verify who had won the election where the results were challenged, the House of Representatives did not seat at least five black candidates. At least ten representatives had their terms abbreviated or interrupted by challenges from disgruntled opponents. Louisiana whites, in 1869, rejected the election results of James Lewis and John Willis Menard, who had won seats in the House of Representatives. The state also refused to recognize the election of Pinckney B.S. Pinchback to the Senate. Many other white congressmen initially opposed the Civil Rights Bill proposed by Senator Charles Sumner, a white Republican. Congress finally adopted the measure as a memorial to him in 1875, only to have its key provision voided by the Supreme Court in 1883. (The Court limited the Civil Rights Act to cases where a state used its authority to deny civil rights to blacks. It ruled that protecting private acts of discrimination by individuals was beyond the scope of Congress.) Nevertheless, the legacy of these officeholders provides a living testimony to the world; after over two centuries of slavery, African-American politicians rose to the challenge of leadership as soon as the halls of government opened to them. Their competence had not held them back before the Civil War; federal and state laws had done so.

This documentary history will show that these congressmen were able politicians. They were loyal to the United States in spite of its history of slavery and discrimination. They did not want to punish whites who had been slave owners, and it is clear that a few of them (to the dismay of their colleagues), as a gesture of their good will, were willing to grant amnesty to former Confederates. Many of them favored federal policies that would indemnify African American investors who had lost money in the Freedmen's Savings and Trust Company. They called for the redistribution of land seized by the Union Army during the Civil War as partial reparation for slavery. They favored enlarging educational opportunities and appropriating federal funds to support public schools. They opposed the Chinese Exclusion Bill, condemning racial profiling in American immigration policy. Their most compelling arguments came in defense of the Civil Rights Bill proposed by Charles Sumner. They saw the legislation as vital to securing the rights that were due African American citizens. Their support for the bill went beyond their race. As Robert Brown Elliott of South Carolina pointed out, a civil rights law would secure the rights of all minorities, including women. Southern whites, along with some northerners, opposed passage of the bill. They also made reversing Congressional Reconstruction a top priority.

To drive blacks from office and discourage their involvement in politics, southern whites resorted to a range of extra-legal tactics. They formed terrorist groups such as the Ku Klux Klan, rifle clubs, and White Leagues that committed violent acts against blacks. They obstructed the electoral process by closing Republican polling places in areas where blacks held a majority, frequently making them walk twenty or more miles to Democratic strongholds in order to cast a ballot. They devised a complicated voting scheme called the eight-box law, requiring African-American voters to place each ballot into separate boxes for each of their candidates. Such a convoluted scheme was designed to confuse black voters. They also adopted poll taxes, literacy tests, and other measures to disenfranchise blacks. While these tactics were effective in weakening the black vote in the South, the fall of Reconstruction came in the disputed election of 1876.

Both Republican Rutherford B. Hayes and Democrat Samuel J. Tilden claimed to have won the election of 1876. Republican and Democratic leaders struck a compromise, with Hayes agreeing to withdraw federal troops from the South once in office. With the infamous Compromise of 1876, Reconstruction virtually ended. Black involvement in state and federal elections declined progressively, until none were left in Congress or in state legislatures. Indeed, in states and counties with large African-American populations, blacks held on to their seats until whites had rendered their votes useless.

While they successfully neutralized black voters temporarily, African Americans apparently had never forgotten what had occurred during Reconstruction. As George H. White, a black congressman from North Carolina, told his colleagues in the House upon the end of his term in 1901, a day would come when African Americans would return to the hallowed halls of Congress. His prophecy came true in 1929 when Oscar S. De Priest was elected in Illinois, becoming the last black Republican to serve in Congress until 1967. In 1935, Arthur Wergs Mitchell was elected to the Seventy-fourth Congress, giving him distinction as the first black Democrat to serve in the House. Indeed, these party labels—Republican and Democrat—mean different things today than they did in the nineteenth century, or even early in the twentieth century for that matter. One thing is sure: the Republican party that freed the slaves and gave blacks the ballot changed during the early days of the New Deal, to become a conservative, big business-oriented party. Ironically, the Democratic party, easily the most conservative political party in the nation after 1854, is today the political party of the masses, including African Americans.

Some critics of black Reconstruction congressmen quibble because they did not successfully push their legislative agenda through Congress. Others complain that some black lawmakers were inarticulate and ineffective. These arguments are flawed, and they obscure important considerations. They assume that the majority of white legislators wrote successful bills, and that they all were enormously articulate. Such a viewpoint is erroneous. Certainly they had limitations; they were not demigods. Some of them were overtly conciliatory, and a few of them held conservative views. At least ten of them were themselves slaves or the children of slaves. They were a diverse group, and it is unreasonable to demand that they all should have been college-educated lawyers. Such a high standard is not imposed upon other lawmakers who served in state and federal offices before 1900.

Perhaps the Constitutional Convention of 1787 is a fitting contrast to any one of the Congresses with black lawmakers. While fifty-five delegates attended the meeting, only thirteen of them engaged fully in any debates. George Washington, the president of the Convention, hardly participated in discussions on the floor; nor did the venerable Dr. Benjamin Franklin, whose greatest spoken contribution was to offer a prayer. My point is that officeholders will always choose when they should engage in debates and often will merely cast an informed ballot. The significance of the African-American congressmen who appear in this book goes beyond the number of bills they pushed through Congress. The majority of them proposed legislation, presented petitions from constituents, debated their colleagues, and presided over Senate and House sessions.

Something magnificent happened between 1870 and 1901, when black Americans served in Congress. It is a phenomenon worth remembering and discussing; it is a period as dramatic as any other in American history. Black congressmen drew black and white spectators to the House and Senate galleries like a magnet, and journalists who wrote about them gave them high marks. Many of them had careers, which did not end with their tenures in Congress. Senator Bruce toured in Europe; Langston, Revels, and Miller were college presidents; Langston was also a diplomat; Lynch and Murray were writers; White was a banker; and others were lecturers and farmers. Many more remained active in party affairs until they were no longer welcomed. They served their communities in important ways. Their voices are recorded here to provide a wider audience an opportunity to judge for themselves whether these politicians merit high accolades for their achievements and bravery, and for their quest to make the United States a true representative democracy.

1

Blanche Kelso Bruce
(1841–1898)
Senate, Mississippi

Republican

Forty-fourth and Forty-fifth Congresses
March 4, 1875, to March 3, 1881

Blanche K. Bruce emerged from the Civil War as one of the most prominent African Americans in the United States. He was the first black American to serve a full term in the United States Senate. His birth, however, was symbolic of slave life. His mother was a victim of an illicit affair forced upon her by the farmer who held her in bondage. She would give birth to ten other children, with Blanche becoming her most famous son. He was born into slavery in a small Virginia town on March 1, 1841. From his childhood, he performed a variety of odd jobs on the plantation, including a stint as servant to his white half-brother. Blanche benefited from this relationship in several important ways. A precocious lad, he sat in while a tutor instructed his half-brother. At age nine, he was taken to Missouri where he learned the printing trade. Blanche spent most of his spare time reading. With his sights aimed high, the Civil War brought other possibilities within his grasp.

The war changed Bruce when his owner volunteered for the Confederate Army. Bruce, whose birth name was "Branch," seized the opportunity to flee slavery at the age of twenty, and took on a new identity in Kansas. While there he tried to enroll in the Union Army but the military had not yet decided to enlist blacks. Concerned for the welfare of his race, Bruce opened a school in Kansas, to begin his odyssey as a teacher. The school survived for only three years; afterwards, Bruce returned to Missouri. Committed to educating children he opened a school in Hannibal, thus establishing the first institution in the state dedicated to teaching African-American children. Teaching, however, was not his life's work. The end of the Civil War brought other opportunities. Although he would not take a degree, Bruce attended Oberlin College in Ohio from 1865 to 1867. He then worked aboard a steamboat on the Mississippi River, an odyssey that carried him to the state where he ultimately launched his political career.

Bruce settled in Mississippi in 1869, and soon became a prosperous landowner in the Delta. Congressional Reconstruction also enabled him to begin his meteoric rise in politics. Mississippi, like the rest of the rebel states, was under military occupation. General Adelbert Ames, who commanded the military district there, appointed Bruce registrar in Tallahatchie County, where he supervised elections. He later landed several other positions such as supervisor of education in Bolivar County where he also served as a tax collector and sheriff. In 1874 on a visit to the capital in Jackson, Bruce caught the eye of Mississippi Republicans, and they quickly made him one of the most recognized politicians in the state. General Ames pressed him to run for lieutenant governor, an offer he declined, but in 1874 the state legislature elected him to the United States Senate, where he served until 1881. The office did not come without controversy. According to custom, the senior senator would present his junior colleague to be sworn in. Senator James L. Alcorn declined the honor, unwilling to approve an African American as a member of the Senate. New York Senator Roscoe Conkling stepped in for the ceremony, and by doing so became a trusted friend and ally. Bruce named his son Roscoe Conkling Bruce in honor of the senator.

Senator Bruce took his seat on March 5, 1875, serving on committees such as Pensions, Manufactures, and Education and Labor in the Forty-fourth Congress. He also served on the Select Committee on the Levee System of the Mississippi River in the Forty-fifth Congress. Bruce held other important positions in the Senate, including chairman of the Committee on River Improvements and the Select Committee to Investigate the Freedmen's Savings and Trust Company. Senator Bruce did not restrict himself to issues that affected his race. He represented all the people of Mississippi, and served the broader national interest such as urging Congress to recognize American Indians as citizens. When he presided over the U.S. Senate during the debate on the Chinese Exclusion Bill of 1881, he vehemently argued against its passage. Senator Bruce urged Congress to pay damages to Americans whose property had been destroyed by the Union Army. He also supported some form of national prohibition on the manufacture and sale of alcohol. He backed programs to help impoverished citizens needing relief, and supported appropriating federal funds for public education. Finally, he defended federal economic programs that would develop the economy of the South, including favorable federal policies for railroad companies.

Understandably, Bruce vigorously defended civil rights legislation. He criticized southern whites for intimidating black voters. He also supported the seating of Louisiana Republican Pinckney B.S. Pinchback, an African American, during a contested senate election that dragged on for three years after Pinchback had apparently won. In defense of his Louisiana challenge, Bruce argued that blacks were in the majority in the State and that it had been their intention to elect Pinchback. Only the corruption of white politicians, he asserted, and intimidation by the Ku Klux Klan, could give a white minority victory at the polls.

Bruce's political career in the Senate ended in 1881, when Southern Democrats regained control of Mississippi politics. However, his future in politics was not over. The Republicans nominated him as ambassador to Brazil, a position that Bruce declined because the country had not yet abolished slavery locally. Republicans also supported him for a cabinet position with President James A. Garfield, but Bruce instead took a position in the Treasury Department where he served until 1885. In 1884, he was appointed chairman of an exhibit at the World's Cotton Exposition in New Orleans, highlighting black achievement since emancipation. He returned to government service in 1889, serving as recorder of deeds for the District of Columbia and trustee of its public schools. During the final years of his distinguished career, Bruce became a lecturer, writer, and community organizer. He died in the nation's capital in 1898.

Bruce explained that a white minority in Louisiana and Mississippi had successfully subordinated the votes of a black majority by resorting to fraud, intimidation and violence. Democrats, Bruce argued, had thus stolen elections from Republican candidates in those states. He believed that in Louisiana it was a mathematical impossibility that whites disloyal to the Union could have defeated Pinckney B. S. Pinchback, a Republican. Bruce also pointed out that violence against African-American voters was pervasive in those states and he urged the federal government to restore order there. Bruce also presented statistical evidence to explain that blacks were successfully making the transition from slavery, using as an example data showing that large numbers of blacks were marrying and maintaining traditional American families.

CONTESTED ELECTION IN LOUISIANA
March 3, 1876

I desire briefly to lay before the Senate my views upon the question under consideration.

When I entered upon my duties here as a Senator from Mississippi, the question had ceased to be novel, and had already been elaborately and exhaustively discussed. So far as opportunity has permitted me to do so, I have dispassionately examined the question in the light of their discussion, and I venture my views now with the diffidence inspired by my limited experience in the consideration of such questions and by a just appreciation of the learning and ability of the gentlemen who have already attempted to elucidate and determine this case.

I believe that whatever seeming informalities may attach to the manner in which the will of the people was ascertained, that Pinckney B.S. Pinchback is the representative of a majority of the legal voters of Louisiana, and entitled to a seat in the Senate. In the election of 1872, the white population of the State exceeded, by the census of 1872, the colored population by about two thousand, including in the white estimate 63,000 foreigners, only half of whom were naturalized. This estimate, as the same ratio in each race, would give a large majority of colored voters. The census and registration up to 1872 substantially agree, and both sustain this conclusion. The census of 1875, taken in pursuance of an article of the State constitution after including the foreign population in the white aggregate, gives a majority of 45,695 to the colored population.

This view of the question is submitted, not as determining the contest, but as an offset to the allegation that Mr. Pinchback does not fairly represent the popular will of the State, and as a presumption in favor of the legal title of the assembly that elected him. The State government elected in 1872, and permanently inaugurated in January 1873, in the face of contest and opposition, obtained for its authority the recognition of the inferior and supreme courts of the State. When organized violence threatened its existence and the United States Government was appealed to for troops to sustain it, the national Executive, in pursuance of his constitutional authority and duty, responded to the demand made for help, prefacing said action by an authoritative declaration, made through the Attorney on December 12, 1872, that said Pinchback was "recognized as the lawful executive of Louisiana, and the body assembled at Mechanics Institute as the lawful Legislature of the State"; and similar recognition of his successor was subsequently given. When, in September 1874, an attempt was made to overthrow this government, the President again interposed with the Army and Navy for its protection and the maintenance of its authority.

This government has proceeded to enact and enforce laws for more than three years which not only affect life, liberty, and property, but which have received the general obedience of the citizens of the State. The present government also had frequently been brought in official contact with the United States Congress—through its Legislatures of 1873 and 1875, by memorials and joint resolutions addressed to the respective Houses; and through its executive, by credentials, borne by Congressmen and by Senators—and in no case has the legitimate authority of the Legislature been excepted to save in its action of electing a United States Senator; and in no instance had the sufficiency of the executive's credentials been questioned, in either House, except in the matter of the senatorial claimant.

Now, shall we admit by our action on this case that for three years the State of Louisiana has not had a lawful Legislature; that its laws have been made by an unauthorized mob; that the President of the United States, actively, and Congress, by non-action at least, have sustained and perpetuated this abnormal, illegal, wrongful condition of things, thereby justifying and provoking the indignant and violent protests of one portion of the people of that State, and inviting them to renewed and continued agitation and violence? Such action by us would be unjust to the claimant, a great wrong to the people who sent him here, and cruel even to that class who have awaited an opportunity to bring to their support the overwhelming moral power of the nation in the pursuit of their illusion—which has so nearly ruined the future of that fair State—a Government based upon the prejudices of castes. I respectfully ask the attention of Senators to another view of this subject, which is not without weight in determining the obligations of this body to the State of Louisiana and in ascertaining the title of the claimant. If the assumption that the present government, inaugurated in 1873, is without legal authority and a usurpation is true, the remedy for this state of things was to be found in the exercise by Congress through the joint action of the two Houses of the powers conferred under the guaranteeing clause of the Constitution relative to republican forms of government in the several States.

Failing to exercise her power and perform her duty in this direction, and thus practically perpetuating the present government, I submit that, in my judgment, we cannot now ignore our obligation to give the State her full representation on the score of the alleged irregularity of the government through which she has expressed her will; and there does seem to me, in this connection, something incongruous in the proposition that we may impose upon the people a government without legal sanction and demand their obedience to and support thereof said government meanwhile determining the character of its successors and thus perpetuating its taint, and yet are powerless to admit a Senator elected thereby. In my judgment, this question should at this juncture be considered and decided not on abstract but practical grounds. Whatever wrongs may have been done or mistakes made in Louisiana by either party, the present order of things is accepted by the people of the State and by the nation, and will be maintained as a final settlement of the political issues that have divided the people there; and no changes in the administration of public affairs can or will be made, except by the people, through the ballot, under the existing government and laws of the Commonwealth.

Under these circumstances, holding this question in abeyance is, in my judgment, an unconstitutional deprivation of the right of a State, and a provocation to popular disquiet; and, in the interest of good will and good government, the most judicious and consistent course is to admit the claimant to his seat. As a father, I know him to be affectionate and worthy; as a husband, the idol of a pleasant home, and cheerful fireside; as a citizen, loyal, brave, and true. And in his character and success we behold an admirable illustration of the excellence of our republican institutions.

Bruce explained that in Mississippi blacks faced violence and intimidation at the polls. Given their numbers and support for the Republican party he believed that only violence and fraud could explain a Democratic victory in most elections. He cited newspaper articles that called for Democratic victories at any cost. Bruce pointed out that only federal intervention would secure the peace and protect voters from mob violence. Bruce believed that liberation from slavery was a grave challenge for the American people. He believed that blacks were making progress. He included in this speech statistical data to show that blacks were making the best of their new lives and citizenship.

ELECTION IN MISSISSIPPI
March 31, 1876

I had hoped that no occasion would arise to make it necessary for me again to claim the attention of the Senate until at least I had acquired a larger acquaintance with its methods of business and a fuller experience in public affairs; but silence at this time would be infidelity to my senatorial trust and unjust to both the people and the State I have the honor in part to represent. The conduct of the late election in Mississippi affected not merely the fortunes of partisans—as the same were necessarily involved in the defeat or success of the respective parties to the contest—but put in question and jeopardy the sacred rights of the citizens; and the investigation contemplated in the pending resolution has for its object not the determination of the question whether the offices shall be held and the public affairs of that State be administered by Democrats or Republicans, but the higher and more important end, the protection in all their purity and significance of the political rights of the people and the free institutions of the country. I believe the action sought is within the legitimate province of the Senate; but I shall waive a discussion of that phase of the question, and address myself to the consideration of the importance of the proposed investigation.

The demand of the substitute of the Senator from Michigan proceeds upon the allegation that fraud and intimidation were practiced by the opposition in the late State election, so as not only to deprive many citizens of their political rights, but so far as to practically defeated a fair expression of the will of a majority of the legal voters of the state of Mississippi, resulting in placing in power many men who do not represent the popular will. The truth of the allegations relative to fraud and violence is strongly suggested by the very success claimed by the democracy. In 1873 the Republicans carried the State by a 20,000 majority; in November last the opposition claimed to have carried it by 30,000; thus a Democratic gain of more than 50,000. Now, by what miraculous or extraordinary interposition was this brought about? I can conceive that a large State like New York, where free speech and free press operate upon intelligent masses—a State full of railroads, telegraphs, and newspapers—on the occasion of a great national contest, might furnish an illustration of such a thorough and general change in the political views of the people; but such a change of front is unnatural and highly improbable in a State like my own, with few railroads, and a widely scattered and sparse population. Under the most active and friendly canvass the voting masses could not have been so rapidly and thoroughly reached as to have rendered this result probable.

There was nothing in the character of the issues or in the method of the canvass that would produce such an overwhelming revolution in the sentiments of the colored voters of the State as is implied in this pretended democratic success. The Republicans—nineteen twentieths of whom are colored—were not brought, through the press or public discussions, in contact with Democratic influences to such an extent as would operate a change in their political convictions, and there was nothing in democratic sentiments nor in the prescriptive and violent temper of their leaders to justify such a change of political relations. The evil practices so naturally suggested by this view of the question as probable will be found in many instances by the proposed investigation to have actually occurred. Not desiring to anticipate the work of the committee nor to weary Senators with details, I offer the single county of Yazoo to illustrate the effects of the outrages of which we complain. This county gave in 1873 a Republican majority of nearly two thousand. It was cursed with riot and bloodshed prior to the late election, and gave but seven votes for the Republican ticket, and some of these, I am credibly informed, were cast in derision by the Democrats, who declared that Republicans must have some votes in the county.

Lawless outbreaks have not been confined to any particular section of the country, but have prevailed in nearly every State at some period in its history. But the violence complained of and exhibited in Mississippi and other southern States, pending a political canvass, is exceptional and peculiar. It is not the blow that the beggared miner strikes that he may give bread to his children, nor the stroke of the bondsman that he may win liberty for himself, not the mad turbulence of the ignorant masses when their passions have been stirred by the appeals of the demagogue; but it is an attack by an aggressive, intelligent, white political organization upon inoffensive, law-abiding fellow-citizens; a violent method for political supremacy, that seeks not the protection of the rights of the aggressors, and the destruction of the rights of the aggressors, but the destruction of the rights of the party assailed. Violence so unprovoked, inspired by such motives, and looking to such ends, is a spectacle not only discreditable to the country, but is dangerous to the integrity of our free institutions.

If honorable Senators ask why such flagrant wrongs were allowed to go unpunished by a Republican State government, and not resented by a race claiming a 20,000 majority of the voters, the answer is at hand. The civil officers of the State were unequal to meet and suppress the murderous violence that frequently broke out in different parts of the State, and the State executive found himself thrown for support upon a militia partially organized and poorly armed. When he attempted to perfect and call out this force and to use the very small appropriation that had been made for their equipment, he was met by the courts with an injunction against the use of the money, and by the prescriptive element of the opposition with such fierce outcry and show of counter-force, that he became convinced a civil strife, a war of races, would be precipitated unless he stayed his hand. As a last resort, the protection provided in the national Constitution for a State threatened with domestic violence was sought; but the national Executive—from perhaps a scrupulous desire to avoid the appearance of interference by the Federal authority with the internal affairs of that State declined to accede to the request made for Federal troops.

It will not accord with the laws of nature or history to brand the colored people as a race of cowards. On more than one historic field, beginning in 1776 and coming down to this centennial year of the Republic, they have attested in blood their courage as well as love of liberty. I ask Senators to believe that no consideration of fear or personal danger has kept us quiet and forbearing under the provocation and wrong that have so sorely tried our souls. But feeling kindly toward our white fellow-citizens, appreciating the good purposes and offices of the better classes, and, above all, abhorring a war of races, we determined to wait until such time as an appeal to the good sense and justice of the American people could be made.

A notable feature of the outrages alleged is that they have referred almost exclusively to the colored citizens of the State. Why is the colored voter to be proscribed? Why direct the attack upon him? While the methods of violence, resorted to for political purposes in the South, are foreign to the genius of our institutions as applied to citizens generally—and so much is conceded by even the opposition—yet they seem to think we are an exceptional class and citizens, rather by sufferance than right; and when pressed to account for their bitterness and proscription toward us they, with more or less boldness, allege incompetent and bad government as their justification before the public opinion of the country. Now, I declare that neither political incapacity nor venality are qualities of the masses of colored citizens. The emancipation of the colored race during the late civil strife was an expression alike of the magnanimity and needs of the nation; and the subsequent and early subtraction of millions of industrial values from the resources of the insurrectionary States and the presence of many thousand additional brave hearts and strong hands around the flag of the country vindicated the justice and wisdom of the measure.

The close of the war found four millions of freedmen, without homes or property, charged with the duty of self-support and with the oversight of their personal freedom, yet without civil and political rights! The problem presented by this condition of things was one of the gravest that has ever been submitted to the American people. Shall these liberated millions of a separate race, while retaining personal liberty, be deprived of political rights? The practical sense of the American people definitely settled this delicate and difficult question, and the demand for a more pronounced loyal element in the work of reconstruction in the lately rebellious States furnished an opportunity for the recognition of the political rights of the race, both in the interest of justice and good government.

The history of my race since enfranchisement, considered in connection with the difficulties that have environed us, will exhibit hopeful progress and attest that we have been neither ungrateful for the civil and political privileges received nor wanting in appreciation of the correspondingly weighty obligations imposed upon us. As evidence, not only of our aptitude for improvement but of our actual progress since 1865, I submit a partial but nevertheless illustrative statistical statement gathered from the census of 1860 and 1870 and from data obtained by the State authorities in the interval between these periods. The statistics cover the questions of marriage, churches, and industrial pursuits. The statistics cover the questions of marriage, churches, and industrial pursuits. I will avail myself of exhibits and comments on these points found in the annual message of my colleague, an ex-slaveholder, to the Legislature of Mississippi, session of 1871:

Marriage Statistics

Class/Race	Population		Marriage Licenses Issued					
	1860	1865	1866	1867	1868	1869	1870
White	189,654	2,708	3,129	2,829	2,546	2,655	2,204
Colored	239,930	564	3,679	3,524	2,802	3,584	3,427

The Percentages of those white marriages to the total number of the whites, and of those colored marriages to the total number of the colored, are as follows, namely:

Class/Race	1865	1866	1867	1868	1869	1870
White	1.43	1.64	1.49	1.34	1.40	1.16
Black	.023	1.53	1.47	1.17	1.49	1.43

Governor Algorn, in commenting on the marriage statistics that represent fully thirty-one counties of the State, says:

A people trained under circumstances precluding the marriage contract stood exposed, when released from restraints of force, to the danger of running into extreme sexual license. Our constitution anticipated such a social evil, and therefore dignified all who had been living together in the intercourse of the sexes under slavery by giving them in law the status of husband and wife.

These figures are full of encouragement to men who doubted the practicability of educating the great body of our labor to the moral level of freedom. They will be read with surprise, when taken in connection with the fact that up to the close of the war the Negro was incapable of making a contract of marriage. They prove conclusively that the colored people are striving to rise to the moral level of their new standing before the law to the extent of a strict adherence, at all events, to the formularies of sexual propriety.

But the marriage contracts of the Negroes are not mere formularies. Taking the production of children as evidence of marital fidelity—which it is held to be—the census of the six counties selected as a basis of my inquiries bears the following evidence to the general good faith of the colored people in contracts of marriage:

Population by Ages

Class/Race Total		1 year	1-5 years	5-10 years	10-60 years	60 + years
White	33, 092	6.02	10.52	13.13	66.92	3.38
Black	43,748	7.31	11.16	14.57	63.25	3.70

The table of population embraces six counties, and is submitted to show the purity of the marriage relations among the colored people. The governor on commenting thereon adds:

The fact remains on the face of the national inventory that the colored people show in the proportion of their infants a rate of production, which constitutes an incontestable proof, that Negro marriages are, as a rule, observed with encouraging fidelity.

Number of Churches

Class/Population in 1860		1865	1866	1867	1868	1869	1870
White	138,991	510	505	528	531	548	563
Colored	179,677	105	125	165	201	235	288

Number of Preachers Employed

Class/Population in 1860		1865	1866	1867	1868	1869	1870
White	125,629	328	339	343	349	373	354
Colored	162,733	73	102	134	177	194	262

These tables embrace returns from twenty-two counties, and the governor commenting says:

The religious progress among the Negroes shown in this table, in corroboration of that shown in the table next preceding, is full of good omen for the perfection of the work you, gentlemen, have inaugurated for crowning the State of Mississippi with the peace and prosperity of a well ordered society of free labor.

Number of Shoemaker's Shops

Class/Population in 1860		1865	1866	1867	1868	1869	1870
White	105,023	99	104	101	94	93	99
Colored	165,169	21	28	24	49	54	63

Number of Smith's Shops

Class/Population in 1860		1865	1866	1867	1868	1869	1870
White	105,896	128	128	145	152	157	182
Colored	6,556	40	63	74	83	98	113

The exhibit shows not only the enterprise of the colored man under great embarrassment, but his aptitude for skilled and diversified labor, and is so far favorable, not only to his diligence, but intelligent capacity.

Tenant Farming   *(Bales Produced)*

Class/Race	1869	1870
White	27,075	20,893
Colored	40,561	50,978

The governor very appropriately selects this form of agricultural endeavor as illustrative of the thrift of the Negro, and in connection therewith adds:

Tenant farming has expanded among the whites since 1860 about 100 per cent. In that year it was, of course, unknown among the Negroes.

The improvidence of the Negro is another subject of popular apprehension as to his future under freedom. The laws of 1865 had excluded him from putting that accusation to trial by having made him a pariah.

A military government is certainly not a very favorable school for the development of industry and thrift. And yet the inauguration of that rule was the first moment at which the Negro had, in fact, had the opportunity of realizing wealth. Four years have passed since that time, and but one of four years had been blessed with civil government; and now, at the expiration of that brief period, what evidence do we find on which to found an opinion as to the future identity of the Negro with the direct interests of property?

Negro Property Owners in Seven Counties

69 colored people own real estate to a gross value of	$30,680
3,798 colored people own personalty to a gross value of	630,860
178 colored people own both realty and personalty to a gross value of	220,700

The governor adds:

Among the forty-three thousand Negroes of Washington, Madison, Holmes, Rankin, Neshoba, Jones, and Lauderdale, who had been plucked penniless four short years ago from the clutches of the unwise legislation of 1865, three thousand four hundred and forty-one accumulated wealth—what the economists hold to represent the political virtue of "denial"—to the enormous amount of $882,240! And here again is undoubted proof that the industry and thrift of the Negro are developing with extraordinary rapidity the production of a mass of property-owners who constitute an unimpeachable guarantee that reconstruction goes forward to the consolidation of a society in which the reward of labor goes hand in hand with the safety of property.

The data here adduced, though not exhaustive, are sufficiently full to indicate and illustrate the capacity and progress of this people in the directions specified, and the fuller statistics, derived from subsequent and later investigations, and exhibiting the operation of the more liberal and judicious legislation and administration introduced since 1870, will amply sustain the conclusion authorized by the facts I have adduced. I submit that the showing made, relative to the social, moral, and industrial condition of the Negro, is favorable, and proves that he is making commendable and hopeful advances in the qualities and acquisitions desirable as a citizen and member of society; and, in these directions, attest there is nothing to provoke or justify the suspicion and proscription with which he has been not infrequently met by some of his more highly favored white fellow-citizens.

Again, we began our political career under the disadvantages of the inexperience in public affairs that generations of enforced bondage had entailed upon our race. We suffered also from the vicious leadership of some of the men whom our necessities forced us temporarily to accept. Consider further that the States of the South, where we were supposed to control by our majorities, were in an impoverished and semi-revolutionary condition—society was demoralized, the industries of the country were prostrated, the people were sore, morbid, and sometimes turbulent, and no healthy controlling public opinion was either existent or possible—consider all these conditions, and it will be seen that we began our political novitiate and formed the organic and statutory laws under great embarrassments.

Despite the difficulties and drawbacks suggested, the constitutions formed under colored majorities, whatever their defects may be, were improvements on the instruments they were designed to supersede; and the statutes framed, though necessarily defective because of the crude and varying social and industrial conditions upon which they were based, were more in harmony with the spirit of the age and the genius of our free institutions than the obsolete laws that they supplanted; nor is there any just or any sufficient grounds upon which to charge an oppressive administration of the laws. The State debt proper is less than a half million dollars and the States taxes are light. Nor can complaint be reasonably made of the judiciary. The records of the supreme judicial tribunal of the State will show, in 1859–1860, 266 decisions in cases of appeal from the lower courts, of which 169 were affirmed and 97 reversed. In 1872–1873 the records show 328 decisions rendered in cases of appeal from below, of which 221 were affirmed and 107 reversed; and in 1876, of appeals from chancellors, appointed by Governor Ames, up to date, 41 decisions have been rendered, of which 33 were affirmed and 8 reversed. This exhibit, whether of legislation or administration, shows there have been no adequate provocation to revolution and no justification for violence in Mississippi. That we should have made mistakes, under the circumstances, in measures of both legislation and administration was natural, and that we have had any success is both creditable and hopeful.

But if it can be shown that we have used the ballot either to abridge the rights of our fellow-citizens or to oppress them; if it shall appear that we have ever used our newly acquired power as a sword of attack and not as a shield of defense, then we may with some show of propriety be charged with incapacity, dishonesty, or tyranny. But, even then, I submit that the corrective is in the hands of the people, and not of a favored class, and the remedy is in the honest exercise of the ballot, and not in fraud and violence. I do not hold that all the white people of the State of Mississippi aided and abetted the White League organizations. There is in Mississippi a large and respectable element among the opposition who are not only honest in their recognition of the political rights of the colored citizen and deprecate the fraud and violence through which those rights have been assailed, but who would be glad to see the color line in politics abandoned and good-will obtained and governed among all classes of her people. But the fact is to be regretted that this better class of citizens in many parts of the State is dominated by a turbulent and violent element of the opposition, known as the White League—a ferocious minority—and has thus far proved powerless to prevent the recurrence of the outrages it deprecates and deplores.

The uses of this investigation are various. It will be important in suggesting such action as may be found to be necessary not only to correct and repair the wrongs perpetrated, but to prevent their recurrence. But I will venture to assert that the investigation will be most beneficial in this, that it will largely contribute to the formation of a public sentiment that, while it restrains the vicious in their attacks upon the rights of the loyal, law-abiding voters of the South, will so energize the laws as to secure condign punishment to wrong-doers, and give a security to all classes, which will effectively and abundantly produce the mutual good-will and confidence that constitute the foundations of the public prosperity.

We want peace and good order at the South; but it can only come by the fullest recognition of the rights of all classes. The opposition must concede the necessity of change, not only in the temper but also in the philosophy of their party organization and management. The sober American judgment must obtain in the South as elsewhere in the Republic, that the only distinctions upon which parties can be safely organized and in harmony with our institutions are differences of opinions relative to principles and policy of government, and that differences of religion, nationality, or race can neither with safety not propriety be permitted for a moment to enter into the party contests of the day. The unanimity, with which the colored voters act to the contrary, they invite the political cooperation of their white brethren, and vote as a unit because proscribed as such. They deprecate the establishment of the color line by the opposition, not only because the act is unwise and wrong in principle, but because it isolates them from the white men of the South, and forces them, in sheer self-protection and against their inclination, to act seemingly upon the basis of a race prejudice that they neither respect nor entertain. As a class they are free from prejudices, and have no uncharitable suspicions against their white fellow-citizens, whether native born or settlers from the Northern States. They not only recognize the equality of citizenship and the right of every man to hold, without proscription, any position of honor and trust to which the confidence of the people may elevate him; but owing nothing to race, birth, or surroundings, they, above all other classes in the community, are interested to see prejudices drop out of both politics and the business of the country, and success in life proceed only upon the integrity and merit of the man who seeks it. They are also appreciative, exhibiting the liveliest gratitude for counsel and help in their new career, whether they come from the men of the North or of the South. But withal, as they progress in intelligence and appreciation of the dignity of their prerogatives as citizens, they, as an evidence of growth, begin to realize the significance of the proverb, "When thou doest well for thyself, men shall praise thee"; and are disposed to exact the same protection and concession of rights that are conferred upon other citizens by the Constitution, and that, too, without the humiliation involved in the enforced abandonment of their political convictions.

We simply demand the practical recognition of the rights given us in the Constitution and laws, and ask from our white fellow-citizens only the consideration and fairness that we so willingly extend to them. Let them generally realize and concede that citizenship imparts to us what it does to them, no more and no less, and impress the colored people that a party defect does not imperil their political franchise. Let them cease their attempts to coerce our political co-operation, and invite and secure it by a policy so fair and just as to commend itself to our judgment and resort to no motive or measure to control us that self-respect would preclude their applying to themselves. When we can entertain opinions and select party affiliations without proscription, and cast out ballots as other citizens and without jeopardy to person or privilege, we can safely afford to be governed by the considerations that ordinarily determine the political action of American citizens. But we must be guaranteed in the non-prescribed exercise of our honest convictions and be absolutely, from within or without, protected in the use of our ballot before we can either wisely or safely divide our vote. In union, no division is strength, so long as White League proscription renders division of our vote impracticable by making a difference of opinion opprobrious and an antagonism in politics a crime. On the other hand, if we should, from considerations of fear, yield to the shotgun policy of our opponents, the White League might win a temporary success, but the ultimate result would be disastrous to both races, for they would first become aggressively turbulent, and we, as a class, would become servile, unreliable, and worthless.

It has been suggested, as the popular sentiment of the country, that the colored citizens must no longer expect special legislation for neither their benefit nor exceptional interference by the National Government for their protection. If this is true, if such is the judgment relative to our demands and needs I venture to offset the suggestion, so far as it may be used as reason for a denial of the protection we seek, by the statement of another and more prevalent popular conviction. Back of this, and underlying the foundations of the Republic itself, there lies deep in the breasts of the patriotic millions of the country the conviction that the laws must be enforced, and life, liberty, and property must, alike to all and for all, be protected. But I allege that we do not seek special action in our behalf, except to meet special danger, and only then such as all classes of citizens are entitled to receive under the Constitution. We do not ask the enactment of new laws, but only the enforcement of those that already exist.

The vicious and exceptional political action had by the White League in Mississippi has been repeated in other contests and in other States of the South, and the colored voters have been subjected therein to outrages upon their rights similar to those perpetrated in my own State at the recent election. Because violence has become so general a quality in the political canvasses of the South and my people the common sufferers in each instance, I have considered this subject more in detail than would, under other circumstances, have been either appropriate or necessary. As the proscription and violence toward the colored voters are special and almost exclusive, and seem to proceed upon the assumption that there is something exceptionally offensive and unworthy in them, I have felt, as the only representative of my race in the Senate of the United States, that I was placed, in some sort, upon the defensive, and I have consequently endeavored to show how aggravated and inexcusable were the wrongs worked upon us, and have sought to vindicate our title to both the respect and goodwill of the just people of the nation. The gravity of the issues involved had demanded great plainness of speech from me. But I have endeavored to present my views to the Senate with the moderation and deference inspired by the recollection that both my race and I were once bondsmen; today we are debtors largely to the love and justice of a great people for the enjoyment of our personal and political liberty. While my antecedents and surrounding suggest modesty, there are some considerations that justify frankness, and even boldness of speech.

I represent, in an important sense, the interest of nearly a million of voters, constituting a new, hopeful, permanent, and influential political element, and large enough to affect in critical periods the fortunes of this great Republic; and the public safety and common weal alike demand that the integrity of this element should be preserved and its character improved. They number more than a million of producers, who, since their emancipation and outside of their contributions to the production of sugar, rice, tobacco, cereals, and the mechanical industries of the country have furnished nearly forty million bales of cotton which have yielded $2,000,000,000, a sum nearly equal to the national debt; producers who, at the accepted ratio that an able-bodied laborer earns, on an average $800 per year, annually bring to the aggregate of the nation's great bulk of values more than $800,000,000.

I have confidence, not only in my country and her institutions, but also in the endurance, capacity, and destiny of my people. We will, as opportunity offers and ability serves, seek out places, sometimes in the field of letters, arts, sciences, and the professions. More frequently mechanical pursuits will attract and elicit our efforts; more still of my people will find employment and livelihood as the cultivators of the soil. The bulk of this people—by surroundings, habits, adaptation, and choice—will continue to find their homes in the South, and constitute the masses of its yeomanry. We will there probably, of our own volition and more abundantly than in the past, produce the great staples that will contribute to the basis of foreign exchange, aid in giving the nation a balance of trade, and minister to the wants and comfort and build up the prosperity of the whole land. Whatever our ultimate position in the composite civilization of the Republic and whatever varying fortunes attend our career, we will not forget our instincts for freedom or our love of country. Guided and guarded by a beneficent Providence, and living under the genial influence of liberal institutions, we have no apprehensions that we shall fail from the land from attrition with other races, or ignobly disappear from either the politics or industries of the country.

Allow me here to say that, although many of us are uneducated in the schools, we are informed and advised as to our duties to the government, our States, and ourselves. Without class prejudice or animosities, with obedience to authority as the lesson and love of peace and order as the passion of our lives, with scrupulous respect for the rights of others, and with the hopefulness of political youth, we are determined that the great Government that gave us liberty, and rendered its gift valuable by giving us the ballot, shall not find us wanting in a sufficient response to any demand that humanity or patriotism may make upon us; and we ask such action as will not only protect us in the enjoyment of our constitutional rights, but will preserve the integrity of our republican institutions.

Senator Bruce eulogized Oliver P. Morton in Chambers. He described Morton as an able politician who made significant contributions to the nation as a governor and senator. Bruce explained that though Morton was born in the South, he did not practice sectional politics. Bruce rated Morton along with Abraham Lincoln and Charles

Sumner in his regard for civil rights. African Americans revered Oliver P. Morton, he said. Yet, Morton did not support enfranchising blacks. As Bruce understood it, Norton believed that uneducated voters could not cast ballots responsibly. Bruce accepted this view, casting the suffrage question as a difficult one, that came at a time of crisis and controversy. Morton believed that black people would eventually assume their rightful position as citizens in the United States; thus, Bruce gave him high marks as a leader of all the people.

THE DEATH OF OLIVER P. MORTON
January 17, 1878

The strong true men of a people are always public benefactors. They do work, not only directly beneficial to their communities, but by the utterance of noble thoughts and the infusion of a manly spirit of life and administration they put in operation forces which in their effects are of greater moment to their fellow-citizens than the immediate and specific labors performed. The death of such men is a public calamity because there are lost to the country, not only their active energies but the influence and stimulus of their personal presence. As a compensation for the evil that death works upon a people in the removal of its great leaders there remain behind the memory of their public services, the effect of their example, and the subtle influence of the truths uttered and illustrated by their lives. Occasions like this furnish, therefore, not only appropriate opportunities to commemorate the services and virtues of the dead, but of instruction and profit to the living by calling attention to those characteristics and qualities that have made the lives of the departed useful and memorable.

My estimate of Oliver P. Morton embraces mainly the ideas of his character formed from personal contact in the Senate and personal observation of him while discharging the duties of his public life. He impressed me as a man of catholic spirit and judgments. Born and reared in a section whose type of thought on both political and moral questions differed from the ideas of the South, receiving his distinctive and permanent character from a period in which the conflicting thought of the country had been intensified and more clearly articulated by the passions and struggles of a great civil conflict, he was a representative of his section upon both the civil and ethical questions of the day; but in no offensive sense was he, as a public man, sectional.

In all of those great judgments which entered into the formation and administration of government, that were the basis of the legislation enacted in the interests of the whole country, there was neither sectional temper nor purpose.

Among the manly and honorable qualities exhibited by the deceased Senator was the kindly and considerate temper manifested personally toward those who were his opponents in the contests and discussions growing out of party differences or the policies and measures of government. So prominent an actor in the public life of his day, so earnest in his thought and aggressive in his endeavors to further what he conceived to be right, it would be singular if the angular points in party life had not sometimes originated unpleasant personal differences and collisions. Such collisions, however, were rare in his case, because he was just and fair in his treatment of those whose ideas he not infrequently was compelled to combat and whose measures he felt impelled to pronounce unwise and hurtful.

A man of mature and positive thought he was decided in the maintenance of any opinion he expressed and sincere in maintaining any measure he advocated, but he conceded like sincerity of purpose to his opponents. While earnest to severity in his opposition to principles, institutions, and measures that seemed unfriendly to the public interest or dangerous to the rights of the people, he was withal deferential to the personal advocates of the very measures that conscientious considerations led him to oppose and sometimes even to denounce. What to the superficial observer appeared to be personal bitterness was personal earnestness, and what seemed illiberal to his political opponents was no more than stringent judgments entertained by him on questions that affected not only the interests of the individual citizen but the people of all classes. Beneath a severe exterior was a kindly heart and back of the great partisan leader were the broad wise opinions of the patriot and the statesman, who knew that the best interests of the people forbade any concessions to unreasonable prejudices or trifling or tenderness in dealing with those who either lightly esteemed or recklessly invaded the rights of the humblest American citizen.

Whether contemplating Oliver P. Morton as the governor of a great State in the critical period of civil war, exhibiting wisdom in his plans and discretion, energy, and courage in execution thereof, or observing him as a member of the National Senate, in discussion and counsel upon the grave questions of legislation and administration, involving the complex and multiplied interest of a great nation, I was impressed that he understood both the philosophy and practice of wise government, and possessed not merely the qualities of a great political leader, but in a notable and remarkable measure the elements of a great statesman, understanding the genius of our institutions no less than the necessities and demands of our great country. A generation hence and opinions and judgments on fundamental and grave questions will be cited and revered as are now those of the fathers of the Republic.

I would do injustice to my own feelings and that of my race did I not refer to Senator Morton's sustained services rendered in our behalf. No public man in his day, with the possible exception of Abraham Lincoln and Charles Sumner, was better known to the colored people of the South than Oliver P.

Morton, and none more respected and revered. In 1865, before he had entered upon his senatorial career, Senator Morton expressed opinions that suggested grave doubts of the wisdom of the measures that contemplated immediate enfranchisement of my people. These measures were in conflict with the sentiment and estimates of even many of the friends of the Negro, persons who had labored most earnestly for his freedom; were opposed by the ancient prejudices of centuries; and there was no historical precedent authorizing such radical measures or that seemed to give guarantee and promise of their success.

Appreciating the responsibility of his action as a public man and the delicacy and difficulties of the problem of Reconstruction, he did not at that time take the pronounced and forward position, subsequently so ably held by him, in behalf and defense of the rights of this people. The shock to the public sentiment and prejudices of an entire section, involved in the sudden introduction of this large and new element into the politics of the country, was feared and the competency of a people so long enslaved and consequently uneducated and unaccustomed to participate in public affairs to perform satisfactorily the important functions that would be devolved upon them in their new sphere as citizens seemed to him questionable. A more thorough consideration of this question, however, in all of its relations—local and national—led to a revision of the opinions expressed in 1865, and upon theses latter judgments of the question his subsequent public action was based, and by them his public career is to be judged. Two facts prominently challenged attention and demanded recognition in any philosophy that was broad enough to encompass equally the interests of each class and every section of the country. The emancipation of more than four million former bondsmen was an accomplished fact. The political relations of eleven great communities were ruptured and imperatively demanded restoration. The question holding these two determining factors must be settled on a philosophy as broad as the facts embraced. Emancipation—that its beneficent ends might be attained and adequate readjustment of these disturbed relations of the political communities of a great section be made—involved reorganization, to be just, harmonious, peaceful, and fruitful of public content and public quiet, and demanded the enfranchisement of the Negro. The liberties and securities that rendered emancipation valuable to him could only be sufficiently attained when he was clothed with the power of self-protection by becoming a personal and actual participant in the creation and administration of government.

Reconstruction of the Southern States—restoration of these political communities to participate in the Federal Government—could only become real and permanent when all classes of the community are equally protected, and equally cordial in obedience to the law and cheerful in submission to its demands; and this cheerfulness and cordial response to civic obligations, and conscientious recognition of the rights of society and individuals, could only exist among the communities generally when every member, by the possession and exercise of equal and common, personal, civil, and political privileges, should be inspired with content, and supplied with equal motives for the cultivation and practice of personal and civic virtues. In the midst of their vassalage my race had still preserved in full force and vigor, their original love of liberty; and despite the embarrassment of their conditions they had felt the ennobling influences of the Christian civilization that surrounded them. Cast down but not destroyed; disciplined by the painful ordeal through which they had passed; apt to learn; and prompt to appreciate the ennobling ideas of American institutions, they were in a large measure prepared to enter upon the new life presented to them.

On the other hand the American people—with institutions established, yet elastic; a public sentiment whose catholicity was reinforced by the sturdiest conservatism—the nation possessing, in a remarkable measure, the maturity of age without its weakness and the vigor of youth without its ignorance, were prepared to initiate, and, in his judgment, to perfect this great philanthropic movement, which looked not only to the elevation of a race, but the reconstruction of a great country. He knew that more than a hundred thousand Negro soldiers had ventured life to maintain the authority of the Government and the integrity of the soil of the Republic; and it seemed appropriate and just that the nation, emerging from a supreme effort for its own preservation, and elevated by its grand success, should requite these services, and realize the popular aspirations for universal liberty and equality by a commensurate liberalization of the laws and institutions of the country.

He believed the Negro would be equal to the responsibility of his new life, and meet, in reasonable and creditable measure, the demands that it made upon him; and he believed also that the institutions of the country were strong enough to bear with safety the strain that this new venture might make upon them, and that the unavoidable mistakes in government, arising from the enforced ignorance of the new citizen, would suggest their own corrective, and that the Republic mean while would both live and prosper. The sober judgments of Senator Morton embraced all this and more. And standing on this high and philanthropic plane of thought he resolutely contributed to put into organic from those constitutional provisions that specifically protect the rights of five million American citizens, and to enact and enforce equally and alike the statutes that rendered these provisions operative and the tights there under practically enjoyable. Through him and his peers the grand declaration of human equality made by Jefferson in 1776, and for nearly a century a glittering abstraction, had become a part of the fundamental law of the land.

For the great ability and integrity that Oliver P. Morton exhibited in his public life he is entitled to the admiration and respect of his countrymen; and for the fidelity and patience with which he labored for the elevation and protection of the Negroes of the South, he will receive their heartfelt gratitude and reverent love.

> *Bruce supported the passage of legislation that would desegregate the army. He cited as an example the United States Navy that had enrolled sailors on a non-segregated basis. He believed that affirmative legislation was necessary because, if left to men of good will, the segregated army would continue. He believed that equality of opportunity would attract qualified enlistees to fill positions in the infantry and cavalry, and as engineers*

ENLISTMENT OF COLORED SOLDIERS
April 10, 1878

I was necessarily absent from the Senate pending the discussion of this bill a few days ago, and have only by a hurried reference to the Record been able to ascertain the views of Senators touching it. I heartily indorse the bill as reported by the Senator from Rhode Island, with the amendment of the Senator from Maine. I think I comprehend the scope and effect of the measure. I do not see that the passage of this bill will confer any additional rights and privileges upon the colored citizen. Under existing laws, exclusive of sections 1104 and 1108 of the Revised Statutes, they have a right to enlist in any arm of the service, whether artillery, cavalry, infantry, or engineers, subject to the same conditions that are applied to other citizens, but sections 1104 and 1108, which the pending bill proposes to repeal, are supplemental in their character, making mandatory provisions for the creation of four regiments that should be constituted exclusively of colored soldiers. These sections doubtless were enacted after careful consideration and from just and honorable motives and with the belief not only that the efficiency of the public service would be increased, but that protection of this class of citizens from the dangers to which their rights were supposed to be exposed from the prejudice of the recruiting and distributing officers of the service would be secured.

It was evidently apprehended that these officers would not be willing to enlist colored soldiers in the absence of these positive provisions of law, but would rather use their power to prevent such enlistment. I am inclined to believe that this danger of unfriendly discrimination existed and that for a year or two or more these gentlemen will relax their efforts on some instances to secure colored enlistment. But admit the grounds for this apprehension and suppose further that the passage of the bill reported by the Senator from Rhode Island should result temporarily in the elimination to some extent of the colored soldier from the Army, still I am in favor of the bill. I believe that under the influence of a healthy public sentiment this discouraging prejudice against this class of our citizens will pass away, and that the day is not far distant when all men, without regard to complexion or previous condition, will be received into the Army as they are today admitted into the Navy. So far as I am informed, there are no such discriminating provisions of law existing relative to enlistment in the Navy; yet we find the naval crews are mixed, and that, too, without impairment of their efficiency.

There is an additional reason why I am in favor of repealing these sections. If they are stricken from the statutes I believe that a better class of colored men will apply for enlistment. Whatever the purposes of this legislation we have looked upon them as creating an opprobrious distinction. I think I may say safely that there are hundreds of out people who are unwilling to enlist in the Army because these special provisions of law are supposed to limit their enlistment and distribution exclusively to these four regiments. We are American citizens, and are beginning to appreciate the value and dignity of the rights of our citizenship. We believe we are competent for military service and are entitled to enlist in any arm thereof, and I assert that we are willing to stand upon our own merits and rest our fortunes upon the same forces that give success to other citizens.

I am anxious to see the color line drop out of the business and politics of this country. Its introduction thereto is contrary to the genius of our institutions, and when it is obliterated from the legislation of the country every interest of every class will be greatly served. The time has been when it was necessary for the protection of the rights of this class that a peculiar sort of legislation should be provided, but is it to be presumed that this necessity must last always?

Senator Bruce addressed civil rights. Though he appeared idealistic he believed that it was possible for America to become a society where color was no longer significant. He wanted a society where a person would be accepted based upon what he had to offer and not because of race or color. As he put it, in "all matters of public concern [Americans should] forget the question of complexion or previous condition and go forward hand in hand as American citizens."

CIVIL RIGHTS
April 11, 1878

I do not know that I have anything more to say at present, but I may, perhaps, add that we do not ask special legislation now. We believe that, clothed with all the powers and privileges of citizens, we are able, if I may use the expression, "to paddle our own canoe"; and, indeed, if we fail to do so successfully under just and proper laws, I do not know but that it is about time for us to sink. We do not ask particular favors. We believe we have passed that period. We believe now that we must rest our claim upon our manhood, and that our integrity, industry, capacity, and all those virtues that go to make up good men and citizens are to measure our success before the American people. I repeat now the sooner we can get rid of class legislation the sooner the necessity therefore will cease.

We are amenable to the same laws that you are, and we are to be held amenable; and now let every man who wants to go into the Army present himself to the recruiting officer, and let him be accepted or refused, not because he is white or black, but because he fills the requirements of the branch of the military service into which he wants to enlist. Just so long, however, as it is deemed proper and necessary to keep up these distinctions in the Army, just so long will there be found a large class in this country ready to assault the rights of these people. I hope we have passed the critical period in our history in which race distinctions even for protection are to be considered necessary; we will in this and all other matters of public concern forget the question of complexion or previous condition and go forward hand in hand as American citizens.

On July 29, 1995, USA Today ran a story about a black cadet who got his due 100 years too late. The article was about Cadet Johnson Whittaker, one of the first African Americans to attend West Point Military Academy in 1876. The article explained that three masked men assaulted Whittaker with a razor, slashing his face, hands, and ears. Ironically, the Military Academy court-martialed the young cadet, and then expelled him dishonorably on the grounds that he had injured himself. Bruce addressed this matter, arguing that the cadet was a victim of a vicious assault.

MUTILATION OF WEST POINT CADET
April 9, 1880

I endorse every word that the Senator from Indiana has uttered. For three or four days the newspapers have been laden with reports as to the mutilation of this young man at West Point. Now, a theory is being advanced that this young man has mutilated himself. If he did, the country ought to know it, and he should be promptly expelled from the institution. But it is asking entirely too much of me when I am called upon to believe that young Cadet Johnson Whittaker, or any other man under similar circumstances, would thus mutilate himself. To use a very significant phrase, this theory is entirely "too thin." We have for several days been engaged very industriously, and legitimately, I think, in an attempt to pass a bill that would more effectually civilize and Christianize the Indians. I think the Senate would do well if it would devote a little time to the civilization of West Point. For six or seven years scandalous stories have emanated from that institution relative to the treatment received by young men sent there. I know of one instance in which a young man voluntarily abandoned the institution because he was unwilling to be subjected to the outrages that were obtained therein.

The Senator from Rhode Island [Ambrose Everett Burnside] says that West Point is not worse than other institutions. I hope it is not; but I fear that West Point has retrograded in some respects, in administration at least, since the Senator left it. I once said to a young colored man who asked me for my influence to secure him an appointment at this institution, that if he were my enemy, and I desired to inflict a severe punishment upon him, I would send him to West Point. But in cases of this sort it makes no difference whether the cadet is white or colored, and I have not for a moment stopped to consider that phase of the question, and I am glad to see that the Senator from Indiana has not done so. We support this resolution upon higher grounds, and rest it upon considerations of humanity and the good order and efficiency necessary to the administration of this important public trust. The Senate ought to know all the facts in the case, and if any of the parties who belong to the corps of which this young man is a member or if other persons not connected with the institution are the criminals, the country should know it, and the guilty parties should be promptly and adequately punished.

I do not propose to institute a comparison between this and other institutions of learning as to their methods of administration; I do not know that there are other institutions as vicious in the direction under discussion as West Point; but I do know that we are more directly connected with the control of this, a Government and national institution, than of any other of similar character in the country, and that public opinion holds us responsible for the conduct of its affairs. It is hard to conceive that such excesses as have sometimes occurred at

West Point, in the matter of hazing and other irregularities and personal indignities, could happen in a military institute with its exact and stringent discipline, unless there was a vice somewhere in the methods of governing the institution, and I believe this investigation will have a healthy influence upon the officers charged with the administration and control of West Point.

Black migration to the West offered the seductive hope of a better life. Once white Democrats returned to power they persecuted African Americans. Some blacks considered colonization an alternative to racism in the US. Many others turned to the western territory in the United States. However, moving West did not immediately ease their economic woes. Senator Bruce addressed this matter, and urged Congress to adopt laws to relieve suffering among black immigrants, just as they had for foreigners in need of economic assistance. He also argued that if the United States could afford to reach across the waters to help Europeans like the Irish, it could use its resources to assist blacks in western states like Kansas.

BLACK MIGRATION
February 20, 1880

It is not my purpose to discuss this question. I have studiously avoided giving expression to any views on this floor touching the movement of colored people from the South, and I have hoped no occasion would arise for me to engage in that discussion. I shall not do so now. It seems to me that the only question involved now is whether or not we will relieve suffering humanity; whether we will allow these people who are in Kansas—whether they have left their homes for cause or without cause, wisely or unwisely, is a matter of no importance, as far as this question is concerned—to die by hundreds, rather than permit a charity which the English people have sent here to pass through the custom house free of duty. That is all. Money is being collected in this country by thousands of dollars to be sent across the seas to relieve the suffering people of Ireland.

I am glad to say I have been one of the persons who have contributed. Nobody up to this moment I believe has objected to this money being sent; and, if I mistake not, two or three days ago, a joint resolution was introduced, and on the next day reported and passed without a dissenting vote, authorizing the Secretary of the Navy to fit up a ship and use that ship in carrying provisions and clothing to those suffering people. Now, I do not believe that the Senator from Indiana [Daniel Wolsey Voorhees] desires to be understood as opposing a movement simply to relieve these suffering people. It is not now a question of how they came there or why they went there; it is not a question whether they ought to have gone there or not; but they are there and they are in distress, and it seems to me that the honorable Senator from Indiana [Mr. Voorhees], whom I know well and favorably, does not intend to antagonize that these people should have originally gone to that State.

In the name of the hundreds of colored people now starving in Kansas I appeal to the Senate to pass the pending measure that they may receive the immediate benefits of this charity.

Senator Bruce criticized America's treaty-making policy with American Indians, suggesting that it w as a scheme to acquire their land. Bruce believed the treaties had been subordinated to manifest destiny. Whenever the US needed more room, the government simply forced the Indians to revise the treaties that had been ratified. Bruce worried that white politicians would ultimately expel the Indians from the continent. He discussed a new policy that respected Indian culture.

AMERICAN INDIAN POLICY
April 6, 1880

I shall support the pending bill, and without attempting a discussion of the specific features of the measure, I desire to submit a few remarks upon the general subject suggested by the bill.

Our Indian policy and administration seem to me to have been inspired and controlled by a stern selfishness, with a few honorable exceptions. Indian treaties have generally been made as the condition and instrument of acquiring the valuable territory occupied by the several Indian nations, and have been changed and revised from time to time as it became desirable that the steadily growing, irrepressible white races should secure more room for their growth and more lands for their occupancy; and wars, bounties, and beads have been used as auxiliaries for the purpose of temporary peace and security for the whites, and as the preliminary to further aggressions upon the red man's lands, with the ultimate view of his expulsion and extinction from the continent. No set purpose has been evinced in adequate, sufficient measure to build him up, to civilize him, and to make him a part of the great community of States. Whatever of occasional and spasmodic effort has been made for his redemption from savagery and his perpetuity as a race has been only sufficient to supply that class of exceptions to the rule necessary to prove the selfishness of the policy that we allege to have practiced toward him.

The political or governmental idea, underlying the Indian policy, is to maintain the paramount authority of the United States over the Indian Territory and over the Indian tribes, yet recognizing tribal independence and autonomy and a local government, un-American in structure and having no reference to the Constitution or laws of the United States, so far as the tribal government affects the persons, lives, and rights of the members of the tribe alone. Currently with the maintenance of a policy thus based, under treaty obligations, the Government of the United States contributes to the support, equipment, and comforts of these Indians, not only by making appropriations for food and raiment but by sustaining blacksmiths, mechanics, farmers, millers, and schools in the midst of the Indian reservations. This Government also, in its treaties and its enforcement thereof, encourages and facilitates the missionary enterprises of churches to send missionaries to educate the Indians throughout the public domain. The effort, under these circumstances, to preserve peace among the Indian tribes in their relations to each other and in their relations to the citizens of the United States becomes a very onerous and difficult endeavor, and has not heretofore produced results that have either satisfied the expectations and public sentiment of the country, vindicated the wisdom of the policy practiced toward this people, or honored the Christian institutions and civilizations of our great country.

We have in the effort to realize a somewhat intangible ideal, to wit, the preservation of Indian liberty and the administration and exercise of national authority, complicated an essentially difficult problem by surrounding it with needless and equivocal adjuncts; we have rendered a questionable policy more difficult of successful execution by basing it upon a political theory which is un-American in character, and which, in its very structure, breeds and perpetuates the difficulties sought to be avoided and overcome. Our system of government is complex in that it recognizes a general and local jurisdiction, and seeks to protect the rights of the individual and of the different political communities and the great aggregates of society making up the nation, by a division of authority distributed among general and local agencies, which are required, like "the wheels within wheels" of Ezekiel's vision, to so move in their several appropriate spheres as shall not only prevent attrition and collision, but as shall secure unity in the system, in its fullest integrity, currently with the enjoyment of the largest liberty by the citizen.

Our system, I repeat, is complex, but it is nevertheless homogeneous. It is not incongruous; the general and local organisms belong to the same great class; they are both American, and they are moved by the response to the same great impulse—the popular will of the American people. Now, the political system that underlies our Indian policy is not only complex but it is incongruous, and one of the governments embraced in the system, ostensibly to secure the largest license and independence to the red race affected by the subject of this nondescript policy, is foreign in its character; the individuals and the system of laws are not American. All the contradictions, the absurdities, and impossibilities developed and cropping out on the surface of our administration of Indian affairs are referable to this singular philosophy upon which, as a political theory, the Indian policy of the United States rests.

There must be a change in the Indian policy if beneficent, practical results are expected, and any change that gives promise of solving this red-race problem must be a change based upon an idea in harmony, and not at war, with our free institutions. If the Indian is expected and required to respond to Federal authority; if this people are expected to grow up into organized and well-ordered society; if they are to be civilized, in that the best elements of their natures are to be developed to the exercise of their best functions, so as to produce individual character and social groups characteristic of enlightened people; if this is to be done under our system, its ultimate realization requires an adoption of a political philosophy that shall make the Indians, as an individual and as a tribe, subjects of American law and beneficiaries of American institutions, by making them first American citizens, and clothing them, as rapidly as their advancement and location will permit, with the protective and ennobling prerogatives of such citizenship.

I favor the measure pending, because it is a step in the direction that I have indicated. You propose to give the Indian not temporary but permanent residence as a tribe, and not tribal location, but by a division of lands in severalty you secure to him the individual property rights which, utilized, will sustain life for himself and family better than his nomadic career. By this location you lay the foundation for that love of country essential to the patriotism and growth of a people, and by the distribution of lands to the individual, in severalty, you appeal to and develop that essential constitutional quality of humanity, the disposition to accumulate, upon which, when healthily and justly developed, depends the wealth, the growth, the power, the comfort, the refinement, and the glory of the nations of the earth.

The measure also, with less directness, but as a necessary sequence to the provisions that I have just characterized, proposes, as preliminary to bringing the red race under the operations of our laws, to present them the best phases of civilized life. Having given the red man a habitat, having identified the individual as well as the tribe with his new home, by securing his individual interests and rights therein; having placed these people where law can reach them, govern them, and protect them, you propose a system of administration that shall bring them in contact not with the adventurer of the border, not a speculative Indian agent, not an armed blue-coated soldier, but with the American people, in the guise and fashion in which trade, commerce, arts—useful and attractive—in the panoply that loving peace supplies, and with the plenty and comforts that follow in the footsteps of peace, and for the first time in the Indian's history, he will see the industrial, commercial, comfortable side of the character of the American people; will find his contact and form his associations with the citizens of the great Republic, and not simply and exclusively its armed men—its instruments of justice and destruction. So much this measure, if it should be a type of the new policy, will do for the Indian, and the Indian problem—heretofore rendered difficult of solution because of the false philosophy underlying it, and the unjust administration too frequently based upon it—a policy that has kept the Indian a fugitive and a vagabond, that has bred discontent, suspicion, and hatred in the mind of the red man will be settled—not immediately, in a day or a year, but it will be put in course of settlement, and the question will be placed where a successful issue will be secured beyond a peradventure.

The red race are not a numerous people in our land, not equaling probably a half million of souls, but they are the remnants of a great and multitudinous nation, and their hapless fortunes heretofore not only appeal to sympathy and to justice in any measures that we may take affecting them, but the vigor, energy, bravery, and integrity of this remnant entitle them to consideration on the merits of this question.

Our age has been signalized by the grand scientific and mechanical discoveries and inventions that have multiplied the productive forces of the world. The powers of nature have been harnessed to do the work of man, and every hour some new discovery contributes to swell the volume of the physical energies that make a people rich, prosperous, and happy. Yet, in the midst of this affluence of physical energy and its utilization, human ingenuity and thought have already been directed to the conservation, to the economy against the waste, of the physical forces. The man is considered a public benefactor who can utilize waste fuel, who can convert to some practical end some physical energy still lost, to a percent, at least, through the imperfection of the machinery employed.

The Indian is a physical force; a half million of vigorous physical intellectual agents ready for the plastic hand of Christian civilization, living in a country possessing empires of untilled and uninhabited lands. The Indian tribes, viewed from this utilitarian standpoint, are worth preservation, conservation, utilization, and civilization. I believe that we have reached a period when the public sentiment of the country demands such a modification in the Indian policy, in its purposes, and in its methods, as shall save and not destroy these people. There is nothing in the matter of obstructions, as suggested by the opponents of this measure, to convince me that the new policy is either impracticable or visionary. As a people, our history is full of surmounted obstacles; we have been solving difficult problems for more than a hundred years; we have been settling material, moral, and great political questions that before our era had been unsolved, and the possible solution of which, even among the timid in our midst, was questioned.

The Indian is human, and no matter what his traditions or his habits, if you will locate and put him in contact, and hold him in contact, with the forces of our civilization, his fresh, rugged nature will respond, and the fruit of the endeavor in his civilization and development will be the more permanent and enduring because his nature is so strong and obdurate. When you have no longer made it necessary for him to be a vagabond and a fugitive; when you have allowed him to see the lovable and attractive side of our civilization as well as the stern military phase; when you have made the law apply to him as it does to others, so that the ministers of the law shall not only be the executors of its penalties but the administrators of its saving, shielding, protecting provisions, he will become trustful and reliable, and when he is placed in the position in which not only to become an industrial force—to multiply his comforts and those of his people—but the honest, full sharer of the things he produces, savage life will lose its attractions and the hunter will become the herdsman, the herdsman in his turn the farmer, and the farmer the mechanic, and out of the industries and growth of Indian homes will spring up commercial interests and men competent to foster and handle them.

The American people are beginning to reach the conscientious conviction that redemption and civilization are due to the Indian tribes of the United States, and the present popular purpose is not to exterminate but to perpetuate them on this continent. The Indian policy has never attracted so much attention as at the present time, and the public sentiment demands that the new departure on this question shall result in measures, toward the wild tribes of America, that shall be Christian and righteous in their character. The destruction of this vigorous race, rather than their preservation and development, is coming to be considered not only an outrage against Christian civilization, but an economic wrong to the people of the United States; and the people of America demand that the measures and administration of government, relative to these people, shall proceed upon the wise and equitable principles that regulate the conduct of public affairs relative to every other race in the Republic, and when rightful conceptions are obtained in the treatment of the red race, the Indian question, with its costs, anxieties, and wars, will disappear.

> *It is common knowledge today that the Union discriminated against black soldiers during the Civil War. They were paid less than white soldiers. They also received substandard clothing, equipment, and poor medical care. Yet, black soldiers frequently faced hazardous duties, resulting in casualties disproportionate to their numbers. Senator Bruce pointed out another area of discrimination-pensions. He argued that the administrators of the colored pension fund discriminated against the heirs of black soldiers, and he supported legislation to remedy that problem.*

HEIRS OF COLORED SOLDIERS
February 10, 1881

I present the petition of George C. Smith, A.I. Rhodes, and others, praying favorable action on House Bill No. 5562, entitled An act for the relief of the heirs of colored soldiers. The officers executing the laws so as to discriminate against such persons of this class—who were slaves in April 1861—have misconstrued the legislation relative to bounty and pensions of colored soldiers. To relieve claimants of the disabilities, under which this legislation left them, the act of March 3, 1873, was passed, entitled An act to place colored persons who enlisted in the Army on the same footing as other soldiers as to bounty and pensions.

The honorable Secretary of the Treasury construed this act, passed February 13, 1879, to disallow claims of a certain class. The bill now before the Senate committee proposes to construe the act of 1873 so as to remove all disabilities relative to the heirs of colored soldiers.

As explanation of the grounds upon which this legislation is asked, I beg also to submit the following official communication of the Second Auditor of the Treasury:

Treasury Department, Second Auditor's Office
Washington, D.C., January 18, 1881

In reply to your verbal inquiry of the 15th instant, as to the status of the heirs of colored soldiers under the act of March 3, 1873, I have to state:

First. In case of colored soldiers shown by record to have been free April 19, 1861, all bounty has been allowed just the same as in case of white soldiers.

Second. The additional bounty, act of July 28, 1866, and the bounty, act of July 4, 1864, have been allowed in case of colored soldiers, whether slave or free, in the same manner as in the case of white soldiers.

Third. Prior to the act of March 3, 1873, the bounties under act of July 22, 1861, and joint resolution of January 13, 1864, were not allowed in case of colored soldiers who were slaves April 19, 1861.

Fourth. The act of March 3, 1873, was construed by the accounting officers as applicable to discharged living soldiers, not to heirs; but after the decision of the Attorney-General of March 26, 1878, all bounty in case of colored soldiers, slave or free, living or deceased, was until February 13, 1879, allowed by this office in the same manner as in the case of white soldiers.

Fifth. Claims in case of heirs of deceased colored soldiers shown to be slaves April 19, 1861, which were filed and settled prior to the Attorney-General's decision of March 26, 1878, were, under this decision, until February 13, 1879, reopened and considered when such cases were properly referred to, either by the claimants or by their duly authorized attorneys.

Claims of this character filed and disallowed prior to March 26, 1878, were and are now considered under the Attorney-General's decision of said date, when such claims supported by proper evidence are referred to either by claimants or by their authorized attorneys.

Again, claims of this character filed prior to March 26, 1878, that have not been either settled or disallowed, but are now pending as original claims, are considered under the Attorney General's decision of said date.

Sixth. All original claims in case of colored soldiers (in behalf of whom or whose heirs no settlement has ever been made by this office), whenever filed, are now considered, as far as bounty is concerned, on the same footing as claims in case of white soldiers.

Seventh. Therefore, the only claims in case of colored soldiers that are affected by the decision of the honorable Secretary of the Treasury of February 13, 1879, are the claims filed as additional to those that were settled subsequent to the act of March 3, 1873, for all due under laws and decisions then in force; and the additional claims are disallowed on the ground that according to the said decision of the honorable Secretary of the Treasury such cases should not be reopened.

While I have the ear of the Chair I beg to call the attention of the Committee on Military Affairs to the importance of action in this matter. The persons to be benefited by this bill belong to a needy class, a class who has exhibited some patience while waiting for an adjustment of their claims.

I move that the petition with the accompanying communication be referred to the Committee on Military Affairs.

The motion was agreed to.

Following emancipation, blacks made a concerted effort to amass capital to further economic development. Blacks in Baltimore organized the Chesapeake and Marine Railway, as well as the Dry Dock Company. African Americans also established savings and loan associations. The federal government chartered the Freedmen's Savings and Trust Company in 1865, to offer blacks a greater opportunity to save. The management of the bank was left to blacks, and William Booth was named its first president. Headquartered in New York, branches of the Freedmen's Bank sprang up in major cities including Washington D.C., New Orleans, and Philadelphia, but the bank was plagued with problems. It hired white cashiers and bookkeepers who did not carefully manage its funds. A recession in 1873 further eroded public confidence, and the Freedmen's Bank closed its doors in 1874. Bruce watched the bank during these years and played a leadership role in helping investors recover their losses

FREEDMEN'S SAVINGS AND TRUST COMPANY RESOLUTIONS AND PETITIONS
March 26, 1879

I desire to offer a resolution:

Resolved, That the President of the Senate appoint a select committee of five on the Freedmen's Savings and Trust Company, to take into consideration all matters relating to said institution; that said committee be authorized to employ a clerk; and that the necessary expenses be paid out of the "miscellaneous items" of the contingent fund of the Senate.

The resolution was considered by unanimous consent, and agreed to.

May 16, 1879

Resolved, That the Select Committee on the Freedmen's Savings and Trust Company appointed by resolution of the Senate of April 7, 1879, is authorized and directed to investigate the affairs of said savings and trust company and its several branches, to ascertain and report to the Senate all matters relating to the management of the same and the cause or causes of failure, with such other facts relating thereto as may be important to a full understanding of the management and speedy adjustment of its affairs.

Be it further resolved, That said committee, and any sub-committee thereof, shall be authorized to sit during the recess of the Senate, and be empowered to send for persons and papers, to summon witnesses, to administer oaths, and shall be authorized to employ a stenographer and such other experts, accountants, and other assistants as may be necessary; and that the said committee be authorized to have printed, from time to time, for the use of the committee and the Senate all the testimony taken by them, together with the papers laid before it.

May 17, 1879

A petition of R.M. Hall, M.D., and other citizens of Baltimore, Maryland, praying passage of an act requiring the commissioners of the Freedmen's Savings and Trust Company to close up the affairs of that institution and distribute the assets among the creditors thereof; which was referred to the select committee on the Freedmen's Savings and Trust Company.

April 5, 1880

Mr. Bruce, from the Select Committee on the Freedmen's Savings and Trust Company, submitted a report accompanied by a bill (S. No. 1581) authorizing and directing the purchase by the Secretary of the Treasury, for public use, the property known as the Freedmen's Bank, and the real estate and parcels of ground adjacent thereto, belonging to the Freedmen's Savings and Trust Company, and located on Pennsylvania avenue, between Fifteenth and Fifteenth-and-a-half streets, Washington, District of Columbia.

The bill was read twice by its title, and the committee ordered that it be printed report was.

Mr. Bruce, from the same committee, to whom was referred the bill (S. No. 711) amending the charter of the Freedmen's Savings and Trust Company, reported it with an amendment, the report upon Senate bill No. 1581 applying also it this bill.

April 12, 1880

M. Bruce asked and by unanimous consent obtained leave to introduce a bill (S. No. 1619) to reimburse the colored depositors of the Freedmen's Savings and Trust Company for losses incurred by the failure of said company; which was read twice by its title, and referred to the Select Committee on the Freedmen's Savings and Trust Company.

January 14, 1881

To the Freedmen's Bank: I will say further that the original cost of the whole ground was $80,000, the appraisement papers $2,060 aggregating $82,060. The cost of the bank building was $176,255.66. The total cost of the building and the ground, which it occupies, was $207,585.66. I am speaking now of the building and the ground which it occupies. We propose that the Government shall not only purchase the building and the ground upon which it is located, but all the ground and property from that point up to the square

Senator Bruce supported federal appropriations to fund black education. Apparently, there were unclaimed funds in the United States Treasury, and Bruce proposed a bill to release them to help support black institutions. Such schools would include Wilberforce University in Ohio and the Lowery Industrial Academy in Alabama

BLACK EDUCATION
April 5, 1878

Mr. Bruce asked, and by unanimous consent obtained, leave to introduce a bill (S. No. 1285) for the endowment of the S.R. and R. M. Lowery Industrial Academy, in the State of Alabama, and to accept a donation of buildings and lands in aid of the same, and for other purposes; which was read twice by its title, and referred to the Committee on Education and Labor.

December 16, 1879

Mr. Bruce asked, and by unanimous consent obtained, leave to introduce a bill (S. No. 865) to provide for the investment of certain unclaimed pay and bounty moneys now in the Treasury of the United States, and to facilitate and encourage the education of the colored race in the several States and Territories; which was read twice by its title, and referred to the Committee on Education and Labor.

February 22, 1881

Mr. Bruce, from the Committee on Education and Labor, to whom were referred the bill (S. No. 792) to encourage and aid the education of the colored race in the several States and Territories, and the bill (S. No. 865) to provide for the investment of certain unclaimed pay and bounty moneys now in the Treasury of the United States and to facilitate and encourage the education of the colored race in the several States and Territories, submitted an adverse report thereon; which was ordered to be printed, and the bills were postponed indefinitely.

2

Richard Harvey Cain (1825–1887)
House of Representatives, South Carolina

Republican

Forty-third and Forty-fifth Congresses
March 4, 1873, to March 3, 1875
March 4, 1877, to March 3, 1879

Richard Harvey Cain was born free in Greenbrier County, Virginia, on April 12, 1825. With limited opportunities available to free African Americans, his parents moved to Gallipolis, Ohio, in 1831, hoping for more rights than those available in a slave state. Cain attended segregated primary schools established by blacks in Ohio. He also attended Wilberforce University in Ohio, the first institution of higher learning founded by African Americans in the United States. Ohio also offered work on steamboats traveling its major rivers. An ambitious young man, Cain soon realized that careers for black professionals were limited. Religion appealed to him as a matter of conscience; it also offered him the prospect of going as far as his talents would allow. Thus, Cain entered the ministry in the Methodist Episcopal (ME) church in 1844. His first assignment was in a church in Hannibal, Missouri, a slaveholding state. He remained there until 1848, but became disillusioned with ministering in a white congregation that followed a policy of racial segregation. Cain finally left the ME Church, and joined the African Methodist Episcopal (AME) church, founded by Richard Allen, a black clergyman.

The switch benefited Cain in several ways. It offered leadership opportunities, including the prospect of becoming a pastor, and the chance of advancing in church governance. Cain served as pastor of an AME congregation in Muscatine, Iowa, and by 1859 had become an ordained bishop. During the 1860s he relocated to New York to become the pastor of a church in Brooklyn. He also became involved in the civic and political affairs of the community. In 1864, he attended a political convention in New York, organized by African Americans. Once the war ended, he moved to South Carolina as a missionary in the AME church, the only state in the nation with a black majority. That state's large black population offered him greater opportunities for religious service; it also launched his political career during Congressional Reconstruction.

Richard Cain settled in historic Charleston. Cain, along with other leaders in the AME church, established new congregations throughout South Carolina. Bishop Cain also assumed leadership of Emmanuel AME Church in Charleston, a congregation that had an impressive history, but had fallen into disarray during the Civil War. Cain revived it, and made it the largest AME congregation in the state. He also published a newspaper, the *South Carolina Leader* (later renamed the *Missionary Record*), launched in 1866. From this religious base, he became involved in politics. In addition to attending conventions sponsored by black groups, he was elected to the State Constitutional Convention of 1868, to help write its political framework and restore the state to the Union. Once the constitution passed a referendum in the state, and was accepted by Congress, Cain was elected to the state senate in 1868, a position he held until 1870. He ran an unsuccessful campaign for the Republican party nomination for lieutenant governor in 1872.

Cain had also entered the race for a congressional seat in 1872, and upon his election, he entered the Forty-third Congress. He was assigned to the Committee on Agriculture. During these years, the Civil Rights Bill proposed by Senator Charles Sumner was an important measure before Congress. Cain offered his most powerful speeches in defense of that bill. He favored equal access to public places, and the service of African Americans in civic capacities, such as on juries. Though Cain did not seek reelection in 1874, he entered the congressional race in 1876, defeating his Democratic rival and surviving his challenge of the results. He was assigned to the Committee on Private Claims. An opponent of segregation since his days in the ME church, Cain proposed a bill making the federal government responsible for funding public education. He did not have confidence in southern support for mixed schools. He also disputed the notion that the black masses were incapable of learning, and he argued that better schools would benefit all Americans. The House did not pass the bill.

When his congressional term ended in 1879, Cain retuned to local politics, as well as to social and commercial issues that had concerned him since coming to the South. He had already distinguished himself in Charleston, having served as chairman of the Republican party from 1870 to 1871. He was also a member of the state militia, and served with the fire company in Charleston. He was an organizer of the Enterprise Railroad Company, a black-owned organization. Cain also flirted with the back-to-Africa movement, and helped found a steamship company to explore the idea. He promoted commerce between Africa and the United States. Nothing substantial, other than black pride, came from such initiatives. Bishop Cain attempted to demonstrate the importance of amassing assets and, according to the 1870 census, owned over $5,000 in real property.

Cain's activities did not make him popular among whites, who regarded an outspoken black leader as a militant. His message was direct, not inflammatory. He urged the federal government to provide African Americans with land that had been confiscated during the war. He believed the nation owed blacks at least a homestead, as reparation for their years in slavery. He felt that black farmers would help enlarge cotton production in the South, as well as increase its yield of corn, wheat, and other agricultural products. For those comments Cain became an object of threats and violence. As his adopted daughter put it, "We lived in constant fear all the time."

Cain continued to work in the AME church when his tenure in Congress ended. In 1880, he was elected bishop of the Texas-Louisiana Conference, until he was reassigned to the New Jersey Conference (New England, New York, New Jersey, and Philadelphia) of the AME church. Bishop Cain remained committed to black education, and helped establish the Paul Quinn College of Waco, Texas, and served as its president until 1884. Richard Harvey Cain died at his home in Washington, D.C., on January 18, 1887.

Richard Harvey Cain made an impassioned plea in support of the Civil Rights Bill. He reminded his colleagues of what life was like for African Americans following passage of the 1866 Civil Rights Act. They were denied service in public places and were forced to ride in railroad cars reserved for smokers, even if they purchased a first-class ticket. Cain explained that African Americans had served the Union faithfully during the Civil War. Northern blacks waited until they could take up arms top defend liberty; blacks in the South did not put white women and their children in danger. He also explained why some black congressmen voted in for the bill to grant amnesty to ex-Confederates, suggesting that they did not want to discriminate against anyone. They also hoped that by their gesture, southern whites would not oppose the civil rights bill.

CIVIL RIGHTS
January 10, 1874

I feel called upon more particularly by the remarks of the gentleman from North Carolina [Robert Brank Vance] on civil rights to express my views. For a number of days this question has been discussed, and various have been the opinions expressed as to whether or not the pending bill should be passed in its present form or whether it should be modified to meet the objections entertained by a number of gentlemen whose duty it will be to give their votes for or against its passage. It has been assumed that to pass this bill in its present form Congress would manifest a tendency to override the Constitution of the country and violate the rights of the States.

Whether it is true or false is yet to be seen. I take it, so far as the constitutional question is concerned, that if the colored people under the law, under the amendments to the Constitution, have become invested with all the rights of citizenship, then they carry with them all rights and immunities accruing to and belonging to a citizen of the United States. If four, or nearly five, million people have been lifted from the thralldom of slavery and made free; if the Government by its amendments to the Constitution has guaranteed to them all rights and immunities, as to other citizens, they must necessarily therefore carry along with them all the privileges enjoyed by all other citizens of the Republic. The gentleman from North Carolina [Mr. Vance] who spoke on the question stated some objections, to which I desire to address a few words of reply. He said it would enforce social rights, and therefore would be detrimental to the interests of both the whites and the blacks of the country. My conception of the effect of this bill, if it is passed into a law, will be simply to place the colored men of this country upon the same footing with every other citizen under the law, and will not at all enforce social relationship with any other class of persons in the country whatsoever. It is merely a matter of law. What we desire is that our civil rights shall be guaranteed by law as they are guaranteed to every other class of persons; and when that is done all other things will come in as a necessary sequence, the enforcement of the rights following the enactment of the law.

Social equality is a right that every man, every woman, and every class of persons have within their own control. They have a right to form their own acquaintances, to establish their own social relationships. Its establishment and regulation is not within the province of legislation. No laws enacted by legislators can compel social equality. Now, what is it we desire? What we desire is this: inasmuch as we have been raised to the dignity, to the honor, to the position of our manhood, we ask that the laws of this country should guarantee all the rights and immunities belonging to that proud position, to be enforced all over this broad land.

The gentleman states that in the State of North Carolina the colored people enjoy all their rights as far as the highways are concerned; that in the hotels, and in the railroad cars, and in the various public places of resort, they have all the rights and all the immunities accorded to any other class of citizens of the United States. Now, it may not have come under his observation, but it has under mine, that such really is not the case; and the reason why I know and feel it more than he does is because my face is painted black and his is painted white. We who have the color—I may say the objectionable color—know and feel all this. A few days ago, in passing from South Carolina to this city, I entered a place of public resort where hungry men are fed, but I did not dare—I could not without trouble—sit down to the table. I could not sit down at Wilmington or at Weldon without entering into a contest, which I did not desire to do. My colleague, the gentleman who so eloquently spoke on this subject the other day [Robert Brown Elliott] a few months ago entered a restaurant at Wilmington and sat down to be served, and while there a gentleman stepped up to him and said, "You cannot eat here." All the other gentlemen upon the railroad as passengers were eating there; he had only twenty minutes, and was compelled to leave the restaurant or have a fight for it. He showed fight, however, and got his dinner; but he has never been back there since. Coming here last week I felt we did not desire to draw revolvers and present the bold front of warriors, and therefore we ordered our dinners to be brought into the cars, but even there we found the existence of this feeling; for, although we had paid a dollar apiece for our meals, to be brought by the servants into the cars, still there was objection on the part of the railroad people to our eating our meals in the cars, because they said we were putting on airs. They refused us in the restaurant, and then did not desire that we should eat our meals in the cars, although we paid for them. Yet, this was in the noble State of North Carolina.

The colored men of the South do not want the adoption of any force measure. No, they do not want anything by force. All they ask is that you will give them, by statutory enactment under the fundamental law, the right to enjoy precisely the same privileges accorded to every other class of citizens. The gentleman, moreover, has told us that if we pass this civil rights bill we will thereby rob the colored men of the South of the friendship of the whites. Now, I am at a loss to see how the friendship of our white friends can be lost to us by simply saying we should be permitted to enjoy the rights enjoyed by other citizens. I have a higher opinion of the friendship of the southern men than to suppose any such thing. I know them too well. I know their friendship will not be lost by the passage of this bill. For eight years I have been in South Carolina, and I have found this to be the fact, that the higher class, comprising gentlemen of learning and refinement, are less opposed to this measure than are those who do not occupy so high a position in the social scale. I think that there will be no difficulty. But I do think this: that there will be more trouble if we do not have those rights. I regard it as important, therefore, that we should make the law so strong that no man can infringe upon those rights.

But, says the gentleman from North Carolina, some ambitious colored man will, when this law is passed, enter a hotel or railroad car, and thus create disturbance. If it is his right, then there is no vaulting ambition in his enjoying that right. And if he can pay for his seat in a first-class car or his room in a hotel, I see no objection to his enjoying it. But the gentleman says more. He cited, on the school question, the evidence of South Carolina, and says the South Carolina University has been destroyed by virtue of bringing into contact the white students with the colored. I think not. It is true that a small number of students left, but the institution still remains. The buildings are there as erect as ever; the faculty is there as attentive to their duties as ever they were; the students are coming in as they did before. It is true that there is a mixture of students now; that there are colored and white students of law and medicine sitting side by side; it is true that the prejudice of some of the professors was so strong that it drove them out of the institution; but the philanthropy and good sense of others were such that they remained; and thus we have still the institution going on, and because some students have left, it cannot be reasonably argued that the usefulness of the institution has been destroyed. The University of South Carolina has not been destroyed.

But the gentleman says more: The colored man cannot stand, he says, where this antagonism exists, and he deprecates the idea of antagonizing the races. The gentleman says there is no antagonism on his part. I think there is no antagonism so far as the country is concerned. So far as my observation extends, it goes to prove this: that there is a general acceptance upon the part of the larger and better class of the whites of the South of the situation, and that they regard the education and the development of the colored people as essential to their welfare, and the peace, happiness, and prosperity of the whole country. Many of them, including the best minds of the South, are earnestly engaged in seeking to make this great system of education permanent in all the States. I do not believe, therefore, that it is possible there can be such an antagonism. Why, in Massachusetts there is no such antagonism. There, the colored and the white children go to school side by side. In Rhode Island, there is no such antagonism. There, they are educated side by side in the high schools. In New York, in the highest schools, are to be found, of late, colored men and colored women. Even old Democratic New York does not refuse to give the colored people their rights, and there is no antagonism. A few days ago, when in New York, I made it my business to find out what was the position of matters there in this respect. I ascertained that there are, I think, seven colored ladies in the highest school in

New York, and I believe they stand Number 1 in their class, side by side with members of the best and most refined families of the citizens of New York, and without any objection to their presence.

I cannot understand how it is that our southern friends, or a certain class of them, always bring back this old ghost of prejudice and of antagonism. There was a time, not very far distant in the past, when this antagonism was not recognized, when a feeling of fraternization between the white and the colored races existed that made them kindred to each other. But since our emancipation, since liberty has come, and only since—only since we have stood up clothed in our manhood, only since we have proceeded to take hold and help advance the civilization of this nation—it is only since then that this bugbear is brought up against us again. The progress of the age demands that the colored man of this country shall be lifted by law into the enjoyment of every right, and that every appliance which is accorded to the German, to the Irishman, to the Englishman, and every foreigner, shall be given to him; and I shall give some reasons why I demand this in the name of justice.

For two hundred years the colored men of this nation have assisted in building up its commercial interests. There are in this country nearly five millions of us, and for a space of two hundred and forty-seven years we have been hewers of wood and drawers of water; but we have also been with you in promoting all the interests of the country. My distinguished colleague, who defended the civil rights of our race the other day on this floor, set this forth so clearly that I need not dwell upon it at this time.

I propose to state just this: that we have been identified with the interests of this country from its very foundation. The cotton crop of this country has been raised and the hands of our race have tilled its rice-fields. All along as the march of progress, as the march of commerce, as the development of your resources have been widening and expanding and spreading, as your vessels have gone on every sea, with the stars and stripes waving over them, and carrying your commerce everywhere, there, the black man's labor has gone to enrich your country and to augment the grandeur of your nationality. This was done in the time of slavery. And if, for the space of time I have noted, we have been hewers of wood and drawers of water; if we have made your cotton-fields blossom as the rose; if we have made your rice-fields wave with luxuriant harvests; if we have made your corn-fields rejoice; if we have sweated and toiled to build up the prosperity of the whole country by the productions of our labor, I submit, now that the war has made a change, now that we are free—I submit to the nation whether it is not fair and right that we should come in and enjoy to the fullest extent our freedoms and liberty.

A word now as to the question of education: I know that, indeed, some of our republican friends are even a little weak on the school clause of this bill; but, the education of the race, the education of the nation, is paramount to all other considerations. I regard it important that the colored people should take their place in the educational march of this nation, and I would suggest that there should be no discrimination. It is against discrimination in this particular that we complain. If you look over the reports of superintendents of schools in the several States, you will find, I think, evidences sufficient to warrant Congress passing the civil rights bill as it now stands. The report of the commissioner of education of California shows that, under the operation of law and of prejudice, the colored children of that State are practically excluded from schooling. Here is a case where a large class of children is growing up in our midst in a state of ignorance and semi-barbarism. Take the report of the superintendent of education of Indiana, and you will find that while efforts have been made in some places to educate the colored children, yet the prejudice is so great that it debars the colored children from enjoying all the rights which they ought to enjoy under the law. In Illinois, too, the superintendent of education makes this statement: that, while the law guarantees education to every child, yet such are the operations among the school trustees that they almost ignore, in some places, the education of colored children.

All we ask is that you, the legislators of the nation, shall pass a law so strong and so powerful that no one shall be able elude it and destroy our rights under the Constitution and laws of our country. That is all we ask. But the gentleman from North Carolina [Mr. Vance] asks that the colored man shall place himself in an attitude to receive his rights. What attitude can we assume? We tilled your soil during the rude shock of war until our hour came; we were docile during that long dark night, waiting patiently the coming day. In the Southern States during that war our men and women stood behind their masters; they tilled the soil, and there were no insurrections in all the broad lands of the South; the wives and daughters of the slave owners were as sacred then as they were before; and the history of the war does not record a single event, a single instance, in which the colored people were unfaithful, even in slavery; nor does the history of the war record the fact that on the other side, on the side of the Union, there were any colored men who were not willing at all times to give their lives for their country. Upon both sides we waited patiently. I was a student at Wilberforce University, in Ohio, when the tocsin of war was sounded, when Fort Sumter was fired upon, and I never shall forget the thrill that ran through my soul when I thought of the coming consequences of that shot. There were one hundred and fifteen of us, students at that university, who, anxious to vindicate the stars and stripes, made up a company, and offered our services to the governor of Ohio; and we were told that this was a white man's war and that the Negro had nothing to do with it. We returned docile—patient, waiting, casting our eyes to the heavens whence help always comes. We knew that there would come a period in the history of this nation when our strong black arms would be needed. We waited patiently; we waited until Massachusetts, through her noble governor, sounded the alarm, and we hastened then to hear the summons and obey it.

I before remarked, we were peaceful on both sides. When the call was made on the side of the Union we were ready; when the call was made for us to obey orders on the other side, in the Confederacy, we humbly performed our tasks, and waited patiently. But the time came when we were called upon; and, I ask, who can say that when that call was made, the colored men did not respond as readily and as rapidly as did any other class of your citizens? I need not speak of the history of this bloody war. It will carry down to coming generations the valor of our soldiers on the battlefield. Fort Wagner will stand forever as a monument of that valor, and until Vicksburg shall be wiped from the galaxy of battles in the great contest for human liberty that valor will be recognized.

And for what was the Great War made? The gentleman from North Carolina [Mr. Vance] announced before he sat down, in answer to an interrogatory by a gentleman on this side of the House, that they went into the war conscientiously before God. So be it. Then we simply come and plead conscientiously before God that these are our rights, and we want them. We plead conscientiously before God, believing that these are our rights by inheritance, and by the inexorable decree of Almighty God. We believe in the Declaration of Independence that all men are born free and equal, and are endowed by their Creator with certain inalienable rights, among which are life, liberty, and the pursuit of happiness. And we further believe that to secure those rights governments are instituted. And we further believe that when governments cease to secure those ends the people should change them.

I have been astonished at the course that the gentlemen on the other side have taken in discussing this bill. They plant themselves right behind the Constitution, and declare that the rights of the state ought not to be invaded. Now, if you will take the history of the War of the Rebellion, as published by the Clerk of this House, you will see that in 1860 the whole country, each side, was earnest in seeking to make such amendments to the Constitution as would forever secure slavery and keep the Union together under the circumstance. The resolution passed, and the sentiments expressed in speeches at that time, if examined by gentlemen, will be found to bear out all that I have indicated. It was felt in 1860 that anything that would keep the "wayward sisters" from going astray was desirable. They were then ready and willing to make any amendments. And now, when the civil rights of our race are hanging upon the issue, they on the other side are not willing to concede to us such amendments as will guarantee them; indeed, they seek to impair the force of existing amendments to the Constitution of the United States, which would carry out the purpose.

I think it is proper and just that the Civil Rights Bill should be passed. Some think it would be better to modify it, to strike out the school clause, or to so modify it that some of the State constitutions should not be infringed upon. I regard it essential to us, and the people of this country, that we should be secured in this if in nothing else. I cannot regard that our rights will be secured until the jury box and the schoolroom, those great palladiums of our liberty, shall have been opened to us. Then we will be willing to take our chances with other men. We do not want any discrimination to be made. If discrimination is made in regard to schools, then there will be accomplished just what we are fighting against. If you say that the schools in the State of Georgia, for instance, shall be allowed to discriminate against colored people, then you will have discrimination made against us. We do not want any discrimination. I do not ask any legislation for the colored people of this country that is not applied to the white people. All that we ask is equal laws, equal legislation, and equal rights throughout the length and breadth of this land.

The gentleman from North Carolina [Mr. Vance] also says that the colored men should not come here, begging at the doors of Congress for their rights. I agree with him. We do not come here begging for our rights. We come here clothed in the garb of American citizenship. We come demanding our rights in the name of justice. We come, with no arrogance on our part, asking that this great nation, which laid the foundations of civilization and progress more deeply and more securely than any other nation on the face of the earth, guarantee us protection from outrage. We come here, five million people—more than composed this whole nation when it had its great Tea Party in Boston Harbor, and demanded its rights at the point of the bayonet, asking that unjust discriminations against us be forbidden. We come here in the name of justice, equity, and law, in the name of our children, in the name of our country, petitioning for our rights.

Our rights will yet be accorded to us, I believe, from the feeling that has been exhibited on this floor of the growing sentiment of the country. Rapid as the weaver's shuttle, swift as the lightning's flash, such progress is being made that our rights will be accorded to us ere long. I believe that the nation is perfectly willing to accord this measure of justice, if only those who represent the people here would say the word. Let it be proclaimed that henceforth all the children of this land shall be free; that the stars and stripes, waving overall, shall secure to everyone, equal rights, and the nation will say "amen." Let the Civil Rights Bill be passed this day, and five million black men, women, and children, all over the land, will begin a new song of rejoicing, and the thirty-five million noble-hearted Anglo-Saxons will join the shout of joy. Thus, will the great mission be fulfilled of giving to all the people equal rights?

Inasmuch as we have toiled with you in building up this nation; inasmuch as we have suffered side by side with you in the war; inasmuch as we have together passed through affliction and pestilence, let there be now a fulfillment of the sublime thought of our fathers—let all men enjoy equal liberty and equal rights. In this hour, when you are about to put the capstone on the mighty structure of government, I ask you to grant us this measure, because it is right. Grant this, and we shall go home with our hearts filled with gladness. I want to "shake hands over the bloody chasm." The gentleman from North Carolina has said he desires to have forever buried the memory of the recent war. I agree with him. Representing a South Carolina constituency, I desire to bury forever the tomahawk. I have voted in this House with a free heart to declare universal amnesty. Inasmuch as general amnesty has been proclaimed I would hardly have expected there would be any objection on this floor to the Civil Rights Bill, giving to all men the equal rights of citizens. There should be no more contests. Amnesty and civil rights should go together. Gentlemen on the other side will admit that we have been faithful; and now, when we propose to bury the hatchet, let us shake hands upon this measure of justice; and if heretofore we have been enemies, let us live as friends now and forever.

Our wives and our children have high hopes and aspirations; their longings for manhood and womanhood are equal to those of any other race. The same sentiment, of patriotism and of gratitude, the same spirit of national pride that animates the hearts of other citizens, animates theirs. In the name of the dead soldiers of our race, whose bodies lie at Petersburg and on other battlefields of the South; in the name of the widows and orphans they have left behind; in the name of the widows of the Confederate soldiers who fell upon the same fields, I beseech you to let this righteous act be done. I appeal to you in the name of God and humanity to give us our rights, for we ask nothing more.

In response to his southern white colleagues who opposed the Civil Rights Bill, Cain disputed the notion that whites had suffered because of civil rights for blacks following the war. He rejected the argument that the races could not live together in peace. He placed his argument in a rational, economic, and religious context to explain that it was possible for the races to live together in harmony. He pointed out that "Almighty God" had placed blacks and whites on the same continent to show that different people could be united in one community. Cain also denounced the notion that blacks should be returned to Africa. In addition to regarding the United States as the home of African Americans, he argued that they played a vital economic

*role in the South, and whites there did not want to drive
them away.*

CIVIL RIGHTS
January 24, 1874

I had supposed "this cruel war was over," and that we had entered upon an era of peace, prosperity, and future success as a nation. I had supposed that after the sad experience of more than five years, after we had sought to heal the wounds the war had made, after we had passed the amnesty bill, and, as we thought, had entered upon the smooth, quiet road of future prosperity, we would meet on a common level in the halls of Congress, and that no longer would we brood over the past; that we would strike out a line of policy, a new national course, and thus succeed in laying broad and deep the foundations of the future welfare of this country; that every man, of every race, of every section of this country, might shake hands and go forward in national progress.

I regret, however, that it again becomes my lot to answer a member from a neighboring State—North Carolina. It was my misfortune a few Saturdays ago to have to answer a gentleman from the same State [Mr. Robert Brank Vance] in relation to strictures upon my race. I regret that it becomes my duty again, simply in defense of what I regard as a right—in defense of the race to which I belong—to meet the arguments of another gentleman from North Carolina [William McKendree Robbins] to show, if I can, their fallacy, and to prove they are not correct. The gentleman starts out by saying that if we pass the pending Civil Rights Bill it may indeed seem pleasant to the northern people, but to his section, and to the South, it will be death. I do not think he is correct for the reason that they have, in the South, suffered a great many more terrible things than civil rights, and still live. I think if so harmless a measure as the Civil Rights Bill, guaranteeing to every man of the African race equal rights with other men, would bring death to the South, then certainly that noble march of Sherman to the sea would have fixed them long ago.

I desire to answer a few of the strictures which the, gentleman has been pleased to place upon us. He states that the Civil Rights Bill will be death to that section. I cannot see it in that light. We lived together before the war—four million colored men, women, and children, with the whites of the South—and there was no special antagonism then. There might have been some friction in some places and in some cases, but no special antagonism between the two races in the South. I fail, therefore, to see the force of the gentleman's argument. I would like to ask why, in all conscience, after the measures of education, these noble efforts to educate these "barbarians," as he terms us, for two hundred years or more—after all the earnest efforts on their part, with their superior civilization, and all the appliances which the gentleman from North Carolina [Mr. Robbins] claims were brought to bear on these "barbarians"—I ask why there was no such antagonism then, but just at this time? If it were true that such philanthropic efforts have been put forth for the education and improvement of the black race, there would be no occasion for antagonism. It is, I believe, a law of education to assimilate, to bring together, to harmonize discordant elements, to bring about oneness of feeling and sentiment, to develop similarity of thought, similarity of action, and thus to carry forward the people harmoniously. That does not seem to have been the case, if the argument of the gentleman from North Carolina is correct. Now, look at the fallacy of the gentleman's argument. This race of barbarians, in spite of all their disadvantages, had been educated to such an extent that the white community of the South was not afraid of them after their emancipation. Is not that correct?

The gentleman further states that the Negro race is the world's stage actor; the comic dancer all over the land; that he laughs and he dances. Well he may; there are more reasons for his laughing and dancing now than ever before. There are more substantial reasons why he should be happy now than during all the two hundred years prior to this time. Now he dances as an African; then he crouched as a slave. The gentleman further states that not more than eighteen hundred Negroes were killed during the four years of the war. The gentleman forgets some battles; he forgets Vicksburg; I presume he does not remember Petersburg; he does not know anything about Fort Pillow. He knows nothing about all the great achievements of the black men while Sherman's army was moving on to victory. He forgets who entered Charleston first; he forgets who entered Richmond first; he forgets all this in blindness of his prejudice against a race of men who have vindicated themselves so nobly on the battlefield. But I will grant the gentleman the charity of dwelling no longer on that point.

The gentleman states that during the struggle for freedom four million Negroes lifted no hand to liberate themselves; that no stroke was made by them to deliver themselves from their thralldom; yet, a few moments afterward he makes the statement that their kind-heartedness prevented them from rising up and destroying the wives and children of the rebel soldiers who were at the front. I accept the admission. Too much nobleness and charity dwell in the black man's heart for him to strike down helpless women and children when he has a chance to do so. No; though the liberty of our race was dear to us, we would not purchase it at such a dastard price as the slaying of helpless women and children, while their husbands and fathers were away. I would scorn the men of my race forever if they had lifted their hands at such a period as that, against helpless women and children, who were waiting in silent anxiety the return of their natural and lawful protectors. Our strong black arms might have destroyed every vestige of their homes; our torches might have kindled a fire that would have lighted up the whole South, so that every southern man fighting in the

Confederate Army would have hastened back to find his home in ashes. But our race had such nobleness of heart as to forbear in an hour of such extremity, and leave those men their wives and children. I mean no disrespect to the gentleman, but I think the facts will bear me out in the statement that on every occasion on the battlefield where the black man met the white man of the South there was no flinching, no turning back, on the part of the black man. He bravely accepted his part in the struggle for liberty or death.

The gentleman says he still looks upon the whites as the superior race. That may be the case in some respect; but, if they educated us they certainly should not find fault with us if we follow out what they have taught, and show ourselves obedient servants. The gentleman states that we would make no movement to achieve our liberty. Why, the education those gentlemen gave the southern slaves was of a peculiar kind. What schoolhouse in the South was open to the colored race? You cannot point to one institution in the nation that was opened to slaves. You cannot name an academy where you educated black men and black women as lawyers or doctors, or in any other department of science or art. Point out the county that provided such education. Give us the name of the district. Give the name of the school commissioner. Name the teacher. I will name one. Her name was Miss Douglas. And for the attempt to educate those of our race she was incarcerated, and remained there for five years. That is the only instance, so far as I remember, of the education of the colored people of the South.

Examine the laws of the South, and you will find that it was a penal offense for anyone to educate the colored people there. Yet these gentlemen come here and upbraid us with our ignorance and our stupidity. Yet you robbed us for two hundred years. During all that time we toiled for you. We have raised your cotton, your rice, and your corn. We have attended your wives and your children. We have made wealth for your support and your education, while we were slaves, toiling without pay, without the means of education, and hardly of sustenance. And yet you upbraid us for being ignorant—call us a horde of barbarians! Why, it is ill becoming in the gentleman to tell us of our barbarism, after he and his people have been educating us for two hundred years. If New England charity and benevolence had not accomplished more than your education has done we would still be in that condition. I thank the North for the charity and nobleness with which it has come to our relief. The North has sent forth those leading ideals, which have spread like lightning over the land and the Negro was not so dumb and not so obtuse that he could not catch the light, and embrace its blessings and enjoy them. I hurl back with contempt all the aspersions of the gentleman on the other side against my race. There is but very little difference, even now, between the condition of the whites of the South and the condition of the blacks of the South. I have given some attention to the statistics of education in the Southern States. I find this pregnant fact, that there is about 12 percent more ignorance existing among the whites in the South than there is among the colored people in the South, notwithstanding the slavery of the colored race. I wish I had the reports here, that I might show the gentleman how the facts stand in reference to his own State especially, because, if I remember correctly, his State shows there is a preponderating aggregate of ignorance in the State of North Carolina, amounting to 60 percent and upward, compared with the entire number of the inhabitants in that sta t e .

Tell us of our ignorance—the ignorance of the colored race. Why, it appears to me to be presumption on the part of the gentleman to state that we— we whom they have wronged, whom they have outraged, whom they have robbed, whose sweat and toil they have had the benefit of for two hundred years; whose labor, whose wives, whose children, have been at their beck and call—I say it ill becomes them to taunt us now with our barbarism and our ignorance. If he will open to us the schoolhouse, give us some chance, we would not have to measure arms with him now. But even now, although there is such disparity between us and him so far as relates to education and resources, even now we fear not a comparison in the condition of education in the last eight years between the whites and the blacks of North Carolina.

The gentleman, moreover, states that the reason why they did not educate the colored race was that the colored man was not ready. Not ready. If I had that gentleman upon the floor, with my foot upon his neck, and holding a lash over him, with his hands tied, with him bound hand and foot, would he expect that I should boast over him and tell him, "You are a coward. You are a traitor because you do not resist me?" Would he expect me to lash his back while I had him under my foot with his hands tied? Would he tell me that, in conscience, I would be doing justice to him? Oh, no, no! And yet such was the condition in which he had my race. Why, the whipping post, the thumbscrew, and the lash were the great means of education in the South. These were the schoolhouses, these were the academies, and these were the great instruments of education, of which the gentleman boasts, for the purpose of bringing these barbarians into civilization. When men boast, they ought to have something to boast about. When I boast I shall boast of some noble deed. I will boast not of the wrongs inflicted upon the weak; I will boast not of the outrages inflicted upon the indigent; I will not boast of lashing the weak and trampling under foot any class of people, who ought to have my sympathy, nor will I reproach them for being ignorant, when they have been kept away from every weans to educate them.

He says we are not ready for it. How long would it have taken us to get ready under their kind of teaching? H o w long, O Lord, how long! How long would it have taken them to educate us under the thumbscrew, to educate us with the whip; to educate us with the lash, with instruments of torture, to educate us without a home? How long would it have taken to educate us under their system? We had no wives; we had no children; they belonged to the gentleman and his class. We were homeless; we were friendless, although those stars and stripes hanging over your head ought to have been our protection. That emblem of the Declaration of Independence, initiated by the fathers of the Republic, that all men are born free and equal, ought to have been our protection. Yet they were to us no stars of hope, and the stripes were only stripes of our condemnation.

The gentleman talked something, I believe, about buzzards or crows taking the place of our brave eagle. The crow would, I think, more beautifully represent the condition of the South now—the croaking bird, you know. They have been croaking ever since the rebellion came on, and they have been croaking against emancipation and the Constitution ever since. They are a nation of croakers, so to speak. Like the crow they are cawing, cawing, cawing; eternally cawing. The gentleman says the Negro has done less for himself than any other race of men on earth; and he cites the German, the Irishman, the Scotchman, the Englishman, and the Frenchman, as having done something. But he forgets that the men of those nationalities come from stations that are the proud, educated, refined, noble, advancing nations of the earth. He forgets that those nations of which he speaks, from which those men have sprung, have given, and are still giving, to the world some of the brightest minds that ever adorned the galaxy of human intellect.

But he tells us that the Negro never produced anything. Well, it may be that in the gentleman's opinion Negroes have never produced anything. I wonder if the gentleman ever read history. Did he ever hear tell of any persons of the name of Hannibal, of Hannor, of Hamilcar, of Euclid—all great men of ancient times—of Esop, and others? No, for that kind of literature does not come to North Carolina. It flourishes on the free mountain peaks and in the academies of the North. That kind of literature comes to such men as Wendell Phillips, as William Lloyd Garrison, as Charles Sumner, as Benjamin Butler, and other distinguished men, men of the North, men that are thinkers, men that do not croak, but let the eagle ever soar high in the conception of high ideas. They are ideas that belong to a free people; they are not consistent with or consonant with slavery. No, they do not tell the Negro of Euclid, the man that in his joy cried out, "Eureka, I have found it"; no, that is not the language for the slave. No, that is not the language they teach by the whip and the thumbscrew.

The gentleman says that the black men in the South, since emancipation and enfranchisement, have put bad men into office. No one regrets it more than I do, but they were not colored men after all. They were not black men, those bad men in office, who have done so much to deteriorate the value of the country. They did not elect our distinguished friend [Mr. Vance] from North Carolina by black votes. They did not elect Mr. William Steele Holman

[Indiana], or a gentleman of some such name, in North Carolina. They did not run the State in debt. They were not the men who took the cash; they were simply the mudsills that did the voting, while another class of individuals did the stealing. I beg to say that we did the best we could; and one of the results of our education was that we had been taught to trust white men in the South. We trusted them, and if they did wrong it was no fault of ours. I presume the gentleman who addressed the House today had some colored constituents who voted for him and sent him here. I will not dare to say, however, that he is a bad man. He may be one of the very best of men; but I think he has some very bad ideas, so far as my race is concerned.

The gentleman says that this is a white man's land and government. He says it has been committed to them in a sacred relationship. I ask in all conscience what becomes of our black men and women and children, to the number of five million; have we no rights? Ought we to have no privileges; ought we not to have the protection of the law? We do not ask for any more. The gentleman harps upon the idea of social equality. Well, he has not had so much experience of that as I have had, or as my race have had.

We have some objections to social equality ourselves; very grave ones. For even now, though freedom has come, it is a hard matter, a very hard matter, to keep sacredly guarded the precincts of our sacred homes. But I will not dwell upon that. The gentleman knows more about that than I do.

The gentleman wishes that we should prepare ourselves to go to Africa, or to the West Indies, or somewhere else. I want to enunciate this doctrine upon this floor—you have brought us here, and here we are going to stay. We are not going one foot or one inch from this land. Our mothers and our fathers, and our grandfathers, and great-grandfathers have died here. Here we have sweated. Here we have toiled. Here we have made this country great and rich by our labor and toil. It is mean of you now to want to drive us away, after having taken all our toil for two hundred years. Just think of the magnitude of these gentlemen's hearts. After having taken all our toil for two hundred years; after having sold our wives and children like so many cattle in the shambles; after having reared the throne of great king cotton on our labors; after we have made their rice fields wave with luxuriant harvest while they were fighting against the Government and keeping us in bondage—now we are free and they want us to go away. Shame on you!

We are not going away; we are going to stay here. We propose to stay here and work out this problem. We believe that God Almighty has made of one blood all the nations upon the face of the earth. We are made just like whites' are made. I stretch out my arms. I have two of them, as you have. Look at your ears; I have two of them. I have two eyes, two nostrils, one mouth, and two feet. I stand erect like you. I am clothed with humanity like you. I think. I reason. I talk. I express my views, as you do. Is there any difference between us? Not so far as our manhood is concerned, unless it is in this: that our opinions differ, and mine are a little higher up than yours. The gentleman states that this idea of all men being created equal is a fallacy, announced some years ago by Thomas Jefferson, that old foolhardy man, who announced so many ideas that have been woven into the woof of the nation, who announced so many foolish things that have made this nation strong, and great, and powerful. If lie was in error, I accept the error with pleasure. If he was a foolish man, I would to God that North Carolina had been baptized in that foolishness about two hundred years ago.

The gentleman also states that if you pass this bill your power over the South would pass away—that the power of the Republican party in the South would pass away. Let me tell the gentleman that behind this bill are nine hundred thousand voters; that, like the warriors of the tribe of Benjamin, every one of them is left-handed and can "sling a stone at a hair's breadth"; that each will come up stronger and mightier and more infused with power than ever before when you pass this bill giving them their rights, as other men have them. They will come up as never before to the support of the Republican party, and they will make the South a source of joy and gladness. The gentleman also talks about the colored people deteriorating. Who tills your land? Who plants your corn? Who raises your cotton? I have been in the South during the last ten years. I have traveled over the Southern States, and have seen who did this work. Going along I saw the white men do the smoking, chewing tobacco, riding horses, playing cards, spending money, while the colored men are tilling the soil, and bringing the cotton, rice, and other products to market.

I do not believe the gentleman from North Carolina wants us to go to Africa; I do not believe it. It was a slip of the tongue; he does not mean that the black people should leave North Carolina. If they did you would see such an exodus of white people from the State as you never saw before, for they would follow them wherever they might go. We feel that we are part and parcel of this great nation, and we propose to stay here and solve this problem of whether the black race and the white race can live together in this country. I can see no reason why not, if they contribute their quota to the advancement of progress and civilization. The mechanics of the South are almost altogether colored people. The carpenters, the machinists, the engineers—nearly all the mechanics in the Southern States are colored people. Why can we not stay here and work out this problem? I ask Congress to pass this bill for the reason that it would settle this question, once and forever. The gentleman says that he does not desire that the colored people shall be crowded into the schools of the white people. Well, I do not think that they would be harmed by it; some few of them might be. But experience has taught us that it is not true that great harm will come from any such measure. I think, therefore, that if we pass this bill we will be doing a great act of justice, we will settle for all time the question of the rights of all people. And until that question is settled there cannot be that peace and harmony in the country that is necessary to its success.

The gentleman says the colored people and the white people are living together now in North Carolina in amicable relations. I am glad for that admission, for he rounded off all that he had said before by that last sentence. He said that the two races could not live together; yet, at the close of his speech he says that the whites and blacks are now living in North Carolina in amicable relations. If they are now living in peace, why would they not hereafter? Will peace and good order be destroyed because all are to have their rights? I do not think so.

I close with this thought: I believe the time is coming when the Congress of the United States, when the whole nation, will recognize the importance of passing this bill in order to settle this question once and forever. I regard the interests of the black man in this country as identical with the interests of the white man. I would have that set forth so clearly and unmistakably that there should be no antagonism between the races, no friction that should destroy their peace and prosperity. I believe Almighty God has placed both races on this broad theater of activity, where thoughts and opinions are freely expressed, where we may grasp every idea of manhood, where we may take hold of every truth and develop every art and science that can advance the prosperity of the nation. I believe God designed us to live here together on this continent, and in no other place, to develop this great idea that all men are the children of one Father. We are here to work out the grand experiment of the homogeneity of nations, the grand outburst of the greatness of humanity, by the development in us of the rights that belong to us, and the performance of the duties that we owe each other.

Our interests are bound up in this country. Here we intend to stay and work out the problem of progress and education and civilization. I say to the gentleman from North Carolina [Mr. Robbins] and to the gentleman from Virginia [John Thomas Harris] and to the gentleman from New York [Samuel Sullivan Cox] who discussed civil rights the other day and to the gentlemen from the other states that we are going to remain in this country side by side with the white race. We desire to share in your prosperity and to stand by you in adversity. In advancing the progress of the nation we will do our part; and if the country should again be involved in the devastation of war, we will do our part in the struggle. We propose to identify ourselves with this nation, which has done more than any other on earth to illustrate the great idea that all races of men may dwell together in harmony, working out together the problem of advancement and civilization and liberty.

We will drive the buzzards away; we will scare the crows back to North Carolina. We will take the eagle as the emblem of liberty; we will take that honored flag which has been borne through the heat of a thousand battles. Under its folds Anglo-Saxons and African Americans can together work out a common destiny, until universal liberty, as announced by this nation, shall be known throughout the world.

3

Henry Plummer Cheatham (1857–1935)
House of Representatives, North Carolina

Republican

Fifty-first and Fifty-second Congresses
March 4, 1889, to March 3, 1893

Born into slavery in 1857 near Henderson, a town in Vance (formerly Granville) County in North Carolina, Henry Plummer Cheatham stood little chance of becoming an educated citizen. If he had any opportunities at all, it was those afforded him by his prominent white "father," who apparently protected him from some of the horrors of slavery. However, he could never be certain about the care his father would provide. Henry, with a strong desire for learning, worked diligently to make his own dreams come true. As soon as he was able to do so he attended a public school in Henderson. With the help of Robert A. Jenkins, a white friend, Cheatham enrolled in the college preparatory program at Shaw University, Raleigh, one of the first colleges established to educate African Americans. In 1882, he earned the bachelor of arts degree with honors from Shaw, and in 1887 was awarded an honorary master of arts degree. Although Cheatham read law in the office of Robert E. Hancock, Jr., a white Republican, he would never practice law, presumably because he did not have time to do so.

Upon graduation from Shaw, Cheatham began his career as teacher. His first assignment was as principal of the Plymouth Normal School in eastern North Carolina. His first wife, Louise Cherry, who was also a Shaw graduate, taught music at the school. (Laura Joyner was his second wife.) While Cheatham would remain a teacher throughout his life, he began his foray into politics in

Henderson in 1884, where after Reconstruction he was twice elected registrar of deeds for Vance County. Cheatham also used his political influence to help establish an orphanage for black children in Oxford, a community located near his hometown. In 1889, Cheatham entered national politics as a member of the Fifty-first Congress where he served until 1893. By the time of his election black lawmakers were disappearing from Congress. Cheatham was the only black member of the House when the session started, though other blacks elected from Virginia and South Carolina would soon join him.

Cheatham played the "freshman representative" role, and said nothing on the floor during his first session. His background as a teacher landed him on the House Committee on Education. He introduced a bill for the federal government to appropriate funds to support public schools, which would benefit mainly the economically depressed South. While the committee looked favorably upon the bill, the measure did not reach the floor of the House because most congressmen viewed public education as a state responsibility. Cheatham used his experience as a teacher to better inform his white colleagues on the achievements of African Americans. He supported a bill to appropriate $100,000 for the Chicago Exhibition in 1893 to showcase post-emancipation black achievements in industry, the arts, and agriculture. Cheatham said he wanted to "show evidence of the development and progress made by the colored people since their emancipation." The House, however, rejected the bill, possibly because of its unwillingness to sponsor such an event for African Americans.

In the Fifty-second Congress, Cheatham served on the Committee on Expenditures and Public Buildings. He sponsored a bill to appropriate funds to construct public buildings in Henderson. Cheatham also supported such causes as federal aid for public education, an anti-tax lard bill, trust regulation, and the Silver Purchase Bill. He called for federal funds to aid Congressman Robert Smalls and his crew for their meritorious service in the Civil War. Smalls and his men had captured a Confederate vessel, the *Planter*, and sailed it to a Union port. Black congressmen generally believed that Smalls and the crew did not receive equitable compensation for delivering this prize of war to the Union. Cheatham and his black colleagues made repeated, but futile, efforts to pass such legislation. He also introduced legislation to cover the losses of depositors who had money in the failed Freedmen's Savings and Trust Company (or Freedmen's Bank.) He urged the creation of a biracial panel to study black society, recommending that they publish a report on African-American progress. He insisted that the government establish a display in the office of the adjutant general highlighting black military service. Congress, however, did not approve these measures. Cheatham proudly accepted his role as a black leader; yet, he served all of his constituents. As he put it, he did what would "be best not for one race or the other, but for both equally." Like modern-day legislators, Cheatham used his influence to obtain federal appointments for his supporters.

As Reconstruction came to an end, blacks in Congress became a vanishing breed. Cheatham was among the last black American's to serve in Congress during the nineteenth century. He prevailed in the 1890 election over his Democratic challenger. In the election of 1892, however, he lost to Democrat Frederick A. Woodward. Cheatham ran for national office again in 1894, but lost the election to his brother-in-law, George H. White, who would be the last African American to serve in Congress during this era. Nominated by President William McKinley in 1897, Cheatham served a four-year term as a recorder of deeds in the national capital, a position he held until 1901. He returned to Oxford in 1907 to lead the orphanage he had helped to establish. He also served as president of the Negro Association of North Carolina, as well as lecturing and engaging in agricultural pursuits. He died in Oxford on November 29, 1935.

Cheatham defended the interests of small southern farmers who after the Civil War had actually gained new markets for cottonseeds. It was serendipitous. Cholera, a disease that killed off hogs, hit many farmers. Large farmers seemingly benefited from the epidemic, as prices rose in the dwindling lard industry. Once researchers discovered that they could make synthetic lard by combing hog fat with cottonseed, small farmers hoped to cash in on the market. Many producers of compound lard, as they called it, were small black farmers. Mostly large white farmers called for legislation to stamp out compound lard. Cheatham opposed passage of such legislation

COMPOUND LARD
Speech of the Honorable Henry P. Cheatham
August 23, 1890

I do not like to say a word against the report of any committee of this House, nor to differ from the leaders of my party, but I am compelled in this case, representing the constituency I do on this floor, to raise my voice against the adoption of this measure. I wish to indicate why it is that the compounding of cottonseed oil with the other ingredients that go to make up this article of commerce helps the Southern States. Ten or fifteen years ago bacon and lard sold in those States, especially in North Carolina, at prices ranging from 25 to 30 cents a pound, such enormous prices that the poor people could scarcely buy it, the reasons therefore, or at least some of them, being, first, and mainly, on account of their individual poverty and, secondly, on account of the poverty of the communities in which they lived, and, indeed, of the very air which they breathed. Money was scarce and labor had little or no market.

Now, there were two particular things that combined to produce this poverty. They are these: About the time referred to there was a fearful and disastrous epidemic prevailing among the hogs of our section, commonly known as the hog cholera, which in many ways embarrassed and destroyed the flattering and bright hopes of thousands of farmers and mechanics. It devastated the Southern farms, and especially those of the poor men who ordinarily raised their own meat and lard, but who saw their little stock of hogs entirely wiped out by this dreadful and apparently incurable disease. And yet the producers and manufacturers of pure lard, about whom we hear so much in this debate, in the North and West, took advantage of the calamity that thus befell us, and reaped a rich reward in the increased prices they forced us to pay. This, however, we all must admit, is generally the case the world over in business circles. They compelled us to buy their product at their own rates. But after Providence, in its kindness and mercy, placed us in a better shape, taking us out of that suspended and deplorable condition of things, and after the hog cholera had disappeared, when the fattening pens of the country had again been rebuilt and were filled with hogs, the farmers once more commenced to flourish and to prosper, and meat and lard fell to prices ranging from 8 to 10 cents per pound.

But this condition did not last long. A movement was *soon* inaugurated which led to an organization among some of the principal landowners, and a measure was lobbied and railroaded through the State Legislatures commonly known as the "no-fence law." The enactment of this law brought about a radical change in the affairs of the people, compelling the poor farmers of both races, who had hogs from which they expected to raise their meat and cows on which they depended for their milk and butter, to sell or get rid of them, and thus place their food supplies at the mercy of the men who manufactured this commodity or who raised large quantities of pork. Now, I do not think anyone can deny that this class of men took the lead in the movement referred to and maneuvered and almost forced the passage of the "no-fence law." By reason, therefore, of the hardships caused by the passage of this act, many of the poor people of the country were forced to sell out—compelled, almost, to give away their stock. The result was that as the stock of hogs was reduced and the price of lard went up again to 20 to 25 cents per pound.

And go now into certain sections of the cotton belt, especially in my own State, and the disastrous effects of this harsh system are visible on all hands. There you will see the stock of hogs of the poor farmer huddled in pens or tied out on some green spot to find food as best they may, and their cows tied down in the little "meadow patch," both hogs and cows reduced to the smallest number; and few farmers have stock enough to supply their families with meat or lard during the year. In addition to this, by reason of unfortunate crop failures, which have followed each other in almost uninterrupted succession for ten years past, the Southern farmers have been thrown helplessly upon the mercies of the brokers and commission merchants of their sections, and in thousands of cases they have been compelled to mortgage everything, from the farms and stock and growing crops, even to their household and kitchen furniture, for the necessaries of life. Many of them are hopelessly involved, and by reason of the accumulation of indebtedness they have no comfort in the present or hope for the future.

Beside, owing to the disadvantages of the great mortgage and lien system existing in the South, which has brought suffering and even crime to the homes of thousands of our people, which has not been productive of improvement in the condition of the people, but which has begotten suspicions and ill-feeling at home as well as a want of confidence between the moneyed men of the North and the property-owners at the South and has impoverished our people generally, it has become almost impossible for them to get enough, through the system in vogue of the pure-lard men, to provide the necessaries of life for their families. Nevertheless, it is remarkable to see how God, in His own wise way, brought a speedy and timely relief in this new chemical discovery for the benefit of those people, producing to them a substitute from which they could get that of which they were formerly deprived by those high rates. Such was the condition of things until there was introduced in our midst this compound of the cottonseed oil. And today in the Southern States you can get lard, the best and most healthful in the world, suitable for all purposes of domestic consumption, at from 8 to 10 cents per pound.

Our people are, therefore, anxiously waiting to see if their friends in the North will take away from them the last blessing they have in the form of cheap food; a blessing, let me say, which materially affects the colored people's condition at the South, four million of whom were emancipated from the curse of slavery at the close of the late war to live upon their own resources and to commence the race of life without a penny for food or raiment, and without even rented homes to shelter them from the heat of summer or the cold of winter. At the same time they were subjected to all kinds of fraud and rascality, perpetrated upon them, in many instances, by those who pretended to be their friends from the North and who claimed to be sent amongst them for the purpose of seeing that all differences and controversies should be settled fairly and squarely between them and their former masters. In nine cases out of every ten, however, these deceptive and heartless friends, for a few dollars and for the purpose of currying favor with their white brothers, would compromise the poor, ignorant

Negro's interests, to settle the demands and costs of their law courts, and, in fact, seemed determined to carry out literally the divine injunction which says:
For unto every one that hath shall be given, and he shall have abundance: but from him that hath not shall be taken away even that which he hath.

And cast ye the unprofitable servant into outer darkness: there shall be weeping and gnashing of teeth.

These gentlemen were placed at the head of what was then known as the Freedmen's Bureau, the object of which was a good one (to protect the rights of the freedmen); but in nearly every case coming before that bureau it but resulted in deplorable and unfair treatment of him. Notwithstanding all this and other unfriendly and uncalled for brutalities with which the colored people of the South have had to contend and to encounter, they have not at any time become wholly discouraged, nor have they allowed themselves to give up in despair. On the contrary, they have earnestly and incessantly toiled, especially in the great cotton belt of the South, in the hope of a better condition of things. And, although the grand boon of freedom brought with it many responsibilities and hardships, it was still received with hearts overflowing with fervor and gratitude to those who gave it.

The very fact that great sacrifices were necessary to secure and perpetuate the enjoyment of freedom and the rights of citizenship gave a stimulus and impetus to a determined, industrious, and self-reliant policy in business. And in order to give an idea of what the colored people have acquired through their skill, intrepidity, and industry since the war, their many adversities to the contrary notwithstanding, I will here read by States the following statistics. (*The table is not included in this book.*) The amount of property owned by the colored churches in the United States is $16,310,441 and the total amount of property owned by them in all the States is about $263,000,000, and I think there is but little doubt that most of the wealth acquired by the colored people in the South since their emancipation is due to the success of the cotton farms, as their staple product.

The project of manufacturing lard out of cottonseed oil, on account of its superfine qualities, has brought it in competition with the great hog's-lard market of the North and West, thereby causing a decline in those lard markets, which justly places it in the reach of even the humblest and poorest farmer everywhere. It is now one of the most essential necessaries of life, and therefore at this time ought not to be burdened with a tax. That which most oppresses the laboring classes of the South and hinders their advancement more than any other cause is the price they are compelled to pay for their food supplies. Producing as they do inadequate supplies of food, and dependent largely upon other portions of the country, has become a source of no little anxiety and concern. Their food accounts are really matters of most serious import, needing, as they invariably must, their constant watchfulness and attention. And when it becomes apparent to both rich and poor that lard made of cotton seed oil and other pure and nutritious ingredients is as palatable, serviceable, and healthful as hog's lard or any other lard, and at the same time will save the workingman at the end of the month five or ten dollars in his market accounts, he will, in nine cases out of every ten, buy the compound brand. If he is a poor man he will make a payment of that difference of five or ten dollars on his little home every month, while if he is a rich man he will have that five or ten dollars credited to his regular bank account. Thus it is clear that this cheap commodity materially benefits both classes.

The cotton-planter is not only benefited by these cheap rates in lard, but he likewise finds at home a ready and profitable market for his cottonseed. This part of his product, as is well known, was prior to this chemical discovery of but little value to him. In fact, it was used only for compost purposes. It has been estimated that the cottonseed from one bag of cotton will average from $5 to $6 in value, although heretofore the same quantity of cottonseed only brought about $2 per bag. Hence it will be readily seen that the difference in value of cotton seed taken from any one of these farms in the State will purchase for that family a quantity of lard sufficient for only a year's use. I do not object to branding all compound lards, thereby letting them show exactly what they are, but I do seriously object to the passage of any measure the sole purpose of which is to tax one commodity out of existence for the good of one whose market price is more expensive to the consumer and whose quality is in no way superior to the commodity taxed. The gentleman from Iowa [Edwin Hurd Conger] has seen fit to put upon exhibition here samples of the compound lard in question, and although he and other gentlemen who favor this bill seek to disabuse our minds of its high reputation and actual worth, it nevertheless shows, upon a fair examination and upon its merits, that it has forced its way into the markets of the country and justly antagonizes and competes with hog's lard or any other lard compound in the markets of the world.

Up to the present time I had hoped that the tariff provisions in the platform of the Republican party meant to protect all of our home industries, especially when competing with those coming from abroad. But I did not think it was meant to discourage any home industry, no matter in what section of our country the same had been established, nor to discriminate absolutely against one section of the United States to its disparagement and commercial loss to benefit another part of it. The leading incentive of the great tariff system of America has always been to stimulate and protect home industries, and this has become the spirit of the age. If this "lard-compound" industry was flooding the markets of our country from some foreign land and on account of its nutritious and healthful composition it hindered the sale of similar commodities manufactured here, Congress would have both a legal and moral right to enact a law restricting by taxation the privilege to sell it in the markets of this country. But as against two honest and lawful home industries, both contending and rivaling each other for supremacy in the markets of the United States, it is hard to satisfactorily explain to the people of this country reasons for this discrimination, unless it is for the purpose of unfairly preventing and neutralizing the existence of one of the most popular and aggressive enterprises of its kind, so that the so-called pure-lard industry may have the entire and exclusive sway in the food markets of this country.

I do not oppose this measure because I wish to injure or paralyze to do so. I am actuated by a higher motive. I am pleading for the honest and hard-working businessmen in the South, who have spent their time, talent, and money upon this enterprise, and for suffering and impoverished humanity everywhere, whose wants and necessities are so readily and well provided for under the operations of this great industry-lard compound. I am opposed to this bill because it can be clearly seen that it proposes to establish by legislation the standard of a product which it could not have otherwise attained, and defends the cause of an article which needs no defense, especially if the product is as pure as it is claimed to be by the gentlemen on the other side. Now, if these gentlemen will make careful research of the history of the large packing houses of the cities of Chicago, New York, Cincinnati, St. Louis, Kansas City, Boston, Louisville, Omaha, Nebraska City, Sioux City, Indianapolis, Milwaukee, and others, they will find that it is not the lard compound that so seriously attacks their product or that degrades the standard of American lard.

Permit me to read from the minority report of the committee, which I think will bear me out in this statement: (The transcript is excluded from this book.)

In view of these facts and recognizing the importance of this product to the poor people of the southern States, while, as I have already said, I regret to oppose the report of the able committee that presents this proposition, I shall feel compelled to vote against the bill.

Representative Cheatham joined his colleagues in eulogizing the late Leonidas C. Houk, a congressman from Tennessee. Cheatham offered the obligatory praise one would expect from a statesman. He described Representative Houk as someone who elevated himself, then entered public service. Houk, Cheatham explained, remained approachable to the least of his constituents. While he acknowledged that Houk was a conservative,

Cheatham described him as being committed to the idea that an African American was a citizen of the United States. Houk favored legislation to reimburse depositors who had lost money in the federal Freedmen's Bank.

THE HONORABLE LEONIDAS C. HOUK
January 30, 1892

There have already been so many grand and truthful things said about the distinguished deceased that I shall find it difficult to steer clear of the same channels on order to avoid repetition. However, removal of the name of Honorable Leonidas C. Houk from the membership of this body by the great hand of death was not only a sad and deplorable event with the great State of Tennessee, that had so wisely seen fit to honor him, but his brave, though conservative and eventful, national career, together with the sad manner by which he came to his death, caused the whole country to feel keenly his untimely death. Judge Houk was in many respects a wonderful man; he did not only manage, with his limited means and opportunities, to elevate himself from the humble walks and conditions of life to a more honorable and exalted plane and remained with contentment and ease, but he ventured further.

In his struggles along the rugged and thorny pursuits of time, seeking a share of the honors and laurels of this life, he soon reached the station of usefulness where he had a chance to convince men of the moral and intellectual powers that he possessed. He became an able advocate at the bar, in which sphere he gained for himself a lasting and imperishable reputation, and step by step he ascended the arena of responsibilities and public trust in his State. After serving upon the circuit court bench and in the State Legislature with peculiar adaptation and distinction, he was then honored with thirteen consecutive years in this body. Here he tied and endeared to him the hearts of not only his party friends, but all lovers of fair and just legislation, for upon all such issues, in Congress, he was positive, forcible, and outspoken, and on account of his ardent and unqualified devotion to the best interest of the common people of his district and State he was always more than a match for any scheme or combined political forces to defeat him before the people.

I have been familiarly acquainted with Judge Houk for several years, and there was one particular and grand trait of character about him which I very much admired; out of his broad and liberal heart always poured forth indications of sympathy and willingness to encourage and assist the poor and needy classes of the people, and as such they always looked to him for kind words and protection. The humblest peasant upon the streets could approach him with ease. He was perfectly friendly, courteous, and conservative in his views; he often expressed to me his desire to see our Government assist in some way in the elevation of the poor white and black people of our land. He thought Congress could best accomplish it through some educational measure, and although he was thoroughly conversant and alive upon all great issues before this body and the country, he was, nevertheless, awakened and mindful of the small and minor interests of the people.

He always argued with great force and clearness that the black man of this country had rights as an American citizen, and as such they should be respected and protected, and as further example of his interest in the welfare of the colored people, he thoroughly believed that the United States Government should reimburse the depositors the $3,000,000 which they lost in the United States Freedmen's Savings Bank. For these liberal and just views the colored people in his district and State and in the United States, as far as they knew him, wish to pay through me this tribute of respect to his memory. They believe with me that such noble-hearted men, such lovers of right and justice to all classes and conditions of men, cannot miss their reward in the great and sublime hereafter.

Cheatham, a teacher, urged Congress to consider a bill to fund a display on the achievements of African Americans since emancipation. He thought that people wanted to know if African Americans had made progress since liberation. Cheatham believed that they had and he cited statistics to support this perspective. The exhibition, scheduled at the World's Fair in 1893, would have been a testimony of what individuals, regardless of color, could achieve if given an opportunity.

WORLD'S FAIR EXHIBITION
Achievements of the Negro
May 25, 1892

I regret exceedingly that this question has assumed a hot political phase. I am sure that the colored people did not intend that any politics should surround this request they have made. They did not intend that any partisan feeling should be interjected into this discussion, and I am very sorry that politics have been brought in here.

It seems to me that whenever the colored people of this country ask for anything, something unfortunate intervenes to hinder their getting what they ask.

If this appropriation were granted it would be, as has been said on this floor, a great stimulus and a great encouragement to the colored people. There is no doubt about it. All through the South and in portions of the North they are waiting and watching the movements of Congress during the consideration of this sundry civil bill to see whether Congress will do something for them in this connection. I am sure that the gentleman who introduced this amendment had no idea that one word of a political character would be mentioned. The people who come to Chicago from distant lands will, no doubt, be anxious to see the evidences of the development and progress made by the colored people since their emancipation. One of the things that will be conspicuous and watched for at Chicago in 1893 will be the exhibition of what the Negro, lately a slave, has accomplished.

Although an amendment of this may be subject to a point of order, the only chance for such a publication to be made is for Congress itself to make provision for it. The census of the United States does not give the data that we desire. It does not show the progress that the colored people have made educationally, financially, morally, and socially. It is too imperfect. Nothing is shown by the census in regard to the progress of the Negro in these directions. The adoption of this amendment is not asked in order to give politicians positions-to give them, as has been said, places in which they can make money. It is asked in good faith. We want white and colored men, competent persons, appointed to take a census of the condition of the colored people. And let the results be submitted at Chicago, where the world can see what they have done; for I claim that they have made remarkable progress in this country since their emancipation. I claim for them that, although they have gone through years of hardship, although many of them are still low in the scale of education and business capacity, they are today exhibiting to the world great signs of permanent development and improvement.

We have accumulated in North Carolina, for instance, $10,000,000 worth of property; in South Carolina, $12,000,000 worth; in Mississippi, $18,000,000; in Louisiana, $19,000,000, and so I might go all through the South. And if you encourage us, Mr. Chairman, and stimulate our efforts with the strong arm of the Government there is no telling what a people we will be in time. I appeal to you, then, to lose sight of party feeling in the matter; lose sight of all race feelings, and give us this appropriation that is so much needed. Now, if you say it is not proper to put it into this bill, then give it to us in some other way. We need it, and need it badly, and ought to have it as a matter of recognition. The leaders of churches and schools of the country, the whole civilized world, all ask this consideration of their efforts. You Representatives from the South and the North can give the relief if you will.

Do not let technical rules of order stand in the way. I admit when I made the request that the honorable gentleman from Indiana [William Steele Holman] had a perfect right to make the point of order against the amendment, and that the Chairman of this committee had a perfect right to decide as he did. I want the country to understand all of that. But further, I admit and it will not be questioned that Congress can do this by both branches, and that there will not be a word of blame or complaint from anybody. Now give it to us, gentlemen. We are helpless, so to speak, and we have need of this appropriation. I have said but little this session, I have taken but little of your time. But I am exceedingly anxious that the Democratic and Republican parties shall get together when you come to the Negro and that all will be willing to join in the effort to do something for him.

The Democratic party cannot afford to "hew to the line" and cut the poor Negro because he votes the Republican ticket. You will find strong, level-headed colored men all through the South, if you will go through these States, who constitute a majority of the people, and they are conservative, courteous, hard-laboring men, and will put down wrongdoing as quickly as any white man. All they want is a chance; all they want is recognition, and this recognition at the World's Fair must be given through you, for they cannot get it otherwise.

Now, to go there and give these people no recognition, what would be the result? You would hear complaints from all over the country that the Negro has been ignored; that he has not been treated right; that he was not allowed a chance at the World's Fair. The Congress of the United States, knowing their wants, knowing all that has been presented in their behalf, yet ignores and cuts them down. They certainly would feel like leaving the country entirely. Now God, in His way of asking things, asks through the mouths of these people that you do this act of humanity, which is demanded in the name of civilization and of justice; and the people of America ask it, and I hope you will reconsider the point of order, and if not in this bill, in some other shape, grant this reasonable request in regard to the colored people.

Few of Cheatham's remarks in Congress demonstrated his intellectual range more than his comments on options and futures. He supported a bill that would impose a tax on products sold on the options and futures market, and required a license for dealers who sold options. He believed federal regulation was needed to help protect small farmers. Cheatham argued that the federal government would have interceded in a natural disaster, and he thought the crisis over options and futures warranted a swift response. "Future selling," he explained, brought out speculation in the farming industry. Legislation was thus needed to protect the investors.

OPTIONS AND FUTURES
June 28, 1892

On behalf of the farming class of our people in the United States, and especially the poor cotton farmer of the South, I rise to say a kind word in support of the bill now under consideration, and I do this cheerfully, believing as I do that no man upon this floor will ever have an opportunity to espouse a more righteous and just cause than this—the cause of an appreciative and deserving people, whose interest to a great extent has been neglected in many ways.

While the depressions of the farmer are great and many, I am ready to admit that there are burdens and unjust burdens, no doubt, upon every vocation in life; but any fair-minded man who is the least conversant with the condition of the man who gets his living by farming, knows and must confess that there is no comparison between the suffering condition of farming and that of any other business in the United States, especially when the sorry crops and low prices of the last few years are taken into consideration. This can be clearly demonstrated from the fact that their home comforts are more or less embarrassed and their lands depreciated, while almost every other business has flourished and developed; and the very fact that farming has not prospered as other businesses, is beyond any doubt attributable to the unfair and fraudulent methods by which the farmers' products are bought and sold in the markets of the United States. If the farming and agricultural classes of our citizens bear their share of the burdens of the revenue which is required to run the American Government as cheerfully and as willingly as any other taxpaying class, as they certainly do, Congress should for that, if not for other good and constitutional reasons, enact a strong and positive law forbidding and putting an end to any but honest and pure methods of selling and buying the farm products of our country, and thereby foster and stimulate the agricultural interest of our land, which is the staff of life to any civilized country. For the last eight or ten years, by reason of shameful market discriminations and undue impediments thrown in the way by the people who ought to be the farmers' best friends, farm produce has gone down below zero, so to speak, which naturally leaves our Southern and all agricultural sections in a calamitous and almost a starving condition. I speak more especially for the cotton farmer, since I am more familiar with that class of farming.

If after the unhappy and restless suspense in which the farmer is placed during the time of growing and cultivating his crops, although confronted in many cases by unfavorable seasons, losing half or destroying the entire crop by wind and hail storms or some other disastrous visitor, he could get a fair and honest deal and could receive fair compensation for his labor, at the hands of those whose business it is to buy his farm products, he would be better satisfied and encouraged to make larger and better crops for markets; but as it seems to be now, he is met at the markets of our country with prices disgracefully and unreasonably low, made entirely to suit the speculator by what is called "future selling" or short sales, which is an agreement to sell and deliver by a person who is not the owner of the article at the time, or has not acquired by previous purchase the right to the future possession of the article from the owner. I believe the relief and remedy for the farmer can be found in the now pending bill, which protects the following named farm articles—cotton, hops, wheat, corn, oats, rye, barley, grass—seed, flax seed, pork, lard, bacon, as well as other edible products of swine—from the destructive competition to which the farmers are subjected by the offering upon the exchanges of almost limitless quantities of fictitious products, by those who do not own nor have they the right to the future possession of the articles they pretend to thrust upon the markets and to sell.

This unfair competition has been allowed to go on until it has reached a point that there are very few spot sales of cotton upon the great market of the city of New York. As a proof of that fact I will read what Mr. Jacob D. Goldman says upon the subject:

New York is no spot market whatever. I do not suppose that there are 20,000 bales consigned to that market for actual sale. The only cotton that is handled there is bought up by future dealers and stored for the purpose of using it as their interests may appear from time to time, and to whip the market one way or the other, either deliver it against sales or withdraw it, as occasion may require. There have been times that the same stock has been carried in New York for two or three successive seasons, particularly the lower grades of cotton in order to scare off buyers from taking options when tendered as very few mills can use it except to make ropes or the very commonest grades of cotton goods.

The volume of future business, compared with spots, can be best answered by referring to question No. 1: there is no spot business whatever in New York, while the future business will probably amount to 30,000,000 or 35,000,000 bales, buying and selling annually. The effect of speculation in the past few years has been very disastrous to the grower of cotton, for the reason that the combination of probably half a dozen houses in the United States has been able to depress the value fully 15 to 20 per cent more than it should naturally have declined, even in the face of these two large crops. This is an argument easily sustained by the fact that no planter of any size who has raised and does plant cotton can do so at such prices and come out near even. I think the passage of the anti-option bill could only benefit the cotton planters, as the present system of doing business is not based on honest principles, giving the seller all the opportunities and the buyer none.

In the New York future's market "middling" cotton is the base, but if you buy, you must take anything they want to give you at the contract price. The mills cannot buy future cotton because they deliver so many grades, which are worthless for manufacturing purposes. I have known as many as ten grades supplied on one contract. What we complain of here in St. Louis is this very practice. We have written to the New York dealers, but it has had no effect. A mill would sacrifice its contract sooner than take much of the cotton offered.

I think the passage of an anti-option bill would benefit the planters and bona fide handlers, for the following reasons: The South is bullish on cotton whether she has it or not. She does not know how much is raised on account of the great extent of her cotton-producing lands. Hence, the South always buys futures. Not one man out of ten in the South would sell futures, even when stocked up with cotton. There are but two sides to the question, and the South invariably gets on the wrong side. New York, on the other hand, seldom comes out a loser. The commissions paid in New York amount to $15,000 to $30,000 per day. It is a rule that when New York buys the South sells, and vice versa, and the South is cut "a-comin' and a-gwyne." The passage of the bill would stop gambling in futures, and that would certainly be a benefit to the country at large. The manner in which New York futures are managed certainly gives no strength to the spot market.

The intention of this measure is also to restore and protect the law of supply and demand and invest it with that free action which has for some time been taken away by the practice of "short selling." By this practice of "short selling," now so common upon the exchanges, prices are determined for the entire product, and in many cases months in advance of the sowing of the seed on the farm. This is certainly one of the troubles with our Southern farmer; for this debars the farmer and planter of that voice and right in fixing the price to be received for the product of his labor and capital which is accorded to other producers. This bill does much to prevent overloading the markets of our country with fictitious products simply for the purpose of establishing low prices on all farm products. Allow me to read the following from the report of the Committee on Agriculture, which fully sets forth the objects of the bill:

To prevent the overloading of domestic markets and the breaking down of prices of farm products by short sales: made by foreign merchants for the purpose of insuring them against possible loss on the purchases of Indian, Egyptian, South American, Australian, and Russian produce, whereby the American farmer and planter are made underwriters of the commercial risks of the European, by whom no bonus or premium is paid for assuming insurance risks that destroy much of the value of our products.

That by restoring the functions of the law of supply and demand, now inoperative by reason of the limitless offers of the "short seller," a measure of relief will be given and prosperity partially restored to that great class constituting more than 40 percent of our population who inhabit the farms, and whose lack of prosperity, your committee believes, is due, in no inconsiderable part, to the practice of "short selling" whereby the prices of the products of the farm have been determined and fixed, during recent years, at an un-remunerative level.

To restore to the producer an honest market and such prices as will follow the unfettered operation of the law of supply and demand, which the committee believes will be sufficiently remunerative to restore, in part, the power of the farmer and planter to purchase the product of forge, factory, and mill, and thus bring prosperity to the artisan, manufacturer, distributor, and transporter. The first section of the bill now reported defines "options," which are more commonly known as "puts and calls," "privileges," and "curb trading," and while not recognized as "regular" by any board of trade or exchange have been openly dealt in upon the premises of most exchanges and by a great majority of the members of such exchanges and yet no successful effort has ever been made, and but rarely attempted, by any exchange to discipline its members for such trading, the exchange contenting themselves with a refusal to enforce such contracts by the machinery of the exchange.

That the exchanges have looked without disfavor upon such transactions as are defined in the first section of the bill is manifest from the fact that while the protests filed with this committee have not failed to denounce the methods and practices of the "bucket shops," yet but one such protest against the proposed legislation offers a word in reprobation of the practice, so general among the dealers upon the exchanges, of trading in "puts and calls." The reason for the failure to denounce "puts and calls" while denouncing "bucket shops" may be found in the fact that most members of the exchanges deal in "puts and calls," while the "bucket shops" attract a very large and profitable business that with the "bucket shops" suppressed, would go to the brokers operating upon the exchanges, and yet the representatives of the exchanges coming before this committee have not hesitated to state that dealings in "puts and calls" are gambling transactions pure and simple. Since, however, it has become apparent that in response to the almost universal demand of the people for legislation which shall restrict the power of the "short seller" to manufacture prices, and your committee would report some bill having that object in view for the consideration of the House of Representatives, an effort has been made during the pendency of such bill to prevent the members of the Chicago Board of Trade from dealing in "puts and calls" yet so powerless for good is that body that in the *Chicago Inter-Ocean* of March 27, 1892, it is stated that:

The Board of Trade has been trying to stop "cub trading" with only fair success. Their greatest opposition comes from Pardridge. He agreed to stop almost a week ago, but his brokers have continued to trade. Yesterday he informed the directors that he did not care a snap for them and would do as he pleased, and had his brokers sell wheat down in the open board one-half cent after the regular closed.

As the closing "curb" price has much to do in determining the opening price of the product the next day, and often absolutely fixes it, your committee believes that the exchanges being unable to suppress methods of dealing and practices that all admit to be evil and but gambling devices and, yet, determine the prices the farmer shall receive for his products, that it is the duty of the Federal Government, so far as constitutional and practicable, in levying taxes for revenue, to protect the greatest of the industrial classes from the wrong inflicted by this unnatural mode of determining prices. The second section of the bill defines "futures" as being a contract for the sale and future delivery of one of the articles enumerated in the third section made by a party who is not the owner thereof, and had not acquired the right from the owner to the future possession of the article contracted to be sold and delivered. In other words, the makers of "futures" contracts, as defined in this section, are what are known as "short sellers," being men who constantly contract to sell and deliver what they neither own nor have any right to the possession of at a future time, and in order to comply specifically with their contracts depend upon their ability to make a future purchase of the article which they have agreed to deliver.

There is abundant evidence that the outstanding contracts of such "short sellers" at all times exceeded manifold the amount of product available for delivery, and it is very generally reported and accepted that the "short sales" of the one dealer who defies the directors of the Chicago Exchange have, for months at a time, exceeded 20,000,000 bushels of wheat, being about twice as much as there was of that grain in all the warehouses of that city, and the "short line" of this one man being equal to half of the visible supply of the entire country. This one statement shows how impossible it would be to comply with such contracts had compliance ever been contemplated.

While this section defines what shall be deemed a "futures" sale, the provisions of the act are not applicable to contracts with Federal, State, or municipal authorities, nor to contracts made by any farmer or planter for the future delivery of the products of his land, either grown or growing, nor to any contract to furnish any farmer or planter with any of the articles named in the bill which he may require for food, forage, or seed. This section of the bill makes it clear that the farmer and planter are left at entire liberty to contract for the sale and future delivery of the product of their field, as is the merchant to contract with the farmer and planter to furnish and deliver at any future time any article which the farmer or planter may require. While this section of the bill is intended to provide the basis for the taxation of all "short sales" of farm products, and thus protect the producer and legitimate dealer against unfair and destructive competition by the vendors of phantom commodities, there is nothing, and there is intended to be nothing, which will in any wise hamper traffic in actual products, either in possession or to which the contracting party has acquired the right of future possession; but it is intended that this section shall, and your committee believes it will, in connection with other sections of the bill, suppress the vicious practice of "short selling."

Section 4 defines what shall constitute a dealer in "options" and "futures"; stipulates that such dealers shall pay an annual license fee of $1,000 and also pay a tax of 5 cents on each pound of cotton, hops, pork, lard, bacon, and other edible product of swine and 20 cents a bushel on each bushel of the other articles named in section 3 of the bill which are the subject of any "options" or "futures" contract which such dealer, as vendor or assignor, shall make, transfer, or assign, either in his own behalf or on behalf of others.

Section 5 requires every dealer in "options" or "futures" to apply, in form and manner prescribed, to the collector of internal revenue for a license to transact such business and to pay an annual license fee of $1,000, as well as to execute a bond in the sum of $40,000, to ensure the payment of the taxes provided in section 4 and the compliance by such dealer with all the requirements of the act. It also provides that, notwithstanding the possession of a license by such dealer, the holder thereof shall not transact the business of a dealer in "options" or "futures" while any tax on contracts previously made or transferred or assigned shall remain due and unpaid.

Section 6 provides that the collector of internal revenue shall keep a register subject to public inspection, in which shall be recorded all applications for license under this act, and a statement as to whether a license was issued thereon.

Section 7 provides that all "options" and "futures" contracts and agreements (and all transfers and assignments thereof) shall be in writing and signed in duplicate, and state the time at which they expire or mature.

Section 8 requires that every dealer in "options" or "futures" shall keep a book in which shall be recorded the date of each "options" or "futures" contract made by such dealer, the names of the parties thereto, whether they appear as vendor or vendee, the kind and amount of the articles agreed to be sold, and the contract time of delivery, and, when a transfer or an assignment of any such contract shall have been made, the name of the assignee and assignor, and that this book shall at all times be subject to inspection by the officials of the Internal Revenue Department.

Section 9 requires dealers in "options" to make weekly reports to the collector of internal revenue, setting forth the facts and items required to be recorded in the book mentioned in section 8, and thereupon pay to such collector the taxes, as provided in section 4, upon the articles embraced in the "options" and "futures" contracts made, transferred, or assigned by such dealer during the preceding week and included in the report required by this section.

This section also provides that the collector shall enter in a register, open to public inspection, all the facts set forth in the reports made by dealers in "options" and "futures," and that such collector shall, at the expiration of each month, make a report to the Commissioner of Internal Revenue, showing the number of such contracts that had not then expired or matured, and the kind and amount of the articles embraced in such contracts, as well as the amount of taxes levied thereon, and that a copy be available for public inspection.

Section 10 provides that any person who shall deal in "options or futures" without being licensed so to do, or fail to keep any book or record or make any return required by this act, or make any "options or futures" contract while any tax remains due and unpaid, or make any "options or futures" contract in form or manner other than as prescribed, or make any false, fraudulent, or partial record or return, or in any other manner violate the provisions of the act, shall be subject to a fine of from one to twenty thousand dollars or to imprisonment from six months to ten years, or to both such fine and imprisonment.

Section 11 provides that neither the payment of taxes provided in this bill nor the license issued by the collector shall exempt any person from the operation of State, Territorial, or municipal enactments regulating, taxing, or prohibiting the same or like transactions, thus leaving State, Territorial, and local authorities at entire liberty to exercise, unhampered, the powers of the local government either for the regulation, taxation, or suppression of the traffic in "options" and "futures" within State, Territorial, or municipal limits.

Section 12 requires the party intending, as owner or as having acquired the right to the future possession of any of the articles enumerated in section 3, so as to make, transfer, or assign contracts for the sale and subsequent delivery of any of such articles to apply to the collector of internal revenue for a license to conduct such business and pay an annual license fee of $2; whereupon such collector shall issue to the applicant a certificate authorizing the making, transferring and assigning contracts for the sale and subsequent delivery of such articles. It also requires the party so licensed to keep a book, in which shall be recorded all the items and facts in relation to such contracts which are required in section 9 in relation to "options" and "futures" contracts; and it further requires the licensee to make to such collector a weekly report of all such transactions, in manner and form similar to those required from dealers in "options" and "futures"; and providing also that, in case of failure to keep any book or make any record, return, or report by this section required, or failing, when so required, to submit such book or record to the inspection of the officials of the Internal Revenue Department, the party so failing shall be subject to a fine of not less than $100 nor more than $5,000.

Section 13, taken in connection with section 2, wherein are defined "futures," of the illegitimate contracts of the "short seller," and section 12, wherein are defined legitimate contracts for future delivery, made by owners or by those who have by purchase acquired the right to the future possession of the articles contracted to be sold and delivered, provide a ready and practical method, not burdensome to the legitimate seller, of determining the character of outstanding contracts for future delivery, in relation to which question may arise as to their regularity, and whether they are such as to be subject to the tax upon articles embraced in "futures" contracts, as provided in section 4.

Whenever the making of any contract for the sale and future delivery of any of the articles named in section 3 of this bill shall not have been reported as required, or it shall come to the knowledge of the collector of internal revenue, or he shall have reasonable cause to believe that at the time of making, transferring, or assigning any contract for the sale and subsequent delivery of any of such articles that the party making, transferring, or assigning thereof was not the owner of, or not then entitled to the future possession of the article or articles contracted to be sold and delivered, it shall be the duty of such collector to demand from such vendor or assignor proof of such ownership or right to the future possession of such property under and by virtue of a contract with its owner, where it is then stored, and such party shall also show the amount of the articles of the kind embraced in such contract of which the party is then the owner of or entitled to the future possession of and the quantity thereof called for by contracts made, transferred, or assigned by such party and then outstanding and not canceled, such proof and showings to be made in the form and manner prescribed.

Upon such proof being demanded by the collector, and the party making, transferring, or assigning such contract failing to comply with such demand, it shall be held that such contract is a "futures" contract as defined in section 2 of this bill and shall subject the maker thereof, unless he shall have a license as a dealer in "futures" covering the time at which such contract was made, transferred, or assigned, to the payment of the license fee of $1,000, as provided in section 5, as well as to the payment of the taxes provided in section 4, and also subjecting such maker or assignor to the fines and penalties provided in section 10.

Section 12 and 13 give force and validity to the act, and your committee believes they are necessary to its enforcement and the collection of the taxes imposed, as they distinctly draw the line between legitimate and illegitimate contracts for future delivery, and while thus adding to the efficiency of the act as a revenue measure will afford protection against the vicious and destructive competition of the "short seller," to which the farmer and planter are now subjected and which they believe, and which your committee believes, deprives them of much of that remuneration to which they are entitled. While so framing the bill as to ensure considerable revenue, your committee has steadily kept in view the object of affording every facility to buyers and at the same time decreasing the number of such sellers as offer for sale only contracts which they expect to adjust by the settlement of differences.

In behalf of the people I represent on this floor, and of the great bulk of the people of the South who are mainly engaged in agriculture, I appeal to this House to enact into law the wise provisions of this bill, which will do justice to all and injustice to none; and which will enable the small farmer to realize on his products what he should honestly receive for his time and labor.

4

Robert Carlos De Large (1842–1874)
House of Representatives, South Carolina

Republican

Forty-second Congress
March 4, 1871, to January 24, 1873

Robert De Large was born in Aiken, South Carolina, on March 15, 1842. Today, historians still disagree about his background. Certainly his father was a mulatto who kept slaves. Along with his Haitian-born wife, they also owned a tailor shop in Charleston. Their children, therefore, had opportunities most African Americans never dreamed about. While some scholars suggest that De Large was born into a rare mulatto aristocracy that used their "color" for their own benefit, others conclude that he was born into slavery. De Large did have an elitist streak about him, which explains why historians label him an aristocrat. He belonged to exclusive fraternal and civic organizations that admitted only mulattoes. In an era when it was nearly impossible for southern African Americans to obtain an education, De Large managed to attend primary school in North Carolina as well as Wood High School in Charleston, South Carolina. He also learned the barbering trade. De Large used whatever resources were at his disposal to get ahead. In addition to politics, he was diligent in his business affairs, and by 1870 the U.S. Census reported that his real estate holdings exceeded $6,000.

Surprisingly, De Large served in the Confederate Navy during the Civil War. He was not a secessionist; yet, it is reasonable to assume that some African Americans might have initially thought that northern troops had invaded their region. Due to personal pride they might have willingly opposed the Union, at least in the early stages of the Civil War. Moreover, the Confederacy employed slaves, and blacks like De Large were occasionally found among the ranks of Confederates. Once it became clear to enslaved blacks that the Union was their liberator, there was little doubt about where the majority of them would direct their loyalty. Soon after the war, therefore, De Large became an ardent Republican.

De Large made his entry into Republican politics in 1865, as an agent for the Bureau of Freedmen, Refugees, and Abandoned Lands (Freedmen's Bureau). He also joined others in the state to organize the Republican party, which had largely been a northern political organization since its inception in 1854. De Large attended the Colored People's Convention meeting at the Zion Church of Charleston in1865, where he chaired the credentials committee. That same year he signed a petition for a state constitutional convention. As a delegate to the state Republican Convention in 1867 he served on the platform committee. Not surprisingly, he was elected a delegate to the state constitutional convention in 1868, where he served on the Committee of Franchise and Elections and lobbied for universal male suffrage. Yet, De Large, with a conservative streak, did not favor giving the vote to illiterate men of either race.

Once the South Carolina Constitutional Convention complied with Congressional Reconstruction, the state was authorized to elect representatives to the General Assembly. De Large was positioned for state office, and upon his election was named chairman of the Ways and Means Committee. Two years later the legislature appointed him to head the Land Commission of South Carolina, where he supervised the sale of land going to new homeowners. He also served on the board for the mentally ill, and was a member of the State Sinking Fund Commission. By 1870, the Republican party believed that he was ready to compete for a national office, and they nominated him for Congress.

De Large, running in the Second Congressional District, challenged Christopher C. Bowen, a white Republican with a checkered past. Bowen was a former Confederate soldier who had been dishonorably discharged from the army. He was an incumbent, but his reputation for unscrupulous politics haunted him. When De Large won the election by slightly fewer than a thousand votes, Bowen contested the results, and spent the next few months trying to unseat his revival. His challenge was marginally successful, but it did not result in his confirmation by Congress. Meanwhile, De Large assumed his seat in the Forty-second Congress on March 4, 1871. The contested election passed to the Committee on Elections in the House of Representatives, which had scheduled a hearing.

Because of the events that would later unfold, Representative De Large's service in Congress was neither extensive nor meritorious. He was placed on the Committee on Manufactures, and he worked on issues such as securing federal appropriations to rebuild an orphanage in Charleston. Nuns had operated the institution during the late war, and had provided needed care for Union troops.

While many of his colleagues in Congress were seeking measures to enfranchise former Confederates, De Large urged them to consider ways to protect loyal Republicans from intimidation in general, and legislation to protect blacks in particular from racial violence. Nine months after he entered the House, the Committee on Elections considered the complaint of Christopher C. Bowen.

The House Committee on Elections met in December 1871, in the matter of *C.C. Bowen v. R.C. De Large*. In the end, the committee concluded that in the 1870 election South Carolina politics was so was marred with irregularities that it could not determine who had actually won. On January 18, 1873—two months before his term would have officially ended—the House committee removed De Large from office. Though he had served approximately twenty-two months in office, most of his time was taken up defending himself in the contest. With failing health, De Large did not seek reelection in 1872, making way for Alonzo J. Ransier, another black Republican, to succeed him.

Robert C. De Large returned to South Carolina in 1873, with the confidence of his party. He accepted an appointment by the "carpetbagger" Republican Governor Robert K. Scott as a magistrate in Charleston. De Large was a politician of great promise, and he served his state faithfully after 1865. He died prematurely from complications associated with consumption at his home in February 1874, at the age of thirty-two.

Passage of the Fourteenth Amendment and other civil rights legislation did not shield African Americans from persecution. Terrorist organizations such as the Ku Klux Klan sprang up in the South, and launched a systematic campaign to drive blacks away from polling places, and deny them access to public accommodations. De Large urged Congress to pass measures to enforce its civil rights laws already on the books. He insisted that violence in the South had made it necessary for the federal government to intercede to protect blacks.

ENFORCEMENT OF THE FOURTEENTH AMENDMENT
Speech of Honorable Robert C. De Large
April 6, 1871

I had supposed that in the consideration of this matter of legislation for the South party lines would not have been so distinctly drawn, but that we would have at least first endeavored to ascertain whether or not there was any necessity for the legislation, and then decide what kind of legislation would be best. I say I did not expect that party lines would be drawn so distinctly while considering a matter of such grave import. I believe that if there was a single gentleman upon the floor of this House who, before the commencement of this debate, doubted that lawlessness, confusion, and anarchy existed in some portions of the South, he is at least cured of that doubt by this time. Gentlemen upon both sides of the House have in their speeches acknowledged, and, by the evidence produced, proven to my satisfaction, and, I believe, to the satisfaction of a majority of the members of this House, that such a state of affairs does exist in some portions of the southern States.

I am free to say that none can bring the charge to my door of ever having acted in a manner that would be termed illiberal. I am also free to say that I, like other gentlemen upon the floor of this House, have the honor of representing a district in which no case of outlawry has ever occurred. Since the time of Reconstruction no outrage has been committed in my district; and I say frankly to you today that until within the last few months no one upon the face of God's earth could have convinced me that any secret organization existed in my State for the purpose of committing murder, arson, or other outrages upon the lives, liberty, and property of the people; and, I sincerely deplore and lament the abundance of that evidence which so plainly proves the existence of such an organization today. Would to God that the fair name of the State of my birth and that I have the honor in part to represent had not been marred by the wicked deeds of these outlaws, who shrink from no cruelty, who spare no sex nor station to carry out their devilish purposes.

I cannot shut my eyes to facts; I cannot refuse to yield my faith to tales of horror so fully proven; and I am thoroughly convinced that it is necessary to do something to cure these awful wrongs. I am free to admit that neither the Republicans of my State nor the Democrats of that State can shake their garments and say that they have had no hand in bringing about this condition of affairs. Both parties are responsible for it. As a member of the Republican party I may state, while demanding legislation on behalf of all the citizens there, that both parties to a considerable extent are responsible for this condition of things. It is necessary that we should legislate upon this subject. The Governor of my State has called upon the Executive of this country for assistance and protection. He has stated distinctly in that call that he is unable to preserve the public peace in some districts of that State. That is something that we must all admit. That is not denied by the Democrats of South Carolina. Some of them doubtless rejoice in this, because they can throw the blame, as they think, upon the administration of the State, which is in the hands of their political foes. It is not now the question, what is the cause that has brought about this condition of affairs? It is useless, except for the purpose of gaining partisan credit or fixing partisan odium, now to charge the blame here or there. But the naked facts stare us in the face, that this condition of affairs does exist, and that it is necessary for the strong arm of the law to interpose and protect the people in their lives, liberty, and property.

Just here allow me to make a suggestion. If the gentlemen on this side of the House propose to legislate for the benefit of the people of the South, I tell them, and say it fully conscious of the responsibility that rests upon me in saying it, that while legislation is necessary, yet unless they are ready to concede along with this legislation for the protection of the loyal people of the South some accompanying measure to go hand in hand with this and remove as far as in our power rests some of the evils that have brought about the existing condition of things, neither this legislation nor any other that you may pass from now until the hour of doom will be of any benefit. I speak knowing what I say.

When the Governor of my State the other day called in council the leading men of that State, to consider the condition of affairs there and to advise what measure would be best for the protection of the people, whom did he call together? The major portion of the men he convened were those resting under the political disabilities imposed by the Fourteenth Amendment. In good faith I ask gentlemen on this side of the House, and gentlemen on the other side, whether it is reasonable to expect that these men should be interested, in any shape or form, in using their influence and best endeavors for the preservation of the public peace, when they have not her to look for politically in the future? You say they should have the moral and material interest of their State at heart, though even always to be denied a participation in its honors. You say insist that the true patriot seeks no personal ends in the acts of patriotism. All this is true; men are but men everywhere, and you ought not to expect of those whom you daily call by opprobrious epithets, whom you daily remind of their political sins, whom you persistently exclude from places of the smallest trust in the Government you have created, to be very earnest to cooperate with you in the work of establishing and fortifying governments set up in hostility to the whole tome of their prejudices, their convictions, and their sympathies. What ought to be is one thing, what in the weakness and fallibility of human nature will be is quite another thing. The statesman regards the actual and acts upon it; the desirable, the possible, and even the probable furnish but poor basis for political action.

If I had time I would enumerate some of the causes that have brought about the existing state of affairs. I am not here to apologize for murderers; I am not here to defend anyone who has committed any act of impropriety or wrong. But it is a fact and I do not give it as any or even the slightest excuse for the Democrats of my State, who, by their influence secretly or by joining in armed organization, have brought about this condition of affairs—it is a fact, unfortunately for us, that our party has done some things which give color to the charge that it is responsible to some degree for the evils which afflict us.

When I heard the gentleman from New York [Samuel Sullivan Cox] on Tuesday last hurl his shafts against the members of my race, charging that through their ignorance they had brought about these excesses, I thought he should have remembered that for the ignorance of that portion of the people he and his party associates are responsible, not those people themselves. While there may have been extravagance and corruption resulting from the placing of improper men in official positions—and this is part of the cause of the existing state of things—these evils have been brought about by men identified with the race to which the gentleman from New York belongs, and not by our race.

5

Robert Brown Elliott
(1842–1884)
House of Representatives, South Carolina

Republican

Forty-second and Forty-third Congresses
March 4, 1871, to November 1, 1874

Robert Brown Elliott was not a native son of South Carolina, though he made his mark there during the Reconstruction Period. Though Elliott claimed Boston, Massachusetts as his home, the evidence suggests that he was born in Liverpool, England. His misrepresentation of his background went further than this; Elliott claimed to have attended the High Holborn Academy in London, and that he had graduated with honors from Eton College in England in 1859. He also claimed to have served in the Union Army during the Civil War. Most scholars, including Peggy Lamson, his primary biographer, question these details. What is certain is that Robert Brown Elliott was well educated, highly intelligent, and supremely confident. While this is conjecture, Elliott could have surmised that to succeed in politics during Reconstruction he needed a distinguished past. His strategy worked and he acquired a record during the Reconstruction Period that only a few men of any race would achieve.

Elliott was born to West Indian parents in 1842, and possibly lived there until 1866. He was a sailor in the Royal Navy and apparently deserted the service when the fleet visited America after the Civil War. He settled in Boston temporarily where he plied his trade as a typesetter. An ambitious man, Elliott was looking for greener pastures, and he relocated to South Carolina in 1867. South Carolina had a black population that exceeded 60 percent of its inhabitants, and Elliott probably expected greater opportunities for a gifted and educated man of his race. He landed a job as a journalist for the *South Carolina Leader*, a newspaper published by black congressman Richard H. Cain. Elliott also married well, finding a mate in the prominent Rollin family, whose free status predated 1865.

His foray into state politics started in 1868, after Congress passed the Reconstruction Acts and enfranchised black males. Elliott won a seat in the Constitutional Convention. He supported issues such as a state-funded school system and an electoral process free from literacy tests and poll taxes. After the convention he also won a seat in the state assembly where he served from July 6, 1868, to October 23, 1870, and again from 1874 to 1876. The legislature elected him speaker of the house in 1874, succeeding Samuel J. Lee, the first black speaker of the South Carolina House of Representatives. During his first term as a legislator Elliott simultaneously read law, and upon passing the bar in 1869 he joined the law firm of Daniel A. Straker. That same year Elliott caught the eye of South Carolina Republican Governor Robert K. Scott, who appointed him assistant adjutant general, an office Elliott held from 1869 to 1871. In that capacity Elliott worked for an issue he cared deeply about, which was protecting blacks from the terrorism of the Ku Klux Klan and other white vigilantes. He organized state militia units, which the *Charleston Daily News* called the Elliott Guards, and ordered them to protect and secure the civil rights of all citizens. While Elliott executed his duties with few difficulties, he resigned the office in 1870 because he believed Scott was using him to further his own career.

In 1870 Elliott ran for Congress and defeated John E. Bacon, a white Democrat. He took his seat in the House as the representative from the Third Congressional District on March 4, 1871. The Speaker of the House assigned him to the Committee on Education and Labor and, upon his election to the Forty-third Congress, to the Committee on the Militia. Elliott continued his quest for civil rights while in Congress. His most memorable speeches were those delivered in 1874, in defense of the Civil Rights Bill proposed by Massachusetts Senator Charles Sumner. Elliott also gained notoriety in the South because of his vigorous opposition to the amnesty bill, which, if adopted, would have returned the franchise to ex-rebel leaders. He instead favored protecting loyal citizens from the atrocities of the Klan, which had recently included the intimidation and murder of vast numbers of black citizens. He made an unsuccessful bid for the United States Senate in 1872, while a representative in Congress. Elliott then resigned his House seat in 1874, to return to local politics in South Carolina. His fears that Democrats would drive blacks from office motivated his return to lead the Republican party in his home state.

Elliott returned to South Carolina in 1874 as a hero among most African Americans, he easily won reelection to the General Assembly. The legislature elected him speaker of the house, a position he held until 1876. Influenced by a desire to prosecute criminals who used violence to deter blacks from exercising their civil rights, Elliott ran and won the office of state attorney general in 1876. His public service also included a term as a commissioner in Barnwell County, a member of the board of regents for the lunatic asylum, and president of the state labor convention. His public career ended with the election of 1876, when Democrats regained control of the state and ousted blacks and other Republicans from the government.

Elliott's career was dependent largely upon his black constituents. In contrast to many of his prominent African-American colleagues, he was of dark complexion. Most whites also considered Elliott a radical because of his proud demeanor, and his rhetoric in defense of black rights. Without a black base after 1876, his career in elective office was over. He returned to practice law in Charleston, but he faced another problem that he never surmounted: there was little demand for black lawyers. He found work in government again when he accepted an appointment in the U.S. Treasury Department in Charleston, and later in New Orleans. Elliott was unhappy in that post and, apparently, performed so poorly that President James A. Garfield removed him from office in 1882.

While Elliott returned to the practice of law, the color line had defined him. Without doubt he was of enormous talent; the *Chicago Tribune* on November 2, 1872, described him as the most able Negro in the South. Elliott probably considered himself to be among the most talented men in the state. Yet, he did not have the "cross over" like some members of his race, including Hiram H. Revels, Thomas E. Miller, and John M. Langston, whose governors appointed them presidents of black colleges in Mississippi, South Carolina, and Virginia. Elliott was overlooked, possibly because of his dark complexion, as well as his militant persona, which alarmed conservative whites. Elliott succumbed to illness and died penniless in New Orleans on August 9, 1884.

As Congress pondered rescinding its earlier proscription on suffrage to ex-Confederates, Representative Elliott thought the decision was not a prudent one. The amnesty bill would have restored the suffrage to eligible voters, regardless of their participation in the late war. Congress passed the bill over his protest, and the Amnesty Act pardoned most of the disenfranchised rebels. (A joint resolution of Congress had already removed some of the disabilities in the Fourteenth Amendment.) According to some estimates only 500 or so men were still excluded from government service after passage of the act in 1872.

THE AMNESTY BILL
March 14, 1871

The House now has under consideration a bill of vast importance to the people of the section that I have the honor in part to represent. It is a proposition to remove the political disabilities of persons lately engaged in rebellion against the sovereignty of the Government of the United States. I believe that I have been noted in the State from which I come as one entertaining liberal views upon this very question; but, at a time like this, when I turn my eyes to the South and see the loyal men of that section of the country suffering at the hands of the very men whom it is proposed today by this Forty-Second Congress of the United States to relieve them of their political disabilities, I must here and now enter my solemn protest against any such proposition.

It is nothing but an attempt to pay a premium for disloyalty and treason at the expense of loyalty. I am not surprised that the gentleman from Kentucky should introduce such a proposition here. It was due to the class of men that it is proposed to relieve that such a proposition should come from the gentleman from Kentucky [George Madison Adams] and gentlemen upon that side of the House. I can appreciate the feeling of sympathy that the gentleman from Kentucky entertains for these men in the South who are today prohibited from holding Federal offices. They are his allies. They are his compatriots. They are today disfranchised simply because they rushed madly into rebellion against this, the best Government that exists under heaven, at their own instances, with the advice, and with the consent of such gentlemen as the gentleman from Kentucky. But when I hear gentlemen like the gentleman from Illinois [John Franklin Farnsworth], who spoke upon this question on Friday last, advance views and opinions such as that gentleman then advanced I must be allowed to express my surprise, ay, sir, my regret, that at this time such words should fall from the lips of a man whom I have been taught long to regard as one of those who are unflinching in their devotion to the cause of liberty and the preservation and maintenance of this great Government.

The gentleman from Illinois [Mr. Farnsworth] took occasion, in his argument on Friday last, to compare the condition of the man who is today disfranchised and the man who is allowed to hold office in the South. He drew a parallel between the disfranchised old man and his servant, or slave, who today holds office or may do so. He tells you that you should take into consideration the condition of this poor old man who, because he simply happened to join the rebellion after having taken an oath to support the Constitution of the Government of the United States, is prohibited from holding office, while his slave is allowed to hold office under the State and the United States governments. Ay, sir, the reason of this difference between the political status of the two is simply this: that while this old man, with whom the gentleman from Illinois sympathizes in his heart, was rebellious against the Government which had fostered and sustained and protected him, his slave was loyal to that Government, loyal to its Army, and loved its flag, which the man who had been reared under it, had learned only to despise. The difference is this: that while that "poor old man," of whom the gentleman speaks so sympathetically, would only curse the Government, would only ill-treat and murder its loyal adherents, the slave was the friend of that Government, and the protector and defender of those who were endeavoring to uphold it.

In discussing this question, and as a reason why this bill should pass, the gentleman from Illinois [Mr. Farnsworth] stated that the removal of disabilities would do good, and that to maintain those disabilities could effect no good purpose. Sir, I say that this removal would be injurious, not only to the loyal men of the South, but also to the Government itself. To relieve those men of their disabilities at this time would be regarded by the loyal men of the South as an evidence of the weakness of this great Government, and of an intention on the part of this Congress to foster the men who today are outraging the good and loyal people of the South. It would be further taken as evidence of the fact that this Congress desires to hand over the loyal men of the South to the tender mercies of the rebels who today are murdering and scourging the southern States.

The gentleman from Illinois, in his argument, was pleased to ask this question, which he proposed to answer himself: are these men who are disfranchised and prohibited from holding offices the men who commit the murders and outrages of which complaint is made? And his answer to that question was that they are not. But permit me to say to that gentleman that those men are responsible for every murder, responsible for every species of outrage that is committed in the South. They are men who, by their evil example, by their denunciations of Congress, by their abuse of the President of the United States, and of all connected with this Government, have encouraged, aided, and abetted the men who commit these deeds. They contribute to this state of things by their social influence, by their money and the money sent from the northern States—money furnished by Tammany Hall for the purpose of keeping up these outrages in order to insure a Democratic triumph in the South in 1872.

And I am here today to tell you, in the name of the loyal men of the South, that it is the fact that money is sent to the South by the Democratic party of the North to aid these men in keeping up this state of lawlessness for the purpose of overawing the loyal people there and preventing them from expressing their preferences at the ballot box; that the number of arms shipped to the southern States, and which are brought there upon every New York steamer that arrives, is an evidence of the fact that these men who have the means, who have the influence, are responsible for these outrages, and not the poor, miserable tools who are their instruments in carrying them out. I ask this House, I ask gentlemen on this side especially, whether they are willing to join hands with those who propose today to relieve these men of their disabilities? Are they willing to tell the loyal men of the South, whose only offense is that they have been true to the Government, that they have sustained Congress in its just and lawful acts, that they have maintained the authority of Congress; are gentlemen willing to tell these loyal men that Congress is not disposed to protect them, but, on the contrary, is willing at their expense to pay a premium for disloyalty?

I speak not today in behalf of the colored loyalists of the South alone. I wish it to be distinctly understood that I represent here a constituency composed of men whose complexions are like those of gentlemen around me as well as men whose complexions are similar to my own. I represent a constituency as loyal as the constituency of any other gentleman upon this floor. Those men appeal to you today to do justice to them. They ask you to protect them by legislation, instead of placing them under the heel of those men who have ruled in the South with an iron hand since the Reconstruction Acts were passed. I come here backed up by a majority as large probably as that of any gentleman on this floor; I come here representing a Republican district; but unless this Congress will aid those loyal men of the South, unless, instead of passing propositions of this kind, it will turn its attention, and that speedily, to the protection of property and life in the South, the Republican party in this House cannot expect the support of those whom I represent.

Elliott favored using federal power to protect blacks from racial discrimination. He considered the Civil Rights Bill of Senator Charles Sumner a legitimate exercise of federal power. He argued in this speech that such a measure was not unconstitutional, as some of his colleagues in Congress had suggested. He believed that the government had the right under the Constitution to protect its citizens. Moreover, he felt that the government could enforce the exercise of these rights with reasonable force. He favored federal courts having original jurisdiction in matters involving civil rights. In this speech Elliott also demonstrates a keen knowledge of constitutional law and civil procedure.

CONSTITUTIONALITY OF THE CIVIL RIGHTS BILL
April 1, 1871

The argument upon the pending bill has proceeded thus far upon a question of constitutional law and a question of fact. The opponents of the bill deny that its provisions are warranted by the Constitution of the United States, and also deny the alleged facts upon which the proposed bill is founded. The probable efficacy of the bill, as a measure of relief and protection for the loyal men of the South from the extraordinary system of oppression to which they are now subjected, has not been assailed.

I shall therefore confine myself to a necessarily brief consideration of the law and the facts. I will endeavor to prove that the pending bill is not obnoxious to the spirit of the Constitution, and that it is founded in right reason, and that, as a measure of repression and protection, this bill is not only fully warranted, but it is imperatively demanded by the present posture of affairs in the Southern States. The issue of constitutional law evolved thus far by the discussion of the bill resolves itself into the question, has the government of the United States the right, under the Constitution, to protect a citizen of the United States in the exercise of his vested rights as an American citizen by the exercise of a direct force through its Army and Navy, or the assertion of immediate jurisdiction through its courts, without the appeal or agency of the State in which the citizen is domiciled? Those who oppose this bill answer this question in the negative, founding their opposition on section four, article four of the Constitution, which the gentleman from Indiana [Michael Crawford Kerr] made the burden of his very able and elaborate but specious argument the other day upon this subject. This, then, in the judgment of our opponents, is the pivot upon which this whole matter revolves, and to this point I shall address myself at the outset.

In this interpretation I fully concur with him, and I also agree with him that the term "domestic violence" refers to a force exerted within the State, as the term "invasion" relates to a power moving from without. But, sir, I totally dissent from the conclusion of the gentleman that this clause. I deny that it forbids Federal interposition except upon the call of the Executive or Legislature of the State. It is a sound maxim of the law that where a power is given, the necessary means for its execution is implied. In this case the duty imposed upon the Federal Government is to protect the States "against domestic violence." The clause is not inhibitory but mandatory. It was evidently not designed to restrict the rights, but to enlarge the duties, of the Government. Hence, when it declares that the Government shall protect the States against domestic violence on application of the Legislature, or of the Executive, when the Legislature cannot be convened, it means not that such "application" shall always be an essential condition—precedent, but simply *estops* the United States from refusing to give protection when the application is made. Otherwise a faithless and undutiful

Executive, giving his personal aid to or covertly bestowing his official sanction upon the insurgent authors of the "domestic violence," might, by withholding his "application," render the Government of the United States a torpid and paralyzed spectator of the oppression of its citizens and the violent dissolution of the State by the overthrow of the authorities constituted pursuant to its organic law.

Those who defend this construction and its logical consequences imitate, in their ideas of governmental duty, but on a grander and graver scale, the rigid etiquette of the Frenchman, who, on being upbraided for not saving the life of a fellow passenger whom he saw drown before his eyes, attempted to justify himself by pleading that he had "not been introduced to him." No, sir; there are paramount duties devolved upon individuals and upon Governments that in the very nature of things demand prompt performance. No broader or clearer vindication of this view is required than that found in the noble preamble to the constitution itself, which declares that....

How shall one of the great objects of the Constitution, the securing "the blessings of liberty to ourselves and our posterity," be achieved if it be true, as virtually contended by the opponents of this bill, that the majority of the citizens of a State may, by domestic violence, be deprived of "the blessings of liberty," and yet the Federal Government, established chiefly for this object, shall remain a passive observer of the great crime against its fundamental law unless invited to "protect" its own citizens by the "Executive" of the State? That it is not a very violent presumption that the majority of the people of a State may be oppressively subordinated to the minority through "domestic violence" is shown by the following remarks of Justice Joseph Story in his comments upon this very section, in the forty-first chapter of his great work upon the Constitution, a work to which the gentleman from Indiana frequently recurred with profound reverence throughout his cogent effort to "make the worse appear the better cause." I think that to quote Justice Story in defense of the position assumed by the gentleman from Indiana and his political co-actors on this floor is to "steal the livery of Heaven to serve the devil in Hell."

It is worthy of remark that the gentleman from Indiana, in treating this section of the Constitution, which he has made the text of the most fervid portion of his able but ill-timed speech, should have omitted all notice of its opening, and, in this discussion, its most pregnant clause. It is worthy of remark, Mr. Speaker, that the gentleman from Indiana, in treating this section of the Constitution, which he has made the text of the most fervid portion of his able bit ill-timed speech, should have omitted all notice of its opening, and, in this discussion, its most pregnant clause. I refer to the words:

The United States shall guaranty to every State in this Union a republican form of government.

Here, then, is a duty imposed without a condition—precedent, even under the very strict construction asserted by the gentleman from Indiana. The mandate is absolute, recognizing and permitting no discretion, either in the State or the United States. It vests in the Federal Government the right to act in the premises, whenever, in its judgment, "a republican form of government" may be endangered in a "State in this Union" from whatever cause, whether by "invasion" or "domestic violence." To make this clear, let us consider what is "a republican form of government" within the meaning of the Constitution? To furnish a substantial and comprehensive definition of this term, we need not consult the publicists. It must be defined by its attributes. It is a government having a written constitution, or organic law, which provides that persons elected by the majority of its citizens shall exercise its executive and legislative functions. In other words, it is a government for the people and by the people.

Assuming this definition to be correct in substance, I ask, how can a republican government be maintained in a State if the majority of the electors are prevented from exercising the elective franchise by force of arms, or if members of the majority, having thus exercised it according to their consciences, are, for that cause, put in terror and subjected to murder, exile, and the lash, through "domestic violence," organized and operated by the minority for the sole purpose of acquiring a political domination in the State? To deny that it would be the absolute and unconditional right and duty of the United States to intervene for the protection of its citizens "against domestic violence" thus directed, in advance of the "application of the Executive" of a State, and even in defiance of his expressed will, would be to make the United States an absolute guarantor of a "republican form of government," which it has guaranteed is endangered. To argue thus is to violate every sound principle of legal and logical interpretation, and to suppose a great wrong without a remedy in our political system.

I shall not reiterate the argument already so exhaustively applied, as derived from the Fourteenth Amendment, which this bill is explicitly designed to enforce. Is not this bill an "appropriate legislation"? I apprehend that it is obnoxious to the Democratic party chiefly because it is "appropriate," and strikes at the homicidal proclivities which become chronic among the active allies of that party in its late exclusive empire, the so-called Confederate States. But the right of the loyal people of the South to have this or some similar measure enacted into a law for their protection against the perils that environ them is derived from the same consideration in which the Constitution itself originated, and is founded on an integral principle that enters in the very idea of government, whether it relates to subject or citizen. I mean the great paramount duty of the Republic to protect its citizens wherever its flag has the right to wave. Indeed, sir, when you abolish or weaken the right to protection you destroy or diminish the duty of allegiance. I am bound to obey my country and her laws because I am by them protected. When they cease to protect me I can rightly cease to obey them. Says Blackstone:

Allegiance is the duty of all subjects, being the reciprocal tie of the people to the prince in return for the protection he affords them.

More especially should allegiance and protection become corollaries when the very danger from which protection is needed is drawn and incurred on the part of the citizens solely because of his loyalty to the government, at whose hands that protection is demanded? The best Government is that under which the humblest citizen is not beneath the protection of the laws, or the highest above the reach of their authority. But admitting the plain principle of constitutional and governmental law herein enunciated may deny, and does deny, that the facts exist to warrant an armed intervention of the Federal Government for the protection of its citizens, or any extraordinary legislation investing Federal courts with a novel jurisdiction to enforce that protection through judicial agencies. Here, then, we have a square issue of fact, and I propose to meet it with incontestable record. In so doing I shall expose the animus of the Democratic party of the South, as evidenced in the utterances of its recognized organs and leaders, as far back as 1868, coincident with the assembly of constitutional conventions in the South, pursuant to the Reconstruction Acts of Congress. This record, drawn from many States, exhibits the declared purpose to defeat the ballot with the bullet and other coercive means, and also the acts of organized lawlessness perpetrated pursuant to that purpose.

I would also call the attention of this House, Mr. Speaker, to the following extracts from the report of the investigating committee of the Legislature of South Carolina of 1868 and 1869, appointed to investigate thoroughly the disordered state of affairs in the Third Congressional District, and the causes of the intimidation, outrages, and murders perpetrated preceding and at the general election of 1868.

During the Civil War, enslaved African Americans had escaped behind Union lines. After the Civil War many of them, now old and sick, needed public assistance. Some white representatives argued that blacks should not expect the federal government to support them. Elliott debated this issue, insisting that these people were American citizens. He also condemned his white colleagues for making scathing remarks about African Americans. He believed whites had ignored the devastating impact of slavery upon blacks. His legal argument was that the former runaways were now domiciled in the North, and as such were entitled to the privileges and immunities to which any other citizen was entitled.

AID FOR DESTITUTE FREEDMEN
April 12, 1871

In order to submit some remarks upon this question, I move to amend the bill by striking out "$12,000" and inserting "$14,000." It has been stated on this side of the House by gentlemen who have spoken upon this amendment that these destitute and aged persons come here in consequence of the exigencies of the war. That they have been in this District for the past two years is apparent from the fact that I have heard stated that this is not the first time an appropriation of this sort has been acted upon in this House. Gentlemen upon the other side of the House have not denied the statement that these persons have come into the District by reason of the exigencies of the war. The fact, therefore, is established that they are here, and that they are aged, infirm, and destitute.

It has been stated by the gentleman from Indiana [Mr. Michael Crawford Kerr] that the District of Columbia should not allow these people to come here and then ask the national Government to support them. Sir, they are here. If they have been here two years they are domiciled here; and I know of no way in which they could be got rid of, even if this District should pass a law or ordinance providing for the return of persons of this class coming into the District. The fact that they have remained here long enough to become domiciled deprives the District, in my opinion, of the right to require their return to the places whence they came.

It is humiliating to me to hear expressions such as have been used today in relation to a class of people with whom I am by race identified; and I think it ought to be humiliating to every gentleman on this floor that there exists in this District, or in any other portion of the United States, such a class of persons, especially when we recollect the fact that they are infirm and destitute, not on account of their own idleness, but by reason of a system of barbarism which has existed in this country in years past—a system under which they have been abused, scourged, and overworked for the purpose of putting money into the pockets of others, and of building up the wealth and material prosperity of this great Republic of which we boast today. To say that these people now in their old age, when misery and want stare them in the face, should receive no assistance from this government is indeed a humiliating statement for any gentleman on this floor to make.

I cannot see in what way it would be an unjust burden upon the people of the country to make provision for the proper care of this class of persons. It seems to me that humanity alone should dictate this as a matter of duty to every Representative here; and, in my opinion, the constituency of every gentleman, regardless of political opinion, would far more readily indorse an appropriation of this kind than many appropriations which receive the favor of this House.

Another gentleman from Indiana [William Ellis Niblack] who spoke on this question stated that he had been told by Republicans in this District that the appropriation of $12,000 proposed in this bill would encourage this class of persons in idleness. Sir, in every State in this Union there are poor laws, there is legal provision for the care of the aged and infirm that are in need. In all the southern States there are such laws. Yet, legislation of that kind has not led to idleness. The statement made upon the other side of the House, while the bill for the protection of life and property in the South was under discussion here the other day, established clearly the fact that since free labor has been substituted for slave labor in the southern States the material prosperity of those States has been greatly enhanced....

If, then, the people with whom I am by race identified have done so much to increase the production and advance the wealth of the country while these poor laws have existed, I ask, why may not the result be the same in the District of Columbia? It is no excuse to offer when an amendment of this kind is pending; and I hope this amendment will not be made the subject of party consideration, and that partisan feelings will not be appealed to prevent its adoption, thus doing injustice to the people of the District.

This speech deals with the condition of South Carolina after the Civil War. Elliott presented figures to illustrate the debt of the South was traceable to Civil War. He disagreed with leaders who advocated issuing "bayonet bonds," explaining that it was a poorly conceived idea. Elliott suggested that South Carolina needed federal appropriations to pull it out of financial ruin. He also suggests that African Americans in the state needed protection from the violence of the Ku Klux Klan.

FINANCIAL CONDITION OF THE SOUTH
May 30, 1872

It is with reluctance that I at this time rise for the purpose of obtruding myself on the attention of the House.

I am reluctant because I recognize the fact that however brief or circumscribed my remarks may be they must necessarily occupy to some extent a portion of the time of the House which is justly demanded by the multitudinous requirements of the public service. But there is a consideration that impels me to the performance of this task; a consideration that must outweigh my own feelings and that must serve as my only excuse for availing me of the courtesy of this body. That is the consideration of my duty as a Representative.

I know this single word, "duty," carries with it all that need be addressed to right-thinking, right-feeling, and conscientious men. The duties of a Representative can neither be evaded, nor slighted, and all that he can hope for is that by a strict and faithful performance of them he may not only secure the approval and endorsement of those he may represent, but obtain that blessing which is sweeter still, the consciousness of his own rectitude and the quiet repose of his own conscience. With this feeling at my heart, and appreciating, as I do fully, the stupendous responsibility that rests upon me, and recognizing also my own weakness, I desire here and now to vindicate the administration of the State government of South Carolina, to reply to the unjust strictures against the race with which I am so closely identified, and to submit a few facts which, when submitted, I feel assured will at once show up in all its glaring characters the mendacity of the assailants of the Republican party of my State. I shall assert nothing that I cannot at this moment substantiate with the proofs. I shall speak from the records and shall ask you to examine with me those records.

As a member of this House I am sworn not only to the faithful performance of my duties toward the nation, but to take care that my Commonwealth be not injured, and to see, in as far as I may be able, that her public officers suffer no unjust harm. With this statement of my position, by way of preface, I shall now attempt to reply to the allegations made a short time ago by the gentleman from Indiana [Daniel Wolsey Voorhees] reiterated by the gentleman from Kentucky [James Burnie Beck] and often repeated by other gentlemen on the other side of the House. I will pause for an instant to challenge those gentlemen as to their proofs, for I know as well as they can know that they do not have reliable proof.

The gentleman from Indiana [Mr. Voorhees] based his argument upon a report submitted to the General Assembly of South Carolina a few months ago by one of its committee. This report was written, shaped, and manipulated by Benjamin Franklin Whittemore, an ex-member of Congress. Whatever of glory may be achieved by that report ought certainly to go to his credit; whatever of infamy might attach to its bold perversions of fact will surely reach him. I will not attempt to explain to the House who this reputable witness is, for you all know him as well as I do, and you all know him to be indeed an honorable man. I will not ask you to rule out his testimony as doubtful or unreliable, for many of you in the Forty-first Congress (the gentleman from Indiana included) gave your testimonial, by your votes, as to his integrity as a man and to his veracity as a witness. I will not ask you at this late hour to express your views as to his moral conduct in public life, for out of regard for his purity as a man and his uprightness as a Representative, the Forty-First Congress declined to [again] subject him to the contaminating influences of legislation from which he had been mercifully relieved but a short time before.

I do not propose to enter into a controversy with the gentleman from Indiana in regard to the bitter acrimony displayed by him in discussing what he has been pleased to term "the ruin of South Carolina"; but I shall attempt to show how groundless are the charges and how untrue is the evidence upon which the Republicans of South Carolina have been made obnoxious to his harsh criticism. The Report to which he has alluded with singular rashness in the use of figures places the bonded debt of South Carolina at $29,158,914.47. This bold and monstrous exaggeration, with all its glaring untruthfulness and mendacity, was still insufficient for the gentleman's purpose, for, not content with this statement of his own witness, he found it necessary to add $10,000,000 more—perhaps for the purpose of obtaining an aggregate that should be so alarming in its magnitude as would make us so infamous in the eyes of the country as to deprive us of a fair and impartial hearing.

This Report places the bonded debt at $13,391,005.49 in excess of what it can possibly be even though every bond ever placed in the hands of the financial agent and not now in the treasury should become a total loss to the State. This enormous figure is reached by classing as a part of the debt $6,000,000 of sterling loan bonds printed by authority of law, which were never issued, but were canceled by order of the General Assembly at its last session, but a few weeks after the publication of this foul calumny upon the Republican State government of South Carolina; also, $6,787,608.20 of railroad bonds, on which the State appears only as an endorser, paying no interest and liable only for any deficiency after all the property of the roads (which have ample assets) shall have been exhausted. In proof of the assertion that these indorsed bonds cannot in any just or proper sense be considered a part of the actual bonded debt of the State, I call attention to the fact that one of the railroads whose bonds have been thus indorsed has, within the past year, provided for and liquidated its indorsed bonds amounting to $2,093,312.40.

But the amount of endorsed bonds given by the committee is subject to a further deduction of $4,000,000, that being the portion indorsed for the Blue Ridge Railroad Company, and which has never been put upon the market, and has, therefore, not yet formed a part of even the contingent liability of the State. In addition to these remote and purely contingent liabilities, the putative father of this report has improperly embraced the following items which at present form no part of the actual debt, in order to make up an astounding aggregate, namely: bonds held by the sinking fund commission of the State, $200,000; bonds due July 1, 1871, and redeemed and canceled and now in the treasury, $212,000. There should be further deducted the college land scrip bonds, amounting to $200,000, now held in trust by the financial agent, as those bonds, after having been computed by the father of this report in his general debt statement, were again added as if they were an additional issue.

Making these deductions which are clearly proper, even according to the figures given in the report now in question, and admitting that every bond of the State delivered to the financial agent is lost to the State or must be redeemed at its face value, the total bonded debt is shown by this very report, short of its stupendous exaggerations, to be $15,759,306. 27; or $8,602.71 less than is set forth in the treasurer's exhibit as given in the last annual message of the Governor to the Legislature on November 28, 1871. I have, up to this time, confined myself strictly to a critical analysis of this report. I have produced no figures not found within its pages; I have made no statement not based upon its own exhibit. I propose now, however, to produce facts based upon other evidence than this report. I shall produce witnesses whose credibility has never yet been called in question, whose veracity has never yet been doubted, and the correctness of whose testimony cannot be successfully impeached.

Having seen the data upon which the committee based their conclusion as to the amount of the bonded debt of the State, let us now examine the law upon which this committee based their declaration; in other words, let us argue the proposition "that there has been no over-issue of State bonds." An over-issue of bonds is, in a legal sense, an issue made in excess of such an issue as may be authorized by law. There is also another sense in which an over-issue of bonds may be claimed to have been made, and that is, that an amount of bonds has been issued in excess of the amount actually necessary to have borrowed the total amount of money required by the laws authorizing such issue.

Will it be pretended for a moment, after examining the acts under which these bonds were issued, that there has been in this case an over-issue, as understood in a strict legal sense? Will it even be pretended that there has been any over-issue, or illegal or fraudulent issue? Will anyone assume to say that the letter or spirit of the statute under which these bonds were issued has been violated? The statute above quoted, and the one which constitutes the pivot upon which this entire question revolves, and the one in the light of which the legality or illegality of the issue of these bonds must be determined, makes no limitation whatever as to the issue of bonds, but simply fixes the time during which loans may be negotiated. It has never been alleged that any loans have been negotiated subsequent to the expiration of the time to which such negotiations were limited.

The several acts authorizing the negotiation of loans specify the amount of money to be borrowed, but are silent as to the amount of bonds to be hypothecated. Has it ever been alleged that the amount of money called for by those acts was not raised and used for public purposes? Never have such allegations been made. In proof of the fact that the greater part of the moneys so raised by the issue of bonds was devoted to the just and faithful payment of the obligations incurred by former administrations, and to the relief of the creditors of the State who had been long kept out of their dues, I submit the following items of public debt that existed prior to 1868, and which have been paid by the Republican administration since its advent into power.

The foregoing is a statement of the actual amount of money borrowed upon coupon bonds in pursuance of the law to meet accrued liabilities. If it required the sale of a greater amount of bonds than is customary in other States to realize these amounts, the responsibility must rest upon the Board of Trade and Chamber of Commerce of the City of Charleston, united with other influential combinations, who, acting under the belief that to destroy the credit of the State was a sure means of destroying the political party in power, stigmatized in advance the bonds of the State as worthless, and declared that as soon as the Democracy should regain the political control of the State they would repudiate every dollar of debt contracted subsequent to the adoption of the new State constitution. Pretending to represent the people of South Carolina, they boldly proclaimed their wicked and unholy purpose to sacrifice the honor of the State. This wicked determination to destroy the financial credit and to depreciate the securities of the State was recklessly put in execution almost simultaneously with the advent of the Republican party into power, and before it could have rendered itself, by any act of its own, obnoxious to the charges of corruption or improvidence.

The *Charleston Daily News,* the leading Democratic organ of South Carolina, on the 17th of July 1868, but ten days after the new State government went into operation, boldly proclaimed the purpose of its party in the following language. (The newspaper article is excluded from this book.) Such was the language of this influential exponent of the Democracy of South Carolina, repeated with equal force by the press of the State, and commended to the people by priest and politician. Does anyone wonder at the stringency of our finances? Let him turn his eyes to the fruits borne by the incendiary and revolutionary utterances of these Democratic leaders—the political allies of the gentlemen on the other side—these men who so loudly proclaim their honest concern for the interest of the State, and his wonderment will cease.

Does he inquire whether or not these wild threats had the effect of accomplishing the object sought? Let the history of our securities in Wall Street;

let the hardships encountered in raising our annual revenue and in obtaining loans to meet our liabilities; let the rapid decline of our bonds from a market value of eighty-five and ninety per cent to twenty-five and thirty per cent answer the inquiry. Does he ask whether the threat conveyed in these words, "this majority we shall have in less than a year," has ever been put in execution? Let the hundreds of new-made graves in which lie the bones of the victims of midnight assassination; let the lacerated backs of men and women; let the women whose persons have been violated by the fiendish emissaries of Democratic malice; let the dark annals of the Ku Klux Klan dens, which have so foully disgraced the history of Christian America, as unfolded by the confirmed, by the heart-rending, recital of cruelties endured by many of the victims themselves, furnish the true, and conclusive reply.

That is required $9,514,000 in bonds to raise $3,200,000 in money can certainly be a surprise to no one who is in any manner acquainted with the terrible ordeal through which the Republican administration of South Carolina has been forced to pass. That the Legislature of South Carolina could not even assume to affix a market value to the bonds of the State can easily be accounted for by the bold and reckless threats of the Democracy; by the bitter denunciations hurled at the heads of the legally constituted officers of the State through the public press, on the hustings, and even in the pulpit, by the infatuated advocates of the Democratic party of the South. The surprised clergyman, commissioned to preach the doctrine of the new Evangel—"peace on earth and good will toward men," stained and polluted as a man his surplice as a priest. Instead of preaching peace he sowed discord.

The political leaders, instead of evincing a spirit of amity toward their fellow-citizens; instead of lending their statesmanship and their influence toward retrieving the shattered fortunes of the State, advised resistance to the State government, and threatened open opposition to the Federal authority. They fired the hearts of their fanatic followers, and thus sacrificed the lives of hundreds of inoffensive citizens to satisfy the demoniac demands of the blind votaries of a hellish Democracy.

Has the Democratic party of South Carolina evinced a desire to advance the prosperity of the State, to maintain her credit in the financial world, to develop her resources, and to make her "waste places blossom as the rose"? I know that the Republican party, forgetting all political differences, would cheerfully have lent its every effort to the accomplishment of such a laudable and beneficent undertaking. Instead of forming combinations having for their object the crippling of the finances of the State, the driving away of capital from our borders, and the hindering of our commercial advancement, had they listened to the exhortation of the people with whom I am identified, the asperities of the past would have been forgotten, and today, the blessings of peace and amity would pervade our entire State. Instead of arraying one portion of her people against the other; instead of countenancing organized murder and outrage, had they tendered their influence and experience, so often solicited, no man would more readily have accepted their counsels and endeavored to profit more than the Republican Governor of South Carolina, whom they new affect to arraign at the bar of public opinion as a public plunderer.

The race, with which I am identified, has often been forced to stand as a target for the shafts of Democratic hate and prejudice. The sufferings and wrongs we have endured on this continent have been indeed great. The taunts, insults, and bitter cruelties to which we have been subjected have ascended even unto the uppermost heaven. Amid all our sufferings, degradation, and woes, having an abiding faith in our Great Creator, we have been content "to labor and to wait." In behalf of that people, I do here declare that despite the Pelion of outrage of the Negro-hating Democracy of the South piled upon the Ossa of the chronic prejudices of their allies of the North, relying still upon divine Providence, we shall have confidence in the true American heart, and having no interests not in common with those of our white fellow-citizens, we hope to perform well our part in increasing the material wealth of our country, in developing her vast resources, in adding to her prowess, and in making her in all respects the grandest and purest as well as the most powerful Government upon all earth.

We trust the time is not far away when all of our fellow-citizens— whether they be native—born or whether they first drew the breath of life on the banks of the Shannon or of the Rhine; whether they sprang from the Orient or the Occident—no longer swayed by unjust prejudices, no longer controlled by the teachings of a false political faith, shall be touched with the inspiration of a holier sentiment and shall recognize the "universal fatherhood of God and brotherhood of man." To hasten that period we shall contribute whatever of energy, brain, and muscle we may possess, and asking only what is just and fair, performing only what is right, we shall ever cherish the genius of our American institutions, and pour upon them with a lavish hand the rich libations of a more than Roman devotion.

Having submitted these facts in vindication of my Commonwealth, and of the people of my own identity, I ask for them the calm deliberation of this House, and believing them to be true, in the name of that people and of my Commonwealth I invoke the just judgment of the civilized world.

Elliott denied that he supported the Civil Rights Bill merely because he was black, but instead did so because it was the right thing to do. Such a law, he argued, would protect the rights of all Americans, including women. He provided an overview of African-American history, to explain that blacks had been patriots since the American Revolution. He also reviewed the Slaughter-house Cases, where the Supreme Court made a favorable ruling on the purpose of the Fourteenth Amendment.

THE CIVIL RIGHTS BILL
January 6, 1874

While I am sincerely grateful for this high mark of courtesy that has been accorded to my by this House, it is a matter of regret to me that it is necessary at this day that I should rise in the presence of an American Congress to advocate a bill which simply asserts equal rights and equal public privileges for all classes of American citizens. I regret, sir, that the dark hue of my skin may lend a color to the imputation that I am controlled by motives personal to myself in my advocacy of this great measure of national justice. The motive that impels me is restricted by no such narrow boundary, but is as broad as your Constitution. I advocate it because it is right. The bill, however, not only appeals to your justice, but it demands a response from your gratitude.

In the events that led to the achievement of American Independence the Negro was not an inactive or unconcerned spectator. He bore his part bravely upon many battlefields, although not cheered by that certain hope of political elevation which victory would secure to the white man. The tall granite shaft, which a grateful State has reared above its son who fell in defending Fort Griswold against the attack of Benedict Arnold, bears the name of Jordan, Freeman, and other brave men of the African race who there cemented with their blood the corner-stone of the Republic. In the State that I have the honor in part to represent the rifle the black man rang out against the troops of the British crown in the darkest days of the American Revolution.

At the battle of New Orleans, under the immortal Jackson, a colored regiment held the extreme right of the American line unflinchingly, and drove back the British column that pressed upon them, at the point of the bayonet. So marked was their valor on that occasion that it evoked from their great commander the warmest encomiums, as will be seen from his dispatch announcing the brilliant victory. As the gentleman from Kentucky [James Burnie Beck], who seems to be the leading exponent on this floor of the party that is arrayed against the principle of this bill, has been pleased, in season and out of season, to cast odium upon the Negro and to vaunt the chivalry of his State, I may be pardoned for calling attention to another portion of the same dispatch. In quoting this indisputable piece of history, I do so only by way of admonition and not to question the well-attested gallantry of the true Kentuckian, and to suggest to the gentleman that it would be well that he should not flaunt his heraldry so proudly while he bears this bar—sinister on the military escutcheon of his State—a State which answered the call of the Republic in 1861, when treason thundered at the very gates of the capital, by coldly declaring her neutrality in the impending struggle. The Negro, true to that patriotism and love of country that have ever characterized and marked his history on this continent, came to the aid of the government in its efforts to maintain the Constitution. To that Government he now appeals; that Constitution he now invokes for protection against outrage and unjust prejudices founded upon caste.

But the distinguished gentleman from Georgia [Alexander H. Stephens] tells us that Congress has no power under the Constitution to pass such a law, and that the passage of such an act is in direct contravention of the rights of the States. I cannot assent to any such proposition. The constitution of a free government ought always to be construed in favor of human rights. Indeed, the Thirteenth, Fourteenth, and Fifteenth Amendments, in positive words, invest Congress with the power to protect the citizen in his civil and political rights. The rights contended for in this bill are among "the sacred rights of mankind, which are not to be rummaged for among old parchments or musty records; they are written as with a sunbeam, in the whole volume of human nature, by the hand of the divinity itself, and can never be erased or obscured by mortal powers."

The honorable gentleman from Kentucky, always swift to sustain the failing and dishonored cause of proscription, rushes forward and flaunts in our faces the decision of the Supreme Court of the United States in the Slaughter-house Cases, and in that act he has been willingly aided by the gentleman from Georgia. Hitherto, in the contests, which have marked the progress of the cause of equal civil rights, our opponents have appealed sometimes to custom, sometimes to prejudice, more often to pride of race, but they have never sought to shield themselves behind the Supreme Court. But now, for the first time, we are told that we are barred by a decision of that court, from which there is no appeal. If this be true we must stay our hands. The cause of equal civil rights must pause at the command of a power whose edicts must be obeyed till the fundamental law of our country is changed. Has the honorable gentleman from Kentucky considered well the claim he how advances? If it were not disrespectful I would ask, has he ever read the decision that he now tells us is an insuperable barrier to the adoption of this great measure of justice?

In the consideration of this subject, has not the judgment of the gentleman from Georgia been warped by the ghost of the dead doctrines of state's-rights? Has he been altogether free from prejudices engendered by long training in that school of politics that well nigh destroyed this Government? I venture to say here in the presence of the gentleman from Kentucky, and the gentleman from Georgia, and in the presence of the whole country, that there is not a line or word, not a thought or dictum even, in the decision of the Supreme Court in the great Slaughter-house Cases which casts a shadow of doubt on the right of Congress to pass the pending bill, or to adopt such other legislation as it may judge proper and necessary to secure perfect equality before the law to every citizen of the Republic. I protest against the dishonor now cast upon our Supreme Court by both the gentleman from Kentucky and the gentleman from Georgia. In other days, when the whole country was bowing beneath the yoke of slavery, when press, pulpit, platform, Congress, and courts felt the fatal power of the slave oligarchy, I remember a decision of that court which no American now reads without shame and humiliation. But those days are past. The Supreme Court of today is a tribunal as true to freedom as any department of this Government, and I am honored with the opportunity of repelling a deep disgrace that the gentleman from Kentucky, backed and sustained as he is by the gentleman from Georgia, seeks to put upon it.

What were these Slaughter-house Cases? The gentleman should be aware that a decision of any court should be examined in the light of the exact question that is brought before it for decision. That is all that gives authority to any decision. The State of Louisiana, by act of her Legislature, had conferred on certain persons the exclusive right to maintain stock-landings and slaughter-houses within the city of New Orleans, or the parishes of Orleans, Jefferson, and Saint Bernard, in that State. The corporation that was thereby chartered was invested with the sole and exclusive privileges of conducting and carrying on the livestock, landing, and slaughter-house business within the limits designated. The Supreme Court of Louisiana sustained the validity of the act conferring these exclusive privileges, and the plaintiffs in error brought the case before the Supreme Court of the United States for review. The plaintiffs in error contended that the act in question was void, because, first, it established a monopoly which was in derogation of common right and in contravention of the common law; and, second, that the grant of such exclusive privileges was in violation of the Thirteenth and Fourteenth Amendments of the Constitution of the United States.

It thus appears from a simple statement of the case that the question which was before the court was not whether a State law which denied to a particular portion of her citizens the rights conferred on her citizens generally, on account of race, color, or previous condition of servitude, was unconstitutional because it was in conflict with the recent amendments, but whether an act which conferred on certain citizens exclusive privileges for police purposes was in conflict therewith, because imposing an involuntary servitude forbidden by the Thirteenth Amendment, or abridging the rights and immunities of citizens of the United States, or denying the equal protection of the laws, was prohibited by the Fourteenth Amendment. On the part of the defendants in error it was maintained that the act was the exercise of the ordinary and unquestionable power of the State to make regulation for the health and comfort of society—the exercise of the police power of the State, defined by Chancellor Kent to be "the right to interdict unwholesome trades, slaughterhouses, operations offensive to the senses, the deposit of powder, the application of steam power to propel cars, the building with combustible materials, and the burial of the dead in the midst of dense masses of population, on the general and rational principle that every person ought so to use his own property as not to injure his neighbors, and that private interests must be made subservient to the general interests of the community."

The decision of the Supreme Court is to be found in the 16th volume of Wallace's Reports, and was delivered by Associate Justice Samuel F. Miller. The court holds, first, that the act in question is a legitimate and warrantable exercise of the police power of the State in regulating the business of stock-landing and slaughtering in the city of New Orleans and the territory immediately contiguous. Having held this, the court proceeds to discuss the question of whether the conferring of exclusive privileges, such as those conferred by the act in question, is the imposing of an involuntary servitude, the abridging of the rights and immunities of citizens of the United States, or the denial to any person within the jurisdiction of the State of the equal protection of the laws.

That the act is not the imposition of an involuntary servitude the court holds to be clear. They proceeded to examine the remaining questions arising under the Fourteenth Amendment. Upon this question the court holds that the leading and comprehensive purpose of the Thirteenth, Fourteenth, and Fifteenth Amendments was to secure the complete freedom of the race, which, by the events of the war, had been wrested from the unwilling grasp of their owners. I know no finer or more just picture, albeit painted in the neutral tints of true judicial impartiality, of the motives and events that led to these amendments. These amendments, one and all, are thus declared to have as their all-pervading design and end the security to the recently enslaved race, not only their nominal freedom, but their complete protection from those who had formerly exercised unlimited dominion over them. It is in this broad light that all these amendments must be read, the purpose being to secure the perfect equality before the law of all citizens of the United States. What you give to one class you must give to all; what you deny to one class you shall deny to all, unless in the exercise of the common and universal police power of the State you find it needful to confer exclusive privileges on certain citizens, to be held and exercised still for the common good of all.

Such are the doctrines of the Slaughter-house Cases—doctrines worthy of the Republic, worthy of the age, worthy of the great tribunal that thus loftily and impressively enunciates them. Do they—I put it to any man, be he lawyer or not; I put it to the gentleman from Georgia—do they give color even to the claim that this Congress may not now legislate against a plain discrimination made by State laws or State customs against that very race for whose complete freedom and protection these great amendments were elaborated and adopted? Is it pretended, I ask the honorable gentleman from Kentucky or the honorable gentleman from Georgia—is it pretended anywhere that the evils of which we complain, our exclusion from the public inn, from the saloon and table of the steamboat, from the sleeping-coach on the railway, from the right of sepulture in the public burial ground, are an exercise of the police power of the State? Is such oppression and injustice nothing but the exercise by the State of the right to make regulations for the health, comfort, and security of all her citizens? Is it merely enacting that one man shall so use his own as not to injure another's? Is the colored race to be assimilated to an unwholesome trade or to combustible materials to be shut-up within prescribed limits? Let the gentleman from Kentucky or the gentleman from Georgia answer. Let the country know to what extent even the audacious prejudice of the gentleman from Kentucky will drive him, and how far even the gentleman from Georgia will permit him to be led captive by the unrighteous teachings of a false political faith.

If we are to be likened in legal view to "unwholesome trades," to "large and offensive collections of animals," to "noxious slaughter-houses," to "the offal and stench which attend on certain manufactures," let it be avowed. If that is still the doctrine of the political party to which the gentleman belongs, let it be put upon record. If State laws which deny us the common rights and privileges of other citizens, upon no possible or conceivable ground save one of prejudice, or of "taste," as the gentleman from Texas termed it, and as I suppose the gentleman will prefer to call it, are to be placed under the protection of a decision which affirms the right of a State to regulate the police of her great cities, then the decision is in conflict with the bill before us. No man will dare maintain such a doctrine. It is as shocking to the legal mind as it is offensive to the heart and conscience of all who love justice or respect manhood. I am astonished that the gentleman from Kentucky or the gentleman from Georgia should have been so grossly misled as to rise here and assert that the decision of the Supreme Court in these cases was a denial to Congress of the power to legislate against discriminations on account of race, color, or previous condition of servitude, because that court has decided that exclusive privileges conferred for the common protection of the lives and health of the whole community are not in violation of the recent amendments. The only ground upon which the grant of exclusive privileges to a portion of the community is ever defended is that the substantial good of all is promoted; that in truth it is for the welfare of the whole community that certain persons should alone pursue certain occupations. It is not the special benefit conferred on the few that moves the legislature, but the ultimate and real benefit of all, even of those who are denied the right to pursue those specified occupations. Does the gentleman from Kentucky say that my good is promoted when I am excluded from the public inn? Is the health or safety of the community promoted? Doubtless his prejudice is gratified. Doubtless his democratic instincts are pleased; but will he or his able coadjutor say that such exclusion is a lawful exercise of the police power of the State, or that it is not a denial to me of the equal protection of the laws? They will not so say.

But each of these gentlemen quote at some length from the decision of the court to show that the court recognizes a difference between citizenship of the United States and citizenship of the States. That is true, and no man here who supports this bill questions or overlooks the difference. There are privileges and immunities that belong to me as a citizen of the United States, and there are other privileges and immunities that belong to me as a citizen of my State. The former are under the protection of the Constitution and laws of the United States, and the latter are under the protection of the constitution and laws of my State. Are the rights, which I now claim—the right to enjoy the common public conveniences of travel on public highways, of rest and refreshment at public inns, of education in public schools, of burial in public cemeteries—rights which I hold as a citizen of the United States or of my State? Or, to state the question more exactly, is not the denial of such privileges to me a denial to me of the equal protection of the laws? For it is under this clause of the Fourteenth Amendment that we place the present bill, no State shall "deny to any person within its jurisdiction the equal protection of the laws." No matter, therefore, whether his rights are held under the United States or under his particular State, he is equally protected by this amendment. He is always and everywhere entitled to the equal protection of the laws. All discrimination is forbidden; and while the rights of citizens of a State as such are not defined or conferred by the Constitution of the United States, yet all discrimination, all denial of equality before the law, all denial of the equal protection of the laws, whether State or national laws, is forbidden.

The distinction between the two kinds of citizenship is clear, and the Supreme Court has clearly pointed out this distinction, but they have nowhere written a word or line which denies to Congress the power to prevent a denial of equality of rights, whether those rights exist by virtue of citizenship of the United States or of a State. Let honorable members mark well this distinction. There are rights that are conferred on us by the United States. There are other rights conferred on us by the States of which we are individually the citizens. The Fourteenth Amendment does not forbid a State to deny to all its citizens any of those rights that the State itself has conferred, with certain exceptions, which are pointed out in the decision that we are examining. What it does forbid is inequality, is discrimination, or, to use the words of the amendment itself, is the denial "to any person within its jurisdiction the equal protection of the laws." If a State denies to me rights which are common to all her other citizens, she violates this amendment, unless she can show, as was shown in the Slaughter-house Cases, that she does it in the legitimate exercise of her police power. If she abridges the rights of all her citizens equally, unless those rights are specially guarded by the Constitution of the United States, she does not violate this amendment. This is not to put the rights which I hold by virtue of my citizenship of South Carolina under the protection of the national Government; it is not to blot out or over look in the slightest particular the distinction between rights held under the United States and rights held under the States; but it seeks to secure equality, to prevent discrimination, to confer as complete and ample protection on the humblest as on the highest.

The gentleman from Kentucky, in the course of the speech to which I am now replying, made a reference to the State of Massachusetts which betrays again the confusion which exists in his mind on this precise point. He tells us that Massachusetts excludes from the ballot box all who cannot read and write, and points to that fact as the exercise of a right which this bill would abridge or impair. The honorable gentleman from Massachusetts [Mr. Dawes] answered him truly and well, but I submit that he did not make the best reply. Why did he not ask the gentleman from Kentucky if Massachusetts had ever discriminated against any of her citizens on account of color, or race, or previous conditions of servitude? When did Massachusetts sully her proud record by placing on her statute book any law which admitted to the ballot the white man and shut out the black man? She has never done it; she will not do it; she cannot do it so long as we have a Supreme Court which reads the Constitution of our country with the eyes of justice; nor can Massachusetts or Kentucky deny to any man, on account of his race, color, or previous condition of servitude, that perfect equality of protection under the laws so long as Congress shall exercise the power to enforce, by appropriate legislation, the great and unquestionable securities embodied in the Fourteenth Amendment to the Constitution.

But a few more words as to the suffrage regulation of Massachusetts. It is true that Massachusetts in 1857, finding that its illiterate population was being constantly augmented by the continual influx of ignorant emigrants, placed in her constitution the least possible limitation consistent with manhood suffrage to stay this tide of foreign ignorance. Its benefit has been fully demonstrated in the intelligent character of the voters of that honored Commonwealth, reflected so conspicuously in the able Representatives she has today upon this floor. But neither is the inference of the gentleman from Kentucky legitimate, nor does the statistics of the census of 1870, drawn from his own State, sustain his astounding assumption. According to the statistics we find the whole white population of that State is 1,098,692; the whole colored population 222,210. Of the whole white population who cannot write we find 201,077; of the whole colored population who cannot write, 126,048; giving us as will be seen, 96,162 colored persons who can write to 897,615 white persons who can write. Now, the ratio of the colored population to the white is as 1 to 5, and the ratio of the illiterate colored population to the whole colored population is as 1 to 2; the ratio of the illiterate white population is to the whole white population as 1 is to 5. Reducing this, we have only a preponderance of three-tenths in favor of the whites as to literacy, notwithstanding the advantages which they have always enjoyed and do now enjoy of free school privileges, and this, too, taking solely into account the single item of being unable to write; for with regard to the inability to read, there is no discrimination in the statistics between the white and colored population. There is, moreover, a peculiar felicity in these statistics with regard to the State of Kentucky, quoted so opportunely for me by the honorable gentleman; for I find that the population of that State, both with regard to its white and colored populations of the United States; and, therefore, while one Negro would be disfranchised were the limitation of Massachusetts put in force, nearly three white men would at the same time be deprived of the right of suffrage—a consummation which I think would be far more acceptable to the colored people of that State than to the whites.

Now having spoken as to the intention of the prohibition imposed by Massachusetts, I may be pardoned for a slight inquiry as to the effect of this prohibition. First, it did not in any way abridge or curtail the exercise of the suffrage by any person who at that time enjoyed such right. Nor did it discriminate between the illiterate native and the illiterate foreigner. Being enacted for the good of the entire Commonwealth, like all just laws, its obligations fell equally and impartially upon all its citizens. And as a justification for such a measure, it is a fact too well known almost for mention here that Massachusetts had, from the beginning of her history, recognized the inestimable value of an educated ballot, by not only maintaining a system of free schools, but also enforcing an attendance thereupon, as one of the safeguards for the preservation of a real republican form of government. Recurring then, to the possible contingency alluded to by the gentleman from Kentucky, should the State of Kentucky, having first established a system of common schools whose doors shall swing open freely to all, as contemplated by the provisions of this bill, adopt a provision similar to that of Massachusetts, no one would have cause justly to complain. And if in the coming years the result of such legislation should produce a constituency rivaling that of the old Bay State, no one would be more highly gratified than I.

I have neither the time nor the inclination to notice the many illogical and forced conclusions, the numerous transfers of terms, or the vulgar insinuations, which further encumber the argument of the gentleman from Kentucky. Now referring to the venerable and distinguished gentleman from Georgia [Mr. Stephens], who has added his remonstrance against the passage of this bill; permit me to say that I share in the feeling of high personal regard for that gentleman which pervades this House. His years, his ability, and his long experience in public affairs entitle him to the measure of consideration I cannot and I will not forget—the welfare and rights of my whole race in this country are involved. When, therefore, the honorable gentleman from Georgia lends his voice and influence to defeat this measure, I do not shrink from saying that it is not from him that the American House of Representatives should take lessons in matters touching human rights or the joint relations of the State and national governments.

While the honorable gentleman contented himself with harmless speculations in his study, or in the columns of a newspaper, we might well smile at the impotence of his efforts to turn back the advancing tide of opinion and progress; but, when he comes again upon this national arena, and throws himself with all his power and influence across the path which leads to the full enfranchisement of my race, I meet him only as an adversary; nor shall age or any other consideration restrain me from saying that he now offers this Government, which he has done his utmost to destroy, a very poor return for its magnanimous treatment, to come here and seek to continue, by the assertion of doctrines obnoxious to the true principles of our Government, the burdens and oppressions which rest upon five millions of his countrymen who never failed to lift their earnest prayers for the success of this Government when the gentleman was seeking to break up the Union of these States and to blot the American Republic from the galaxy of nations.

It is scarcely twelve years since those gentlemen shocked the civilized world by announcing the birth of a government that rested on human slavery as its cornerstone. The progress of events has swept away that *pseudo*-government which rested on greed, pride, and tyranny; and the race whom he then ruthlessly spurned and trampled on are here to meet him in debate, and to demand that the rights which are enjoyed by their former oppressors—who vainly sought to overthrow a Government which they could not prostitute to the base uses of slavery—shall be accorded to those who even in the darkness of slavery kept their allegiance true to freedom and the Union. The gentleman from Georgia has learned much since 1861; but he is still a laggard. Let him put away entirely the false and fatal theories that have so greatly marred an otherwise enviable record. Let him accept, in its fullness and beneficence, the great doctrine that American citizenship carries with it every civil and political right which manhood can confer. Let him lend his influence, with all his masterly ability, to complete the proud structure of legislation which makes this nation worthy of the great declaration which heralded its birth, and he will have done that which will most nearly redeem his reputation in the eyes of the world, and best vindicate the wisdom of that policy which has permitted him to regain his seat upon this floor.

To the diatribe of the gentleman from Virginia [John Thomas Harris] who spoke yesterday, and who so far transcended the limits of decency and propriety as to announce upon this floor that his remarks were addressed to white men alone, I shall have no word of reply. Let him feel that a Negro was not only too magnanimous to smite him in his weakness, but was even charitable enough to grant him the mercy of his silence. I shall, sir, leave to others less charitable the unenviable and fatiguing task of sifting out of that mass of chaff the few grains of sense that may, perchance, deserve notice. Assuring the gentleman that the Negro in this country aims at a higher degree of intellect than that exhibited by him in this debate, I cheerfully commend him to the commiseration of all intelligent men the world over-black men as well as white men.

Our republic mandates equality before the law as a universal and glorious rule. No State can violate that. Kentucky and Georgia may crowd their statute—books with retrograde and barbarous legislation; they may rejoice in the odious eminence of their consistent hostility to all the great steps of human progress which have marked our national history since slavery tore down the stars and stripes on Fort Sumter; but, if Congress shall do its duty, if Congress shall enforce the great guarantees which the Supreme Court has declared to be the one pervading purpose of all the recent amendments, then their unwise and unenlightened conduct will fall with the same weight upon the gentlemen from those States who now lend their influence to defeat this bill, as upon the poorest slave who once had no rights which the honorable gentlemen were bound to respect.

Not only does the decision in the Slaughter-house Cases contain nothing which suggests a doubt of the power of Congress to pass the pending bill, but it contains an express recognition and affirmation of such power. No language could convey a more complete assertion of the power of Congress over the subject embraced in the present bill than is here expressed. If the States do not conform to the requirements of this clause, if they continue to deny to any person within their jurisdiction the equal protection of the laws, or as the Supreme Court had said: "deny equal justice in its courts," then Congress is here said to have power to enforce the constitutional guarantee by appropriate legislation. That is the power that this bill now seeks to put in exercise. It proposes to enforce the constitutional guarantee against inequality and discrimination by appropriate legislation. It does not seek to confer new rights, nor to place rights conferred by State citizenship under the protection of the United States, but simply to prevent and forbid inequality and discrimination on account of race, color, or previous condition of servitude. Never was there a bill more completely within the constitutional power of Congress. Never was there a bill that appealed for support more strongly to that sense of justice and fair play that has been said, and in the main with justice, to be a characteristic of the Anglo-Saxon race. The Constitution warrants it; the Supreme Court sanctions it; justice demands it.

I have replied to the extent of my ability to the arguments that have been presented by the opponents of this measure. I have replied also to some of the legal propositions advanced by gentlemen on the other side; and now that I am about to conclude, I am deeply sensible of the imperfect manner in which I have performed the task. Technically, this bill is to decide upon the civil status of the colored American citizen; a point disputed at the very formation of our present Government, when by a shortsighted policy, a policy repugnant to true republican government, one Negro counted as three-fifths of a man. The logical result of this mistake of the framers of the Constitution strengthened the cancer of slavery, which finally spread its poisonous tentacles over the southern portion of the body politic. To arrest its growth and save the nation we have passed through the harrowing operation of an internal war, dreaded at all times, resorted to at the last extremity, like the surgeon's knife, but absolutely necessary to extirpate the disease which threatened with the life of the nation the overthrow of civil and political liberty on this continent. In that dire extremity the members of the race which I have the honor in part to represent—the race which pleads for justice at your hands today, forgetful of their inhuman and brutalizing servitude at the South, their degradation and ostracism at the North—flew willingly and gallantly to the support of the national Government. Their sufferings, assistance, privations, and trials in the swamps and in the rice fields, their valor on the land and on the sea, is a part of the ever-glorious record which makes up the history of a nation preserved, and might, should I urge the claim, incline you to respect and guarantee their rights and privileges as citizens of our common Republic. But I remember that valor, devotion, and loyalty are not always rewarded according to their just deserts and that after the battle some who have borne the brunt of the fray may, through neglect or contempt, be assigned to a subordinate place, while the enemies in war may be preferred to the sufferers.

The results of the war, as seen in Reconstruction, have settled forever the political status of my race. The passage of this bill will determine the civil status, not only of the Negro, but of any other class of citizens who may feel themselves discriminated against. It will form the capstone of that temple of liberty, begun on this continent under discouraging circumstances, carried on in spite of the sneers of monarchists and the cavils of pretended friends of freedom, until at last it stands in all its beautiful symmetry and proportions, a building the grandest which the world has ever seen, realizing the most sanguine expectations and the highest hopes of those who, in the name of equal, impartial, and universal liberty, laid the foundation stones.

The Holy Scriptures tell us of a humble hand-maiden who long, faithfully and patiently gleaned in the rich fields of her wealthy kinsman; and we are told further that at last, in spite of her humble antecedents, she found complete favor in his sight. For over two centuries our race has "reaped down your fields." The cries and woes that we have uttered have "entered into the ears of the Lord of Sabbath," and we are at least politically free. The last vestiture only is needed—civil rights. Having gained this, we may, with hearts overflowing with gratitude, and thankful that our prayer has been granted, repeat the prayer of Ruth: "Entreat me not to leave thee, or to return from following after thee; for whither thou goest, I will go; and where thou lodgest, I will lodge; thy people shall be my people, and thy God my God; where thou diest, will I die, and there will I be buried; the Lord do so to me, and more also, if aught but death part thee and me."

6

Jeremiah Haralson
(1846–1916)
House of Representatives, Alabama

Republican

Forty-fourth Congress
March 4, 1875, to March 3, 1877

Jeremiah Haralson was born into slavery on April 1, 1846, near Columbus, Georgia. While he might not have been Jeremiah's original owner, John Haralson apparently owned him in 1859 when he took him to Alabama. John had given no thought to manumitting the slaves when the Civil War broke out, and Jeremiah remained in bondage until 1865, when Congress adopted the Thirteenth Amendment to emancipate his race. He had been bought and sold, and had worked as a field hand. He understood bondage well, and would devote the rest of his life to further the cause of freedom and equality for African Americans. When Congress freed him from physical bondage, he freed himself from illiteracy. Although self-educated, he pursued a career in politics soon after emancipation, and he emerged as an able public servant in Alabama during the Reconstruction era. Writing in 1940, Samuel D. Smith considered Haralson a "natural politician."

As with some of his black colleagues during Reconstruction, few records exist on Jeremiah Haralson's early life. He claimed to have been a minister, but historians have not identified his affiliation. Certainly he had gained valuable experience working with African Americans, and in using words to rouse them to demand their civil rights. His friends considered him an effective stump speaker and campaigner. Frederick Douglass regarded him as a gifted debater with a talent for using humor in his rhetoric. His portrait is deceiving for it suggests a quiet demeanor. Contemporaries described him as a "ready, shrewd debater, full of wit and sarcasm." An Alabama journalist offered this assessment: "He is perhaps feared more than any other colored man in the legislature in Alabama." His adversaries questioned his qualifications, for he was neither college educated nor a lawyer. One of his harshest critics described him as an inarticulate field hand. Haralson was not lacking in confidence, and that same critic observed that he was "shrewd and fully aware of the strength of his people."

While many of his black colleagues in Congress had prominent European features Haralson was unmistakably of African stock. An Alabama reporter proclaimed that he was as "black as the ace of spades." Ironically, his dark complexion worked to his benefit in Alabama, a state with a large black population. Whites understood that once blacks obtained the vote, they surely would elect a member of their race to national office. White Democrats, therefore, wanted to give the black electorate the illusion of their full participation in the affairs of the state; and they preferred someone of Haralson's hue. By supporting him, they closed the door to other ambitious black politicians who might have been better educated, or more radical than Haralson. At any rate, Haralson plunged into the political arena soon after Alabama returned to the Union.

Haralson made an unsuccessful bid for Congress in 1868, at the age of twenty-two. Possibly recognizing that he was not yet connected politically, he thrust himself into state politics. In 1871 he was elected president of the Alabama Labor Union Convention. An organizer for the Republican party under Congressional Reconstruction, he quickly became a rising star in Alabama. Haralson launched a campaign for the Alabama General Assembly, and landed his first elective office, serving in the state house and senate from 1870 to 1875. From this base, he turned to national politics, defeating Frederick G. Bromberg, a white Republican, in the 1874 election. Bromberg tried to unseat him, alleging voter tampering. The Democratic-controlled House Committee on Elections did not agree and affirmed Haralson the winner. Haralson took his seat on March 4, 1875, and served on the Committee of Public Expenditures.

Haralson's congressional career was not spectacular. Certainly the Civil Rights Bill of Senator Charles Sumner occupied a great deal of attention in Congress. Haralson had pledged to his black constituents during the campaign that he would vote in its favor. He unequivocally favored equal opportunity for all people, but he stopped short of calling for social integration among the races. He favored separate schools for blacks and whites, and he did not advocate interracial marriages. He chided his Democrats, telling them he "would not marry a white woman unless she was rich. A poor white woman he wouldn't look at twice." As an advocate for his constituents in the Twenty-first Congressional District, Haralson presented several petitions and bills to support their interests. He wrote a bill on behalf of Mobile residents who wanted the Freedmen's Bureau to pay for the use of supplies and facilities provided them. He also submitted a petition from Clarke County residents seeking a postal route from Bay Minette to Suggsville.

Haralson also supported a bill to appropriate federal funds for the Medical College of Alabama, and to help fund compulsory public education in the state. As he had in the election of 1874, when he challenged a liberal Republican, he offended blacks again by supporting amnesty for ex-Confederate officers, and urging blacks to oppose the reelection campaign of President Grant. He had been an independent since 1870, and since he favored causes popular among white Democrats, Haralson faced harsh criticisms from Alabama Republicans. He issued a statement in his defense on January 29, 1876, stating, "We must drive out these hell hounds and go in for peace between the two races in the South." He did not satisfy Radical Republicans, and Haralson faced new challenges on the national and state level when he ran for reelection in 1876, and when he entered the race in 1878. His conservative politics, in part, ultimately ruined his political career.

The Republican party nominated former congressman James T. Rapier, another black politician, hoping to unseat the incumbent. Haralson entered the campaign as an independent. Once Charles M. Shelly, a white Democrat, entered the race, Haralson and Rapier were poised to neutralize their core constituency of black voters. Shelly easily *won* the election. Haralson contested the results to no avail because the state board of elections immediately certified Shelly. Haralson made his final bid for Congress in 1884, but with the state solidly in the hands of Democrats, he never reclaimed the status he had during the era of black political power in Alabama.

Jeremiah Haralson ended his political career holding appointive positions in the nation's capital. He was a customs agent in Baltimore, worked in the Department of the Interior, and for the Pension Bureau during the early 1880s. By the late 1880s, he turned to farming and joined others in the Black Exodus to the West, where they hoped to find better opportunities. Haralson took up farming temporarily in Louisiana, then Arkansas, and finally in Colorado he found work as a coal miner. Apparently an avid sportsman, he was killed in 1916, while hunting near Denver.

Jeremiah Haralson did not deliver any speeches from the House floor. The transcript on the election of 1874 is the most extensive official document connected to him in the Congressional Record. It summarizes the challenge filed by Frederick G. Bromberg, who charged Haralson with fraud, stealing votes, and intimidating voters. The Committee on Elections found evidence irregularities but concluded that they unlikely changed the results. They confirmed Haralson but it was too late in the term for him to participate in any debates.

CONTESTED ELECTION
Reported by Representative John Thomas Harris of Virginia
April 18, 1876

I desire to call up the case of *Bromberg v. Haralson*, from the First Congressional District of Alabama.

In this case I am happy to inform the House that the committee is unanimous in their report, and that, too, in a full committee composed of all its members; and therefore the committee deems that no debate would be necessary upon this question to enlighten the House. But I must add that I desire the House and I desire the country to read the report that the committee has made in this case. While it retains the sitting member in his seat, it will show frauds as flagrant and abuses as violent as ever have been committed in this country upon the elective franchise. Moreover, it will show that when two years ago this House was called upon to extend its charitable hand to relieve the sufferings of the colored people of Alabama caused by the floods in their rivers, and large quantities of bacon were provided for them, that bacon was taken by the Government officials and used, not in the district where the distress existed, but in the high lands where the people were prosperous, to influence and control the elective franchise.

It will be shown, moreover, that the colored voters were intimidated by their own race against voting for the contestant in this case. It will show, also, undue and unwarrantable interference on the part of the military to secure the election of the sitting member.

But notwithstanding all these acts of fraud, of undue military interference, and of the perversion of the bounty of the Government, still the large majority of the sitting members of 2,700 could not, in the opinion of the committee, be legitimately and properly overcome. Had the committee been disposed to act in a partisan way, there was heretofore in this House to have unseated the sitting member and to have seated the contestant. But the committee acting in the spirit of judicial officers, strictly analyzed the vote, and having thrown out a large number of votes illegally and improperly cast, they still found that the sitting member was entitled to his seat, and therefore they offer the resolutions which I desire the Clerk to read, and on which I call the previous question.

The Clerk read as follows:

Resolved, That Frederick G. Bromberg was not elected a member of the Forty-fourth Congress from the first congressional district of Alabama, and is not entitled to a seat in this House.

7

John Adams Hyman
(1840–1891)
House of Representatives, North Carolina

Republican

Forty-fourth Congress
March 4, 1875, to March 3, 1877

The Second Congressional District (the Black Second) in North Carolina elected three African-Americans to Congress during the late nineteenth century. John Adams Hyman was the first successful congressional candidate, as well as the first African American in North Carolina to be elected to the House of Representatives. Born to slave parents in Warren County, on July 23, 1840, Hyman at an early age experienced one of the horrors of slavery. While he worked for a Warrenton jeweler sympathetic to his desire to learn to read, his white neighbors objected when they caught him with a spelling book. They forced the jeweler out of town, accusing him of "corrupting" the slaves. The jeweler sold Hyman to an Alabama slave owner. Hyman apparently vowed to continue his quest for knowledge. As the Alabama farmer discovered, John sought to become literate. Fearing his attitude would influence other slaves the planter sold him. Hyman later recalled that he was sold at least eight times for expressing his thirst for learning.

John Adams Hyman, at the age of twenty-five, was finally freed by the Thirteenth Amendment. He returned to North Carolina to be with his family and for the first time enrolled in school. He acquired the equivalent of an elementary education. As with most southerners, farming was the primary mode of making a living, so Hyman purchased land and planted crops. He also opened a country store. He joined civic associations, such as the Colored Masons of North Carolina. As Hyman established himself, he emerged as a black leader. He was appointed the trustee of a first segregated public school in Warrenton. He was also elected a delegate to the State Equal Rights Convention in 1865, and helped to organize blacks for the political opportunity available to them during Reconstruction. He became an active member of the Republican party, and in 1867 was appointed a registrar in Warren County to enroll black voters. He was also elected to the state Constitutional Convention in 1868, joining15 other African Americans to make up the delegation of 133 charged with writing the new constitution required by Congressional Reconstruction.

North Carolina delegates drafted a progressive constitution in 1868. They called for public education and universal male suffrage; they also proposed ending property qualifications for suffrage and advocated state funded welfare for the destitute. In compliance with the Reconstruction Acts of 1867, the Convention sent the proposed constitution to the people. With mostly Republicans and black males casting ballots, the constitution won approval in spite of intimidation by the Ku Klux Klan. The Republican party was solidly in control, and when voters elected a legislature, they chose members of the party. John Adams Hyman was among them.

While the legislature was primarily white, Hyman was elected to the state senate in 1868, serving until 1874. He served on the Penitentiary Committee, and unluckily for him the committee was embroiled in a scandal. Some of its members had allegedly accepted bribes in a deal to purchase land. Indeed, the entire legislature at one time or another was accused of corruption. Hyman also was accused of selling his votes in a railroad scheme, an accusation he denied. He admitted that he had borrowed money from a railroad lobbyist to finance his campaign but asserted that he had repaid the debt. Though his tenure in the senate was turbulent, Hyman had his eyes set on national office. With a large black electorate in his district, he had made an unsuccessful bid for Congress in 1872, losing to white Republican Charles R. Thomas. He launched another campaign in 1874, this time beating George W. Blount, a white Democrat, and Garland H. White, a black Republican. Blount contested the election, thus delaying Hyman taking his seat in the Forty-fourth Congress. A congressional committee ultimately confirmed his election in August 1876. The term ended before Hyman was thoroughly acclimated to the office. Though he ran for reelection in 1876, he was a one-term representative, losing the election to former governor Curtis Brogden, a white Republican. After being spurned by the Republican party in the 1878 election, Hyman gave up on elective office.

Congressman Hyman defended many causes in Congress. He pursued legislation to appropriate federal funds for a courthouse in Jones County destroyed by Union troops during the Civil War. He introduced a bill to reimburse depositors who had lost money in the Freedmen's Bank. He supported legislation to establish a lighthouse at Gull Rock on Pamlico Sound in North Carolina; and he favored appropriating federal funds for indigent Cherokee Indians. As with legislation by other black congressmen, his white colleagues did not endorse these measures. Hyman served on the Committee on Manufactures, a body that offered him little opportunity to serve his constituents in the agricultural Black Second.

John Adams Hyman was a shy, quiet, and reserved man; he did not make any speeches in Congress or participate in House debates. Given the election contest that shortened his term, he did not have the opportunity to make a mark in Congress. He was a responsible lawmaker who attended most sessions, and he voted on issues based upon his conviction. He voted against a bill forbidding federal employees from contributing to national elections. He opposed general amnesty to ex-Confederates, though he voted in favor of a bill that would have only denied Jefferson Davis amnesty. Nothing exists in the *Congressional Record* other than his roll call votes, a few bills and the fourteen petitions calling for relief of poor people in his state. Upon losing the election in 1876, he returned to North Carolina at the end of his term. He served as special deputy collector of internal revenue for the Fourth District of North Carolina for one year. In 1878 Hyman returned to farming; he also opened a grocery and liquor store in his hometown of Warrenton.

Hyman fell of favor in North Carolina during the late 1870s. His liquor business was a casualty of the temperance movement spreading across the nation, and he watched his sales dwindle. His church excommunicated him for selling whiskey to members of the congregation. His critics also alleged that he had embezzled church funds. He left North Carolina, accepting a job in 1879 as a postal clerk in Maryland. In 1889, Hyman returned to the national capital to work in the Department of Agriculture. On September 14, 1891, at the age of fifty-one, John Adams Hyman died from a stroke in Washington, D.C

8

John Mercer Langston
(1829–1897)
House of Representatives, Virginia

Republican

Fifty-first Congress
September 23, 1890, to March 3, 1891

John Mercer Langston was born in Louisa, Virginia, on December 14, 1829. While most historians agree that he was born in bondage, others claim that he was never a slave. The confusion stems mainly from the status of his mother, Lucy Jane Langston, a black woman of mixed ancestry, possibly American Indian. The assertion that Lucy was free at the time of John's birth is not convincing, though it would add credence to the assertion that John was born free. Under the slave codes of Virginia, an offspring followed the status of his or her mother; if Lucy had been free so would John. Recent historians have concluded that Lucy was a slave, and this suggests that John was also born into slavery.

There are other circumstances that corroborate this thesis. Ralph Quarles, a wealthy white farmer, owned Lucy. He might have had affection for her, but did not regard her as his wife. From their relationship John came into the world, the "son" of a slave owner. Quarles took an interest in his "son," but would not claim him as such, or immediately emancipate him. Quarles might have kept him as a slave to protect him; Virginia law might have forbidden unilateral manumission. John's fate improved in 1834, when his "father" died. Quarles left instructions in his will that the executor of his estate should free Langston and provide him with an education. Unable to do so in Virginia, the executor sent the young man to Chillicothe, Ohio, and placed him in the home of an abolitionist family. Langston began his schooling there, and then was sent to the black high school at Oberlin College. He later enrolled in the college curriculum, earning the bachelor and master degrees. Upon graduation from Oberlin in 1849, he began an apprenticeship in law with Cleveland attorney Sherlock J. Andrews. For reasons that are not clear, Langston switched tutors and studied in the office of attorney Philemon Bliss of Elyria, Ohio. Upon passing the bar exam in 1854, he became the first African-American attorney in Ohio.

Langston joined the abolitionist movement during the 1840s while a student at Oberlin College, a center of antislavery fervor in northern Ohio. He became the first African-American president of the Ohio Anti-Slavery Society. He was also tempted by the prospect of colonization, because the pain of racism caused him to doubt that blacks would ever achieve civil rights in the United States. These were only periods of despair, and Langston was never committed to the colonization movement. Langston held various public offices as well as offices in civic and professional associations before the Civil War. He was probably the first African American to hold an elective office in Ohio. As *Fredrick Douglass's Paper* reported, Langston was the only "colored man" living in Brownhelm, a township in Ohio, which elected him clerk. In 1856, soon after he returned to Oberlin, he was elected to the city council, and also the board of education.

Langston's public service continued when the Civil War started, and he held various appointive and elective positions for the rest of his life. In 1863, he recruited black soldiers for the Union Army, and played a key role in organizing the famous Massachusetts Fifty-fourth and Fifty-fifth, as well as the Fifth Ohio, regiments. He was elected president of the National Equal Rights League in 1864. Following the war, he relocated to the nation's capital, and opened a law practice there. He was elected to the board of education in the capital. The Freedmen's Bureau also hired him to tour the South to assess living conditions of African Americans. In 1871, President Ulysses S. Grant appointed him to the Board of Health of the District of Columbia. Active in business, Langston was elected president of the Richmond Land and Financial Association, a company that purchased property to resell to African Americans seeking to purchase a home or business.

Langston rose to prominence as an educator, and he reached a high level as an administrator. He helped establish the law school at Howard University, and from 1868 to 1875 served as its first dean. Later, he was appointed vice president of the university, as well as its acting president. He aspired to become president of the school but never received the post, presumably because of his race. In 1885, however, he was appointed president of the Virginia Normal and Collegiate Institute in Petersburg, where he served until 1887.

Langston entered national politics when President Rutherford B. Hayes appointed him to diplomatic posts in Haiti and Santo Domingo. A citizens committee in Farmville, Virginia, asked him to run for a seat in the Fourth

Congressional District in 1888. Having been an active Republican, he sought the party nomination. However, when the state party chairman, William Mahone, opposed the nomination of a Negro, Langston entered the election as an independent. Frederick Douglass, the most prominent black leader in America, also opposed his candidacy, claiming that Langston had used what amounted to a race card by appealing to blacks to vote for him. Langston also called on prominent supporters, and one, Bishop James T. Holly came from Port-au-Prince, Haiti to defend Langston, asserting that it was "treason to the cause of the colored race, for anyone of that race, under any pretext whatsoever, to oppose" Langston's election to Congress. White Republicans and Democrats resorted to other schemes, hoping to dilute the votes of the black majority in the Fourth. They obstructed the election process by making black voters wait as long as three hours to cast a ballot. In the end, election officials declared Edward Venable, a white Democrat, the winner. Langston successfully contested the election, and took his seat at mid-term. Congressional Democrats, still smarting because of the election, boycotted the induction ceremony for Langston. Once his shortened term ended he made an unsuccessful race for reelection. Convinced that he had lost the election due to fraud, Langston recognized that the Democrats now in Congress would not confirm him, and thus he did not challenge the results.

Langston had set his sights high, and he mingled in prominent circles. He married Caroline M. Wall, the Oberlin—educated "daughter" of Stephen Wall, a wealthy white North Carolinian, who had sent her to Ohio to be educated. Their family included two children, and they easily merged with the black elite in Ohio and the rest of the nation. Having amassed a small fortune after several decades of public service, he turned to public speaking and writing during the 1890s. After publishing his memoir, *From the Virginia Plantation to the National Capitol*, and several articles, he died in the District of Columbia on November 15, 1897.

Langston made the argument that black people are citizens of the United States and are entitled to civil rights. He couched his argument in the Declaration of Independence and the Ten Commandments of Moses. He opposed colonization, insisting blacks would never leave the United States. He predicted that the African-American population in the United States would grow, notwithstanding racial oppression. He considered the Democratic party the enemy of black freedom. He implored his colleagues in Congress to recognize the citizenship of all Americans.

THE ELECTION BILL
January 16, 1891

If there is anything that I would gladly see, it is "our country first on land, and first on sea," and it is natural for me, coming into this body, as I do, from the Old Dominion that gave life to Washington and birth to Jefferson to come with the sentiment I have just expressed. I have seen American masters of ships wronged in foreign countries, and finally successfully defended by the Government through the vigorous and manly efforts of our representatives abroad. I recollect among the very last things that occurred when I had the honor of representing this Government abroad was this fact, first, that an old shipmaster said to me in our legation, "When you go home, if you ever have the opportunity to say a word for us, say it, say it freely and say it positively, and so emancipate us, that on the great sea, as well as at home, we may feel the consciousness that we are Americans."

I promised that shipmaster that if ever I had the opportunity of speaking for our shipping I would do it, and do it fearlessly and thoroughly. One of these days, in this august body, I trust that I shall have the opportunity of saying a word. But how can we make our land and our Government great in the estimation of others, except as finally we plant ourselves as a nation on those fundamental, far-reaching eternal principles underlying all democracies and perpetuating all republics? I would speak to you today not in any other wise than as I would defend the Constitution of my country and planting myself on those doctrines of the Declaration of Independence so clearly and forcibly enunciated in these words: We hold these truths to be self-evident, that all men are created equal. Ah, the day has come to us now when we are to recur in our thoughts and reach in our purposes those olden times of this Republic when our fathers built, as Christ did, "on the rock," that his Church might stand, and now that our government may stand. Why, the feeling in the country seems to be today that silver is the thing; and a man said to me the other day, when the silver bill had been laid aside for the time being, "Ah, your cause has been sold for thirty pieces of silver." I mean when the election bill was laid aside. But I said: "Not so, for we live in the United States of America, in the midst of schoolhouses, in the midst of schools, in the midst of churches, in the midst of Christians, and we have built our nation on other material than that which shall find any class of our population, politicians or statesmen, finally willing to sell the cause of our liberty, the rights of the humblest citizen of our Government, for anything like a compromise, even in silver."

Our nation is built first on those fundamental laws given in the midst of the flame and smoke of Sinai and in the light of this law slavery has gone. We find that there was in the same law, enunciated so clearly and so beautifully by Him "who spoke as never man spoke," the maxim: "Whatever you would that men should do unto you, do ye even so unto them." And we built on that afterwards. But here is the declaration which we have built on, and that is this Constitution, which we have amended, not because it needed amendment, but that there might be no mistake as to the question of whether a black man might be free or slave; whether he should continue ignorant and a discredit to you by having been born in this country. In his nativity he finds the fact that he is an American, and the law must protect him in that character.

But my friend on the other side of the House the other day referred to what was done in 1815. He alluded to the fact that great men moved in that day, and I watched for him to come down to the position of General Andrew Jackson on the Negro question, because I wanted to hear him on that; but he tarried at the Hartford convention and did not come on down to the victory that was won at New Orleans, when the great general of that day called his troops about him and gave utterance to sentiments that the Negro loves and some men hate even up to this hour. Ah, General Jackson was not a bad man, although he was a Democrat in some senses of the word. I would that the Democrats of the United States would accept the doctrines of that great and venerable man who, firm and true to the last, was able to see, beyond a curl of a man's hair and beyond the color of his face, the fact that he was a man and the fact that he could be a patriotic American. Ah, my white fellow-citizens in the House and Senate, and my white fellow-citizens in every section of the country, black as we are no man shall go ahead of us in devotion to this country, in devotion to its free institutions, for we hold our lives, our property, and our sacred honor in pledge to the welfare of our country and of all our fellow-citizens. Do you want men to fight; call us and we will come. Do you want men to tarry at home and take care of your wives, take care of your children, take care of your homes and protect your interests; call on us. And when the time is past, if you can find a Negro who has betrayed you in a single case put your finger on him and we will aid you in lynching him.

What a wonderful chapter that is, that the men who lived near where General Jackson uttered these words, in the State of Louisiana, and in the States of the South, all along the line of battle, could go away leaving everything in the hands of the Negro and come back and find that it had been guarded, thoroughly protected. For that alone, if for no other reason, the Negro might well be accorded the freedom and justice that are his right, and he would be if those men had only been fair and true to him. This is our native country. We do not have to go abroad to find our native country, for Jackson has told us we need not go. Some men want us to go to Africa and to the isles of the sea, but, blessed be the name of this grand old Democrat, he has taught us another lesson; he has taught us that this is our home; and in the name of Jackson, whose shade is about me now, I declare in this sacred place that we are here to stay and never will go away. Why, we cannot go. How can I get out of this country? I undertook to leave Virginia, and the first thing I knew I was back there. I moved away and located in Ohio, but I could not stay. I came to the District of Columbia, but I could not stay here. I went abroad, but I could not stay there. When I returned and undertook to go away again, by a curious adjustment of Providence I found myself in Virginia; and today, by a curious adjustment of Providence, I find myself standing in this august and wonderful presence. We cannot control ourselves in these things.

Do you think that the Negro would have come to this country to find slavery when the white man came here to find liberty? Yet, when the white men were landing on the eastern shores of the continent and beginning to build our nationality, the Negro came in chains to the south-ward; and, as the white men became great in numbers, the Negroes multiplied, until finally, in the great struggle for liberty, when, in its far-reaching and broad sweep slavery had stricken down the liberties of the people, and the fight had to come, the Negro, in the midst of the thunder of the great contest, is called from his slumbers, comes forth from his rages a free man, and enters upon real life the equal of his white fellow-citizens. Here we are and here we are to stay. And I give my Democratic friends warning that they may oppress us as much as they will, but still we shall remain. Abuse us as you will, gentlemen, we will increase and multiply until, instead of finding every day five hundred black babies turning up their bright eyes to greet the rays of the sun, the number shall be five thousand and shall still go on increasing.

We are simply fellow-citizens. We have always been fellow-citizens. We are nothing but fellow-citizens today, and fellow-citizens in permanent residence in this our native country. But this is not the only testimony. I can offer on this subject Southern testimony that goes further than this. Gentlemen are very timid about us—not only timid, but anxious. But where do you find the very first judicial opinion, broad and comprehensive, recognizing the Negro of this country not only as a citizen, but also as an elector? Suppose I should state here that in this matter we must follow the lead of the South? Suppose I should say that as a matter of fact the enunciation in that behalf, clear and distinct, was made not by a Northern judge, but by a Southern judge, and that this judge was the first lawyer of the State of North Carolina? I will say so; and I will astonish you by reading (if you have not read it) from the learned opinion of Chief Justice Gaston, as given in the case of the *State v. Manuel*. A Negro boy, having assaulted a white boy, was brought to trial and found guilty; and punishment adjudged was thirty-nine lashes at the whipping post. A young white lawyer said to gentlemen of Fayetteville, N.C.: "Raise a little purse and I will take this case before the supreme court of the State; I will ask Judge Gaston to pass on the case, and I believe he will decide that no colored man, even though born a slave, if subsequently emancipated, as Manuel has been can be punished at the whipping post, because by reason of his nativity he is an American citizen." The money was raised and the case carried to the Supreme Court. Judge Gaston sat in that case and delivered the opinion.

Being citizens, being electors, we are confronted today as distinctly as in 1861 to 1865 with the question of slavery or freedom, with the question whether every American citizen may wield the ballot in this country freely and according to his own judgment in the interest of the welfare of our common country. It does not matter how black we are; it does not matter how ignorant we are; it does not matter what our race may be; it does not matter whether we were degraded or not; the question presented today under our amended Constitution, as under the Constitution without amendment, is, shall every freeman, shall every American citizen, shall every American elector in the North and in the South, everywhere in the country, be permitted to wield a free ballot in the interests of our common country and our free institutions? Here lies the difference: The old Democratic party used to maintain that this right should be accorded to every American citizen; the new Democratic party is fighting it. But, thank God, the genuine Americans—mainly found in the Republican party—some few in the Democratic party, but through mistake—are standing up bravely and truly today to meet this question intelligently and patriotically.

"Oh," but the Democrats say, "You got beaten at the last election." In one sense we did, and in one sense we did not. We have only been chastened a little to make us more firm, and more solid, and the more certain in the high march that is before us to the "promised land" in the midst of our own homes to which God would lead us in the establishment of an all-comprehensive freedom and equality of right. How dark it was in 1861! How dark it was in 1850! Ah! Compromises were made; the great orators spoke; the great parties resolved; and the friends of freedom came well-nigh to despair. But the voice of the faithful and the true was still heard; and finally in the thunder of great guns, in the midst of terrible smoke as of the Mountain of Sinai, and in the flashes of light that made every slave in the land glad, emancipation was declared and the country was saved.

It is sneeringly said that the Republican party laid aside the elections bill in the Senate. But it was only for a little while; it was only to take it up again; that was all. And they have taken it up now in earnest. And if the elections shall come around shortly you will see the change when the people have been forgotten who failed to do their duty in connection with the matter. Yes, they have taken up the elections bill again, and those people who yielded it for awhile, who laid it aside to address themselves to other matters, have gone back to the solid, patriotic conviction that at last liberty is the whitest and brightest jewel in the firmament, and that the greatest heritage of American citizenship is to be free.

The Democrats talk of carrying the election in 1892. How could they carry it? They could not do it by any fair means. But our Democratic friends do not talk of fair means any more. They avoid all that. A gentleman who spoke the other day, and talked of free ballots and all that sort of thing, was asked against whom he made the charges. He said "The Democratic party." Why should we not so charge it under the circumstances? I would like to see somebody put his finger on something that the Democratic party has done from the beginning that looks like favoring freedom or favoring the colored men in this country. How peculiarly our friends are characterized! You can hardly believe the language that is used towards them. I have some of it here before me; studied, selected, written, and rewritten as it must have been, but yet very peculiar language.

Eight million people stand behind me today, a few in the West and all over the South, command me to say to you that so long as there is a name akin to that of Hoar in New England we will honor and revere it because that man has been true to us in the Senate. But it would not have made any difference. We do not forget our friends. You recollect that there was a Hoar who went South once, and he went to Charleston, S.C., going there as the agent of the great State of Massachusetts. He appeared in the name of the sovereignty of that great State as a lawyer, not to "steal Negroes," but to inquire in the courts of that State as to whether it was legal for a colored citizen of the State of Massachusetts, sailing into the harbor of Charleston on a Northern vessel, to be arrested and imprisoned and adjudged not to be a free Negro and sold into interminable slavery. His sweet, elegant, charming daughter, a young lady of Boston, accompanied him. He appeared, and very soon a committee of gentlemen of property waited on him. "What is your business here?" He said, "I have come," as I have described, "in the name of the Commonwealth in which I live, to look after matters of interest to the great body of the people of our State." "We give you one hour's notice to take your trunk and leave this city, and if you are not gone within that time we will tar and we will feather you." And at the end of that time the committee waited on him again. He was a little behind time. And it is record in history that the presence of his daughter alone saved him from their clutches. This spirit does not know white man or black man. All stand equal before it, as they should stand equal before the law. When I stand here today speaking for the cause of the people of my State, my native State, the State of Virginia, I am pleading for her people both white and black. I am speaking for white men as well as for Negroes; for white men in my State are proscribed, and they are denied a free ballot, though their "locks be flaxen and their eyes blue."

And that is no uncommon or isolated case. But go into another county, if you will. Go with me to my beautiful city of Petersburg. They sometimes say I do not live there, but if you will go with me down there I will show you that I do live there and live at home. One man said, "I do not believe you live in Petersburg, because you have a house in Washington." Well, unfortunately, I have got a house in Washington, because it sometimes happens that a colored man can have two houses, one in which he lives and one where he does not live. White men, of course, may have three or four without question. But most Negroes now have their own homes. Come down there with me. Let me introduce you to a fine-looking man with splendid hair, noble face, fine bearing, and the picture of intelligence.

He went and voted. What was the result? The next morning at 5 o'clock, when he stepped out of his door, he found it all draped with crape. What was going to be done? Why, he voted for a Republican yesterday, and this crape was significant. What was the result? He was proscribed and his children were proscribed. They point their fingers at these children as they are on the way to school and when they get to the school they call his children names. And I plead the cause here today not only of 7,000,000 Negroes of the South, but of the white men in the entire South who have accepted the principles of the fathers and dedicated their faith to Republican doctrine. I appeal to any and every Democrat on this floor, if it is not true, that I state hastily here, too hastily to make myself well understood, the doctrine, first, that the white men of the South have maintained that Negroes are citizens upon their nativity; secondly, the decision of Judge Gaston, who ruled that we are entitled to the elective franchise upon a property qualification in North Carolina; and then, thirdly and lastly, if it is not true today in the South that white men may not vote the Republican ticket with greater facility or larger freedom from proscription than Negroes themselves? Oh, you ought to come down there and see it. You ought to see an intelligent, fine looking white girl, well dressed, and well behaved, bearing herself like a lady, passing along the street with a rabble of white men saying, "Your father voted for a damned Negro and we will show you," and frightening that sweet American girl.

Do you like that spirit? I do not. I will never be the coward to say that I do. And I would pass bills and pile up penalties and put behind every bill soldiers until they rose to the top of the mountain and kissed the stars, to put these women and these men in the sure consciousness of their protection by law. Now, oppress Negroes if you must, but for God's sake stop oppressing white voters. Deny to the Negro the ballot if you will, but for God's sake do not take the ballot from your own brother with flaxen hair and blue eyes. Now, another speaker says, "Why don't you make Blanche Kelso Bruce President? Why don't you make John Mercer Langston President?" I want to plead guilty to some things here. I think we have honored Mr. Bruce a good deal. He is a splendid gentleman. He is one of the classes of good-looking colored men on this continent, and you will excuse me if I tell you we have got some of the finest looking Negroes on this continent that you ever saw. And then we have got so many. You think you have got millions in the United States, but go with me where I used to live when I was your representative, and let me show you hundreds of thousands there, so black on one side of the island and so light on the other, and let me introduce you to that living monument of fine appearance and culture and magnificent appointments in every respect, the man who used to be president of the Republic of Haiti.

When Rear Admiral Cooper visited me on his ship, the *Tennessee,* I said, "Admiral, do not you want to see a splendid man; do not you want to see the best-looking black man in the world; do not you want to see a great man, the impersonation of learning and culture, a man who many a day escorted Mrs. Dix to dinner in Paris, who towered up there in all his beauty as a gentleman admired by every representative of every foreign country?" The old admiral said, "I would like to see him." That will be your national air one of these days, in the good time coming. Our bands shall play it, our choristers shall sing it, and we as a Christian nation shall march on under the banner of the Republican party to national and local victory under the impulse and purpose that that song will awaken in our souls. We entered the palace, and very soon we were in the presence of this magnificent man of more than 300 pounds' weight. His hair was as white as the snow, his face as black as the night, his face the face of Webster, his manner polite, genteel, and elegant; like the manner of Wendell Phillips. He was the impersonation of culture. And when I said to him in French: "I have the honor to present to you a rear admiral of the American Navy," the bow he made, out of his high regard for our free institutions and our noble country and our magnificent nation, was charming in the extreme.

And shortly we took the usual elegant drink of magnificent champagne without ice, as is the custom in this country. When the rear admiral was about ready to go, he said, "Now, minister, make my speech to the President. Tell the President that my goodly ship the *Tennessee,* has carried me into the waters of every civilized nation; that I have looked into the faces of kings and queens, emperors and empresses, and the executives of all sorts of men and governments; and say to him that I seem now, in the presence of this President, to stand in the presence of the man whom we call the Father of our Country, 'First in war, first in peace, and first in the hearts of his countrymen.' I feel that I stand in the presence of Washington himself." I threw it into French, as I could then, and then these great men advanced with tears in their eyes and gave each other the warm palm; and I said to them, "Ah! Gentlemen, this is the Great Republic of the North extending her warm palm in sympathy to this Negro republic."

It is prophetic of what? That American influence shall prevail with reference to the Negro race of this country on the continent and in the isles of the sea. We are here on the continent; we are here living on the continent as a part of a great nation. God is with us; the people are with us, and we are with you, and we are in the South to remain; coming gently towards the North, increasing day by day, to wield the ballot, the free ballot, given to us by the Government that we defended in its possession, and we will wield it to make our country great on the land and great on the sea, matchless in the ship, and matchless in industry, with mankind in our endeavors to realize the glory and distinction which the fathers knew this country would attain in the future; and to that end may God help us.

Langston urged Congress to adopt legislation to protect the shipping industry. He believed that the United States had lost ground in commerce since the beginning of the century. He hailed the great cities and ports in Virginia, including the Cities of Petersburg, Newport News, and Norfolk. Langston described his personal experience on American ships while he was a minister to Haiti. From his contact with captains of American vessels he concluded that the fleet needed more funding. He used statistical data to argue that the United States merchant marine had fallen behind its competitors around the world. Langston explained that the chambers of commerce in the cities he represented shared this point of view and they wanted Congress to act in this matter

---

SHIPPING ON THE HIGH SEAS—THE TONNAGE BILL
February 27, 1891

I come to a duty that I am about to perform as directed by the people of the State that I have the honor in part to represent on this floor. And yet it is after no inconsiderable observation with regard to the condition of our shipping on the high seas that I answer this duty with a great deal of pleasure and satisfaction.

You are aware that I have the honor of representing a district of the State of Virginia in which is located the city of Petersburg. That city and the country around about the city have expressed themselves in very decided and positive language in favor of the shipping interests of our country, and of the measure now pending for consideration before this House. I could read to you the words of the Chamber of Commerce of the city of Richmond, the great city of our State. I could read to you the language of the Chamber of Commerce of Norfolk, and Newport News is already characterized as the rival of New York in a future not very distant. All the people of my section favor this measure. It is not because I am influenced by any undue consideration, partisan or sectional or selfish, that I stand here to represent my section of the country in respect to this bill.

When during a residence of five years in a foreign port, where I had the honor to represent this Government, I saw not a single American steam vessel riding into that harbor and anchoring on business. Here was the great English vessel, here the great German vessel, here the great French vessel, here the Spanish. All these nations were represented there, but not a single steamship from our country. Why was this? We had conceded away to the English Government the freedom of our seas. And at New York there has been established a line of ships now large in its property, rich and commanding in its influence on the sea, on whose ships, as the American minister and consul general going to the West Indies, I was obliged to ride. I went out in 1877 on the best ship in that line. In 1885, having sent my resignation to President Arthur, I returned to my country riding in the best ship in that line. Now, what has that company done? They own large property in their wharves; they own large property in their office buildings; they have established not three ships upon the high seas to do the carrying business of New York City, but twenty. When I asked officers of that company, "What is the condition of your company?" they said to me, "We have paid for all these ships, and we have now over $200,000 in the hands of the company as a reserve fund."

On one occasion, going to the West Indies, I was ship-wrecked in one of their vessels. For eighty-six days we were kept there at Matthew-town, and when that ship was floated from the rock on which she had struck she was carried for repairs, not to New York but to Liverpool, where she had been manned. And now nothing is done for American shipping, but our seas are given up and our carrying business surrendered to vessels of other nations. We are now told that when the Government has thus given away our privileges on the seas that she is not to help the ship-building interest to again master the sea as we master the land. I am here to ask, we having legislated away so largely our interests on the sea, so that we are not where we were in 1825, when Webster said, "We have a commerce which explores every sea, and navies which take their law for no court," how shall we recover our former position? That is the question. If it is necessary for this purpose to give $5,000,000 a year, or even more, let us establish ourselves upon the high seas; let us do it firmly and thoroughly, so that as we are now the greatest nation on the face of the earth we shall be the greatest nation on the mighty deep. The judgment and voice are well-nigh universal among our people that anything which the Government can legally do to rehabilitate, improve, and establish our marine in power upon the high seas should be done at once, in the interest as well of trade and commerce as the general welfare and defense of American interests.

As showing public feeling and purpose in the character and to the extent indicated, letters and papers, the recent proceedings of the chambers of commerce, and the opinions of distinguished statesmen may be cited, and did time permit be read, with great benefit in our discussions. Such expressions reflect the old judgment of Virginia on this subject, with respect to this subject; and had the policy which they inaugurated, in such behalf, been maintained, it is entirely probable that the American flag had never lost its character as the symbol of power upon the mighty deep. The State of Virginia, always interested in this matter, specially by reason of her situation, both as regards the land and the sea, is able to facilitate the movement of exports and imports on the one and upon the other; is especially now interested therein when a new impulse, under the pressure of an improved popular purpose, promises enlarged commercial enterprises, with improved and profitable shipbuilding and navigation, which must bring into requisition every facility and advantage which her situation commands.

Such impulse our State is feeling, as evidenced in the improvements which are being made with reference to general business, not only in the State generally, but in the ports of Norfolk and Newport News preeminently. But the recent developments of business interests throughout the South would indicate upon the least reflection how deeply that whole section of our country must sympathize with the State of Virginia as respects her movements as indicated, and how deeply it must appreciate all efforts which are being made for the easy, profitable transportation of her accumulating products, so immense in quantity and of such character that they must sooner or later figure largely in general commerce. It must have been with the whole field of its present immense interests within the compass of the vision of his magnificent statesmanship, with the possibilities of our future trade at home and abroad in his contemplation, that the late Honorable William Windom made his dying bequest to the country in an utterance matchless and wonderful in the breadth and profundity of its sentiments and counsels. In four years we lost of import carriage 10 percent, and of export carrying 2 per cent of total traffic. Our shipping increased its business 59 percent, but foreign vessels added to their traffic 177 per cent, exactly three times the gain of American transportation. Of course this enormous rate of growth was for British business mainly. From 1849 to 1853, both inclusive, British arrivals of tonnage in our ports increased 70 percent. In the presence of facts like these it is palpable our shipping legislation and commercial treaties have not covered the ground of national economics, and much less of patriotism.

The first have shown apparent want of real interest and sympathy on the part of the Government with our merchant marine, while the latter, discovering the disposition and purpose of foreign powers to profit, often by imposition of undue burdens upon our shipping, have tended to drive our seafaring class from the ownership and use of vessels employed in the foreign trade. Often American seamen have felt the impositions and exactions here referred to so deeply to their injury that while they have not quitted the sea and the service to which they had become inured, they have sought emancipation there-from by putting their ships under foreign flags.

Heretofore, certainly for many years past, the American Navy has been without such name and power upon the high seas as to give assurance of certain protection and defense to our navigation, and hence those who would have invested in great ships and made their use, perhaps, profitable, have refused to invest in such way and risk their property upon the ocean in the foreign trade, subject to the impositions of foreign governments. Fines imposed on American ships have often been exceedingly annoying and unjust, and have often been imposed and collected in such manner, in such outrage of the rights of American citizens, as to require prompt and decisive action by the Government in the use of such means and with such circumstances as to discover its purpose and power in their behalf. Three American ships were once fined, as the record will show, as they lay at anchor in the same foreign harbor, under the same government, without the least authority of law, but according to an unjust custom, which, for the want of suitable protection, had been endured by American ship owners so long that it was claimed to be and enforced as in fact the law. These ships were fined each $50, and had it not been that our consular officer was positive and determined in the action taken by him in behalf of his citizens, the fines would not have been returned to the captains in these cases and this vile custom abrogated.

It has often been the case that captains of American ships have been illegally and improperly arrested and imprisoned. A case of this sort, which figures in conspicuous and noted manner in the records of our State Department, is worthy of special reference and mention here. Without naming the party in this case, it may be stated that his Government did not neglect the American citizen who was thus wronged and outraged. For the foreign government whose officer was arrested and imprisoned $5,000 in American gold in the case, constituting reasonable compensation for all damage done.

Facts and Conditions That Promise Well to Our Merchant Marine

Leaving such considerations, and not referring to others that have had much to do with driving our merchant marine from the seas, we reach the more agreeable task of dwelling upon those facts and conditions that promise its re-establishment thereupon at no distant day. At peace now with the world; freed at home from those unnatural conditions of sectional life, aggravated by a peculiar institution which cast its blighting shadow once across the whole country; with our great industrial and manufacturing interests far on the way toward completed development; with our railroad, our telegraphic, our banking, our educational, our governmental systems well established, working out the highest good of the people, we are prepared as a nation to give attention to such master-hood of the sea as comports with our dignity and power on the land.

Our day of improving manufacturing, mining, agricultural, and general enterprises and interests shall prove, as we must all hope, to be the returning dawn of that day of our mastery of commerce and navigation, in power, dignity, yand glory like that which makes us grand and matchless on the land.

9

Jefferson Franklin Long (1836–1901)
House of Representatives, Georgia

Republican

Forty-first Congress
December 22, 1870, to March 3, 1871

Jefferson Franklin Long was born into slavery in Knoxville, Georgia, on March 3, 1836. His light complexion easily identified his mulatto background. His white "father" made no provisions for him, and only his ambition enabled him to get ahead. Long was obviously resourceful, because he learned to read and managed to become a tailor when these opportunities were limited for blacks. He opened a tailor shop in Macon, Georgia, and over time attracted a clientele of mostly white shoppers, who could afford to buy tailor-made clothing. His business acumen led him into prominent circles and into the Republican politics during Reconstruction.

During the late 1860s, Jefferson Long worked as a political organizer for the Republican party. He was a member of the Macon Union League, a grass roots political action group. A recognized orator, the Republican Congressional Committee in Georgia also hired him as its speaker. According to one journalist, his "appeal to the poor whites was so forceful and convincing, that several converts were drawn" to the Republican party. In 1869 he was elevated to the Republican state executive committee. He had been involved in literacy programs for African Americans since 1866, when he joined the Georgia Educational Association. He also represented black laborers, and was one of the main organizers of the Georgia Labor Lonvention, which sought jobs, better pay, and improved working conditions. These experiences made him a standout in the

Republican party, and by 1870 Jefferson Long won a campaign from the Fourth District for a seat in Congress.

Long was preceded to the House of Representatives by Joseph H. Rainey, a black politician from South Carolina. Consequently, Long was the second African American to be elected to Congress. His term in Congress was too short to judge it in any significant way. The white-controlled government in Georgia intentionally supported his candidacy for a "shortened term," and Jefferson Franklin Long took his seat on January 3, 1871, for a term that ended in March. Many southern states had elected blacks to the shortened terms, hoping to placate African-American voters. Most whites in the South, including native Republicans or "scalawags," had no intention of helping blacks win re-election. Long did not seek it because Georgia whites had made it clear through intimidation and violence that blacks should not become candidates.

Though his term in the House was brief, Jefferson Long had a few memorable moments in the national legislature. On February 1, 1871, he became the first African American to make a speech in the United States House of Representatives. A journalist for the *New York Tribune* reported favorably, indicating that Mr. Long "in manner was perfectly self possessed. His voice is full and powerful, filling the Hall with ease while his enunciation was quite good." He opposed enfranchising unrepentant ex-Confederates upon whom the Fourteenth Amendment had placed political disabilities. He did so not from bitterness; rather, he believed that the ex-rebels were the leaders of the Ku Klux Klan in Georgia and elsewhere, and had led and sanctioned assaults on blacks throughout the South. A Georgia correspondent, writing for the *Savannah Republican*, criticized Long by claiming that he eagerly supported the disenfranchisement of whites. He claimed that Long had lied about white conduct in the South in order to frighten Congress into denying the old citizens the vote. In addition to such criticism, organized groups of whites threatened Long, and he needed armed guards for protection.

In addition to opposing the amnesty bill, Long supported civil rights measures. He spoke in favor of legislation to enforce the Fifteenth Amendment and defended universal suffrage in the District of Columbia. Once his term in Congress was over, Long never again sought public office, and it would be over a century before Georgia would elect another black to Congress. Nonetheless, Long remained active in the Republican party and in state politics. While he attended party conventions, he antagonized white Republicans by urging blacks to be independent in their party affiliations.

When his term in Congress ended, Long returned to his tailor business. Before he had entered politics his tailor shop was reputedly one of the finest clothing stores in Georgia. As he discovered, his politics adversely affected his business. As Theophilus G. Steward, pastor of the Macon A.M.E. church put it, "His stand in politics ruined his business with the whites who had been his patrons chiefly." They did not take kindly to a Negro who advocated civil rights legislation and equal opportunity for all Americans. Though they stopped spending money at his shop, Long, a determined businessman, turned to other ventures. He opened a liquor store and a dry-cleaning business—the first, a luxury with mass appeal, and the second, a necessity. He remained self-employed until his death on February 4, 1901.

Congressman Long opposed amnesty for ex-Confederate military and civil officers. He further believed that some southern whites were feigning loyalty to the Union only to get back into politics. He argued that these people were likely supporters of the Ku Klux Klan, and other terrorist groups responsible for murdering southern blacks.

AMNESTY BILL
February 1, 1871

The object of the bill before the House is to modify the test-oath. As a citizen of the South, living in Georgia, born and raised in that State, having been there during the war and up to the present time, I know the condition of affairs in that State. Now, we propose here today to modify the test-oath, and to give to those men in the rebel States who are disloyal today to the Government this favor. We propose to remove political disabilities from the very men who were the leaders of the Ku Klux Klan and have committed midnight outrages in that State.

What do those men say? Before their disabilities are removed they say, "We will remain quiet until all of our disabilities are removed, and then we shall again take the lead." In my State since emancipation there have been over five hundred loyal men shot down by the disloyal men there, and not one of those who took part in committing those outrages has ever been brought to justice. Do we, then, really propose here today, when the country is not ready for it, when those disloyal people still hate this Government, when loyal men dare not carry the "stars and stripes" through our streets, for if they do they will be turned out of employment, to relieve from political disability the very men who have committed these Ku Klux Klan outrages? I think that I am doing my duty to my constituents and my duty to my country when I vote against any such proposition.

I do mean that murders and outrages are being committed there. I received no longer ago than this morning a letter from a man in my State, a loyal man who was appointed postmaster by the President, stating that he was beaten in the streets a few days ago. I have also received information from the lower part of Georgia that disloyal men went in the midnight disguised and took a loyal man out and shot him; and not one of them has been brought to justice. Loyal men are constantly being cruelly beaten. When we take the men who commit these outrages before judges and juries we find that they are in the hands of the very Ku Klux Klan themselves who protect them. I propose, as a man raised as a slave, my mother a slave before me, and my ancestry slaves as far back as I can trace them, yet holding no animosity to the law-abiding people of my State, and those who are willing to stand by the Government, while I am willing to remove the disabilities of all such who will support the Government, still I propose for one, knowing the condition of things there in Georgia, not to vote for any modification of the test-oath in favor of disloyal men.

Gentlemen on the other side of the House have complimented men on this side. I hope the blood of the Ku Klux Klan has not got upon this side; I hope not. If this House removed the disabilities of disloyal men by modifying the test-oath, I venture to prophesy you will again have trouble from the very same men who gave you trouble before.

10

John Roy Lynch
(1847–1939)
House of Representatives, Mississippi

Republican

Forty-third, Forty-fourth and Forty-seventh
Congresses
March 4, 1873, to March 3, 1883

John Roy Lynch was born into slavery on September 10, 1873, on Tacony Plantation in Concordia Parish, Louisiana. Tacony had for years been the home of his mother, Catherine, and an Irish-born slave driver named Patrick Lynch. John Roy was the offspring of this affair. Apparently, Patrick took his responsibility to Catherine and their son seriously; he promised to buy their freedom. Unfortunately, Patrick died in 1849, before he could make the arrangements. Before his death, Lynch urged the plantation owner to carry out his wishes; instead, the farmer sold the Lynch family to Alfred Davis, who owned a plantation in Mississippi. Davis carried them to Natchez, just east of the Mississippi River.

Living in the Deep South when Abraham Lincoln announced the Emancipation Proclamation in 1863, Davis ignored the declaration that the slaves in the states in rebellion were free. Lynch remained in bondage until 1864, when Union forces invaded Mississippi. At age fourteen, he joined the army as a cook, and then served briefly aboard a Union gunboat. While these experiences broadened his horizon, Lynch had already shown great promise. He had willed himself to read and write, and had a strong desire to take advantage of every opportunity to advance. While in the army he studied photography, and after the war opened a studio in Natchez. When northern philanthropists opened a school for Negroes there in 1865, John enrolled. His interest in education remained strong throughout his life. During the 1890s he read law and started a practice in Mississippi. In 1898 at the age of fifty-one, Lynch was appointed an army major, and served as paymaster in the United States Army. Later in his long life he moved to Chicago, opened a law office, hoping for better opportunities for a black attorney.

Lynch, like most blacks following the Civil War, became an organizer for the Republican party. From this base he caught the eye of the military governor Adelbert Ames of Mississippi, who in 1869 appointed him a justice of the peace in Natchez. Lynch, always ambitious, won a seat in the state legislature in 1870 and, at the youthful age of twenty-five, was elected speaker of the state house in 1872. He was among the first African Americans to hold a seat in the Mississippi General Assembly, and the first, and for a hundred years the only, black congressman from that state. As a legislator Lynch helped establish the state's first public school system. While he acquiesced in segregated schools, he prevailed in the argument that in areas where only one school existed children would be admitted on a non-segregated basis. In 1873 Lynch won a seat in Congress where he served for ten years. Representative Lynch sat on the Committee on Mines and Mining and the Committee on Expenditures. He also supported civil rights legislation, defending the Civil Rights Act of 1875. He spoke favorably on bills that would benefit his district and the state of Mississippi. He supported legislation calling for federal appropriations for health care, and improved navigation on the Mississippi River. Lynch also wanted to indemnify investors who lost money in the failed federal Freedmen's Bank. His congressional career ended in 1883 when Democrats regained control of Mississippi politics.

Lynch's public service did not end with his tenure in Congress. He remained a loyal Republican, serving as chairman of the state party from 1881 to 1892. He was a delegate to every national party convention from 1872 to 1900 (except 1896) and in 1884 was its temporary chairman. He was the first African American to deliver a keynote address at a convention for a national political party. (Fannie Lou Hamer was the second African American to speak at a national party convention.) Appointed by President Benjamin Harrison, he served as fourth auditor of the treasury, holding the position from 1889 to 1893.

During his twilight years Lynch dedicated himself to writing his memoirs and to producing scholarly works on Reconstruction. From his speeches and investments he had amassed enough money to afford a life of leisure. He was reputedly worth over $100,000 at the turn of the twentieth century, not a small sum for that period. Lynch also had an active social and family life. He married Ella Somerville, the daughter of a distinguished black official in Alabama. After a divorce in 1900 he married Cora Williamson. Relocating to Chicago soon after his second marriage Lynch died there on November 2, 1939, the last surviving black congressman of the Reconstruction era. The *New York Times* eulogized him as "one of the most fluent and forceful speakers in the seventies and eighties." The *Chicago Tribune* said that Lynch was "the grand old man of Chicago's Negro citizenry."

> *Lynch opposed reducing the pay of the vice president of the United States and the Speaker of the House. He also favored fixing the annual salary of members of Congress at $6,000 per year. He explained that his constituents would not object to a pay increase for members of Congress. However, they were against making such an increase retroactive. Lynch suggested that debate over a pay raise revolved around the regional divide in the country.*

AMENDMENT TO THE BILL
Salary of Vice President of the United States
Salary of Speaker of the House of Representatives
December 9, 1873

It will be seen that the amendment I offered contains several propositions. One is to strike out that portion of the bill that contemplates a reduction of the pay of the Vice-President and the Speaker of the House. The other is to fix to the pay proviso, that the change shall not take effect during the present Congress.

Now, I will state the reason why I propose that amendment. I am satisfied that, so far as the people of the district I represent are concerned, they are satisfied with the law as it now stands. They do not object to $7,500 per annum for a member of Congress, but what they did object to was the clause making the increase retroactive. That was what they thought was wrong. I am satisfied myself that Congress ought not to alter the compensation of members so as to affect the members of the Congress making the change. That is the position that I stand upon, and I am now ready, and will be whenever the opportunity presents itself, to vote for an amendment to the Constitution of the United States prohibiting any Congress from hereafter altering the compensation of its own members. That is what I favor; and although I know the precedents have been the other way, yet I am in favor of changing the precedents. But it occurs to me that if it is wrong in principle for Congress to increase its own pay, it is also wrong for Congress to reduce its own pay. I think that the principle applies both ways.

It has been intimated by some gentlemen that we of the South, the Southern Representatives, as a general thing, are opposed to repealing the increased pay. Now, I do not admit that, as a general thing, we are opposed to the repeal, although it may be true that a great many of us are. If we are opposed to repealing the increased pay it is not because we defy public sentiment, but because we have the privilege and the high honor of representing a constituency that is more liberal on this question than are the constituencies of some of our Western brethren. That is the reason why we do it. I am satisfied that the southern people have not made so much fuss about this question as some of the northern people have. You will have noticed that the southern newspapers have not denounced the members of the Forty-second Congress so severely as the northern newspapers have, and you will have noticed that the political conventions of the two parties in the southern States have not denounced the members of the Forty-second Congress as severely as the political conventions of the North have done. We, consequently, cast our votes in accordance with what we believe and know to be the sentiment of the people that we represent. And now I say that the people, so far as I have been able to ascertain, are satisfied with the pay as it stands. They did believe, and do, that the retroactive clause was wrong. I think so, too, and that is the reason why I do not want Congress to change the compensation now. If we believe the pay is too high, reduce it, but do not let the reduction apply to ourselves. If we believe that is to too small, then increase it, but do not let the increase apply to ourselves. The Forty-second Congress fixed the salary at $7,500 per annum. I say, let us provide that Congress shall not hereafter increase the salary of it own members. If the members of the Forty-second Congress had fixed the pay at $4,000 instead of $5,000, had reduced instead of increasing it, I would still have been opposed to members of the Forty-third Congress adding to it so as to affect themselves; that is my position.

But I have been thinking during the discussion of this question that some gentlemen are making a mistake in what they believe to be public sentiment in this matter. They seem to think that the people of the country require a reduction of the pay of members below what it was before the last increase. Now, I am satisfied that the people do not require that; I am satisfied that not even the people of the Western, and Northern, and Eastern States require a reduction of the pay of Congress below what it was prior to the last increase. The members of the Forty-second Congress, and of each prior Congress for several years, drew $5,000 salary, mileage at the rate of 20 cents a mile each way, and had the benefit of the franking privilege, beside a proper allowance for newspapers, stationery, &c. Now, to put the salary back to $5,000 without those prerequisites would be to reduce the pay below what it was prior to the last increase. I am satisfied that the people do not demand that; and when Representatives go that far they go beyond public sentiment. My friend from Ohio [William Lawrence], the boanerges of this debate, says that the Republican party had been defeated in many States, and has had its majority reduced in others, in consequence of this measure for the increase of salaries; and yet he says that the party is not responsible for it. Well, if there is any force in that argument it amounts to this, that the people have condemned the Republican party for doing one thing, and have indorsed the Democratic party for doing the same thing. I cannot see the force of such an argument.

Now, although I am satisfied from my knowledge of southern feeling that our constituents will indorse our action if we vote to keep the pay what it is, yet I offer a proposition, which I think is fair and Liberal, to make the pay $6,000 per annum, the increase of $1,000 over the $5,000 to be in lieu of mileage, stationery, and the franking privilege; in other words, that we abolish mileage, that we abolish stationery allowances, that we abolish every perquisite that members of Congress have heretofore enjoyed, and add $1,000 to the $5,000 to make up for that. If that amount does not quite equal it, then reduce the pay that much; if it exceeds it, then we increase it that much. That is my proposition; and I make it apply to future Congresses and not to this one, in order to be consistent in the proposition I have assumed on this question, that a Congress ought not to interfere with its own pay.

Lynch objected to a newspaper article that misrepresented his comments on civil rights. The journalist suggested that blacks were neither interested in reconciliation nor integrity; they would vote for anyone. The writer maintained the view that blacks were inferior to whites and thus unfit for the franchise. Lynch countered by arguing that civil rights legislation was an act of simple justice.

THE CIVIL RIGHTS BILL
June 13, 1874

I only ask the attention of the House for a few minutes while I make an explanation on a matter that is somewhat personal to me. It is not often that I deem it necessary to call public attention to anything that I may see in a newspaper; but an editorial in a recent number of the *New York Tribune* has been brought to my notice that I think is of sufficient importance to justify an explanation. Had the speech alluded to in this editorial been delivered in the House where it could have been reported, or if I were satisfied that the writer of the editorial intended a willful misrepresentation, I would not have deemed this course necessary. But it is due to my able and distinguished colleague on the other side of the House [Lucius Q.C. Lamar] as well as to myself that I make this explanation, because those who may have heard his very eloquent speech on Monday last and who may have read this editorial will agree with me in the opinion that it did him injustice as well as myself. But he of course is sufficiently competent to take care of himself. I ask the Clerk to read the paragraph that I have marked in an editorial of the *New York Tribune* of June 10.

I have not quite such a poor opinion of my colleague, as that seems to infer. But the idea I intended to convey upon that occasion and the substance of what I said was simply this: that whatever may be the nature of the reports that have been circulated about some of the Southern States, and whatever may be true of the governments of other States, I know that such unfavorable reports are not true of the State of Mississippi, the State which I have the honor in part to represent on this floor. The idea I intended to convey was this, and I want to impress it upon my friends on the other side of the House, because I regard some of them as my friends personally if not politically, that for the evils complained of in some of the southern States they themselves are responsible and not the colored people. It is in consequence of the continued uncompromising, repulsive attitude of the Democratic party toward the colored people that they are necessarily compelled on many occasions to vote for men whom they would otherwise vote against. The position of the Democratic party toward the colored people had been and is such that their rights and their privileges to a certain extent are involved in every election. If gentlemen on the other side of the House will bear this fact in mind, they will agree with me in these conclusions. I want to see the day come when the colored people of this country can afford to occupy an independent position in politics; but that day, in my judgment, will never come so long as there remains a strong, powerful, intelligent, wealthy organization arrayed against them as a race and as a class. That is my judgment. When this state of things shall have passed away, then they will be more independent than they now are.

I ask for a national civil rights bill full and complete, not only because it is an act of simple justice, but because it will be instrumental in placing the colored people in a more independent position; because it will, in my judgment, be calculated to bring about a friendly feeling between the two races in all sections of the country, and will place the colored people in a position where their identification with any party will be a matter of choice and not of necessity. And while I reiterate the opinion that the great majority of the colored people will remain true to the Republican party so long as that party maintains its present friendly attitude towards them, yet I know and believe that all true Republicans are ready, willing, and anxious to place the colored people in a position where they can be more independent in the management, government, and control of their local affairs.   I will, if the opportunity shall ever present itself, give my views at length upon the important question of civil rights and civil government at the South.

> *The proposed Civil Rights Bill of Senator Charles Sumner faced many challenges. Its opponents used the states' rights argument against it. Lynch argued that the bill was merely misunderstood. He blamed its opponents for this, likening them to the Calhoun school of state sovereignty. He pointed out that the Civil War had settled some of these issues, but that it could not make anyone recognize the centralization of federal power. He urged Congress to pass the bill that would endorse the Civil War Amendments.*

THE CIVIL RIGHTS BILL
February 3, 1875

I was not particularly anxious to take part in this debate, and would not have done so but for the fact that this bill had created a great deal of discussion both in and outside of the halls of Congress.   In order to answer successfully the arguments that have been made against the bill, I deem it necessary, if my time will allow me to do so, to discuss the question from three standpoints—legal, social, and political.   I confess that it is with hesitancy that I shall attempt to make a few remarks upon the legal question involved; not that I entertain any doubts as to the constitutionality of the pending bill, but because that branch of the subject has been so ably, successfully, and satisfactorily discussed by other gentlemen who have spoken in the affirmative of the question.   The importance of the subject, however, is my apology to the House for submitting a few remarks upon this point in addition to what has already been said.

Constitutionality of the Bill

It is a fact well known by those who are at all familiar with the history of our Government that the great question of state's rights—absolute State sovereignty as understood by the Calhoun school of politicians—has been a continuous source of political agitation for a great many years.   In fact, for a number of years anterior to the rebellion this was the chief topic of political discussion.   It continued to agitate the public mind from year to year and from time to time until the question was finally settled upon the field of battle. The war, however, did not result in the recognition of what may be called a centralized government, nor did it result in the destruction of the independent functions of the several States, except in certain particulars.

It did result in the recognition, and I hope the acceptance, of what may be called a medium between these two extremes; and this medium position or liberal policy had been incorporated in the Federal Constitution through the recent amendments to that instrument. But many of our constitutional lawyers of today are men who received their legal and political training during the discussion of the great question of State rights and under the tutorship of those who were identified with the Calhoun school of impracticable state's rights theorists; they having been taught to believe that the Constitution as it was justified the construction they placed upon it, and this impression having been so indelibly and unalterably fixed upon their minds that recent changes, alterations and amendments have failed to bring about a corresponding change in their construction of the Constitution. In fact, they seem to forget that the Constitution is not in every respect the Constitution it once was.

We have a practical illustration of the correctness of this assertion in the person of the distinguished gentleman from Georgia [Alexander H. Stephens] and I believe my colleague who sits near me [Lucius Q.C. Lamar] and others who agree with them in their construction of the Constitution. But believing as I do that the Constitution as whole should be so construed as to carry out the intention of the framers of the recent amendments, it will not be surprising to the House and to the country when I assert that it is impossible for me to agree with those who so construe the Constitution as to arrive at the erroneous conclusion that the pending bill is in violation of that instrument. It is not my purpose, however, to give the House simply the benefit of my own opinion upon the question, but to endeavor to show to your satisfaction, if possible, that the construction which I place upon the Constitution is precisely in accordance with that placed upon it by the highest judicial tribunal in the land, the Supreme Court of the United States. And this brings us to the celebrated Slaughter-house Cases. But before referring to the decision of the court in detail, I will take this occasion to remark that, for the purposes of this debate at least, I accept as correct the theory that Congress cannot constitutionally pass any law unless it has expressed constitutional grant of power to do so; that the constitutional right of Congress to pass a law must not be implied, but expressed; and that in the absence of such expressed constitutional grant of power the right does not exist.

I repeat that for the purposes of this debate at least, I accept as correct this theory. After having read over the decision of the court in these Slaughter-house Cases several times very carefully, I have been brought very forcibly to this conclusion: that so far as this decision refers to the question of civil rights—the kind of civil rights referred to in this bill—it means this and nothing more:

that whatever right or power a State may have had prior to the ratification of the Fourteenth Amendment it still has, except in certain particulars. In other words, the Fourteenth Amendment was not intended, in the opinion of the court, to confer upon the Federal Government additional powers in general terms, but only in certain particulars. What are those particulars wherein the Fourteenth Amendment confers upon the General Government powers that it did not have before? The right to prevent distinctions and discriminations between the citizens of the United States and of the several States whenever such distinctions and discriminations are made on account of race, color, or previous condition of servitude; and that distinctions and discriminations made upon any other grounds that these are not prohibited by the Fourteenth Amendment. As the discrimination referred to in the Slaughter-house Cases was not made upon either of these grounds, it did not come within the constitutional prohibition. As the pending bill refers only to such discriminations as are made on account of race, color, or previous condition of servitude, it necessarily follows that the bill is in harmony with the Constitution as construed by the Supreme Court. I will now ask the Clerk to read the following extract from the decision upon which the legal gentlemen on the other side of the House have chiefly relied to sustain them in the assertion that the court had virtually decided the pending bill to be unconstitutional.

But there are some democrats, and if I am not mistaken the gentleman from Georgia [Alexander H. Stephens] is one among the number, who guarantee to the colored citizens all of the rights, privileges, and immunities that are enjoyed by white citizens. But they say that it is the province of the several States, and not that of the Federal Government, to enforce these constitutional guarantees. This is the most important point in the whole argument. Upon its decision this bill's guarantee of equal rights is conceded, which is an important concession for those calling themselves Jeffersonian Democrats. The question that now presents itself is has the Federal Government the constitutional right to enforce by suitable and appropriate legislation the guarantees herein referred to. It will be seen from the above that the constitutional right of Congress to pass this bill is fully conceded by the Supreme Court. But before leaving this subject, I desire to call attention to a short legal argument that was made by a distinguished lawyer in the other end of the Capital (if it is parliamentary to do so) when the bill was under consideration before that body:

The position assumed by the eminent lawyer is so unreasonable, untenable, and illogical that it would have surprised me had an ordinary village lawyer of inferior acquirements taken it. There is nothing in this section that will justify the assertion that it contemplates regulating State juries. It simply contemplates carrying into effect the constitutional prohibition against distinctions on account of race or color. There is also a constitutional prohibition against religious proscription. Let us suppose that another section conferred the power on Congress to enforce the provisions of that article by appropriate legislation; then suppose a State should pass a law disqualifying from voting, holding office, or serving on juries all persons who may be identified with a certain religious denomination; would the distinguished Wisconsin Senator then contend that Congress would have no right to pass a law prohibiting this discrimination, in the face of the constitutional prohibition and the right conferred upon Congress to enforce it by appropriate legislation? I contend that any provision in the constitution or laws of any State that is in conflict with the Constitution of the United States is absolutely null and void.

As the Supreme Court has decided that the above constitutional provision was intended to confer upon Congress the power to prevent distinctions and discriminations when made on account of race or color, I contend that the power of Congress in this respect is applicable to every office under the constitution and laws of any State. Some may think that this is extraordinary power; but such is not the case. For any State can, without violating the Fourteenth or Fifteenth Amendment and the provisions of this bill, prohibit any one from voting, holding office, or serving on juries in their respective States, who cannot read and write, or who does not own a certain amount of property, or who shall not have resided in the State for a certain number of months, days, or years. The only thing these amendments prevents them from doing in this respect is making the color of a person or the race with which any person may be identified a ground of disqualification from the enjoyment of any of these privileges. The question seems to me to be so clear that further argument is unnecessary.

Civil Rights and Social Equality

I will now endeavor to answer the arguments of those who have been contending that the passage of this bill is an effort to bring about social equality between the races. That the passage of this bill can in any manner affect the social status of any one seems to me to be absurd and ridiculous. I have never believed for a moment that social equality could be brought about even between persons of the same race. I have always believed that social distinctions existed among white people the same as among colored people. But those who contend that the passage of this bill will have a tendency to bring about social equality between the races virtually and substantially admit that there are no social distinctions among white people whatever, but that all white persons, regardless of their moral character, are the social equals of each other; for if by conferring upon colored people the same rights and privileges that are now exercised and enjoyed by whites indiscriminately will result in bringing about social equality between the races, then the same process of reasoning must necessarily bring us to the conclusion that there are no social distinctions among whites, because all white persons, regardless of their social standing, are permitted to enjoy these rights.

See then how unreasonable, unjust, and false is the assertion that gentlemen on the other side of the House means when they say, when they admit, as they do, that the immoral, the ignorant and the degraded of their own race are the social equals of themselves, and their families. If they do, then I can only assure them that they do not put as high an estimate upon their own social standing as respectable and intelligent colored people place upon theirs; for there are hundreds and thousands of white people of both sexes whom I know to be the social inferiors of respectable and intelligent colored people. I can then assure that portion of my democratic friends on the other side of the House whom I regard as my social inferiors a seat at the same table with you or the same seat in a car with you, but do not think that I have thereby accepted you as my social equal. But if any one should attempt to discriminate against you for no other reason than because you are identified with a particular race or religious sect, I would regard it as an outrage; as a violation of the principles of republicanism; and I would be in favor of protecting you in the exercise and enjoyment of your rights by suitable and appropriate legislation.

It is not social rights that we desire. We have enough of that already. What we ask for is protection in the enjoyment of public rights-rights that are or should be accorded to every citizen alike. Unlike our present system of race distinctions a white woman of a questionable social standing, yea, I may say, of an admitted immoral character, can go to any public place or upon any public conveyance and be the recipient of the same treatment, the same courtesy, and the same respect that is usually accorded to the most refined and virtuous; but let an intelligent, modest, refined colored lady present herself and ask that the same privileges be accorded to her that have just been accorded to her social inferior of the white race, and in nine cases out of ten, except in certain portions of the country, she will not only be refused, but insulted for making the request.

I appeal to your sensitive feelings as husbands, fathers, and brothers, is this just? You who have affectionate companions, attractive daughters, and loving sisters, is this just? If you have any of the ingredients of manhood in your composition you will answer the question most emphatically, No! What a sad commentary upon our system of government, our religion, and our civilization! Think of it for a moment; here am I, a member of your honorable body, representing one of the largest and wealthiest districts in the State of Mississippi, and possibly in the South; a district composed of persons of different races, religions, and nationalities; and yet, when I leave my home to come to the capital of the nation, to take part in the deliberations of the House and to participate with you in making laws for the government of this great Republic, in coming through the God-forsaken States of Kentucky and Tennessee, if I come by the way of Louisville or Chattanooga, I am treated, not as an American citizen, but as a brute. Forced to occupy a filthy smoking car both night and day, with drunkards, gamblers, and criminals; and for what? Not that I am unable or unwilling to pay my way; not that I am obnoxious in my personal appearance or disrespectful in my conduct; but simply because I happen to be of a darker complexion. If this treatment was confined to persons of our own sex we could possibly afford to endure it. But such is not the case. Our wives and our daughters, our sisters and our mothers, are subjected to the same insults and to the same uncivilized treatment. You may ask why we do not institute civil suits in the State courts. What a farce! Talk about instituting a civil-rights suit in the State courts of Kentucky, for instance, where the decision of the judge is virtually rendered before he enters the courthouse, and the verdict of the jury substantially rendered before it is impaneled. The only moments of my life when I am necessarily compelled to question my loyalty to my Government or my devotion to the flag of my country are when I read of outrages having been committed upon innocent colored people and the perpetrators go unpunished.

If this unjust discrimination is to be longer tolerated by the American people, which I do not, cannot, and will not believe until I am forced to do so, then I can only say with sorrow and regret that our boasted civilization is a fraud; our republican institutions a failure; our social system a disgrace; and our religion a complete hypocrisy. I have an abiding confidence in the patriotism of this people, in their devotion to the cause of human rights, and in the stability of our republican institutions. I hope that I will not be deceived. I love the land that gave me birth; I love the Stars and Stripes. This country is where I intend to live, where I expect to die. To preserve the honor of the national flag and to maintain perpetually the Union of the States hundreds, and I may say thousands, of noble, brave, and truehearted colored men have fought, bled, and died. And now, I ask, can it be possible that that flag under which they fought is to be a shield and a protection to all races and classes of persons except the colored race? God forbid!

The School Clause

The enemies of this bill have been trying very hard to create the impression that it is the object of its advocates to bring about a compulsory system of mixed schools. It is not my intention at this time to enter into a discussion of the question as to the propriety or impropriety of mixed schools; as to whether or not such a system is essential to destroy race distinctions and break down race prejudices. I will leave these questions to be discussed by those who have given the subject a more thorough consideration. The question that now presents itself to our minds is what will be the effect of this legislation on the public-school system of the country, and more especially in the South? It is to this question that I now propose to speak.

I regard this school clause as the most harmless provision in the bill. If it were true that the passage of this bill with the school clause in it would tolerate the existence of none but a system of mixed free schools, then I would question very seriously the propriety of retaining such a clause; but such is not the case. If I understand the bill correctly (and I think I do) it simply confers upon all citizens, or rather recognizes the right which has already been conferred upon all citizens, to send their children to any public free school that is supported in whole or in part by taxation, the exercise of the right to remain a matter of option as it now is—nothing compulsory about it. That the passage of this bill can result in breaking up the public school system in any State is absurd. The men who make these reckless assertions are very well aware of the fact, or else they are guilty of unpardonable ignorance, that every right and privilege that is enumerated in this bill has already been conferred upon all citizens alike in at least one-half of the States of this Union by State legislation.

In every Southern State where the Republican party is in power a civil-rights bill is in force that is more severe in its penalties than are the penalties in this bill. We find mixed school clauses in some of their State constitutions. If, then, the passage of this bill, which does not confer upon the colored people of such States any rights that they do not possess already, will result in breaking up the public school system in their respective States, why is it that State legislation has not broken them up? This proves very conclusively, I think, that there is nothing in the argument whatever, and that the school clause is the most harmless provision in the bill. My opinion is that the passage of this bill just as it passed the Senate will bring about mixed schools practically only in localities where one or the other of the two races is small in numbers, and that in localities where both races are large in numbers separate schools and separate institutions of learning will continue to exist, for a number of years at least.

The question had been asked what effect would the civil-rights bill have on the public school system of our State if it should become a law? Our opinion is that it will have none at all. The provisions of the bill do not necessarily break up the separate school system, unless the people interested choose that they shall do so; and there is no reason to believe that the colored people of this State are dissatisfied with the system as it is or that they are not content to let well enough alone. As a people, they have not shown a disposition to thrust themselves where they are not wanted, or rather had no right to go. While they have been naturally tenacious of their newly acquired privileges, their general conduct will bear them witness that they have shown consideration for the feelings of the whites.

As to our public school system, so far as it bears upon the races, we have heard no complaint whatever. It is not asserted that it is operated more advantageously to the whites than to the blacks. All share its benefits alike; and we do not believe the colored people, if left to the guidance of their own judgments, will consent to jeopardize these benefits in a vain attempt to acquire something better. The question may be asked, however, if the colored people in a majority of the States are entitled by State legislation to all of the rights and privileges enumerated in this bill, and if they will not insist upon mixing the children in the public schools in all localities, what is the necessity of retaining this clause? The reasons are numerous, but I will only mention a few of them.

In the first place, it is contrary to our system of government to discriminate by law between persons on account of their race, their color, their religion, or the place of their birth. It is just as wrong and just as contrary to republicanism to provide by law for the education of children who may be identified with a certain race in separate schools to themselves, as to provide by law for the education of children who may be identified with a certain religious denomination in separate schools to themselves. The duty of the lawmaker is to know no race, no color, no religion, and no nationality, except to prevent distinctions on any of these grounds, so far as the law is concerned.

The colored people in asking the passage of this bill just as it passed the Senate do not thereby admit that their children can be better educated in white than in colored schools; nor do they admit that white teachers are better qualified to teach than colored ones. But they recognize the fact that the distinction when made and tolerated by law is an unjust and odious proscription; that you make their color a ground of objection, and consequently a crime. This is what we most earnestly protest against. Let us confer upon all citizens, then, the rights to which they are entitled under the Constitution; and then if they choose to have their children educated in separate schools, as they do in my own State, then both races will be satisfied, because they will know that the separation is their own voluntary act, and not legislative compulsion.

Another reason why the school clause ought to be retained is because the Negro question ought to be removed from the politics of the country. It had been a disturbing element in the country ever since the Declaration of Independence and it will continue to be so long as the colored man is denied any right or privilege that is enjoyed by the white man. Pass this bill as it passed the Senate, and there will be nothing more for the colored people to ask or expect in the way of civil rights. Equal rights having been made an accomplished fact, opposition to the exercise thereof will gradually pass away and the everlasting Negro question will then be removed from the politics of the country for the first time since the existence of the Government. Let us be just as well as generous. Let us confer upon the colored citizens equal rights, and, my word for it, they will exercise their rights with moderation and with wise discretion.

Civil Rights from a Political Standpoint

I now come to the most important part of my subject—civil rights from a political standpoint. In discussing this branch of the subject, I do not deem it necessary to make any appeal to the republican members whatever in behalf of this bill. It is presumed, and correctly, too, I hope, that every republican member of the House will vote for this bill. The country expects it, the colored people ask it, the Republican party promised it, and justice demands it. It is not necessary therefore for me to appeal to republicans in behalf of a measure that they are known to be in favor of. But it had been suggested that it is not necessary for me to make an appeal to the democratic, conservative, or liberal republican members in behalf of this measure; that they will go against it to a man. This may be true, but I prefer to judge them by their acts. I will not condemn them in advance. I desire to call the attention of the democratic members of the House to one or two things in connection with the history of their organization. Your party went before the country in 1872 with a pledge that it would protect the colored people in all of their rights and privileges under the Constitution, and to convince them of your sincerity you nominated as your standard-bearer one who had proved himself to be their life-long friend and advocate.

The colored people did not believe that you were sincere, and consequently did not trust you. As the promise was made unconditionally, however, their refusal to trust you does not relieve you from the performance of the promise. Think for a moment what the effect of your votes upon this bill will be. If you vote in favor of this measure, which will be nothing more than redeeming the promises made by you in 1872, it will convince the colored people that they were mistaken when they supposed that you made the promise for no other purpose than to deceive them. If you should vote against this bill, which I am afraid you intend to do, you will thereby convince them that they were not mistaken when they supposed that you made the promise for no other purpose than to deceive them. It can have no other effect than to increase their suspicion, strengthen their doubts, and intensify their devotion to the Republican party. It will demonstrate to the country and to the world that you attempted in 1872 to obtain power under false pretenses. I once heard a very eminent lawyer make the remark that the crime of obtaining money or goods under false pretenses is in his opinion that next crime to murder. I ask the democratic and conservative members of the House will you, by voting against this bill, convict yourselves of attempting in 1872 to obtain power under false pretenses?

I will take this occasion to say to my democratic friends, that I do not wish to be understood as endeavoring to convey the idea that all of the prominent men who were identified with the so-called liberal movement in 1872 were actuated by improper motives, that they made promises which they never intended to redeem. Far from it; I confess that some of the best and most steadfast friends the colored people in this country have ever had were identified with that movement. Even the man whom you selected, from necessity and not from choice, as your standard-bearer on that occasion is one whose memory will ever live in the hearts of the colored people of this country as one of their best, their strongest, and most consistent friends. They will ever cherish his memory, and the consequence of his life-long devotion to the cause of liberty, humanity, and justice—for his earnest, continuous, persistent, and consistent advocacy of what he was pleased to term manhood suffrage. In voting against him so unanimously as the colored voters did, it was not because they questioned his honesty, or his devotion to the cause of equal rights, but they recognized the fact that he made the same mistake that many of our great men have made—he allowed his ambition to control his better judgment. While the colored voters would have cheerfully supported him for the Presidency under different circumstances they could not give their votes to elevate him to that position through such a questionable channel as that selected by him in 1872. But since he had passed away, they are willing to remember only his virtues and to forget his faults. I might refer to several other illustrious names that were identified with that movement and whose fidelity to the cause of civil rights can never be questioned, but time will not allow me to do so.

I will now refer to some of the unfortunate remarks that were made by some gentlemen on the other side of the House during the last session— especially those made by the gentleman from North Carolina [William McKendree Robbins] and those made by the gentleman from Virginia [John Thomas Harris]. These gentlemen are evidently strong believers in the exploded theory of white superiority and Negro inferiority. But in order to show what a difference of opinion exists among men, with regard to man's superiority over man, it gives me pleasure to assure those two gentlemen that if at any time either of them should become so generous as to admit that I, for instance, am his equal, I would certainly regard it as anything else but complimentary to myself. This may be regarded as a little selfish, but as all of us are selfish to some extent, I must confess that I am no exception to the general rule. The gentleman from North Carolina admits, ironically, that the colored people, even when in bondage and ignorance, could equal, if not excel, the whites in some things—dancing, singing, and eloquence, for instance. We will admit, for the sake of the argument, that in this the gentleman is correct, and will ask the question, Why is it that the colored people could equal the whites in these respects, while in bondage and ignorance, but not in others? The answer is an easy one: You could not prevent them from dancing unless you kept them continually tied; you could not prevent them from singing unless you kept them continually gagged; you could not prevent them from being eloquent unless you deprived them of the power of speech; but you could and did prevent them from becoming educated for fear that they would equal you in every other respect; for no educated people can be held in bondage.

If the argument proves anything, therefore, it is only this: That if the colored people while in bondage and ignorance could equal the whites in these respects, give them their freedom and allow them to become educated and they will equal the whites in every other respect. At any rate I cannot see how any reasonable man can object to giving them an opportunity to do so if they can. It does not become southern white men, in my opinion, to boast about the ignorance of the colored people, when you know that their ignorance is the result of the enforcement of your unjust laws. Any one would suppose, from the style and the manner of the gentleman from North Carolina that the white man's government of the State from which he comes makes it one of the best States in the Union for white men to live in at least. But I will ask the Clerk to read, for the information of that gentleman, the following article from a democratic paper in my own State.

We do not see the point of the joke. The "white men who moved from Cabarrus will doubtless report" that they have not realized, and do not expect to, any serious inconvenience from the election of Bruce. It is better to be endured than the inconvenience of eking out a starveling existence in a worn-out State like North Carolina. Besides, when we look to the executive offices of the two States we will find that the governor of North Carolina claims to be as stanch a republican as his Excellency of Mississippi. And then contrast the financial condition of the two States. There is poor old North Carolina burdened with a debt of $30,000,000, with interest accumulating so rapidly that she is unable to pay it much less the principal. The debt of Mississippi, on the other hand, is but three millions, and with her wonderful recuperative powers it can be wiped out in a few years by the economical management solemnly promised by those in charge of her State government. So far as the gentleman from Virginia is concerned, the gentleman who so far forgot himself as to be disrespectful to one of his fellow-members, I have only this remark to make: Having served in the Legislature of my own State several years, where I had the privilege of meeting some of the best, the ablest, and I may add, the bitterest democrats in the State, it gives me pleasure to be able to say, that with all of their bitterness upon political questions, they never failed to preserve and maintain that degree of dignity, self-respect, and parliamentary decorum which always characterized intelligent legislators and well-bred gentlemen. Take, for instance, my eloquent and distinguished colleague [Lucius Quintus C. Lamar] on the other side of the House, and I venture to assert that he will never declare upon this floor or elsewhere that he is only addressing white men. No; Mississippians do not send such men to Congress, or even to their State Legislature. For if they did it would be a sad and serious reflection upon their intelligence, and a humiliating disgrace to the State.

Such sentiments as those uttered by the gentleman from North Carolina and the gentleman from Virginia are certainly calculated to do the southern white people a great deal more harm than it is possible for them to do the colored people. In consequence of which I can say to those two gentlemen, that I know of no stronger rebuke than the language of the Savior of the world when praying for its persecutors: "Father, forgive them; for they know not what they do."

The South Not Opposed to Civil Rights

The opposition to civil rights in the South is not so general or intense as a great many would have the country believe. It is a mistaken idea that all of the white people in the South outside of the Republican party are bitterly opposed to this bill. In my own State, and especially in my own district, the democrats as a rule are indifferent as to its fate. It is true they would not vote for it, but they reason from this standpoint; the civil rights bill does not confer upon the colored people of Mississippi any rights that they are not entitled to already under the Constitution and laws of the State. We certainly have no objections, then, to allowing the colored people in other States to enjoy the same rights that they are entitled to in our own State. To illustrate this point more forcibly, I ask the Clerk to read the following article from the ablest conservative paper in the State; a paper, however, that is opposed to the White League. This article was published when the civil-rights bill was under discussion in the Senate last winter.

The Clerk read as follows:

A civil rights bill is before the Senate. As we have civil-rights here in Mississippi and else where in the South, we do not understand why southern representatives should concern themselves about applying the measure to other portions of the country; or what practical interest we have in the question. On the 29th, Senator Thomas Manson Norwood of Georgia, one of the mediocrity to whom expediency has assigned a place for which he is unfitted, delivered himself of a weak and driveling speech on the subject upon which he did what he was able to do to keep alive sectional strife and the prejudices of race. We will venture to say that his colleague, General Gordon, who was a true soldier when the war was raging, will not be drawn into the mischievous controversy which demagogues from both sections, and especially latter-day fire-eaters who have become intensely enraged since the surrender, take delight in carrying on.

It will be seen from the above that if Mr. Garland means what he says, which remains to be seen, the democratic or conservative party in Arkansas is in favor of civil rights for the colored people. But if the Legislature had failed to pass it, as in Alabama for instance, White League demagogues would have appealed to the passions and prejudices of the whites, and made them believe that this legislation is intended to bring about a revolution in society. The opposition to civil rights in the South therefore is confined almost exclusively to States under democratic control, or States where the Legislature has failed or refused to pass a civil rights bill. I ask the republican members of the House then will you refuse or fail to do justice to the colored man in obedience to the behest of three or four democratic States in the south? If so, then the Republican party is not made of that material which I have always supposed it was.

Public Opinion

Some well-meaning men have made the remark that the discussion of the civil-rights question has produced a great deal of bad feeling in certain portions of the South, in consequence of which they regret the discussion of the question and the possibility of the passage of the pending bill. That the discussion of the question has produced some bad feeling I am willing to admit; but allow me to assure you that the opposition to the pending bill is not half as intense in the South today as was the opposition to the reconstruction acts of Congress.

As long as congressional action is delayed in the passage of this bill, the more intense this feeling will be. But let the bill pass and become a law and you will find that in a few months reasonable men, liberal men, moderate men, sensible men, who now question the propriety of passing this bill will arrive at the conclusion that it is not such a bad thing as they supposed it was. They will find that democratic predictions have not and will not be realized. They will find that there is no more social equality than before. Whites and blacks will not intermarry any more than they did before the passage of the bill. In short, they will find that there is nothing in the bill but the recognition by law of the equal rights of all citizens before the law. My honest opinion is that the passage of this bill will have a tendency to harmonize the apparently conflicting interests between the two races. It will have a tendency to bring them more closely together in all matters pertaining to their public and political duties. It will cause them to know, appreciate, and respect the rights and privileges of each other more than ever before. In the language of my distinguished colleague on the other side of the house, "They will know one another, and love one another."

Conclusion

I say to the republican members of the House that the passage of this bill is expected of you. If any of our democratic friends will vote for it, we will be agreeably surprised. But if republicans should vote against it, we will be sorely disappointed; it will be to us a source of deep mortification as well as profound regret. We will feel as though we are deserted in the house of our friends. But I have no fears whatever in this respect. You have stood by the colored people of this country when it was more unpopular to do so than it is to pass this bill. You have fulfilled every promise thus far, and I have no reason to believe that you will not fulfill this one. Then give us this bill. The white man's government— Negro-hating democracy will, in my judgment, soon pass out of existence. The progressive spirit of the American people will not much longer tolerate the existence of an organization that lives upon the passions and prejudices of the hour.

When that party shall have passed away, the Republican party of today will not be left in undisputed control of the Government; but a young, powerful, and more vigorous organization will rise up to take the place of the democracy of today. This organization may not have opposition to the Negro the principal plank in its platform; it may take him by the right hand and concede him every right in good faith that is enjoyed by the whites; it may confer upon him honor and position. But if you, as leaders of the Republican party, will remain true to the principles upon which the party came into power, as I am satisfied you will, then no other party, however just, liberal, or fair it may be, will ever be able to detach any considerable number of colored voters from the national organization. Of course, in matters pertaining to their local State affairs, they will divide up to some extent, as they sometimes should, whenever they can be assured that their rights and privileges are not involved in the contest. But in all national contests, I feel safe in predicting that they will remain true to the great party of freedom and equal rights.

I appeal to all the members of the House republicans and democrats, conservatives and liberals—to join with us in the passage of this bill, which has for its object the protection of human rights. And when every man, woman, and child can feel and know that his, her, and their rights are fully protected by the strong arm of a generous and grateful Republic, then we can all truthfully say that this beautiful land of ours, over which the Star Spangled Banner so triumphantly waves, is, in truth and in fact, the "land of the free and the home of the brave."

Lynch eulogized former Vice President Henry Wilson as a friend to all people. He rated Wilson as a public servant on the same level as Henry Clay. Lynch explained that Wilson favored abolition because he considered slavery a moral wrong. He praised Wilson for giving support to Radical Reconstruction. Wilson had also used his influence to win state support for Congressional Reconstruction.

THE DEATH OF HENRY WILSON
January 21, 1876

Not long since the sad intelligence was flashed from one end of the country to the other that Henry Wilson, late Vice President of the United States, was dead. This sad news carried a pang of sorrow and grief to the heart of every lover of his country and to every friend of liberty and justice. I shall not attempt to do justice to the memory of this great and good man. I shall refer more especially to his achievements as a public man—as a representative man. Mr. Wilson was known and recognized throughout the civilized world as a man of acknowledged ability and admitted capacity. The period in which he lived was one that enabled him to make for himself a record that is in every respect worthy of emulation. He was a man of broad, liberal, and conservative views upon public questions.

In the person of Henry Wilson the poor have lost a true and consistent friend, the oppressed an able advocate, and the country a faithful public servant. He dedicated his entire life to the cause of liberty, justice, and equal rights. He regarded the institution of slavery as a foul blot upon our system of government, our civilization, and our Christianity. Recognizing the fact as he did, that the tree of liberty had been planted upon American soil and watered with the precious blood of thousands of patriotic advocates of freedom, that we could not consistently tolerate and sustain an institution that was more aggravating and disgraceful than that of which the founders of our Government complained, and against which they were justified in rebelling, he did not entertain any feeling of ill-will toward those who did not agree with him in his views, nor toward those who were personally interested in perpetuating the existence of that institution which he regarded as a national disgrace, and to the destruction and abolition of which he devoted a long, useful, and successful life. But he was actuated by higher, nobler, and purer motives. He regarded the toleration of an institution which recognized the right of property in man as not only destructive of our system of government, subversive of true democracy, and as having a tendency to demoralize society, disturb the labor of the country, corrupt the morals of the masses, and retard the progress, happiness, and material prosperity of the people, but he also regarded it as contrary to the laws, useful and eventful life. He never failed to raise his voice, to use his pen, and to cast his vote in the defense of those principles which he so consistently and persistently advocated.

During the memorable contest of 1856 over the admission of Kansas as a State in the Union, with the friends of freedom upon one side and the advocates of slavery upon the other, Henry Wilson was one of the few members of the United States Senate at that time who took a bold, independent, outspoken position in favor of freedom for the slave. He did not oppose slavery simply from a standpoint of political expediency, but because he believed it to be morally and religiously wrong, as will appear from the following quotation from one of his great speeches that he delivered when the Kansas question was before the Senate. Henry Wilson was an ardent and devoted lover of his country. As chairman of the Senate Committee on Military Affairs during the late war he displayed such remarkable ability as to make his power and influence felt, acknowledged, and respected throughout the country. His advice and counsel were often sought by the Government, and seldom if ever rejected. His admonitions and remonstrance were seldom disregarded but often heeded, and never disrespected. He was justly looked upon by the country as one of the chief pillars of the government during that important period of our country's history. His able speeches, his patriotic utterances, his statesman-like declarations, had the effect of giving renewed life and vigor to the cause of the Union and of strengthening the Union soldiers upon the field of battle. The Union soldier knew that in the person of Henry Wilson he had a true friend, an able advocate, and a strong defender.

Since the beginning of reconstruction Henry Wilson had occupied a very conspicuous position. He was among the first to advocate the adoption of a broad, liberal and comprehensive system of Reconstruction. I well remember his earnest appeals to the old-line Whigs of Virginia, shortly after the adoption of the congressional plan of reconstruction, to join with the newly enfranchised element of the grand old Commonwealth in rehabilitating their State government upon a firm, lasting, and solid foundation. He appealed to them to lay aside their passions and prejudices of race, the existence of which is known and generally admitted to be the result of the toleration of slavery and not from natural causes, and join in with this new element that had been incorporated in the body politic of the Commonwealth in reconstructing their State government upon a basis that would prevent a repetition of previous mistakes. His advice to the old-line Whigs of Virginia was no less applicable to the same element in every one of the States similarly situated.

It is doubtless a source of serious regret to thousands of those he addressed that they did not accept his advice. They now recognize the fact that his object was to prevent the formation of parties upon the race issue. He could foresee the disastrous results that would follow a bitter political contest between antagonistic elements, whether it be based upon race, religion, or nationality. He could foresee that, if reconstruction was made an accomplished fact upon the basis of antagonism between the two great elements of which southern society is composed, passion and prejudice would take the place of reason and argument, and that the material interests of the people, the development of the resources of the country, and the cultivation of friendly relations between the sections would be made subordinate to the ambition of unscrupulous politicians. The results that have followed the rejection of Mr. Wilson's advice by those to whom it was given have very clearly demonstrated the wisdom of his position.

The serious apprehensions entertained by him as to the disastrous results that would be likely to follow the adoption of any other course have been unfortunately realized to an extent that is almost irreparable. It cannot be denied by those who are at all familiar with southern politics that the present unfortunate condition of affairs in that section of our country is due more to the existence of this antagonism between the two great elements in the South than to the faults and shortcomings of local, temporary, and periodical administrations. I believe there are but few who will not agree with me in asserting that had the views of

Henry Wilson been accepted and generally acquiesced in, the southern states would be in a prosperous and flourishing condition today. During the last two or three years of Mr. Wilson's life he saw proper to advance a few ideas upon what may be called the southern question which subjected him to a little unfavorable criticism on the part of a few of those who are identified with the same political organization of which he was a distinguished leader; but they evidently did not understand his purpose nor appreciate his motives. Those who knew Henry Wilson, who have carefully watched his career since the beginning of reconstruction, could see in his recent utterances upon that subject that same consistent determination to bring about, if possible, a union of the best elements from the two great masses of which southern society is composed. They could see the same manifestations of an extreme anxiety on his part to bring about harmony and a reciprocity of feeling between the two races in the south, which all must admit is the most effectual if not the only remedy for the evils complained of in southern politics.

Henry Wilson was a conscientious public man and a true Christian. His character for honesty and integrity could never be questioned. His public career, though long and eventful, was one that was particularly free from everything that was impure or even suspicious. His example is one that is in every particular worthy of emulation. The only thing that is consoling in the death of this great and good man is the fact that he left behind him a glorious record, and that, having lived the life of a pure and devoted Christian, he was enabled to say, "I have fought a good fight, I have finished my course, I have kept the faith." Let us hope, Mr. Speaker, that we may live the life that Wilson lived, and die the death he died.

Lynch objected to the way Congressman Singleton described the states under Congressional Reconstruction. Singleton, a Democrat, argued that men without integrity were in power in the South, and that they had stolen money from the good white men. Lynch pointed out that he too was a southern man, and that his election to Congress was not a result solely of black or Union loyalists. He argued that his election resulted from a mixed constituency of the people in Mississippi. He urged his colleagues to avoid the politics of division. Instead he told them that what the South needed was better control over hate groups, such as the Ku Klux Klan and White Leagues.

RECONSTRUCTION
February 10, 1876

I regret that it is necessary for me to make any remarks upon this subject at all. I certainly would not have done so but for some remarks that fell from the lips of my honorable colleague [James Washington Singleton] who reported this bill from the committee; a gentleman, by the way, for whom I have the highest regard, and in whose judgment, upon some things, I have unlimited confidence. He is doubtless aware of the fact that there is not a member upon this floor from whose views upon any subject I dissent with more reluctance than his. I confess that I shall not confine myself to the subjects contained in this bill, but will endeavor to combat some of the arguments that were so forcibly and eloquently presented by my colleague in favor of the passage of this bill as reported from the committee.

To give additional emphasis, doubtless, to the above, my colleague remarked that he is a southern man, every inch of him, from the crown of his head to the sole of his foot. To this I have no objection. I, too, am a southern man. I admit, however, that I am not in the ordinary acceptation of that term. I am aware, in its ordinary acceptation that it includes only that portion of the white people who resided south of the Mason and Dixon line anterior to the rebellion. But, to speak practically and not theoretically, I can say that I too am a southern man—by birth, education, inclination, and interest. I will say that it is not my purpose in discussing this subject to attempt to revive any of the unpleasant feelings engendered by the war. Far from it; I am anxious to see the day come when all those unpleasant feelings that were created by that struggle, when everything in the nature of race prejudices, will be buried in the grave of forgetfulness never again to be remembered. I am anxious to see the day come when the rights and privileges of all classes of citizens will be recognized and universally acquiesced in from one end of the country to the other, so that we all can gladly and truthfully say, this is our beloved country, with which we are well pleased.

I am not unmindful of the fact that I occupy a seat upon this floor to-day not by the votes of colored men alone, but by those of white men as well; not by the votes of those who fought the battles of the Union alone, but by the votes of a large number of those who fought bravely the battles of the Confederacy as well; not by the votes of outspoken, pronounced republicans alone, but by the votes of a large number of those whom we are pleased to designate liberal and moderate conservatives as well. I hope therefore that my colleague will not object when I claim the right to speak not only for the colored people, not only for republicans, but for a large number of liberals and conservatives as well. Let us see something about what my colleague said in regard to the imposition of taxes by adventurers—by persons who have no interest in the soil. In speaking of carpetbaggers—those who have imposed heavy, oppressive, and unreasonable taxes upon the people of the South—I cannot believe that my colleague intended to include the State he had the honor so ably to represent in part upon this floor. I ask is he aware of the fact that nine-tenths of the offices in the State of Mississippi are now and have been ever since the re-admission of that State into the Union held by southern men—men who are to the manor born, many of whom fought bravely the battles of the confederacy, and who, according to what they say, are not ashamed of it!

I regret that my colleague is not better informed. He can say that Republicans hold a majority of them, but if he says Carpetbaggers hold them it is a mistake. Some of them are, but southern men hold about nine-tenths of them. And I ask him is he not aware of the fact that these men, representing a large percentage of the wealth, the intelligence, and the virtue of the people of that State—is he not aware of the fact that they are a class of men whom the Democratic party were proud to acknowledge in days passed and gone as among their brightest intellects and their ablest leaders? When we speak of men who are holding offices in the South, and especially in the State of Mississippi, we will find a large majority of those offices held by this class of men. Although not identified with my colleague's party now, yet they upheld the cause of the South—that cause for which he no doubt fought, or at least with which he sympathized—as bravely as those who are identified with the political organization of which he is an honorable member.

I commend my colleague in his zeal to inaugurate economy, retrenchment and reform. He has my cooperation and support as long as he confines himself within the bounds of reason and moderation. I am with him heart and soul to bring about economy, retrenchment, and reform, wherever it can be affected. But when he comes forward and tells us that the passage of this bill is demanded in consequence of the heavy taxes under which the people of the South and Mississippi especially are laboring, this demands some little reply, some notice. Let us see what these taxes are of which my colleague so eloquently complained. Let us see why it is that he comes forward and asks that a large number of our important consulships shall be abolished and that the compensation of our foreign ministers shall be reduced in order to relieve the overburdened taxpayers of the South and of Mississippi especially. Let us see wherein that statement can be substantiated and sustained.

The taxes in the State of Mississippi levied for the support of her government are nine and a quarter mills, or $9.25 on each $1,000 worth of taxable property, of which only four mills are for the support of the State government, two mills for educational purposes, and the other three and a quarter mills to pay the interest on the public debt and to create a sinking fund for its liquidation. Now my colleague says that this is a heavy burden, and appeals to the House to come to the relief of the tax payers of the South, and especially of the State of Mississippi. He says that if you could stand where he stood, if you could see the anxious countenances of the tax-payers of Mississippi, when the tax collector was crying off their property to the highest bidder, and see the tears falling down their pallid cheeks, you would sympathize with them, and reduce the pay of these officers for their relief. He says that the people of the South are suffering, and we must make these retrenchments, these reforms, even though it be done at the expense of the honor of this great nation, and I hope my friend from Virginia [John Randolph Tucker] will pardon me for using the word nation in this connection, but the word had become so familiar to me that I cannot help it.

But my colleague says that the people must be relieved, that these burdens must be taken off their shoulders, and that the way to do it is to abolish these important consulates and reduce the compensation of our foreign ministers. The people of Mississippi pay directly comparatively nothing to support the General Government. I admit that, according to the theory of the gentleman from New York [Samuel Sullivan Cox]—and I do not wish to be understood as combating it—we pay doubtless a great deal indirectly, in consequence of the tariff imposed upon articles necessary for home consumption. We pay something in that way, but so far as direct taxes are concerned, I repeat, the people of Mississippi pay comparatively nothing. Still that is no reason why we should not be in favor of retrenchment; but that was not my colleague's line of argument. His argument was that it was local taxation imposed upon us by those who came there in the floodtide of reconstruction, for the purpose of living upon the substance of the people. For my colleague's benefit, I have had a little comparison made, a comparison of the tax system of Mississippi in 1865, when my colleague's party held undisputed control of the State government, and in 1875, when the party with which I am identified had control of it.

My colleague says that we can raise seven million bales of cotton in one part of the State alone, which is about three millions more than I suppose we could raise in the whole State; I presume he is better informed on this subject than I am. My colleague also spoke of the public debt, the debt under which the people of the South are groaning and laboring, especially in Mississippi. Mr. Chairman, the public debt of my State is today less than half a million dollars exclusive of what is called the Chickasaw and common school fund, and yet he asks us to go to work and relieve the burdens of the people of Mississippi by reducing the appropriations for the diplomatic and consular service of the Government. I wish to tell my colleague what I believe to be the true remedy for the evils complained of in the Southern States. The true remedy, I think, is for a public opinion to be inaugurated that will crush out mob law and violence and enforce obedience to the laws of the country. What we want in the South is a public opinion that will cause every man, wherever he may have been born, whatever may be his color, whatever his politics, to feel perfectly safe and secure in the exercise of his rights and privileges as an American citizen.

I can assure any colleague that what we want more than anything else is to have these political agitators, these instigators of strife, these promoters of confusion and disturbers of public peace, forced to take back seats. What we want is to bring about a public sentiment that will render impossible the existence of the White League, Ku Klux Klan, and other dangerous, mischievous, and rebellious organizations. It is in consequence of an unsettled state of affairs, of an unhealthy public opinion that has tolerated the existence of these dangerous organizations and justified these crimes that have been committed upon the rights of private citizens, that the development of that portion of our country had been prevented. You may make as many reductions in the appropriations as you please. But until there shall be brought about by a revolution in the public sentiment of the South a better condition of affairs, that part of our country will never prosper as it should. What we need is to have the people of that portion of our country, the taxpayers, those who are interested in the soil, to rise up in their might and to declare that these men who go about from place to place appealing to the passions and prejudices of race and riding into power upon the demerits of others and not upon any merits they may themselves possess shall be forced to that position which they deserve. That is what we want, and I hope my colleague agrees with me that we must have the good men of the South of both races unite so as to render impossible the elevation to power of a class of men who go about creating confusion, stirring up strife, and trying to keep the country all the time in an unsettled condition.

When this shall have been brought about, then and not until then will merit, honesty, capacity, efficiency, be made the test of political preferment, and not a man's capacity to appeal successfully to race prejudices and the baser instincts of mankind. I can assure my colleague that what we want is to have his party inaugurate a liberal, fair, generous, reasonable policy that will tolerate an honest difference of opinion upon political organization. I express it as my honest opinion that the identification of the colored people as a mass with one political organization, especially so far as local matters are concerned, is not so much a matter of choice as it is, in consequence of democratic hostility to them as a race, a matter of necessity. The affiliation of the masses of the white people in the South with one political organization is not so much a matter of choice with them as it is the result of the existence of a public opinion which in some localities does not tolerate an honest difference of opinion upon political questions except at the sacrifice of social position and success in business.

These are the evils that must be removed. White men must be allowed to disagree upon political questions without being socially ostracized and destroyed in business. Colored men must be convinced that they too can divide in political matters without running the risk of losing their rights and privileges under the government. When this can be done all will be well and the South will prosper, but not till then. We hear a great deal about emigration to the South, but how can we get emigrants to go there? How can we get capital there when men must know before they go that their status in society—their success in business—will depend upon their political affiliations? How can you get them to go there when it is understood beforehand that a public expression of an honest political opinion, unless it happens to be in accordance with the popular views of the hour, means social ostracism and destruction in business. How can you get capitalists to invest in southern communities when they are informed beforehand that public opinion there will sustain and tolerate a class of men who made it their business to ignore the Constitution, disregard the laws, defy the decrees of courts, outrage the rights of private citizens, and revolutionize State, county, and municipal governments?

I say let us have peace, let us have toleration, let us have an honest difference of opinion without being socially ostracized and without being destroyed in business, and then the South will prosper as other sections of the country do, and not till then. These are the evils under which we are laboring and under which we are now struggling. Now let me appeal to my colleague [James Washington Singleton] for he is aware of the fact that I look upon him as one of the best men in the House; that I have the highest respect and admiration for him; that I love him; I hate to disagree with him; it pains me to be compelled to dissent from him—let me appeal to him to endeavor to get his party leaders and party managers to re-adopt and faithfully adhere to that grand old democratic doctrine of former days "the Union, the Constitution, and the enforcement of the laws."

Lynch explained that as a southerner he shared many of the interests of others in the South. His views on southern issues would be free from prejudice. He would not try to advance the Republican party, or any other interest group. Lynch believed the main problem in the South was partisan politics, which brought blacks and whites into conflict. Furthermore, he argued that the immediate enfranchisement of blacks was a necessity for the Union. He believed the country depended on the loyalty of black men, and their vote was essential to Congressional Reconstruction.

THE SOUTHERN QUESTION
June 13, 1876

I do not rise for the purpose of discussing the pending bill, but as the Army had a direct bearing upon southern affairs, I did not think it would be inappropriate for me to take advantage of this occasion to discuss in a general way what is commonly called "the southern question." It is a source of deep regret to me that this is still the most important question agitating the public mind. It is important, because it was out of the discussion of this question that sprang up some of the most serious political troubles that have occurred in this country since the organization of the Government. It is important, inasmuch as it was the immediate cause of the recent Civil War, which cost the country many millions of dollars and thousands of lives. It is important, because the results of the late war were supposed to have been made secure under the system of Reconstruction that was finally adopted.

In discussing this subject I desire to have it understood that I speak not as a casual observer of passing events, but from thorough practical knowledge. It is a subject with which I am not only familiar in consequence of my identity with southern people and southern interests, as I understand them, but it is one that had occupied no little portion of my most serious consideration. The spirit of my remarks I hope will be such as will satisfy the House and the country that I am entirely free from passion and prejudice. Having been born upon southern soil and raised under the influences of southern society, it is nothing more than reasonable to suppose that I would have a very strong attachment for its people, even though I could not as much as respect some of its peculiar institutions. The peculiar relation which I occupy toward a large class of white citizens in my State makes it a source of deep regret to me to give utterance to some things which nothing but a sense of public duty would cause me to utter. Believing as I do that the best and truest friend that any people can have is the friend that will tell them of their faults as well as of their virtues I shall proceed to discharge what I believe to be a plain duty, regardless of consequences personal to myself.

It is not my purpose to speak with a view of advancing the interest of the Republican party, except so far as its interest may be advanced by the truth of history impartially told. It is a fact well known by those who are familiar with my public career thus far that I am not one of that number, if there be such, who are anxious that the Republican party at the South or elsewhere should retain or regain its ascendancy more in consequence of the demerits of others than any merit it may possess itself. I hope to see the day come when public opinion will be such that no party can be successful in the Government or in any State of this Union unless it deserves success.

Although the Republican party is not as free from faults as it should be yet its claim upon the gratitude and support of the American people is sufficiently strong, in my judgment, to commend it to their approbation upon its own merits, and not as the least of two admitted evils. As anxious as I am that this great party shall remain in the ascendancy in the Government, yet if I could be induced to believe that this ascendancy can only be made an accomplished fact at the expense of good government, friendly and amicable relations between the different elements of which southern society is composed, and that democratic ascendancy would being about the opposite result, then I would be willing to at least try the experiment of a change. But I am thoroughly convinced that republican ascendancy in the government is not the cause of political troubles at the South, and that democratic ascendancy is not the remedy for the evils thus complained of.

Nor am I one of that number—if there be such—who take pleasure in referring to political troubles at the South with a view of controlling public opinion at the North. It would be to me a source of personal pride and congratulation if I could declare upon the floor of the House of Representatives today that mob-law and violence do not exist in any part of the South and are not tolerated by any portion of its citizens. That circumstances are such that the facts would not sustain me in making this declaration is to me a source of deep mortification and profound regret. If the political troubles at the South were not unusual and exceptional, and were such as are common on excitable and extraordinary occasions, and would be just as likely to occur in one section of the country as in the other, for the purpose of preserving the good name of the people whom I have the honor in part to represent, as well as the section of country from which I come, I would cover them over with the mantle of charity rather than expose them to the public gaze.

The chief cause of political troubles at the South, in my judgment, is, as I have said on a former occasion, the result of the existence of a public sentiment which renders it necessary for the masses of the two races to identify themselves with two different political organizations and thus bring themselves into an apparent, if not real, antagonism with each other. Every sensible man must admit that, if, in any government, State, or community, the material elements composing the society of which consist of different races, nationalities, and religions, political parties should be organized upon the basis of race, nationality, or religion, the result will be disastrous, not only to the parties to such a contest, but also to the entire community where such organizations may exist. It was certainly not the intention of the original advocates of the system of reconstruction that was finally adopted to make race or color the basis of political organizations at the South, but they evidently believed and were justified in believing that the incorporation of the colored element into the body-politic was not only essential to secure to the Government the fruits of its victory upon the field of battle, but that a combination of the Union and liberal element among the whites with that of the colored would be most certain to follow.

That the anticipations of those who thus believed have not been fully realized presents to the American people questions that demand the most serious attention and careful consideration of the statesmen of today. The causes that have conspired to prevent a realization of these anticipations and to keep up race organizations at the South are questions that I propose briefly to touch upon at this time. There are in brief just two causes that have brought about this result: First, the continuous and unnecessary opposition of the bourbon or impracticable element inside of the ranks of the democracy to the system of reconstruction that was finally adopted by Congress and a stubborn refusal to willingly and cheerfully acquiesce in the results of the war (and this element had unfortunately controlled the democratic organization and shaped its policy); second, the persistent and uncharitable opposition of the same element to the civil and political rights of the colored people.

I now ask the careful attention of the House while I enlarge somewhat upon these two points. I admit that the unconditional enfranchisement of the colored men at the South may have been brought about as much from necessity as from choice; yet, as I said before, no other plan, in my judgment, would have secured to the Government the fruits of its victory upon the battlefield. The success of the Johnson plan of reconstruction would not only have placed the colored man in a condition worse than abject slavery, but it would have restored to power and position in the Government the very class of men who inaugurated the rebellion and brought on the war. The loyal people of the nation saw the danger, and the cry came up from one end of the country to the other, "Give the colored man the ballot." The colored was the only material element at the South that the country could depend upon. Although the masses of them were known to be ignorant, yet it was also known that they were true to their Government. Whatever else may be said of the colored man, it can never be truthfully said of him that he was ever disloyal to his Government or ungrateful to his friends, in consequence of that I feel justified in appealing to the generous heart of the American people. Condemn not the colored man for his unintentional mistakes when he had stood by you so firmly in the hour of need.

I see nothing in the congressional plan of reconstruction to condemn. The fact that the South is in an unsettled condition today is not the result of the adoption of that policy, but the fault is in the people of that section. The same conduct on their part would produce precisely the same results under any system. If the congressional plan of reconstruction is a failure in consequence of the opposition of those from whom opposition was expected, then the war was a failure, because the rebellion was crushed out by force, and not by the voluntary consent of the confederate authorities. To admit that a plan must be agreed upon that will be satisfactory to the bourbon element at the South will be admitting everything for which the northern democracy contended in 1864. The plan of Reconstruction that was finally adopted was not only the policy of the

Republican party but it was also the policy of the Government, for it involved everything which was supposed to have been accomplished as the result of the war.   The colored people, being loyal to the Government and friendly to its policy aside from the fact that they were the immediate beneficiaries of that policy, could not be expected to identify themselves with an organization the aims, the purposes, the tendencies, and the public declarations of which were in opposition to that policy even though they may have been assured that their right and privileges would not be interfered with.   The loyalty of the colored man to his Government is not measured by his personal interest.   Even to admit that the promises made by the democracy to the colored voters were made in good faith and would have been carried out, still the colored man would not have been justified in affiliating with that organization so long as its policy was in opposition to that of the Government.

The opposition of the democracy to the policy of the Government would not bring about such disastrous results, but for the fact that this opposition is so intense and intolerant as to render independent action on the part of white as well as colored men almost an impossibility.   Except in some counties and localities, the bourbon element inside of the ranks of the democracy at the South controls that organization and shapes its policy and as a natural consequence there is a morbid public sentiment that renders life, liberty, and property comparatively insecure.   In consequence of this intolerance, colored men are forced to vote for the candidates of the Republican arty, however objectionable to them some of these candidates may be, unless they are prevented from doing so by violence and intimidation.   White men are compelled to vote for the candidates of the Democratic party, however objectionable to them some of these candidates may be, or else suffer the consequences of being outcasts from society and destroyed in business.

As an aristocracy that was antagonistic to every principle of true republicanism governed the South even for a number of years anterior to the rebellion, it is not strange that the public sentiment of that section should be hostile to the principles embodied in the system of reconstruction that was adopted by the government.   As republican governments can only be sustained by the public sentiment of the people, however strange it may seem to some or humiliating to others, it is a fact, nevertheless, that until there shall have been a revolution in public opinion at the South—until an honest difference of opinion upon public questions shall be tolerated in white and colored men alike—until malice, passion, and prejudice shall give way to reason, argument, and persuasion, civil governments in harmony with the system of reconstruction that was adopted by the General Government can only be sustained and upheld by the power of the General government—the power that crushed out the rebellion. And yet to sustain or tolerate a governmental system at the South hostile or inimical to the principles embodied in the reconstruction acts of Congress will be to acknowledge practically that the war was a failure, and that the policy of the Government toward the Southern States had been from the beginning a mistaken one.

Democratic Opposition to the Civil and Political Rights of the Colored People

The facts of history will bear me out in asserting that the repulsive attitude of the Democratic party toward the colored man has had more to do with preventing the political affiliation of the two races than anything else; that united political action on the part of colored men had been and is still a matter of necessity in consequence of democratic opposition to them as a race and as a class is what every unprejudiced man must admit; that there is any necessity for united political action on the part of white men as such is what every fair-minded man must deny; that any considerable number of colored men can ever be induced to affiliate with the Democratic party of to-day is just as unreasonable as it is unnatural. Colored men can no more affiliate with the Democratic party, as at present organized, than Catholics and foreign-born citizens could affiliate with the Know Nothing party during the existence of that organization.

I can say to the democrats of the House and of the country, that the colored people are asking you every day to allow them to occupy an independent position in politics; to allow them to make their identification with a political organization a matter of choice and not of necessity; but this far you have repulsed them on nearly every occasion. You tell them in nearly all of your political platforms; in nearly all of your leading papers; in nearly all of your political speeches; in nearly all of your political votes as members of Congress or of State Legislatures that they shall not be allowed to affiliate with any other than the Republican party without self-humiliation and disgrace. Thus, I appeal to the leaders of the democracy in the name of humanity and justice: why continue this unjust, unnecessary and uncharitable opposition to this powerless and defenseless race? You know that they are not your enemies; they do not seek to harm you, or to deprive any of you of any of the rights and privileges that you are entitled to under the Constitution and laws of the country. They have been and are still cultivating the soil of the southern portion of this great country, and have produced with their labor the wealth that many of you are enjoying today. And now, what do they ask or demand of you: nothing but a fair chance in the race of life—protection and security through a healthy public opinion in the enjoyment of their rights and privileges as American citizens. It is strange, remarkably strange, that the Democratic party should maintain such persistent and uniform opposition to the colored people.

Shame upon this once grand, noble, and patriotic organization; it has so degenerated that it can have no nobler aim, no grander object, no higher aspiration than the degradation, humiliation and political subjugation of an innocent, harmless, powerless (as compared to whites) and inoffensive race. May I exclaim: "Oh democracy, where is thy generosity, where is thy magnanimity!" It is true that a number of the leaders of your party profess to be in favor of protecting the colored people in the enjoyment of their rights. A number of these gentlemen I believe to be honest and sincere in these professions; but it is an unfortunate, a lamentable, fact that every proposition that had been presented thus far having for its object the elevation, advancement, and promotion of the colored race in the scale of civilization and morality, as we understand it, had met with your solid, united and unbroken opposition.

I listened carefully and attentively not long since to a very able and eloquent speech that was delivered by the honorable gentleman from New York [Mr. Cox] in defense of the Indians, every word and sentence of which, so far as it related to the Indians, met with my hearty and cordial approval. But while he was delivering that speech this thought occurred to me: What a pity it is, how unfortunate it is, that some gentleman on that side of the House cannot be recognized as the advocate and defender of the colored race of America. So far as the gentleman from New York is concerned I have no hesitation in expressing it as my opinion that he personally wishes the colored people no harm. I look upon him as a kind, generous, benevolent man—as much so as it is possible for a democrat to be. But the aims, the purposes and the tendencies of his party are such, the policy of his party is such, that he dare not stand upon the floor of the House of Representatives as the advocate and defender of the colored race of his country without placing himself in hostility to and in antagonism with the political organization with which he is at present unfortunately identified.

An Appeal to Republicans

I desire to make what may be my final appeal to the republican members of the House. I use the word final because, as little as you may think of it, the condition of the colored people of the South are standing upon the brink of our political and personal destruction. When we look to the right, we find the angry billows of an enraged democracy seeking to overwhelm us. When we look to the left, we find that we are crushed to the earth, as it were, with an unjust and an unchristian prejudice. When we turn to the rear we find the assassin in certain portions of the country ready to plunge the dagger into our hearts for a public expression of our honest conviction. We turn our faces to you then as our friends, our advocates, our defenders, and our protectors.

Some of you may say that the colored man having been invested with the same political rights that are enjoyed by the whites ought to be able to take care of himself. To this we would have no objection if we were allowed to exercise and enjoy the rights and privileges thus conferred. But in some localities we are not. The Democratic party has an armed military organization in several of the southern States today called the White League. This organization had been brought into existence for the sole and exclusive purpose of accomplishing with the bullet that which cannot be accomplished with the ballot; for the purpose of controlling public opinion and carrying popular elections by violence and force of arms; for the purpose of destroying the freedom of speech, the freedom of opinion, the freedom of the press, and the protection of the ballot. Its mission is to accomplish practically within the Union that which could not be accomplished through the madness of secession. Not to establish an independent confederacy with slavery as its chief cornerstone, but to use in substance the language of the gentleman from Georgia [Benjamin Harvey Hill], it is to crush out northern fanaticism at the South and to eliminate the Negro from the politics of the country. The election held in my own State in November last is a striking illustration of the purpose for which this organization had been brought into existence.

I do not propose to go into details upon that subject at this time. It is sufficient for me to say that that election was a sad and serious commentary upon our elective system and upon our republican form of government. Here is a State that would be just as certain to vote for the nominees of the Cincinnati convention in November next as any State in the Union if we could have toleration of opinion and a free, fair, orderly election. But under existing circumstances this State, with its known, acknowledged, admitted, unquestionable Republican majority of from twenty to thirty thousand votes, will be just as certain to vote for the nominees of the Saint Louis convention as any State in the Union, simply because the republican organization has been crushed practically out of existence by the terrorism that has been inaugurated by this White-League organization. In several of the largest counties in that State today the Republican party cannot as much as have an organized existence.

I ask the question in all seriousness, can the public sentiment of the country afford to sustain and tolerate this condition of affairs? If so, then the war was fought in vain and the billions of dollars spent for the preservation of the Union have been thrown away. To use the language of the honorable gentleman from Tennessee [John Ford House], "the Union has only been restored in name, and the mighty conflict waged professedly to save it, is a terrible and melancholy failure." We will have civil government in name but not in fact. I do not wish to be understood as endeavoring to convey the idea that all of the white people of my State who are not identified with the Republican party are in sympathy with the White-League or bourbon element—far from it. There is a large intelligent and respectable element among the whites of that State who are opposed to mob-law and violence and in favor of maintaining law and order and having every citizen protected in the enjoyment of his rights. It gives me pleasure to be able to bear testimony to the fact that there is not a more peaceable, orderly, and law-abiding people anywhere in the United States than those of the county and city in which I live. But, taking the State as a whole, it is an unfortunate fact that this liberal, moderate, conservative element is controlled and domineered over just as the Union element was in 1861.

I can fully recognize and appreciate the fact that there is a strong desire in the northern mind to blot out all of the unpleasant recollections engendered by the recent war. I am aware of the fact that there is a strong desire in the northern mind to have the issues growing out of the war dropped from the politics of the country. I confess that I share in this desire; for every man who knows anything about southern politics is aware of the fact that, if we ever expect to have a permanent republican organization in this section, it must be composed of men who fought the battles of the Confederacy as well as those who fought the battles of the Union. And in this connection I will remark that the men who are instrumental in bringing into existence White Leagues and other dangerous and mischievous organizations are not, as a rule, those who fought in the rank and file of either army, but they are men who never smelled powder in their lives, men who are particularly anxious to fight in times of peace but have no desire in that direction in times of war. While you are anxious to forgive everything in connection with the war, let me admonish you, be careful that you do not allow your desire in that direction to become so intense as to render it possible for you to lose, practically, that which you are supposed to have accomplished as the result of the war.

Conclusion

I will say that the colored man does not ask his Government to protect him from violence as a colored man but as an American citizen. He does not ask to be protected in the right to vote the republican ticket, but to exercise the rights and privileges appertaining to American citizenship. It is a fact perhaps not generally known that the white man at the south who affiliates with the Republican party, whether he be of northern or southern birth or whether he fought on the side of the Union or the side of the confederacy, is as much in need of this protection as the colored man. The colored man of the South appeals to the generosity of this great nation today to save him from personal if not political destruction. He appeals to the generous heart of what he believes to be a patriotic, just, and magnanimous people. He cannot believe that his appeal will be made in vain, but that the people of this great country will gratefully remember that, when the Union was threatened with dissolution, when the Constitution was ignored and the flay of the country was draped in mourning, the colored man remained true to his country, true to the Constitution, and loyal to the flay of this country.

In making this appeal, it is nothing more than proper that I should state, as one who knows whereof he speaks, that, if you should desert us in this the hour of our troubles; if you leave us to perish at the hands of those who seek our destruction for no other reason than because of our devotion to principle, if not loyalty to the Government, you will have destroyed our hopes, banished our ambition, crushed out our energies, and buried our aspirations beneath the sod of political degradation, to which you will have so ungenerously assigned us. I will not believe that it is possible for the American people to be guilty of such ingratitude as this until I am forced to do it. In considering this subject I hope you will be governed by the same motives that actuated Patrick Henry when he gave utterance to that noble and patriotic declaration, "Give me liberty or give me death."

Lynch defended Congressional Reconstruction, and praised the legislature for enfranchising blacks. He explained that Democrats were responsible for violence against African Americans in southern states like Mississippi. He argued that violence and intimidation were designed to keep blacks away from the polls. He urged Congress to end the violence with appropriate legislation.

CONDITION OF THE SOUTH
June 15, 1876

I am very thankful to the gentleman from New Jersey [Frederick Halstead Teese] for his courtesy in allowing me to submit a few remarks at this time. I will require only a very few minutes to correct some one or two errors that he has fallen into with regard to the condition of affairs in the State which has the honor so creditably to be represented [by Mississippi Representative Charles Edward Hooker] in part on this floor.

I recognize the fact and none can deny it, that we have had in the Republican party in several of the Southern States men whose records it would not be a credit to any one to attempt to defend. We have had some such men in my own State. I do not propose now—I never have had any desire and never have expected—to defend all the men who are identified with the Republican party. In my judgment no honest man would attempt to defend all of the members of the party with which he may be identified. I do not think it would be to the credit of my honorable colleague to attempt to defend all of the members of his party in the State of Mississippi or elsewhere, for no one knows better than him that all of the bad men in Mississippi are not identified with the Republican party. In speaking of carpetbaggers—of that class of men who came to the State for no other purpose than to fill their pockets—my colleague seems to have entirely forgotten that his own party did not only set the example for the colored people to follow in this respect, but the hostility of his party toward the colored voters was such that it was possible for them to get in. Is it strange, then, that they put some of that class of men in office? But let me explain what I mean when I say the Democratic party set the example for the colored people to follow in this respect.

The gentleman ought to be aware of the fact that that very class of men have been taken up by the Democratic party and elevated to power and position whenever they would consent to serve that party. I have witnessed with sorrow and regret that the very class of men whom the Democratic party would denounce, repudiate, and condemn in one election would be taken up by them at the very next election and eulogized to the skies, although they were carpetbaggers, provided they would join their party. Does my colleague desire me to make an illustration? I will not do it by referring to my own State. I will not be so uncharitable as to do that, but I will take a case from another southern State, and refresh his memory in that particular. He will perhaps remember that there never was a carpetbagger in the South that was more universally denounced, repudiated, and condemned by the Democratic party than was Ex-Governor Warmoth of the State of Louisiana. They said so many bad things about him, accused him of so many bad things, that I among others was induced to believe that at least some of them were true. But yet when that gentleman decided to join the democracy, or rather decided to affiliate with them at that election, I was surprised to find that the party that had denounced, repudiated, and condemned him had opened wide its doors for his reception. They did not only receive him immediately into their ranks but they regarded him as one of their most notable and trusted leaders, one of the shining lights of their party, and they were ready to honor him with the highest office in the gift of the people of the State.

It is believed that when the important announcement was made that Governor Warmoth intended to affiliate with the democracy they had a grand jollification meeting in honor of that important event, and the chief mogul of the party, I imagine, took the young political convert by the right hand and exclaimed solemnly in these words: "Warmoth, we have regarded you as a bad man; we have accused you of being a corrupt man, a dishonest man, a public plunderer of our people; but we now confess that there is only one sin of which we considered you guilty: affiliation with the Republican party. As you have left that organization it makes no difference with us now how much you may have stolen, how much you may have plundered us, how much you may have corrupted the morals of our people. These little sins will be charged against you no more forever. Enter thou into the joys of the democracy, for as you have been found faithful over a few things we will now make you ruler over many." That is in brief the history of the Democratic party in the southern states on the Carpetbag question, in consequence of which I think it comes with very bad grace from the leaders of that party to complain of carpetbag rule at the South.

So much for carpetbaggers; as I said before, I will not refer to my own State; I will be too generous to my honorable colleague to do that. I will let that pass; for he knows as much about it as I do. Now I want to refer to the question of violence resorted to at the last election in the State of Mississippi, and which my colleague so eloquently denies. I had hoped there would be no necessity for referring to it at length. In the few remarks which I delivered here day before yesterday, I made only brief reference to that point. But, in speaking of violence, I say now with sorrow, with regret, with mortification, that it is true that an armed military organization exists in the State of Mississippi in behalf of the Democratic party; and my colleague took particular pains not to deny it, because he cannot deny it. If he thinks he can, I am willing to yield him the floor now to do it. There is an army in the State of Mississippi today called the White League. It is a military organization.

I will not say violence was resorted to in all the counties of that State, for it is not true. The election was fairly, peaceably, and honestly conducted in almost every democratic county in that State. The election was fairly, peaceably, and honestly conducted in some of the republican counties in that State. Violence and intimidation were confined on the part of the democracy chiefly to the republican counties. The reason, I suppose, will readily suggest itself why they were confined to republican counties. I say the colored people of my own State especially have been particularly anxious to be placed in a position where they could be justified and sustained in voting against their own party when it put up men whose honesty is open to question, but they have never been placed in that position in consequence of the hostile attitude of the party which my colleague so ably represents. He says they are all friendly, no ill will, no bad blood, when he knows, wherever the White League organization had an existence, that the public declarations of the men who belong to it as well as the paper which represents it declare in their speeches and in the columns of those papers that that organization has been brought into existence for the very purpose of bringing about white supremacy, and to crush out the Negro because he is a Negro and for no other reason.

That is true of the White League. It is not true of all of the white people of the State because they all do not belong to it. It is not true of all of the Democrats, for they do not all belong to it. But it is true of that organization which has been brought into existence by the bad men in the Democratic party for the purpose of securing position by the power of the bullet and not by the power of the ballot. I will make one illustration to substantiate it—as my colleague referred to one county—will refer to another. In the county of Claiborne in my State, one of the counties of my district, a county containing about 3,000 votes, 500 of which or thereabouts are democratic and the balance republican—that county, in 1872, out of a total vote of about 2,500, gave 1,752 Republican majority. That is just about the average republican majority of that county in an ordinarily fair election. At the last election the White-League organization, being in existence, was armed for the purpose of intimidating the colored people. They borrowed cannon, so I was informed, from some of the steamboats, and had some men from Louisiana come over for the purpose of assisting them in the work of intimidation. They carried that county for the Democratic party by a majority of 556, as they said, out of a total vote of about 1,500. They would not let the colored people vote at all at a majority of the voting-places in the county, unless they would vote the democratic ticket. They had men armed for the purpose of preventing them from doing it, and they did prevent them. And yet the gentleman would have you believe that the election in that county was fairly and honestly conducted and that no violence was resorted to, when he knows the reverse to be true.

And I will tell you today and say to my honorable colleague that it is to the interest of his party if it is in favor of good government; it is for the interest of all law-abiding men to put down this lawlessness, this violence, and allow men to vote without being intimidated. If he can induce the colored men to vote for him, or for any member of his party, of their own free will, by their own choice, I for one will have no objection to their doing it. In fact, I will be glad to see the day come when the colored man will incur no risk in voting the Democratic ticket whenever he wants to do so. But I do not want you to shoot him down if he does not vote the way you want him. And the White League is brought into existence for that very purpose. I do not want you to say, as some of the democratic papers in our State have said, "If you cannot vote him down, knock him down." That is the language of one of the democratic papers in Mississippi.

Now, with all candor, with all fairness, with every feeling of goodwill to the white people as well as to the colored, I will say that I want to see the honest white men of that State who are opposed to mob law and violence rise in their might against this rebellious organization that has been brought into existence for the purpose of carrying elections by violence and not by votes. I assert that this is true of the White League organization. The Democratic party, in my judgment, exists in Mississippi today for the purpose of carrying elections by violence; and no man can deny this assertion, for Mississippi could not be carried by that organization in any other way. Let me refer now to the question of taxation in that State. My honorable colleague said in effect that the taxation in Mississippi that had been brought about by the republican administration justified what had been done for the purpose of turning that party out of power. He asserted in effect that they were determined to defeat the Republican party in consequence of the corruption, the extravagance, and the taxation that had been heaped upon the people. Now, as a citizen of that State, as a taxpayer, I say that the charge cannot be sustained. I have some figures here in regard to the public debt in Mississippi. I did not know that I would have occasion to use them today.

Prior to the inauguration of the administration of Governor Ames in the State of Mississippi the total tax rate was about fourteen mills on the dollar, $14 upon each $1,000 of taxable property. During the two years that Governor Ames had the privilege of serving as governor in that State the taxes were considerably reduced, so that in 1875, instead of being fourteen mills, the tax rate was nine and one-fourth mills on the dollar. Now I ask any member of this House, regardless of party, dose he consider that an exorbitant tax—a tax of nine and one-fourth mills—only four mills of which were for what we call general purposes, two mills for a teacher's tax, and three and one-fourth mills to pay the interest on the public debt and to create a sinking fund for its redemption? I never thought that was an exorbitant rate. I never thought it extravagant. And during the two years that Governor Ames served as governor the public debt, as I have above shown, was decreased to about half a million dollars, leaving out what is called the Chickasaw and common school fund debts; debts the principal of which cannot be paid, the interest of which has to be paid every year. Leaving out the Chickasaw and common school fund debts, the debt was decreased to the amount that I have already stated.

Such was the extravagance—the profligacy of which my colleague spoke—our debt decreasing each year! The value of the State paper increased from 10 to 15 percent on the dollar when Governor Ames went out over what it was when he went in. And yet my colleague says that we had extravagance and profligacy to an extent that justified violence and mob law to turn what he is pleased to call a corrupt party out of power. I hold that that charge cannot be substantiated. I do not believe that the public sentiment of the country will justify the means that were resorted to for the purpose of carrying an election against the known wishes of a majority on such a flimsy pretext as that. I admit and confess that a large element inside the ranks of the democracy in that State are honestly in favor of vindicating the majesty of the law in protecting every citizen in the exercise and enjoyment of his rights, while I acknowledge this, it is with sorrow and regret that I am compelled at the same time to acknowledge that the public sentiment there sustains and tolerates an organization that has been brought into existence for violence, and violence alone. And I am utterly surprised that my colleague, for whom I have the highest respects, should allow his love of party to carry him so far as to attempt to justify the deeds of violence, the deeds of bloodshed that were resorted to by this organization for the purpose of overcoming the popular majority in that State.

Let the investigation reveal what it may, I stand upon the platform of honest government and honest men to administer the laws; and when the Democratic party will recognize the complete equality of the colored man before the law, which they have not yet done, then the colored man will be justified in voting against the Republican party when the candidates of that party do not come up to the Jeffersonian standard of honesty and capacity. Now let me admonish gentlemen on this floor from other sections, let me admonish the democrats from the North, and I would appeal especially to my honorable friend from New York [Mr. Cox.] who so gracefully occupies the chair in the absence of the honorable Speaker—a gentleman for whom I have the highest regard, because I look upon him as a man of moderate views except on some questions—let me say to him, as a leader of his party, and a creditable one, too, at this; let me say to others from the North who are leaders of the Democratic party, to put your power, put your votes, put your organization upon record against mob law and violence, and try to gain the colored vote by honest means, by argument, persuasion, and reason.

When you succeed in gaining the colored vote by those means no one will regret it. I will not regret it, but I will rejoice to see the day come when they will be enabled to vote as they please without personal risk to themselves by doing so. I trust that the northern democrats will try and get our southern brethren to come up to the standard that you keep at the North, to tolerate differences of opinion, and try and educate them up to the necessity of allowing men to vote how they please and for what party they please. When you do that we shall have peace and goodwill at the South. But under existing circumstances that cannot be done. No government can be sustained and upheld by the public sentiment of a people when one portion of the country is controlled and governed by a band of men organized into an army for the purpose of intimidating men who do not belong to the party they are identified with.

Now I appeal to the public sentiment of the country to crush the mobs in the South; to vindicate freedom of speech, freedom of opinion, freedom of the press, and the purity of the ballot box. That is what I am in favor of, and I trust the gentlemen from the North will see the necessity of this course. Otherwise you will lay the foundation for the dissolution of this Republic. I could say more if I had more time, for this is a subject that I could speak upon for hours. It is a subject that my honorable colleague knows I am as deeply interested in as he is, and while I take pleasure in saying that a large number of the white democrats in my State did not countenance the violence resorted to for the purpose of overcoming the Republican party, yet, it is an unfortunate fact that that party could not have been wiped out of existence as it has been by any other means than by violence and intimidation.

Lynch expressed surprise that after passage of the Civil War Amendments black people still did not enjoy civil rights. He had hoped that protection of the race would have been the aim of both political parties. He pointed out that blacks in Mississippi favored a general amnesty for all former rebels. They asked only that former rebels renounce secession and pledge their support for civil rights reform. He believed that while the Republican party needed them, blacks needed the support of southern whites.

POLITICAL STATUS OF THE COLORED RACE
August 12, 1876

I am very grateful to the House for its courtesy in allowing me to occupy the floor for an hour. It is not my purpose to reply to the speech that was made by my colleague from the fifth district [Charles Edward Hooker] but to reply to some of the points which were so ably and so eloquently presented by my colleague from the first district [Lucius Q.C. Lamar]. It is not my purpose, however, to refer to the first part of his speech, as I have no disposition or inclination to discuss the theory of our Government, the constitutional limitations of power, the propriety or impropriety of Federal interference in the domestic affairs of a State. I shall endeavor to confine myself to what I believe to be the living issues of today—those that are now agitating the public mind.

The political status of the colored race of this country is in some respects an unfortunate one. In my humble judgment it is unfortunate that the status of that race is necessarily made the subject of political discussion. I had hoped that after the last three amendments to the Constitution had been ratified, and the colored people invested with all of their rights, civil and political, so far as that all political parties would acquiesce in these results to such an extent as to remove from the politics of the country this race question. I had hoped that the elevation, the advancement, and the protection of this race would be the aim, the object, and the aspiration of all political parties. This race issue will not be removed from the politics of the country, in my judgment, until that is done, and that it should be done I believe every honest man must admit. Before proceeding to answer the points that were so forcibly made by my colleague from the first district, I hope I will be pardoned for digressing a little, for the purpose of explaining to the House and the country why it is that the colored people in the State of Mississippi are in favor of general amnesty. I have been desirous of making a remark or two on this point ever since the amnesty debates of last winter, but have not had an opportunity to do so. As this question had a direct bearing on the southern situation, I presume it will not be inappropriate for me to do so now.

After the passage of the reconstruction acts by Congress conferring upon the colored people the right to vote, we found ourselves in a very peculiar position. The voting population of the South was composed of three distinct elements: the ex-confederate soldiers and those who sympathized with them, the ex-Federal soldiers who had concluded to locate at the South, and the colored race. These elements have been, and were at that time, politically antagonistic to each other. The colored men could not be expected to identify themselves with any other than the Republican party, and yet they could not fail to see and realize the fact that the party, to have a permanent existence and a firm and solid foundation, must include in its membership a large percentage of the wealth and the intelligence of the State, some of those who fought on the side of the confederacy.

How to bring the Republican party into existence in that State upon such a basis as would render possible a harmonious union of theses conflicting elements and at the same time be in harmony with the great Republican party of the Union was the task we had before us. To make this union possible, the colored men very generously and magnanimously, traits for which I presume all will admit they are particularly characterized, declared in language which could not be misunderstood that if those who had fought and upheld the "lost cause" would renounce all allegiance to that cause, announce it as their determination to stand by and defend the Union, and concede to the colored men every right and privilege they claimed for themselves—in other words, identify themselves with the great Republican party—if they would do this then they, the colored men, would support them just as heartily, just as earnestly, and just as enthusiastically as they would support those who fought for the cause of the Union; and to give emphasis to this declaration they were willing to incorporate in the platform of the Republican party of that State, and did incorporate, a plank pledging the party to this doctrine of equal rights for every man and amnesty for the late rebels.

Upon this platform the Republican party of Mississippi was brought into existence; and I stand upon the floor of the House of Representatives today for the purpose of declaring what I know to be true, that this party as thus organized, including in its membership as it does not less than nineteen-twentieths of the colored men of the South; including in its membership as it does not less than nineteen-twentieths of the ex-Federal soldiers in the State; including in its membership as it does not less than one-fifth and possibly more of the ex-confederate soldiers in the State; this party as thus organized includes in its membership a majority of not less than thirty thousand of the qualified voters of that State. It was so strong, so powerful, so overwhelming in numbers that nothing short of organized terrorism and armed violence, such as was unfortunately resorted to by the Democratic party of that State last year, could crush it out of existence or defeat it at the polls.

I may be pardoned for remarking here that the white men who are identified with the Republican party of the State, of Mississippi, not northern men merely but southern men, ex-confederates, represent a large percentage of the wealth, the intelligence, and the moral worth of the white people of that State. They are as a class, men who would be accepted in any community as high-toned, honest, honorable citizens and valuable members of society. They are as a class men whom the democracy in former days delighted to honor with the highest positions in the gift of the people of the State. They are admitted to be men of character, men of ability, men of standing and of unquestionable reputation. None of my democratic colleagues—I venture to assert—will deny this—for they know it to be true. This is why we have placed ourselves upon this broad, liberal, and conservative platform in addition to the fact that the colored people are particularly desirous of showing to their white brethren that they have no disposition to oppress them or deprive them of a single right they claim for themselves.

I will now refer to some of the points made by my honorable colleague. In giving his reasons for the present unfortunate condition of affairs at the South, there was one remark made by him that touched my sensitive feeling. And that was the comparison, apparently at least, of the colored people with the Mongolian race that has been imported from China to American. It is certainly known by southern as well as northern men that the colored people of this country are thoroughly America; born and raised upon American soil and under the influence of American institutions; not American citizens by adoption, but by birth; worshiping the same God that the white men worship; identified with; imbued with every sentiment of love of country, devotion to the Constitution, and loyalty to the flag that the white race is imbued with; identified in every conceivable particular with American institutions and with American liberty. For my honorable colleague, unwittingly as I believe, to compare this race with the untutored, the uncivilized, the non-Christian, and the un-Americanized Mongolian, that has been imported from China to America, was unjust, ungenerous, and unfair. I do not wish to be understood as detracting any thing from that great and powerful race, but it is known that they are not American; and that cannot be said of the colored race, for they are.

Reconstruction

Now, let me say something with regard to the policy of reconstruction. It will be remembered by those who heard the speech of my colleague that he made the remark that the reconstruction policy of the Government was the foundation of all of the political evils at the South; that that was the foundation of the color-line in politics because the reconstruction policy of the government enfranchised the colored men and disfranchised the white men; and that therefore there was a gulf between the two races, and that was the cause of the race struggles of the South and all the evils of which we complain. Before answering that argument let us see what the logical deductions that can be drawn from it are. If it be true, as he asserted, that the enfranchisement of the colored men at the South was the cause of all of our troubles there, it seems to me that we can draw no other deduction from that argument (if there is anything in it) then that the only effectual remedy is to remove the cause; that you cannot remove it unless you disfranchise them and remand them back to their former condition. That seems to me to be the logical deduction to be drawn from the argument, though he did not say so, and I do not wish to be understood as placing him in the attitude of advocating that proposition. I am merely stating what seems to be the only conclusion to be arrived at as the logical result of the argument.

    Let us inquire whether there is anything in that view of the case. I take issue with my honorable colleague in that respect, and will endeavor to show by referring to my own State that he is entirely mistaken. Why, my colleague seems to have forgotten that the State of Mississippi we have never had any serious troubles between the two races since the re-admission of that State into the Union until the latter part of 1874 and during the campaign of 1875. Until then we never had any serious troubles whatever. The two races got along well together and never had any serious difficulty of any kind, the Democratic party sometimes putting colored men on their own ticket. If, then, enfranchisement of the colored men was the cause of all the troubles in the South, is it not remarkably strange that it took the Democratic party from five to eight years to find it out? Is it not remarkably strange that we could get along so well together for five or eight years without finding out that the incorporation of the colored element into the body politic was the cause of our difficulties? The democratic victories at the North in 1874 so encouraged and exasperated the lawless and turbulent elements at the South as to give them the entire control of the party machinery in the Democratic party.

    The democratic victories at the North so strengthened this element of lawlessness as to give them power to control the democratic organization and to shape its policy; and therefore the color line was drawn in politics, not because the colored men first drew it, as is sometimes charged, but because this element felt that they would be sustained by the public sentiment of the country in resorting to violent measures for the purpose of accomplishing what they could not accomplish by peaceful means. The incorporation of the colored element into the body politic had nothing to do with it, because the two races had lived as peacefully, as quietly, as orderly together prior to that time as they possibly could have done. Every election held in Mississippi since the re-admission of the state was peaceable; quiet, orderly and, except possibly in one or two localities that were not general in their character, fair. We never had occasion to call on the Federal Government for Federal interference; we never had an occasion to bring up charges for violence in any election held in the State until the general election last year and in a local election the fall previous. Is it not strange that the argument is now brought forward that what was done five or eight years ago was the foundation of the violence of last year? Why, the argument is fallacious, it is unsound, it is unreasonable, and cannot be substantiated.

Democratic Rule in Mississippi

Let us see what has been done in the State of Mississippi under this policy that has been inaugurated. It will be remembered that my honorable colleague in his very eloquent speech referred to the State of Louisiana, and in so doing he held up republican rule in that State as typical of republican rule in the other southern States. But he did not make any allusion to Mississippi especially. Now, then, when holding up republican rule in the State of Louisiana as typical of republican rule in other southern States, he certainly must have known that republican rule in Louisiana, as understood and explained by himself, is not typical of republican rule in Mississippi. But I presume that none of our democratic friends will object to having democratic rule in the State of Mississippi under the new order of things held up as typical of democratic government in the other southern States. I cannot speak of all of it, for I have not the time to do so. As the result of the election in the State of Mississippi in November last we had a Legislature brought into existence which had characterized its proceedings by greater blunders than any that were ever complained of by any of its republican predecessors. This Legislature having been brought into existence through questionable channels—that is a mild phrase, for I have too much respect for the feelings of my colleagues to use harsh phrases in their presence—but that Legislature having been brought into existence through questionable channels, what did it do?

Among the first of its proceedings was to revolutionize the entire State government, by taking forcibly the possession of the other two departments—the executive and judicial—by turning out of office every man who stood as a stumbling block in the way of a complete democratic ascendancy in the State. Well, they say they did it in a legal and constitutional way. Let us see about that. To get control of the executive and judicial departments of the government, it was necessary for them to impeach and remove from office both the governor and lieutenant governor, so that the democratic president of the senate could became the acting governor. The first thing then was to get rid of the lieutenant governor. He was impeached and removed from office on a charge of bribery. He was charged with having been bribed by two eminent lawyers to pardon a convict out of the State penitentiary; a very grave offense, for which he deserved impeachment, if true. Under the laws of Mississippi a man who proposes a bribe is just as guilty as the one who accepts it.

Those two lawyers who were charged with having bribed the lieutenant governor happened to be very eminent and able democrats. The charge was made several months before the election and several months before the assembling of the Legislature. During that time the grand jury of Lowndes County, the county in which all three of the parties resided, thoroughly we are told, investigated this matter. This grand jury, composed of a majority of democrats, made a report to the court that all the parties to the transaction were innocent. No evidence could be produced to establish the guilt of any of them. The Legislature had no jurisdiction over the two democratic lawyers, they being private citizens. But they did have jurisdiction over the lieutenant governor, he being a civil officer of the State. They then proceeded to investigate his conduct upon the charges upon which he had been acquitted by a democratic grand jury, no other charge being preferred against him, and pronounced him guilty, and he was accordingly impeached and removed. Now I do not say he was innocent, for I do not know; I did not investigate the matter, and I am not prepared to express an opinion upon that subject. Perhaps he was guilty; it is not necessary to answer my purpose to defend him. But the point I make is that the Democratic grand jury failed to discharge its duty for the purpose of shielding the two Democratic lawyers from justice or else the Legislature was guilty of persecuting an officer for political purposes; one of the two is true, and it is not very favorable to the Democratic party either way.

After getting rid of the lieutenant governor, the next thing was to get rid of the governor. Charges of impeachment were preferred against him. My time will not permit me to go over all of them, but I will give a skeleton of some of them. He was impeached in one article for failing to remove a man from office who in the judgment of the Legislature ought to have been removed. He was impeached in another article because he called on the President of the United States for troops to put down what he believed to be domestic violence. He was impeached in another article because he leased out the penitentiary convicts to his partisan friends. The law expressly authorized him to lease them out; there was no crime at all in leasing them out; the offense was in leasing them out to his partisan friends. The inference of course is that if he had leased them out to his partisan enemies no offense would have been committed.

These were the principal charges that were preferred against him. He was impeached on these articles and driven from his office for the sole purpose of getting a democrat in his place. After the articles had been drawn up, some of the democratic members of the Legislature had some conscientious scruples on the subject. They did not desire to vote for these articles, and therefore a public pressure had to be brought to bear upon them. What was done now to accomplish that? The leading democratic paper published at the capital of the State came out with flaming headlines: "This man must be impeached and removed from office!" Upon the law and the evidence that may be presented? Then how are you to get rid of him? He must be impeached and removed, said the Democratic paper, "as a party measure." I defy any of my colleagues to deny that. The paper said that the governor must be impeached and removed from office as a party measure. No matter what the constitution may declare, no matter what the law may provide, no matter what the evidence may be, the people demand it at their hands, and they must obey the command of the people. I ask the Clerk to read what I have marked, and be careful and emphasize the words I have underscored.

Yes, it is the official organ of the party, and its proprietors are the public printers of the State. I suppose my colleague [Mr. Singleton] has had some experience in the matter of public printing. Now, having demanded the impeachment of this man as a party measure, of course the articles of impeachment were put through the House, but one democrat, I believe, dissenting. After the impeachment articles had gone through the house, it was found out that there were some conscientious democrats in the senate who were not altogether prepared to vote for conviction. So the next thing was to prepare the senate for conviction. But the only way to do that was to turn out enough republicans and put in enough democrats to make conviction sure. They then proceeded to turn out republican senators. They turned out one man upon the ground that he was a foreigner, although he was ready to swear that he was born in New York. But it made no difference where he was born; a democratic vote was needed and they must have it. Therefore the republican was turned out and a democrat put in his place; who had not been elected even in the peculiar manner by which they carried the elections there last fall. He had not been elected, and had no right or title to the seat. Yet they turned out the republican and put in the democrat.

After having prepared the senate for conviction we are told that a committee waited on the governor. And I suppose some such conversation as this took place: "Governor, you have been impeached; your conviction is but a question of time. If you will resign your office, then you will save money to the State and some money to yourself." To that I suppose the governor replied something like this: "If I resign, will you withdraw your articles of impeachment?" Judging from the result the reply to that was, "Yes, certainly we will." And that was agreed upon. The committee went back, made their report, and the articles of impeachment were immediately withdrawn, the resignation was sent in, and the proceedings thereupon came to an end. Now, in what attitude does this place them? I am not a lawyer, but it seems to me that the Democratic party in that Legislature proved itself guilty of one or two things: they either acknowledged that the charges were groundless and false, without a shadow of foundation in fact, or else they were guilty of what the lawyers would call compounding a felony. I would like any democrat to deny that. One of the two must be true. Either that Legislature was guilty of compounding a felony by allowing this man to escape as a consideration for his office, or else it was a confession on their party that he was innocent of the charges brought against him. They said: "All that we want is your office; it is immaterial to us what you may have been guilty of; the sole objective point we have in view is to get a republican out and a democrat in."

In a speech of my honorable colleague [Mr. Lamar], which he delivered here when some proposition relative to the impeachment of the late Secretary of War was before the House, he took the very strong ground that the object of impeachment is not merely to get rid of an objectionable officer, but to punish him besides. He did not represent his Legislature in that sentiment; for they took the position that the object of an impeachment with them is to get a republican out and a democrat in. I would like to know whether the democrats on the other side of this House from the other southern states are willing to have the Mississippi democracy held as typical of the democracy in their States. I hope for their sakes that they are not.

The Color Line-Violence

In referring to this question of the prevalence of violence and the drawing of the color line in politics, I am willing for one to give my colleague credit for everything that he says on that point. I am willing to give him credit for sincerity in deprecating the drawing of the color line and the inauguration of brute force and violence. The only thing upon which I take issue with him in that respect is this: He believes, honestly, no doubt, that in giving utterance to conservative sentiments here and elsewhere, in deprecating the drawing of the color line and the inauguration of violence, he represents the controlling element in the ranks of the Democratic party in Mississippi. I believe (and I presume he will give me credit for honesty and sincerity in this opinion) that he does not.

I am willing to admit, as I said upon a former occasion, that there are in the State of Mississippi numbers of white men who are not identified with the Republican party and whom I believe to be honestly opposed to these violent measures and to drawing the color line in politics. I may be pardoned for mentioning the names of one or two of these gentlemen, because their names are somewhat national; the country knows them. I will mention for instance the present speaker of the House of Representatives of Mississippi, Honorable H.M. Street. I will also mention Honorable J.W.C. Watson, of Marshall, the editor of the paper that opposed the impeachment of the governor upon party grounds; General A.M. West, of the same town; ex-Governor Charles Clarke; and ex-Governor and ex-United States Senator Albert G. Brown, of Hinds. These men, I believe, are honestly opposed to this policy of violence and the drawing of the line of politics. I have always believed that my colleague [Mr. Lamar] was one of that number. I am willing to give him credit for it, but when he asserts that in his conservative utterances he reflects the sentiments of the controlling element of his party, I take issue with him. His position cannot be substantiated, for it is not correct.

It is sometimes said that these violent measures are sometimes necessary to get rid of bad government, heavy taxes, and dishonest officials. I have asserted on this floor more than once that this cannot be truthfully said of Mississippi. I did not make groundless assertions and empty declarations, but presented facts and figures to substantiate what I said. Not one of my democratic colleagues has denied or can deny my position on this question. In that State there was no occasion whatever for the inauguration of violent measures on the ground that bad, incompetent, or dishonest men had control of the government.

Inefficiency of State Governments

One other point that has been made very forcibly is the inefficiency of republican State governments at the South. It is very often said that we have violence only in the State under republican rule. Without admitting that there is any foundation for this statement, (for it is not altogether true), I say that admitting it for the sake of argument, what does it prove? It proves that the democrats will obey the laws only when made and enforced by men of their own choice, while republicans will obey the laws whether they are made and enforced by men of their own choice or by democrats. Let us admit that violence exists only in republican localities; why is it so? Simply because democrats say, "Let us have the government and we will obey the laws; if you do not, we will not." That is precisely the argument upon which the rebellion was inaugurated.

I presume no gentleman in this Hall who is familiar with the history of our government will deny for a moment that had John C. Fremont been elected President instead of James Buchanan in 1856, the war would have been inaugurated four years sooner than it was. And I presume no one familiar with our history will deny that had John C. Breckinridge, or even Frederick Douglass, been elected in 1860 instead of Lincoln, the war would have been postponed at least four years later. Why, my colleague might just as well come before the American people and contend that the election of Samuel J. Tilden and Thomas A. Hendricks is essential to the peace of the country; he might just as well say: "Elect Tilden and Hendricks and you will have peace; elect Hayes and Wheeler and you will have war." If the argument is good as applicable to a single State, it must be equally good as applicable to the nation. If the country is ready to accept this condition of affairs, then it can do so, but it seems to me that it would be death and destruction to what are recognized as the results of the war.

Civil Service Reform

My colleague lays great stress upon civil-service reform in the government. That is the controlling idea, he says. Let me say to the House and the country that civil service reform does not occupy one-twentieth part of the consideration of the southern democrats. Civil service reform does not enter into their composition. They have not got it to think about. The sole objective point with the Democratic party of the South, and I presume at the North, is democratic success. It is immaterial to them what the attitude of their candidate may be on any of the public questions now before the people. It is immaterial to them whether their candidate for the presidency is in favor of contracting the currency or expanding it. It is immaterial to them whether he is in favor of free trade or protection. It is immaterial to them whether he is really in favor of administrative reform or whether he is, as their candidate for the presidency is now believed to be, the earnest advocate of gigantic corporations. They are willing to subordinate all other questions to the one great object of democratic success. They are willing to subordinate all other questions without accepting the honor, the integrity, and the plighted faith of the nation. They only ask, "Give us the Democratic party; that is what we want. The sole objective point with us is to get the Government into our hands and let us get our fingers on the purse-strings of the Treasury."

They have not only drawn the color line in politics for the purpose of appealing to the passions and prejudices of race, but they have drawn the sectional line for the purpose of rolling up the southern vote in behalf of the Saint Louis nominees. Civil service reform amounts to nothing in the estimation of the Democratic party south of the Mason and Dixon Line. I speak of them knowingly. It may also be true of those living north of it; but I speak of those south, for I know whereof I speak. The order has already gone forth from Tammany Hall, as represented by the chiefs of that organization, saying to the Democratic party of the South, "Put this party into power, elect the ticket nominated at Saint Louis, and all things else will be added unto you." I tell you that it is the only issue in the South today. No other public question agitates the public mind there. You may be divided at the North on questions of currency or of administrative reform, but they do not enter into politics at the South, because the democrats do not care anything about them.

Conclusion

Let me say that the Democratic party is supposed to carry the South. Every Southern State they propose to carry as they carried Mississippi last year— a state with a 30,000 Republican majority—was reversed by nominally giving the votes to the Democrats. They propose to carry all the others the same way, not by the power of the ballot, but by an organized system of terrorism and violence. That is the way they propose to do it.

Now let me say, in conclusion, that I am satisfied, I am convinced, that the public sentiment of the people of this country is sufficiently aroused now to see the danger we are in. I am satisfied that the people of this country are beginning to realize the importance of the situation we are in. I am satisfied that when these questions are known, when they are fully understood, the people will be determined to rise in their might and declare in language which cannot be misunderstood that this great, grand, glorious Republic must and shall be preserved. It is no pleasure for me to be compelled to admit the violence which is in my own State. I would be happy if I could say truthfully that such is not the case. It gives me no pleasure to be compelled to acknowledge perfect toleration of opinion does not exist in the State of Mississippi. I have friends there on both sides. My home is there. My interests are there. My relatives are there; and I want to see the State prosperous and happy.

I want to see perfect toleration of opinion everywhere, and especially in the State where I live. I am anxious for that to be the case, and nothing would give more pleasure than to be able to declare on the floor of the House of Representatives that perfect toleration of opinion is allowed to all classes. The fact that I am compelled to acknowledge that such is not the case in many counties in the State fills me with pain, mortification, and regret, for I want to see the two races living in harmony and in peace, and friendly relations existing between both parties. That is the object of my aspiration, and it is what I hope the better judgment of the whole body of the people of that State will see is for the general good. For I can realize the fact that since the State of Mississippi has been in its present condition of turmoil our commerce has been practically destroyed, the friendly relations between the two races arrested, emigration to the State retarded, and the State itself almost in a disorganized condition, with a lawless class controlling it to a great extent.

In conclusion, let me warn the House and the country, not with any feeling of malice, not with any feeling of hatred, for I have none, that if you expect to preserve the constitutional liberties of the people as well as to uphold the perpetuity of republican institutions you must see to it that lawlessness is crushed out at the South. I say to the northern democrats, you must see to it, with my honorable friend from New York [Mr. Lord], that your party stands upon the platform which that gentleman made in the resolutions introduced here yesterday to crush out mob law and violence at the South, whether proceeding from political friends or from political enemies. If the Democratic party had a legitimate majority in the State of Mississippi or any other State, it is entitled to the vote of that State and ought to have it. If the Republican party had a legitimate majority in that State or in any other State, it is entitled to the vote of that State and ought to have it. This is what honest men of all parties ought to be willing to say. And now I am satisfied that the people of this great Republic, realizing the necessities of the situation, will see to it that this grand and glorious Union of ours must, shall, and will be preserved.

> *Lynch objected to the notion that Congress could only count votes and report results in contested elections. He believed the process would give the president of the Senate powers the framers did not intend. He thought the framers intended for Congress to act as a supervisory body in disputed elections. Lynch was concerned that in the name of state sovereignty the states could restrict black suffrage and the federal government would be powerless to stop them. He concluded that the framers created a federal system, which gave the national government and the states shared sovereignty.*

REMARKS ON THE POINT OF ORDER BILL TO PROVIDE FOR AND REGULATE THE COUNTING OF VOTES FOR PRESIDENT AND VICE PRESIDENT, AND THE DECISION OF QUESTIONS ARISING THEREON, FOR THE TERM COMMENCING MARCH 4, 1877
January 26, 1877

I desire to present briefly some of the reasons why I shall vote in the negative on the pending proposition. It is an unfortunate fact that the Constitution, in many of its most essential provisions, is susceptible to different and conflicting interpretations. This is due, in my judgment, to the fact that the Constitution itself, in many respects, is a compromise upon some of the most vital questions that were before the people when that instrument was framed. It is a compromise between State sovereignty, upon the one hand and what may be called federalism on the other. It is a compromise between pro-slavery upon the one hand and anti-slavery upon the other. Whatever is agreed upon as the result of a compromise it necessarily follows that the language employed is ambiguous and uncertain. The reason for this is plain. Whenever there is a conflict of ideas upon any subject and a compromise is agreed upon as the result of a consultation, the document is usually so worded as to justify both parties in contending that it is susceptible of a construction that will be in harmony with their views.

I am satisfied that the strongest advocates of the complete sovereignty of the several States are, as a rule, just as honest and sincere in their interpretation of the Constitution as the most enthusiastic advocates of what may be called the Hamiltonian school of federalists. It is no doubt true that the ambiguous and uncertain language that is used in the Constitution in describing the powers and duties of the President of the Senate and of the Congress in counting the electoral votes was the result of a conflict of ideas with regard to the limitations of power upon the Federal Government and that of the several States. The clause as finally agreed upon was no doubt the result of a consultation, which satisfied both parties, that the language used could be so construed as to conform to their particular ideas. Under these circumstances, it seems to me that the safest rule of action that we can adopt is to ascertain as far as possible the intention of the framers of the Constitution and govern ourselves accordingly. Upon this point, however, I find that I am compelled to take issue with some gentlemen on this side of the House who have presented their views with a great deal of force and eloquence.

It is contended by some, for instance, that when the two Houses meet in joint convention that they are there simply as spectators, with no power or authority over the subject, and that the President of the Senate is to open the certificates, count the vote, and declare the result, and that his action is final. To this I certainly cannot give my assent. It seems to me that this would be a centralization and concentration of power in the hands of one man that was never contemplated by the framers of the Constitution. The two Houses do not, in my judgment, meet simply as spectators, but they are there as representatives of the people to see that the will of the people as expressed in the manner prescribed by law is carried out. It is clear to my mind that the framers of the Constitution intended that the Congress should have some supervisory power in counting the electoral votes, and that this power can be exercised whenever the opportunity presents itself.

I shall endeavor to give as briefly as possible some of the grounds upon which this opinion is based. The honorable gentleman from Ohio [James A. Garfield], in his very able and eloquent speech upon this subject a few days since, stated that there are five express or implied limitations upon the power of the States, and that if Congress has any authority whatever to interfere with the action of the States in the appointment of electors, that authority must be found in some one or more of the five limitations. And these limitations in brief are, first, that it must be a State that elects the electors; second, no State can have more electors than the number of Senators and Representatives to which it is entitled in Congress; third, no one can be an elector who is ineligible under the Constitution; fourth, Congress can fix the day when the States shall vote for electors; fifth, Congress can fix the day when the electors shall give their votes. My friend from Ohio will pardon me for expressing it as my opinion that this is not a reasonable construction of the Constitution with regard to the limitations of power between the Federal Government and that of the several States upon this subject. I agree with him that the constitutional power of Congress over this subject is not unlimited, and it may be that the framers of the Constitution intended that the Congress should be confined to the limitations referred to by him whenever the fundamental principles of republican government have not been violated by the action of a State. But to hold that the action of the State is final, subject only to the five limitations or exceptions referred to, would have the effect of depriving the Federal Government of all power to uphold, preserve, and maintain its national existence. The sovereignty of the Federal Union would become practically subordinate to the sovereignty of the several States.

If it is made the duty of the United States to guarantee to every State in this Union a republican form of government, does it not necessarily follow that the United States is to be the judge as to what constitutes a republican form of government? And do not the five limitations of power referred to by the gentleman from Ohio have the effect of depriving the Federal Government of the power to pass upon such a question, even when our national existence as a people is involved? It seems clear to me that this is the logical deduction to be drawn from the argument. The Fifteenth Amendment to the Constitution declares that "the right of citizens of the United States or by any State on account of race, color, or previous condition of servitude," and that "the Congress shall have power to enforce this article by appropriate legislation." Let us suppose (and the supposition is by no means an unreasonable one) that a state legislature, in providing for the appointment of electors, should declare that none but white citizens should participate in such election. Would this action on the part of the Legislature be in violation of any one of the five conditions or limitations referred to by the gentleman from Ohio? I think not. I take it for granted that there would be no question as to the State being a State in the Federal Union. The number of electors chosen will not be in excess of the number of Senators and Representatives to which the State is entitled in the national Congress. There will be no question as to the qualification of the electors. They will have been chosen on the day prescribed by law for that purpose, and they will cast their votes in the manner prescribed by law, and on the day appointed by law for that purpose. Will not the five conditions have been complied with and at the same time the last amendment to the Constitution ignored and completely disregarded?

It may be said that in that event the representation in Congress would be reduced in proportion to the whole number of citizens thus disfranchised. True, this maybe done at the next succeeding apportionment of Representatives, but not before; for if the Federal Government has no power under the Constitution to enforce the provisions of the Fifteenth Amendment in the election of presidential electors, then it has no power to enforce the provisions of the Fourteenth Amendment relative to the reduction of representation in Congress and in the electoral college in consequence of such disfranchisement. It is clear to my mind that, when a State shall have violated the fundamental principles and conditions of republican government in choosing its electors, the United States Government through its legislative department has ample power to inquire into the validity of such an election, and if necessary set it aside.

Let us now inquire as to the limitations of this power. No one, I presume, will contend that the powers and duties of Congress in this respect are unlimited, for the several States have certain powers conferred upon them by the Constitution which are entirely independent of the General Government or any department thereof. It is claimed by some that the vote of no State can be counted unless both Houses of Congress will agree to the same. This position seems to me to be both unreasonable, and unsound. To say that the vote of no State can be counted unless both Houses of Congress will so decide will have the effect of completely destroying the independent functions of the several States. It would be a centralization of power, not in the Federal Government, not in the Congress of the United States, but in either House thereof. It would then be in the power of a party majority in either House of Congress to prevent an election of President by the people. It seems to me that no one who has the slightest conception of the proper constitutional limitations of power between the General Government and the several States can for a moment assert that the Constitution, as ambiguous and uncertain as it is in this respect, is susceptible of such a dangerous construction. Moreover, the rule of evidence in that case would be at war with every principle upon that subject that is known to our English and American jurisprudence. For the presumption would be that every State, in casting its electoral votes, would have done so in violation of law. The burden of proof in such a case would rest with the party objected to, and not with the party making the objection. I certainly cannot give my assent to such a proposition.

What then are the powers and duties that the framers of the Constitution intended to confer upon the Congress in this respect? It is clear to my mind that, when the electoral votes of a State shall have been cast according to the forms of law, they then present a *prima facie* case. They are presumed to be lawful, and must stand until they are set aside or rejected by competent authority. The certificates having been opened by the President of the Senate, my opinion is that it is competent for any member of either House to enter an objection to the counting of the electoral votes of any State. But, the votes having been cast according to the forms of law, they present a *prima facie* case, and the burden of proof therefore rests with the objecting party; and unless both Houses sustain the objection the votes must be counted. To make my position upon this point clearer I will make this illustration: Should I be permitted to do so, I, as a member of the present Congress, will be certain to enter my solemn protest against counting the electoral votes of the State of Mississippi, because the election was carried by fraud and violence and therefore the result does not reflect the sentiments of a majority of the voters of that State. But the votes have been cast according to the forms of law, and they are presumed to be correct. Unless, therefore, both Houses of Congress sustain the objection, the votes must be counted. But the next and most important question involved is in cases where there are two or more sets of returns from the same State.

It is true that the President of the Senate, in his ministerial capacity as custodian of the returns, has no power to inquire into the legality of the election or the qualification of electors. In fact he has no power whatever conferred upon him, either in expressed terms or by necessary implication, to pass upon any question affecting the legality of the election or the qualification of electors. Still, it seems to me that some discretion was intended to be conferred upon the President of the Senate as to what are the returns of a State, subject, of course, to the action of Congress. This interpretation of the Constitution with regard to the powers and duties of the President of the Senate is not only reasonable and necessary, but is absolutely essential to prevent inextricable confusion. It is made the duty of the Clerk of the House of Representatives to place upon the rolls of the House the name of every congressman-elect who presents credentials signed by the governor or the person or persons authorized by the laws of the several States to certify to the election of officers. He, like the President of the Senate, has no right to inquire into or pass upon the legality of the election or the qualification of electors. His duties in that respect are simply ministerial. But, when two or more persons present credentials, claiming to be the member-elect from the same district and the credentials are signed by different persons, all claiming to be authorized by law to discharge that duty, the Clerk must exercise some discretion as to what names shall go upon the rolls, subject to the action of the House, and his decision stands and is legal and valid until the same shall be reversed by the House.

The President of the Senate having presented to the joint convention what he considers to be the returns of the several States, they thus present the *prima facie* case and must be regarded as the lawful returns until his decision shall be reversed by the concurrent action of both Houses. To make my position upon this point clearer, I will suppose that the President of the Senate will, in February next, lay before the joint convention the certificates from the State of Louisiana, signed by John McEnery, claiming to be the governor of that State, as the certificates of that State attest. This action on his part would give the certificates of that State. This action on his part would give the certificates thus presented the *prima facie* case and they would stand as the votes of that State unless objection is sustained by both Houses of Congress. This is a great power, I admit, but it is not plenary; it is subject to revision and reversal. The rights and liberties of the people are, presumptively at least, protected by their immediate representatives. I shall not enter into a detailed explanation of the pending bill, as other gentlemen have already done that in a very elaborate manner. It is sufficient for me to say that I shall vote in the negative solely upon constitutional grounds. This is to my mind a political, and not a judicial, question

Even if it should be conceded that Congress can by legislation confer upon a different tribunal than that prescribed by the Constitution for the settlement of this question the power which is contemplated being conferred upon this proposed tribunal, the composition of the tribunal opens it to serious constitutional objections. The bill provides that this proposed tribunal should be composed of a portion of two of the independent departments of the federal government. This, I believe, to be in violation of the spirit of the Constitution. The framers of the Constitution were particularly anxious to keep separate and distinct from each other the independent departments of the federal government.

I earnestly hope that the highest anticipations of those who advocate this bill may be fully realized and that the country may be saved from the consequences of a disagreement between the two Houses of Congress. It is to be hoped that the decision of this tribunal, if created, will give general satisfaction and that the people of all parties and sections will willingly acquiesce in the decision. I do not oppose the passage of the pending bill from a standpoint of equity. I am, as a republican, perfectly willing that the rights of the candidates of my choice should be submitted to the decision of a fair and impartial tribunal, and I would cheerfully give my vote for this bill if I could be induced to believe that it is warranted by the Constitution. I am apprehensive that the passage of this bill will establish a precedent that will be more dangerous in the future and will be more injurious in its application than the temporary evils that it is intended to remedy.

While he detested corruption in Mississippi, Lynch affirmed his love for the state and the South. He accused Democrats of endorsing terrorist acts against blacks. He charged that the Democrats had committed fraud and violence to dissuade blacks from voting. He dispelled the notion that suffrage was merely a favor to be granted or withheld. Voting was a right given to all eligible citizens, he said. Lynch clearly marked the escalation of violence against blacks in Mississippi with the withdrawal of federal troops following the Compromise of 1876.

THE LATE ELECTION IN MISSISSIPPI
March 1, 1877

On the Report of the Select Committee on the Late Election in the State of
Louisiana

I do not rise for the purpose of making a partisan speech. I recognize the fact that we are still in the midst of an important crisis, in consequence of which it behooves every lover of his country to put patriotism above party. It is not my purpose to speak with regard to the manner in which the late election was conducted in Louisiana, except in an incidental way. My main purpose is to call public attention to some of the grave irregularities that were committed in the State that I have the honor in part to represent upon this floor. It is hardly necessary for me to say that this is to me anything else but a pleasant duty. Every consideration of love of home, of section and people, would necessarily cause me to be anxious to throw the mantle of charity over the faults and shortcomings of that people rather than expose them to the public gaze. I confess that my inclination is in this direction. But when the offenses of a people or a portion of them are sufficiently grave to bring reproach upon our institutions and demoralize society, then their concealment will be more in the nature of a crime than a charitable act. It is in obedience, therefore, to a sense of public duty that I shall lay before the country some of the causes that produced what is called by some the great political revolution, in the State of Mississippi. But I shall not do this because the electoral votes of that State have been cast for the candidate of the Democratic party. However anxious we may be that the man of our choice should be successful, yet I hold that it is the duty of every true American citizen to cordially and cheerfully acquiesce in the will of the people when legally and fairly ascertained according to the forms of law, whether it be in accordance with our wishes or not. I presume there are none who will deny that the perpetuity of our system of Government depends upon the sacredness and security of the ballot-box, and that whenever our elective system ceases to be pure and sacred, then the foundation-stone of our governmental system will have been destroyed and the final dissolution of the government, possibly through a bloody revolution, will be but a question of time.

I have not the slightest hesitation in asserting that if elections such as the one held in Mississippi in November last are to be accepted by the people of this country as a legal and valid expression of the will of the people of a State, then indeed our elective system will have come to be a convenient medium for giving legal effect to the most outrageous frauds that were ever committed upon the ballot-box in that State at the last election in the interest of the Democratic party, to say nothing of terrorism and violence, which were carried so far and were made so general in their application that they have not in my judgment, a parallel in the history of a State in this Union. These frauds were carried so far beyond the bounds of reason, decency, and propriety that no man who has the slightest regard for his reputation, who believes in maintaining and upholding our governmental system, can for a moment defend them, countenance them, or indorse them. The frauds that were committed in the Sixth Congressional District alone, to say nothing of violence, made a change in the vote of the State of not less than 10,000; and the frauds that were committed in that district, in connection with violence, made a change in the vote of the State of not less than 20,000. Some may think that these are extravagant assertions, but I make them upon my knowledge as a citizen of the State. Every assertion that I have made is susceptible of the clearest proof. To give some idea as to how the election was conducted, I will call particular attention to the sixth district.

In 1875 fraud and violence were confined chiefly to four counties— Coahoma, Washington, Warren and Claiborne. Otherwise the result would have been about the same that year as at previous elections. In 1876 the frauds that were committed in the four counties above named were made applicable to every county in the district, with possibly one or two exceptions. It will be seen from the above that the revolution in favor of democracy and "reform" was confined exclusively to two precincts—Washington and Kingston. The returns from the other precincts were just about as the Republicans had calculated. What, then, was the cause of this great and unexpected change at Washington and Kingston? The answer is an easy one. There were over 600 Republican tickets taken out of the ballot boxes at those two precincts, and the same number of democratic tickets substituted in their stead. I went to Kingston on Election Day myself, and remained there from the time the polls were opened until two o'clock in the afternoon, at which hour the election officers took a recess for dinner. Up to that time 361 votes had been polled, and to my own personal knowledge over 300 of that number were straight republican tickets. One hundred and twenty-six votes were polled after dinner, about 85 of that number being Republican. When the votes were counted at night there were just 91 votes in the box for the Republican electoral ticket and 85 for the congressional candidate, thus showing clearly that all, or nearly all, of the republican votes that were polled before dinner were taken out of the box when they went to dinner and the same number of Democratic tickets substituted in their stead. At the Washington precinct they took no recess for dinner, but after the polls were closed at night they counted a few tickets and then took a recess until the next morning.

When they met the next morning to proceed with the count it was ascertained that between two and three hundred republican tickets had been taken out of the box and the same number of democratic tickets substituted in their stead. The objective point, however, was to carry the election for Congressman. In changing the tickets, therefore, they were generous and magnanimous enough to put in about fifty tickets containing the names of the republican candidates for presidential electors with that of the democratic candidate for Congress. This accounts for the material difference in the vote for President and congressman. It is perhaps proper to state that the Republicans were allowed but one inspector of elections at each box, and the ballot box remained in the possession of a Democrat.

Public Opinion

It will perhaps be remembered by some that in a speech that I had the honor of delivering in this Hall during the last session of Congress I stated that the election of 1875 in the State of Mississippi brought to the front the worst element in the ranks of the Democratic party in that State. The election of 1876 fully substantiated that assertion. Democrats who reside in counties that were allowed to go Republican in 1875 have been tantalized ever since and characterized as cowards. Public opinion has become so demoralized that the commission of the most outrageous frauds upon the ballot box is encouraged, tolerated and justified; it is absolutely demanded as a condition—precedent to recognition in the party of reform according to the modern acceptation of that term. These frauds are apparently committed without the slightest compunction of conscience and without the slightest regard for any law, moral or statutory. To carry elections with or without votes, peaceably and fairly if possible, forcibly and unfairly if necessary, have now come to be settled maxims with the element that is now in the ascendancy in the Democratic party in that State. Honesty and fairness in the management and conduct of elections on their party are the exception, and not the rule. But they did not seem to be satisfied with the inauguration of the policy of fraud, but deemed it essential to inaugurate or rather continue the policy of violence as well. Nearly every Democratic club in a number of counties in the State is an armed military organization, brought into existence for aggressive political purposes. The violence and terrorism was so intense in some counties that not a Republican meeting was allowed to be held nor a Republican speech to be made at any time during the campaign. It is hardly necessary to say that in such locations lawlessness reigns supreme. Republicans who reside in such localities are permitted to do so simply as a matter of favor and not as a matter of right. The only law that is recognized or respected is the law of force. There is absolutely no security for life, liberty, or property except such as may be afforded as a gracious favor by these armed clubs. I now call attention to Warren County.

Warren County

In Warren County there are about seven thousand voters, and over five thousand of them are colored Republicans. In 1876 over three thousand

Republicans were positively denied the rights to register and consequently the rights to vote.

The elections held in 1869 and in 1872 were conducted with perfect fairness, and can therefore be accepted as a fair test of the strength of the two parties. The election held in 1875 is generally admitted to have been a fraud and a swindle. Senators Thomas Francis Bayard, Sr. and Joseph Ewing McDonald, as members of the Senate committee that investigated the election of 1875, declared in their minority report that the election was a fraud, and that a ticket had been declared elected that had been not voted for by any one in the county. The charge that over three thousand Republican voters were denied the right to register and consequently the right to vote is fully substantiated by the official returns. In county districts, where the colored voters are largely in the majority, the registrars would make affirmative answers to certain unlawful and unauthorized questions a condition—precedent to registration. Whenever a voter would fail to give an affirmative answer to any one of these questions he was told to step aside. But in the city of Vicksburg, where the bulk of the Democratic vote of the county is, no such questions were asked, and thus every white man who desired to do so was allowed to register, while thousands of colored voters were denied that right. But even if those whom they allowed to register had been allowed to vote, and the votes counted as polled, the result in the county would have been different, for we find the registration, thought incomplete and fraudulent, to be about as follows: whites 2,019, blacks 1,689.

It will be seen from the above that the Democratic vote is only 24 in excess of the whole number of white men registered, while the republican vote is 1,074 less than the whole number of colored men registered. This result was brought about by refusing to receive the votes of a large number of colored men, and it is also believed that frauds were committed at several precincts, similar to those that were committed at Washington and Kingston, in Adams County. The registrars for alleged irregularities, where over 400 Republican votes were polled, and not more than about 5 Democratic votes were polled, rejected the Davis Bend box. They did not pursue the same course in this county that was pursued in a majority of the Republican counties. In a majority of the Republican counties they allowed the colored men to register and vote, but before proceeding with the count they would take out Republican tickets by thousands and substitute Democratic tickets in their stead, and then telegraph over the country that the colored men had voted the Democratic ticket. In Warren County they thought it would be more convenient, and perhaps more honorable, to disfranchise the Republican voters, and not allow them to vote at all. They were satisfied that the colored men were Republicans, and if allowed to vote at all, would vote for the candidates of that party. Every effort that had been made to induce them to join the democracy had proved unsuccessful.

The devotion manifested by the colored voters for the Republican party under such circumstances is certainly worthy of the highest possible commendation, even though the wisdom or propriety of this devotion may sometimes be open to question. The democrats of Warren County know that the colored voters of that county are Republicans, and therefore they concluded to disfranchise them by thousands. Here are more than three thousand sovereign citizens of this country; men who are clothed by the Constitution of their country with the right to participate in the choice of their own rulers; men who laid their lives upon the altar of their country in the hour of its need; and yet these men were positively denied the right to vote, for no other reason than because they are Republicans. It cannot be said that they failed, refused, or neglected to conform to the requirements of law, for they did everything that the law required of them. Their disfranchisement was the result of a settled determination to deprive them of their rights and privileges of American citizens.

Claiborne County

In Claiborne County not less than 1,000 Republican voters were positively denied the right to register. Terrorism and violence were inaugurated by the Democrats and continued up to the election. The election was also characterized by great frauds. It will be seen that the total vote polled was only 272 less than the whole number of voters registered, while the Democratic vote is 581 more than the whole number of white men registered and the Republican vote is 853 less than the whole number of colored men registered. Admitting that the 272 voters who failed to vote were colored men, it will be seen that there were still 581 colored men who did vote, and whose votes were counted as having been polled for the Democrats. That the number of colored men voted the Democratic ticket is what no reasonable man who is familiar with the politics of the county will affirm.

Jefferson County

In Jefferson as in Adams County the registration was conducted with fairness and impartiality; but the Democrats inaugurated a reign of terror throughout the county. Republicans were not allowed to hold public meetings under any circumstances. The Democratic party of the county is an armed military organization. Armed bodies of Democrats would attend and interrupt the election. The election was a farce from beginning to end, as will be clearly seen by comparing the election of 1875 with several preceding elections. There were registered in 1876 2,940—voters 2,154 colored and 786 whites. It will be seen that the total vote polled was 975 less than the whole number of voters registered. The Democratic vote was 759 more than the whole number of white men registered. Admitting that the 975 voters who failed or were denied the right to vote were colored men and Republicans, still it will be seen that the difference between the Republican vote and the whole number of colored men who voted was 759. The conclusion is irresistible that an organized system of frauds and swindles upon the ballot box was inaugurated in nearly every Republican county in the State. It was the settled determination of the democracy to carry the election peaceably and fairly if possible, forcibly and unfairly if necessary.

Washington County

In Washington County the Republicans were positively denied representation on any of the boards that were appointed for holding the elections at the several voting-precincts. There were registered in 1876 4,648 colored men, and 1,264 whites. Republican clubs were organized throughout the county with a membership of over three thousand, and yet the official returns as counted and officially promulgated are as follows: Democratic, 2,295; Republican, 1,591; Democratic majority, 1,314.

It will be seen from the above that the total vote polled in 1876 is 1,416 less than the total number of voters registered. Admitting that the 1,416 voters who failed, or were denied the right, to vote were colored men and Republicans, still the Democratic vote is 1,641 more than the whole number of white men registered, while the Republican vote is 1,640, one less than the whole number of votes polled by colored men were counted for the Democrats. I am satisfied that not less than one thousand republican tickets, and perhaps two, were taken out of the ballot boxes before they were counted and the same number of democratic tickets substituted in their stead. This system of fraud and swindling seems to have been inaugurated and successfully carried out in a majority of the republican counties in the State. I have selected four counties in the sixth district only for the purpose of giving an idea as to how the election was conducted throughout the State.

The Future of the South

As I have said on a former occasion, there is, in my judgment, a large element among southern white men who are honestly opposed to revolution, to violence, and to frauds in elections. So far as Mississippi is concerned I know this to be true. The element that supported H.S. Foote for governor as against Jefferson Davis; the element that earnestly opposed the secession of the State, but finally acquiesced in what they believed to be the will of the majority—this element is still strong in that State, but it has never yet been utilized. They have been made to believe that the policy of the Republican party is inimical to southern interests, in consequence of which the mass of them have affiliated with an organization which had been the bane of the South for the last quarter of a century. It is to be hoped that the inauguration of a new administration will render possible the utilization of this element and thus prevent the ultimate destruction of that section of our country. If the present lawlessness is allowed to continue; if mob law is allowed to take the place of civil law; if fraud is accepted as the popular method of carrying elections, and violence as the legitimate plan of controlling public opinion, then the decay of that section will necessarily follow. In this connection I will make quotation from the minority report of Senators Bayard and McDonald, who, as members of a Senate committee, investigated the Mississippi election of 1875, which I cordially indorse.

Having thus stated the limitations upon the power of Congress, which a respect for the Constitution of our Government and to the decisions of its highest judicial tribunal have dictated, we cannot refrain from an expression of our abhorrence and hearty reprobation of every act of lawlessness and so often brutal interference with the rights of citizenship which were related by witnesses in our presence. Prosperity and happiness can never thrive in a community where such scenes of violence can be enacted without condign punishment. By a law higher than man's the "wages of sin is death," and it will be vain for the people of Mississippi to look for the advancement of their State to that position in the ranks of wealth, influence, and reputation which those who love her would desire to see her occupy, until the spirit of law shall be strengthened and assert itself over the "dangerous classes," who have brought disrepute upon her good name.

Lynch defended his victory at the polls in the election of 1880, arguing that votes for him had been destroyed. He cited newspaper clippings where whites admitted that they wanted to win the election at any cost. He stopped short of saying that racial prejudice during elections was a southern problem. He naively assumed that well-qualified and well-known African Americans such as Frederick Douglass or John Mercer Langston could win a presidential election in some southern states. Lynch reminded his colleagues that African Americans would survive the problems they now faced. He admitted that whites could deny blacks work and access to certain accommodations, and even deprive a black person of life. Yet, Lynch affirmed that no man could deprive another of his essence.

ELECTION CONTEST
April 27, 1882

In presenting this case to the House and to the country I will not discuss the legal questions that are involved; nor will I review the testimony that has been taken. These points have been and will be forcibly presented by members of the committee who have familiarized themselves with the case. I will content myself with calling public attention to the disreputable system of elections of which the pending case is a natural and necessary outgrowth.

Out of 21,143 votes polled the contestee actually received about 5,000. In the counties of Adams, Claiborne, Jefferson, Washington, and Wilkinson approximately 5,000 votes were counted and returned for him that were polled against him. Giving him the benefit of these frauds, he was still defeated by a majority of 663. His pretended claim to the seat is based upon the action of election commissioners or county returning boards in several counties in throwing out over 5,000 Republican tickets that had been received, counted, and returned by the precinct inspectors. Over 3,000 of these tickets were thrown out for the alleged reason that the election officers failed to comply with some technical requirements of the law; such, for instance, as a failure on the part of the election clerks to send up with the returns a list of the names of those who voted.

Warren County

In Warren County all of the Republican tickets except those polled in the first ward of the city of Vicksburg were thrown out, for the alleged reason that they had on their face the usual and ordinary printers' dashes, which the contestee claimed to be a disgraceful act in the whole questionable business. Warren County, which includes the city of Vicksburg, is the county and city in which General Chalmers now claims to live and where he lives is not favorably known. Although the election machinery in Warren, as in all the other counties in the district, was in the hands of his partisan friends and supporters, but where, I am pleased to be able to say, the election was fair and the count honest, up to the time the returns were made to the county commissioners, the county gave a majority of 1,052 against him. No one supposed for a moment that the commissioners could be induced or even seduced into committing this great outrage; especially as the precinct inspectors had positively refused to reject these tickets in spite of the appeals that were made to them to do so.

But General Chalmers, who seems to be equal to any emergency when his personal interests are at stake, appeared before this board in the person of his law partner, and without notice to his opponent, without allowing the other side an opportunity to take exceptions to the jurisdiction of the board or to present the other side of the question on the merits of the case, insisted upon the commission, without delay, of this great wrong, although they had ten days under the law in which to make their returns to the secretary of state. The opinion is prevalent in Warren County today that this board of election commissioners, which consisted of three men of only ordinary intelligence, would not have committed this outrage upon popular suffrage, as one of them frankly admitted to me, had both sides of the question been presented at the time. But the contestee, through his law partner, made them believe that it was their sworn duty to act exactly in accordance with his advice and agreeably to his instructions. In fact it can be truly said that he virtually decided the case himself; and as his modesty is not equal to his ambition, it is perhaps not strange that he decided the case in his own favor.

But there is another fact in support of the assertion that the commissioners acted agreeably to instructions furnished from General Chalmers's law office. The result of the election in the first ward of the city of Vicksburg was as follows: Chalmers, 168; Lynch, 57. The 57 Republican tickets polled in that ward were exactly like those that were declared by the commissioners to be unlawful, and yet these 57 tickets were declared to be lawful and were therefore counted and returned as such. If all of the other tickets voted by the Republicans in the county were unlawful on account of the printers' dashes, then these were unlawful also, for they were all exactly alike. When the commissioners were asked why they did not throw these out also, their answer was because they were not protested against. The reason they were not protested against is no doubt due to the fact that the contestee had a large majority in that ward. The charge, therefore, made by the *Vicksburg Herald*, the ablest Democratic paper published in the State, that the Republican tickets in that county were not thrown out because they had a few printers' dashes on them, but because they did not have the name of Chalmers on them, is unquestionably true. The assertion that the illiterate Republican voters were enabled to distinguish between the tickets of the two parties by these dashes is untrue, because every ward in the city and every precinct in the county was supplied with counterfeit Republican tickets, the only difference between the genuine and counterfeit Republican tickets was that the latter had the name of Chalmers instead of Lynch on them for Congress.

The words "short of violence" and "short of open bribery" were no doubt used for purposes of embellishment and smooth reading. The facts would have been more accurately stated, as expressive of the purposes and methods of the element of which that gentleman is a recognized exponent, had these qualifying words been omitted. But the language the gentleman is reported to have used, as quoted above, is hardly less than a libel upon the most intelligent and respectable white people of Mississippi. That General Chalmers is authorized to speak for the bourbons of Mississippi, I unhesitatingly admit. That he is authorized to speak for the conservative white people of Mississippi, I most emphatically deny. That he does not and has not expressed their feelings, sentiments, and wishes, either in his utterances or methods, I most positively assert. No one, I presume, will deny that whenever there is a conflict between wealth and intelligence upon the one side and poverty and ignorance upon the other; the former can always wield a controlling influence or at least hold the latter within legitimate bounds without resorting to any lawless or questionable means for that purpose. Whenever fraud and violence are resorted to, upon the plea that they are necessary to prevent the ascendancy of ignorance over intelligence, the impression that is naturally created upon the public mind is that the order of intelligence is either very inferior or else there is no antagonism or conflict between these elements.

I deny that race prejudice had anything to do with fraud and violence at elections in the Southern States. There is not half as much race feeling at the South as many of the bourbon leaders of that section would have the country believe. The antagonisms that exist there today are not based on antipathies of race, but they are based on antipathies of parties. The race feeling was strong shortly after the war, but it has now very nearly died out. Colored men are not now persecuted in the section from which I come on account of their color, but Republicans, white and colored, are persecuted in many localities on account of their politics. More colored than white men are thus persecuted, simply because they constitute in larger numbers the opposition to the Democratic party. The opposition to me as the candidate of the Republican party for Congress was no more intense than it would have been had the Republicans nominated an aristocrat of the ante-bellum period who fought on the side of the confederacy during the late war. The barrier to my success was not due to my color; it was due to my politics.

Bruce, Douglass, Langston, or any other reputable colored man, as the candidate of the Republican party for the Presidency in 1880, would have come just as near carrying Mississippi, as did General Garfield. The southern bourbons are simply determined not to tolerate honest differences of opinion upon political questions. They make no distinction between those who have the courage, the manhood, and the independence to array themselves in opposition to bourbon methods and measures. The name of the opposition assumes doesn't matter or the elements that make up the opposition. They may call themselves Republicans, Greenbackers, Independents, or Re-adjusters. The fact that they oppose the ascendancy of bourbon Democracy makes them, from a bourbon standpoint, enemies to the South, to its interests and to its people. All that is needed at the South today is the inculcation of a just and liberal public sentiment that will destroy political proscription and intolerance. That being done, a full vote, a free ballot, and a fair count will necessarily follow for it is an indisputable fact that fraud and violence have, as the basis of their existence, proscription and intolerance.

The Solid South

That the South is solidly Democratic at the expense of the purity of elections is no longer a disputed question. Every intelligent man knows it and every candid man admits it. Many of those who defend the methods of Southern bourbons do so upon the plea that wealth and intelligence ought not to be governed by poverty and ignorance, and, as the wealth and the intelligence of the South are identified with the Democratic party, it necessarily follows that Democratic success is essential to the ascendancy of the intelligent and property-owning classes. According to their reasoning, therefore, the country ought to countenance and justify fraud and violence on their part. Let us inquire into this a little. The claim that the Democratic party at the South embraces within its membership all of the wealth and the intelligence of that section had not the slightest foundation in fact. I know whereof I speak when I assert that the opposition to the Democratic organization, in the State of Mississippi for instance, embraces within its membership a large percent. It is equally true that the Democratic party embraces within its membership some of the most ignorant and depraved of our population.

True, the Republican party at the South has a larger percentage of the illiterate voters than has the Democratic party, but it is also true that both parties contain a sufficient number of each of these classes to prevent either from being accepted as the exclusive representative of either class. Under the existing order of things it is impossible to make wealth and intelligence the basis of party organization in any one of the southern States. If it be true that the Democratic organization at the South is the exclusive representative of the wealth and the intelligence of that section, why is it they do not establish by law an educational or a property qualification for electors? I think I can inform the country why it is they have attempted nothing of the kind. It is because they know they cannot disfranchise the illiterate Republican voter without disfranchising at the same time and in the same way the illiterate Democratic voter. It is because they know they cannot disfranchise the poverty-stricken Republican voter without disfranchising at the same time and in the same way the poverty-stricken Democratic voter. This is the "self-preservation" which they consider to be the "first law of nature."

I admit that a much larger number of Republican than Democratic voters would be thus disfranchised, but a sufficient number of Democrats would be disfranchised to create a public sentiment that would destroy the Democratic organization and drive the party from power. As to that party being the exclusive representative of political morality, the facts presented in this case have gone far to disprove that claim. I assert with feelings of deep mortification and profound regret that in the official person of the contestee in this case the country is presented with a living monument of rifled ballot boxes, stifled public justice, and a prostituted suffrage. Although the gentleman had occupied a seat upon this floor during the last five years, yet no one knows better than he does himself that he had never, with possibly one exception, 1878, when the Republicans made no organized opposition, received as many as one-third of the votes polled at any election at which he was a candidate. With all of their boasted intelligence and independence it is an unfortunate fact that Southern Democrats are particularly noted for their subservience to party leadership. They rely chiefly upon their party leaders and local newspapers for political instruction and direction and they generally do allow to be done whatever their leaders and party papers advise, whether it be right or wrong, fair or unfair. Under these circumstances it can be truly alleged that the contestee in this case is more responsible for the frauds and outrages that were committed in his behalf and for his benefit than any one else.

I am satisfied that had he gone before the people of the sixth district and told them that while he was ambitious to represent them in Congress, yet as an honorable man he could not afford to countenance or encourage any fraudulent or questionable methods to bring about that result, the election would have been fair and the count honest throughout the district. But it is an unfortunate fact that no such words as these were ever known to fall from his lips. On the contrary, the fraudulent acts that were committed by a portion of his friends and supporters, and which resulted in his being returned to a seat upon this floor, were received by him with either silent acquiescence or public approval. His chief aim, his sole object, seems to have been to occupy a seat upon this floor, regardless of the means by which that result might be brought about. I can assure the House and the country of the fact that it gives me no pleasure to feel compelled, in vindicating the cause of truth and justice, to use such strong language in referring to my distinguished opponent, because, aside from his questionable election methods, he is a gentleman whose ability, eloquence, and genial disposition are calculated to commend him to the appreciation and respect of those with whom he may be officially or socially connected. Gladly would I acquit him of ever having countenanced or encouraged the commission of election frauds if the facts would only warrant me in so doing.

But, Mr. Speaker, must it be assumed that the commission of these crimes and these outrages are encouraged by the wealth and the intelligence of the sixth of Mississippi? In the name of those who in ante-bellum days gave tone and character to southern society, under the supervision and direction of some of whom I received my early training, and by whom I was taught to seek through a laudable and commendable ambition the realization and accomplishment of those things which can be honorably achieved only by those who are imbued with and actuated by the highest, noblest, and most exalted aspirations, I must enter my earnest and emphatic protest against such an unjust, unfair, and unreasonable assumption. While I admit that the late war, which was disastrous in its results so far as many of the Southern white people were concerned, produced a marked and lamentable decadence in the public morals of that section, yet I know, of my own personal knowledge, that there are, even in the sixth district of Mississippi, white men and Democrats who are admitted by all who know them to be men of honor, character, and integrity. When, therefore, the contestee attempts to make it appear that these men indorse and defend the methods by which he was returned to a seat upon this floor, he thereby becomes a maligner of his section and a traducer of the most intelligent and respectable portion of his own people.

I can assert whereof I know to be a fact that there are thousands of Democrats in the sixth district of Mississippi, many of whom voted for the contestee, but who know and admit that he was fairly and honestly defeated, and that he reflects no credit upon himself, his party, and his State in claiming a seat upon such a flimsy and ridiculous plea as the one set up by him in this case. The worst that can be said about these law-abiding Democrats is, that through a mistaken zeal for the success of their party they remain, as a rule, reticent and inactive, while the ignorant and immoral are allowed to debauch the suffrage in the interest of the Democratic party, and thus bring odium and disgrace upon their State and party. Both of the great political parties of the day are no doubt anxious to bring about a cessation of the agitation of sectionalism. They differ only as to the basis upon which this agitation shall cease. The Democrats who are in favor of upholding and defending the bourbon system of fraudulent elections, as illustrated in this case, for instance, are anxious to bring about a cessation of sectional agitation upon the basis of a violent and fraudulent suppression of the popular will. The Republicans, on the other hand, and I am pleased to be able to say thousands of honest Democrats as well, are anxious that this agitation shall cease, upon such conditions as will secure to all citizens the equal protection of the laws, and a willing acquiescence in the lawfully expressed will of the majority. As a humble member of the great Republican party, I have no hesitation in declaring it to be the unchangeable determination of that party to continue to wage a persistent way upon bourbon methods at the South until the right of every citizen to cast his ballot for the man or the party of his choice and have that ballot fairly and honestly counted shall have been acquiesced in from one end of the country to the other.

So far as this case is concerned it is not a question of party. It is one that appeals to the patriotism and justice of the American people. You are called upon to determine in this case whether or not 10,000 voters of one party in a district shall be allowed through systematic frauds and ballot-box manipulation to be equal to 20,000 voters of the other party in a district where the election is fairly and honestly conducted. You are called upon to determine whether or not on a district containing about 40,000 voters 30,000 of them shall be allowed through the commission and perpetration of flagitious crimes to be practically disfranchised and the 10,000 alone to have voice and representation upon this floor. You are called upon to determine whether or not these grave offenses against law, justice, and public morals shall receive the condemnation or approbation of the national House of Representatives; to the Democratic members of the House who are the chosen representatives of a willing constituency and whose titles are not saturated with the crime of fraud, I have this to say: that you will accept the fraudulent methods and practices that were resorted to in behalf of the contestee in this case as your standard of political morality is what I have been too charitable to believe and too generous to assert. That any considerable number of representatives of any party can give these offenses the sanction of their approval is what I cannot and will not believe until that fact has been unmistakably demonstrated.

I am aware of the fact that Southern Republicans are sometimes reproached because they do not make forcible resistance to the perpetration of these frauds; but it must be remembered that the frauds are always committed under some sort of color of law. Men whose sworn duty it was to make true and correct returns of all the votes polled in their respective counties threw out the five thousand and more Republican tickets that were thrown out in the sixth district of Mississippi. In counties where not less that than 5,000 votes were counted and returned for the contestee that were polled against him, the frauds were either committed by the sworn officers themselves or by accomplices who had been selected for that purpose. The frauds are always committed either by the sworn officers of the law or by others with their knowledge and approval. What lawful redress have Republicans, except to do just what I am now doing?

You certainly cannot expect them to resort to mob law and brute force, or to use what may be milder language, inaugurate a revolution. My opinion is that revolution is not the remedy to be applied in such cases. Our system of government is supposed to be one of law and order, resting upon the consent of the governed, as expressed through the peaceful medium of the ballot. In all localities where the local public sentiment is so dishonest, so corrupt, and so demoralized as to tolerate the commission of election frauds, and shield the perpetrators from justice, such people must be made to understand that there is patriotism enough in this country and sufficient love of justice and fair play in the hearts of the American people to prevent any party from gaining the ascendancy in the government that relies upon a fraudulent ballot and a false return as the chief source of its support.

Bravery and Fidelity of the Colored People

The impartial historian will record the fact that the colored people of the South have contended for their rights with bravery and a gallantry that is worthy of the highest commendation. Being, unfortunately, in dependent circumstances, with the preponderance of the wealth and intelligence against them in some localities, yet they have bravely refused to surrender their honest convictions, even upon the altar of their personal necessities. They have said to those upon whom they depended: you may deprive me for the time being of the opportunity of making an honest living; you may take the bread out of the mouths of my hungry and dependent family; you may close the schoolhouse door in the face of my children; yea, more, you may take that which no man can give, my life, but my manhood, my principles you cannot have! Even when the flag of our country was trailing in the dust of treason and rebellion; when the Constitution was ignored, and the lawfully chosen and legally constituted authorities of the Government were disregarded and disobeyed; although the bondsman's yoke of oppression was then upon their necks, yet they were then true and loyal to their Government, and faithful to the flag of their country.

They were faithful and true to you then; they are no less so today. And yet they ask no special favors as a class; they ask no special protection as a race. They feel that they purchased their inheritance when upon the battlefields of their country they watered the tree of liberty with the precious blood that flowed from their loyal veins. They ask no favors; they demand what they deserve and must have an equal chance in the race of life. They feel that they are a part and parcel of you, bone of your bone and flesh of your flesh. Your institutions are their institutions and your government is their government. You cannot consent to the elimination of the colored man from the body politic, especially through questionable and fraudulent methods, without consenting to your own downfall and to your own destruction. That the colored people of the United States have made and are making material progress in the acquisition of knowledge, the accumulation of wealth, and in the development of a high order of civilization are facts known, recognized, and admitted by all except those who are too blind to see them or too prejudiced to admit them.

The condition of the colored people of this country today is a living contradiction of the prophecies of those who have predicted that the two races could not live upon the same continent together upon terms of political equality. In spite of these predictions we are here today, clothed with the same rights, the same privileges, and the same immunities, with complete political assimilation; loyal to the same laws, revering the same institutions; actuated by the same patriotic impulses, imbued with the same noble ambition; entertaining the same hopes, seeking the gratification and satisfaction of the same aspirations; identified with the same interests, speaking the same language; professing the same religion, worshiping the same God. The colored man asks you in this particular instance to give effect to his ballot, not for his sake alone, but for yours as well. He asks you to recognize the fact that he has the right to assist you in defending, protecting, and upholding our Government and perpetuating our institutions. You must, then, as I am sure you will, condemn the crimes against our institutions, against law, against justice, and against public morals that were committed in this case.

Conclusion

In conclusion, I regret to be compelled to say that it seems to be the settled determination of the bourbon party at the South that we must either have a centralized government or no government at all. They seem to be determined that if they cannot destroy the government in one way they will in another for it is an incontrovertible and indisputable fact that the sanctity and the purity of the ballot is the chief pillar in our governmental structure. Destroy that pillar, and the structure must necessarily fall. I speak today not in behalf of my party, but in behalf of my country. I hope that I speak not as a partisan, but as a patriot. If the party to which I belong and to which I feel that I owe allegiance cannot commend itself to the approbation and support of a majority of the American people upon its merits, then it does not deserve success. Political parties under our system of Government are supposed to be organized for the purpose of advocating certain political principles and to carry into effect certain public policies. Upon all such questions we may honestly differ and make such differences the basis of party organization. But upon questions affecting the stability of the Government and the perpetuity of our institutions we are at least presumed to be a united, harmonious, and indissoluble people.

This disgraceful system of election frauds in several of the Southern States through and by which that section was made solid in its support of one of the great political parties of the day ought, must, and will be destroyed. The people of this great country are too intelligent and patriotic to tolerate a continuance of such outrages upon our elective system. Such methods and such practices are contrary to the spirit of the age in which we live and to the civilization of the nineteenth century. That there may exist in all parts of our country—North, South, East, and West—and among all races and classes of our people peace, happiness, concord, and fraternal feeling upon such conditions as will secure to all exact justice and the equal protection of the laws is the aim, the object, the hope, and the aspiration of every patriotic American citizen. For the accomplishment of these grand and noble purposes and the attainment of these commendable and patriotic ends, I invoke, in the language of the immortal Lincoln, the considerate judgment of mankind and the gracious favor of almighty God.

Lynch appealed to the House to revise the statutory amount available to candidates who incurred a loss in a contested election. His argument was that if the $2,000 maximum rule applied only a wealthy contestant would challenge a vote. He believed that federal law enabled Congress to decide if any award could be made. Congress could also decide to lift any maximum payment allowable.

CONTESTED ELECTIONS
July 13, 1882

What I wish to say in explanation of this amendment is this: I am aware of the fact that a law is in existence limiting the amount to be paid to contestants and contestees to $2,000. In my judgment that law is inoperative, and has no binding force upon the House.

My reasons are these: each House of Congress, under the Constitution, is the sole judge of the election, returns, and qualifications of its own members, and any expense which may be incurred by a contestant or contestee in asserting his right to a seat on this floor necessarily involves the question as to the right of the House to pass on the question of its own membership. For instance, if the House of Representatives of the Forty-seventh Congress, with the concurrence of the Senate, can decide that the House of Representatives of the Forty-eighth Congress shall not be allowed to pay a contestant or a contestee for expenses incurred to an amount not exceeding $2,000 they can also decide that nothing whatever shall be allowed. And if we admit they can pass a law or decide by bill or resolution, or order that a succeeding House of Representatives shall not have the power to pass on any such question, that, in my judgment, is practically deciding that the House of Representatives of a succeeding Congress shall not be permitted to exercise the right which the Constitution says it shall exercise in passing on the question of its organization and its membership.

If the House of Representatives of a preceding Congress can say that the House of Representatives of a succeeding Congress shall not pay a contestant or contestee anything whatever in the way of reimbursing him for expenses incurred in the prosecution of the contest, or in the defense of the case, it is equivalent to saying that this House will not allow the next House practically to pass upon any such question; for the effect will be to prohibit any man from making a contest for a seat in the House unless he happens to be a man in opulent circumstances. No one but a rich man could make a contest for a seat in the House of Representatives should one House decide that the next House would allow nothing whatever for it; and if one House shall say such expense shall be limited to $2,000, it can, as I have said, say with equal propriety that nothing whatever shall be allowed. Now, my judgment is, Mr. Chairman, that this is a question that the House ought to be allowed to determine for itself, and that no previous House, no preceding Congress, can bind a succeeding House or Congress as to what shall be done with regard to the organization of that House or with regard to its membership, or whether anything shall be allowed in making contests or defending them.

The Senate of the United States acts upon this principle. I believe the custom of that body in matters of contest is to pay the expense, whatever it may be, out of the contingent fund of the Senate, just as was formerly done by the House, and therefore the Senate determines that for itself without asking anything of the House in regard to it. And according to the remarks made by the distinguished gentleman from Kentucky this morning, even on an amendment to an appropriation bill, upon its right to fix the compensation of its own officers and employees, it does not concede to the House the right to restrict that body in fixing the salaries of its own officers. The gentleman from Kentucky admitted that. After all the only thing that can be said in support of the contrary proposition and the only argument that is made in favor of restricting or limiting the amount to be paid in any case, is that it sometimes encourages parties to make contests where they have no merit. I cannot see that there is anything in that position from my own experience.

I only desire to say in answer to the argument which had been presented here that, unless this limitation as to the amount to be paid in cases of contest shall be made, contests may be instituted by parties before they know the case is without merit and without foundation. There is nothing in that point, for I have had some experience in contested elections. If the Houses should determine in each case to allow the contestant and the contestee the exact amount which he personally will swear that he had paid out, and no more, then I cannot see why that presents an inducement to anybody to institute a contest. For when a man institutes a contest and it costs him from $1,000 to $2,000 in it prosecution, and at the expiration of twelve or fifteen months the House will vote him the exact amount paid out only, it seems to me that it is nothing more than equivalent to a businessman investing that amount of money for twelve or fifteen months without interest, and that is what no prudent businessman would do. Hence I cannot see any inducement or where the inducement comes in for a man to institute a contest, unless the House pays interest upon the money invested. Now, if the House does not pay interest on money, and if it pays back only the exact amount which a man has expended, then I fail to see where the inducement exists to institute contests.

While asking for money to improve the Mississippi River, Lynch told his colleagues that this issue was different from the Civil Rights Bill. While blacks expected opposition in Congress, whites did not. Whites, Lynch argued, would be devastated by an unfavorable vote. The Democratic party was solidly in control of the House of Representatives, and this was the party of most southern whites. He urged the House to vote favorably on federal appropriations for internal improvement in Mississippi.

RIVERS AND HARBORS
March 1, 1883

On the bill (H.R. 7631) making appropriations for the construction, repair, and preservation of certain works on rivers and harbors, and for other purposes

Before the vote is taken upon the final passage of this bill I desire to make a few remarks in behalf of the section from which I come and in behalf of the constituency I have the honor to represent upon this floor. I desire to speak especially in behalf of the proposed appropriation for the improvement of the channel of the Mississippi River. This is a measure that deserves and should receive the united support of representatives of all parties and from all sections. Is it claimed that this appropriation is not warranted by the Constitution? My answer is that it is supported by some of the ablest constitutional lawyers in the country; but even if it is a doubtful question the people should be given the benefit of the doubt. Is it claimed that the appropriation should not be made for the reason that the owners of private property will be incidentally the beneficiaries thereof? My answer is that the owners of private property along the lines of the great Pacific railroads were no doubt the incidental beneficiaries of the construction of said roads, and yet no one, I presume, claimed that the government should not aid the construction of these roads for that reason. This work is not local but national; not sectional, but general.

To the Democratic members of the House I feel that it is my duty to address a few remarks. You have no doubt accepted the result of the late elections as an expression of confidence in your party, if not an endorsement of your principles. So thoroughly convinced are you of this that you will be sadly and seriously disappointed if the country is not turned over to your care and keeping at the next national election. Whether your expectations in this respect will be realized or not, all must admit that important trusts have been confided to your keeping and grave responsibilities have been placed upon you. So far as the colored people at the South are concerned, perhaps it is well that I should frankly tell you that nothing you might do or fail to do will be to them a serious disappointment. But with a large majority of the white people of that section it is different. They have supported you with a self-sacrificing devotion, which entitles them to your gratitude, your friendship, and your support. They have supported you when they believed you deserved it, and they have stood by you when they believed it to be to their interest to do otherwise. They have been true and faithful to you even when you were false and faithless to them. They have rejoiced with you in the hour of your victory and they have sympathized with you in the hour of your adversity.

If it is possible for any people to have a claim upon a party which ought not, can not, and must not be ignored, it must be admitted by all that the southern white people have that claim upon the Democratic party of this country. Will you ignore their wishes, disregard their claims, and reject their demands? If so, my prediction is that they will refuse to smile at the witticisms and facetious jokes of my friend from New York [Samuel S. Cox] nor will they be satisfied with the masterly eloquence of the gentleman from Kentucky [Mr. John Griffin Carlisle] nor will they follow the sagacious leadership of the gentleman from Pennsylvania [Samuel Jackson Randall]. Already the murmuring sounds of discontent are distinctly heard and perceptibly felt throughout the Mississippi Valley. Southern white men did not receive the news of Democratic victories at the North at the late elections with the same satisfaction and delight as at previous elections. Why? Because they saw that prominent men in both parties at the North had been defeated because they voted at the last session of Congress for the passage of the river and harbor bill which, in their opinion, contained a just, fair and equitable recognition of the claims of their section. When they saw that their friends in both parties had been slaughtered they received the news with many misgivings, with serious apprehensions, and in many instances with deep regret. The impression was created upon their minds that the result was due in a great measure to hostility to and a war upon their section and its interests, not by Northern Republicans alone, but by Northern Democrats as well.

But again, they do not believe that the late election was an endorsement of the principles of the Democratic party but that it was, in addition to a feeling of hostility to their action, a condemnation of the methods and practices of one party rather than an endorsement of the purposes and tendencies of the other. There are thousands of white men at the South who have voted the Democratic ticket at every election since the war, not because they love Democracy but because they distrusted Republicanism. There are thousands of others who have voted the same way during the same time not because they are Democrats but because they believed, as between the two parties, the Democratic was friendlier to their section and to their interests. I speak whereof I know when I say that this state of affairs is being rapidly changed; and it must be admitted by all that in proportion as these things change the white as well as the colored man will become more independent and the attachment of either to any political party will depend more upon the attitude of parties to the questions and issues of the day than upon the passions and prejudices of the past.

To the Republican members, and especially those who through the partiality of your respective constituents will occupy seats in the Forty-eighth Congress, I feel that I should make a few parting admonitory remarks. Race prejudice and sectional hatred are not only on the wane throughout the South, but in spite of the fact that many grave frauds are committed in the management and conduct of elections in some localities there is a strong sentiment, which is growing in strength every year, in favor of fair and honest elections and in opposition to political intolerance and proscription. Do you ask me for evidences of the growth of this sentiment? I have only to point to the late election in the district where I had the honor of being the candidate of the Republican party. The registration books of the various counties in this district show that there are about 1,500 more white than colored voters, and previous elections show that the usual Democratic majority in the district is between 1,500 and 2,000; and yet at the late election one of the strongest and ablest Democrats in the district was elected by a majority of about 600. As the candidate of the Republican party, I am proud to be able to say that I was the recipient of the cordial and hearty support of some of the most substantial and respectable white men in Southern Mississippi.

Let the leaders of the Republican party pursue such a course as will satisfy these men that, while the Republican party will defend and protect all citizens in the exercise and enjoyment of their rights as far as it has the power to do so, and while it will not under any circumstances countenance or encourage the commission of election frauds, yet under its administration justice will be done to all sections of our country and to all classes of our people—that the Republican party is national and not sectional, that it is as much the party of the South as it is the party of the North, that every man, without regard to race or color, who believes in the National Union, the equal rights of men, the purity of elections, and an economical government, will find in the Republican party his friend, his advocate, and his protector.

While the following entries on the Freedmen's Bank are not extensive, they are important in establishing the economic thrust of the civil rights movement during the nineteenth century. Black congressmen urged their colleagues to aid investors who lost their deposits due to mismanagement of the bank.

FREEDMEN'S SAVINGS AND TRUST COMPANY
January 29, 1883

I ask to have entered in the Journal a motion to reconsider the vote by which the House referred to the Committee on Appropriations the bill (H.R. No. 6204) to reimburse the depositors of the Freedmen's Savings and Trust Company for losses incurred by the failure of said company.

February 28, 1883

Mr. Lynch, by unanimous consent, from the Committee on Education and Labor, reported back with a favorable recommendation the bill (H.R. 6204) to reimburse the depositors of the Freedmen's Savings and Trust Company for losses incurred by failure of said company, which was referred to the Committee of the Whole House on the Private Calendar, and the accompanying report ordered to be printed

11

Thomas Ezekiel Miller
(1849–1938)
House of Representatives, South Carolina

Republican

Fifty-first Congress
September 24, 1890, to March 3, 1891

Thomas Ezekiel Miller was born on June 17, 1849, in Ferrebeville, a small town in Beaufort County, South Carolina. Although he was the son of free parents, Thomas lived with a racial stigma for his entire life. His mother was a mulatto of light complexion, and the daughter of Thomas Heyward, Jr., a signer of the Declaration of Independence. With a white father, Thomas naturally inherited prominent Caucasian features but the "one-drop" law in South Carolina made anyone with a hint of African blood black. Thomas did not find acceptance among his white family. They did not approve of the relationship of his parents, and they persuaded his biological father to give him up for adoption. Thomas's birth mother, apparently, did not have a say in the matter. As rumor had it, Richard and Mary Miller, a black family, adopted Thomas. Due to these factors his racial status remained a subject of controversy for him for his entire life.

As a biracial child, Miller had trouble fitting in as an African American. He actually had a better chance of asserting his white background, if he had only moved to an area where his ancestral past was unknown, but he refused to do so. African Americans who did not know him assumed that he was white and, as Thomas matured, blacks were also suspicious, wondering if he was claiming to be black solely for political reasons. Thomas would gain little political benefit for acknowledging that his birth mother was black under state law. At the end of his life he offered the answer to his conscious decision to assert the African traits in his family lineage. "Not having loved the white less, but having felt the Negro needed me more" is carved into his tombstone as a lasting memorial of his interest in promoting civil rights reform.

Richard and Mary Miller, his adoptive parents, were poor, but hardworking people. More than likely, they were once slaves. Mary, whose birth name was Ferrebe, is associated with a prominent slave-owning farmer and businessman in Beaufort County, for whom the town was named. Evidently, Mary and Richard were freed sometime before 1850, and were available to raise Thomas. There is no evidence to link them directly to Thomas's biological parents, though it is likely that they were on the same plantation. What is certain is that Richard and Mary left for Charleston in 1851, hoping to find greater opportunities among blacks in the city. After a few years in Charleston, they enrolled Thomas in schools opened exclusively for free blacks. Living conditions were still difficult, so they moved to New York, expecting to better their chances in the North. Education was obviously a priority for the Millers, and they enrolled Thomas in a New York school. He was college trained, graduating from Lincoln University in Pennsylvania in 1872. Apparently, Thomas attended law school at the University of South Carolina when it temporarily admitted African Americans, but he did not take a degree there. He completed his apprenticeship in law under solicitor P.L. Wiggin and Chief Justice Franklin J. Moses, and upon passing the bar examination in 1875, he opened a law practice in Beaufort.

Miller began his public career in Beaufort in 1872, winning a seat on the board of education. From his base in Beaufort, Miller was elected to the General Assembly in 1874, serving three terms in the house and one term in the senate. He was also the Republican nominee for lieutenant governor, until Democrats persuaded white Republicans that the state should not put a black man in that position. He would serve in the state militia, and as a U.S. customs inspector. Active in the Republican party, he was elected chairman of the state organization in 1884. The highpoint of his political career came with his election to Congress in 1888.

When Miller entered the national political arena, whites throughout the South had already begun to weaken the black vote. One strategy aimed at disenfranchising blacks was the eight-box law. Election officials would place eight boxes for voters to place their ballots. Seven of them would be for candidates running for state offices with one for a candidate seeking a federal office. Obviously this technique was designed to confuse black voters, as whites were steered through the maze. The officials working the polls used a variety of other schemes, such as inflating the count of white voters. When Miller allegedly lost the 1888 election to white Democrat William Elliott in a heavily black district, he charged fraud and contested the election. The House of Representatives Committee on Elections agreed with him, naming Miller the winner. The contest, however, had lasted more than a year, and Miller actually served only a few months, from September 24, 1890, to March 3, 1891. He was appointed to the House Committee on the Library of Congress. Seeking election in 1890, Miller had apparently won again, but this time he lost the contest in a ruling by the state supreme court.

The chances of a black politician winning an election in South Carolina were slim after the Compromise of 1876. Whites united as a political bloc, no matter their differences, in order to neutralize the black majority. Democrats in the legislature closed majority Republican precincts. In addition to making Republicans walk long distances to polling places in order to vote, whites organized rifle clubs to intimidate black voters. Yet, in spite of these tactics, blacks held on to their political rights in counties where they held a majority. Following the leadership of its newly elected governor Ben Tillman in 1895, whites at the state constitutional convention meeting that year determined to destroy the last vestiges of black suffrage. Thomas E. Miller, Robert Smalls, and George Washington Murray worked diligently to make the elections fair, but the white-dominated convention officially disfranchised African Americans by adopting literacy and property tests for voting, as well as the eight-box law to confuse voters on election day.

With his political career over, Miller turned to educational leadership. He was one of the guiding lights behind the Colored Normal, Industrial, Agricultural and Mechanical College founded in 1896 in Orangeburg, South Carolina. He served as its first president, from 1896 to 1911. (The state legislature later renamed the school South Carolina State College.) Upon his retirement Miller returned to Charleston where he lived until 1923, when he moved to Philadelphia. As the end of his life drew near, Miller returned to Charleston in 1934, where he died four years later.

Miller explained that white officials had charged that blacks had acquired elective office by inappropriate means. Yet, he argued, office-holding was not the most important issue to blacks. African Americans were concerned about violence against them. Miller told of blacks going off to work, fearing that they might be lynched before they could return home; or of black workers toiling for white farmers and then having their pay withheld on unfounded charges of stealing. These were the issues, Miller concluded, that were important to his black constituents.

CIVIL RIGHTS
January 12, 1891

It is late in the day and in the session, but some things are being said to which I should like to reply. To hold office is a precious gift and the race to which I belong is desirous of it, but there are gifts superior to office. Gentlemen talk about the North and about it not giving Negroes representation on their tickets. That is not the thing we are suffering most from in the South. There are other things of more importance to us. First is the infernal lynch law. That is the thing we most complain of. It is a question of whether when we go to work we will return or not. Second, they have little petty systems of justice who rob us of our daily toil, and we cannot get redress before the higher tribunals. Third, we work for our taskmasters, and they pay us if they please, for the courts are so constructed that Negroes have no rights if those rights wind up in dollars and cents to be paid by the white taskmasters.

They speak about pure elections and call the election law a force law. Do not gentlemen from the South boast here in their speeches that it is the white man's right to rule and to control elections, and if they cannot control them by a majority vote they will control them by force or fraud? Take the speech delivered by my colleague from South Carolina [John James Hemphill] and you will see his brazen faced boast that it is his right to remain here even without votes; and then when we have an appropriation bill the North is to be taunted with not giving Negroes representation upon their tickets.

Yes, we want offices; but the first and dearest rights Negroes of the South want are the rights to pay for his labor, his right of trial by jury, his rights to his home, his rights to know that the man who lynches him will not the next day be elected by the State to a high and honorable trust; his right to know that murderers shall be convicted and not be elected to high office, and sent abroad in the land as grand representatives of the toiling and deserving people. These are rights that we want; and we call upon you gentlemen of the North to speak for us and ask the Chamber over yonder to give us an election law—not a force law—a national law, Mr. Chairman, that will compel the people of the South to register the votes of the Negro and the white man alike, and count them as they are cast, and let the wishes of those people in this American country be expressed here by duly elected Representatives of their States. The sickly sentiment about not giving Negroes positions in the North! The Negroes of the North have their schoolhouses. Taxes are levied and schoolhouses supported. What do we find in South Carolina, where the Democrats rule? First, the newly elected governor, who claims to stand upon the platform of the principles of Thomas Jefferson, denies that all men are born free and equal and endowed with equal rights by their Creator. In his annual message to the Legislature he asks for the annihilation of the public school system that is bringing South Carolina out of the bog of ignorance that she is in to day and fast placing her along in the phalanx of other states in prosperity.

The governor in his annual message, to re-establish ignorance, desires to close the schoolhouse door against the poor children by creating class schools. What does he recommend? He recommends that the constitutional guaranty of a 2-mill tax be abolished; that communities be left to themselves to levy school taxes; and to the community shall also be left the right to say whether the education of the rich man's son or the education of the poor man's son shall be supported by the taxes levied. How do they seek to do it? The largest taxpayers are those people generally who have not many children and as they are compelled by the state law to pay a tax, it is to be left to them whether it shall be used to educate the poor man's children. It amounts to having no educational system at all and is the destruction of the school system down there. Then they come to the North and speak about the bitterness of sectionalism, while right there in our southland country, for want of experience, the governor of South Carolina recommends the destruction of the school system, which has been erected upon the promise of universal education.

What else does he do? He recommends the abolishment of two colleges established by my assistance to educate black young men that they may know how to lead the Old State up out of poverty and ignorance. Ah, gentlemen, what we need in this land are not so many offices. Offices are only emblems of what we need and what we ought to have. We need protection at home in our rights, the most important of which is the right to live. First, we want the right to live; and next the right to own property, and not have it taken from us by the trial justices. I will read you an illustrative chapter, if gentlemen will allow me the time. A Democratic lawyer from my state, Mr. Monteith, speaking about the trial-justice system as sustained by the Democratic Party of that State, says that under it no man is secure in his rights, and he gives a picture like this.

I hope gentlemen will listen. A Negro was employed to plow for a white man for $10 a month. This man had a game hen. The hen was lost, and simply because the Negro was plowing there he was assumed to be guilty of stealing her, was tried and sentenced to imprisonment, and they chained him by his hands to the plow, but before the thirty days of his sentence expired the good ole game hen, with fourteen chicks, came out from under the barn where she had been "setting." The same gentleman gives another illustration that will bring the blush of shame to the face of every white man. A Negro woman, in the absence of her husband, got into a dispute with a white neighbor concerning a boundary line, a question which the trial justices have no right to settle; but they take such a question when it comes before them and whip it around and whip it around until they manage to work it into a criminal case. They put this woman on trial in his absence, and, although her attorney pleaded that she was in a condition in which women can not go to court, she was tried, convicted, and sentenced; and a white constable went to her house, two hours after she had become a mother, dragged her from a sick bed and carried her 15 long miles, to the very seat and center of the intelligence of our State, old Columbia. There, to the honor of the jailer and his white wife, they called together several women, white, and black, and they ran that inhuman constable away from the jail and took the poor woman and made her an object of charity.

These are some of the outrages that are inflicted upon my people in the Southland that this "force" bill, as you call it, will protect them from; because, if we get it, instead of seeing South Carolina represented as she has been in this Congress by seven Democrats, you will find six or seven Republicans here. The offices will not go around among the Democrats, and then the spirit of fight that made them secede will make them break up the Democratic Party and we shall have peace.

> *Miller urged his colleagues to support civil rights reform, reminding them that he was elected from South Carolina, a state that had fostered sectional conflict and supported the subordination of blacks. He disputed those congressmen who blamed blacks for the economic problems of the southern states.*

ELECTION DAY
February 14, 1891

Coming as I do from a State that has been first in all strife looking toward the suppression of human rights or the destruction of republican institutions, it is expected that I should be moved, like others from that State in the last forty years, by passion founded upon sectionalism and local aggrandizement. But that is not my purpose. I am here, first an American, second a South Carolinian; as an American for Americans, living in the present with hopes for the future, I am here to speak to this question.

With regret I have witnessed the acrimony, criminations, and recriminations indulged in by those from my section against the legally chosen Representatives of a people and a party whose views are broad, liberal, humane, and merciful. I have read all the speeches delivered by the Senators and Representatives from the South against the passage of an election law, a law which is intended to protect the humblest American in the discharge of the duties of freemen at the elections, a law which promises the absolute protection of republican institutions, a law which aims at the obliteration of sectionalism, caste prejudice, and the hatred that is manifested by the Representatives from the South.   There is nothing in these speeches, bereft of malignant hatred and statements unfounded in history and political economy.   Every one of them savors of the same stale tale that has been announced, either in this Chamber or in the next, or over the entire country in the last fifty years, by arrogance and ignorance.

But there is one speech to which I must invite the attention of the American people; I refer to the speech of a Christian friend from Georgia [Alfred Holt Colquitt]. Its importance does not lie in the fact that he announces any new doctrine, but because he represents himself as a self-constituted sponsor of the Negro in religion and political economy.   He claims to speak for us as our religious adviser, political and personal friend.   Standing out in bold relief from the others is that clever theological politician.   With gloved hand he holds the Bible in a most theological way while he lays down his badly mixed syllogisms, but in that gloved hand is the stiletto, the dagger, which, as he advances in his argument, he inserts into the very vitals of the Negro, and along with him he drags down the representatives of the party of constitutional liberty, the party that has driven from the North sectionalism and clannish hate, the party that has planted north of the Mason and Dixon line a civilization founded upon "Do unto others as you would have others do unto you," the like of which has never been known under the canopy of heaven.

The presence of the Negro does not retard the development of the South. It is not his fault that the South has remained bottled up, yes, literally bottled up, within her circumscribed sphere feasting upon sectional hate, seeking to destroy all that is good on our institutions, falsifying and misrepresenting her countrymen, and playing the part of Kilkenny cats among themselves. There is no people in the world more self-opinionated without cause, more bigoted without achievements, more boastful without a status; no people in the world so quick to misjudge their countrymen and misstate historical facts or political economy, and impugn the motives of others. History does not record a civilized people who have been contented with so little and who can feast so long upon a worthless buried past. While I am crying for mercy and attempting to speak as an ambassador of peace, there are no people in the world who are more vituperative than her leaders.

It is not the Negro that keeps northern capital and western energy from within the borders of the southland, but it is the revolutionary spirit of the white citizens, it is the clannishness of the white citizens, it is the petty prejudices of the white citizens, it is the continuing to dwell upon past uselessness of the white citizens, it is the mean jealousy of the white citizen, it is his love of misjudging and misrepresenting historical achievements that drive from our borders thrift, capital, energy, and inventive genius. Caucasian energy and enterprise will seek wealth in any clime, and the color of a man's skin cannot keep them from coming; but men of refinement will not go to a country where the rights of property are not secure; men of religious convictions will not go among a people who, Pharisaical-like, consider themselves the superior of the influx; men of business habits will not go in a country until by the laws of that land investments are secure. The Negro beyond any people from a barbarous state assimilates readily. Full of gratitude, trained to obey, it is his nature to lovingly serve those by whom he is employed; he never attempts to cross the boundary of established social lines; but, like the hewer of wood that he is in the South, he toils, obeys, and develops his section. His habits are those of the white man, his religion is that of the white man, he has not an obtrusive nature. Then in God's name I ask Christian statesmen not to mix their theology and their political economy, and state to the world that the presence of the Negro is the cause of the non-development and the lack of progress, energy, and prosperity of the South.

Why, capital is shy, the prosperity of the country is great; the invitation to investments is too general in the North and West, where laws are strong and protect the capitalists against the adventurer. In some of the southern States laws are enacted today to entrap investments and to inveigle men with their cash, only to ruin the investor. Think of a State enacting a law empowering townships to issue railroad bonds and under that act inviting capitalists to invest the savings from their toil, and as soon as those bonds are all upon the market the supreme court of that State invalidating the act that created the bonds and thereby robbing the investor, and, as soon as the original holders of the bonds have sacrificed them, have lost all, at the next session of the Legislature the invalidated bonds being by another act validated again. Now, I do not speak for every Southern State, for I plead ignorance as to the exact form of robbery practiced by most of them. But this case is not a hypothetical one; it is taken from the records of the courts and the Legislature of South Carolina during the recent past. Who wants to come to a county or a town where, because he is a Swede, a German, an Englishman, an Irishman, a Frenchman, or a Yankee, the tax assessor assesses his property on account of his nationality or his politics. And yet, there is a case where a Union soldier, because he was a Yankee, was outrageously overtaxed by a local assessor; because he braved the dangers of a battlefield and exposed his breast to the bullet of the traitor his property was outrageously assessed by a local assessor not twelve years ago.

Not even five years ago, but in the near past this has been done in my native county. One of our largest merchants was outrageously assessed, in comparison with his neighbors. What think you? A letter was unearthed, written by the local assessor to a member of the State board of tax rebates, stating that the taxpayer was a Yankee and for that reason he was over-assessed, and for that reason the county officer asked that the rebate should not be allowed. The person alluded to is Captain N. Christensen, of the town of Beaufort, S.C. And yet, when the guardians of the peace of our country, when the guardians of our homes, when the natural protectors of the rights of American citizens formulate a law for the betterment of the condition of the whole country and the protection of the black and white citizens of the South in their rights as electors, they are branded in this and the other Chamber, yes, everywhere, as kindlers of strife, as promoters of sectionalism, and seekers of mal-administration; they are branded as champions of the Negro race, seeking to plant in the Southland the supremacy of the inferior over the superior, and the obliteration of the social line, as destroyers of the business energy and the domestic happiness of the Caucasians confined therein.

The charge is false; they aim at no such achievement, no such attempt has been made. But, this institution is founded upon the common brotherhood of man and the inalienable rights of the citizens of a common country, and the protection of each and every citizen in the enjoyment of all the rights with which he is commonly endowed by a common Creator, coming as men do from an original creation. The same friend, Senator Alfred Holt Colquitt, of Georgia, states that the second barrier to the improvement of the South "is the action of the Government." If he alludes to the action of the southern government for the fifty years, I plead guilty to the indictment drawn; but if he refers to the government administered by the founders of the Constitution, the government of Thaddeus Stevens, Charles Sumner, William H. Seward, Salmon P. Chase, and Abraham Lincoln; if he refers to the government of Oliver P. Morton, Ulysses S. Grant, and John Sherman, I would repel it with indignation. Take the utterances of the leaders of the Government to whom I refer, take their actions whenever in authority, take their votes whenever cast, and I call upon civilization to witness that there has been no people entrusted with the government of humanity who have been more merciful, more watchful, more forbearing, and more humane.

There is a time when to indulge the child makes the parent guilty of a crime, when to be merciful to the criminal sinks the judge beneath the weight of the law; for mercy is founded upon the principles of justice. What think you of a people and a portion of this Union, placed as they are upon their record as secessionists and nullifiers, continually crying and playing upon the harp of sectionalism under the guise of injured innocence? Think of a people whose record at the polls for the last twenty-five years is recorded in the innocent blood of voters; think of a people whose history records the massacre of white citizens for opinion's sake in the time of peace; think of the murder of Chisholm's family in Mississippi and the assassination of white and black citizens without cause in every Southern State; think of a people who drive property holders from within the borders of their State for no crime other than that they support the Republican ticket, giving such property holders the choice of but two alternatives, to remain and die or to leave their property with their lives only.

Think of a people who are ever ready to nullify the acts of this great Government standing up at any and all times ready to brand the protectors of

American homes and the guardians of our Treasury as a band of enemies to their progress and hypocritically crying sectionalism and enmity to the South. The sectionalism and the enmity to republican institutions are all upon the other side. And our party leaders sit here, and over yonder, too, and submit from year to year, and from day to day to the virulence that is hurled in their very teeth. Speak of our Government as a government of the few, for the few, and by the few! Speak of our National Government as a Government of plunder and the Government of misrule! Why, all Europe, yea, the whole civilized world, especially where monarchies are tottering, point to the triumph of universal rights, point to the republican institutions established by my party, point to the "Government for the people, of the people, and by the people," with pride and certain hope, and the only spot that mars this country is that spot, unfortunately for me and mine, that is circumscribed within the narrow limits of the slave States, where intolerance and the suppression of the rights of mankind have been common for more than a century.

The above quotation sounds eloquent, looks well in print, but what does it mean? As shown further on in his speech, it means nothing, no, absolutely nothing, politically, for the Negro. Who is to be the judge of the capacity of the Negro? By what measurement is his right to citizenship to be meted out? Should this self-constituted friend be entrusted with that task? Oh, no, he is not, for he sees the Negro through eyes that are ignorantly prejudiced; he falsifies his position in the South and arraigns him as unjustly, though with guarded words, as those here in this building who have made their record, not as teachers of the Negro in morals and political economy, but as leaders in other fields, leaders on election day... and every other persecution to which the poor American Negro has been subjected. Now, is that quotation ethnologically true? And, if true, what does it prove? What does the history of man teach? Why, it teaches the absolute certainty that races locked up to themselves remain in a barbarous, and, if not in a total, in a semi-barbarous state. I challenge any student of ethnology to point to a race, a tribe, or a clan that ever rose to permanent civilization without the assisting hand of another superior civilization. Tacitus faithfully portrays the uncivilized and degraded condition of the Germans and Gauls at the beginning of the Roman conquest of their lands. Pliny portrays the degraded condition of the Britons, and speaks of the women of this parent stock of Caucasian English civilization as attending their religious feasts in nude phalanx.

Some writers think that they were cannibals. Now, these races, touched by the magic hand of Roman civilizations, rose from their degradation and immorality to the highest specimens of Christian civilization the world over. The incestuous British parent stock has evolved and improved to so high a degree that, whenever we speak of a woman of constancy, Christian morality, and absolute virtue, we go, without stopping to think, among the English-speaking Caucasians. I truthfully say this without disparity to other civilized Christian women. I am dealing with ethnology and history as recorded by the English-speaking world. This friend [Mr. Colquitt] thinks the Negroes incompetent of the achievements that are common to Caucasians. Why, the Romans held the same views about the Gauls, Germans, and Britons. When sending cargoes of slaves from the British Isles to Rome, Caesar said, "I send a race that will require a century of education to be made fit to become house servants." Ah, the science of ethnology is perfect, the philosophers of this school have been faithful, and they all agree that the primitive state of an excluded people from the influx of a world's advancement is no proof of their inherent and unchangeable inferiority, but proves the absolute certainty of the common brotherhood of man, created by a common Creator, with equal faculties and moved by a universal impulse. Will the friend from Georgia [Mr. Colquitt] charge the poor Negro with his ignorance of this unerring, divine law?

Will the friend from Georgia [Mr. Colquitt] point to a single race of slaves who were strangers in a strange land, separated, absolutely separated, as the American Africans have been from the protection which men instinctively look to on their native soil, who have achieved their own freedom, who have been so obediently true to their masters, and have done as much to secure their freedom, or who have done so much for the protection of free institutions as the American Negro? No, the Negro as a class in America is not the mutinous, riotous element of our community, but at all times he has labored faithfully to obtain his emancipation and to better his condition. And, also, he speaks lightly of the morals of the women; yet he speaks as a teacher and friend of the Negro. If you found ignorance, incest, superstition and barbarism, you have the condition of the English-speaking people at the time of the Roman invasion, but they had all their rights secured, with the Book of Christ in their hand beholding their grandeur today. And God knows it; man knows it; the Southern people know it, that there was no barbarity, as natural history understands it and records it, common to the American Negro at the breaking out of the war. He was ignorant and illiterate, but never barbarous at the period mentioned by this learned friend [Mr. Colquitt].

He was the custodian of what little peace and happiness were enjoyed by helpless women and children, while this friend from Georgia [Mr. Colquitt] and others who speak of him as a barbarian at that time were acting like barbarians, drenching their hands in the blood of a common ancestry, and with all the ferocity of primitive barbarians striving to pull down the very temple of education, protection, life, and liberty. And, if it is not true, what position must a Christian statesman, professing to be the friend of my people, occupy in the estimation of that people? Great God is there no limit to the slander and malignant utterances of these self-constituted friends of a toiling, deserving, plodding portion of the American people? Stand up and indict a race of males as the invaders of the sanctity of Caucasian home ties, as the brutal destroyer of that in woman that is her very existence. The charge is groundless, mean, slanderous, and most damnably false, as false as the elements that constitute the infernal regions.

I live in the blackest belt in the South, where in numbers the whites are few. My district covers a country of hundreds of miles. The large plantations, with dense population of black illiterates, are there, and nestled among them are isolated white homes, miles apart. Many of these homes are peopled by widowed mothers, half-grown and grownup girls, without the protecting hand of a male of their race. The girls often go alone from neighbor to neighbor or to the store or to church or to school, and I challenge the pleader at the bar or the custodian of the criminal records to point to a single case where these walking emblems of American purity have been assaulted or raped by a Negro in that district or any portion of it since emancipation.

The records of the courts of the South prove that the crime is not indulged in and the charge is never laid at the door of the Negro where he is powerfully strong in numbers and the morals of the white women are certain. Whenever it is hurled at him the crime is laid in a locality where the numbers of the whites and the Negroes are nearly equal, where the whites and the Negroes are equal in morals; and, even after the poor unfortunate victim has been lynched and his spirit gone to the eternal world, letters or verbal admissions coming from the supposed victim of licentious brutality invariably absolve the innocent dead man from the crime charged.

There is not a Christian mother in the South but knows the utter falsity of this charge. I call upon white women who are left alone from day to day and from night to night in their struggling homes in the South to deny it. I call upon the ministers of the gospel who are not political demagogues to deny it. I call upon the white struggling son of toil, whose hand has never been stained with the innocent blood of the ex-slave, to deny it. I call upon the young white girls budding into womanhood, with their voluptuous charms, who travel the lonely country roads of the South, without the nearing hand of a male friend, to deny it. I call upon the statistician of crime to investigate the charge and stamp it false. I call upon all lovers of truth, in the South and North, all protectors in this Christian land of the purity of women, to be a witness for us that it is false, absolutely false.

I have learned a great deal during the vicissitudes of a stormy life, but the lesson taught me by this religious friend of my people is unexampled in the history of lessons taught. A religious, Christian, Caucasian, self-constituted friend of the Negro thus falsely records him in history, and justifies lynch law in the South, and uses it as a cause of the denial of the boon of citizenship to a deserving, competent citizen. Yes, I say competent citizen, for in the South the Negro is the equal of the poor illiterate white citizen in every element that constitutes an American, Christian citizen. And in devotion to the National

Government, in love for the Stars and Stripes, in regard for the laws as expressed by majorities and as a protector of constitutional liberty, history records him as the superior of his white master, never a nullifier, never a carping hypocrite with foul treason in his heart.

Now, what does he mean by "an untrained moral intelligence"? Let us see how this quotation fits the master class of the South. The poor white men of my State who were property-holders, and thereby could vote before the war, were treated by the master class quite differently from the way in which Republican managers of election dealt with their voters. We know that the Negro instinctively is a law-abiding citizen and he votes for constitutional liberty at all times. And the same is true of the struggling portion of the white citizens of the South. They were unlearned, many of them untrained in morals, but they instinctively knew that the Whig party was their protector. They struggled at all times to vote the ticket, and to prevent them from voting against the master class. The old southern barons, in intelligence and morals trained, would coax these illiterate white men, weeks before election, and cage them in places called bull pens, drug them with bad whisky, and keep them there to vote against their convictions on Election Day, drunk and brutalized by the master class. History records it that at elections around Columbia, S.C., when the men became unmanageable, lewd women were procured and placed among them to satisfy the licentious passions of the brutalized men.

Think of a people, who have at all times sustained an oligarchy by force, or bribery, or fraud, or by degrading her voters with bad whiskey, or through the instrumentality of lewdness, talking about a government for the few or talking about the control of an illiterate ballot. It has always been the other way down there. Oh, erring Southern brethren, behold our vote. Now what is true of the Negroes of Georgia is true of them in every state of the South. Suddenly becoming citizens, without shelter or food, they have struggled in a land where they receive little assistance from the courts and where the juries are systematically formed to oppress them; where they work often on the promise to pay; where they receive no protection from the labor law; yet they have achieved a success founded upon material prosperity and accumulated wealth the equal of which has never been accomplished by pauperized serfs or peasants in any part of the universe. In my State, if the employer states verbally that the unpaid laborer of his plantation contracted to work for the year no other farmer dares employ the man if he attempts to break the contract rather than work for nothing; for down there it is a misdemeanor so to do, the penalty is heavy, and the farmer who employs the unpaid, starving laborer of his neighbor is the victim of the court.

In my county for the last ten years the same set of citizens with very little variation has been jurors from year to year. I have scanned the names of the jurors of my county for the last five years; it speaks for itself. I shall ask leave to print it as a part of my remarks. On the rice plantations in many counties checks for labor are issued in lieu of money, the laborer never seeing a cent. They are made redeemable in two or three years after their issuance, and very often the planters fail or the business changes hands before their maturity, and if the laborer lays them up as the fruits of toil he awakes to hear that his former employer has failed and his earnings are gone; and yet these people are acquiring property; they are becoming owners of their little cabins. This system is not confined to one plantation. I have checks here from many plantations, some of which I will append to my remarks. No one knows, but God, how many heartaches and disappointments these promises to pay have caused the innocent holders, for in many cases the employers failed long before the time for their redemption, and left the laborer poor indeed, with no possession other than the remembrance of how he toiled and how magnificently his master entertained upon the fruit of his labor.

Now, is the above quotation true? Ethnologically true? Let us see. Is there here a student of history who can point me out a single State, community, or municipality where the people who have remained unmixed have amounted to anything, who have been eminent in self-government, literature, inventive genius, art, or science? I pause for the student of ethnology to name the people. The Egyptians, say the Greek writers, were of a mixed race. Deeds to property by Egyptians are in the museums of Europe from Egypt during the Ptolemaic period that proved conclusively that the vendors and vendees were of a mixed race. Her literature and art prove that her citizens were of a mixed race. The same thing is ethnologically true of the Babylonians; the same is true of the Romans; the same is true of the Jews; the same is true of the Caucasians.

The converse is true, that where people remain for centuries unmixed, although they were originally mixed, or of several races, they retrograde. There is decay in virtue and in brains; such people have become vicious and debased. Compare the North of our great country with the South. What is the cause of the North's triumphant rank at the head of civilization? What is the cause of her wealth, prosperity, inventive genius, great cities, peace, happiness, and universal prosperity? What is the cause of her virtue and great brain development? Show me a city that has grown within the last fifty years in manufacturing, shipping, banking, or business prosperity, show me a city where the law is obeyed, and I will show one that is peopled by every nationality under the sun, rubbing and jostling against each other in the race of life. But show me a city that has retrograded or barely held its own during that period, and I will show you a citizenship that has been excluded from the world's progress and from the influx of the nations of the world.

Men discussing this question glibly point to Mexico as a place where a mixed race has retrograded, but that is not the cause; the cause lies in the fact that Mexico has remained an excluded people. What she suffers from is want of new blood, the assisting hand of other nations. She needs what New York and the Great West contain; the admixture of every people of the universe. The South has actually retrograded in many things, and the localities that are noted for improvements, or can be styled the "New South," are places where enterprises are conducted by Northern, Western, or European capital, honesty, and industry. Take the personality of the representative men of that section and it bears the mark of decadence. Some of the old names are here, but none of the old learning and eloquence. Which of the two Breckinridges can take the place of the original Breckinridge among American statesmen and orators? Who can succeed Clay or Benton? Who from South Carolina can equal Henry Lawrence, Rutledge, Pinckney, Calhoun, McDuffee, Barnwell, or Rhett? Who from Georgia is to be the equal to Stephens or Toombs? Who from Virginia is the equal of any of her great men? The South is possessed of an inferior order of statesmanship today simply because their school is founded upon a buried past and because she has remained an exclusive people.

It is not alone for the Negro that this law is needed; it is necessary to protect the white citizens of the South. It is not the fear of Negro supremacy in the South that causes the Southern election officers to suppress the Negro vote, but it is the fear of the rule of the majority regardless of race. The master class does not want to surrender to the rule of the people, and they use the frightful bugbear of Negro rule to scare the white man and drive him under the yoke that has been bearing heavily upon him for more than a century. At no period in the history of reconstruction has there ever been Negro domination in the South. White men occupied all the good offices. There never was a Negro governor, attorney general, and comptroller general. All of the judges save one or two were white men. Ninety-five percent of the tax collectors were white men. Ninety percent of the tax-assessors where white men. Eight-tenths of the Republican Congressmen from the South were white men, and still they talk of Negro supremacy and really make the North believe that it existed, when in reality it never existed, and at every election the candidates of the native whites, if they sought the vote of the Republican party, have received the same treatment that Negroes or carpetbaggers received.

Colonel R.P. Blair of South Carolina was the candidate of the Independent White Republicans and Greenbackers in 1880, a native South Carolinian from one of our first families in blood and wealth, had no Negroes on his ticket, but announced himself as the candidate of a party that was opposed to the oligarchy established and was succeeding to divide the white people. For that reason and one other, he was notified to come off the ticket. He refused, and a citizen of his town killed him at noonday. The governor who was counted in rewarded the slayer of his competitor by appointing him the high sheriff of his county. Those who lynch innocent people are elected to high offices in my State.

A veritable set of fools a few of our party leaders have been. They will listen to all the cheap sentimentality sounded under the name of Negro domination and business prostration, be swerved from a plighted duty to a faithful constituency the country over. The elections bill cannot and will not prostrate business. It cannot and will not retard the development of the South. But it will go a long way towards the protection of republican institutions; it will protect those voters; it will count those votes; it will establish an equilibrium between both sections and secure honest representation; it will make both races who are loyal to the Republican party in the South feel that they are protected in their rights of citizenship by the party to which they have clung, blindly followed and supported, even with their lives.

I absolve the President and our party leaders in this branch from the charge of dereliction to party or a contemptible desertion of Southern Republicans. Without favor to any at all time this majority has done its simple duty to us. But what must I say, what can I say for the action of a few of those in the other end of this building? Ah, they have too readily accepted the false pleas rendered and the apparent social courtesies extended by the enemies of republican institutions and the universal rights of man; they have been led astray, and they have violated every pledge by which they have stood and to which our party is tied.

What is to be the result? I tremble for it; to think about it fills me with awe and causes me to shed bitter tears of anguish for the future, for right is right. "Justice, like a volcanic fire, may sleep suppressed awhile, but can not expire." What is to become of us when the slumbering embers of a smoldering volcano rekindle and burst forth with all its horrors in a not very distant future? The wheels of progress cannot be reversed; every right, because it is right, must be secured sooner or later; to postpone it is to quadruple its violence and the dire consequences that are bound to follow. The Revolutionary fathers submitted to the planting of slavery in new territory against the protests of Jefferson; their yielding was a crime. Future historians will record the weak, sickly yielding of Senators here to a false sentiment as a crime against the rights of man. False leaders may deceive an entire people; men deluded by false ambition may mislead, may beguile, and entrap an entire section, but the day of reckoning must come, and to delay an evil is to augment the volume and increase the horrors.

Now, it would be a hardship on the gentleman from South Carolina [Mr. Hemphill] to hold him responsible for the truthfulness of the above statement, for I believe he thought he was repeating history as it had been made by my party; he really believed that seventy-three Union soldiers were a thousand. The gentleman from South Carolina [Benjamin Tillman] in a great speech before the braves in his district warned them not to say too often anything that was not true, for if they repeated it too often they were liable to believe it. He reminded them that the Senator from South Carolina [Wade Hampton] had stated so often, for the purpose of deceiving the North, that Negro voters had elected him in 1876, that he (the Senator) actually believed it.

Perhaps the gentleman from South Carolina [John James Hemphill] had stated so often to his Northern friends that he had faced a thousand Union soldiers bayonets, on the day of the election in 1876 in his county, and with the assistance of those thousand Union soldiers' votes he was elected to the South Carolina Legislature in 1876, that he had really got into the habit of believing it; but the simple truth is he was not elected at all in that year. Chester County gave a majority for the Republican party in that year. There were not seventy-five soldiers in the gentleman's county on the day of election in 1876. The number of soldiers on duty in South Carolina in November 1876 is herein shown. It is taken from the record of the War Department and not from the vivid imagination of irresponsible representatives from the South. The above editorial is not worthy of a comment. The Administration of Mr. Benjamin Harrison compares favorably with that of any of our great presidents. His state papers are as broad, as liberal, as scholarly, and as thoughtful as any of the papers of Jefferson, Jackson, or Lincoln. His plea for the protection of citizens in the enjoyment of rights that are universal and common to all is as conclusive as anything that has ever been written by any of the champions of the rights of mankind.

The sickening part of the editorial is this, that, while the writer seeks to incense the South against its Chief Executive, should the President pass through Charleston the writer of that editorial would break his neck to get upon the reception committee to play the part of a coxcomb the equal of which has never been seen upon the continent of Europe. He would be chief among the President's flatterers while there and damn him the moment his back was turned. They have been playing at this game for the last fifty years, and they do succeed admirably in making dupes of our great Northern national leaders.

If our party had passed the elections law previous to the last election, a majority of the Representatives from the South in the next Congress would have been from my party. I was elected; my votes were received, canvassed, and returned by Democratic election officers, but because the word "for" was on my ballots (notwithstanding the word "for" had been placed upon the ballots during the last eight years under the same statute and all of them had been counted) they were thrown out and the certificate was given to a man who had received little over 3,000 votes in the whole district. My majority under the seal of Democratic officers is greater than the whole vote cast for my competitor. And still I am a contestant before the next Congress. By the way, I have been reminded that to make this speech may cost me my seat. If it should lose me a single vote, I will accept it. I have stated nothing but the truth; I have done nothing but my duty; I would not for anything do less. I may be defeated in the contest. The man who was not elected to it may retain the office, but I leave here possessed of the consciousness that I have endeavored to defend, in this Chamber, my people and my party.

I shall not be muffled here. Muffled drums are instruments of the dead. I am in part the representative of the living; of those whose rights are denied; of those who are slandered by the press, on the lecture platform, in the halls of legislation, and oftentimes by men in the livery of heaven, and I deem it my supreme duty to raise my voice, though feebly, in their defense.

12

George Washington Murray (1853–1926)
House of Representatives, South Carolina

Republican

Fifty-third and Fifty-fourth Congresses
March 4, 1893, to March 3, 1895
June 4, 1896, to March 3, 1897

George Washington Murray was born into slavery on September 22, 1853. He grew up in a community located near Rembert, a small town in Sumter County, South Carolina. George was orphaned at a young age, and knew nothing about his birth parents. Virtually penniless but rich with motivation, George taught himself to read; the first schoolhouse he ever entered was the one where he was the teacher. George taught school for fifteen years. Obviously gifted, George passed an examination in 1874 that allowed him to attend the University of South Carolina in Columbia while it was still racially integrated during Reconstruction.

In 1876, following the presidential contest of Rutherford B. Hayes and Samuel J. Tilden, and the end of Congressional Reconstruction, whites again excluded blacks from the university. Murray was forced out and continued his education on a part-time basis at the State Normal School for Negroes in Columbia. Despite these restrictions, Murray had an active career, serving as a customs inspector at a federal port in Charleston, dabbling in real estate, writing, lecturing, and farming. He represented the Colored Farmers' Alliance, providing black farmers with new innovations in agriculture as well as advice on the marketing of their crops. As an inventor, Murray received eight patents for producing agricultural implements, such as a fertilizer distributor, cotton chopper, and a combined furrow opener and stalk knocker. A tireless campaigner, he worked for Benjamin Harrison, the Republican presidential candidate in 1888. Because of his varied interests, G.W. Murray gained the reputation as the "most intellectual Negro in the country."

As a Republican partisan, Murray made an unsuccessful bid for Congress in 1890. Undeterred by defeat, he ran again in 1892 and won, though the initial count suggested that he had lost to white Democrat E.W. Moise. Represented by Thomas Ezekiel Miller, a black lawyer, Murray prevailed in the election contest, and took his seat in the House in 1893. He ran for reelection in 1894, but white legislators so gerrymandered the districts that they virtually negated the black vote. Murray lost the election to William Elliott, a white Democrat. Thereupon Murray again charged election irregularities and successfully contested the results. The contest, however, lasted for most of the term, and Murray did not take his seat until June 4, 1896. His interest in public education led to his appointment to the Committee on Education. (He also served on the Committee on Expenditures.) Convinced that white prejudice was a result of ignorance, Murray endeavored to educate whites on African-American life and history. To that end, he asked Congress to appropriate money for the Cotton States and International Exposition in Atlanta in 1895. He defended the bill on grounds that the exposition offered an opportunity to showcase black achievement. Murray pointed out various statistics on African Americans, including the fact that black inventors had received ninety-two federal patents by 1894, including eight by Murray himself. In addition to an interest in education, Murray defended the use of silver, insisting that the people he represented did not favor inflated greenbacks as legal tender. His congressional career ended in 1897.

Murray, considered the "Black Eagle of Sumter" by his contemporaries, fought for passage of federal civil rights legislation, feeling that as the only black official in Congress, it was a duty. As he told his colleagues in the House of Representatives, "standing before you today, the lone spokesman for my race, I hear voices which you do not hear; I see faces which you cannot see. I see their wants and I feel their needs, and every fiber of my body vibrates in sympathy with the people—the common people." Murray also embraced the self—help and the educational philosophy of Booker T. Washington. The "Wizard from Tuskegee" was rapidly gaining prominence for advocating industrial education for blacks. Murray believed that Hampton Institute in Virginia and Tuskegee Institute in Alabama were good models for black education. He insisted that the establishment of more schools providing an industrial education would better prepare black youths to enter the mainstream of American society.

As the century came to a close, Murray paid close attention to politics in South Carolina. When the state constitutional convention met in 1895, Murray worried that whites might disenfranchise black voters. He joined six other black delegates at the convention, but their voices were not enough to defeat disenfranchisement. The convention adopted residency laws, poll taxes, and property and literacy tests that effectively denied black suffrage. The Supreme Court in 1898 in effect approved the convention's actions when it decided that the poll tax did not violate the equal protection or due process clause in the Fourteenth Amendment.

With his political life over, Murray and his wife, Cornelia, concentrated on farming. They also opened a real estate office and marketed their service to blacks. As a landlord, he was sued and convicted in a contract dispute with a tenant. Murray believed that racist whites were determined to put him in jail, so he left South Carolina in 1905 to live in Chicago. He continued to be active in Republican politics, attending national conventions, and lecturing. During this time Murray wrote two books—*Race Ideals: Effects, Cause and Remedy for the Afro-American Race Troubles* (1914) and *Light in Dark Places* (1925). He died in Chicago on April 21, 1926.

In discussing the legal tender issue, Murray identified three classes of Americans: the business and professional class, miners, and workers. He said his constituents were primarily in the third class. Since the supply of gold was diminishing, he believed that the federal government should pursue a monetary policy that would produce economic stability. He suggested that a combination of gold and silver might be appropriate. He favored a policy that would be balanced, whereby neither the working class nor the wealthy class would have an advantage.

MONETARY POLICY
August 24, 1893

The speeches on this floor remind me of the custom among persons of the Methodist persuasion, when called upon in experience meetings to give expression to the reasons upon which their faith is predicated.

As my first important vote in this House will be on the pending bill, I deem it necessary to give expression to the reasons impelling me to cast it, as I shall. The casual observer very readily perceives that upon the settlement of the pending question the American people are divided into three distinct and somewhat antagonistic elements. Upon its settlement the miner, producer, and laborer are becoming no less interested than the merchant prince and millionaire. The first class is composed of capitalists, bankers, and commercial men, who own and control nearly all the currency, and are desirous of making and keeping it dear by keeping this volume as small as possible. The second class is composed of those who own the silver miners and all the un-coined bullion not in possession of the Government, and are using all their power to establish free coinage, I fear, mainly to enhance the value of their possessions. The third class is composed of the toiling and producing millions, who are neither gold bugs nor silver bugs, and who realize so little from their labor and investments that each year finds them less able to meet the obligations of the former, in consequence of which they are forced to sink deeper and deeper under threatening billows of mortgages and debts, beneath which many of the giant ships of their fellows, bringing the bread and necessaries of life from the shores of nothingness, have sunk to rise no more, leaving their overburdened barks in raging seas of debts. I am in favor of a change in our monetary policy, but not such a one as has been suggested by the advocates of the gold standard.

To the last named class nearly all of my constituents, and the whole race of which I am the sole representative, belong. In two respects I represent the largest constituency of any member of this House, a district of two hundred and seventy thousand, and a race of nearly eight million. Speaking for them I do not believe that the great evils with which they are afflicted are owing to the operations of the so-called Sherman Law. They had been hurtfully feeling the mailed hand of the unrighteous financial policy of their country long before the silver-purchasing bill of 1890 became a law. They believe and know that the primary cause of the direful disease which has been making paupers of them and their children for more than a dozen years lies deeper than the recent superficial, and in some respects, designing unrest in money circles. They trace it to a contraction of the circulating medium that, like a viper with its victim in its coils, has been drawing its cords tighter around their prosperity, until it is dead. I am of the opinion that the only sure and permanent remedy is a lengthening of the cords, an enlargement of the volume of money.

Unlike the other classes, my constituents combine patriotism with self-interest. They want the volume of money increased by the use of those substances in which their Government would have the greatest security. While they want and must have more and cheaper money, they demand that it be made of such substances as have the greatest intrinsic value, and as the supply of gold is inadequate and growing less, are in favor of making up the deficiency with silver, and to that extent favor free coinage and bimetallism, and no one, in the course of this debate, has even pretended to prove that there is more than a sufficiency of both gold and silver obtainable to supply the monetary use of the world. I submit that the true measure of the superabundance or insufficiency of the circulating medium is the price of labor and productions of one period compared with those of another.

For example, let us compare the war period, when circumstances forced a superabundance of money into circulation, in consequence of which the price of labor and productions rose on the Federal side from two to three, and on the Confederate side from thirty to forty times their nominal price with the present period, in which contraction, causing an insufficiency of money, has forced down the price of productions and labor to such an extent that one dollar is buying from two to three times as much of them as it should. We want neither of these extremes, but a mean ratio between them in which neither products and labor on the one hand or money on the other would have the advantage. I believe that their condition would be vastly improved by the remonetization of silver and the use of that substance in which the Government would be secured with liabilities that could be sold in the markets of the world for 60 per cent of their nominal value, even at the present suppressed price of silver bullion.

The Negro, as patriotic and devoted as when dying on the plains of Boston, bleeding on Bunker Hill, or suffering the horrors of war through cold and heat, in hunger and nakedness, amidst northern snows or the malarial swamps of the South, under the lead of Marion, Sumter, and Washington, or repelling the formidable army of Lord Packenham, under the lead of the gallant and indomitable Jackson, in the war of 1812, or turning the tide of war in favor of the Stars and Stripes, under the commands of Butler, Hunter, Shaw, Logan, Hancock, and Grant, in the Civil War, in such a way as caused each star to assume such brilliancy and each stripe such strength as to daze the eyes and successfully resist the great battering rams of the Confederacy, is in favor of the remonetization of silver as a means of increasing the circulating medium, because it would tend to made America the happy home of all Americans. I can proudly say that history does not reveal the fact where a black hand was ever voluntarily raised to strike down the flag of his country, nor is the vote of the black man ever knowingly cast against its interest. Notwithstanding the ill treatment received at the hands of his countrymen, he is always found voting and shouting for America and Americans, and on this currency question he is in favor of an American, instead of an English, German, French, or Belgian policy. I am especially in favor of silver, because it so fittingly illustrates the condition of the colored Americans.

Driven out of competition with gold in paying custom dues and the principal and interest on the bonded debt, which it so largely aided in making, and is not even allowed to redeem its creature, the silver certificate, there are those who ask why, does it not stand up on terms of equality in the marts of trade with gold? It is dishonest to ask, or expect, a slave to compete on terms of equality with a free man. I remember seeing, in my peregrinations through my native State, placarded in many nooks and corners, "White is king," which I was inclined to believe. But in the case of gold and silver it seems that that doctrine has been exploded. The little, yellow, gold man, so small and circumscribed, has, by special training and baneful education in later years, become so strong and malevolent that he is spitefully driving this large, useful, humane, and philanthropic white man (silver) from nearly every place of honor, usefulness, and amusement.

Every lover of fair play and justice, every sympathizer with the toiling millions in adversity and demoralization resulting from the lost and patronizing care of their best and ever present friend, silver, is called upon to assist in restoring his ancient power and glory, that he in turn might being prosperity and happiness to the homes of the poor as well as those of the rich. As I am placed in a similar position, common misery makes us one, and impels me to come to the rescue of and to use all my power to defend this white man, who has ever been the friend of the poor, white or black, the world over. I sincerely trust that the lovers of the white metal will hereafter have more sympathy, even for human beings when suffering and dying under the fell blows of hateful prejudice and discrimination. Each member of society, finding his wants so varied and many, and without the power, machinery, skill, or climate to supply them all, is forced to the necessity of producing enough of that substance which nature and education have enabled him to produce at least cost to himself, to supply his own wants of it and sufficient to spare for barter with others to furnish him all the necessaries of life; but as those with whom he would exchange are distant and inconvenient to reach, he needs an abundant medium of exchange that will not only measure the value of his products, when compared with the products of those with whom he would exchange, but will ever honestly measure itself when compared with the value of the products for which it is mediating.

I deny that the American people have such a medium of exchange today, and contend that any other is dishonorable to a great nation, and tends to rob its principals at both ends. We are prepared to prove that such is the character of our present circulating medium. Is the gold dollar of today an honest dollar? The suffering and deplorable condition of all labor and productions, outside of manufacturing industries, answers no. Our prostrate silver mines in anger and woe answer, no. The one who buys another's products at the lowest price possible, and while in transit to other sections, where he would exchange them for other products, destroys their value and takes them at his own price by murdering his competitors, is a scoundrel, that should be hung to the first limb; and yet this is the character of this so much honored gold dollar. In competition with silver, which forced the market down, he bought up millions of national and local bonds, and mortgages covering the railroads and homes of the people some dozen or more years since, and now when the time has arrived for another exchange he is making the final attempt to murder his competitor, the silver dollar, in order to be taken at the boastful and bloated estimate that he puts upon himself; and honorable Senators and Congressmen stand within the legislative halls of the greatest nation on earth and aid and abet him in the performance of his dastard deed. I heard a gentleman say, in the course of his remarks on this floor the other day, that the only class affected by the appreciation of gold is that having long contracts.

It seems to me that his deductions will not hold good, for it is evident that when money appreciates to such an extent that $1 will purchase twice as much at a given time as it did at the time of its acquirement, the individual owning it is twice as rich at the latter period as he was when he came in possession of it. Therefore when money appreciates to the extent of 50 percent its owner is 50 percent richer and every other class is 50 percent poorer, because his property will buy 50 percent more of the property of all other classes than at the time of acquirement, and theirs 50 percent less of his. Each of two citizens twenty years ago engaged in the same employment acquired $10,000. One invested his money in bank stock, while the other invested his in real estate outside of some boomed town or city. Now the one investing in bank stock has not only the accumulated interest of his money, but his property is worth, at the lowest estimate, 40 percent more than that of his co-laborer. The one investing in real estate finds that $6,000 of his neighbor's bank stock will purchase all his ten thousand dollar of real estate property, notwithstanding that the property of the one cost as much sweat and blood as that of the other. This is the great wrong of which there is so much complaint. The same amount of gold that was purchased with one day's labor, 1 pound of cotton, 1 bushel of wheat twenty years ago will buy from two to three times as much of the same commodities today. Any system of finance that will add such an inflated and dishonest value to the property of one man, at the destruction of the value of other men's property, should find no abiding place on this earth, and especially in the so-called land of the free and home of the brave.

If the organized labor of our manufacturing industries had been paid the same scale of wages as the scattered and disorganized labor of the farm we would have had anarchy and revolution long since. In 1866, the circulating medium, when the 7-30 notes, which ex-Treasurer, General Spinner, says, was a part of the currency are added, was $1,728,872,668-$80,839,010, the amount reserved in the Treasury, leaving $1,648,043,658, as the volume of circulation, which when divided by the population for that period 35,460,000, gives a per capita circulation of $46.40, and it is conceded on all sides that the period during and after the war was the most prosperous period ever known in this country. While the volume of money of 1886 was $1,808,559,694-$555,859,169 Treasury reserve, which leaves a balance of $1,252,700-525 as the volume of circulation, which divided by 57,404,000, the population for the period gives a per capita circulation of $21.82. But it seems to me that the reserve funds of our national banks are just as much out of circulation as those of the Treasury, and should not be any more regarded as a part of the dividend in finding the per capita circulation. According to the statistical reports of 1886, the reserve fund in all the national banks, amounting to $225,055,019, which, when deducted from $1,252,700,525, the dividend used by Treasury authorities, leaves a balance of $1,027,645,506 as a new dividend, and, divided by the population, gives us a per capita circulation of $17.88, instead of $21.82. When we consider the vast amount of money lost and destroyed and hoarded up by misers, which is as much out of circulation as that locked up in the Treasury, even the $17 per capita circulation is entirely too high an estimate. I verily believe that when everything is considered, that even $21 is a high estimate for the circulating medium per capita at present.

During a speech as far back as 1874 that gallant general and great statesman, Senator John A. Logan, who has gone to his grave wearing two honors, and whose memory is so dear to the men he led, as well as those he freed, said that "contraction has gone on until the whole amount of currency of every kind now outstanding is only $742,000,000." We can very readily perceive why we are forced to sell our products for less than cost when you came to us in 1886 with less than a billion dollars to do the business of our country, while it took at least one billion and four hundred millions of dollars in 1866. You brought a billion dollars in 1886 to do the business of 57,000,000 people, when it took for 35,000,000 people some fourteen hundred million in 1866. In 1873, when we had a bimetallic standard and a silver dollar was worth as much as a gold dollar, an ounce of silver bringing $1.32, the average price of wheat was $1.31 per bushel and that of cotton 18.08 cents per-pound; when now the gold dollar, through favored legislation and contraction, has appreciated some 40 percent per-pound; when now the gold dollar, through favored legislation and contraction, has appreciated some 40 percent when compared with the silver dollar and every other species of property and productions, we are brought to the awful dilemma of a silver dollar worth 60 cents buying the same amount of cotton, corn, wheat, and every class of property, while gold buys the same as it did when silver was worth its face value anywhere in the world, thereby forcing us to take 7 cents for our cotton and 68 cents a bushel for wheat, subscribing in the use of productions to the silver standard and in the use of money to the gold standard.

The former is the standard of the producers; the latter that of moneylenders and speculators. It seems that because a comparatively few bankers and large business concerns are failing, the metropolitan press having stirred and alarmed the nation, this Congress was speedily and gravely called into extraordinary session to furnish means of relief. Yet when we who have a patient and long-suffering constituency, which has been on bended knee for years begging for aid, enter objections to aiding gentlemen representing banking and moneyed constituencies, unless some measure is coupled with theirs to give relief to ours as well, we notice intimations in a portion of the metropolitan press, which disclose a design to charge us with disloyalty, recreantcy, and negligence. If we seek no deeper than the immediate cause which brought about the present crisis, and provide only for its relief, we shall have given a dose of opiate to our country, the dying patient, in order that it may pass away without apparent pain, in a fit of stupor and resigned demoralization. We shall have occupied the position of the foolish architect, who is extremely careless concerning his foundation, but takes alarm at the slightest leakage from the top. Through an inequitable financial system, the foundation of this grandest of all republics is being consumed in a flame of debt, but we seem alarmed only at the falling in of the gilded top.

What should alarm us most is the decay and utter ruin of the million pillars, the producing and laboring masses, and the hardy foundation upon which our gilded financial and commercial superstructures are erected. More than half of the mortgages on the farms of our country are a true index of failures. In making comparisons of the ratios of increase and decrease in the circulating medium, population, rates of interest, productions, and mortgages of one period and section of country with another, cold and lifeless figures grow eloquent in depicting the reasons for the sufferings of the masses at one time and in one locality when compared with their prosperity in another. Yet, when the great masses, too busily engaged in winning the bread of life and beating back the great waves of mortgages and debts beneath which they are sinking from day to day, to study finance or monetary institutions in order to see their need, and to understand in what way to demand protection to themselves through legislation, ask those in whom they have confided, and from whom they are expecting relief, what is the cause of such a state of affairs as has brought them to the very vortex of ruin, the answer is, almost uniformly, "overprotection."

What nonsense! What an unpatriotic and un-statesman-like answer! Instead of furnishing the country with sufficient currency to form an honest medium of exchange, to carry on its great, varied, and growing business, one class of doctors say raise less, when hardly a sufficiency is now raised to satisfy the demands of consumption; another class prescribes diversification of culture, which means, in a great measure, the raising of such crops as the soil is least adapted to, thereby entailing a loss on the diversification and destruction of the market for the products of those whose soil, machinery, and experience best fit them to cultivate; and still another, that money is not scarce and that there is abundance of it in England, Germany, and Belgium, seeking and longing for investment, and all that is necessary to secure it is a restoration of confidence in the business world, and an exhibition of honesty and ability to pay at the expiration of the term of loans.

How unreasonable it is, while continually holding up the enormous amount of bonds and mortgages belonging to this country and citizens, in the hands of foreigners, to urge our citizens to place more bonds and mortgages with them by borrowing more of them; when even if a small portion of the principal and interest on those already placed were demanded, all the gold reserve in your national Treasury and national banks would be depleted, all that we have to construct a financial system upon, should we yield to the advocates of a gold standard. Such a course is liable to lead to complications and war with foreign powers, for if ever the American people come to the conclusion that they are being ground to nothingness under the shrewd and skillful manipulations of a moneyed clique, a period of revolution and repudiation will speedily follow, in which our country, while in a state of chaos and anarchy, will be humiliatingly forced to conciliate, or fight some foreign power demanding the return of principal with interest of the loans of its citizens to our Government and citizens. I believe in an American policy throughout our financial and economic legislation, and would take no note of the surplus foreign capital, even if their cities were walled in with it. In 1870 our gold was regarded only as commodity commanding a high price. In 1880 we had $255,695,779 of gold in circulation, and in 1890, $374,258,923—a slight increase during the ten years; but we observe that from 1887 to 1890 the amount of gold coin in circulation steadily decreased while the general stock that was coined or issued increased. During the same period the amount in the Treasury increased.

Debt and Mortgages

The census of 1890, in its investigation of ownership and debt, gives a clear idea of the burden that bears upon our farmers and upon the working class in general. In its investigation of mortgage indebtedness it shows clearly the advantages that the East has over the South and the West in obtaining and retaining loans; and a comparison of the rates of interest paid by the borrowers discloses the fact that for the last ten years money has been scarce and dear. Fifty-two and sixty-one-hundredths per cent of all the families in South Carolina are farmer families, and 61 per cent of all these hire the farms that give them bread. No State has yet been shown by the census statistics to have so high a percentage of tenancy as South Carolina. Upon the farms of that State there are liens amounting to $3,363,679, which is more than 50 per cent of their value; and this great mortgage debt bears an average rate of interest of 8.57 per cent; and each owned and encumbered farm is subject to an average debt of $930.

I appeal to the grand old party, which has always stood for what is greatest and best in freedom and progress, which has labored for the freedom of my race and has been loud in its protestations against its oppressors, to reflect before consigning us to the gold standard, for fear that in bearing us away from Scylla it may bear us upon Charybdis. The only difference between the physical and financial masters is that our personality was the property of the former, while our labor and production is the slave of the latter. The one was among us, the other at a distance. The former fed and clothed us, because we represented so much property; the latter cares little for our welfare, because their interest is in our personal and real property. Under certain conditions great real estate mortgages are signs of wealth, business, and prosperity. This is the case in rich New England, in busy New York, and in the Eastern States generally. Their interest is low and the life of their mortgage is long. When this is the case, mortgages show wealth in a section.

This is not true of my own state or of the South in general; nor is it true of the great West. In those two sections rates of interest are high, and men clamor to foreclose their mortgages on the poor farmer at the end of one or two years. The real fact is that money, like human beings, will not seek distant company as long as its pleasure is satiated at home. Our census special investigation has shown that capitalists in New England and the East allow mortgages to run and live for six, seven, and eight years. Why should I pay 8.57 percent interest in South Carolina and have my property sold for debt in a year or in two years, while the citizen of Massachusetts can borrow at 5½ per cent and is given six years in which to pay? If we turn to the State of Missouri, the great State represented by that gallant friend and champion of silver [Mr. Bland], we find in the last ten years that the people have been paying on their mortgage debt seventy-two different rates of interest, varying from 1 per cent up to 80. The poor hard-working class pays this interest. Now, why do I say this? The statistics show that 48 per cent of all the mortgages were for amounts of less than $500. Only the poor man, the toiling farmer, wants these little amounts to improve his property and to keep his business going.

In Arkansas twenty-five different rates of interest are recorded, for 1 percent up to 60 per cent. In Minnesota we find forty different rates, and there again we step from 1 percent to 80 per cent. In Indiana we find forty-three different rates-from 1 percent to 40 percent. Everything connected with our debt question shows that the South and West need more money. If I compare the farmer families of Massachusetts and those of South Carolina, I find that only 4.80 percent of those of Massachusetts have to pay interest greater than the State rate of 6 per cent. In South Carolina I find that 39.65 per cent of farmer families must pay more than 8 per cent on the money that they borrow in order that they might live. I have contrasted my own State with a rich Eastern State. What the South needs today is more money; there is coal beneath its surface, there is iron in the ribs of its mountains, and its fields can be made fertile and fruitful. We need some remedy for the ills that are now upon us. I do not speak alone for the South, today, but I plead for the half million idle men who are looking to us and begging to be allowed to dig in our mines, to plow our fields, to work in our shops and factories, and to have honest wages paid in honest dollar. Standing before you today, the lone spokesman for my race, I hear voices that you do not hear; I see faces that you cannot see. I have visited the farmer in his cabin; have tilled the soil and followed the furrow side by side with the humblest; I have spoken and discussed with the businessmen, and the ruling class of my State. I see their wants and I feel their needs, and every fiber of my body vibrates in sympathy with the people—the common people.

They call to us today for help; call from the mines that close them out and deny them bread; call from the factories that have hushed their busy hum, but have not stilled the cry of the child for bread. I shall be criticized for the stand which I have taken on this question, but as between the monopolist and the gold bugs on the one side and the common people on the other I stand with the people, feeling myself their creature and their servant and ready to do their bidding, especially while standing on one of the principal planks of my party in two national conventions, which indorsed the bimetallic standard and condemned the Democratic Party for the attempted demonetization of silver. I submit to gentlemen demanding the repeal of the purchasing clause of the silver-purchasing bill of 1890, as a means of relief to their constituency, unless some measure is coupled with it to bring relief to mine as well, whose business contraction has made a vast heap of ruin, I can never give it my approval. Outside of manufacturing institutions the industrial classes everywhere are justly dissatisfied.

The very employment of bankers, usurers, and speculators gives them an insight into the workings of financial institutions, which supplies them with offensive and defensive weapons, used and ready for use at all times, when their interests demand protection, while that of all other classes is such that they have little opportunity to learn anything of their operations, except their baneful effects upon their lives and property. Such is the case now, and while they do not understand the cause, they are beginning to attribute it to harmful legislation, for which they held the Republican party responsible last year; and if this Administration strikes down a protective tariff, and deny the laboring and producing millions better prices for their labor and products, through the medium of an enlarged currency, a political cyclone of such dimensions and power will sweep through the ranks of the Democratic party in 1896 that it will take a quarter of a century to get its broken and scattered fragments together. But our opponents contend that free coinage will only benefit the owners of silver mines and silver bullion. It seems to me that that proposition is fallacious, inasmuch as the increase of money in any one section of a country lessens its use in another, and tends to make it more plentiful everywhere. That system of finance that produces a small crop of millionaires and an abundant harvest of paupers is antagonistic to every principle of the religion of God, and to every form of republican government, and should, and ultimately will, be wiped from the face of this beautiful earth, in which the Creator decreed every individual the enjoyment of freedom and the full fruition of his labor.

As the price of everything that we own or produce, except gold, is so much in sympathy with that of silver that its ratio of increase or decrease is in almost exact proportion with the ratio of increase or decrease in the price of silver, a fall in the price of the latter commodity should be of alarming concern to all but owners of bonds and bank stock. If the ratio in the price of everything else keeps pace with the ratio in the fall off the price of silver when compared with gold, as has been the case for the past twenty years, and this Congress joins with England and Germany in the complete demonetization of silver, which must inevitably drop to some 30 to 40 cents per ounce, cotton will go at 4 cents per pound, and wheat at 35 cents per bushel. It does not take a prophet to foretell that revolution and repudiation will speedily follow. The South needs $400,000,000 of it each year to move her cotton crop alone, and billions more to build its much-needed manufactories, dilapidated cities and towns, and to bring into activity the inexhaustible resources of its soil, forests, and waters.

I am in favor of silver versus gold, because three-fourths of the people of the world who are not our competitors in manufactured and various other products use it, while those owning the gold of the world are our fiercest competitors, both in commerce and manufacture. The remonetization of silver means 10 instead of 7 cents for cotton, which in turn means $120,000,000 to the producers of cotton with which to lighten the great mountains of debt that are pressing the last drop of blood out of them. It means the appreciation of silver to such an extent that the government will realize the full amount of its investment in silver bullion. It means the payment of contracts in money of the same value as when the contracts were made. If we remonetize silver it will be worth more in our market than those of demonetized England and Germany, and the money of Mexico, Central America, all South America, India, China, and Russia, being worth more in our markets than theirs, will find investment here and make our manufacturers and producers masters of the commercial situation. New York, and not London, will speedily become the great commercial mart of the world. Our competitors will either have to close a part of their industrial establishments or hurriedly follow us in the remonetization of silver. I shall vote for the free and unlimited coinage of silver, because I am for the betterment of the miserable condition of my countrymen, and for America first and the entire world afterwards.

This question, like the great question of abolitionism, which made new converts among honest men everywhere it was studied in the light of truth, until it resulted in a tidal wave of freedom, is beginning to be discussed in every cabin and hovel, as well as mansion and palace, and the history of this country furnishes abundant evidence of the fact that when the people become alive to their interests on any subject they will rise in their manhood and vote or shoot down any man or party who would strike down their property or liberty. I adjure you who are in favor of doing something to help the masses sometimes, instead of the classes always, not to be coerced or flattered into submission, but trust in the righteousness of God and the patriotism of the American people, and the day will come when you will be as proud as Abraham Lincoln was when the Stars and Stripes again floated from the parapet of Fort Sumter.

I call upon the Democratic party, which claims to be of and for the masses, to show its colors now, while laboring under the greatest responsibility that it has carried in thirty-odd years, before it is eternally too late. I call upon the Republican party, founded upon the bedrock of human freedom, which had inscribed in letters of living light in its initial banner, unrestricted human rights and equality before the law: every deviation from which principles marks its failure to remember the pristine valor of its heroes and martyrs, and assume the cause of the masses in this struggle, and the white angel of hope and victory will hover over our camp, exhibiting the pillar of cloud by day and fire by night that will inevitably lead us from one victory to another until our victorious campfires shall keep burning in every State from the Lakes to the Gulf, from the Atlantic to the Pacific. In the words of Lord Chatham, if I were an Englishman, as I am an American, I would never cease war until every creature in every land should bow to the golden calf that was erected by and sustains and maintains the honor and glory of my country.

Murray charged that state leaders were using a variety of methods to disenfranchise black voters. While southern whites argued that African Americans were pleased with their representatives and re-elected them, Murray believed that the elections were fraudulent. He argued that qualified black voters were often not given the opportunity to register to vote. Murray complained that such practices obviously violated federal law.

ELECTION LAWS
October 5, 1893

While I do not think it becoming in any public man to take notice of all the pusillanimous charges against his ability, integrity, or honesty on the part of irresponsible persons, I do not think that I would either be doing justice to myself or constituents to allow the charge, made by one of my colleagues from my own State during my remarks on yesterday, that I was delivering the productions of another party to remain unanswered. In reply, I will state that I neither think that another can express my sentiments as well as myself, nor find space to quote very largely from the productions of others. I do not think that the alleged imputation comes from my friend with good grace, who has so recently suffered from similar misrepresentations, being charged by the local press with quoting in a recent speech in this House from the late Henry W. Grady without giving due credit. The descriptions given of the wild scrambles and sacrifices made for homes when a Government reservation is opened up to settlement are the only parallels of the scenes around the offices of the supervisors of registration in South Carolina in the year 1882, and I call on angels and men to witness the great outrage upon the boasted citizenship of America when the guardians of liberty, joining in with the enemies of their wards, would strike down the walls of protection instead of strengthening their weak places.

What honest man would knowingly vote to dispense with officers proven so useful and necessary in aiding citizens to become qualified as these Federal supervisors? Though section 6 of the election laws of South Carolina requires the supervisors of registration to open their offices for the purpose of issuing, renewing, and making transfers of certificates of registration on the first Monday in each month after each election, to and including the first Monday in July preceding the next election, in mine and neighboring counties, and I believe, upon information received, throughout the State, they have failed to follow these directions since the control of the present Administration. The practice heretofore has been to open the offices of registration only in election years, beginning with the first Monday in January and ending with the first Monday in July, thereby cheating the electors out of thirteen of the twenty days allowed by law between the periods of election.

As precinct and county chairman of my party during nearly the entire period covered by the present registration and election laws in my State, which required my presence and active participation in all the registrations and elections during the period, which afforded my exceptional opportunities to become acquainted with all the practices, methods, and manners current in them, in the presence of God and this Congress, I declare to you and the people of America, that no gambler nor conjurer has ever planned more or meaner tricks and schemes to beat his competitor or victimize his companion than have been used by the sworn officers of the law to deceive American citizens (if there be any) in the qualification of the right of franchise, or to destroy the effectiveness of their votes on election day. With nearly four-fifths of the electors disfranchised through such methods as I have outlined in the conduct of registration, and with the wrongdoers derisively jeering and laughing in the faces of the openly and intentionally disfranchised citizens, in plain violation of all constitutional and statutory laws, both local and Federal, the Southern press is wont to answer the question as to why the Southern vote is always so small by a repetition of the old worn-out answer that the Negroes are so well pleased with the government that they do not try to vote. There is a wonderful change for the better in many respects under the present administration is South Carolina; but, actuated as it has shown itself to be by lofty patriotism and a desire to right many of the prevailing wrongs, you shall have destroyed half of its safeguards should you annul the Federal election laws, for with one or two rare exceptions custom has made it an unwritten law during the past twelve years for the governor to appoint only his partisans as commissioners of election, who in turn appoint the same class managers of elections which denies the opposition, of whatever kind of class, the right of any witness within the election booths.

In the conduct of elections the managers have been known to put a number of ballots for the candidates of their partisans into the ballot boxes before the opening of the polls, to make out fraudulent poll lists accounting for the same, to deny persons legally qualified the right to vote, to tamper with the labels on the ballot boxes, to obstruct or allow the obstruction of the way into the election booths, to vote nonqualified partisans, to put false votes into the ballot box intermittently during the entire period of voting, and at the close of the polls on the second count when the first votes have been found in the box in excess of the names on the poll lists, by putting the votes of their partisans to the bottom and those of their opponents on top, to draw out the legal ballots of their opponents and count the fraudulent ballots of their partisans in their stead, thereby giving their partisans a majority instead of a minority.

I submit that the Federal supervisors act as a check on all such malpractices, but, mark you, only as a check. Armed with their commissions, instructions, and blank poll lists they enter the election booths. Before the voting begins they have the ballot boxes opened for inspection, to see that they are clear of everything. Mark "the outs" can only do this under federal, not state control, notwithstanding the practice of placing bundles of partisan ballots in the boxes previous to voting as has been so largely advertised. They secure positions as near to the ballot boxes as possible, and arrange for keeping their poll lists, which fact impairs their scrutiny very much, but which they are forced to do themselves, as they are not allowed to carry assistance into the booths. It may be observed that the managers generally arrange to throw the supervisors of opposing political views as far from the ballot boxes as possible. The supervisors of opposing political views to the managers, without leaving the polls, unless permitted to substitute a man of their own selection, remain in their places and watch the conduct of the elections during their entire periods. At their posts of duty, they protest here, correct there, challenge in another place, threaten to report when forced to do so, until the polls are closed, votes counted, and returns made. Sometimes they report managers for opening the polls too early or too late or closing them during the election, each one of which practices has been regarded by the county and State boards of review as sufficient cause to throw the returns, where they occur, out of the count.

Time fails me to enumerate the many ways in which their presence prevents the violation or evasion of the law, but suffice it to say, humble though they be, armed with the authority of this great government, for which even erring managers of elections have not quite lost all respect and fear, they exercise a wonderful influence in the interest of fair play and honest elections. These supervisors, representing both parties, generally perform their duties pleasantly together, at times even aid each other in keeping their poll lists, and at the close of the elections sign each others' returns, when in their judgment the election has been free and fair, and their returns similar. What honest man can object to the appointment of officers aiding so materially in efforts to have free and fair elections? This is the most insidious and diabolical bill that has been reported by a committee of this House in thirty years. It strikes at the very root of popular government, inasmuch as it seeks to destroy the very arms by which the nation can protect its rights and citizenship. It truly appears that every man who votes for this bill has entered into a conspiracy with ballot-box stuffers, perjurers, and murderers, whom he has promised to shield by destroying the light by which their deeds are exposed.

I appeal to all honest and brave men from the South, to look beyond the dim political present into the buoyant hopeful future, when advancing civilization and Christianity, annihilating ignorance and wrong, will cause all men to appear in their true light, and to ponder long and earnestly before voting for this bill, which must have been conceived in sin and born in iniquity. I appeal especially to my colleagues, all of whom are respectful, generous, and magnanimous men, to give no aid and comfort to this measure. I appeal to Northern Democrats, who are free from some strong influences which force some honest and true men from other sections to support this measure, and who partially acquired their seats by the votes of black men, not to give aid and comfort to this unholy, but yet legitimate offspring of State sovereignty. I appeal to the Populists from the great West, who claim their mission to be the freedom of the human family, not only from financial but industrial and political slavery, to give no aid in untying the hands of the ballot-box stuffer and election conjurer, for he will nip in the bud the beautiful plants now budding and blooming in their hopeful fields of the South, where in time they will secure their greatest strength.

I appeal to Republicans from everywhere, standing true to the principles of Sumner, Seward, Lincoln, and Grant, the great saints of the grand old party, to resist this nefarious measure with all their power and resources; and though for the time being the banner of their party—always a bow of promise, leading the advancing columns of civilization and progress from the dark, gloomy, despondent period of the greatest rebellion of authentic history for thirty years to a position that challenges the admiration of the world—may trail in the dust, as sure as God and truth live, the nation witnessing its own stultification, embarrassment, and confusion, brought on by the lowering of that banner, will triumphantly raise it again, and march to its destined haven of freedom, citizenship, prosperity, and victory. To further illustrate the harm that is being wrought on a majority of the electors in some sections of the country, and incidentally on those of the whole country, as regards the suffrage, let us compare the votes cast in the last congressional election in three Southern States with those in three Northern or Western States having approximately the same representation on this floor.

I have selected for this illustration the States of South Carolina, Louisiana, and Mississippi in the South, and Minnesota, Kansas, and California in the West. The three former States, with a nominal voting population of 711,867, in the last Congressional election cast only 213,603 votes; while the latter three, with a nominal voting population of 787,510, cast at the same time 767,265 votes. In comparing the votes in certain districts of South Carolina or Mississippi with those in certain districts of Kansas or Minnesota, the results are still more startling. The Seventh District of South Carolina, which I have the honor to represent, has a nominal voting population of 43,300, and cast and had counted in the last election only 9,995 votes; while the First District of Minnesota, with a nominal voting population of only 37,100, cast and had counted 35,774 votes. Again, the Third District of Mississippi, with a nominal voting population of 36,800, cast and had counted only 2,654 votes, while the Sixth District of Kansas, with a nominal voting population of 35,800, cast and had counted 38,916 votes. When it is asked what caused this state of affairs, in which such a disparity between the votes of different sections could exist, the answer of modest apologists is that the people of the South are so satisfied with the Government that they do not care to vote, while that of the bold annihilator of the elective franchise is that it means white supremacy or a rule of intelligence. I desire it to be distinctly understood that I am not here to apologize for the rule of ignorance but I do claim that when the condition of suffrage is fixed by national and local law, that every citizen, irrespective of race or color, should be held strictly to the gauge of franchise. Neither of the two reasons stated above is tenable, for it is seen that the total vote cast in the three southern States in the above comparison is far below the total nominal white voting population.

Again, if the suffrage is based upon intelligence, there is still too great a disparity between the votes cast in the two sections; for deducting the number of notes representing the percentage of illiteracy from the nominal voting population in the three Western States, leaves us a nominal voting population of 740,250, and there were actually cast in the last election 767,265 votes; while, after deducting the number of votes represented by illiteracy in the three Southern States from the nominal voting population, we have still a voting population of 348,782, casting only 213,605 votes in the late election. In the nominal voting population based upon intelligence, we still have a discrepancy of 145,000 votes in the three Southern States, and an excess of 25,000 votes in the three Western

States. The suffrage is not only denied colored men, but in some sections white men, differing from the Administration's party, knowing that their votes will not be counted as cast, remain away from the polls. I submit that as long as such conditions obtained in those laws should remain, so that white as well as black men lose confidence in the fairness and integrity of local governments they can invoke the majesty of their chief Government. In our form of government there can of right be nothing but a manhood suffrage; for, as the voters are the rulers and by their votes they protect their lives and property, persons denied the suffrage are in some respects worse off than slaves, because they are permitted to live and hold property simply by sufferance, while even a slave's master's ballot protects him. I would commend to the careful consideration of the gentleman from Illinois [Mr. Black] the foregoing comparisons of the votes in the different States and districts compared, as he, during his remarks upon this bill, boastfully flaunted the great Democratic majority in the late elections in the face of the minority.

I earnestly beseech him to put his hand on his troubled heart and go to his God in prayer and ask Him what would that majority be if the voters of the South had been allowed the same freedom to vote, and honesty in the count, as those of the North and West. He said that his party got over "6,611,00 votes in the recent election, a majority of a million and a quarter in favor of the repeal of this bill." Again, he asserted that the Populists united with the Democratic Party on this issue, which I respectfully deny, so far as the South is concerned. While the Populists of the West, without knowledge of the true condition of affairs in the entire country, might have joined in this demand for the repeal of these most important of all laws on the Federal statute books, those of the South did not; for, in the State of Alabama and elsewhere, they asked for the enforcement of these very laws, to enable them to have some friend, at least, at the Federal polls to see what would become of their votes. Now, it is preposterous to say that these people voted for the destruction of laws that they regarded as their only safeguard at the time of voting.

Before boasting again, I would suggest that he examine the returns of thirteen States counted for his party, Maryland, Virginia, West Virginia, North Carolina, South Carolina, Georgia, Florida, Tennessee, Alabama, Mississippi, Louisiana, Texas, and Arkansas, which with a nominal voting population of 3,874,017 counted only 2,679,800 votes in the recent election. Can the gentleman say for whom the 1,200,000 suppressed votes would have been cast? Now, if the gentleman will add to these 1,200,000 suppressed votes those of the People's party of the South, he will discover that his million and a quarter majority will vanish away into a minority of several thousand less than the majority of the defeated party. I certainly admire the Democratic party in one respect. It has made the road to the ballot box for all its adherents throughout the length and breadth of this country as free from obstruction as the path to Hades, but the way there for the adherent of any other party in sections of this country is as rugged and dangerous as the road to Heaven. The gentleman from Illinois further said "that these laws were intended to benefit only the most ignorant class of all American citizens." The assertion is erroneous. A man brought up under the inspiration of American institutions, even devoid of theoretical education, is better prepared and entitled to vote than the alien, ignorant alike of our language and our institutions, fresh from some foreign land, who is hurriedly made a citizen and permitted to vote without question. There is another important feature involved in the question of suffrage that should find more play in the patriotism and devotion of the American people than any other: the right of those who are taxed to be represented.

According to the late census returns the black men of the State of South Carolina pay taxes on more than $12,000,000 of property, which is about one-thirteenth of the taxable property of the State, and those of the entire country own $265,000,000. When this country was a mere suckling babe they fought the Seven Years War with the mother country for taxing the colonies without allowing them representation, at the end of which victory perched upon its banner. American orators in words that burned said "that taxation without representation is tyranny." How unjust it is to deny others the right you claim for yourself. But, regardless of the fact that we of right have been citizens of the country from its birth; that our forefathers joined with yours in making it what it is; that we have aided in winning every battle celebrated in this same history: that we are taxed to support this Government, and that in hours of danger we are required to stand between it and the guns of its enemies in obedience to the wish of the friends of this iniquitous measure, ascending the mound beneath which are buried not only the fetters and liberty of more than six million black people, but the heroes and martyrs who died to strike off their shackles, I request you to let those laws remain for the sake of white men in opposition to the local administration parties in the South.

With the picture and history of many brave and true men who have died in defense of right fresh on my memory, I could paint a picture from which all patriots and Christians would turn in sorrow and shame; but, letting the curtain of silence fall over the scene, and the tears of their orphans and widows keep the grass moistened and green on their graves, and turning to the hopeful future, I beg all true men to forget party and partisanship and right the great wrongs perpetrated upon humble and unoffending American citizens. With all the local governments in the hands of white men—and black men have scarcely any participation in them in any way—there are those who have the brazen effrontery to request the repeal of these laws in the interest of white supremacy. What a monstrous proposition! Oh, boasted religion of God, guardian angel of liberty and humanity, that teaches men to do as they would be done by, whither hast thou departed? We need thy presence and wonderful influence. I declare that no class of people has ever been more misrepresented, slandered, and traduced than the black people of the South. Judged in the light of the religion of God, which teaches obedience to law, forgiveness of wrongs, and charity to all, you would search in vain to find a class of people more submissive to law, more forgetful of wrong and more charitable to all men than they. But, whenever robbery, perjury, and murder are sought to be justified the old familiar hymn, sweet to the ears of misanthropists of Negro domination, is chanted, and large sections of the press of the country join in the song, and we stand helpless and amazed. I declare that the patient, long-suffering, generous black man has never attempted to domineer anywhere in this country.

At the very dawn of freedom, when the refusal to act on the part of the master class placed the reins of Government in his hands with only a handful of white men in his party, he gave nearly every position of honor and emolument to them, and there are numerous instances where, when there were not enough white men belonging to his party to fill the offices, he even elected Democrats rather than appear to dominate the white race. Even now, ruthlessly stripped as he is of almost all participation in the government of his State and country, with only the shadow of the party of his choice left in his section, and with still a handful of white men among hundreds of thousands of black men, many of whom are fitted to fill almost any position in the gift of the nation, he almost uniformly gives the places of honor to that handful of white men. Yet gentlemen, with these facts staring them in the face, talk to this House of Negro domination. I assert without fear of successful contradiction that the black man is generally the most law-abiding citizen in America. He is required and does obey the laws in the strictest sense, while white men in many parts of this country, regardless of the Constitution and laws, are obeying the only king that has ruled among savages in the history of the world, public opinion. Whenever public opinion is stronger than written law then you have a sign of the weakening of civilization. What more can savages do than make and execute their laws at the same time for every emergency?

I would remind my colleagues of the South of the fact that when their State governments were in the hands of black men, in peace and war their friends, and they were backed by the strong arm of the National Government, not yet forgetful of the services they rendered in saving its life, that they met them everywhere; and in the sweet tongue of a flirting maiden persuaded them to vote for them and to place the governments in their hands, and promised them that their rights should be ever sacredly guarded in their care and keeping. You said that they were your brothers and that you wanted them to join with you not only in building up the waste places of the South, but in making the governments what they should be. Many believed and aided you in obtaining control, and how have your promises been kept?

Let the hundreds and thousands of their number be disfranchised, and the almost daily occurrence of the savage and diabolical murders in the very hands of the law testify. Having by foul means driven them from almost all participation in the government of their State and country, and having fooled and flattered them in the States where they could vote, and have their votes counted as cast, to aid you in obtaining control of the Federal Government, some of you are heartless enough to propose and press the passage of this bill, which does not only complete the destruction of their political liberty, but is a real step in the direction of the abrogation of the Thirteenth, Fourteenth, and Fifteenth Amendments.

I request my people everywhere to take the roll when it shall have been called on the passage of this bill, mark the name of every man casting an affirmative vote, and regard him as their perpetual enemy. I further request that precious care be taken of that roll, and after nominating conventions in their localities everywhere to compare it with the ticket nominated, and if it contains the names of any man who shall vote for this bill, use all means to defeat it. But even if you repeal these laws, I do not despair. The tardy vengeance of God will sooner or later overtake you. The same omnipotent power that heard the prayers and groans of black fathers and mothers away down in the valleys of the cotton and rice fields and brought awful retribution upon you for the wrongs committed upon a helpless people, by arraying one section of this country against the other in a disastrous war, is not asleep, and those suffering people are still praying. While I cannot persuade myself that there can be found there and in the Senate enough cruel and wicked men to make this law effective, still if I am disappointed in that, I still indulge the hope that this bill will never become law.

I hope that that broad-soul and philanthropic man occupying the Executive chair is too brave and humane to join in this cowardly onslaught to strike down the walls impaling the last vestige of liberty to a helpless class of people. I know that the Charles Sumners, John Logans, Abraham Lincolns, Thomas Jeffersons, Ulysses Grants, and Roscoe Conklings are dead and sleeping beside the liberty of a class of their countrymen in whose behalf they have spoken and labored, and I do not despair.

13

Charles Edmund Nash
(1844–1913)
House of Representatives, Louisiana

Republican

Forty-fourth Congress
March 4, 1875, to March 3, 1877

Charles Edmund Nash was born free on May 23, 1844, in Opelousas, Louisiana. He was educated in the public schools for free blacks, and took up a trade as a bricklayer. When the Union army opened its ranks to African Americans in 1863, Nash enlisted as a private in the Eighty-second Regiment, United States Volunteers. By the end of the Civil War he had reached the rank of sergeant major. Nash was engaged in many battles during his tour of duty, and sustained a serious injury to his right leg at the battle of Fort Blakely in Alabama.

Like most African Americans, Charles Edmund Nash considered the Republican party his emancipator and defender. His interest in Republican politics continued after the war, and he landed an appointment as a U.S. customs inspector in New Orleans in 1869. He also drew the attention of Republicans who agreed to give blacks a token representation in Congress. Indeed, Louisiana had a black majority, but it would never develop into a political force as it had in South Carolina. Louisiana, therefore, elected only one black representative— Nash—during Reconstruction. Black Republican Pinckney B.S. Pinchback came close to winning a seat in the national Senate but he lost in an election contest to a Democratic rival. So Charles Edmund Nash was the lone African American to represent his state in Washington during an era of black political involvement in state and national politics.

Nash served one term in the House of Representatives, and was appointed to the Committee on Education and Labor. He was not a skilled orator, as were many of his black colleagues. He wielded little influence in Congress. Nash did stand out in one respect. The House leadership initially refused to allow black members to address the assembly. Any remarks they made were printed in the appendix of the journal. Nash objected to this practice, explaining that he wanted his remarks heard, not read. The House granted his request, and Nash made a few speeches from the floor. He praised the Republican party for emancipating the slaves and providing rights. In his speeches he particularly defended civil rights legislation and promoted public education for all people. He also proposed a bill to authorize a survey of the Courtableau Bayou in Louisiana. Upon completion of his term Nash made an unsuccessful bid for reelection in 1876. He then accepted an appointment in the U.S. postal service to round out his career in public service.

Upon his retirement Nash returned to Louisiana to resume masonry work. His trade as a bricklayer was hard physical work, and he soon discovered that the injuries from war made it too difficult for him. As his health grew progressively worse, he opened a cigar shop in New Orleans. Nash died there on June 21, 1913, a few weeks past his sixty-ninth birthday.

Following speeches of Democratic congressmen who made scathing comments about blacks, Nash admitted to them that he was an inexperienced speaker. Yet, he could not allow their remarks to go unchallenged. He reminded them that the Republican party had enfranchised blacks in order to restore the Union. Nash argued that had southern whites approved Congressional Reconstruction, Republicans would have not granted black suffrage. In addition, Nash objected to the notion that black Republicans were corrupt. He pointed out that critics of black politicians were too quick to label them as incompetent and unethical.

POLITICAL CONDITION OF THE SOUTH
June 7, 1876

It was not my purpose to crave the indulgence of the House during the present session, in view of my inexperience in public legislation, and especially in public speaking, but the recent speech of the honorable member from North Carolina [Jesse J. Yeates] is such an extraordinary production in its reflections upon the State government of Louisiana and the character of many of its citizens that I feel that I would be false to my public trust were I to remain silent and fail to refute the many glaring misrepresentations of the distinguished gentleman's production. The gentleman from North Carolina has given the caption to his speech, "Economy, Retrenchment, and Reform," and the House now being in committee of the whole on the state of the Union I shall follow with a like caption as the text for my remarks.

Now, General James Longstreet needs no defense at my hands, being a representative man of that class of our reconstructed citizens who immediately after the close of hostilities patriotically came to the front, accepted the situation, put their shoulders to the burdens and responsibilities of bringing order out of chaos by reestablishing the practical relations of the insurrectionary States and the people to the Federal Government. He had political sagacity and independence of character to be among the advanced guards in this patriotic labor of reconstruction. The Democratic party in like spirit and for like purposes as evidenced by the remarks of the gentleman from North Carolina, have made General Longstreet a target of their displeasure and attack. The gentleman admits that General Longstreet performed valiant services for the Confederacy, and I will tell him that he has done equal service for the reconstruction of the Federal Union; and I do not understand why he should be specially assaulted for the performance of his duties as a citizen. But it seems the special pleasure of the Democratic party to assault the character and impugn the motives of all white men who act in concert with the policy of the Republican party in the Southern States, as well as to doubt the integrity and ability of the few colored men called to the performance of the public trusts therein.

So, in due course, when they could not get our votes then they turned the colored people loose and let them vote. What else did they do? They multiplied offices and filled those offices with ten thousand carpetbaggers, who came down and prejudiced the colored people against us. They poisoned the minds of the colored people; they left the country a howling waste and wilderness; they destroyed liberty in Louisiana and in all the States where they had the power to do it. I am willing to admit with this gentleman that the colored race owe their freedom rather to the providence of Almighty God, who took His own good time and adopted His own means to accomplish this great result, than to any party. Being one of that proscribed race which has been benefited by the results of the War of the Rebellion in the providence of God, I take this occasion to publicly offer up my thanksgiving and heartfelt prayer of gratitude to Him who is the Giver of all good for the emancipation of my race in view of the anticipated future which I trust awaits them as citizens of this Republic. I cannot agree with the gentleman in that portion of his speech where he announces that the colored race owes nothing to the Republican party for the enjoyment of the political rights conferred upon us.

I may be no historian, but this much of history I do know, because I have been an actor in its scenes. Let me remind the gentleman what the Democratic party has done for us in the past. When the Thirteenth Amendment, abolishing slavery, was proposed, the Democratic party, both in Congress and throughout the country, opposed it; when the Fourteenth Amendment was proposed the Democratic party opposed it; when the Fifteenth Amendment was proposed the Democratic party, with a vehemence only equal to its assaults upon the life of the nation, opposed it. Why, when arming the Negroes was proposed, the Democratic party opposed it; when paying pensions to Negroes was proposed, the Democratic party opposed it; when giving the right of suffrage to the colored people of the District of Columbia was proposed as an experiment, the Democratic party came forward with its usual philanthropy and opposed it.

Now, tell me where any measure of constitutional law or general legislation has been proposed or enacted for the benefit of the emancipated black race which the Democratic party had not strenuously opposed; and, not satisfied after the popular verdict had been rendered in favor of the rights which we have thus far secured, this same Democratic party in the South, encouraged and backed by its brethren of the North, has kept a continual warfare upon the advancement, peace, and prosperity of our people. Therefore, I propose to give a timely warning to these stirrers up of strife, of what they may expect if they continue this war of races. It is not difficult to comprehend the effect of a combination like that named by Pinckney B.S. Pinchback. When it shall be made, if it ever shall be, the day will be a sorry one for southern society. So far it has been for the interests of the ruffians and outlaws of the South to work with the white-leaguer. But the moment the scramble for spoils shall have fairly commenced there will be a division, and in that division white respectability must be re-enforced by colored decency or the cotton States will be handed over to a rule as shameless and scandalous as the imagination can conceive. There has been a great deal of opposition manifested by the native southern whites to the education of the colored people.

Wherever the republicans have had control, as in Texas, Louisiana, and Mississippi, a system of schools has been put in operation that would have honored the New England States themselves. But the moment any of them fall into the hands of the democracy, that moment public education meets with discouragement. This is such egregious folly that it is surprising that the people of the South do not see it. The danger to that section is and has been in the ignorance of the masses. Designing demagogues can influence the uneducated and thus direct their ends; if intelligence were universal, any combination of vice and ignorance would be impossible. Let the South realize this fact and encourage popular education. The race issue is the issue of ignorance. Education dispels narrow prejudices as the sun dispels the noxious vapors of the night. The South needs more and better schools than the North, for she has a wider field for them.

Not only has she a large colored population groveling in the dust of intellectual squalor, but also a majority of her white citizens are without the facilities for mental improvement. Let a spirit of progress in this respect be manifested, and the southern people will find the North giving them a helping hand and bidding them Godspeed in the work.

There are other portions of the gentleman's speech that I might take notice of, but I hardly deem it necessary, inasmuch as I have already noticed those parts of it, which apply more particularly to the interests and people of my State. As to a defense of the whole Republican party, which he has seen fit to arraign, there need little be said. We have before us today a living and useful illustration of the wise forethought and broad philanthropy of the men of 1776. Today it is the boast of the Republican party that every man born in this country or naturalized, no matter what his condition in life, his race, or color, is an American citizen, and, as such, is entitled to equal rights before the law, and to a participation in the elective franchise. The Republican party, which has achieved much for the country, has wrought no greater work than this. It is a proud day for us. Although we have passed through a sanguinary struggle in which thousands of our brave and patriotic citizens have yielded up their lives, yet we cannot lose sight of the fact that at the close of the conflict the immortal principles so happily announced in the Declaration of Independence have not only been preserved, but have grown into practical and living reality. This is the essential creed of the Republican party.

It is true we have not yet seen unqualified acquiescence in this grand result on the part of our democratic fellow-citizens, but the time is not far distant when even the people of the South must lay aside the prejudices engendered by the late war, and accept in its fullest sense the freedom of citizenship and equality before the law of all men. Democratic conventions may be silent on this subject, and a democratic House may be criminally neglectful of its highest duty; the people themselves may be misled and deceived by political leaders; the "still, small voice" of reason may be hushed and silenced by the turbulent passions of the hour, yet the day is not far distant when this underlying principle of the Republican party will be fully acknowledge and accepted by all the people. When this shall be done, the first great purpose of the Republican party will have been accomplished; and it will then be the duty on that party to preserve intact its own great power.

The mission of the Republican party is not yet ended. The loyal people of this country, who preserved the Government in war and have maintained its honor in peace, are not yet ready to hand it over to the party that conspired to destroy it and has resisted every effort to make it indestructible. At no time in our history has the cause of civil and religious liberty made such progress as in this decade under the fostering care of the Republican party. In giving freedom with civil and political rights to one race it has not been unmindful of the rights and liberties of the other. The same constitutional provision that gave freedom to the black man makes it forever impossible to enslave any portion of the white race. The citizenship secured by the fourteenth article of amendment to all persons born or naturalized in the United States applies alike to all persons, rich and poor, white and black. The inhibition upon the States to make or enforce any law which shall abridge the privileges or immunities of the citizens of the United States, or to deprive any person of life, liberty, or property without due process of law, or to deny to any person within their jurisdiction the equal protection of the laws, is a bulwark of safety to every citizen and a protection against the oppressors that might otherwise be created by sectional jealously or local hate. All these constitutional provisions were passed in the interest of personal liberty and individual security. The love of liberty is inherent in human nature. It may be stifled, but not without much difficulty. Whenever it is not gratified there is danger to the state. Gratify it and you insure the safety of society. Neither these constitutional provisions nor any statute passed in conjunction with them oppresses or harms any human being. A government that cannot protect its humblest citizens from outrage and injury is unworthy of the name and ought not to command the support of a free people.

These are the works of the great Republican party of the nation, which saved the country in war and is able to preserve it in peace. This is the party that must control the destinies of this free country for years to come. The awful scenes of the late war are passed, and forever. The battle cry is no longer sounded; war's thunderclouds have rolled muttering away, and the skies are bright after the storm. The heroes of one side are sleeping side by side with those whom they withstood in battle, and they sleep in peace. The grave has closed over their animosities and a truce has been proclaimed between them forever. Let the living strike hands also, for we are not enemies but brethren. A man with the noblest instincts may succumb to a temporary madness, but he is nevertheless a man, and when the cloud has passed away he is to be restored to a man's loves and rights and privileges. Brother, late our foe in battle but our brother still, this country is our joint inheritance, this flag has always been our joint banner. The glories of our past belong to both of us.

This purified land, this great, united people, these broad acres stretching from ocean to ocean, yet bound by the cord of commerce, which makes of oceans near neighbors and of mountains level plains—this boundless wealth, this tireless energy, this hunger for progress, this thirst for knowledge—it is yours, it is ours, and no power can despoil us of it. We alone by our dissension can destroy this rich inheritance. Over brothers' graves let brothers' quarrels die. Let there be peace between us, that these swords, which we have learned to use so well, may if used again strike only at a common foe. Let us sing anthems of peace; let the song be taken up throughout the land; by the shores of the great lakes, by the waters of the Gulf, in the land of the loom and spindle, in the land of gold, on broad prairies, on sunny savannas, let the chorus again and again break forth, "Peace on earth, good will toward men." We have had enough war. Too many widows' weeds are scattered in this land; too many orphan children are gazing upon and lamenting the past. It was a just and righteous war, bravely fought and nobly won. Thank God it is over; and let us hope it will be revived only in memory.

I think the time has arrived for the ravages of this war to entirely disappear. Where any turbulent elements still exist the law should have its just sway, however much we may dread such necessities. And unto every citizen is there a duty assigned. As to what that is no honest patriot can doubt. The elimination of bias and bigotry and the general education of the high and low of every section will be found to be the true source of our national prosperity; and as the mind is expanded, reason will come forth from the dark obscurity of ignorance to balance with a nice hand the scales of justice.

America will not die. As the time demands them great men will appear, and by their combined efforts render liberty and happiness more secure. The people will be ready and answer in every emergency that may arise. If they have been able to direct and manage affairs wisely in the past, how much additional power will they have in the future with which to mold and invigorate the mighty fabric of the Republic. The union of national prosperity with social harmony, which is sure to come, will be indicated by one rapid reconstruction. Wisdom and knowledge from their highest pinnacles must no longer view the progress of national greatness, but its perfection. From Maine to Alaska will resound the shouts of rejoicing that will arise from millions of intelligent and happy freemen. With such watchwords as freedom, equality, and fraternity no factor of discord will be apparent. The seed has been sown and the harvest shall be reaped, and such a one as has never been known before in the history of nations—a harvest of peace, prosperity, and virtue.

But before this millennium dawns there will be still much to accomplish. However, we may comfort ourselves with the reflection that the path of virtue is sometimes dark; if we follow it steadily difficulties and embarrassments will melt away. The cloud will one day roll off, and the bow of hope and promise will be found in its place. Let us surrender no vital principle; neither let us waste precious time in the idle discussion of obsolete issues. The policy to be adopted must be one that will build up our waste places, cover our broad acres with waving grain, send our ships into every sea, start out factories, bridge out streams, and make the hum of industry resound on all sides. Let us go on as an orderly, law-abiding people, and wait patiently for the time when the reward cometh; for the time when a sense of justice shall once more animate the hearts of all, and malice and hate shall give place to brotherly love.

14

James Edward O'Hara
(1844–1905)
House of Representatives, North
Carolina

Republican

Forty-eighth and Forty-ninth Congresses
March 4, 1883, to March 3, 1887

James Edward O'Hara was born free in New York City on February 26, 1844. He was the son of an Irish merchant and a West Indian mother. Soon after James was born his parents left the United States and returned to the West Indies to raise their children. James returned to New York with his parents during the 1850s, and later joined missionaries who went to North Carolina to teach. James visited the camps of African Americans who had fled the plantation, and dedicated himself to their causes, as well as to his own educational development. O'Hara studied law temporarily at Howard University, and completed an apprenticeship in law in North Carolina. He passed the North Carolina bar examination in 1871, and opened a law office in Enfield. His association with officers in the Union Army in North Carolina led him into Reconstruction politics.

O'Hara's first significant political activity came in 1866 when he was appointed secretary of the North Carolina Colored Convention in Raleigh. In 1867, he attended the first state convention of the Republican party, setting the stage for his election to the state constitutional convention in 1868, where he served not only as a delegate but also as its secretary. After the convention, O'Hara was elected to the state legislature. In 1873 he was elected chairman of the Halifax County Board of Commissioners. Two years later he returned as a delegate to a new state constitutional convention. In addition to his interest in politics, he was involved in a number of causes to further the progress of African Americans in North Carolina. He was a leader in the Freedmen's Educational Association, and he supported civil rights reform.

James Edward O'Hara lost the 1874 Republican nomination for Congress to John A. Hyman, who was also a black politician. Undaunted, he launched the next campaign, this time winning the nomination in 1878, only to lose the election to William Hodges Kitchin, a white Democrat. O'Hara lodged a complaint against Kitchin, alleging election fraud, but he also lost the contest. During the campaign Republicans and Democrats made unflattering remarks about his character, such as accusing O'Hara of bigamy. Democrats also asserted that O'Hara was not a citizen of the United States, claiming instead that he was a native of the Virgin Islands. O'Hara admitted that he had applied to become a naturalized citizen but withdrew the application when he learned that he had actually been born in New York City before his parents relocated to the West Indies. Finally in 1882, he prevailed in the election, beating his Democratic rival by over 18,000 votes. O'Hara took his seat in Congress as the representative from the Second District of North Carolina on March 4, 1883.

By the 1880s, North Carolina, and the rest of the South, had virtually, though not yet legally, disenfranchised black voters. Hence, black politicians stood little chance of success at the polls. O'Hara, for example, was the only black congressman at the beginning of this decade until 1884, when Robert Smalls was elected from South Carolina. O'Hara won reelection that year, defeating Democratic candidate Frederick A. Woodward. He served on various committees, including Invalid Pensions, Mines and Mining, and Expenditures on Public Buildings. He wrote a bill calling for special commendations for Robert Smalls, who during the Civil War had commandeered the *Planter*, a Confederate vessel, and then sailed it to the Union side. O'Hara urged the House to continue the pension that had been given to Smalls and his crew. While a House committee looked favorably upon the bill, the measure never reached the floor for consideration.

Racial violence greatly disturbed O'Hara. He was an articulate spokesman against lynching, a crime that had become rampant throughout the South. He urged Congress to pass a bill to make lynching a federal offense. The need for such legislation became more apparent to O'Hara on March 17, 1886. A white mob stormed into the courthouse in Carrollton, Mississippi, where seven whites were on trial for assaulting two blacks. The assailants opened fire upon black spectators in the courtroom, killing eleven and wounding at least nine. O'Hara called for a special House committee to investigate the murders, but the matter died there. O'Hara was also interested in gender equity. In 1887, he introduced a bill to outlaw discrimination in salary decisions based upon the gender of teachers who had similar credentials and performed similar duties.

Representative O'Hara's greatest efforts were made to strengthen the nation's civil rights laws. The Supreme Court in 1883 had virtually voided the Civil Rights Act of 1875, when it decided that Congress could legislate only on matters involving state action aimed at racial discrimination. When Congress extended the law to private citizens the Supreme Court concluded that it had gone beyond the scope of the Fourteenth Amendment. O'Hara proposed another civil rights amendment, hoping to reverse the effects of the Court decision. Congress took no action; nor did it act upon O'Hara's bill to make racial discrimination in the capital a federal crime. O'Hara vigorously reminded his colleagues in the House that black officials could not eat in white-owned restaurants in the District of Columbia. In addition, Representative O'Hara proposed an amendment to the Interstate Commerce Bill that would allow travel across state lines on a non-segregated basis. The Interstate Commerce Act passed, but did not address interstate travel, and segregation on trains traveling across state lines continued. O'Hara also unsuccessfully called for federal appropriations to reimburse depositors who had lost money in the failed Freedmen's Bank.

O'Hara sought a third term in 1886, but faced a formidable challenge from Israel B. Abbott, a black Republican. With the black vote divided in the Second District, O'Hara lost the election to Furnifold M. Simmons, a white Democrat. Eric Anderson, in an exhaustive analysis of race and politics in North Carolina, concluded that James O'Hara "had represented his district well during his four years in Congress. One can only wonder how much stronger his legislative record would have been had his party been in the majority." With Reconstruction over, O'Hara returned to North Carolina and joined Raphael, his son, in a law practice in New Bern. He died from a stroke on September 15, 1905.

O'Hara offered an amendment to a bill that would require railroads to end discrimination in interstate travel. He asked only that black travelers be assigned seating by the class of ticket they purchased. O'Hara pointed out that Congress had regulated domesticated animals that were transported across state lines. If animals could be subject to federal protection, he declared, the government should also secure the rights of its citizens to travel on a nondiscriminatory basis. O'Hara believed it was the "duty of Congress to protect all classes of citizens from discrimination."

INTERSTATE COMMERCE
The Civil Rights Amendment
December 16, 1884

I offer this amendment, which I send to the desk. The Clerk read as follows:

And any person or persons having purchased a ticket to be conveyed from one state to another, or paid the required fare, shall receive the same treatment and be offered equal facilities and accommodations as are furnished all other persons holding tickets of the same class without discrimination.

The amendment I have offered provides that whenever any person purchases a ticket or pays an amount of money as fare to the officer or agent of any railroad corporation in the United States for a continuous passage from one State to another, that person shall be entitled to the same facilities, privileges, accommodations, and advantages that any other person or persons holding the same class of ticket is accorded and entitled to, this and nothing more. Congress has legislated for the protection of property; it has provided by law how dumb brutes shall be cared for, as evidenced by section 4386 of the Revised Statutes, which reads as follows:

No railroad company within the United States whose road forms any part of a line of road over which cattle, sheep, swine, or other animals are conveyed from one State to another, or the owners or masters of steam, sailing, or other vessels carrying or transporting cattle, sheep, swine, or other animals from one State to another, shall confine the same in cars, boats, or vessels of any description, for a longer period than twenty-eight consecutive hours, without unloading the same for rest, water, and feeding, for a period of at least five consecutive hours.

In the bill now under consideration and so ably championed by the honorable gentleman from Texas [John Henninger Reagan] he and his friends ask this House (and properly so) to protect shippers of goods, wares, and merchandise from unjust charges, conditions, and discriminations now imposed upon them by the railroad corporations of the country, and daily, for the several days on which this bill has been considered, its friends almost with one accord have proclaimed to the country their intention to abate and stop what they term the inequality of rates between the "long and short haul." In the face of the many decisions of the Supreme Court of the United States in favor of the right of Congress to regulate commerce between the States none can deny at this date the constitutional right of Congress so to do, nor will any member upon the floor of this House presume to deny the constitutional right of Congress to engraft the provisions of this amendment to the laws of the United States, and particularly to the bill now under consideration.

In the celebrated Passenger Case, *Norris v. Boston*, Supreme Court Justice Peter V. Daniel uses this language:

The power to regulate commerce includes the regulation of the vessel as well as the cargo and the manner of using the cargo.

If Congress had the right to regulate the using of the vessel it certainly has the right to regulate the use of freight cars, a proposition that every friend of the bill admits, then it must certainly follow that it unqualifiedly has the same right to regulate the use of passenger cars. Would time and opportunity permit I might cite a large number of decisions and authorities in strict accord with the two already cited. Now an evil exists, and none will deny that discriminations are made unjustly, and to a great disadvantage, between persons holding the same class of tickets who are compelled to travel on business from one State to another, and perchance across several States, en route to their destination in another State. I therefore hold it to be not only within the power but the imperative duty of Congress to abate the evil and protect all classes of citizens from discrimination in any and every form.

This amendment simply proposes that, should any person purchase a first-class ticket or a ticket of any of the several classes sold by a railroad corporation in the United States for a passage over its road of any it its connections for a continuous passage to some point in an adjacent or some other State, whenever he or she arrives within any of the States necessary to be traveled over they shall not be subjected to any discrimination or molestation not imposed upon all other persons holding tickets of the same grade or class or who have paid the same amount of money for transportation. This is not class legislation. I do not nor would I ask such. It is not a race question, nor is it a political action. It rises far above all these. It is plain, healthy legislation, strictly in keeping with the enlightened sentiment and spirit of the age in which we live; it is legislation looking to; and guarding the rights of every citizen of this great Republic, however humble may be his station in our social scale.

Having theretofore provided (as we ought to have done) for the protection of dumb brutes while in transit, and as we are now providing against discriminations in freight rates by the railroad corporations of the country, let us come nobly forward and in this bill also throw a shield around the citizen's rights.

December 17, 1884

I regret exceedingly that this color question has arisen in this debate. I for one hold that we are all Americans; that no matter whether a man is white or black he is an American citizen, and that the aegis of this great Republic should be held over him regardless of his color. The day is too late, public sentiment and the healthy influence of the nineteenth century all stare us in the face—it is too late for the American Congress to legislate on the question of color. My amendment proposes nothing in regard to color; it merely says the white man who may not occupy so high a social position as some of his more favored brethren shall not be discriminated against. It is an amendment in a healthy direction, an amendment appealing to the common sense and patriotism of the entire people of this land.

The gentleman from Alabama [Hilary Abner Herbert] has suggested that I introduced the amendment or rather inserted the words in it "without discrimination" for a political purpose. I am not in the habit of raising a political purpose. I am not in the habit of raising a political issue two years before a campaign begins. The campaign has ended, and others who agree with me will abide by the result. And far be it from me at this period to raise anything for political purpose. All I ask of the American Congress is that while you are protecting the property of men, while you are protecting dumb brutes, while you are protecting every other interest, you shall at the same time give voice and expression to the protection of the rights of American colored citizens.

"Without discrimination" seems to be the words that hurt. If, as the gentleman has said, upon the statute-book of Georgia and upon the statute-book of Alabama there are laws which provide no discrimination can be made, or in substance the same thing, then why in the name of common consistency, why in the name of fairness and justice should there be a desire now to place this "ride" upon my amendment? Why, you gentlemen of the North, you gentlemen of Ohio, of New York, of Indiana, and of every other Northern State, yea, gentlemen from my own State of North Carolina, we ride together, we ride according to the fare we pay or feel able and disposed to pay. If I am not able or disposed to pay for or buy a first-class ticket I buy a second-class ticket, and I go right along and there is no trouble.

If the gentlemen mean what they say, that it is the idea and the firm conviction of every man in the length and breadth of this land to accord to all men their rights and privileges, why then is this amendment to the amendment needed? The very amendment itself bears a negative assertion on its very face. When gentlemen come here and say the words "without discrimination" should be stricken from my amendment, it shows a deliberate purpose to discriminate. I do not believe there is a single railroad in the land; I do not believe there is a single corporation in this country that desires to foster any discrimination. Let the man be white or black, humble or great, plebian or aristocratic, if he pays his fare, if he decently behaves himself, he is entitled to the same right as his money and desire prompt him.

O'Hara wrote this resolution in response to the massacre of blacks in Carrllton, Mississippi. He condemned the atrocity and chastised the state for turning its back on the victims. He called for a federal investigation, and urged the government to take appropriate actions upon capturing the assailants.

RESOLUTION
MURDER OF CITIZENS IN CARROLLTON, MISSISSIPPI
March 29, 1886

I desire to introduce a resolution and ask its immediate consideration:

Whereas it is a matter of public information that on the 18th of March, 1886, in the town of Carrollton, the county seat of Carroll County, Mississippi, a lawless band of persons rode to the courthouse and there indiscriminately murdered, by shooting, a number of peaceful citizens of the United States; and

Whereas it is alleged that the governor of said State of Mississippi has absolutely refused to take effective measures to bring to justice said murderers; and

Whereas it is alleged that the grand jury in and for said county of Carroll has neglected to act in such manner as would bring said murderers before the courts to answer for their crimes; and

Whereas the Constitution of the United States guarantees to each and every one of its citizens full and adequate protection of his life and the enjoyment of his property:

Therefore,

Be it resolved, That a committee of five members be appointed by the Speaker to investigate the facts connected with said alleged murders, and to report, by bill or otherwise, such measure as will check or prevent in future the wanton and barbarous destruction of human life.

Resolved, That said committee, when appointed, shall have power to subpoena witnesses, administer oaths, and do all other acts necessary to a full investigation of the subject-matter; that said committee may appoint a subcommittee to visit the State of Mississippi to take testimony, and do such other acts as may be necessary in the premises; and that the expenses of the committee shall be paid from the contingent fund of the House, not to exceed __ dollars.

O'Hara argued against passage of an arbitration bill, which would have enabled a third party to settle disputes between employer and employee. While he supported arbitration in principle, he recognized that the majority of his constituents came from the working class. O'Hara apparently envisioned that labor unions would advocate for laborers.

THE LABOR ARBITRATION BILL
April 2, 1886

It is true that this bill came up in the House before the members thereof had time to consider it. I have not given the bill that consideration I desired to give to it, and yet I am in favor of it, believing it is a step in the right direction. It is an earnest effort, at least on the part of the House of Representatives, to show to the laboring men of this country that they are in favor of assisting them in settling their difficulties by arbitration. It has been said upon this floor that the spirit of our civilization is strongly pointing toward settling not only difficulties between capital and labor, but also all differences between nations by arbitration. I represent a constituency upon this floor composing a large class of unorganized labor, but which must in the very near future be organized for its own protection; and in its clash with other great interests which it must meet, it regards as earnest this sentiment of arbitration receiving its expression here, so that when the time comes when it shall clash with other interests that sentiment will have gone forth to the country and arbitration may be called upon to settle that great difficulty.

When that time comes then I shall expect to hear great constitutional lawyers here get up and invoke the shades of the Constitution; but thank God, the spirit of the times will say to these gentlemen that the Constitution is broad enough and strong enough to allow the Congress of the United States to step in and assist the people in their difficulties by arbitration. I am not one of those who is afraid that we are going to retrograde; that this great movement which is now on foot, this settling of difficulties between labor and capital, because we pass this bill, will retrograde, as has been said by the gentleman [John Joseph Adams] from New York. Nor am I afraid that the great spirit of liberty will be crushed out because so asserted by the gentleman [William Campbell Preston Breckinridge] from Kentucky.

But however much I may be in favor of this bill I must protest in the name of the ignorant, the unlettered people of these United States, against the innuendoes thrown out by the friends of this measure that we are for taking $77,000,000 of the people's money for the purpose of educating a certain class. I say that is a false idea. That seventy-seven million when taken from the Treasury of the United States will return in bounties fifty-fold. It will be for the education not of a certain class of people, but for all the people of these United States; and it will be one of the greatest levers that can be used to bring about a settlement between these two mighty interests, labor and capital. It will educate the laborer of the country to that extent that he will be enabled to maintain his rights within the law. It will enable him to justly appreciate such settlement as may be made by arbitration, and thus tend to elevate the entire masses of the people.

O'Hara did not believe that this bill would ensure the safety of the food supply it was ostensibly designed to protect. He believed the bill would harm the butter industry and benefit another industry. He also objected to the new bureaucracy the bill would create. He believed that the funding required to implement the law would be excessive and misdirected. He disputed his colleagues who claimed that the bill would help the poor. O'Hara believed industrial leaders supported the bill because it would advance their interests.

THE FOOD SAFETY BILL
June 2, 1886

No member of this House will go further than I am ready to go to protect the people from the adulteration of food. But this bill, as I understand it, proposes not to prevent the adulteration of food as such. On the contrary, under the guise of protecting the poor man from oleomargarine and spurious butter, it seeks to destroy one industry of the country for the purpose of building up another. More than that, it proposes to create a number of new offices and to revivify and set in motion all the odious features of the internal-revenue system. The fourteenth section of this bill, which I propose to strike out, does not only create additional officers at large salaries, but it gives to the Commissioner of

Internal Revenue the power, whenever in his judgment the necessity of the service may require it, to add to this already large army of officers other officers.

The number of these will be limited, say gentlemen on the other side, by the appropriation; but every member on this floor knows that the appropriation does not limit the number of the public offices of the Government when the administrative official sees fit to go beyond the authority of existing law. At every session we are met by demands from the Treasury Department, from the Internal Revenue Bureau, from the Department of Justice, and from almost every other Department asking Congress to pass "urgent deficiency appropriation bills." We murmur; but the executive officers come to us and tell us that the service had been performed, that when we passed our appropriation bills we were mistaken as to what the public exigencies required; and murmur though we may, we always pass such bills when their passage is demanded. Thus, Congress after Congress, we find that these administrative officers go beyond the appropriations. Therefore, the so-called limitation involved in the appropriation of money is no limit at all.

If places are needed for party favorites let gentlemen say so. Let the country so understand it. Let us all understand that such is the scope of the pending measure. Let us make it clear and sure there should be no attempt here to throttle any interest or to strangle any industry of the country. I am no advocate of oleomargarine; but it is said that this bill is made in the interest of the poor man, and I ask, where are the petitions of poor men crying out against this abuse? The poor man is not here clamoring for this proposed legislation, but it is the rich dairymen of the country who by this bill are saying you shall have only what we desire to give you at whatever price we may demand, whether it be butter made from pure milk of fancy and well-kept cows, or from milk of diseased and swill-fed cows as they do from oleomargarine or any of the other manufactures mentioned in the bill.

The crowning piece of infamy of the bill, however, is found in the nineteenth section. This section proposes to give a premium to every spy and informer in the land who shall become a self-appointed guardian of this law; it offers a reward, holds out an inducement, to the lazy and worthless to spy upon his neighbor's action, that he may satisfy his avarice and cupidity by securing one-half of the penalty imposed by the bill. It has a tendency to create an army of Jean Valjeans to follow with sleuthhound tenacity every imaginable violator of this law. I do not think that I overdraw the picture when I warn this House that the passage of this bill will add at least one-fourth more officers to the already long list of special United States marshals, assistant prosecuting attorneys, and henchmen to be employed and paid from the hard-wrung taxes of an already overtaxed people.

I have heard the cry of the Democratic party for the past ten years: "Reduction of taxes!" "Relief of the masses from an army of officeholders!"

"Help from the merciless red-legged grasshoppers and 'golden-winged butterflies,'" as the revenue officers were once called in my State. But, I suppose all this has changed, and the cry of war taxes has changed to the cry of protection to the people from spurious and death-dealing food, and the slogan of reform. The revenue officer, the spy, the accuser of his neighbors, the United States prosecuting attorney is no longer tyrants but guardian angels to the health and liberty of the poor man.

The hard-wrung tax to keep up and feed this vast additional army of cormorants becomes a free-will offering of spices and ointment of sweet-smelling savor. I do not believe that the people of my State or of any State in this Union are in favor of this bill; it savors of class legislation, of favoritism to one industry and oppression to another; it is not protection—it is destruction; and as such it must work to the detriment of the poorer classes. I will willingly go as far as any gentleman upon this floor to protect the people from adulterated food, and I say here and now that whenever the Committee on Agriculture, or any committee of this House, shall bring in a bill to remedy that evil, placing its enforcement with the ordinary courts of the country, without the creation of additional officers and spies and informers, separate and apart from the Internal Revenue Bureau, I am ready to give it my hearty approval. As between natural butter and the manufactured article I am decidedly in favor of natural butter, and am of the opinion that if the dairymen of the country need protection they ought to have it; but I would ask the friends of the bill, a large number of whom are in favor of State rights, are not the respective State Legislatures competent to deal with this question? Has an effort been made by the dairymen of any particular State or number of States to secure protection against this so-called false representation of butter and refusal by the Legislature? If not so, why, then, not let them first apply to the States for the necessary legislation?

It cannot be urged that for any needs of the Government the revenue derived from this source is necessary, for we have heard, and the world was made to believe, that there was a large surplus of money lying idle in the Treasury of the United States, to the great detriment of the poor laboring man. Is it now proposed to augment this surplus? That a single industry shall be crushed out, or that a rival industry, both to the manner born, shall be protected, or that political favorites, henchmen, and bosses shall have places? If for either of these, I think we have done enough, and it is full time that our faces and footsteps were turned in another direction. By all means protect the poor from adulterated and deleterious food, but in the name of common fairness let us do it in one general bill. Enact a law that will made no invidious distinction, but one that will bear alike upon all, that will be wise and beneficial, but let not this engine of favoritism and injustice mar the pages of our statutes.

O'Hara criticized the chairman of the House Ways and Means Committee for duping the House into thinking that they would discuss the tariff bill. Instead, the chairman turned to the pension fund, seeking to deny the Committee on Invalid Pensions an opportunity to do their job. O'Hara believed that Union soldiers were entitled to receive payments from the pension fund.

THE INVALID PENSIONS BILL
June 22, 1886

From the announcement made the other day by the gentleman from Illinois [William R. Morrison], the chairman of the Committee on Ways and Means, we were led to expect that he would this morning again undertake to call up his tariff bill. But much to our surprise, we are met here with a proposition to make the pensions of the soldiers odious in the eyes of the masses of the American people. The gentleman from Indiana [Courtland Cushing Matson], the chairman of the Committee on Invalid Pensions, has told this side of the House that yesterday when by a motion to suspend the rules it was intended to deprive the Committee on Invalid Pensions of its day for the consideration of pension bills we on this side rose as a man to advance that proposition. Every member of the Committee on Invalid Pensions on this side of the House expected to see its chairman stand up and combat that proposition and resist the attempt to have the Committee on Invalid Pensions give way. But among the first men to yield to the effort to deprive the soldiers of a day in this House was the chairman of the Committee on Invalid Pensions.

We hear a great deal of talk about the arrears-of-pension bill and of the necessity of putting riders on our pension legislation. The arrears-of-pension bill was reported to this House early in last March. There has been plenty of time to consider it; yet the chairman of the Committee on Invalid Pensions has never tried to bring it up; or if he has tried, those on this side who stood ready and willing to assist him have never been able to discover that effort on his part. The gentleman tells us that it will take two, or three, or four, or five hundred million dollars to pay these arrears of pensions; and it would appear from the statement that this vast amount of money was to be expended at once. But the Commissioner of Pensions, General Black, told the Committee on Invalid Pensions in a conference which he had with that committee—and I betray no secrets of the committee—that his office could not expend more than $50,000,000 per annum, that he thought the revenues of the country sufficient, and that the demands of the soldiers required the expenditure.

This question of pensions is not such a bugbear to the people of the country, as some gentlemen here seem to suppose. It is not a bugbear to the people of my own State; for today North Carolina, although one of the States which gentlemen on the other side are in the habit of saying was robbed and crushed into the dust by the Republican "Carpetbaggers" and "scalawags," levies a large tax upon the property-holders of the State—for what? For the purpose of paying pensions to Confederate soldiers. And every man, black and white, pays the tax cheerfully; not a murmur has arisen. More than that, in my own county some of these pensioners on the Confederate rolls are today occupying federal positions; and nobody complains. The federal soldier in that State contributes his mite.

James O'Hara eulogized General John A. Logan as a great politician and soldier. He expressed admiration for Logan as a man who embraced truth, loved his country, and honored his God.

THE DEATH OF SENATOR JOHN A. LOGAN
February 16, 1887

The man who so conducts the order of his life that when the summons comes, bidding him join the majority beyond, and leave vacant his chair at the family board, the social circle, or the nation's council where he was wont to be met, as to leave behind him indelibly impressed upon his age marks or traits of character worthy of emulation, that man has not lived in vain; the world and his fellows are benefited by his being, and such a life may fitly be said to be like unto "a tree planted by the rivers of water that bringeth forth his fruit in his season, whose leaves shall not wither," and whom no evil can befall, whether he be alive or dead.

Today the House of Representatives pauses and for the time being sets aside the work of legislation that must for weal or woe affect the living, and with bowed heads and hearts filled with sympathy face the stern realities of death, and recognize that a great light has gone out from among the nation's counselors, no more to raise his voice in defense of right, or lift an arm to strike a blow in behalf of justice and protection to the weak and humble poor, who from every city, village, and hamlet in the land bewail his loss, and join with us at this hour in placing to his memory from the storehouse of thought ointments of sweet-smelling savor, mingled with fragrant flowers, plucked from the garden of kindness, sown by the noble deeds of him whom they called friend.   My acquaintance with the late Senator Logan was not such a one as would entitle me to speak of his many great and noble qualities as father, husband, or friend, or soldier. This I leave for those who enjoyed a place in his social circle, and whose contact with him in everyday life gave them the opportunities to speak as they have of him in that regard.

Hence in the brief remarks that I shall submit I will speak of the illustrious deed from that portion of his life that shines forth with such effulgence as to strike the admiration of all, whether friend or foe. If there was any one trait of that strong character that appeared stronger than the other it was his great love for his country and the deep and abiding faith that his country was destined by God himself to be that country in which liberty in its broadest and most comprehensive term should find its greatest fulfillment. It was this love of country that made him search after truth, and when found, according to the lights before him he disregarded party tenets or dictation; yea, even the counsel of friends if they in the least appeared to jar with what his reason and his heart suggested to be for the interest of his whole country. He may be charged by those who are accustomed blindly to follow leadership or to look only upon the surface for results of being sometimes harsh and impetuous with those who did not agree with him. Yet such, if they would delve deep for causes and effects, will find that such a nature as his, accustomed to reach results by direct reasoning with truth, avoiding ingenious methods, could have no patience nor tolerance for that sophistry which would endeavor to make the worst appear the better reason; and having himself a strong and determined will, abject submission to the will or dictation of others when in conflict with what he believed right could not be understood or appreciated by him.

No greater example of love for one's country can be found than Logan's patriotic act when he exchanged a seat upon this floor for a common soldier's lot amid the stern realities and severity of camp life when the well-being of his country was threatened, the Union endangered, and sound to arms for the right was heard all over the land. How well he kept that pledge he then made let the answer be given by the fifty-two well-fought battles in which he was successfully engaged from July 21, 1861, to April 26, 1865. Deeds like these will live in song and story and be recounted when and wherever the bards or historians gather to recite noble deeds for the emulation of the youth of this or any other land. Next to General Logan's great love for his country was his love and veneration for his comrades in arms, a love and veneration so pure and holy that it blessed both him that gave and him that received, so that when the dread summons came that bade that noble soul sunder the golden chord of life and leave its cerements of clay, to put off mortality and put on immortality, every one of his late comrades in arms felt that not only their great volunteer leader had crossed the river invisible to mortal view, but also that a friend, and advocate, and, yea, almost a father, had been taken from them.

This ceremony is not solely in honor of the dead, for neither "storied urn, nor animated bust"; but it is that the lesson of this noble life, ended so suddenly, yet filled with honor and usefulness, may be emphasized and adorned as far as we are able to emphasize and adorn it; that the same love of country, love for one's fellow, may be held up as a noble example to those who may come after us, and that posterity may know that the American Republic has and can produce heroes equal to if not surpassing in valor, fidelity, and patriotism the fabled heroes of ancient Greece or Rome.

> O'Hara chastised the government for refusing to pay the heirs of black soldiers their due pensions. He charged that the federal government denied them compensation solely because of their color. He complained that black soldiers had faced discrimination in pay in the Civil War; white soldiers received higher pay.

THE DEPENDENT SOLDIERS PENSION BILL
February 24, 1887

In the limited period to which I am confined in the discussion of this measure it will be a matter of impossibility to intelligently present my views in regard to this veto message. There is one feature of it, however, to which I shall attempt to address myself.

There is one portion of the bill about which the President has been silent, and that is the first section, providing for the relief of dependent parents. That class of people who gave their sons to their country at the time of its greatest peril, a class of people that I particularly represent, are debarred by an unjust ruling in the Department. The mothers of Negro soldiers who gave their sons to their country are met with this ruling when they approach your Pension Office. The mother says: "I gave to a country which looked upon me with scorn my sons as her defenders, and I am today without strength to support me because those men gave their blood and their lives that their country might live." There is a decision of this Government, through its Pension Office, saying to them, "You were slaves, and, therefore, although your sons may have died upon the battlefield your country will turn you aside with scorn."

This is unjust—unjust to that noble band who though they knew their country spurned them, came forward and gave their lives for its defense. It is not as the President would indicate that these men went for dollars and cents. The Forty-fourth and Forty-fifth Massachusetts Regiments, composed entirely of colored men, went out and nobly did their duty; but when the paymaster of the government met them he said: "You are soldiers of this Government, but your skin is black, and we will give you less than we give your white comrades." They spurned it and said: "No; we are in this contest for liberty, and if you cannot pay us the full measure you pay to other soldiers, we will fight for our flag and our country without compensation." The colored soldiers in our late Civil War were not bummers, camp followers or were specially provided for with bomb-proof positions, yet they discharged their duties faithfully. Is it possible to believe that the dependent parents of men like these shall be denied by this act of the President that relief and succor in their old age that a fateful country would willingly accord to them? It is enough for this first clause of the bill, which the President of the United States had not even offered to the country a lame excuse for his disapproval.

As to the second clause of this bill, upon which the President of the United States based his veto, I beg to state that the President can not be sincere in his veto message on this bill when he approved, as far as we know without hesitancy, the "Mexican pension bill," a bill with far larger opportunities for fraud, and pensioning a larger class of persons who may not be in need at all. I regard this veto as a blow aimed at the patriots who at their country's call responded in person and did not send a substitute, and a declaration on the part of the President that he has no sympathy with the men who defended their country in the day of its need. Thus, I am willing to stand by the action of the committee, and believing that the country will sustain us, I shall vote to pass the bill, the veto of the President to the contrary notwithstanding

15

Joseph Hayne Rainey (1832–1887)
House of Representatives, South Carolina

Republican

Forty-second, Forty-third, Forty-fourth and Forty-fifth Congresses
December 12, 1870, to March 3, 1879

Joseph Hayne Rainey was born into slavery in Georgetown, South Carolina, on June 21, 1832. He was the son of racially mixed parents, and was officially labeled a mulatto by the state. While his father Edward Rainey was a slave, he was also a barber by profession. It was a common practice in the South for an owner to allow a slave to work for money, so long as the person shared the profits. Edward's owner allowed him to work independently, and from the money he saved he purchased his freedom and that of his family. In 1846, Edward moved the family to Charleston. While he was industrious, Edward Rainey could not afford to send Joseph and his other children to the school opened for free blacks. Joseph Rainey, who was also ambitious, decided to take up barbering; he moved to Philadelphia to ply his trade and broaden his horizons. He met Susan there, and after their courtship they were married in 1859. Now facing the responsibilities of a husband, Rainey returned to Charleston to be among his family and open a barbershop.

During the Civil War, the Confederate Army impressed Rainey and Susan, making them work menial jobs, such as cooking and cleaning. Apparently, southern vessels made periodic runs to Bermuda and the West Indies for supplies. Rainey and his wife were aboard one of these ships and escaped while in Bermuda. Slavery had been abolished in the former British colony since 1834, and Rainey was automatically considered free. He opened a barbershop in St. Georges, and remained there until the end of the war. Upon returning to South Carolina in 1866, Rainey joined politically active blacks. He attended the state labor convention, and joined the Union League, a political organization loyal to the Republican party. In 1868, Rainey was elected to the South Carolina constitutional convention, and then to the state senate, serving from 1868 to 1870; he chaired the Finance Committee. He later served as a brigadier general in the militia, and as a U.S. census taker in Georgetown, South Carolina.

Rainey won election to Congress in 1870, to fill the seat vacated by Representative Benjamin F. Whittmore, whose tenure was cut short amid charges of corruption. Rainey was the first black representative to sit in the U.S. House of Representatives, serving four terms from the First District in South Carolina, from 1870 to 1879. Representative Rainey was appointed to the committees on Freedmen's Affairs, Invalid Pensions, and Centennial Celebration. He spoke in favor of the Ku Klux Klan bill of 1871, calling for the protection of blacks from racial violence. Rainey also urged the federal government to use the army to protect blacks from Klan terrorism. He supported a bill mandating appointments to juries on a nonracial basis. He also supported the Civil Rights Bill of 1875, as well as other measures that would protect blacks from any form of racial segregation in public accommodations, public education, and public transportation. He denounced the massacre of black militiamen in Hamburg, South Carolina, on July 4, 1876.

Representative Rainey became a national symbol in 1874, when he temporarily replaced James G. Blaine as Speaker of the House. Rainey presided over a session on the Indian appropriations bill. Newspapers carried the story, hailing Rainey as the first black to preside over the House of Representatives.

Rainey struggled to manage his personal and business affairs after his congressional term. He worked for the U.S. Internal Revenue Service and became involved in a financial brokerage and banking firm. While he was an active investor holding stock in various railroad companies, he never acquired great wealth. His wife Susan also tried to build a financial base by operating a clothing shop for women, but the business foundered. Frustrated by racial violence against blacks and limited economic opportunities for them, Rainey supported the Black Exodus to the West during the 1880s. With his health declining by 1886, Rainey retired from all business activities and returned to Georgetown where he died in 1887.

Rainey denounced the violence and persecution of African Americans in the South. He compared them to whites who had been besieged by Native Americans. Black women and orphans were forced to drift about their states, foraging for food and seeking aid from impoverished people who could not help them. He also explained that elderly blacks were frequently murdered for their political opinions.

ENFORCEMENT OF THE FOURTEENTH AMENDMENT
April 1, 1871

In approaching the subject now under consideration I do so with a deep sense of its magnitude and importance, and in full recognition of the fact that a remedy is needed to meet the evil now existing in most of the southern States, but especially in that one which I have the honor to represent in part, the State of South Carolina. The enormity of the crimes constantly perpetrated there finds no parallel in the history of this Republic in her very darkest days. There was a time when the early settlers of New England were compelled to enter the fields, their homes, even the very sanctuary itself, armed to the full extent of their means. While the people were offering their worship to God within those humble walls their voices kept time with the tread of the sentry outside. But it must be borne in mind that at the time referred to civilization had but just begun its work upon this continent. The surroundings were unpropitious, and as yet the grand capabilities of this fair land lay dormant under the fierce tread of the red man. But as civilization advanced with its steady and resistless away it drove back those wild cohorts and compelled them to give way to the march of improvement. In course of time superior intelligence made its impress and established its dominion upon this continent. That intelligence, with an influence like that of the sun rising in the east and spreading its broad rays like a garment of light, gave life and gladness to the dark and barbaric land of America.

Surely it was reasonable to hope that this sacred influence should never have been overshadowed, and that in the history of other nations, no less than in our own past, we might find beacon-lights for our guidance. In part this has been realized, and might have reached the height of our expectations of it had not been for the blasting effects of slavery, whose deadly pall has so long spread its folds over this nation, to the destruction of peace, union, and concord. Most particularly has its baneful influence been felt in the South, causing the people to be at once restless and discontent. Even now, after the great conflict between slavery and freedom, after the triumph achieved at such a cost, we can yet see the traces of the disastrous strife and the remains of disease in the body-politic of the South. In proof of this witness the frequent outrages perpetrated upon our loyal men. The prevailing spirit of the southerner is either to rule or to ruin. Voters must perforce succumb to their wishes or else risk life itself in the attempt to maintain the simple right of common manhood.

The suggestions of the shrewdest Democratic papers have proved unavailing in controlling the votes of the loyal whites and blacks of the South. Their innuendoes have been evaded. The people emphatically decline to dispose of their rights for a mess of pottage. In this particular the Democracy of the North found themselves foiled and their money needless. But with a spirit more demon-like than that of a Negro or a Caligula, there has been concocted another plan, destructive, aye, diabolical in its character, worthy only of hearts without regard for God or man, fit for such deeds as those deserving the names of men would shudder to perform. Is it asked, what are those deeds? Let those who liberally contributed to the supply of arms and ammunition in the late rebellious States answer the question. Soon after the war, there was widespread willingness in the South to comply with the requirements of the law. But as the clemency and magnanimity of the General Government became manifest once again did the monster rebellion lift its hydra head in renewed defiance, cruel and cowardly, fearing the light of day, hiding itself under the shadow of the night as more befitting its bloody and accursed work.

I need not recite here the murderous deeds committed both in North and South Carolina. I could touch the feelings of this House by the story of widows and orphans now wandering amid the ravines of the rural counties of my native State seeking protection and maintenance from others who are yet unable, on account of their own poverty, to grant them aid. I could dwell upon the sorrows of poor women, with their helpless infants, cast upon the world, homeless and destitute, deprived of their natural protectors by the red hand of the midnight assassin. I could appeal to you, members upon this floor as husbands and fathers, to picture to yourselves the desolation of your own happy firesides should you be suddenly snatched away from your loved ones. Think of gray-haired men, whose fourscore years are almost numbered, the venerated heads of peaceful households, without warning murdered for political opinion's sake.

The gentleman to whom reference is made in the article read is certainly one of the most inoffensive individuals I have ever known. He is a gentleman of refinement, culture, and sterling worth, a Carolinian of the old school, an associate of the late Honorable John C. Calhoun, being neither a pauper nor a pensioner, but living in comparative affluence and ease upon his own possessions, respected by all fair-mined and unprejudiced citizens who knew him. Accepting the situation, he joined the Republican party in the fall of 1870; and for this alliance, and this alone, he has been vehemently assailed and murderously assaulted. By all the warm and kindly sympathies of our common humanity, I implore you to do something for this suffering people, and stand not upon the order of your doing. If I could exhume the murdered men and women of the South and array their ghastly forms before your eyes, their presence would appeal in tomes of plaintive eloquence which would be louder than a million tongues.

It has been asserted that protection for the colored people only has been demanded; and in this there is a certain degree of truth, because they are noted for their steadfastness to the Union and the cause of liberty as guaranteed by the

Constitution. But, on the other hand, this protection is equally desired for those loyal whites, some to the manner born, others who, in the exercise of their natural rights as American citizens, have seen fit to remove thither from other sections of the States, and who are now undergoing persecution simply on account of their activity in carrying out Union principles and loyal sentiments in the South. Their efforts have contributed largely to further reconstruction and the restoration of the southern States to the old fellowship of the Federal compact. It is indeed hard that their reward for their well-meant earnestness should be that of being violently treated, and even forced to flee from the homes of their choice. It will be a foul stain upon the escutcheon of our land if such atrocities are allowed to tamely continue.

In the dawn of our freedom our young Republic was widely recognized and proudly proclaimed to the world the refuge, the safe asylum of the oppressed of all lands. Shall it be said that at this day, through mere indifference and culpable neglect, this grand boast of ours is become a mere form of words, an utter fraud? I earnestly hope not! And yet, if we stand with folded arms and idle hands, while the cries of our oppressed brethren sound in our ears, what will it be but a proof to all men that we are utterly unfit for our glorious mission, unworthy of our noble privileges, as the greatest of republics, the champions of freedom for all men? I would that every individual man in this whole nation could be aroused to a sense of his own part and duty in this great question. When we call to mind the fact that this persecution is waged against men for the simple reason that they dare to vote with the party which has saved the Union intact by the lavish expenditure of blood and treasure, and has borne the nation safely through the fearful crisis of these last few years, our hearts swell with an overwhelming indignation.

The question is sometimes asked, why do not the courts of law afford redress? Why the necessity of appealing of Congress? We answer that the courts are in many instances under the control of those who are wholly inimical to the impartial administration of law and equity. What benefit would result from appeal to tribunals whose officers are secretly in sympathy with the very evil against which we are striving? But to return to the point in question: If the Negroes, numbering one-eighth of the population of these United States, would only cast their votes in the interest of the Democratic party, all open measures against them would be immediately suspended, and their rights, as American citizens, recognized. But as to the real results of such a state of affairs, and speaking in behalf of those with whom I am conversant, I can only say that we love freedom more, vastly more, than slavery; consequently we hope to keep clear of the Democrats! In most of the arguments to which I have listened the positions taken are predicated upon the grounds of the unconstitutionality of the bill introduced by the gentleman from Ohio [Samuel Shellabarger]. For my part I am not prepared, Mr. Speaker, to argue this question from a constitutional standpoint.

16

Alonzo Jacob Ransier (1834–1882)
House of Representatives, South Carolina

Republican

Forty-third Congress
March 4, 1873, to March 3, 1875

Alonzo Jacob Ransier was born free in Charleston, South Carolina, on January 3, 1834. He was considered a mulatto under state law, the product of a liaison between a French and Haitian couple. While his early education was limited, Ransier managed to obtain work as a shipping clerk for a white Charleston merchant. However, the owner of the business had violated a state law, which had barred African Americans from the profession, for which he was prosecuted and convicted. While the court levied a fine for the infraction, it clearly did not consider the hire an egregious violation of state law. The judges apparently surmised that though the statute had restricted free black employment, it did not entirely exclude employing shipping clerks. The 1850s were good economic times in Charleston, and such a "black law" was not rigidly enforced.

Ransier's employment as a clerk had given him sufficient experience to hold other administrative offices. In 1865, he was a delegate to the convention of the Friends of Equal Rights meeting in Charleston. Convention delegates drafted resolutions, and selected Ransier to deliver them to Congress. In 1866, he landed a job as associate editor of the *South Carolina Leader*, a black-owned newspaper. Ransier also accepted a position as registrar of elections under the provisional military government of General Daniel Sickles. In addition he served as chairman of the state Republican Central Committee, and in 1868 he was chosen as a presidential elector for Ulysses S. Grant. That same year the registrar of elections was elected as a delegate to the state constitutional convention.

Ransier won elective office for the first time in 1868, serving in the state assembly from 1868 to 1870. He was chairman of the Committee on Privileges and Elections. He was also the county auditor for Charleston, and a trustee of the state orphan asylum. In 1869, Ransier helped charter the Amateur Literary and Fraternal Association of Charleston. In 1870, he was elected lieutenant governor under Governor Scott. As the second in command in South Carolina, he headed the Southern States Convention that met in Columbia in 1871. He was a delegate to the Republican National Convention that met in Philadelphia in 1872. Having earned the reputation as an honest and fair politician, Ransier won support from the state Republican party and made a successful bid for Congress in 1872. Upon taking his seat on March 3, 1873, he was appointed to the Committee on Manufacturers. Congressman Ransier supported such measures as erecting a federal building in Beaufort, and making federal appropriations of at least $100,000 to develop Charleston Harbor. He also sought federal support to rebuild a wing at the Citadel military academy, which had been destroyed in the Civil War.

Representative Ransier defended federal civil rights protections for all American citizens. He specifically challenged his colleagues in the House of Representatives when they made disparaging comments about African-Americans, disputing the assertion that blacks were genetically inferior to whites. Ransier used conflicts between blacks and whites in the House of Representatives to highlight racial strife in the country at large. He argued that the 1875 Civil Rights Bill of Senator Charles Sumner would bring about greater racial harmony in the nation. He believed that blacks had earned "civil rights" by having fought and sacrificed their lives in the Civil War. Ransier asserted that all people were human beings, and he insisted that there was no justification for racial segregation. He supported integrated schools, citing black achievements in education and successful experiments at mixed schools at Harvard, Yale, and Oberlin University.

Ransier and his wife Louisa had eleven children. Unfortunately, his wife died soon after giving birth to their last child. For that reason he wanted to make the child's name special, while he simultaneously honored a great civil rights leader. He gave the child the name, Charles Sumner Ransier. Once his congressional career ended, Ransier worked respectively for the United States Internal Revenue Service, as a guard at the Customs House in Charleston and as a street sweeper for the Charleston Sanitation Department. While Ransier had become relatively prominent and modestly wealthy in the 1870s, his life took a turn upon the death of his wife. He slid into a depression, lost his money, and soon died at the age of forty-eight.

Ransier defended the Civil Rights Bill, disputing whites who argued that most blacks were not interested in the measure. He explained that although African Americans were willing to forget past abuses, they demanded equal protection of the laws. Ransier reminded his colleagues that over 180,000 black soldiers had fought for the Union in the Civil War and had given their lives for freedom and equal rights.

CIVIL RIGHTS
February 7, 1874

But for some remarks made by the gentleman from Georgia [Henry Richard Harris], the gentleman from North Carolina [William McKendree Robbins], and the gentleman from New York, our learned and genial friend [Samuel Sullivan Cox], during the protracted debate on civil rights, made before and subsequent to the recommission of the bill on the subject to the Judiciary Committee, which in my judgment calls for a specific reply, I would not again ask the attention and indulgence of the House for myself.

Statements have been made by one or all of these gentlemen, and others who oppose such a bill, as many of us think ought to pass, that ought not to go to the country un-contradicted, and a condition of affairs pictured by them as likely to follow its enactment into law which if true or likely to occur ought to go far toward the defeat of such a measure. If, on the other hand, these statements are shown to be untrue and to rest upon no foundation in point of fact, and that the enactment of such a law by Congress will be of benefit to all classes of our people and promote the ends of justice, of concord, and harmonious relationships, as we think we can show, then we cannot pass this measure a day too soon. This measure has been presented to us in masterly efforts in its constitutional aspects, and we are asked to consider it now in the light of practical statesmanship. We are asked to consider what would be the effect of its operation as to our school system and upon the relationships between the races. To these inquiries I propose to address myself as briefly as possible, and to this end I ask the indulgence of the House.

Before proceeding I desire to express my regret that anything should have occurred calculated to create ill feeling between members of this House during this debate, and which the press of the country has characterized as contravening the legitimate limits of parliamentary courtesy. I am satisfied that a very large majority of the republican members of this House do not understand the true condition of affairs in the South. For if they did, and are sincere in their avowals of solicitude for the welfare of the country, and especially for the prosperity and advancement of the colored race, I am very sure that they would indicate it in some better way than the adoption of legislative enactments which in my judgment, when tried, will not only prove unacceptable to the masses of colored people at the South, but alike destructive of the harmony and great interests of both races.

I am sure that a very large majority of the republican members of this House do know the true condition of affairs in the South, hence the desire on their part for the passage of such a measure. As to the remark that such enactments, "when tried, will not only prove unacceptable to the masses of colored people at the South, but alike destructive of the harmony and great interests of both races," he evidently misunderstands the situation himself. He is not the only member who has said during this debate that the colored people, the masses of them, are not asking for the passage of such a bill. The gentleman from Texas [De Witt Clinton Giddings] suggested the same thing.

The Colored People: A Unit for Civil Rights

There are organizations in nearly every State in the Union the object of which, in part at least, is to endeavor to secure for the colored people of the country their equal rights. They have been asking this of the country, through individuals with delegated authority to act, through State and county organizations, and through national conventions assembled for the purpose. A convention subsequently held at New Orleans, Louisiana, which was composed of delegates from all parts of the country, issued a similar address, as did the one recently held in this city. I have similar papers from meetings held all over this country to the same import. I will call attention to the following, which has been adopted by the Legislature of my own State; and be it known that in that Legislature there are about thirty-five democrats. The *News and Courier* newspaper, published in the city of Charleston, where I live, one of the leading democratic organs of the South, commenting upon the adoption of these resolutions, says that the democratic members, with a single exception, in both houses, voted for them.

I affirm that, so far from the masses of the colored people not desiring civil rights, no man could, having made known his object, obtain without intimidation or coercion in some form the signatures or assent of one hundred colored men in any State of the Union against the passage of a full and complete civil-rights bill by Congress, or to indicate a disapproval of it "when tried." The gentleman from Georgia [Mr. Harris] suggests that such a measure "will not only prove unacceptable to the masses of the colored people at the South, but alike destructive of the harmony and great interests of both races." Just here he thinks, and very properly so, is a wide field for practical statesmanship. Not only since the rebellion, passing through some terrible scenes during and since reconstruction, (if indeed that work is completed), and during the terrible four years when the country groaned amid the throes of rebellion, but during the entire two hundred and fifty years, whether as slave or freeman, has the black man in our country exhibited a patience under long suffering, a forbearance under most provoking circumstances, and a forgiving and friendly disposition, that make him at once a good and peaceable citizen and perhaps a study. He is taunted for his conduct during the war by the honorable gentleman from North Carolina [Mr. Robbins] because he did not lay in ashes the home of his master and murder the women and children while he (the master) was engaged in that which the gentleman seems to glorify.

I have nothing to say in reply to those remarks as to the conduct of the colored people during the rebellion. Upon this and some other points he has been answered by my colleague [Richard Harvey Cain] except that if (and I say this in the kindliest spirit) those with whom the gentleman acts politically had shown during the years of the agitation of the question of slavery in this country, especially in the past fifteen years or so, that patience, Christian spirit, and I might add good sense, exhibited by the Negro during the rebellion, the country would not have been called upon to mourn the loss of three hundred thousand of her sons, cut off by the casualties of war, and to groan today under a debt of over $2,000,000.

The gentleman from North Carolina uses language that is calculated to keep alive whatever of sectional feeling there may be existing between the people of the North and the people of the South, which it is the business of the statesmanship of today to allay and to bury in the oblivion of the past, if possible, in the interest of both sections and of all classes and colors. This language I shall not repeat; it is found in the concluding sentence of the extract of his speech just quoted.

When I plead for the passage of a full and complete civil rights bill that shall seek to prevent and punish discriminations against the citizen, I know that I speak for five million people, and ask for that which is a necessity to them; and when I say that these five million people desire to live on terms of amity with their white fellow-citizens, I know that I correctly represent them. The Negro desires to forget the wrongs of the past, and has imposed no disabilities upon those who held him as a slave, when he has been in a position to do; and he rejoices today, both from motives of patriotism and self-interest, that the bitter feeling against him in the South, especially on the part of those who were his owners, which found expression in acts of violence and butchery, is fast dying out; that a better state of feeling exists, which must increase as he becomes educated, and, therefore, better acquainted with his duties and responsibilities as a citizen, and as the other unlearns some of the teachings of the past.

The Negro Desires Harmonious Relationship With All Other Races

If I believed with the gentleman from Georgia [Mr. Harris] that such a measure as the bill we are now discussing would be "destructive of the harmony and great interest of both races," I, for one, would not insist upon its passage. I insist upon it, not only because it is right in the abstract, but also because I feel that it will remove from the field of politics that which goes far to array one class against the other, in the South especially, I mean those class and caste distinctions, and would go far to disarm the mere political demagogue who is ever on the alert to use the colored vote, indifferent as to the ultimate results so long as their selfish purposes can be best served thereby. It will increase his opportunities for learning and make him a more intelligent and independent voter, and make him feel a deeper interest in those questions affecting his material welfare and that of the community in which he lives.

He will then have no animosities to feed or nourish, or at least no occasion for any, and as he advances in the scale of intelligence and usefulness, and acquires wealth through the unobstructed avenues to the school-house and to the industrial marts, and finds his undisputed way to the witness-box, the jury-box, and the ballot-box, which is his right, then the prejudices against him will melt as does the snow under a burning sun. Then, and not until then, will a more harmonious relationship be brought about between him and his more favored brother, the Caucasian, to whose interest it is, especially in the South, that this desirable result should be brought about. Permit me to say we want peace and good-fellowship in the South and throughout the country; we want race lines and sectional feelings blotted out and buried forever. We want new life and vigor infused into the arteries of our industries in the South; we want assistance in the direction of developing our vast and hidden material resources, and to rebuild our waste places, and to this end I ask in the name of the black man and in the name of the white man of the South alike, the generous aid and encouragement of the powerful North, the great and liberal East, and the sturdy and growing West.

Vindication of the Colored Man as a Soldier During the War of the Rebellion

The honorable gentleman from North Carolina [Mr. Robbins] said in his speech the other day, in which he compared the colored man to somebody's "merry-Andrew," referring to the dissimilarity of the races, "this is a question which has puzzled the brains of scientists for centuries." Now, I doubt not that if that gentleman undertook to discuss that subject, "which has puzzled the brains of scientists for centuries," in a lyceum, he would find as many fools, judged by his standard, among his audience as he must have noticed here when he made this modest exhibition of his prodigious attainments in the direction indicated. I beg to refer the honorable gentleman to the fifth chapter of the Acts of the Apostles, and to call his attention to the terrible fate of the persons therein spoken of [Ananias and Sapphira]. The gentleman is indeed fortunate in having escaped a similar fate while uttering the words just quoted from his speech.

As to the other remark, that the Negro is no fighter, in proof of which he says that only fifteen hundred of them were killed in action during the rebellion, I have a word to say. I cannot in the time allowed, read over or quote the opinions of those who have made this very question raised by the gentleman a matter of study at any considerable length. Nor was the conviction that the colored men could be employed to advantage as soldiers during the rebellion confined to the officers of the Union Army. The confederate government passed an act, approved March 30, 1865, authorizing the employment of Negroes as soldiers. This law was never put in force, the rebellion having collapsed before colored men were mustered in that service *vietarmis* [with force and arms]. This action is the one remarkable instance where the southern people were perhaps a unit in favor of the doctrine of no discrimination on account of races, color, or previous condition of servitude.

A study of the opinions expressed by one hundred and fifteen surgeons engaged in the examination of both black and white recruits who are ethnological authorities, namely, that no race is equally adapted to all circumstances of life; that mankind obeys the same general laws that govern the distribution of florae and faunae upon the earth; and that the isotherms between which are limited the health and development of the Negro do not comprehend less space upon its surface than those within which the others are confined. It may be confidently affirmed that the statistics of the Medical Bureau, which refer principally to physico-geographical influences and to the effects of the intermixture of blood upon the Negro, when taken in connection with those parts of the Surgeon—General's forthcoming report in which he is regarded as amenable to the vicissitudes of war, will form a more complete and reliable physical history of this race than exists at this time.

It would not be in accordance with the plan of this report to enter upon a discussion of the comparative aptitude for military service exhibited by the two types of mankind of which I have been speaking without the accompanying tables as evidence of the data upon which my opinions were based.

It appears, however, that of the surgeons of boards of enrollment five have given their opinion that the Negro recruits and substitutes examined by them were physically a better class of men than the whites; nineteen that they were equal; two that they were inferior. A favorable opinion as to their fitness for the Army is expressed by seventeen; a doubtful one, because of insufficient data on which to ground the decision, by forty-three; an unfavorable opinion by nine; and by twenty a statement of not having come to any conclusion upon this subject. The question of the prevalence of disease among the Negro inhabitants of different sections of the country is one upon which, at present, no specific opinion can be expressed. As in the case of the white race it may be shown hereafter that their maladies conform to those general principles that have been heretofore established. The discussion of the physical characteristics of the Negro, as involving the propriety of his use in war, only belongs to this department. It is difficult and, in the present state of science, most uncertain to erect upon any general characteristics of organization anything but the most general rules concerning the effect of that structure upon the moral and intellectual nature. It may be said, however, that there are not more instances of disqualifying causes of this nature among the Negroes in proportion to the numbers examined than are to be found in the records of exemption among the white race.

Again, the total number of white troops, regulars and volunteers, in service during the rebellion in the Union Army is put down at 2,041,154. Of this number 42,724 are reported killed in action, 1 1/2 percent. The total number of colored troops in service during the rebellion was 180,000. Of that number 1,514 are put down as killed in action; to which number are added 896 reported missing by competent authority, who were evidently killed, making 2,410 or about 1 1/3 percent, showing on the whole a difference of about 1/6 of one percent. When it is considered that the colored soldier participated in no battle because he was not admitted into the service until some of our heaviest battles were fought, is it not fair to strike off this difference of 1/6 of one percent? This done, would it not be fair to say that the white and the colored troops in the Union Army during the rebellion in the direction indicated by the gentleman from North Carolina, stand upon about the same footing?

The most objectionable feature of the bill to many gentlemen is the provision prohibiting discriminations in the public schools on account of color or race. It is feared, and so said by some gentlemen who favor the bill, that to incorporate this feature in the bill, and to attempt to enforce it, will destroy the school systems in the South especially, and operate as a check upon the education of the children of both races. It does not seem to me that these fears are well founded. About the same line of argument was urged by many good people as to the abolition of slavery and clothing the colored man with the elective franchise, and at every step in the grand march toward freedom. Yet, in nearly every instance these objections and apprehensions vanished, and were in a great part lost sight of upon trial. In addition, the principle upon which you concede, if you please, the right of the colored man to the privileges of the car, the inn, the theater, the witness and the jury box apply in this case as well.

The learned gentleman from New York [Mr. Cox] whose speeches are always to be read with interest and profit, well said in a speech delivered here recently:

Is it not irrefragable that if the right to the inn, railroad, theater, and cemetery be conceded to the black (as provided in the civil rights bill) to the same extent as to the white to enjoy them, (though the enjoyment of the grave-yard is perhaps a melancholy hilarity,) that the same right should be extended to them as to the schools? The colored members are correct in their reasoning, assuming these premises. Indeed, all the amis des noirs who have spoken, if right at all, are right in demanding equality alike in school and inn, in cemetery and car. When you debar them from the school you as much keep up the bar sinister as by keeping them from the playhouse. Would it not be a craven logic, unworthy of the struggling blacks and their admirers, to insist on the one and not the other?

Non-Proscriptive Schools Promotes Harmony

As to the practical working of non-proscriptive schools, or, in other words, schools where blacks and whites are taught in the North and East as well as in the South, it does not appear that either race is injured, or that the cause of general education suffers. At Yale, Harvard, Wilberforce, Cornell, Oberlin, the testimony is that both races get along well together. Nor is the South without such schools. It is needless to add that the danger was averted by this prompt and imposing array of force, and Yale College was saved to New Haven, and Connecticut, and the country. In 1831 the delicate nerves of Yale College could not endure the shock of seeing black boys educated a mile away; now she takes them to her own arms and bids them call her alma mater, and to our notion she looks quite as fair and buxom as ever. We are not a bit surprised to hear Mr. Harris, of Virginia, talk in the same wild strain as did Mayor Kimberly in 1831; for we knew him to be forty-three years behind the times. Let the doors of the public school house be thrown open to us alike, if you mean to give these people equal rights at all, or to protect them in the exercise of the rights and privileges attaching to all freemen and citizens of our country.

The Colored Vote

It is true that these people, the colored people of our country, compose a very small minority of the American people, yet they contribute largely toward its industrial interests and at times play an important part in political affairs. For instance, President Grant's popular majority in the last presidential election was 762,991. The total color vote is put down at 900,000. Now, allowing 10,000 of this vote to have been cast for Mr. Horace Greeley, and 50,000 of these voters as not voting at all, which I am satisfied is in excess of the number of this class not voting, making 60,000, then deduct the 60,000 from the 900,000, and the result will show a colored vote polled of 840,000 for General Grant; yet the popular majority of General Grant as taken from the *Tribune Almanac* for 1873 was not more than 762,991, as already stated.

To the curious in such matters, and to those who seriously consider our institutions in this respect, this might be considered as not unworthy of a passing notice.

Ransier responded to his colleagues who argued that the Civil Rights Bill was not necessary, pointing out that if it was not essential, over five million African Americans would not have urged its passage. He also explained that its author, Charles Sumner, on his deathbed, had urged his colleagues to adopt it.

THE CIVIL RIGHTS BILL
February 12, 1874

I am obliged to my friend for yielding a portion of his time to me, while I am sorry that by doing so he has interrupted himself in his eloquent speech. I had intended, if I had had the opportunity, to say something on this occasion by way of reply to a part of a recent speech by the gentleman from Mississippi [Lucius Q.C. Lamar] and that of the gentleman from Tennessee [Roderick Randum Butler]. The few minutes allowed me, however, are not sufficient to enable me even to briefly sketch what I have hoped to be able to say.

The remarks on yesterday of the distinguished Mississippian [Mr. Lamar] who somewhat electrified the House, and who by the way seems to be somewhat in advance of those for whom he spoke in the matter of a sincere and hearty acquiescence with some of the results of the late war, attracted my attention for more reasons than one. The first was because to many of his utterances importance ought to be attached, coming from the gentleman who spoke. But when he said that the Negroes in this country were possessed of all the rights and privileges attaching to other citizens, I cannot admit that he stated what was exactly true. For if that were the fact five millions of people would not be asking, the Congress of the United States today for the passage of the civil rights bill. Nor would the dying words of Charles Sumner, addressed to Mr. George Frisbie Hoar, have been uttered, "Do not let the civil rights bill fail." Nor would the Senate of the United States sit twenty consecutive hours to pass a useless measure. Hence I say that the statement of the distinguished Mississippian that the colored people of this country possessed all the rights attaching to American citizenship, followed up by the imploring appeal that we ought to pay some attention to the rights and interests of the white people of the South, was not exactly true; else we would not be here today asking the Congress of the United States to pass the civil-rights bill; nor would we be here today reminding the Republican party of the country of their solemn obligation to pass such a bill, nor would we be here to remind the Republican party today that if Congress adjourns without the passage of such a bill, to which it is committed, they will demoralize nine hundred thousand voters in this country and withhold an act of justice from five millions of people. I repeat that the statement of the gentleman from Mississippi is not exactly true, as has already been abundantly proven.

But it is a sign of the rapid strides of progress we have made as a nation that the distinguished gentleman from Mississippi, identified in the manner he is with the past, is now seeking to blot out that past, so far as clinging to its dead issues is concerned. I hail the spirit of his speech as indicative of the progress and advancing strides we are making as a nation. But I say today, and I speak, if I can, to the country, that so far as there is an impression that the colored man in this country has obtained all that attaches to American citizenship; or that the passage of the civil rights bill will work injuriously to either whites or blacks, there never was a greater mistake made. If that were the fact, I say again there never was a more useless or unnecessary imploration uttered than that embodied in the dying words of Charles Sumner, "Take care of the Civil Rights Bill."

Let me say in the brief moment allowed me that what pains me most in this matter is that men coming from the South, from Tennessee and from Virginia, indebted for their elevation to the position of members of Congress on this floor in part at least to colored votes, are to be found declaring that colored men do not want the civil-rights bill. They misrepresent that portion of their constituencies. I say to them, in the language of Charles Sumner to a Senator of the United States, "They are not your constituency; they are mine." You misrepresent them and have added insult to the injury you would inflict. When the gentleman from Tennessee [Mr. Butler] said that the colored people did not want civil rights, that portion of his constituency almost at that same moment were, in a State convention called for the purpose, engaged in making a protest against the position assumed by Mr. Walter Preston Brownlow of Tennessee who had written against the bill. I ask for the passage of the civil rights bill before we shall adjourn. We ask it as a measure of justice to those people who have been true to the nation and to the party in power. We ask it as the hands of President Grant and the Republican party. We also ask it as a matter of sound public policy in the interest of the Republican party and the country. To say that the intelligent colored people do not desire this measure is, I repeat, adding insult to injury. We ask it; we are not in a position to demand it. We plead for it respectfully, but in no uncertain voice, and confidently look for its early passage.

The condition of affairs in South Carolina, Arkansas, Louisiana, and elsewhere in the South is lugged into these debates here and into the writing of newspaper articles as evidences of the unfitness of the Negro for the franchise and for civil rights. That the affairs in some of these States are not in a satisfactory condition is unfortunately true; but these people have done as well under all the circumstances as any other race similarly situated could have done. They have made mistakes and are alive to the fact, and so far as they are concerned are endeavoring to rectify them. They have been deceived in men whom they elected to fill important positions, as the too confiding colored people of portions of Tennessee and Virginia and elsewhere have been deceived and are being misrepresented by some of those towards whose election they contributed largely.

As to affairs in my own State I could wish that there were no grave constitutional obstructions in the way of an investigation into our affairs, as is asked for by a portion of our people. The masses of our people, white and black, would rather invite investigation and a thorough understanding of our affairs than shrink from it. None but those who may be guilty of such practices as are charged against them, and are or may be directly responsible for the misuse of the public moneys and abuses in other directions, could reasonably object. But, because some officials in these States have abused the public confidence and prostituted their office should violence be done to a great principle of justice and a whole race denied therein equal rights in a government like our? It cannot be. Let justice be done though the heavens fall.

17

James Thomas Rapier
(1837–1883)
House of Representatives, Alabama

Republican

Forty-third Congress
March 4, 1873, to March 3, 1875

James Thomas Rapier was the son of free parents, and was born free in Florence (Lauderdale County), Alabama, on November 13, 1837. His father, John H. Rapier, was emancipated in 1829, and operated a successful barbershop in Florence while his wife Susan worked the farm with their four boys. John and Susan managed to circumvent Alabama laws against educating blacks by hiring tutors to teach their children in the privacy of their home. Fortunately, they had the financial resources to provide them with a formal education. John and his wife enrolled James and his brother at Franklin College, a private school in Nashville. To further their education, they sent the children to study at Montreal College in Canada, and at the University of Glasgow in Scotland. During the 1850s, James earned a teaching certificate in Canada and read law. While he had passed the Canadian bar exam, he had decided to dedicate his life to a career in teaching. Upon returning to the United States in the spring of 1864, James worked as a schoolteacher and as a correspondent for a northern newspaper. By the time the Civil War ended Rapier was an educated and well-established farmer in Tennessee.

Rapier began his political activities in Nashville, Tennessee, in 1865, where he attended a convention on black rights. He was a staunch advocate of universal male suffrage. He had lived with his slave grandmother, who operated a laundry business in Nashville. Rapier had also launched a farming business in Maury County, Tennessee, and rented over 200 acres of land. Due to the illness of his father in Alabama, Rapier returned to the state of his birth in 1866, where he immediately began to make his mark in state politics. That year, he rented 550 acres of land in the Tennessee Valley of Alabama. He was also appointed a notary public. By the 1870s, he had begun to earn an annual income of approximately $7,000.

In 1867 at the start of Congressional Reconstruction, Rapier entered Republican politics. He attended the first Republican party convention held in Alabama, and helped develop the platform. He was a delegate to the state constitutional convention in Montgomery in 1867 and ran for secretary of state in 1870, losing to a white Democrat. His first public office came in 1871, from a federal appointment as assessor of internal revenue for the Second District in Alabama. Obviously proud of the appointment, Rapier declared, "No man in the state wields more influence than I." While his assertion is questionable, he was indeed the state's most prominent African American. His travels on official business enabled him to establish his presence among black leaders, and he earned the reputation as a smart and articulate politician. A reporter for the *New National Era* wrote, "Mr. Rapier is the best intellect under a colored skin in Alabama." The journalist also observed that Rapier was well connected politically.

Rapier held other appointive positions for the federal and state governments. In 1867, he traveled to Paris, France, as a federal commissioner for the World Fair. In 1873, Alabama appointed him commissioner to an exposition in Vienna. As he toured Western Europe he broadened his views on the common plight of workers. Rapier also represented civic organizations, recruiting sharecroppers and tradesmen to join the Colored National Labor Union. He served as secretary for the Alabama Equal Rights League, and defended such civil liberties as free speech and a free press. These constitutional guarantees, he frequently declared, were vital in a representative democracy. He also pushed for public school education for whites and blacks, and universal male suffrage. He urged the state and national government to secure the civil rights of African Americans. He published a newspaper, the *Montgomery Sentinel*, along with a partner, Nathan H. Alexander. With these credentials, Rapier set his eyes on a seat in Congress.

At the Republican party convention in 1872, Rapier was nominated to run for Congress. He defeated an ex-Confederate candidate in the election, capturing nearly 3,000 more votes than the opposition. Though the Ku Klux Klan threatened his life and seized his property, Rapier remained diligent in his quest for political office. He took his seat in Congress in 1873, joining six other African Americans. He was appointed to the Education and Labor Committee. As a result of his efforts, President Grant made Montgomery a federal port of delivery in 1874. Rapier also labored to obtain federal funds to dredge Alabama rivers, improve postal services, and restore federal buildings in the state.

The Civil Rights Bill of Charles Sumner was a burning issue in Congress during the mid-1870s, and Rapier joined the battle. In addition to caucusing with his African-American colleagues on the bill, he attended a national civil rights meeting held in the nation's capital in 1873. Delivering his maiden speech in the House of Representatives on June 9, 1874, Rapier defended the Civil Rights Bill. "I cannot willingly accept anything less than my full measure of rights as a man, because I am unwilling to present myself as a candidate for any brand of inferiority." A reporter for the *New National Era* praised him. Rapier, the correspondent declared, delivered a brilliant speech that would surely be read with great pride by black Americans. His only achievement in the House, however, was passage of the port bill.

When Congress spurned the Civil Rights Bill and disregarded its black members, they emboldened white Democrats in Alabama. The white press and politicians called for driving blacks from government. It was a choice between white rule and Negro rule, the *Mobile Daily Register* announced. Another newspaper proclaimed that the 1874 state election would decide white supremacy forever. Still others threatened black Americans with violence. Republicans and Democrats united to drive blacks out of office. Rapier went to Washington, pleading for federal protection, but the government had also begun its retreat from defending blacks. With blacks staying at home on election day, Rapier stood little chance of winning. Once Democrats regained control of the state government, they gerrymandered areas heavily populated by blacks. Rapier made one final bid for Congress in 1876, but when Jeremiah Haralson, another black Republican, entered the race they divided the black vote. This made it possible for Charles Shelly, a white Democratic, to win the election.

After 1876, Rapier would never again seek political office. He continued to be active in business, and in 1878 was again appointed U.S. collector of internal revenue for the Second District of Alabama. Yet, he continued to face the humiliation of living in a state that enforced racial segregation. Though more articulate and better educated than most whites he encountered, his color identified him as a man inferior to whites. None of his efforts to enforce the Reconstruction constitutional amendments had prevailed. The wealth of his uncle James P. Thomas, whose assets exceeded a quarter of a million dollars, did not shield them from racial discrimination. Rapier became bitter, and during the final years of his life he began to consider black emigration to the North as a real alternative to racial oppression in the South.

As his health declined, he offered a glimmer of hope to African Americans. He urged them to fight on, assuring them that they would one day achieve success. He told them that the "war" they were fighting was between truth and a lie. Looking to the future, Rapier said, "a wide, deep sea of prosperity awaits our beloved State and nation." He died in Montgomery, Alabama, on May 31, 1883, at a relatively young age.

> *Rapier disputed the notion that black congressmen defended the Civil Rights Bill solely because it applied to them. His arguments in favor of civil rights legislation included: (1) immigrants would be surprised to discover that blacks were not free in America. (2) that although he was a public servant, he was denied access to public places such as first-class railroad cars and restaurants. (3) whites argued that blacks were inferior, but by denying African Americans access to schools they seemed to doubt the assertion of black inferiority. and (4) mainly poor whites wanted to hold down African Americans.*

CIVIL RIGHTS
June 9, 1874

I had hoped there would be no protracted discussion on the civil rights bill. It has been debated all over the country for the last seven years; twice it has done duty in our national political campaigns; and in every minor election during that time it has been pressed into service for the purpose of intimidating the weak white men who are inclined to support the Republican ticket. I was certain until now that most persons were acquainted with its provisions, that they understood its meaning; therefore it was no longer to them the monster it had been depicted, that was to break down all social barriers, and compel one man to recognize another socially, whether agreeable to him or not.

I must confess it is somewhat embarrassing for a colored man to urge the passage of this bill because if he exhibits earnestness in the matter and expresses a desire for its immediate passage, straightway he is charged with a desire for social equality, as explained by the demagogue and understood by the ignorant white man. But, then it is just as embarrassing for him not to do so, for, if he remains silent while the struggle is being carried on around, and for him, he is liable to be charged with a want of interest in a matter that concerns him more than anyone else, which is enough to make his friends desert his cause. So in steering away from Scylla I may run upon Charybdis. But the anomalous, and I may add the supremely ridiculous, position of the Negro at this time in this country compels me to say something. Here his condition is without comparison, is parallel alone to itself. Just think that the law recognizes my right upon this floor as a lawmaker, but that there is no law to secure me any accommodations whatever while traveling here to discharge my duties as a Representative of a large and wealthy constituency. Here I am the peer of the proudest, but on a steamboat or car I am not equal to the most degraded. Is not this most anomalous and ridiculous?

What little I shall say will be more in the way of stating the case than otherwise, for I am certain I can add nothing to the arguments already made in behalf of the bill. If in the course of my remarks I should use language that may be considered inelegant, I have only to say that it shall be as elegant as that used by the opposition in discussing this measure; if undignified, it shall not be more so than my subject; if ridiculous, I enter the plea that the example has been set by the democratic side of the House, which claims the right to set examples. I wish to say in justice to myself that no one regrets more than I do the necessity that compels one to the manner born to come in these Halls with hat in hand (so to speak) to ask at the hands of his political peers the same public rights they enjoy.

And I shall feel ashamed for my country if there be any foreigners present, who have been lured to our shores by the popular but untruthful declaration that this land is the asylum of the oppressed, to hear a member of the highest legislative body in the world declare from his place, upon his responsibility as a Representative, that notwithstanding his political position, he has no civil rights that another class is bound to respect. Here a foreigner can learn what he cannot learn in another country, that it is possible for a man to be half free and half slave, or, in other words, he will see that it is possible for a man to enjoy political rights while he is denied civil ones; here he will see a man legislating for a free people, while his own chains of civil slavery hang about him, and are far more galling than any the foreigner left behind him; here will see what is not to be seen elsewhere, that position is no mantle of protection, in our "land of the free and home of the brave"; for I am subjected to far more outrages and indignities in coming to and going from this capital in discharge of my public duties than any criminal in the country providing he be white. Instead of my position shielding me from insult, it too often invites it.

Let me cite a case. Not many months ago, Francis L. Cardozo, treasurer from the State of South Carolina, was on his way home from the West. His route lay through Atlanta. There he made request for a sleeping berth. Not only was he refused this, but he was denied a seat in a first-class carriage, and the parties went so far as to threaten to take his life because he insisted upon his rights as a traveler. He was compelled, a most elegant and accomplished gentleman, to take a seat in a dirty smoking-car, along with the traveling rabble, or else be left, to the detriment of his public duties. I affirm, without the fear of contradiction, that any white ex-convict (I care not what may have been his crime, nor whether the hair on the shaven side of his head has had time to grow out or not) may start, with me today to Montgomery, Alabama, and that all the way down he will be treated as a gentleman, while I will be treated as the convict. He would be allowed a berth in a sleeping car with all its comforts, while I will be forced into a dirty, rough box with the drunkards, apple sellers, railroad hands, and next to any dead that may be in transit, regardless of how far decomposition may have progressed. Sentinels are placed at the doors of the better coaches, with positive instructions to keep persons of color out; and I must do them the justice to say that they guard these sacred portals with a vigilance that would have done credit to the flaming swords at the gates of Eden. Tender, pure, intelligent young ladies are forced to travel in this way if they are guilty of the crime of color, the only unpardonable sin known ill in our Christian and Bible lands, where sinning against the Holy Ghost (whatever that may be) sinks into insignificance when compared with the sin of color. If from any cause we are compelled to lay over, the best bed in the hotel is his if he can pay for it, while I am invariably turned away, hungry and cold, to stand around the railway station until the departure of the next train, it matters not how long, thereby endangering my health, while my life, and property are at the mercy of any highwayman who may wish to murder and rob me.

And I state without the fear of being gainsaid, the statement of the gentleman from Tennessee [Roderick Randum Butler] to the contrary notwithstanding, that there is not an inn between Washington and Montgomery, a distance of more than a thousand miles, that will accommodate me to a bed or meal. Now, then, is there a man upon this floor who is so heartless, whose breast is so void of the better feelings, as to say that this brutal custom needs no regulation? I hold that it does and that Congress is the body to regulate it. Authority for its action is found not only in the Fourteenth Amendment to the Constitution, but by virtue of that amendment (which makes all persons born here citizens), authority is found in Article 4, Section 2 of the Federal Constitution, which declares in positive language "that the citizens of each State shall have the, same rights as the citizens of the several States." Let me read Mr. Brightly's comment upon this clause; he is considered good authority, I believe. In describing the several rights he says they may be all comprehended under the following general heads: "Protection by the Government; the enjoyment of life and liberty, with the right to acquire and possess property of every kind, and to pursue and obtain happiness and safety; the right of a citizen of one State to pass through or to reside in any other State for purposes of trade, agriculture, professional pursuits, or otherwise."

It is very clear that the right of locomotion without hindrance and every thing pertaining thereto is embraced in this clause; and every lawyer knows if any white man in *antebellum* times had been refused first-class passage in a steamboat or car, who was free from any contagious disease, and was compelled to go on deck of a boat or into a baggage-car, and any accident had happened to him while he occupied that place, a lawsuit would have followed; and damages would have been given by any jury to the plaintiff; and whether any accident had happened or not in the case I have referred to, a suit would have been brought for a denial of rights, and no one doubts what would have been the verdict. White men had rights then that common carriers were compelled to respect, and I demand the same for the colored men now.

Whether this deduction from the clause of the Constitution just read was applicable to the Negro prior to the adoption of the several late amendments to our organic law is not a question, but that it does apply to him in his new relations no intelligent man will dispute. Therefore I come to the national, instead of going to the local, legislature for relief, as has been suggested, because the grievance is national and not local; because Congress is the lawmaking power of the General Government, whose duty is to see that there is no unjust and odious discrimination between its citizens. I look to the Government in the place of the several States, because it claims my first allegiance, exacts at my hands strict obedience to its laws, and because it promises in the implied contract between every citizen and the Government to protect my life and property. I have fulfilled my part of the contract to the extent I have been called upon, and I demand that the Government, through Congress, do likewise. Every day my life and property are exposed, are left to the mercy of others, and will be so as long as every hotelkeeper, railroad conductor, and steamboat captain can refuse me with impunity the accommodations common to other travelers. I hold further, if the Government cannot secure to a citizen his guaranteed rights it ought not to call upon him to perform the same duties that are performed by another class of citizens who are in the free and full enjoyment of every civil and political right.

I submit that I am degraded as long as I am denied the public privileges common to other men, and that recognizing my political equality while I occupy such a humiliating position correspondingly degrades the members of this House. What a singular attitude for lawmakers of this great nation to assume, rather come down to me than allow me to go up to them. Did you ever reflect that this is the only Christian country where poor, finite man is held responsible for the crimes of the infinite God whom you profess to worship? But it is; I am held to answer for the crime of color, when I was not consulted in the matter. Had I been consulted, and my future fully described, I think I should have objected to being born in this gospel land. The excuse offered for all this inhuman treatment is that they consider the Negro inferior to the white man, intellectually and morally. This reason might have been offered and probably accepted as truth some years ago, but no one now believes him incapable of a high order of culture, except someone who is below the average of mankind in natural endowments. This is not the reason, as I shall show before I have done. There is a cowardly propensity in the human heart that delights in oppressing somebody else, and in the gratification of this base desire we always select a victim that can be outraged with safety. As a general thing the Jew has been the subject in most parts of the world; but here the Negro is the most available for this purpose; for this reason in heart he was seized upon, and not because he is naturally inferior to anyone else. Instead of his enemies believing him to be incapable of a high order of mental culture, they have shown that they believe the reverse to be true, by taking the most elaborate pains to prevent his development. And the smaller the caliber of the white man the more frantically has he fought to prevent the intellectual and moral progress of the Negro, for the simple but good reason that he has most to fear from such a result. He does not wish to see the Negro approach the high moral standard of a man and Gentleman.

Let me call your attention to a case in point. Some time since a well-dressed colored man was traveling from Augusta, Georgia, to Montgomery, Alabama. The train upon which he was traveling stopped at a dinner-house. The crowd around the depot seeing him well dressed, looking fine, and polite, concluded he must be a gentleman, (which was more than their righteous souls could stand), and straightway they commenced to abuse him. And he had to go into the baggage-car, open his trunks, show his cards, faro-bank, dice, etc., before they would give him any peace; or in other words, he was forced to give satisfactory evidence that he was not a man who was working to elevate the moral and intellectual standard of the Negro before they would respect him. I have always found more prejudice existing in the breasts of men who have feeble minds and are conscious of it, than in the breasts of those who have towering intellects and are aware of it. Henry Ward Beecher reflected the feelings of the latter class when on a certain occasion he said: "Turn the Negro loose; I am not afraid to run the race of life with him." He could afford to say this, all white men cannot; but what does the other class say? "Build a Chinese wall between the Negro and the school-house, discourage in him pride of character and honest ambition, cut him off from every avenue that leads to the higher grounds of intelligence and usefulness, and then challenge him to a contest upon the highway of life to decide the question of superiority of race." By their acts, not by their words, the civilized world can and will judge how honest my opponents are in their declarations that I am naturally inferior to them. No one is surprised that this class opposes the passage of the civil rights bill, for if the Negro were allowed the same opportunities, the same rights of locomotion, the same rights to comfort in travel, how could they prove themselves better than the Negro?

It was said, I believe by the gentleman from Kentucky [James Burnie Beck], that the people of the South, particularly his State, were willing to accord the colored man all the rights they believe him guaranteed by the Constitution. No one doubts this assertion. But the difficulty is they do not acknowledge that I am entitled to any rights under the organic law. I am forced to this conclusion by reading the platforms of the Democratic party in the several States. Which one declares that that party believes in the constitutionality of the Reconstruction Acts or the several amendments? But upon the other hand, they question the constitutionality of every measure that is advanced to ameliorate the condition of the colored man; and so skeptical has the democracy become respecting the Constitution, brought about by their unsuccessful efforts to find constitutional objections to every step that is taken to elevate the Negro, that now they begin to doubt the constitutionality of the Constitution itself. The most they have agreed to do is to obey present laws bearing on manhood suffrage until they are repealed by Congress or decided to be unconstitutional by the Supreme Court.

I will, however, take the gentleman at his word; but must be allowed to ask if so why was it, even after the several amendments had been officially announced to be part of the Federal Constitution, that his State and others refused to allow the Negro to testify in their courts against a white man? If they believed he should be educated (and surely this is a right) why was it that his school houses were burned down, and the teachers who had gone down on errands of mercy to carry light into dark places driven off, and in some places killed? If they believe the Negro should vote (another right, as I understand in the Constitution), why was it that the Ku Klux Klan organized to prevent him from exercising the right of an American citizen, namely, casting the ballot-the very thing they said he had a right to do? The professed belief and practice are sadly at variance, and must be intelligently harmonized before I can be made to believe that they are willing to acknowledge that I have any rights under the Constitution or elsewhere. He boasts of the magnanimity of Kentucky in allowing the Negro to vote without qualification, while to enjoy the same privilege in Massachusetts he is required to read the constitution of that State. He was very unhappy in this comparison. Why, his State does not allow the Negro to vote at all. When was the constitution of Kentucky amended so as to grant him the elective franchise? They vote there by virtue of the Fifteenth Amendment alone, independent of the laws and constitution of that Commonwealth; and they would today disfranchise him if it could be done without affecting her white population.

The Old Bay State waited for no "act of Congress" to force her to do justice to all of her citizens, but in *antebellum* days provided in her constitution that all male persons who could read and write should be entitled to suffrage. That was a case of equality before the law, and who had a right to complain? There is nothing now in the amended Federal Constitution to prevent Kentucky from adopting the same kind of clause in her constitution. When the convention meets to revise the organic law of that State, I venture the assertion that you will never hear a word about it; but it will not be out of any regard for her colored citizens, but the respect for that army of fifty-thousand ignorant white men she has within her borders, many of whom I see every time I pass through that State, standing around the several depots continually harping on the stereotyped phrase: "The damned Negro won't work." I would not be surprised though, if she should do better in the future. I remember when a foreigner was just as unpopular in Kentucky as the Negro is now; when the majority of the people of that State were opposed to according the foreigner the same rights they claimed for themselves; when that class of people were mobbed in the streets of her principal cities on account of their political faith, just as they have done to the Negro for the last seven years. But what do you see today? Kentucky's chief Representative upon this floor is one of the proscribed classes. Is not this an evidence of a returning sense of justice? If so, would it not be reasonable to predict that she will in the near future send one of her now proscribed class to aid him in representing her interests upon this floor?

There is another member of this body who has opposed the passage of this bill very earnestly, whose position in the country and peculiar relations to the Government compel me to refer to him before I conclude. I allude to the gentleman from Georgia [Alexander Stephens]. He returns to this House after an absence of many years with the same old ideas respecting States' rights that he carried away with him. He has not advanced a step; but unfortunately for him the American people have, and no longer consider him a fit expounder of our organic law. Following to its legitimate conclusion the doctrine of States' rights (which of itself is secession), he deserted the flag of his country, followed his State out of the Union, and a long and bloody war followed. With its results most men are acquainted and recognize; but he, bourbon-like, comes back saying the very same things he used to say, and swearing by the same gods he swore by in other days. He seems not to know that the ideas which he so ably advanced for so many years were by the war swept away, along with that system of slavery which he intended should be the chief cornerstone, precious and elect, of the transitory kingdom over which he was second rule

18

Hiram Rhodes Revels
(1827–1901)
Senate, Mississippi

Republican

Forty-first Congress
February 23, 1870, to March 3, 1871

Hiram Rhodes Revels was the first African American to serve in the Senate of the United States. On September 27, 1827, he was born free to mixed parents in Fayetteville, North Carolina. Revels was considered a "quadroon," a person who is one-fourth black. He attended various schools for free blacks in Fayetteville, including barbering school. He owned a barbershop in Lincolnton, North Carolina. Once he became a minister, Revels enrolled in the Beach Grove Seminary, a Quaker school in Indiana. Apparently feeling isolated as the only black seminary student, he transferred to a black seminary in Drake County, Ohio. Revels also attended Knox College in Indiana. In 1845, he was ordained as a minister in the African Methodist Episcopal (AME) church. He would develop an impressive resume, serving as a teacher, pastor, lecturer, and public servant. He also joined Frederick Douglass, John Mercer Langston, and other prominent figures in recruiting blacks for the Union Army during the Civil War. Revels helped establish black regiments in Maryland and Massachusetts. He also served as an army chaplain.

His civil rights record preceded Reconstruction. He intentionally violated state law in Missouri in 1854 when he preached the Gospel of Jesus Christ to free African Americans. He was jailed for the offense but did not surrender the conviction that the Gospel was available to all men. He continued to embrace these principles after the Civil War. While traveling by train with his family in Kansas, they were ordered to a smoking coach on the grounds that state law required it. Revels objected, explaining that he had purchased a first-class ticket. He also objected because the language used by travelers in male-dominated smoking coaches was coarse. "I do not wish my wife and children to be there and listen to such language." The conductor relented, and allowed the Revels family to defy the Jim Crow law of Kansas.

After the war, Revels continued his public service. He helped establish churches and schools throughout the South. He also worked for the Freedmen's Bureau. Revels settled in Natchez, Mississippi, in 1866. He landed his first elective office in 1868 as an alderman. He was also the interim secretary of state. In 1867, Adams County voters elected him to the state senate. In 1870, Republicans in the state legislature chose Revels to fill the unexpired congressional term of Jefferson Davis. Revels faced opposition in Washington. Some of his future colleagues in the Senate tried to deny him a seat by questioning his citizenship before passage of the Fourteenth Amendment. Hence, they contended, Revels had not yet satisfied the nine-year residency requirement for senatorial service. Article 1, Section 3 of the Constitution states that "no person shall be a Senator who shall not have been nine years a citizen of the United States." Others argued that Mississippi had not yet established a legitimate civil government following the war, and was not authorized to elect a senator. They also claimed that the governor had not signed Revels's credentials. After extensive debate the majority in the Senate confirmed Revels on a vote of forty-eight to eight, and he assumed his seat on February 25.

Senator Hiram Rhodes Revels was appointed to the Committee on Education and Labor and the Committee on the District of Columbia. He remained true to his principles on temperance, religious education, equality, and self-help. He surprisingly favored the amnesty bill for individuals who held high offices in the Confederacy. Revels insisted only that they make a pledge of their future loyalty to the United States. Although he had conservative views, Revels did not abandon civil rights. He supported black participation in government and denounced the states that barred African Americans. When Georgia refused to seat its duly elected black lawmakers, Revels persuaded Congress to insist upon their certification. He also nominated Michael Howard, a black student, to West Point, though the applicant was denied admission. Revels backed legislation to develop the economy of the South. He supported federal appropriations to increase cotton production, proposing a $2 million package. He also favored desegregation of public schools in the District of Columbia. However, he did not necessarily back social integration. He believed that mixed schools would not automatically lead to social integration. He likened schools to churches, where mixed congregations went their separate ways after worship. He defended black workers who were denied jobs at the Navy Yard in Washington.

Once his brief term in the Senate ended, Revels returned to educational and religious leadership. He was appointed president of Alcorn Agricultural

College in 1871 (future Alcorn University), the first land grant university for blacks. He resigned from Alcorn in 1874, believing Adelbert Ames, the new Republican governor and a political opponent, would fire him. He returned to church work and accepted a pastorate in Holly Springs. During the 1876 gubernatorial campaign Revels supported Democratic candidate John M. Stone who, upon winning the election, returned him to lead Alcorn. Revels had hoped for this result, although he lost favor among black Republicans. Revels died in Aberdeen, Mississippi, on January 16, 1901.

Revels urged the Senate to adopt legislation to protect the loyal black and white people of Georgia. He reviewed the history of Reconstruction politics in Georgia, arguing that the majority of whites had boycotted its election. The voters had determined the outcome of the elections there, and had established a republican government. Democrats wanted to subvert the wishes of the voters. He explained that blacks had earned the right of federal protection. He considered it noble that enslaved African Americans had remained loyal to the United States during the Civil War.

THE STATE OF GEORGIA
March 16, 1870

I rise at this particular juncture in the discussion of the Georgia bill with feelings that perhaps never before entered into the experience of any member of this body. I rise, too, with misgivings as to the propriety of lifting my voice at this early period after my admission into the Senate. Perhaps it were wiser for me, so inexperienced in the details of senatorial duties, to have remained a passive listener in the progress of this debate; but when I remember that my term is short, and that the issues with which this bill is fraught are momentous in their present and future influence upon the well-being of my race, I would seem indifferent to the importance of the hour and recreant to the high trust imposed upon me if I hesitated to lend my voice on behalf of the loyal people of the South. I therefore waive all thoughts as to the propriety of taking a part in this discussion. When questions arise which bear upon the safety and protection of the loyal white and colored population of those States lately in rebellion I cannot allow any thought as to mere propriety to enter into my consideration of duty. The responsibilities of being the exponent of such a constituency as I have the honor to represent are fully appreciated by me. I bear about me daily the keenest sense of their weight, and that feeling prompts me now to lift my voice for the first time in this Council Chamber of the nation; and, I stand today on this floor to appeal for protection from the strong arm of the Government for her loyal children, irrespective of color and race, who are citizens of the southern States, and particularly of the State of Georgia.

    I am well aware that the idea is abroad that an antagonism exists between the whites and blacks, that that race which the nation raised from the degradation of slavery, and endowed with the full and unqualified rights and privileges of citizenship, is intent upon power, at whatever price it can be gained. It has been the well-considered purpose and aim of a class not confined to the South to spread this charge over the land, and their efforts are as vigorous today to educate the people of this nation into that belief as they were at the close of the war. It was not uncommon to find this same class, even during the rebellion, prognosticating a servile war. It may have been that "the wish was father to the thought." As the recognized representative of my downtrodden people, I deny the charge, and hurl it back into the teeth of those who make it, and who, I believe, have not a true and conscientious desire to further the interests of the whole South. Certainly no one possessing any personal knowledge of the colored population of my own or other States need be reminded of the noble conduct of that people under the most trying circumstances in the history of the late war, when they were beyond the protection of the Federal forces. While the Confederate Army pressed into its ranks every white male capable to bearing arms, the mothers, wives, daughters, and sisters of the southern soldiers were left defenseless and in the power of the blacks, upon whom the chains of slavery were still riveted; and to bind those chains the closer was the real issue for which so much life and property was sacrificed.

    And now, I ask: how did that race act? Did they in those days of confederate weakness and impotence evince the malignity of which we hear so much? Granting, for the sake of argument, that they were ignorant and besotted, which I do not believe, yet with all their supposed ignorance and credulity they in their way understood as fully as you or I the awful import of the contest. They knew if the gallant corps of national soldiers were beaten back and their flag trailed in the dust that it was the presage of still heavier bondage. They longed, too, as their fathers did before them, for the advent of that epoch over which was shed the hallowed light of inspiration itself. They desired, too, with their fathers, to welcome the feet of the stranger shod with the peaceful preparation of good news. Weary years of bondage had told their tale of sorrow to the court of Heaven. In the councils of the great Father of all they knew the adjudication of their case, albeit delayed for years, in which patient suffering had nearly exhausted itself, would in the end bring to them the boon for which they sighed—God's most blessed gift to His creatures—the inestimable boon of liberty. They waited, and they waited patiently. In the absence of their masters they protected the virtue and chastity of defenseless women. Think for a moment about what the condition of this land would be today if the slave population had risen in servile insurrection against those who month by month were fighting to perpetuate that institution which brought to them all the evils of which they complained. Where would have been the security for property, female chastity, and childhood's innocence? The bloody counterpart of such a story of cruelty and wrong would have been paralleled only in those chapters of Jewish history as recorded by Josephus, or in the still later atrocities of that reign of terror which sent the unfortunate Louis XVI and Marie Antoinette to the scaffold. Nay, the deeds in that drama of cold-blooded butchery would have out-Heroded the most diabolical acts of Herod himself.

I maintain that the past record of my race is a true index of the feelings, which to say, animates them. They bear toward their former masters no revengeful thoughts, no hatreds, and no animosities. They aim not to elevate themselves by sacrificing one single interest of their white fellow-citizens. They ask but the rights which are theirs by God's universal law, and which are the natural outgrowth, the logical sequence of the condition in which the legislative enactments of this nation have placed them. They appeal to you and to me to see that they receive that protection which alone will enable them to pursue their daily avocations with success and enjoy the liberties of citizenship on the same footing with their white neighbors and friends. I do not desire simply to defend my own race from unjust and unmerited charges, but I also desire to place upon record an expression of my full and entire confidence in the integrity of purpose with which I believe the President, Congress, and the Republican party will meet these questions so prolific of weal or woe, not only to my own people, but to the whole South. No spirit of petty tyranny has so far as I can read the history of the times, influenced them.

And how have they used that power lodged in them by the people? In acts of cruelty and oppression toward those who sought to rend in twain this goodly fabric of our fathers, the priceless heritage of so much hardship and endurance in revolutionary times? Let the reconstruction enactments answer the interrogation. No poor words of mine are needed to defend the wise and beneficent legislation that has been extended alike to white and colored citizens. The Republican party is not inflamed, as some would fain have the country believe, against the white population of the South. Its borders are wide enough for all truly loyal men to find within them peace and repose from the din and discord of angry faction. And be that loyal man white or black, that great party of our Republic will, if consistent with the record it has already made for posterity, throw around him the same impartial security in his pursuit of liberty and happiness. If a certain class at the South had accepted in good faith the benevolent overtures that were offered to them with no niggard hand, our land today would not still be harassed with feuds and contentions.

I remarked that I rose to plead for protection for the defenseless race that now send their delegation to the seat of Government to sue for that which this Congress alone can secure to them. And here let me say further, that the people of the North owe to the colored race a deep obligation that it is no easy matter to fulfill. When the Federal armies were thinned by death and disaster, and somber clouds overhung the length and breadth of the Republic, and the very air was pregnant with the rumors of foreign interference in those dark days of defeat, whose memories even yet haunt us as an ugly dream, from what source did our nation in its seeming death throes gain additional and new found power? It was the sable sons of the South that valiantly rushed to the rescue, and but for their intrepidity and ardent daring many a northern fireside would miss today paternal counsels or a brother's love.

I repeat the fact that the colored race helped save the noble women of New England and those in the middle states upon whom they lean today for security and safety. Many people of my race who represented the Union on the field of battle now sleep in countless graves in the South. If those quiet resting-places of our honored dead could speak today what a mighty voice, like to the rushing of a mighty wind, would come up from those sepulchral homes! Could we resist the eloquent pleadings of their appeal? I think that this question of immediate and ample protection for the loyal people of Georgia would lose its legal technicalities, and we would cease to hesitate in our provisions for their instant relief. Again, I regret this delay on other grounds. The taunt is frequently flung at us that a Nemesis more terrible than the Greek impersonation of the anger of the gods waits her hour of direful retribution. We are told that at no distant day a great uprising of the American people will demand that the reconstruction acts of Congress be undone and blotted forever from the annals of legislative enactment. I ask if this delay in affording protection to the loyalists of the State of Georgia does not lend an uncomfortable significance to this boasting sneer with which we so often meet. Delay is perilous at best; for it is as true in legislation as in physics that the longer we procrastinate to apply the proper remedies the more chronic becomes the malady that we seek to heal.

I favor the motion to strike out so much of the bill under debate as tends to abridge the term of the existing Legislature of Georgia. Let me, then, as briefly as possible, review the history of the case that so urgently claims our prompt action. In the month of November 1867, an election was held by the authority of the reconstruction policy of this Congress in the State of Georgia. Its object was to settle by the ballot of her whole people, white and colored, whether it was expedient to summon a convention that should frame a constitution for civil government in that State. A certain class of the population declined to take any part in the election. The vote cast at that election represented thirty thousand white and eighty thousand colored citizens of the State. It was a majority, too, of the registered vote, and in consequence a convention was called. A number of the delegates who formed that convention were colored. By the authority of the convention they helped frame a constitution that was just and equitable in all its provisions. Race, color, or former condition of servitude found no barrier in any of its ample enactments, and it extended to those lately in armed rebellion all the privileges of its impartial requirements. This constitution was submitted to the people of the State for ratification. Every effort which human ingenuity could call into requisition to defeat its adoption was resorted to. The loyal population of the State was victorious; and notwithstanding the determination of some to defeat the constitution that same class sought under its provisions to procure the nomination for all the offices within the gift of the people. A number were declared elected as county officers and members of the General Assembly.

Under the authority given by the act of Congress of June 25, 1868, the Legislature thus elected convened on the 4th of July of the same year in Atlanta. The act of Congress to which I refer reaffirmed certain qualifications that were demanded from all persons who were to hold office in the reconstructed States. After some delay the Legislature of Georgia adopted a resolution declaring that that body was duly qualified, and thus began the civil government in the State. Peace and harmony seemed at last to have met together; truth and justice kissed each other. But their reign was of short duration. By and by the reconstruction acts of Congress began to be questioned, and it was alleged that they were unconstitutional; and the legislature which was elected under the constitution framed and supported by colored men declared that a man having more than an eighth of African blood in his veins was ineligible to hold office or a seat in the Legislature of the State of Georgia. These very men, to whom the Republican party extended all the rights and privileges of citizenship, whom they were empowered if deemed expedient, to cut off forever from such beneficent grants, were the men to deny political equality to a large majority of their fellow-citizens.

In the month of September 1868, twenty-eight members of the Legislature were expelled from that body, and upon the assumption of the strange and startling hypothesis just mentioned they continued to legislate in open violation of the constitution. That constitution required by its provisions the establishment of a system of free schools. Such provisions were wholly abortive, indeed a dead letter, for none were established. The courts of law, at least so far as colored men were regarded, were a shameless mockery of justice. And here an illustration, perhaps, will the better give point to my last remark. A case in which was involved the question whether or not a colored man was eligible to one of the county offices was taken before the superior court, and the judge upon the bench rendered as his judicial opinion that a man of color was not entitled to hold office. I am told that the colored man in question is a graduate of Oberlin,

Ohio, and served with honor as a commissioned officer in the Union Army during the late war. Is any comment needed in this body upon such a condition of affairs in the State of Georgia? I trust not.

Then, again, these facts were presented for the calm consideration of Congress in the following December, and the results of their deliberation may be seen in the report of the Committee on the Judiciary toward the close of January of last year. Congress took no action to remedy this state of affairs and aid the people of Georgia in obtaining the rights clearly guaranteed to them by the provisions of their State constitution. In December last, at the earnest recommendation of the President, the act of the 22nd of that month was adopted. It provided for the reassembling of the parties declared to have been elected by the general commanding that district, the restoration of the expelled persons of the Legislature, and the rejection of disqualified persons by that body. The present Legislature of Georgia has adopted the Fourteenth and Fifteenth Amendments to the Constitution of the United States and the fundamental conditions required by the act of June 25, 1868. The state of Georgia now offers herself through the constitutionally elected Senators for the recognition and admission by this Congress.

I have thus rapidly gone over the history of the events, which have transpired in the State of Georgia till I have come to the legislation of the present time. The Committee of Reconstruction in the other House prepared and presented a bill providing for the admission of the State on similar grounds to those on which my own State and Virginia were allowed to take their places in the Union. An amendment, however, was proposed in the House and adopted, the aim and purport of which is to legalize the organization of 1868, and declare that the terms of the members of the Legislature, who have so recently qualified for a fair and just recognition by Congress, shall expire before they have completed their full term of two years under the constitution. Again, this amendment seeks to retain in office, whether approved by the Legislature of the State or not, the judges who have declared, in opposition to the constitution and the law, that in the State of Georgia at least there exists a distinction as to race and color, so far as civil and political rights are concerned. If there be any meaning in the words of the constitution of that State no such class distinction as this exists; and I am at a loss to determine upon what grounds we are called upon to hedge in by congressional enactment any public servant who may still give utterance to such doctrines, which are part and parcel of the effete civilization of our Republic. If the Legislature of Georgia thinks it right and proper to place in positions of trust and responsibility men of this school of political thought, certainly I shall not offer one objection. But let that Legislature assume the risk, as it is its true province, and let it also bear the consequences.

I do not believe that it can be proved that the State of Georgia has ever been beyond the control of Congress, nor that she has ever become fully admitted into the Union or entitled to representation since her impotent efforts to promote rebellion; and that therefore, when the act now under consideration and properly amended shall have been adopted, the government of that State and the Legislature of that State will enter upon the terms of office, will assume the powers for good and right and justice which are prescribed in the constitution of that State, and that under the circumstances the Senate will not deny to the loyal men of Georgia the recognition of their recent victory. And now, I protest in the name of truth and human rights against any and every attempt to fetter the hands of one hundred thousand white and colored citizens of the State of Georgia. I now leave this question to the consideration of this body, and I wish my last words upon the great issues involved in the bill before us to be my solemn and earnest demand for full and prompt protection for the helpless loyal people of Georgia.

I appeal to the legislative enactments of this Congress, and ask if now, in the hour when a reconstructed State most needs support, this Senate, which hitherto has done so nobly, will not give it such legislation as it needs.

Revels supported removing all disabilities imposed upon ex-Confederates. His only criterion was their making an oath of their future loyalty to the United States. He praised his state for conforming to Congressional Reconstruction. He claimed that blacks and whites lived in harmony in Mississippi. He did not believe that there were compelling arguments against passing the amnesty bill.

THE AMNESTY BILL
May 17, 1870

I did not intend to take any part in this discussion. It was not my desire to do so. I do not rise now for the purpose of doing so, but merely to explain my position and that of the State that I in part represent, in regard to the question of general amnesty. I have been referred to by quite a number of honorable senators who have already addressed the Senate on this subject, and at last I have been called upon to define my position and that of my State. I am in favor of removing the disabilities of those upon whom they are imposed in the South just as fast as they give evidence of having become loyal and of being loyal. If you can find one man in the South who gives evidence that he is a loyal man, and gives that evidence in the fact that he has ceased to denounce the laws of

Congress as unconstitutional, has ceased to oppose them, and respects them and favors the carrying of them out, I am in favor of removing his disabilities; and if you can find one hundred men that the same is true of I am in favor of removing their disabilities. If you can find a whole State that this is true of I am in favor of removing the disabilities of its entire people.

Now, my position ifs fully understood. Often I receive petitions from citizens of my State asking Congress to remove their disabilities; and how much I regret that it is not in our power to take that class of persons and put them by themselves and remove the disabilities of all of them at once. I would be glad to see this done, but we can only do it by the process adopted by Congress. In regard to the State of Mississippi I have this to say: the Republican party, now dominant there, pledged itself to universal amnesty. That was in their platform; the speakers pledged themselves to it; and the Legislature redeemed that pledge by unanimously adopting a resolution asking Congress to remove the political disabilities of all the citizens of Mississippi, which resolution they placed in my hands, and made it my duty to present here, and which I have presented.

Now, I can say more, I believe, for the State of Mississippi than I can say for any of the other lately insurrectionary States. I do not know of one State that is altogether as well reconstructed as Mississippi is. We have reports from a great many other States of lawlessness and of violence, and from parts of States we have well-authenticated reports to this effect; but while this is the case, do you hear one report of any more lawlessness or violence in the State of Mississippi? No; the people now I believe are getting along as quietly, pleasantly, harmoniously, and prosperously as the people are in any of the formerly free States. I think this is the case. I do not think my statement exaggerates anything at all. I hope that I am understood. I am in favor of amnesty in Mississippi.

Revels opposed a bill that would prohibit mixed schools in the nation's capitol. He argued that mixed schools would not lead to social equality. Revels pointed out that in churches and at family celebrations the races would remain separate. He asserted that segregation was a policy problem, and not a people problem. Revels believed that whites would share "space" with blacks if the law did not prohibit it. He shared stories from his own life on how segregation was humiliating to blacks, and on how some whites did not object to being in the same room with African Americans.

SEPARATE SCHOOLS IN THE CAPITAL
February 8, 1871

In regard to the wishes of the colored people of this city I will simply say that the trustees of colored schools and some of the most intelligent colored men of this place have said to me that they would have before asked for a bill abolishing the separate colored schools and putting all children on an equality in the common schools if they had thought they could obtain it. They feared they could not; and this is the only reason why they did not ask for it before. I find that the prejudice in this country to color is very great, and I sometimes fear that it is on the increase. For example, let me remark that it matters not how colored people act, it matters not how well they behave themselves, how well they deport themselves, how intelligent they may be, how refined they may be—for there are some colored persons who are persons of refinement; this must be admitted—the prejudice against them is equally as great as it is against the most low and degraded colored man you can find in the streets of this city or in any other place. This I do seriously regret. And is this prejudice right? Have the colored people done anything to justify the prejudice against them that does exist in the hearts of so many white persons, and generally of one great political party in this country? Have they done anything to justify it? Can any reason be given why this prejudice should be fostered in so many hearts against them, simply because they are not white? I make these remarks in all kindness, and from no bitterness of feeling at all.

If this prejudice has no cause to justify it, then we must admit that it is wicked, we must admit that it is wrong; we must admit that it has not the approval of Heaven. Therefore I hold it to be the duty of this nation to discourage it, simply because it is wicked, because it is wrong, because it is not approved of by Heaven. If the nation should take a step for the encouragement of this prejudice against the colored race, can they have any grounds upon which to predicate a hope that Heaven will smile upon them and prosper them? It is evident that it is the belief of Christian people in this country and in all other enlightened portions of the world that as a nation we have passed through a severe ordeal, that severe judgments have been poured out upon us on account of the manner in which a poor, oppressed race was treated in this country. This prejudice should be resisted. Steps should be taken to discourage it. Shall we do so by taking a step in this direction, if the amendment now proposed to the bill before us is adopted? That step will rather encourage, will rather increase this prejudice; and this is one reason why I am opposed to the adoption of the amendment. Let me here remark that if this amendment is rejected, so that the schools will be left open for all children to be entered into them, irrespective of race, color, or previous condition, I do not believe the colored people will act imprudently. I know that in one or two of the late insurrectionary States the

Legislatures passed laws establishing mixed schools, and the colored people did not hurriedly shove their children into those schools; they were very slow about it. In some localities where there was but little prejudice or opposition to it they entered them immediately; in others they did not do so. I do not believe that it is in the colored people to act rashly and unwisely in a matter of this kind.

Let me say that it is the wish of the colored people of this District, and of the colored people over this land, that this Congress shall not do anything that would increase that prejudice which is now fearfully great against them. If this amendment be adopted you will encourage that prejudice; you will increase that prejudice; and, perhaps after the encouragement thus given, the next step may be to ask Congress to prevent them from riding in the street cars, or something like that, I repeat, let no encouragement be given to a prejudice against those who have done nothing to justify it, who are poor and perfectly innocent, as innocent as infants. Let nothing be done to encourage that prejudice. I say the adoption of this amendment will do so.

I desire to say here that the white race has no better friend than I. The southern people know this. It is known over the length and breadth of this land. I am true to my own race. I wish to see all done that can be done for their encouragement to assist them in acquiring property, in becoming intelligent, enlightened, useful, valuable citizens. I wish to see this much done for them, and I believe God makes it the duty of this nation to do this much for them; but at the same time, I would not have anything done which would harm the white race. During the canvass in the State of Mississippi I traveled into different parts of that State, and this is the doctrine that I everywhere uttered: that while I was in favor of building up the colored race I was not in favor of tearing down the white race. The white race need not be harmed in order to build up the colored race. The colored race can be built up and assisted, as I before remarked, in acquiring property, in becoming intelligent, valuable, useful citizens, without one hair upon the head of any white man being harmed.

Let me ask, will establishing such schools as I am now advocating in this District harm our white friends? Let us consider this question for a few minutes. By some it is contended that if we establish mixed schools here a great insult will be given to the white citizens, and that the white schools will be seriously damaged. All that I ask those who assume this position to do is to go with me to Massachusetts, to go with me to some other New England States where they have mixed schools, and there they will find schools in as prosperous and flourishing a condition as any to be found in any part of the worlds? They will find such schools there; and they will find between the white and colored citizens friendship, peace, and harmony.

When I was on a lecturing tour in the State of Ohio, I went to a town, the name of which I forget. Whites in the town raised the question of whether it would be proper or not to establish mixed schools there. One of the leading gentlemen connected with the schools in that town came to see me and conversed with me on the subject. He asked me, "Have you been to New England, where they have mixed schools?" I replied, "I have." "Well," said he, "please tell me this: does not social equality result from mixed schools?" "No; very far from it," I responded. "Why;" said he, "how can it be otherwise?" I replied, "I will tell you how it can be otherwise, and how it is otherwise. Go to the schools and you see there white children and colored children seated side by side, and reciting their lessons, and perhaps, in walking to school, they may walk along together; but that is the last of it. The white children go to their homes; the colored children go to theirs; and on the Lord's day you will see those colored children in colored churches, and the white children in white churches; and if an entertainment is given by a white family, you will see the white children there, and the colored children at entertainments given by persons of their own color." I aver that mixed schools are very far from bringing about social equality.

I hold that establishing mixed schools will not harm the white race. I am their friend. I said in Mississippi, and I say here, and I say everywhere that I would abandon the Republican party if it went into any measures of legislation really damaging to any portion of the white race; but it is not in the Republican party to do that. In the next place, I desire to say that school boards, and school trustees, and railroad companies, and steamboat companies are to blame for the prejudice that exists against the colored race, or to their disadvantage in those respects. Go to the depot here, now, and what will you see: A well-dressed colored lady, with her little children by her side, whom she has brought up intelligently and with refinement, as much so as white children, comes to the cars; and where is she shown to? Into the smoking car, where men are cursing, swearing, spitting on the floor; where she is miserable, and where her little children have to listen to language not fitting for children who are brought up as she has endeavored to bring them up, to listen to. Let me ask, why is this? Is it because the white passengers in a decent, respectable car are unwilling for her to be seated there? No, not as a general thing; it is a rule that the company has established, that she shall not go there.

Let me give you a proof of this. Some years ago I was in the State of Kansas and wanted to go on a train of cars that ran from the town where I was to St. Louis, and this rule prevailed there, that colored people should go into the smoking car. I had my wife and children with me, and was trying to bring up my children properly, and I did not wish to take them into the smoking car. So I went to see the superintendent who lived in that town, and I addressed him thus: "I propose to start for St. Louis tomorrow on your road, and wish to take my family along; and I do not desire to go into the smoking car. It is all that I can do to stand it myself, and I do not wish my wife and children to be there and listen to such language as is uttered there by men talking, smoking, spitting, and rendering the car very foul; and I want to ask you now if I cannot obtain permission to take my family into a first-class car, as I have a first-class ticket?" He said, "You can do so; I will see the conductor and instruct him to admit you." And he did admit me, and not a white passenger objected to it, not a white passenger gave any evidence of being displeased because my family and I were there.

Let me give you another instance. In New Orleans, and also in Baltimore, cities that I love and whose citizens I love, some trouble was raised some time ago because colored people were not allowed to ride in the streetcars. The question was taken to the courts; and what was the decision? The court decided that the companies should make provision for colored passengers to go inside of the cars. At first they had a car with a certain mark, signifying that colored people should enter. I think the words were, in Baltimore, "Colored people admitted into this car"; and in New Orleans they had a star upon the car. They commenced running. There would be a number of white ladies and white gentlemen who wanted to go in the direction that this car was going, and did not want to wait for another; and notwithstanding there was a number of colored persons in the car, they went in and seated themselves just as if there had not been a colored person there. The other day, in Baltimore, I saw one of these cars passing along with the words, "Colored persons admitted into this car." The car stopped, and I saw a number of white ladies and gentlemen getting in, and not one colored person there. It was the same way in New Orleans. Let me tell you how it worked in New Orleans. The company finally came to the conclusion that if white persons were willing to go into the car appropriated to colored and ride with them without a word of complaint, they could not consistently complain of colored persons going into cars that were intended for white persons; and so they repealed their rule and opened the cars for all to enter. And ever since that time all have been riding together in New Orleans, and there has not been a word of complaint. So it will be I believe in regard to the schools. Let lawmakers cease to make the difference, let school trustees and school boards cease to make the difference, and the people will soon forget it.

19

Robert Smalls (1839–1915)
House of Representatives, South Carolina

Republican

Forty-fourth, Forty-fifth and Forty-ninth Congresses
March 4, 1875, to March 3, 1879
July 19, 1882, to March 3, 1883
March 18, 1884, to March 3, 1887

Robert Smalls was born into slavery in Beaufort, South Carolina, on April 5, 1839. He was the son of mixed parents, fathered by the man who held his mother in bondage. In 1851, the slave owner carried Robert to the waterfront at the Charleston harbor to work in seaport trades in sail making and navigating. Smalls gained a reputation for knowing the waters along the coast and for piloting ships. Once his owner allowed him to hire himself out, Smalls began to earn money for his own benefit. By 1861, he had earned over $700, and saved it to purchase his freedom. The Civil War altered his plans, and the circumstances that befell Smalls put him in the history books.

The Confederate Army did not overlook talents such as those of Smalls. The rebel Navy impressed him into service, assigning him to pilot a ship called the Planter. Smalls, as was the case of the majority of black slaves under the Confederacy, was not a secessionist. Hence, as soon as the opportunity presented itself, Smalls sailed the vessel to a Union port where he turned it over to the government. Robert Smalls and his all black crew became war heroes in the

North. Smalls joined the Union navy as a lieutenant, rising to the rank of captain by 1866. Smalls later used the reward he obtained for turning over the Planter to the Union to purchase land in Beaufort and open a store. By 1870, he had amassed over $6,000 in real property and $1,000 in personal property.

Captain Smalls supported a variety of programs aimed at developing the black community. During the Civil War and Reconstruction, he sought funds to establish schools for blacks in South Carolina. The most well known of these educational schools is commonly called the Port Royal Experiment, where emancipated blacks were settled and taught to read and write. He supported black economic development, becoming the director of the Enterprise Railroad, a black-owned company. Smalls was also an officer in the South Carolina militia, and he was the publisher of the *Beaufort Standard*, a local newspaper. In 1864, he staged one of the first sit-ins in the United States when he boarded a Philadelphia streetcar reserved for whites. Other African Americans joined in the protest, and the city later integrated its public transportation.

Smalls admitted that due to slavery the vast majority of African Americans were illiterate. Unable to read or write, he hired a tutor in 1865. A few years later he considered himself fit for elective office. His first opportunity came in 1868, when he was a delegate to the state constitutional convention. He favored compulsory school education and helped to write in the constitution a provision for the state's first public school. Next, he won a seat as a state representative, serving from 1868 to 1870. He also served in the state senate from 1870 to 1874. An active member of the Republican party, he attended seven national conventions and was twice elected vice-chairman of the state party convention.

Smalls entered Congress in 1875, serving three consecutive terms in the House of Representatives. He was appointed to the Committee on Agriculture and worked diligently for his district, presenting a bill to designate Port Royal Harbor as a docking station for the U.S. Navy. He urged the federal government to keep troops in the South to protect black Americans from racial violence. White Democrats in South Carolina targeted Smalls, accusing him of taking bribes. In the 1878 election, armed whites threatened black voters to keep them away from the polls. White intimidation worked again in 1880, and Smalls lost the election. However, Smalls contested the results and the House Committee on Elections confirmed him.

After an unsuccessful bid for reelection to the Fiftieth Congress in 1886, Smalls left national politics for good. Once whites in South Carolina had successfully disenfranchised black voters at the turn of the century, his political career ended in South Carolina. He accepted a presidential appointment as a U.S. collector at the port of Beaufort in South Carolina, serving from 1897 to 1913, leaving the position only when local racist politicians forced his resignation.

Smalls retired in 1913 and died on February 22, 1915. Smalls was laid to rest at the Tabernacle Baptist Church Cemetery in Beaufort.

Smalls accused Democrats in South Carolina of supporting terrorism and murder. Due to slavery, Smalls asserted, most whites had acquired a domineering spirit and would not voluntarily submit to any government they did not control. He alleged that whites believed that they were the superior race. He charged that whites in South Carolina had used fraudulent means to drive blacks from the political arena.

AN HONEST BALLOT IS THE SAFEGUARD OF THE REPUBLIC
February 24, 1877

As a Representative of the State of South Carolina, I rise to submit my views regarding the investigation of the election by a committee of this House. The unfortunate division existing among the people of my State as to who is the lawfully elected governor of the State and who were the lawfully elected presidential electors has led to this investigation. I am happy to say the committee is unanimous in their conclusion that the Hayes electors received a majority of the votes cast and I regret to have to add that they are divided politically upon the governorship.

Under ordinary circumstances I would be content to allow the report of the committee to go upon the record with no further opposition than to record my vote against the majority report, believing, as I do, that the report of a partisan committee cannot and will not be accepted by the people of my State as an honest conclusion based upon the results of the investigation. The committee having divided upon the important question of who is the legally elected governor, the question remains an open one, to be accepted or denied according to party opinion.

I therefore propose at this time to submit to this House and the American people, in as concise shape as possible, the facts relating to the late political campaign and election in my State. The Democratic party pursued a policy calculated to drive from the State every white man who affiliated with the Republican party or who would refuse to join them in their attempts to deprive the Negro of the rights guaranteed him by the Constitution of South Carolina and of the United States, the manifest intention being to reduce the Negro to a condition of political dependence upon the former slaveholder; to place him in the power of the men who had degraded his manhood, who had reduced him to a condition of ignorance through centuries of enforced subjection. The Democratic party adhered to such a policy with these results: they committed large numbers of murders, resorted to violence and outrages, and terrorized entire counties. Thus, the political rights of 10,000 Negroes and access to the ballot box were denied by means of fraud.

The white race of the South possesses intelligence and courage. The existence of the institution of slavery cemented their personal interests and compelled them to act in concert in political matters. The relation of master to slave produced in the ruling class a domineering spirit, a disposition to ignore and trample down the rights of those they could not control. They became in a large degree cruel, refusing education to and ignoring the sanctity of the family relations of their slaves; they assumed the slave had no rights and denied the fact of his being a brother man and entitled to his personal liberty. They never learned to recognize such a principle and would tolerate no free expression of opinion. Such qualities provoked the late civil strife between the North and the South, and are today responsible for the unhappy condition of the South. The late slaveholding class will not submit peacefully to a government they cannot control, believing they are a superior race; and, not recognizing the rights of the colored man, they feel justified in resorting to any means or power to accomplish their end. To achieve their purpose they take human life with impunity, drive citizens from their homes, and perpetrate fraud against them.

Such is the policy and character of the men who, having disgraced the name of South Carolina by their acts, now ask to be sustained in the result accomplished. On the other hand, the Negro race, under ordinary circumstances is gentle, patient and affectionate; possessed of no cruel impulses, they are a harmless race, generous to a fault; their confidence is easily won. These qualities are the outgrowth of long years of suffering and have become engrafted in their natures by the bitter lessons of experience. The granting of suffrage to them originated a new and controlling element in the Southern States. This, Mr. Speaker, has led to all the sorrows and the cruelties they have felt in the last ten years. The determination of the former slaveholding class to control them has prompted the many scenes of cruelty that make the history of the new South one of blood and form the subject for one of the darkest pages in American history. The blood of the innocent freedman, shed by southern democrats, will in the future prove to be one of the dark spots upon the fair name of the American Republic.

It is manifest that two political elements so widely different in their character would provoke much antagonism, but I do not think it ever entered the mind of the most apprehensive that the white race would resort to such inhuman brutality to recover power. If the Negroes had been as a race their equals in courage there might possibly be some palliation for so inhuman a policy, but when it was considered their cruelty was against a harmless race, it affords no defense, and their course becomes the blacker in comparison with their boasted chivalry, their claim of superior gentleness, and of those virtues which adorn the human race. The oppressed colored race can ask no greater punishment upon their persecutors than to call the attention of the civilized world to the history of the South for the last ten years, and to a comparison of the manner by which a rebellious people were treated by a generous Government, and in turn the treatment of the Negro race by the pardoned class, and they challenge the annals of civilization to show a people who have maintained a more peaceful policy under such trying circumstances.

The late campaign and election in South Carolina have attracted the attention of the country. Great efforts have been made by the Democratic party to win the ear of the American people. I now, in behalf of the colored race, to which I belong and who have under the sun of liberty suffered by the lash of slavery, who were objects of contention when a price was placed upon their heads, as well as when vested with the right of suffrage, call attention to the following facts which I propose to prove: I charge upon the Democratic party of South Carolina murder, violence, and intimidation, specifying that in the several counties of the State, more especially Aiken, Barnwell, Abbeville, Edgefield, and Laurens, murder was openly committed with the sanction of that party; violence was resorted to everyday during the campaign; intimidation was practiced by the party in nearly every county; to sum up in a few words, the entire party went into the canvass resolved to win under any circumstances, and to do so resorted to means which ought to bring a blush of shame to the face of every honest citizen. I charge upon the Democratic party the crime of creating a necessity for protection to peaceful citizens in a time of profound peace. I charge upon the Democratic party the greater crime of turning the day of election into a carnival of bloodshed and violence. This day of all others when the public peace should be most sacredly maintained was by their efforts made a day for the infliction of every cruelty necessary to change the result desired by the honest majority of the voters of South Carolina. I charge upon the Democratic party the crime of violating the purity of the ballot box by unblushing fraud, sanctioned by the entire party, from candidate down to voter. I charge them with the crime of striking a second blow at the perpetuity of American institutions by inaugurating in the centennial year the practice of securing by fraud and murder what could not be obtained by honorable means.

In support of these charges I invite a careful examination of the facts given in the following pages, each and every one having been taken from the sworn testimony before the committee appointed for that purpose. It will be observed that comparisons have been made of the voting strength of the two parties, and of the votes cast by each race, between the elections of 1874 and

1876. To fully explain this I will say that the election officers of the various precincts make a registry of the color of the voter, white or colored, which is transmitted with the returns to the secretary of state. To further obtain an intelligent estimate of the strength of the two parties and of the votes cast at previous elections the tables taken by the committee in evidence are given entirely. The impression may arise in the minds of some persons that the increase of the democratic vote can be attributed to colored men supporting that party with their ballots. The registry taken on the day of election shows how many white and colored men voted, there being blanks for that purpose, with the poll-lists. An examination of these returns is given in the following pages for the various counties, and it will be observed that the increase of 30,000 votes for the democratic ticket was cast by white men almost entirely, showing conclusively that the frauds committed by white men were enormous, and caused the very large increase in the democratic vote.

In this connection it may help to enlighten the minds of some by calling attention to the fact that in Georgia the difference between votes cast by the Democratic party in the October and November elections amounted to 25,000. The fact is that an immense number of Georgian voters cast ballots in South Carolina. This explains the decrease in Georgia votes and the increase in the votes in South Carolina. The following data sufficiently establishes this fact, and it should convince even the most skeptical person:

At the October election the Democratic party of Georgia rolled up an astonishingly magnificent majority of 75,000 votes, while the result of the November election shows a majority of only 50,000. What became of the remaining 25,000 Georgia democrats on the 7th of November? There would be room for speculation as to the answer to this query were it not for the fact that we find them in the official election returns of their adjoining sister State of South Carolina, where they went to make up the 25,000 of which the South Carolina democracy knew it was short. To support this assertion with statistical facts we need only to point at the election return of one of the border counties of South Carolina, the county of Edgefield, where the preponderance of the white vote over the census return of the same for 1875 is so wonderfully striking that the mere figures will point at once at the manner in which the South Carolina democracy obtained their majority in that county.

The white male population of Edgefield in 1875 was twenty-nine hundred and seventy-three, and the democratic election returns one year later pretend to show a vote of over 6,000 white males for that county alone. The State of South Carolina is divided into thirty-two counties. In the year 1875 an official census of the population in the State was taken. The number of whites and colored were carefully noted. The population was also classified in regard to age. The total number of inhabitants returned by this census was 925,145, of which number 574,391 were colored and 350,754 white. The number of white males over twenty-one years of age was 74,199; colored over twenty-one years of age, 110,744.

A general election is held in the State every two years, at which time the following officers are elected: Governor, lieutenant-governor, secretary of state, State treasurer, comptroller-general, attorney-general, adjutant and inspector-general, superintendent of education, solicitors for eight circuits, one half of the State Senate, and one hundred and twenty-four representatives. The following county officers are also elected: Ninety-six county commissioners, thirty-two sheriffs, thirty-two clerks of courts, thirty-two probate judges, and thirty-two school commissioners. For the purpose of giving some idea of the manner in which the State government has been administered the following facts are furnished: The tax for the last year was eleven mills, three mills for the purpose of paying the public debt, two mills for the interest fund, one and a quarter to pay unpaid salaries, a portion of a mill to support penal and charitable institutions, penitentiary, deaf and dumb asylum, the lunatic asylum, and the orphan home, and so forth. This tax is the smallest that has been imposed since reconstruction, and it is due to Governor Chamberlain to say that the taxes have been reduced a full one-fourth under his administration. The State debt is $7,000,000 and the assessed value of real estate $140,000,000, and the assessment is very fair.

The administration of Governor Chamberlain had been one of marked reform, of a character to command the admiration of every citizen. Reductions have been made in the expenditures and salaries have been reduced. The abuse of the pardoning power has been corrected, men of better character have been appointed to office, faith has been kept with the public creditor, a savings of $400,000 to the State effected, the tax laws have been amended to secure unanimity of assessment and taxation, a savings of $101,200 in the contingent fund of the executive has been effected, the legislative expenses have been reduced $350,810, the contingent expenses of the government $355,000, the expense of public printing reduced $512,418, and taxes reduced from thirteen and one-half mills to eleven mills. The deficiencies in his administration were $291,024 less that those of 1872 and 1873, and $233,315 less than those of 1873 and 1874, making a grand total of savings under the administration of Governor Chamberlain of $1,719,488; and let it be added that this is the testimony offered by the organ of the Democratic party in the State. The *Charleston News and Courier* published in its columns the following testimony to the reform character of Governor Chamberlain's administration.

And the voice of the *Charleston News and Courier* was the voice of the majority of the democrats in the State. Evidence from the leading democrats who testified before the committee can be found all through the investigation bearing testimony to the excellent character of the administration of Governor Daniel H. Chamberlain. It was the pet project of these men to have him nominated as their candidate for governor, and they never wearied of sounding his praises; he was accredited with doing more to give South Carolina good government than any other citizen within her borders, and up to the time of the nomination of Wade

Hampton it was an open question what party would bear in the campaign the name of Governor Chamberlain with his prestige of reform; and let it be said here that with all their democratic abuse of carpetbag government in the South, it is a part of the political history of that section that whenever a man rose superior to the corruption in his party, be he a native republican or otherwise, he became an object for abuse and vilification.

The more he endeavored to accomplish for good government the worse the abuse he would receive, and often the crime of doing good for himself and his people merited the punishment of death. Governor Chamberlain still lives, and nothing but the protecting hand of Providence has saved his life. The abuse, the vilification, has been heaped upon him out of the mouths that a few months ago bore testimony to the great reforms he had accomplished. Threats of assassination have been uttered every day and night during the campaign and since its close. Today his life is preserved for the reason alone because it would not be good policy at this time, when Hampton is seeking to win the confidence of northern people, to murder him. The Republican party has endorsed the reforms accomplished by Governor Chamberlain, and it entered the campaign to reform a good government. South Carolina, under the Republican party, in the future will be governed wisely in the interests of her people.

Before going into the question of general intimidation in the State, a brief reference will be made to the unblushing attempt made to buy one of the republican presidential electors elect to cast his vote for Samuel J. Tilden for President. By reference to the very full testimony taken by the committee, it will be seen that the sum of $50,000 was offered to Charles Edmund Nash, as elector, as a bribe to have him vote for Tilden. Further, it was attempted to bribe Mr. Nash to have him secure for the democrats four republican state senators by paying $10,000 for each one, $40,000 for all. It is needless to say this base attempt to accomplish by bribery what had failed through fraud and intimidation failed of its purpose; Mr. Nash, a colored man, declining the bribe. The four State senators, had they been purchased, would have given the democrats a majority in the State senate and enabled them to set up an administration in opposition to the regular State government. The purchase of the presidential elector would have placed Tilden's election beyond doubt.

The various methods of intimidation resorted to by the democrats were as follows: The killing of colored men; making threats of personal violence; sending threatening letters, coffins, bullets, etc.; by riding armed through the country, by day and by night; by firing into the houses of republicans; by breaking up republican mass meetings; by forming armed bodies, dressed in red shirts, called rifle clubs; by discharging employees who refused to promise to vote the democratic ticket, etc. All of these various measures of intimidation were rigidly carried out in order to produce, by an organized system, a reign of terror among the Republicans of the State. When the various counties are referred to it will be conclusively shown that men have been murdered, driven from home, discharged, beaten, etc. The republicans, with few exceptions, could hold no political meetings. When such would be called, armed rifle clubs, on horseback and on foot, would surround the republicans and demand control of the meeting. If this was not accorded the meeting was broken up. The "preference policy," or, on other words, discharging employees who voted the Republican ticket, was openly advocated by the democratic press, who published their news in the following shape.

The Easterlin's Mill Democratic Club adopted resolutions carrying intimidation to its most extreme limit. Democratic vengeance was visited upon the innocent families of republicans; even little children were made to suffer by these chivalrous people because their father was a republican. Think of a party—a party professing the name of "democracy" resolving against women and children—and remember at the same time these are the men who boast of their chivalry, of their manly courage, of their ancestry. If any man supposes for a moment that my language is not justified by the facts, let him read the annexed testimony. An ex-governor of the State, a professed gentleman, called upon his hearers to refuse social intercourse with a radical; and this gallant gentleman demands that the innocent family "be made to feel the brand of infamy, the moral pestilence surrounding them." I again call the attention of the people of the country to these sentiments, to their full extent. Here is an ex-governor of a State, a representative citizen, who in a public meeting asks that the innocent family of a man guilty of republicanism receive the same condemnation as a convicted felon.

I now call attention to the law upon the subject of intimidation of voters, and do so in order that it may be fully understood that Governor Chamberlain was only executing his sworn duty when he called upon the Federal Government for necessary support in enforcing the laws of South Carolina. An examination of the extract from the revised statutes will show how completely and thoroughly the men who have announced to the country their purpose to "redeem" the State have violated the laws of South Carolina. These men respected no law upon the statute books, if in any way it interfered with the plans they had adopted to carry the State. They knew no law, human or divine, that interfered with their purposes. The democrats in their different meetings would adopt resolutions to the effect that republicans could receive no work from them. These threats had great significance when it is considered that the democrats or former slaveholders own nearly all the land. It literally meant starvation to the laboring republicans. The testimony of General M.C. Butler shows that the democrats were determined upon such a policy, and it further shows that it was the practice of the democrats to carry arms.

The Democrats proceeded so far in their intimidation policy that on the 7th day of October, 1876, the governor was forced to issue a proclamation disbanding the rifle clubs, on order that the peace of the State and the authority of its laws should be maintained. At and before this time the laws of the State were powerless to protect its citizens in their rights, and the sheriff of Aiken County telegraphed September 19, 1876, to the governor that he was unable to disperse the white democrats who were under arms in that county. It had been reported that the colored people had armed and commenced a riot.

Smalls urged the House to appropriate funds to develop Port Royal Harbor. He described the harbor as accessible to merchants and of strategic value to the navy. Port Royal Harbor could also accommodate large ships. Naval officers and the navy and merchant marine recognized its value. Failure to develop the port would deprive them of one of the best areas on the Atlantic to dock their vessels.

THE COALING STATION AT PORT ROYAL
August 5, 1882

I desire to say but a few words in advocacy of Senate amendment No. 145 that the committee of conference recommended. It is as follows:

For establishing and completing a coaling-dock and naval storehouse at Port Royal Harbor, South Carolina, $30,000, the site for said coaling-dock and naval storehouse to be located by a board of naval officers appointed by the Secretary of the Navy for that purpose.

I would have preferred the original amount of $30,000 with which the Senate amended the bill. But the House refused to concur yesterday in that amendment. The committee now recommends twenty thousand. I am willing to accept that amount, and do earnestly hope that the House will reconsider its action of yesterday whereby it refused to concur in the Senate amendment granting $30,000 for this purpose, and will now concur in the committee's report and grant the twenty thousand recommended. Port Royal Harbor is one of the best, if not the best, harbor on the Atlantic coast south of Hampton Roads, and I might include the harbors of the Gulf of Mexico. I might appropriately add what is now of historical importance, that Port Royal Harbor was selected by the late distinguished Rear Admiral Dupont as the base of his operations during the early part of the late war and that it was the headquarters for important operations both by land and sea during the entire continuance of the war.

Since the war Port Royal had been practically a "coaling-station and naval storehouse," though not designated such formally by law. One or more vessels have been lying there continually, so that the building of this coaling-dock and naval storehouse on land owned by the Government will be really a matter of economy and will dispense with the necessity of vessels lying there continually in the stream for this purpose, subject to constant decay. The *Pawnee* has been lying in the harbor for more than a year, and is there still; and it is reportedly to be greatly injured by worms. The *Wyoming* is also lying in Port Royal Harbor at present. The building of this dock and storehouse will prevent the necessity of the *Pawnee* lying in the harbor or any other vessel for that purpose. The distinguished officers whom I have already quoted say: "it is a wonder that the advantages of Port Royal Harbor were so little known prior to 1861."

I will state that its advantages are now well known. Port Royal Harbor has more water on its bar at low tide than either Charleston or Savannah has at the highest spring tide. And it is yet destined to be the great port of outlet for the immense grain products of the West on their way to Europe. It is a harbor, moreover, that the Government will not be annually called upon to make large appropriations to keep in a condition to allow large ships to enter, as it is required to do both at Charleston and Savannah. It is a harbor furnished by nature for the largest ships in the world, and can easily contain the entire Navy of the United States. I speak from personal knowledge and experience, Mr. Speaker, for it was my good fortune during the late war to be engaged as a pilot in the Navy in their harbor and afterward as a captain in the Quartermaster's Department.

Port Royal Harbor, with its twenty-one feet of water on her bar at low tide and twenty-eight feet at high tide, is destined to rise to the position which her great natural advantages entitle her at an early day, although she lies between the two old and well-established sea-ports of Charleston and Savannah; her railroad to Augusta and thence to the great West will give her the facilities which she needs, and she will yet eclipse all the South Atlantic ports.

Smalls urged the House to vote against a bill that would segregate blacks and whites in interstate travel. He asserted that segregation was humiliating to blacks. Black travelers who purchased a first-class ticket in one state could be moved to another car upon entering a Jim Crow state. Black women and their children were seated in coaches where men smoked, used foul language, and insulted them.

CIVIL RIGHTS
December 17, 1885

I hope that the amendment just offered will be voted down. I am glad that this amendment comes from a Representative of Georgia. I know, as the gentleman says, that we have no objection to riding in a separate car when the car is of the same character as that provided for the white people to ride in. But I state here to the House that colored men and women do have trouble in riding through the State of Georgia. In Georgia they have a car called a second-class car; and, notwithstanding a colored man may buy a first-class ticket here in Washington, or anywhere else, to go perhaps to New Orleans, yet when he reaches the State of Georgia he is compelled to go into a "Jim Crow car," which is placed next to the locomotive. The railroad officers do not object, as they state, to furnishing us fair and proper accommodations; but when we get to a certain station on the road, and the conductor goes out, as is claimed to attend to business of the road, we always find a crowd coming into the cars and asking us, not very politely, to go out; and if we do not go out peaceably we are put out by force. This has been done time and again in Georgia.

I have no reason to speak of such things, thank God, as occurring in my own State, for we have a statute in that State providing for proper accommodations for the colored people; and I wish to say, to the credit and honor of the people of the State of South Carolina, that no distinction is made in that State among persons traveling through the State. But when you come to the State of Georgia there is a difference; and for that reason a Representative of that State asks that this amendment be made. He had referred to the statute law of that State. Why, that statute, so far as concerns any colored man or lady riding through that State in a first-class car, is as dead as some law that never was thought of.

I hope the amendment would be voted down by this House. I believe the good sense of the House, and especially the good sense of those Democrats who are now crying out they are going to be the best friends of the colored man are not going to allow the State of Georgia to come in here at this last hour with any such discrimination as has been proposed. No, you cannot fool the people any longer. If you mean what you say, start doing it now. I believe the same good sense of the House that adopted the amendment offered by the gentleman from North Carolina [James Edward O'Hara] will vote down this amendment moved by the gentleman from Georgia [Charles Frederick Crisp]. I first thought it would be better to move that the amendment be laid upon the table, but supposing other gentlemen wish to have something to say on it, I will for the present withhold that motion. And I believe further that this amendment will be voted down by the right-thinking Democrats of the House, by those who are hallooing and crying out that there is no trouble about this matter; that great and good man Governor Cleveland, who is going to be our next President, will do all that is best for the welfare of the colored people. I do not believe those men are going to say here now today the colored people shall have nothing but a "Jim Crow" car in Georgia under the action of the railroad commissioners.

Smalls addressed discrimination in dispersing monies from the pension fund. He argued that a pension to the widow of a fallen soldier was a way to honor him for his military service and heroic deeds. The pension had nothing to do with need. He admitted that he had voted favorably on giving pensions to the widows of deceased veterans in the past. Apparently, the House had not treated the claim of Maria Hunter, the widow of General David Hunter, as it had other cases. They discriminated against her because General Hunter was a friend of the Negro. He charged hypocrisy in this case and stated that Mrs. Hunter deserved the pension

A BILL FOR THE RELIEF OF MRS. MARIA HUNTER
July 30, 1886

In the consideration of the pension claims passed by this Congress and vetoed by the President I have thus far remained silent and should have continued so, contenting myself with the expression of my opinions by the vote I should feel constrained to cast; but having introduced this bill and the peculiar relations I bore to this distinguished soldier and patriot for whose widow this bill provides, I would be doing injustice to myself, injustice to history, and an unpardonable injustice to my constituents, constituting most largely that race of American citizens of which I am one, if I longer remained silent or neglected as a member of this body to state the reasons why this bill should become a law notwithstanding the objections of the president.

It is due the beneficiary of this bill that I should say that it was introduced without consultation with or knowledge on her part. I knew it was the custom to pension the widows of eminent soldiers, not so much because of the necessities of their condition but as the grateful tribute of a country saved by their heroism and valor. During my service in Congress I had invariably voted for such bills. With pride and pleasure I favored the pension to the widow of that magnificent soldier and courtly gentleman, General Hancock, whose death was lamented throughout the land. Who today regrets that legislation? Who today would not have been indignant at so ungracious and unpatriotic an act as a veto? It was the nation's tribute to the heroic dead. He was the country's pride while living, and it is just that his bereaved widow should be the nation's ward; and actuated by these sentiments I felt that the claim of General Hunter's widow had been forgotten or neglected, and therefore introduced this bill.

I knew that the pittance of $50 per month was more than would have been allowed by existing law, and yet fell far short of a proper estimate of the eminent services rendered by General Hunter during a long, eventful, and illustrious career, but it was an expression of national gratitude, and it accorded with the almost universal precedent of the Government since the close of the war. So just and meritorious was the claim regarded by the Committee on Pensions that it was unanimously reported and passed both Houses without criticism or apposition. To me and to my people the circumstances surrounding this case is singularly exceptional. Less than a quarter of a century ago that class of which I am a representative was the "hewers of wood and drawers of water." Our importance seemed to consist in the money value we represented. Ownership in our blood and of our labor had long existed. Our lives were one long eternal night, not even an occasional silver lining in the sky of our existence to bid us hope for a more useful and grander experience in the affairs of life. We heard words of hope even amid the din of battle and the clash of arms. We were told and began to realize we were human beings made after God's image, and possessed of the same inalienable rights attaching to other citizens of a great and free Republic.

We are not an ungrateful or unappreciative people. We can never forget the Moses who let us out of the land of bondage, and when the following order was issued it sounded like silver bells upon our startled ears. Can it be that there is secret and sinister motive either personal or political? Is it because of his hostility to slavery before and during the war? Is it because of his proclamation freeing the slaves? Is it because of his official action as a member of the court-martial that tried and convicted Fitz-John Porter for treason to a government, which General Hunter aided to preserve? Can it be that this is your revenge for all his patriotic conduct? The future historian of this country's legislation will not be charitable toward you for your treatment of this bill. But after all the action of the Democratic party in this House is not without a useful lesson. It exposes the hypocrisy of its assurances of friendship for the colored man by striking a blow at the nation's brave defenders and the colored man's best friend.

I trust I may be excused in referring to my personal intercourse with General David Hunter. After I surrendered the Confederate steamer, the *Planter,* to the United States naval authorities under the command of that noble gentleman and splendid officer, Admiral Samuel F. Dupont, I met General Hunter, then in command at Hilton Head, South Carolina, where he had organized a regiment of colored troops. Not having been authorized to do so, they were disbanded.

General Hunter then entrusted me with a letter to our country's great War Secretary, Stanton. Proceeding to Washington I was honored with several interviews with President Lincoln and Stanton, and from them bore an official letter to General Hunter authorizing the formation and mustering on of several regiments of colored soldiers. Their records are part of the country's history that I need not repeat here, further than to say that as we were faithful to the Union then we will be true to its defenders now.

By the variations and methods of modern politics, my race of approximately seven million people is represented on this floor by the honorable gentleman from North Carolina [O'Hara] and myself. How long this injustice will be tolerated I will not dare to prophesy; but so long as one of us be permitted on this floor our voice and our vote will not be withheld from any measure of legislation which will add to the prosperity and happiness of all the people, without regard to color or condition, and permanence and greatness of a common country.

20

Benjamin Sterling Turner
(1825-1894)
House of Representatives, Alabama

Republican

Forty-second Congress
March 4, 1871, to March 3, 1873

Benjamin S. Turner was born into slavery on March 17, 1825, in Weldon, North Carolina. In 1830, his owner, along with Benjamin and his mother, relocated to Alabama. As a playmate of the white children in the family, Benjamin sat in on lessons taught by their tutor and gained a rudimentary education. Once better educated, the children became his teachers. When his owner sold him at the age of twenty, Turner could already read and write. This early preparation worked to his advantage. His new owner allowed him to hire himself out for profit, and Turner managed to earn a good deal of money by managing a hotel and a livery stable in Selma, Alabama. He had saved over $8,000 when the Civil War began, and had purchased property. Turner, like his white neighbors, suffered financial losses during the war, when Union troops destroyed southern crops and buildings. Once elected to Congress during Reconstruction, he urged the Southern Claims Commission to restore lost property to its owners. Turner continued to apply his business acumen after the war and succeeded as a merchant and farmer. In 1870 the federal census reported that he owned $2,500 in real estate and $10,000 in personal property, a remarkable achievement in view of his pre-war status, and the depression following the war.

Appreciating the difference an early education had made for him, Turner became a teacher. In 1865, he helped establish a school in Selma. He also became active in local politics. In 1867, he attended the Republican State Convention. Republican officials soon named him to local offices, including tax collector in Dallas County. In 1868 he was elected to the Selma City Council. Armed with this experience, it was only natural for Turner to run for national office. He was the first black in Alabama to be elected to the House of Representatives. Taking his seat in 1871, Representative Turner found himself in opposition to most Radical Republicans when he proposed a bill to grant amnesty to ex-rebels who took an oath of loyalty. The House, still solidly under Republican control, did not consider the measure. His less controversial proposals included a bill to construct federal buildings in Selma at a cost of about $200,000. In addition, he sought relief for St. Paul's Episcopal Church, also located in Selma, for damages it sustained during the war.

Appointed to the Committee on Invalid Pensions, Turner was instrumental in helping Union veterans of the war secure pensions. He believed that the federal cotton tax had harmed farm workers in the South, many of whom were poor black tenant farmers. In a petition presented on February 20, 1872, Turner argued that the tax had violated the Constitution. On May 31, he asked the House to refund the cotton tax that had been assessed from 1866 to 1868, claiming that the South had lost approximately $250,000,000 in revenue, which was probably a reasonable estimate of the losses.

While his views on the loyalty test were conservative, Turner supported civil rights. He advocated racially mixed schools and he called for reparations for ex-slaves. He asked the House to appropriate land to be divided into 160-acre plots and sold to black farmers at discounted rates. While these clearly were not radical measures, the House ignored them.

Turner faced a formidable challenge in the Republican Party when he ran for its nomination in 1872. Apparently, some individuals did not see him as a member of the black elite. While Turner was literate, he was not college educated. Prominent blacks criticized him for supposedly lacking the social graces of the upper class. His challenger, black politician Philip Joseph, had always been a free man and believed he was in a higher class than Turner. Joseph was a newspaper editor and highly regarded among black voters. His class status did not secure him a seat in Congress. Turner and Joseph divided the black vote, and white Republican Frederick G. Bromberg won the election.

When he returned to Selma in 1874, Turner remained interested in public issues. He attended the convention of the Alabama Labor Union and the Republican National Convention in 1880 but failed to revive his political career. He resumed his business activities, operating a bar and a livery stable in Selma. When Alabama and the rest of the nation experienced a depression during the 1870s Turner lost his businesses. He returned to farming to make a living but this was not enough to pull his family out of poverty. He died virtually penniless on March 21, 1894.

> *Turner proposed a bill to construct public buildings in Selma because the city had been virtually destroyed in the Civil War. It was now a time to build it up again and he believed federal funds were necessary. In defending the bill Turner made conciliatory remarks about the South. He considered the Civil War a great sin, and was ready to forgive and forget.*

PUBLIC BUILDING IN SELMA
May 30, 1872

In April last I had the honor to introduce a bill in this House providing for the erection of public buildings in the city of Selma, Alabama, suitable for the pressing demands of business and commerce in that growing city. That bill has been referred to the Committee of Public Buildings and Grounds, and without knowing what their report may be, I desire to offer some reasons to this House why the bill should pass at once. And before proceeding further let me say to the members of the House that I am earnest and pressing for the passage of this bill, and I shall not relinquish one foot of ground until I shall have succeeded in my efforts. The people of Selma have been magnanimous toward me; they have buried in the tomb of oblivion many of those animosities upon which we hear so many eloquent appeals in this Chamber; and I intend to stand by to labor for them in their need and desolation. In this I repay personal kindness, resent wrong by upholding right, and at the same time advocate a measure of necessity to the Government of my country.

In the year 1865 two-thirds of the city of Selma was reduced to ashes by the United States Army. Churches, schoolhouses, manufactories, stores, workshops, public buildings, barns, stock pens, and a thousand or more private residences were swept away by the destroying flames. In short, nearly the whole city was burned. The Government made a display in that unfortunate city of its mighty power and conquered a gallant and high-toned people. They may have sinned wonderfully, but they suffered terribly. War was once the glory of her sons, but they paid the penalty of their offense, and for one, I have no coals of fiery reproach to heap upon them now. Rather would I extend the olive branch of peace, and say to them, let the past be forgotten and let us all, from every sun and every clime, of every hue and every shade, go to work peacefully to build up the shattered temples of this great and glorious Republic.

But to proceed: From 1865 until quite recently that city lay prostrate in the dust. I now ask Congress, in behalf of the people of that ruined city, to be as bountiful toward them in mercy as the Army was vigorous and ambitious in reducing them to subjugation.   I introduced the bill asking Congress to appropriate $200,000 for the erection of public buildings in that city:

First, because there is a great and absolute need for these buildings for Government use.

Second, because the erection of the buildings will give work to many who need and deserve it, and who, without sinning, have suffered from the sins of others.

Third, because this is a growing city, and if aided in this manner by the Government will soon become flourishing and an honor to the commercial growth of our country.

Already the city has a population of over ten thousand inhabitants. Nine railroads radiate from its center, manufactories, stores, and private residences are springing up everywhere, the result of private enterprise. The city is situated upon the Alabama River, where steamboats and other watercraft can reach it at all seasons of the year with safety. It is within three miles of the center of the State, and is in the midst of the largest and most prosperous cotton-growing region in the whole United States. More cotton and property were destroyed in this city than in any other place in the reconstructed States. The future of the city is brilliant, and I do hope that Congress will see the necessity of making this appropriation. All that is required to make this place the "queen-city" of the South is for "Uncle Sam" to wield the scepter of "peace and plenty" around her with the same determination and vigor as he did the fiery sword in time of war. The passage of this bill will convince my people that you mean forgetfulness of the bloody past, and only want harmony and peace with the proffers of your aid.

And now, in conclusion, let me say that when Chicago, that proud city of the West, was swept away and her noble people left in penury and want, this same little city of which I have spoken, destitute and impoverished as she was, was among the first in the South to respond to the call of humanity and send her heartfelt tribute to her fallen sister of the West. The people of the city claim nothing for this act of kindness; but they do ask that while with lavish hands you rear your magnificent edifices in other places, you will not quite forget them who need so much, and for whose honesty and sincerity in their attachment to the Government I am proud to boast.

Turner analyzed the tax clauses in the federal constitution, asserting that the cotton tax of 1866 was invalid. From this review he argued that the constitution requires that taxes on property must be uniform. He also argued that mostly poor people were adversely affected by the act.

REFUNDING THE COTTON TAX
May 31, 1872

On a Petition and Memorial Praying Congress and the Country to Refund the Cotton Tax I had the honor on the 20th day of February last to present a petition and memorial to Congress praying Congress and the country to refund the cotton tax. The understanding of the people is that this tax fell upon a certain section and class. It did not fall upon the owner of the land, nor upon the merchant, nor upon the consumer, but directly upon the laborer who tilled the soil and gathered the cotton with his bloodstained fingers from the pods. The seventh section of the Constitution of the United States authorizes Congress to levy a uniform tax. Our understanding of uniformity is that every State in the Union shall pay a tax in proportion to its population and wealth; hence we claim that the cotton tax falling upon a special section of the country and upon a certain class of citizens is unconstitutional; because, in the first place, it is detrimental to one section of the country and beneficial to another; next, it is a direct tax upon industry in that part of the country where cotton is made. And, instead of paying the people a premium for their industry it is a direct prohibition of cotton making.

In 1866, 1867 and 1868 there was a cotton tax levied amounting to $70,000,000. We claim that this tax was unjust, inequitable, and unconstitutional. This law was the creature of Congress, for it was not supported by the people in any section of the county; and we hold now that Congress has the same power to refund this tax as it had to collect it. This tax wrought a more serious influence and destructive consequence than seems to be understood by Congress and the people in general. The war through which we have passed stopped cotton making for a time, and thus caused cotton to be scarce and high in other markets of the world. Other nations, looking upon cotton as one of the chief necessities of life, went into cotton making in self-defense, and continued so to do till the war was over in the United States. During the war cotton went up as high as eighty cents per pound; and as soon as the war ended and cotton was shipped from the United States it began to go down and was as low as forty-three cents in 1866. This was no doubt caused by other nations taking the idea that American cotton was coming into the markets of the world, and could be purchased for less than they could make it at their homes. But when Congress imposed the prohibitory tax in 1866, it caused the people of the world to believe as before that it would be impossible to purchase cotton from the United States at any reasonable price; therefore, they again made an effort to defend themselves by going into cotton making and bringing their cotton in competition with that of the United States.

These nations, by their energy, industry, and success, glutted the markets of the world with cotton, so much so that it reduced the cotton of the United States from forty-three cents in 1866 to thirty-one cents in 1868. And when the cotton tax was repealed in 1868, the outside influence began to decrease and the price of our cotton to increase, and has been getting higher and higher ever since. A fair calculation will show that if there had been no tax upon cotton the minimum value would never have gone below thirty-five cents per pound. And, as I have said before, the Government collected $70,000,000 upon cotton, thereby bringing about the influence of which I have spoken before, namely, increasing competition, glutting the markets and reducing the price of our cotton to an additional amount of $250,000,000, besides the $70,000,000 paid on cotton. This $250,000,000 fell into the hands of other nations by the prohibitory influence of our own Government, consequently the whole loss to the cotton-making section of the country by the direct tax and its indirect influence amounts to $820,000,000.

To prove my argument to be true, I will refer to other products of industry than cotton. For instance, take away the tariff from iron and place a prohibitory tax of three cents per pound for making iron. What would be the effect? I am satisfied that such would be the effect that iron-masters from all parts of the world would be bringing iron to the United States, while the iron-masters in our country would have to abandon their business or starve. The tariff men of Pennsylvania upon this floor will, not dispute this I know. I will place any other article in the same situation that cotton has been placed. Salt, for instance. Take away the tariff and impose a tax of one cent per pound, and the effect will be the same as upon cotton. Or take sugar, and impose the prohibitory tax of three cents per pound upon it, and the effect upon it will be the same as that upon cotton.

According to the Constitution, I deny that this tax is uniform, since it would have been as fair to tax either of the just-named articles, as it was to tax cotton, for custom and the present status of civilization recognize these articles to be the prime necessities of life. Cotton is a necessity according to custom, decency, civilization, and under rules and regulations of society. There are no rules nor regulations laid down by law, neither constitutional, statute, common, nor municipal law, that compels any man to eat or drink; but, on the other hand, municipal law, moral customs, and influences of every civilized community, compel every man to properly clothe himself, making it a penal offense for him to appear in the street unless his nakedness is thoroughly concealed; nor does custom stop with a mere concealing of nakedness, but even a superfluity of clothing is necessary, so as to add to his personal appearance. Cotton, therefore, being an indispensable article of dress, and an absolute necessity to protect us from the many changes of weather, should not be placed in the same category with tobacco and whiskey, recognized and acknowledged poisonous luxuries of life.

Again I refer to the class of people who make cotton. The statistics will show that twenty-nine bales of cotton out of every thirty made in the United

States are made directly by the Negroes in the southern states, and to them this tax is due. I will say for them that when they were set free they found themselves without homes, without clothes and without bread; with all their means of subsistence in the North and northwestern states, thousands of miles from them, slandered and abused, said to be too lazy to make cotton unless a will superior to their own were placed over them to control, they united themselves and determined to make cotton under their own direction in order that they might refute the base slanders which had been heaped upon them. And but for this tax which I have mentioned they would have been able to purchase one-eighth of the land upon which this cotton was made. Further, this three cents per pound came directly from the labor of the man who made the cotton. In addition to this tax, he pays large freights upon all substances, meat, bread, and other articles, such as are shipped to him from the great distances above mentioned. He must pay the freights on cotton to and from the New England mills, also the manufacturer's percentage and the merchant's profit.

Now, I plead in behalf of the poor people of the South, regardless of caste or color, because this tax had its blighting influence. It cut the jugular vein of our financial system, bled it near unto death, and wrought a destructive influence upon every line of business. It so crippled every trade and industry that our suffering has been greater under its influence than under that of the war. That tax took away all the income and left us no profit and very little circulating medium. I therefore beg Congress to correct the error and refund the cotton tax to that class of people from whom it was taken and for whom I wish to please in my imperfect way. And further, I had the honor to introduce bill No. 2277, which cannot be reached in the regular order of business during this session of Congress, and I therefore ask the indulgence of members for a few minutes, while I make some remarks in relation to this bill. The bill purports to authorize the United States Land Commissioners to bid for large tracts of private land, when sold at public auction, with the right to secure titles to these lands in the name of the United States, in the same manner as they are secured by private individuals; and to subdivide these tracts into small tracts containing not more than one hundred and sixty acres, and as much less as suits the convenience of the purchaser. The latter shall have the right to receive from the Land Commissioner a certificate of entry, and shall pay to the United States, at the time of purchase, ten percent on the cost, and shall continue to pay annually ten percent on cost until the whole is paid. When the final payment has been made the Land Commissioner shall be required to give to the purchaser a warrantee title to the land purchased.

I ask Congress to make this appropriation, and I ask it in behalf of the landless and poor people of our country. In that section of country that I have the honor in part to represent upon this floor the people are extremely poor, having been emancipated from slavery after hundreds of years of disappointment and privation. These people have struggled longer and labored harder, and have made more of the raw material than any people in the world. Notwithstanding the fact that they have labored long, hard, and faithfully, they live on little clothing, the poorest food, and in miserable huts. Since they have been free they have not slackened their industry, but have materially improved their economy. While their labor has rewarded the nation with larger revenue, they have consumed less of the substance of the country than any other class of people. If dressing less, eating little, and hard and continued labor means economy, these people are the most economical in the world. And, it is a universal understanding among themselves that they are not to live in any extravagant way so far as eating and dressing is concerned. They are laboring and making every effort to secure land and houses. It is next to impossible that this generation will accomplish it without such aid, as I now ask from the Government.

I am frequently met on the floor with the argument that the Government should be just before it is generous. Then, I call the attention of the gentlemen of the House to the fact that we should look to our own interests before we care for those of our neighbors. What has been the result of our legislation? We have subsidized for the people of China; we have subsidized for the people of Japan; we have subsidized to feed the wild Indians, roaming over the domains of the West, pillaging, robbing, and murdering our citizens. These subsidies are sucking vampires upon our people, for not one of those who are benefited by them pay to the United States a single dollar of taxes, while the people in whose behalf I plead pay annually $70,000,000 taxes to the United States Government.

While we pay gratuitously to Chinese, Japanese, and Indians, millions of dollars annually, we hesitate to even lend to the landless but peaceable and industrious citizens of the South $1,000,000 annually to help them aid themselves and at the same time greatly develop the resources of the country. Nor can this loan be attended with the least risk to the Government, for it is secured by the best of security placing a small portion of the surplus money of the Treasury to profitable use, at the same time paying the Government large interest.

I thank the gentlemen for their attention, and again beg them to give us a united vote on the bill to refund this cotton tax.

21

Josiah Thomas Walls
(1842–1905)
House of Representatives, Florida

Republican

Forty-second, Forty-third and Forty-fourth
Congresses
March 4, 1871, to January 29, 1873
March 4, 1873, to March 3, 1875
March 4, 1875, to April 19, 1876

Writing in 1940, Samuel D. Denny stated that Josiah T. Walls was born free. Later historians are uncertain of his claim. By giving family histories, he was responsible for the confusion. While Walls claimed that his parents were manumitted in 1842, he also reported that he had lived in bondage until the Union Army freed him during the Civil War. Without convincing evidence to the contrary, there is little reason to believe that Josiah was never a slave. He was born on the plantation of Dr. John Walls in Winchester, Virginia, on December 30, 1842. Apparently Dr. Walls, who practiced medicine in Winchester, was Josiah's father. He and Josiah remained in contact, and continued their relationship upon his election to Congress.

Scholars are more certain about his status at the start of the Civil War. By one account he was impressed into service by the Confederate Army and assigned to an artillery detail. He was not a soldier in any sense of the word. He was a slave of the army, ordered to haul equipment and dig drenches. His fate changed in 1862 when the Union Army captured him at the Battle of Yorktown and carried him to Harrisburg, Pennsylvania. The Union did not consider him a prisoner of war, so they immediately emancipated him. Walls attended school in Pennsylvania, and volunteered for the army after the Emancipation Proclamation authorized black enlistment. He enrolled in the Third Infantry Regiment of the United States Colored Troops, and he quickly rose to sergeant major and then instructor of artillery; otherwise his military career was largely undistinguished. He received no medals or special commendations; he was mustered out of the army without fanfare, and with only $118.66 to his name.

Walls adopted Florida as his home following the Civil War because his military career ended there. His platoon leader gave him a job in a lumber mill. Walls also turned to farming, and began to build a modest financial base. Soon greater opportunities opened for him in public service and he was elected to the state constitutional convention from Alachua County in 1868. That same year Walls was elected to the state legislature as a Republican. In 1870, he won the only congressional seat in Florida, becoming the first and only black official to be elected during Reconstruction. He also has the distinction of being the only black legislator to represent an entire state. The Speaker of the House appointed Walls to the committees on the Militia, Mileage, and Expenditures in the Navy Department. Having had limited schooling, he believed that an education was the surest way to solve some of the nation's social problems. Like other black congressmen and some white Republicans, Walls urged the federal government to become involved in public education by creating a national education fund. He doubted that southern states could be relied upon to educate blacks–or had the financial means to do so.

His service in the House did not have his complete attention. During his tenure, Walls was involved in two contested elections. White Democrat Silas L. Niblack contested Wall's election of 1870, charging that the people who had voted for him had their ballots rejected at the polls by Republican workers. Walls argued that Niblack was trying to steal the election. On January 29, 1873, the House of Representatives removed Walls with only two months left in his term, and seated Niblack. Since Walls had already won reelection in 1872, he immediately returned to Congress and held on to his seat until he faced a new contest from white Democrat Jesse J. Finley. Walls had narrowly defeated Finley in 1874 by a margin of 371 votes. Finley successfully contested the election and for the second time the House removed Walls from office.

His controversial tenure in Congress notwithstanding, Walls provided dynamic leadership. He pressed for passage of Sumner's Civil Rights Bill and he condemned lynching. He favored relief for Seminole War veterans, and improving the harbors in Florida, and supported turning over public lands in Florida to railroad companies. He believed that laying additional railroad tracks would facilitate travel and expansion. He also supported the anti-colonial movement in Cuba, and denounced Spain for enslaving over 500,000 blacks there. Walls ran for the Republican congressional nomination in 1876, but lost.

With his national political career over, Walls returned to state politics and won a seat in the Florida senate. Walls continued to press for mandatory public education. Frustrated by failure, he took a leave from the senate, and later gave up politics. Walls ended his career as an educator, joining the faculty at Florida Normal College (Florida A & M University). He headed the agricultural department, and demonstrated improved methods of growing lettuce and oranges. Walls also returned to lumbering. He died in Tallahassee on May 15, 1905.

Walls favored making federal appropriations to support public education. His opponents claimed that national education was contrary to state sovereignty. Walls insisted that as long as the Ku Klux Klan burned black schools and churches African Americans would need the support of the federal government.

THE NATIONAL EDUCATION FUND
February 3, 1872

My remarks will be principally directed as an answer to the remarks made by the gentleman from Georgia [Archibald Thompson MacIntyre] who it appears was in opposition to the bill establishing a national educational fund as proposed by the Committee on Education and Labor. If we did not understand those who keep up this great clamor for State rights, we might be constrained to believe as the gentleman from Georgia, that no one had any interest in their respective State governments but those who duly warn us against the infringements upon the rights of the States. But we understand them. We know what the cry about State rights means and more especially when we hear it produced as an argument against the establishment of a fund for the education of the people.

Judging from the past I must confess that I am somewhat suspicious of such rights, knowing, as I do, that the Democratic party in Georgia, as well as in all of the other southern States, have been opposed to the education of the Negro and poor white children. And I can, without doing that party any wrong, safely and truthfully state that the Democratic party today in Georgia, as well as in Florida is opposed to the education of all classes. We know that the Democratic party used to argue that to educate the Negro was to set him free, and that to deprive him of all the advantages necessary to enable him to acquire an education was to perpetuate his enslavement. Their argument against educating the poor whites was that the Negro more directly associated with the poor whites than with that class who controlled the destinies of slavery. So fearful were they that the Negro would become educated, either through his own efforts or by the aid of some poor white person, they enacted laws prohibiting him from being educated even by his own master; and if a poor white person was caught teaching a Negro, he was whipped, or in some States sold or compelled to leave the State; and if by chance a Negro did learn to read, and it was found out, he was whipped every time he was caught with a book, and as many times between as his master pleased. We must remember that this state of affairs existed only about six years ago, and this being the case, is it unreasonable for us to suppose that the Democratic party of Georgia is opposed to the Negro being included in the bill that proposes to establish an educational fund and his being educated out of the public money? I think not.

The gentleman from Georgia also tells us that he is in favor of seeing the schools of the country promoted, and we believe he is but he wishes to promote them under the old system, which has so far been a failure in the South, and every fair-minded and unprejudiced man will admit it. He informs us also that the Georgia Legislature has within the last twenty days appropriated $300,000 for the purpose of education and that the educational system is not confined to the whites alone. He then informs us that the "colored people of his State are entitled under the law to the same rights that the whites will enjoy." Mark his words, "entitled to the same rights that the whites will enjoy." This is very true; but will the colored people have an opportunity, or be permitted to enjoy the same rights that the whites enjoy? This is the question. The echo of the past answers no–Not while the Ku Klux Democracy is permitted to burn the schoolhouses and churches belonging to the colored people of Georgia; not while they shut the doors of the schoolhouses against the colored children, will the colored people of Georgia enjoy the same educational advantages that the whites enjoy.

We find that in July 1783, the Georgia Legislature appropriated one thousand acres of land to each county for the support of free schools. In 1784 the General Assembly appropriated forty thousand acres of land for the endowment of a college or university. In 1792 an act was passed by the Legislature appropriating one thousand acres of land for the endowment of each of the county academies; $250,000 was appropriated in 1817 for the support of poor schools. We see that the Georgia Legislature prior to 1868 appropriated thousands of acres of land for the support of colleges, county academies, and free schools, but did Georgia have a free-school system in operation prior to 1870? Again, we see that the Georgia Legislature appropriated $250,000 for the support of what they called "poor schools." If this appropriation was applied to the establishment of schools, did the poor white and colored children get an equal benefit of it? We are informed by Colonel J. R. Lewis that Georgia had indeed a very "poor school" system prior to 1870, and no free schools in operation at all; Savannah and Columbus were the only places where they had any schools worthy of the name. I suppose he refers to that patriotism existing among the colored people, or that which the whites have inculcated since May 1865. Now, if we judge of the patriotism existing among the Democratic party in Georgia today from the course that party has pursued in that State relative to free schools and the education of the Negro, our conclusion will be that Georgia is now opposed to free schools, and the education of the Negro and poor white children, as heretofore.

It is useless to talk about patriotism existing in those states in connection with free schools under the democratic system, and in connection with those who now and always have believed that it was wrong to educate the Negro, and that such offenses should be punishable by death or the lash. Away with the patriotism that advocates and prefers ignorance to intelligence! Let us look into the patriotism of Florida's sister state, Georgia. My state has been very retrogressive in connection with free schools, but she is still ahead of Georgia in this respect. I am indeed sorry I cannot say as much for the patriotism of the Democratic party of my State as the gentleman has about Georgia, when I know that in 1845 the General Government donated to Florida, while under Democratic rule, 908,503 acres of the public domain of that State for common-school purposes. And what did they do with it? They enacted a common-school law that did not mean anything, which was enacted only to obtain the possession of the lands donated. In this same law they created a common-school fund, and under the operation of this bogus law they obtained fraudulent possession of the lands, sold them, and applied the proceeds to everything else except that for which they were donated. Is this the kind of patriotism to which the gentleman alluded in his remarks?

I am in favor of not only this bill, but of a national system of education, because I believe that the national Government is the guardian of the liberties of all its subjects. And having within a few years incorporated into the body-politic a class of uneducated people, the majority of whom, I am sorry to say, are colored, the question for solution and the problems to be solved, then, are: can these people protect their liberties without education; and can they be educated under the present condition of society in the States where they were when freed? Can this be done without the aid, assistance, and supervision of the General government? No, it cannot. Were it not that the prejudice of slavery is so prevalent among the former slaveholder against the education of the Negro it would be superficial to say that the Negro could not protect his educational interests, or could not be educated without the establishment of a national system of education. This prejudice is attributable to the fact that they were compelled to keep the Negro in ignorance in order to hold him in slavery. Moreover, with the advantages of education and enlightenment available to whites they were enabled to successfully keep blacks in bondage. As everyone knows that the advantages of education are great.

We are told that the Persians were kept for ages in slavery from the power of intellect alone. Education constitutes the apprenticeship of those who are afterward to take a place in the order of our civilized and progressive nation. Education tends to increase the dignity and self-respect of a people, tends to increase their fitness for society and important stations of trust, tends to elevate, and consequently carries with it a great moral responsibility. This is why the Democratic party in the South so bitterly opposes the education of all classes. They know that no educated people can be enslaved. They know that no educated people can be robbed of their labor. They well know that no educated people can be kept in a helpless and degraded condition, but will arise with a united voice and assert their manhood. Hence, to educate the Negro in the South would be to lift him to a state of civilization and enlightenment that would enable him not only to maintain and defend this liberty, but to better acquit himself as an honorable and upright citizen, and prove himself more worthy of the rights conferred upon him.

I cannot believe that the democracy of Georgia or any other state manifests this patriotism or has taken this sudden departure. They know the Negro is loyal, and while their present educational institutions are fosterers of disloyalty and nurseries of enmity and hatred toward the government of the loyal blacks and whites, I cannot hope to ever see this Democratic party endowed with sufficient patriotism and justice to lend their energies and support in favor of the education and elevation of my people. While the Democratic party adheres to the ideas and principles that they have now it would be against their interests to educate the Negro; not only against their interests, but entirely inconsistent with their faith. Can we then suppose that these firm adherents to slavery and State rights are willing to educate the Negro and loyal whites, who are opposed to their principles, and thereby enable them to wield the controlling power of the South? No, I should think not so. They are more consistent and patriotic toward the principles of the lost cause than this. The Democratic party is opposed to any system that will have the effect of making a majority of the present or rising generation loyal to the government. It had been admitted by every lover of free government that popular education, or the education of the masses, is necessary to and inseparable from a complete citizenship. Then let the nation educate her subjects. It is to the interest of the Government, as also to the people, to do so. An educated people possess more skill, and manifest more interest and fidelity in the affairs of the Government, because of their chance to obtain more general information, which tends to eradicate the prejudices and superstitions so prevalent among an ignorant people.

Educated people seek always to improve their condition, not only at home, but in all their surroundings. Educated people are more social, more refined, and more ready to impart their knowledge and experience to others; more industrious because more ambitious to accumulate and possess property;

while the ignorant and uneducated are more prone to idleness, more addicted to low habits and dissipation, more careless and less ambitious, being more of a "turn" to content themselves and let things go about as they are. The uneducated person cannot have the influence among his fellow men that educated persons have. As knowledge is power, in short, education is the panacea for all our social evils, injustices, and oppression. The general diffusion of education among the whole people of the South would render them less submissive to the social and political stigmas under which they are today laboring. Now that our whole people throughout this broad land are free, it yet remains for this Government to give them that which will not only enable them to better enjoy their freedom, but will enable them to maintain, defend, and perpetuate their liberties. Imagine your race, Mr. Speaker, as having been in bondage for over two hundred years, subjected to all the horrors of slavery, deprived of every facility by which they might have acquired an education, and in this ignorant and helpless condition they were emancipated and turned loose in the midst of their enemies; among those who were opposed to not only seeing them educated, but opposed to their freedom, among those who possessed all the wealth, controlled all the educational facilities of the country; among those who believed your race to be naturally inferior to themselves in every particular, and fit only to be considered as goods and chattels.

Imagine, I say, your race today in this deplorable situation. Would you be considered as comprehending their desires and situation were you to admit that their former enslavers would take an impartial interest in their educational affairs? I think not. Hence, I cannot believe that the Democratic party in the South would provide equal educational advantages to all classes. The gentleman from the District of Columbia [Norton Parker Chipman] had correctly said that the lately enfranchised people are peculiarly the wards of the government. Still, we ask that equal advantages, impartial protection, and the same educational facility may be extended to all classes, to the whole people. Give us this, and we will further endeavor to remove the ignorance from our people, and about which so much had been said by those who have occasioned it and who are justly responsible for it; they who have imposed it upon us through the operation of that once loved and cherished institution, slavery–that institution which has cost the nation millions of dollars and many of her best and bravest men, and has stamped upon the Negro a curse which this generation will fail to obliterate.

I might here pay a passing notice to the arguments generally used against the Negro, and against his being educated. It has been said that the Negro is an inferior race, with minds unfit for cultivation, with no traits of science, skill, or literature; with no ambition for education and enlightenment; in short, a perfect "booby brain." But these arguments fell to the ground many years ago, and have been rendered insignificant from the fact that notwithstanding all the laws enacted prohibiting the Negro from being educated, in spite of the degradation of over two hundred and forty-seven years of the most inhuman and barbarous slavery ever recorded in the history of any people, and coupled with five years subjugation to the reign of terror from the Ku Klux Klan, the dastardly horrors of which those only know who have been the victims, and those who commit the deeds. Notwithstanding all theses obstacles and opposition, we find in nearly every town and village, where the whipping-posts and auction-blocks were once visible, school-houses and freedmen's savings banks erected in their stead, which are the growth of only five years, and which stand today as living refutations to the foul, malignant, unjust, and untrue arguments used against the Negro. We still find him, however, loyal to his Government and friendly toward his former master, today looking to this Congress for the passage of a measure that will aid in increasing the educational facilities throughout the country for the benefit of all classes, and thereby enable him to rear his children to truly comprehend their relations with and duties toward their Government.

Believing, then, as I have before said, that the national government is the guardian of all the liberties of her subjects; I think we should lend all our aid to the establishment of a national educational fund. I think it behooves us, as the guardians of the rights and liberties of the people of this nation, to do so; for we are told that all there is of a nation that is good, that is mighty, that exercises influence and promotes prosperity, are the products of the education of its citizens. Then, let us make provisions for the education of all classes; and if the State governments are unwilling to provide equal facilities for all, then let the national Government take the matter in hand.

Walls urged Congress to appropriate $3 million for the centennial celebration of the United States and the international exhibition. Walls, as did other black congressmen, believed that by displaying the achievements of African Americans since emancipation, whites, upon being better informed, would become enlightened on the subject of race and discontinue their persecution of blacks. Furthermore, he believed the exposition would lure peoples from abroad to come to the United States.

Centennial Celebration
May 7, 1874

From what I have seen of the wide discussion of the proposed centennial exposition in the public press, and from the course of the debates upon the subject in these Halls, it seems to me that a misapprehension of the origin and character of the enterprise has from the beginning taken largely from the dignity of the discussion, and has largely and without necessity added acrimony and bitterness to the evident feeling attending it.

The exposition has in the press, even of this capital, been sneeringly alluded to as "The Philadelphia Job," as though it were an evident attempt on the part of the people of Pennsylvania, and especially of the city of Philadelphia, in an improper and unwarrantable manner, from motives of selfish greed, to foist upon an indifferent and an unwilling people a scheme foreign to their interests and in opposition to their wishes, and all for the petty gains and notoriety that by the adoption of the proposed plan would inure to the local benefit of a particular section. It is only upon the supposition of the existence of some such opinion that I can account for an acerbity of feeling and a harshness of language in the newspaper discussion of the centennial that to me seemed utterly uncalled for and unworthy of the theme. From my recollection of the congressional action heretofore, and in which I participated, the place of holding a proper national celebration of the one hundredth birthday of this Government and of this people, as a separate and independent nationality, was, previous to the fixing of a definite location for its celebration, in no sense of the word considered as a job attempted to be put up by anybody. From and indeed previous to any action whatever being had on the part of Congress, the whole subject had been widely agitated in all parts of the country; and congressional action was proposed and was had, not in advance of the popular wish and sentiment, by in response to a general popular demand, and in conformity with the popular wish of the whole people, as evinced in the numerous petitions presented to us.

Indeed, I can but feel that the mere selection and designation of the city of Philadelphia as the place in which the exposition should be held did a great deal to further our cause. But aside from all these minor and incidental considerations, the aid of Congress having already been granted to some extent to the centennial by such legislation as was asked; and more, its former assistance having been solicited in a proper manner by a very numerous and respectable portion of the people at large as well as by the centennial representatives selected and commissioned by the Government from every State and Territory of the Union, and certainly very plausible reasons having been offered for the grant of further national assistance, we have a plain duty before us.

And accordingly it seems to me that, under all the circumstances of the case and in view of the large share of public attention already excited toward the centennial, and partly in consequence of the very decided encouragement drawn to it from the congressional action already had, the very least that we can with propriety do is to give the whole matter full consideration, in justice to ourselves as well as to a matter appealing so directly to the patriotic sentiments of our whole people, and by a full and fair discussion endeavor to ascertain the actual merits of the place proposed, the probable success of the undertaking, the benefits that may be expected to result from it both to ourselves and to the world, the propriety upon general principles of a grant of national aid, and whether or not the extension of such national aid is by our previous action already pledged. First, then, what are the real merits of the proposed international exposition? In reference to this point, the mere recital of the preface to the act of Congress to which the centennial owes its corporate existence would seem to summarize the whole matter in its authoritative announcement of "Whereas it behooves the people of the United States to celebrate by appropriate ceremonies the centennial anniversary of this memorable and decisive event, which constituted the 4th day of July, 1775, the birthday of this nation."

From the very first, then, a dominant and not discreditable feature of the centennial seems to have been that it contemplated a public, emphatic, and comprehensive expression by a whole people, who for a hundred years had enjoyed a more than usual share of the ordinary blessings of human life under the genial but powerful influences of an essentially popular government based upon the organic and paramount doctrines of the Declaration ascribing to every man born of woman an entire and absolute equality of political rights, of their gratitude for the blessings attending their lot, and their profound appreciation of the adequacy of a free government to the protection of the social, political, and personal rights of all within its scope. Such recognition of advantages received from the practical operation of existing systems of government has characterized the people of all the various known governments that have existed from time immemorial, so much so as to have become a custom well-nigh universal. Recognized thus as proper and becoming under monarchical and even despotic governments, will any say that it is any less proper and becoming to the happy people who exult in the possession of the only literally free government upon the face of the broad earth? Indeed, there would seem to be a peculiar propriety in such a national exhibition to the nations of the world of our own satisfaction with the capacities and excellencies of our own system of government thus approved, tested, and favored, to be both sufficient and satisfactory, by the dangers and reverses as well as the sometimes more dangerous successes of a century of practical trial.

It may all be very true that no absolutely new truth and no thereto unheard of discovery in political science was announced in the Declaration as a novel and starting base upon which to found governmental structure that should challenge the admiration of the nation. Such admitted fact in no whit derogates from the value or force of that noble document. Right there, in the very fact that in the Declaration was nothing intrinsically new, but that it simply gathered up and arranged in systematic order and for a practical purpose in the promotion of human happiness and progress those simple, forcible, and undoubted political truths which had long been acknowledged as true in the abstract, but never practically embodied in any actual and existing form of government, consists the real power of the Declaration. It was this very novelty of making practical application of what had previously been considered only abstract prepositions for the discussion of philosophers, and to serve as themes for sentimental preachers and visionary theorists, to the protection of every-day rights and privileges, and their incorporation into an actual system of government for living men, which aroused the skeptical curiosity, and awakened the incredulous but zealous attention of the political world.

Thus proclaiming nothing actually new to philosophers and theorists the announced determination to base upon the truths of the Declaration an actual government of living men, and to place it in competition with existing governments of a variously but totally different character, startled and at first alarmed the nations. Organically strange, and, in its application, of necessity essentially aggressive and practically threatening, the newly organized Government met with but chary courtesy from other nations, and early excited an alarm and a proclivity to opposition that to this day has not entirely disappeared. While other nations thus so gladly welcome and celebrate those memorial days which remind them of the glorious deeds of their own noble and beloved ancestry, and delight to sound their praise, shall we, a happy and prosperous nation of forty millions, exulting in the possession of a Government by the people, for the people, of the people, entirely adequate to all our wants, and, however otherwise differing, united in common satisfaction without political heritage, decline upon an appropriate occasion to manifest our gratitude to our fathers and our pride in the quality of their work?

What measure of success may be expected to attend an enterprise begun in the spirit and with the purposes alluded to is a question with which in fact we have little to do, for the purposes of this discussion, as to the propriety of lending our aid; and yet it is a question the discussion of which will help to influence the action of many in reference to it. No little weight, however, should attach to the evident truth, that our action upon the matter, whether favorable or the reverse, will be apt to exert a very strong, if not a conclusive influence upon the success or failure of the proposed undertaking. The commission, as an organized body, owes its existence as such to the action of Congress which gave the first effective impetus to its life, and in its every stage, so far, has been led on and encouraged by governmental co-operation and congressional legislation.

The entire nationality of its character as indispensable to its probable success, even as a merely national exposition, was fully recognized by the commission at their first convention, while they were soon convinced that to attempt an international exhibition without the open and emphatic countenance and assistance of the national Government was, from the impossibility otherwise of any formal communication with foreign governments, wholly absurd. Such countenance, which indeed was foreshadowed in the direction of the organic law that the exposition should be held "under the auspices" of the United States Government, was sought in the petition for the incorporation of "the centennial board of finance," and was granted in the enactment of its charter. Thus led on, step by step in its gradual progress, and encouraged by the successive acts of participation by different branches of the national Government, it is scarcely too much to say that the ultimate success of the exposition, as of a full and complete national character, depends upon the determination which we shall reach as to the extension of further national aid. And, as it seems to me, that consideration alone, that the success of an enterprise that originated as an organized undertaking to congressional action, and had been in the same manner steadily encouraged hitherto, will depend very largely upon our future action, and will be marred by our refusal of any further aid, should carry with us great weight.

With such aid as we are now solicited to grant, and which, in view of the many beneficial effects that may reasonably be expected to result from a successful exposition, is really of little account and nearly insignificant, the favorable progress and successful termination of the exposition may safely be predicted. The general interests of the nation as a whole, as well as the particular interests of each State and section, will be so surely and so largely promoted by the intimate intermingling of citizens from every corner and section of the vast extent of our own country, with an opportunity for a prolonged association with the citizens of far-away regions whose very existence has with thousands of our own people secured–from remoteness alone an almost mythical interest in the exposition which from the time of general assurance of its vigorous prosecution will increase day by day up to the close of the exposition. Located, as it is, in the midst of one of the most prosperous and densely populated regions of our country; in a city itself containing nearly one million people, and in the near vicinity of a half dozen others with an aggregate population of two million more, the probable attendance upon the exposition from a circle about its location of a radius of two hundred and fifty miles, or within a single day's travel by rail, may safely be estimated at from two to three millions of our own people.

The immense deposits of mineral resources in this country, of which the simple and truthful report has amazed the world–our incalculable wealth of coal, iron, copper, silver, and gold, of which a thorough and exhaustive exposition will be given, will alone attract the attendance of many thousands from abroad. The admitted perfection in the cultivation of various implements in the mechanic arts, the demonstrated excellence of mechanical skill attained by our American workmen, as exhibited in the European expositions, with the immense extent and wide distribution of our manufacturing establishments, will be of special interest to many other thousands. The wide-spread and familiar use of steam and other machinery in the prosecution of all varieties of agricultural as well as merely mechanical work will constitute a feature of the exposition that will add largely to its attractiveness in the eyes of thoughtful men from all sections. A full exhibition of the immense variety of the natural productions of the United States, stretching as it does from the tepid waters of the Gulf to the northern home of the glaciers, and reaching from the orange and grape of California, the banana, the cocoa-nut, and the Polar circle, will present at one glance so striking and palpable a view of the immense extent of our country with vast range of vegetable production, stretching not in distant colonies, but in what will ultimately and organically, and at no distant period, form a solid continuation of coterminous States, as to sustain universal and irresistible attention.

Indeed, viewed in any probable light, a large attendance and participation from abroad may reasonably be expected to gather at the centennial, if only that aid which is subsequently necessary now in the time of its utmost need be extended, and that its inauguration and an auspicious beginning secured, for after that it can take care of itself. From some, among the many nations of the eastern world, our country has never met with any but the most cordial and kindly support, and their good offices in our behalf have more than once been tendered; for however different in character and tendency may be their own governments, they have been wise enough to recognize the strength that may naturally be made to grow out of organic differences. From all those nations warm sympathy and a large attendance may be counted on with certainty.

And, in the case of nations to whom our own steady and progressive expansion and prosperity have been a matter of disappointment and regret, the very jealousies and even animosities that peradventure may exist, will all work together to enhance the curiosity that will induce many to see with their own eyes the actual sources of weakness of the "Republic of the North," upon which in contemplation they have fed, perhaps, their grudges. On all these accounts, then, and in view of all these inducements and moving causes, I count with confidence upon an attendance upon the exposition that if itself will command its final success. I come next to respond to the inquiry: are there any substantial results or value anticipated from the Centennial Exposition, providing it is fairly successful. The benefits of the kind commonly considered are alone substantial–that is to say that they will bear immediate and tangible fruit within a short time following the celebration. There can be little doubt that exposition we contemplate will be beneficial to the county. It will serve a direct and effective part in promoting the growth our nation–its national strength–as shown in the experiences of its people. It can plainly be seen that immigration has played a vital role in the development of the United States. For the last half century, a mass of humanity has constantly been flooding into this country, and even now, after all the attention that has been given to it, very few people appreciate that many of our most intelligent men came from other continents.

I care not now to go into many of the ascertained facts in regard to that matter in detail, but in this connection will call attention to only one or two. Hiram Casey Young, the chief of the federal Bureau of Statistics, reported an increase in the population of the United States, due to immigration. Young found that "during the entire period from 1820-1870 the increase in each year averaged about 13 percent." In 1870, he estimates that "the total number of aliens who have been permanently added to our population by direct immigration since the formation of the Government will reach 7,803,863." Finally, I desire to close this part of my discussion by asking some bold man among my colleagues upon this floor to give here and now a cash valuation of the value of the life and services in one direction of such men such as Carl Schurz and Louis Agassiz, both emigrants. They show that this country offers an opportunity for manifold progress in areas as social and political; the country also provides an opportunity for material advancement. This country offers these as free gifts to every son of man who chooses to apply in person for them and to demonstrate his sincerity by assuming the obligations of American citizenship, to add a powerful and continuing stimulus to a never-ending tide of valuable immigration—for those reasons alone, were there absolutely none others offered, I am in favor of substantial and direct aid to an enterprise so palpably capable of such valuable results.

I will leave to others such comments as the certain improvement in mechanical and artistic skill, which may reasonably be expected to grow out of such a favorable opportunity for the examination and comparison of the master achievements of the trained and skilled workmanship of the world; for I know that this will be with many a favorite and fruitful subject of full discussion. But I will take the occasion to call attention to a less direct, but to my mind a no less important, effect that may be expected to result from a well-understood national and international exposition. I allude to the tendency of such a gathering as will then occur to revive, invigorate, and stir to vigorous life that feeling of national patriotism in our land which recent occurrences have somewhat weakened. I am well aware of the common inclination to consider patriotism as a sort of myth and a popular delusion, and to look upon any allusion to it as at least bordering upon the ridiculous. Long ago patriotism was said by an eminent English novelist to be "The love of office," and politics "The art of getting it"; and I am not ignorant of the common supposition that, in southern politics particularly, the actual truth of old Fielding's allegation is being continually illustrated; but coming from the South, as I do, I desire to say that the patriotic tendency of the centennial is not the least attractive or least important feature of it in the estimation of southern men, "without respect to previous condition."

In the face of the common drift of the modern general mind toward ridicule of anything in the way of sentiment in the discussion of important questions, I am fully conscious that I am by no means alone in ascribing to a patriotic attachment to one's own country, its people, and its government, a powerful influence in adding to its strength and in increasing the stability of its institutions. This is proved to be true of all the nations of which history has preserved the records, and equally true of all, no matter what may have been the nature of their governments. This is true even of governments of a monarchical character, as is proved in the history of yesterday as well as of a thousand years ago; as is witnessed to-day in the devotion of his adherents to Don Carlos, in the warm affection of Frenchmen of prominence to the prince imperial, and in the undying devotion of the enthusiastic Irishman of the green banner of the Ireland of old.

Instances innumerable in point could easily be adduced, extending through the whole reach of recorded and traditional history from the noble Roman who knowingly gives himself to torture and death for his country's sake to the equally noble American who in the very last extremity "only regretted that he had but one life to lose in the cause of liberty," and within our own personal knowledge has been convincingly exemplified in the unnoted deaths of thousands in our last great struggle, who died and gave no sign of the paramount strength of patriotic and unselfish sentiments and opinions, and sealed the evidence of their power and their sincerity as well in the oozing ebb of their life's blood. The power of a mere sentiment, whether shown in the unchanging faith of the martyr or the constant and undying attachment of the patriot, has, in the shaping of the destinies of this world and the dignity lent to its history, worked greater miracles than any other divine power. And I insist upon it that now, as it ever has been, whatever agency adds to the force or enhances the vitality of the considerate patriotism of the thoughtful and intelligent citizenship ministers directly to the permanent sources of the health and strength of the nation to which it belongs.

Does any man suppose that the founding fathers of 1776, with the halter dangling before their eyes, affixed signatures to the Declaration from deliberate conviction that pecuniary gain to them would there-from result? Was greed the animus of that ever-memorable political announcement of "Millions for defense, but not one cent for tribute?" So I believe that when from every corner of this broad land, from every State and Territory, thousands and millions of the free citizens of a free government shall assemble in the very cradle and place of the birth of all that politically they hold dear, and exchange with each other the mutual grasp and the meaningful glances of a common citizenship, there will be aroused in the bosoms of all a higher and purer sense of the honest and sincere attachment cherished by all in common for those free institutions whose origin and beneficent sway they are now to celebrate than they have ever before been permitted to feel, and which will strengthen all the bonds which can unite freemen to their native land, and kindle a blaze of patriotic feeling in whose dazzling light all questions of minor differences and all hurtful recollections of past disagreements will be blotted out.

Recognizing fully the obligations of a large majority of those to whose suffrages I owe my official presence in this Hall to the tardy but in the end the full and complete vindication of the sublime and sublimely simple announcements of the Declaration, I am willing that others should find amusement in contemplating the centennial as "an overgrown and spread-eagle Fourth of July"; while for myself and at least four millions of the new freemen of this land of liberty, I will hope that, in the mercy of God, my own life may be spared till, among the crowding thousands of exulting freemen, I may on the 4th of July, 1876, stand in the very shadow of Independence Hall, and with glowing heart read the undying words of Webster:

When my eyes shall be turned to behold, for the last time, the sun in heaven may I not see him shining on the broken and dishonored fragments of a once glorious Union; on states dissevered, discordant, and belligerent; our land rent with civil feuds, or drenched, it may be, in fraternal blood! Let their last feeble and lingering glance rather behold the gorgeous ensign of the Republic now known and honored throughout the earth, still full high advance, its arms and trophies streaming in their original luster, not a stripe erased or polluted, not a single star obscured, bearing for its motto no such miserable interrogatory as "What is all this worth?" nor those other words of delusion and folly, "Liberty first and Union afterwards," but everywhere spread all over it in characters of living light, blazing on all its ample folds, as they float over the sea and over the land, and in every wind under the whole heavens, that other sentiment, dear to every true American heart–Liberty and Union, now and forever, one and inseparable!

Entertaining such sentiments and cherishing the hope that the day of the termination of one hundred years from the birth of our government may by common consent and by universal adoption be fixed upon as the day of the definite and emphatic termination of all feelings of harshness and bitterness arising from our recent contentions, I shall not apologize for them, however unfashionable they may be held to be but still continue to hold them, hoping for them a wider adopting and a more commanding prevalence. In the presence of so many who are infinitely better versed in all matters of the legal and constitutional authority of Congress to make a grant of pecuniary aid, I do not propose to occupy much time with that part of the discussion. If the centennial is right and proper in itself, as I think it is; if it will promote the general harmony, increase the fervor of the common patriotism, and so strengthen the sources of national strength; if it will unite more closely together the now somewhat discordant and jarring interests of the North and the South; if it will tend to discourage and extinguish all feelings of sectionalism; if it will stimulate that immigration, to which more than to all other except organic agencies we owe our wonderful national growth; if it will promote and advance our progress in the industrial arts, then I have faith to believe that no specifically permissive power is constitutionally necessary.

In a common-sense way I look about for analogies, and I find them spread around me on every hand. I find national banks established, a circulating medium of paper money created Pacific railroads built, the improvement of internal harbors and rivers effected, vast sections of foreign territory purchased and incorporated with our own, a board of immigration established, provision at large expense for a periodical census, a national observatory establish and supported, and all, so far as I can discover, without any specific permission given in the Constitution, and I am satisfied that the good results expected and attained thereby give, in my opinion, sufficient warrant. I am content to consent to an appropriation for the centennial on the same ground on which the picture of the Father of his Country was placed upon the walls of the Capitol in the city that took his name. And while others may feel at liberty to criticize Congress and the Executive for their decision, or for supposedly taking this step under duress or some other consideration, I cannot regard it as such.

The Commission was inaugurated by and took its organic life from the action of Congress in accordance with the wishes, expressed by direct petition and through the press, of a large portion of the citizens. The commissioners were under government authority, by virtue of congressional action, the acts executives of every State and Territory in the Union, and by the authority of the president of the United States. Thus, the centennial is to be held "under the auspices of the national Government." Its officers are to report regularly to the national Government, and finally, when "all is made ready" for the festival, the Executive of the nation is to proclaim the fact to the nations, and to communicate the regulations that may be adopted for its control to the representatives of such nations. The construction that to me seems the only proper one of all these doings and sayings is that in the ordinary significance of the words used they mean that the various nations of the earth are formally and officially informed of all these things. They were invited by our representatives to be present and participate in this national and international festival, and in an exhibition of natural resources, the products of the shop and the mine, and the evidences of the advancement made in social, educational, scientific, and mechanical progress within the Republic of the western continent. And finally, I am constrained to a hearty support of the centennial from a conviction that whether the effect of the exhibition be great or small, and whether it be entirely beneficial or not upon the northern and eastern states, its results upon the western, and particularly the southern states, will be prolific in great and unmingled good.

With a climate of unexampled mildness, and yet, with the exception of extreme cold, existing in its various sections almost every conceivable grade of temperature between the mild temperate and the tropical; with every known description of soil, the various kinds being intermingled in all desirable ways, and, in large proportion, of a character for fertility equaling the best; with a range of vegetable production, extending from the lime, the cocoa, and the coffee of the fervent climate of the tropic, to the green, the forage, and the fruit of the temperate zone, the South, as a distinct division of our common country, is worthy of vastly more attention relatively than she had yet received. For more than a half century the South as a whole has been given so exclusively to agricultural pursuits, and those of the ruder kinds alone, which were involved in the raising by unskilled labor of the usual crops of corn, cane, and cotton, as now in the time of an entire revolution of her whole system of labor to find herself utterly destitute of those higher agricultural and mechanical employment which have proved so lucrative in the North and West. Again, by the abolition of slavery, in which mainly by her own fault, but also partially through the consenting toleration of the North and West, the South was instantaneously deprived of an incalculable amount of capital actually invested, which has operated as a similar destruction of what stood for property and represented capital that would have operated elsewhere in the world, and had reduced the whole section to comparative, and it may be said actual, poverty.

With all her great variety of valuable productions and all her great wealth of mineral resources; with her abundance of cheap fuel for the operation of steam machinery and plenary water-power abundant through her whole extent, the South may be said to furnish a vast, rich field for profitable development of manufacturing industry, but as yet almost entirely unoccupied. These patent sources of untold wealth remain dormant, because first their existence is only known to a small proportion of the world, who never dream of the advantages there offered; and second, because of a widely prevalent notion that the introduction of capital would not be safe and immigration would not there be welcome. Knowing personally that in my own sunny state as fair and promising fields for agricultural labor, mechanical skill, and manufacturing capital are offered with as much of safety, as hearty a welcome, and as good a prospect of success as can be found anywhere in the North or West, or indeed in the world, and having reason to believe that in these respects, what is true of Florida is true of the South as a whole, I am anxious that she should be better known to our own people and to the nations of the world.

Seeing, then, in the proposed centennial exposition an opportunity, not likely soon to recur, to exhibit to the widest observation the manifold capacities and resources of the Southern States, and to make fully known to the sensible appreciation of the largest number of discriminating observers the thousand rare and valuable inducements to immigration, I have in addition to that general interest, so proper for all, an interest which is, as I trust, of a pardonably sectional character, that my own state and her sisters of the South may have a chance to be more fully and more particularly known for then I know they will be more highly considered.

And now, almost reluctantly, I leave the subject with a closing remark. I desire to say, as of my own personal knowledge, that in my own State very much of the not inexplicable bitterness and hostility of feeling between the different classes of citizens which followed after the war, and not, as it strikes me, unnaturally so, has now for several years been gradually and rapidly disappearing, until now it would not be easy for a northern or western man to discover the fact of his being in a former slave state from any peculiarity of the treatment that he, as a stranger, would there receive–as rapid an interest as could have possibly been anticipated by the most sanguine anti-slavery man of ten years ago.

The sanctity of the Union is tacitly conceded; the majesty of the inherent power of a free government is felt and known, so much so that if in the future any strong tendency to increasing the power of the government by concentration should ever be manifested at will, in my opinion, first develop itself in the southern states. While something of remaining bitterness still rankles in the breasts of a small portion of the "irreconcilable," it does not indicate the general feeling. With the majority, and the best among them, the old government and constitution of the fathers has received an increased sanction from its baptism of blood. The streaming folds of the "flay of the free" has received an increase of force and an added significance. Many, very many of those who once fought against that flay under the delusions of sectionalism are now more fully aware of the extent and folly of their wide political departure than any care in words to admit. But let once more the starry flag be unfurled in a national cause, whatever it be, to convince the world that the whole American continent is to be reserved for the gradual occupation of popular governments, attaining to the stature of strength and national manhood by steady and normal growth and development; or whether it be displayed above a national centennial exposition, as unfurled to celebrate a common and patriotic exultation at the triumphant demonstration by a hundred years of trial and practical use of the wisdom and forecast of our fathers as to the adequacy of popular government for the political necessities of the races, and the spontaneous joy of a free people at their unbroken Union and the restored unity of that nationality, and none will hail the glorious old banner with more joy than the men of the South.

Walls explained his support for the Cuban Revolution by referencing the American Revolution. He argued that the oppression of Americans before independence was pale to what Cubans experienced. Americans did not stand alone after they declared independence; they received aid from France. Walls also reviewed world history to argue that oppressed people had always thrown of the yoke off bondage. He condemned Spain as a colonizing and slaveholding nation.

CUBAN BELLIGERENCY
January 24, 1874

I feel moved to press the adoption of this joint resolution in obedience to what I understand as the prevailing sentiment of the American people–that sentiment which soars above the selfishness of traditional dynasties, or the soulless ordinances of international law. The progress of the human family is indicated all along the line of its march by bright epochs that embody the heroic endeavor of people in the effort of self-government, and in their opposition to the pernicious habit of government under the extinct prerogative of divine right.

Experiments in the establishment of governments of the people have net with almost uninterrupted failure in the past, down to the time when the continental patriots of our own land arose in their honesty, their might and majesty, and their devotion to truth and justice, to throw off the yoke of a tyranny less odious than that under which the Cuban patriots suffer at this moment, and pledged their lives, their fortunes, and their sacred honor to the maintenance of the principle that "all men were created equal," and entitled to life, liberty, and the pursuit of happiness; and that when governments are subversive of these ends, they ought to be altered or abolished. The grand emotion of liberty rekindled in the hearts of the brave men of America in the resolution which brought the nation to life touched a responsive chord in the hearts of patriots the world over; and following in our exemplary path, under the lead of the fearless General Lafayette and other bright spirits of France, came that memorable revolution of the people of that country, which planted the germ of republicanism, the growth of which had made the tenure of kingcraft and imperialism of doubtful duration. And it must not be forgotten that in the dark hours of our struggle for independence such men as Lafayette and Kosciusko, willing to lay down their lives for the principle of liberty, as were the brave Crittenden, Ryan, Fry, and their compatriots, who, educated in the school of the Republic, and appreciating the immeasurable advantages of a government of the people, by the people, and for the people–inspired with nerve, valor, and devotion to humanity–went to the rescue of the intrepid patriots of the Cuban republic.

It is a fact beyond controversy, that the erection of a republic on this continent placed the possessions of European powers on our soil beyond the possibility of rehabilitation, and created the desire for liberty in the hearts of all peoples to whom the glad tidings went, that in this endless waste of the western world, whither the star of empire takes its way, the full fruition of the hopes of mankind was fully realized. Even in the breasts of chattel slaves of Haiti, supposed to be brutalized by the oppression of centuries, the divine inspiration sprouted into patriotism, and out of the revolt there came a brain-power and a capacity which successfully secured emancipation, enfranchisement, the defeat of the great Napoleon, and the final establishment of the Haitian Republic. Then the struggle of the peoples of the Spanish possessions in South and Central America came to throw off the yoke of the tyranny under which the Cuban republic now suffers without encouragement or assistance. These republics, under the genial influences of the sympathies of this and other great governments, came to the front in the struggle for national existence; and by the proffer of belligerent rights, which came to them as the spontaneous offering of the great nations which are the guardians of human rights, achieved their independence and were bidden God-speed in the march upward to the glory and grandeur of equal liberty.

The Greek rebellion is another instance of the revolt of the people against oppression–in which a people struggled heroically for seven years, under untold suffering and privation–for the boon of liberty. The tyranny of the Turkish government toward the Greeks bears a strong resemblance to that of Spain toward the Cubans. The Greeks, like the Cubans, exhibited the noblest qualities of character–bravery, patience under suffering and unconquerable resolution. The bloodshed at Constantinople, the execution of the patriarch, and the massacres of Scio, find their adequate parallels in the repeated and cold-blooded murders of non-combatants, foreigners, women and children, by the Spanish authorities in Cuba. But here the comparison ceases. These acts of the Turkish government toward the Greeks created a profound sympathy for them throughout the world, and summoned to the cause of Greek independence brave spirits and lovers of liberty from every land. Contributions of money, the necessaries of life, and the munitions of war went out to them from all parts of civilization; and our own land was not lacking in this grand benevolence. Under the magnetic influence of the eloquence of Henry Clay, Daniel Webster, Edward Everett, and other statesmen of that time, the nation was equal to the occasion, and the moral effect of her sympathy and recognition contributed greatly toward the final result, decisively accomplished at the battle of Navarino by the destruction of the Turco-Egyptian fleet by the combined fleets of England, France, and Russia.

Thus was the independence of an oppressed people–greatly tyrannized over by a so-called paternal government, but less brutally governed than are the Cubans by Spain–achieved mainly through the aid, comfort, and tangible assistance rendered by governments which created the precedents and conditions of international law, but upon whom its requirements are powerless when in conflict with the God-given privilege of self-government. In these later times, when the space of a century stands between us and the struggle of the fathers for liberty, and the heroism and sacrifices of our own patriots are falling unto forgetfulness, and conditions of neutrality still the best impulses of the heart and paralyze the strong arm that was ever ready to protect the weak and assist the oppressed to a higher plane of manhood, it seems that history has ceased to repeat itself; and we have forgotten the grand principle which underlies our institutions; ceased to have a "manifest destiny"; have given the "Monroe Doctrine" to the winds of heaven; while upon our own soil continued atrocities are committed to violation of every principle we have enunciated in the past. While we honor the fearless commander of the British gunboat, the *Niobe*, and are grateful for his timely and noble defense of our flag, and his protection of the lives of our citizens at Santiago de Cuba, we can but feel the humiliation, and earnestly pray for the time to come when this great Government will return to the duty of protecting its own flay and citizens.

For every effort to achieve independence throughout the world, in the century of the existence of this Republic, the nation is measurably responsible by the proud example of July 4, 1776. And the sympathies of this great people have not been lacking, neither has the government of the country been tardy in recognizing the efforts of peoples striving to attain the form of government proved by trial in the crucible of adversity to be the best instituted among men. That this Congress will immortalize itself by following the traditions of the past, and obey the behest of civilization and humanity, by conceding belligerent rights to the republic of Cuba, there is little doubt; and the friends of Cuban liberty and emancipation are willing to rest their case and trust to the magnanimity and love of equity, individually and collectively characteristic of the war-making power of the land.

Aside from the claims of the brave patriots of Cuba, battling for national existence, there are half a million of people whose race this American nation had started on the high road to equality, and whom they are teaching the world to respect as citizens of the best government on earth, suffering under the galling chains of an abject serfdom, upon which we have placed the stamp of our condemnation in our land, and which continues in all its horrors under Spanish rule in Cuba, in spite of the kindly offices of Christian nations and in flagrant violation of the most sacred treaty obligations. The course of Spain in the matter of emancipation had been one of continued duplicity and fraud, and the institution of slavery is as flourishing today in the Spanish possessions in America as before the time when God, in His mercy, waked this nation to light and life. Existing as a foul blot at our doors and a disgrace and a reproach to the institutions of which we are representative, and a foul stigma upon the civilization of the time, Spain had reveled in the blood-bought wealth of this heinous traffic for more than three centuries; and even now, when Russia and even Brazil have followed in our footsteps in the noble work of emancipation, the Spanish government insults the Christian world by perpetuating human slavery.

The Cuban patriots first incurred the hatred of Spanish officials, and incited their persecution, by their outspoken hostility to the African slave trade, which Spain had solemnly agreed with Great Britain to prohibit, and their advocacy of emancipation in some shape. As early as 1848 an assemblage of Cuban planters, all slave-owners themselves, declared the time had come for the illicit traffic in African slaves to cease, and characterized it as "the scorn of the civilized world, a hideous abyss in which was buried all hope of security and future welfare"; and requested the inflexible prosecution of those engaged in the traffic. "Finally the commissioners from Cuba and Puerto Rico, elected by the city councils of those islands, and sent to Madrid to report upon the reforms which their constituents claimed, demanded, on January 29, 1869, that the African slave trade be declared piracy." In 1865 a private association of Cubans was formed in Havana to suppress the traffic; and the members pledged themselves on their honor not to acquire property, from the date of joining the association, in any African slave landed on the island subsequent to January 29, 1869. And in a constitutional convention assembled at Guaimaro, the provisional capital of the republic of Cuba, in the first year of the declared independence of that republic, a constitution was unanimously adopted, the twenty-fourth article of which provides that "all inhabitants of the republic of Cuba are absolutely free!"

The contest in Cuba is waged on the part of Spain for continued supremacy in her possessions on this continent; pride in the perpetuation of African slavery in the western world is a continued menace to our institutions. The existence of the so-called republic of Spain, professing to be inspired by the *Magna Carta* of American liberty, which pronounced "all men are created equal," is a travesty upon humanity and a libel upon civilization while it extends the protection of the Spanish government to the most pronounced slave oligarchy that has ever existed among men. If, for this reason alone, this Government were to forcibly remonstrate with the Spanish mal-administration in Cuba, and as an act of humanity in consonance with the common law of nations, grant belligerent rights to the young republic of Cuba, Christianity would condone and civilization justify the act. We have reached the proud position occupied by the Republic today by a course which some construe as above the law, yet none will regret that the foul blot of slavery had been removed from our bright escutcheon, and the nation placed in the foremost rank of the nations of the civilized world above the law, according to the technical construction of these who tolerate the violation of all law, human and divine, if a captious selfishness furnishes a pretense. International law is a compact of precedents, the majority of the parties to which are opposed to human progress, and the construction upon its requirements are construed to serve the ends of governments constructed upon the violated rights of the people. The comparatively new idea of republicanism necessitates a new construction of the ordinances and the indefinite provisions of international law, and a republic in its intercourse with the nations of the earth should, while observing equity, pursue a policy which would comport with the dignity of a great nation to conserve and propagate the principles upon which it is founded.

The farce of emancipation had been indulged in by Spain through a series of years, to satisfy the remonstrance of civilization and quiet the conscience of the Christian world. The so-called emancipation act of the Spanish Cortes in 1870 insults peoples of all countries who have striven to have their institutions conform with the requirements of the age by elevating their peasant classes to the plane of manhood equality. This act provides that all those shall be free—

First. Who are born after the publication of the act. (Article 1)

From what we know of Spanish honesty and fair dealing, it is just to presume that either the law was not promulgated in the Spanish sense of publication, or there have been no African children born in Cuba since the publication of the act.

Second. Those who have served in the Spanish army, or have assisted the troops during the present insurrection. (Article 3)

Of course the Spanish officers in power in Cuba will decide in the fullness of their benevolence who have served in the Spanish army or assisted the troops in the present insurrection, and how far this act will relieve them from the chains of slavery, and general emancipation will ensure.

Third. Those who at the date of the publication of the act, may have attained the age of sixty years, and others when they attain that age. (Article 4)

In plain terms, as long as the slave retains capacity to be useful, he or she is under sixty years of age, and cannot be emancipated under the act. When so old as to be unable to earn bread for subsistence, then he or she is considered over sixty, and is emancipated under the act.

Fourth. The slaves of the government and those known as emancipates. (Article 5)

It is rather a reflection upon Spanish officers who have no regard for the lives and property of American citizens, with the protection of this Government shadowing them continually, to give them credit for entertaining consideration for the liberty of the chattel slaves in whom very Spanish official considers he has common property. Neither it is probable that *emancipates*, declared free by treaty with Great Britain, but who have been held in slavery in defiance of treaty obligations, will be benefited more than others supposed to be emancipated by this fraud called a law.

Fifth. Those who have been cruelly punished, and their owners are punished by law for the offense. (Article 17)

This is cool, in view of the fact that slaveholders in Cuba are not held accountable for the most hideous barbarities practiced upon their slaves, or punished for their murder.

Sixth. Those who are not registered as slaves in the census to be taken December 31, 1870. (Article 19)

If a grain of comfort be extracted from the preceding provisions, this clause would invalidate all that goes before. The census, as a matter of course, was in the hands of the Spanish officials, whose sympathies and inclinations are all on the side of the slaveholders, and whose interests required, in their narrow view, the continuance of the institution of slavery in Cuba.

If any one was emancipated by the act promulgated June 23, 1870, we would do gross injustice to these officials if we did not concede their willingness to register every man, woman, and child of the African race within Spanish jurisdiction as slaves, in the register of the census taken December 31, 1870, without the slightest uneasiness of conscience, and by that act invalidate the provisions of the so-called emancipation act, which was prepared and passed for foreign consumption, and not for home use. This legislation of the Spanish Cortes is an excellent example of the buncombe and subterfuge that attempt to foist upon the world a bastard republic, which, under the plea of Spanish pride, tolerates the most horrible crimes against humanity, and protects with all the power of the government an institution repugnant to every sense of decency and right. In addition to this, we have on record, to be placed to the account of Spain, the heinous crimes running through a series of years, committed by the accredited agents of Spain in the suppression of a rebellion which the Spanish government persists in declaring does not exist—the violation of the laws of war and the laws of God and man. These atrocities even antedate the Cuban rebellion. The dance of death opened more than twenty years ago with the assassination of the gallant Lopez and the cold-blooded murder of the brave Crittenden and his followers, and is appropriately supplemented by the thousands of brutal outrages and murders committed in recent years, and is a fitting preparation for the massacre of the school-children two years ago at Havana, the crowning horror committed upon the Virginian prisoners at Santiago de Cuba, and the gross insult to the flag, the honor of which every American ought to defend with his life if need be.

Spain insists that there is no war in Cuba, and proceeds to place her construction upon international law as applied to neutrals in a state of war, and gracefully permits us to rehabilitate her navy, furnish arms and ammunition, and offer legal opinions if you will, to enable her to prosecute a war which is no war, and suppress a rebellion which is no rebellion. The tide of events so well developed by the gallant Cubans persuade us there is a war of some dimensions in Cuba, to suppress which Spain had repeatedly violated the rules of civilized warfare, and to exterminate the men who dare to die rather than accept a questionable liberty under Spanish tyranny, and strengthen the chains of slavery on the limbs of half a million human beings who will never bask in the sunlight of freedom till this Government asserts in its power that no slave shall exist upon this continent. While the republic of Cuba is struggling against the fearful odds of the wealth and munitions of war freely furnished Spain by the peoples of the world without hindrance, with no sympathy but that cheap and safe kind which emanates from mass-meetings and is couched in resolutions; shut out from the light of the world, as it were; fighting like Spartans in the fastness of Cuba; decimated and dying, but never surrendering; the footsteps of her sympathizers are dogged by Spanish spies—even followed within the jurisdiction of neutral powers, and on the high seas captured and murdered in cold blood for the crime of sympathizing with the heroic struggle of a brave people who demand liberty or death.

The Spanish government has continued to suppress the Cuban rebellion, which they persist in claiming is not a rebellion, every year since its inception, at the cost of twenty thousand lives and hundreds of thousands in treasure; and if no argument and no plea will reach this Congress from the voice of the struggling patriots or of the oppressed slaves of Cuba, in God's name let us interpose to save Spain and the so-called Spanish republic. If the continued violation of all law, the confiscation of the property, and the imprisonment of American citizens, and their indiscriminate murder; the unblushing protection of the institution of slavery in its most repulsive form, repugnant to every instinct of free government; the insult to our flay, and the brutal murders of women and children without the forms of law, do not arouse this nation to duty and to action, then, in the name of the Spanish republic, if such an anomaly can exist in the present state of affairs in that unhappy country, I appeal to this Congress to relieve her of one of the insurrections on her hands so that she can have a fair trial in her new-found republican experiment.

Grant belligerent rights to the republic of Cuba, and aside from the inestimable boon of liberty conferred upon a million of people who are with us and of us, we relieve a European republic of entangling alliances, and give their scheme a fairer chance among the crumbling dynasties of the Old World. As a representative in part of the people of the State of Florida, I join my feeble effort with the earnest appeal of the present governor of that State.

With the submission of these earnest declarations, and the facts presented, I commend the question of Cuban recognition; the emancipation of the slaves in the Spanish possessions in America; the guardianship of the free institutions of an advanced civilization; the protection of our citizens, and the vindication of our flag, to the favorable consideration of the Forty-third Congress.

Walls urged whites to accept that federal law had granted black male suffrage. He argued that white southerners who lost the vote had taken up arms against the Union. He also accused southern leaders of attempting to develop a new form of slavery immediately following the war. He disputed the notion that African Americans were now taught to hate whites. Instead he pointed out that the only hatemonger in the South were members of the Democratic party.

CONDITION OF AFFAIRS IN THE SOUTH
March 2, 1875

In attempting to address myself to the condition of affairs in Arkansas and in the South generally, I do so with no intention to misrepresent any class of our people. It would seem to an interested observer of the political affairs of this great nation, one who desires to see her people once more united in one hand of brotherhood, one who desires to see this whole land peopled with none but free men and free women, that the time had come when there should be peace assured to all, irrespective of race, color, or the section in which they live; that property is protected everywhere in this broad land; that complete safety is granted to all in expressing their religious and political sentiments; that life and liberty are as safe in one state as in another, and that all classes shall be free.

But I reluctantly confess, after so many long years of concessions, that unless partisan and sectional feeling shall lose more of its rancor in the future than has been experienced in the past, that unless we shall ere long reach that point in our history when a full comprehension of the true mission of the result of the war will be plain to all public men regardless of party affiliation, Arkansas, Louisiana, Alabama, and Mississippi will not be the only States in this Union in which fundamental law will be disregarded, overthrown, and trampled under foot, and in which a complete reign of terror and anarchy will rule supreme as it does today in Arkansas. But every southern State will follow their example. It was sincerely and earnestly desired I believe by every person who remained loyal to the flag of our country that when the States lately in rebellion had accepted the condition by which they were readmitted into the Union, peace, prosperity, and good feeling had been secured and the results of the war accomplished. For one I desired and still desire better feeling among our people in the South, and here in my place, I appeal to those who claim to be the intelligent and property-holders of that section of our common country to stay their acts of oppression, and in the language of the concluding remarks of the Senator from Georgia, [John Brown Gordon], "As ye would that men should do to you, do ye also to them." But if our experience in the future is to be that of the past, appeals are all in vain; but we shall not cease to appeal until we shall have reached the true sentiment of the American people all over this land.

I am aware that emancipation and enfranchisement of the Negro and his devotion to the Union as well as to those whom he believed to be his friends, are made the pretext for dissatisfaction, and with which gentlemen like the Senator from Georgia [Mr. Gordon], unreconstructed as he is, expects to reach from the bar of the Senate of the United States, or somewhere else, the great public opinion in these United States. But it will be remembered that this all-powerful public opinion is the jury in the pending case; and I am of the opinion that when the American people are honestly made acquainted with the true condition of affairs in the South, that when their attention is called to them, they will clearly understand the different reports which contain the true condition of the southern states, and which present clearly the intention of those who complain loudly about the distraction of the colored laborer of the South by those who may choose to go there for the purpose of "gaining," as they say, "by the ballot that which we lost by the bayonet." This cannot successfully be denied, as it is well known that the democratic newspapers in the South teem daily with such sentiments.

But the grave question that presents itself to the American people, especially those who remained loyal to the Union, is, what was it that this class of people lost by the bayonet that they now expect to gain by what they call the ballot? I hear the answer echoed, by the bayonet we lost our power and our human property, and by the ballot we shall regain what we lost by the bayonet. It will be remembered that they failed to extend slavery, as they desired to do, and finally lost them in the States where they were allowed to hold them under some shadow of law. It will also be remembered that they appealed to arms for the open and avowed purpose of overthrowing or dissolving the Union. Failing in this, is it their intention and purpose to obtain control of the General Government, reinstate and extend slavery in some shape, or overthrow or dissolve the Federal Union? These are two of the things that were lost by their bayonets. Do they intend after their accession into power to vote themselves pay for the slaves emancipated by the proclamation of President Abraham Lincoln, to fix upon the national government of the Confederate States, pay its debt, repeal the Thirteenth, Fourteenth, and Fifteenth Amendments to the federal Constitution? These are questions of great moment to the loyal people of these United States and should command their immediate attention.

I wish to state to the House and the country that I have been connected with every political canvass made in the South since reconstruction, and all the appeals to race, color, and the daily teachings on one class of people to hate the other have invariably come from Democratic orators and their friends. Here in my place I ask is there any place in the history of our country where it can be found that the colored people in any state or county of this land have banded themselves together by such pledges into black leagues to overthrow legislative, judicial, and ministerial offices? The answer is emphatically No! And the argument of the Senator falls to the ground for naught. But in the face of these and other glaring facts let the people, the loyal people of the United States, hear the Senator's defense of and excuse for murder, assassination and outrage.

There is no better evidence of the hatred engendered by those who claim to be the virtuous and intelligent of the South than is shown in this labored effort of the Senator from Georgia [Mr. Gordon] to array the white people of this whole American Union against four millions of lately emancipated colored people. Is it just, I ask, nay is it honorable or brave or logical in an American Senator who boasts so loudly of being the representative of a virtuous, cultured, and great people, to seek to fire the hearts of a powerful nation by gross misrepresentation against a class of people once their slaves? Is it plausible to suppose that the colored people are guilty of one-tenth of the imaginary crimes with which they are charged after one had sought to acquaint himself with the facts in connection with the true condition of affairs in the South? In the face of the living truth, in not one page of the history of our country, indicted as it may be by partial historians, can it be found in fact that the colored people at any time banded themselves together for the purpose of arraying themselves against the white people of the South.

When I say that we cherish no animosity toward those who were once our masters, I speak for all the colored people of this broad land. Yet we demand that our lives, our liberties, and our property shall be protected by the strong arm of the government that it gives us the same citizenship that it gives to those who it seems would, if it were possible, sink our every hope for peace, prosperity, and happiness into the great sea of oblivion. There is yet living, conclusive testimony, which forms the most conspicuous pages of the history of the late war, to show that the colored people did not and do not entertain or cherish any ill-feeling or bitterness against those who one held them as their property. It will be admitted by every fair-minded man, North or South, that there was not a time during that long and bloody war that the colored people could not have swept as it were from existence the women, children, the aged and the infirm, who were entrusted to their care while all of the able bodied of the slave oligarchy were arrayed in arms for the open and avowed purpose of destroying the Union or perpetuating the power of slavery.

It is with pride and the most profound pleasure that I can refer this self-styled virtue and intelligence of the South to these humane acts of a Christian people, and which stands today, and will stand as long as there is a vestige of the archives of this nation, and as a living refutation of the baseless charges and slanders that are sent out from these Halls for no other purpose than to fire the hearts and to embitter the prejudice of the northern people against four million of comparatively helpless people. Is it bravery, I ask of one who prides himself as being an American senator and a Christian gentleman, to so grossly misrepresent the growing good feeling between both classes in the South, the result of which he knows will have the inevitable tendency of perpetuating the oppression of the weaker class and the continuance of an unsettled condition of society generally? Why not let the issues and the result of the war be remembered among the things of the past?

I appeal again to history for argument to show that the unsettled condition of affairs in the Southern States is not caused by the black people arraying themselves against the white people of that section of the country, but that is the same old spirit that inspired the late war, and that the seeming hatred and fear of the ignorance of the colored people is only used in the Halls of Congress for political purposes, by which certain elements that failed to obtain success in the late conflict between the states, may yet succeed. In face of these facts what becomes of the arguments of the opposition, with their terrible tales of falsehood, their reports of Negroes arraying themselves against the whites, influenced and urged to do so, as is falsely charged, by the carpetbagger? I do not wish to be misunderstood. I am not here to apologize for the wrongs that one or two white Republicans may have committed in the South; but, I do affirm that the carpetbaggers, assisted by the loyal white and black men of the South, have done more to enact laws and to erect public institutions that conform more closely to the genius of our American ideas of civilization, in the short period of six or eight years under republican administration, than was done by the democratic slave oligarchy in the South prior to the rebellion.

I present in support of my position, in defense of the outraged and slandered loyal people of the South, an article taken from the *Daily Inter-Ocean*, a highly respectable and widely circulated newspaper published at Chicago, Illinois, which contains some indisputable truths, and which will go far, in my opinion, to relieve the minds of the loyal people of the North of the impression that the so-called carpetbaggers, Unionists, and Negroes have destroyed to utter ruin eleven States in this Union, as would seem to be the case after one had read the apologies for and endorsements of murder, assassination, and outrages contained in the speeches of the opposition on this all important question. A more clear and correct statement of the disposition exercised by the southern democrats, who might have controlled the political affairs of the South from the beginning of reconstruction up to the present hour, could not have been presented to the public. They had the opportunity to make the colored people their political friends by assuring them by constitutional and legislative enactments that they would be protected in their freedom and that the right of suffrage and the right to participate in governmental affairs were as secure to them as they were to the whites. There would have been no real cause to suspect them, if they would have only abstained from enacting under their policy of reconstruction in 1865 such oppressive laws, laws that will ever stand as an index as to what they will do if they should again obtain control of this Government, laws that would virtually reinstate slavery in a different form, that continued in force the whipping-post and the pillory. It is eminently proper, in my opinion, to submit here some of the enactments made by the Legislature of Florida in 1865.

I do not submit these terrible facts for the purpose of embittering or impeding the progress of the growing good feeling that is fast making its appearance among both classes in many sections in the South, but to show beyond successful contradiction the reason why the colored people did and do honor and support those of the white race who respect them as being human and capable of being as cultivated, virtuous, and intelligent a people as they are themselves when endowed with the same rights and advantages. These are but few of the many oppressive and inhumane legislative enactments passed by the Legislature referred to; and as I have said before, attention is not called to them at this time for the purpose of awakening the old animosities, but to prove conclusively to an intelligent people that it is not because the colored people hate or dislike the people who make up the Democratic party of the South that they are opposing their accession to power again, but it is because, with the undisputed history of that party before them, we have no guarantee that that party will not enact laws again equally oppressive, inhumane, and tyrannical.

This kind of legislation by the Democratic party in the South was not confined alone to Florida; it extended all over the South. Now I ask is it reasonable to suppose that a people having been held as goods and chattels for two hundred and forty-seven years would rush headlong into the beautiful glittering generalities of the Democratic platforms and elevate them to power, when a moment's research into the history of that party would reveal the fact that it was and is the avowed purpose of that party to ignore reconstruction and cling to their old States' rights ideas? Daily, you hear it loudly proclaimed upon this floor by the enemies of this Government that "reconstruction" in the South, caused by the enfranchisement of the Negro "is a failure." They go further, and attempt to show that reconstruction is a failure in the South by calling our attention to the unsettled condition of affairs in that unhappy section of our country. But they suggest no remedy for evils that are said to exist, nor do they deny the fact that it is the white-leaguers banded together for the very purpose of overthrowing regularly established State governments by force and fraud.

Ah! Look at poor, suffering Arkansas. Read the reports of the majority and minority of the committee that was appointed and sent to that State by an order of this House, and you will see that her rightfully elected officers have been forced from the positions to which they were legally elected, none will deny, by force and fraud; her fundamental law disregarded, overthrown, and trampled under foot; murderers, assassins, and white-leaguers (not black-leaguers) rule supreme; her rightful governor compelled, with his cabinet, to leave the State; her chief judicial officer outraged and menaced with assassination and ousted from office without cause. And yet it is claimed that Congress should not take any action in restoring the legally elected authorities of that State and enforcing the only fundamental law that the State of Arkansas can have a legal claim to, the constitution of 1868. I am not one of those that believe that Congress should allow the so-called Garland government to remain in power in Arkansas. To do so in my opinion is a complete recognition of the fact that any one of the reconstructed States can with safety disregard the fundamental provision under which they were admitted into the Union, and render inoperative every provision of their constitutions adopted in accordance therewith. These are important features for the loyal people of this country to look at with fear as to the future stability of this Union.

But let us go a little further, and I have done so. Take the evidence of bad faith made in changing the oath of office; the striking out of all provisions asserting that the paramount allegiance of the citizens is due to the Federal Government; the striking out all provisions that assert that no power exists in the people to dissolve their compact with the Federal Government; the striking out of a provision denying the right of secession; the striking out of all provisions asserting that the Federal Government is clothed with power to maintain its existence by force of arms; the striking out of a provision prohibiting the Legislature from compensating for emancipated slaves; the striking out of a provision prohibiting the Legislature from paying any debt or liabilities incurred in support of the rebellion, and let an enlightened, loyal public opinion decide what these things prove.

As I have said, I am not one of those who believe that the people of Arkansas have acquiesced in the adoption of the Garland constitution, or do I believe that they ever will acquiesce in his usurpation, corruption, outrages, and unparalleled rascality. I do not believe that to put an end to the revolutionary and unconstitutional action that has been carried on in Arkansas a general uprising will ensue. Pass the resolution presented by Mr. Elijah Ward from the Committee on the Condition of Affairs in the State of Arkansas; put into operation the common schools; again restore peace to all the people of Arkansas; assure the business men of every kind that there is stability in the State government of Arkansas, and give Garland ten days to retire peacefully to his home, and you will have no further trouble in the South.

All that is required is dare to do right and every true American citizen, from the pine forests of Maine to the golden shores of California, from the ice-bound steppes of Alaska to the sunny coast of the Gulf of Mexico, will hail with joy the news that a new rebellion has been nipped in the bud and the country saved.

22

George Henry White
(1852–1918)
House of Representatives, North Carolina

Republican

Fifty-fifth and Fifty-sixth Congresses
March 4, 1897, to March 3, 1901

George Henry White was born in Rosindale (Bladen County), North Carolina, on December 18, 1852. While historians earlier believed that he was born into slavery, Benjamin R. Justesen, his biographer, argues that White was most probably never a slave. George H. White grew up on a farm in a free working class family. Apparently, by selling produce his family managed to secure a lifestyle that enabled them to enroll George in private subscription schools in Columbus County after the Civil War. While George was precocious and hardworking, he did not hold a high school diploma or earn a college degree. He did not attend law school, even though some early works infer that he did. White was enormously talented and well read; his interest in his personal and professional development remained strong throughout his life. His ambition ultimately led him into national politics, and he was the last African American from the Reconstruction era to hold a seat in the United States House of Representatives.

The road George White took to national prominence ran through schools of varying quality. A public school education was rare for white children before 1870, and an African American stood little chance of gaining such schooling. White claimed that he attended school only about two or three months a year. From 1869 to 1872, he obtained the equivalent of a middle school education. He matriculated at Howard University in 1874, entering the two-year teacher preparation program and the four-year liberal arts program. He contemplated studying medicine, then law, but before he could enroll the law school changed its requirements for admission and made it less likely that they would accept him. He received a Normal Certificate from Howard in 1877, the highest diploma he ever earned, and returned to North Carolina to become principal of the State Normal School for Negroes in New Bern.

Working at a high school was not a full-time job, not even for a principal. White soon applied his talents to law, a profession he hoped would offer greater rewards than public education. He began an apprenticeship in law in the office of William John Clarke, a former officer in the Confederacy, as well as an active Republican and retired judge. Upon passing the bar examination in 1879, George White opened a law practice in New Bern, North Carolina. He would also stay on as principal of the State Normal School. He continued his teaching and administrative duties, such as working on curriculum development, and handling personnel matters. By the time White left the school in 1883, its courses included hygiene, reading, and physics. As a result of his law practice and business ventures, he had become one of the wealthiest black men in New Bern.

When the state Republican party held its convention in 1880, White attended as a delegate. He won the party nomination for the General Assembly. Once he entered the legislature, White quickly wrote five bills, calling for paying jurors, making seduction a crime, amending the charter of New Bern, establishing the Order of the Good Samaritans, and making public education compulsory. He also submitted a series of petitions on prohibition. These early measures died in the committees.

George White considered himself a civil rights leader, and he pursued legislation that would put African Americans in the mainstream. Since "Jim Crow" laws had barred blacks from universities, White proposed legislation to establish segregated colleges in North Carolina that would offer a general education program as well as teacher training. When elected to the state senate in 1884, White remained committed to improving black education. From 1886 to 1894 he also held various offices in North Carolina, ranging from solicitor to prosecutor in the Second Judicial District of North Carolina. He was also the president of the Negroes State Council, the largest black organization in the state.

Active in party politics, White served as a delegate to the Republican National Convention in 1896. He began to set his sights on Congress, and in 1894 launched a campaign for the House of Representatives—which he lost to his brother-in-law and fellow Republican, Henry P. Cheatham. Undaunted, White ran again in 1896, this time winning the nomination and defeating Democrat Frederick A. Woodard and D. Schuyler Moss, the Populist nominee. As the only African American serving in Congress at this time, White assumed the role of spokesman for the black race. From the day he was sworn in on March 15, 1897, until his second term ended in 1901, he reminded his colleagues in the House that he represented the millions of African Americans in the country.

White supported measures that would help African Americans as well as the country at large. On March 31, 1897, he defended passage of a high tariff bill for he believed it would not only protect the nation's industry but also preserve jobs for black workers. "There is a growing sentiment that the industries and the labor of America shall be protected against the cheap labor of foreign countries." He recommended several individuals, white and black, for appointments as postmasters. He proposed measures to protect blacks from racial violence. He condemned lynching and proposed making it a federal crime that carried the death penalty upon conviction. When a white mob in Lake City, South Carolina, lynched a black postmaster, White proposed a bill to aid the family. The House referred these measures to committee, but took no action on them. White also proposed legislation to provide relief for Robert Smalls, who had commandeered the *Planter* during the Civil War and sailed it to a Union port. And he called upon the U.S. Army to establish a black artillery regiment.

Representative White, along with other black leaders, believed that it would help their cause by showcasing the achievements made by African Americans since their emancipation from slavery. They favored an exhibition on black culture and its contribution to American life. White proposed a bill asking Congress to appropriate $15,000, which Congress declined.

Though White ended his political career in 1901, he remained an ardent leader until his death. He opened a law practice in Washington, and then used his money to buy land in New Jersey to establish a town, chartering it as Whitesboro in 1905. Three years later White established the People's Savings Bank of Philadelphia, hoping to provide loans to blacks seeking to buy homes or start businesses. Located on Lombard Street, he converted the third floor of the building into his private residence as well as his law office.

George White delivered many speeches during his career as teacher, politician, and business leader. His farewell address to the House of Representatives was easily one of the most memorable. Speaking on January 29, 1901, he observed that no other member of his race would be left to serve in Congress. Considering his departure a "temporary farewell," he predicted that a day would come when the African Americans would rise up Phoenix-like to become leaders in Congress. Illinois businessman Oscar S. De Priest fulfilled the vision when in 1929 he broke the color barrier in Congress, becoming the first African American elected to the national legislature in the twentieth century. After pleading with national leaders for "an even chance in the race of life" for African Americans, George Henry White succumbed to illness and died at home in Philadelphia on December 28, 1918.

White supported a bill that presumably would protect the southern economy from foreign competition. He believed that it would also provide employment for working-class people. White believed himself the sole representative of African Americans and considered it his obligation to vote favorably on any measure that would protect their jobs.

THE WILSON BILL
March 31, 1897

    I rise to supplement what my colleague [Romulus Zachariah Linney] said during the five minutes I have. I desire not only to add a word in behalf of the articles mentioned by him–coal, iron, mica, cotton, wool, cattle, hogs, and so forth–but wish especially to emphasize a word in behalf of the people of eastern North Carolina on that part of this bill which includes lumber. Under the Wilson bill the contracts which had been entered into by the mill men had in many instances to be forfeited; the mills that had been running day and night, giving employment to thousands and thousands of operatives, were shut down, and those operatives were thus shut out. These men, the heads of families, were forced to see their loved ones pinched with want, with no way for them to earn a dollar. This bill, because of this lumber schedule, as well as others, commends itself especially to the southern people who have to labor to get bread and meat for their families.

    My Democratic friends have amused me in their advocacy of "free trade." Why, they have from time to time advocated "free whiskey" also; and in the last campaign their shibboleth was "free silver." In fact, the Southern element of the Democratic party had advocated "free" everything except free ballots and free Negroes. It is wonderful how solicitous those gentlemen are about the future welfare of the Republican party. The bone and sinew of their arguments are their fears that the place that now knows us will, if we pass this bill, would soon know us no more forever. Well, gentlemen, we will take care of this side of the House. We have heard of the devil teaching scriptures, but never to save a soul. If we are contented, you ought not to be troubled. Gentlemen on the other side of this Chamber have felt themselves called upon to resent some imputations of incompetence that went from this side of the House. Well, I am a Southerner to the manner born and reared, and am usually in sympathy with the South, but when Democratic members on the other side of this House drag into this great Congress of the United States the expressions of the southern plantations in regard to "the darky and heels of a mule," then I think the imputation is a correct one.

I am here to speak, and I do speak, as the sole representative on this floor of 9,000,000 of the population of these United States, 90 percent of whom are laborers. Under this bill they are protected; they are given an opportunity to earn their living. Bread and butter are what we want, not fine-spun Democratic campaign theory. We have had enough of that. We want something now upon which soul and body can be kept together. We want an honest dollar. We want pay for an honest day's work. We believe that this bill may bring about these things or that such may largely be the effect. We are therefore willing to rest our case here. We are willing to go before the American people with this bill even as it is now. When, as the gentleman from Indiana [Henry Underwood Johnson] suggests, it shall have passed under the scrutinizing eye of the United States Senate, we shall have, as I believe, a measure of which every American citizen ought to be proud. My friend from South Carolina said that my colleague [Mr. Linney] did not represent the popular sentiment of the South when he advocated the protective tariff features enunciated in this bill. I think that it comes with bad grace from the gentleman to talk of misrepresentation of the Southern people when he considers the fact that 130,000 people in his State are not allowed to vote at all.

I want to say to him that while I know but little of South Carolina as it now is–I used to know something of it when it was a State in the Union, with the privileges of sister States of the Union–yet I do know something of the sentiment in my own State of North Carolina, and many other States, and I can tell the gentleman from my own knowledge that there is a growing sentiment prevailing with the development of that country that the industries and the labor of America shall be protected against the pauperism and the cheap labor of foreign counties, Democratic campaign thunder to the contrary notwithstanding.

White argued that the pending bill was deficient because it made no provisions for enrolling black soldiers in artillery regiments. He pointed out that federal law had provided for the appointment of black soldiers to the cavalry and infantry. Without federal law requiring it, White argued that the Army would continue to discriminate against blacks. He repeated the mantra of black representatives, affirming that African Americans– his people–deserved "an even chance in the race of life."

THE ARMY BILL
March 7, 1898

I regret exceedingly that under the rules, as I am informed, I have not the privilege of offering an amendment to this bill. There is now in the United States Army no artillerymen whatever enlisted from my race. The troops of the line of the Army as at present constituted consist of 10 regiments of cavalry, 25 regiments of infantry, and 5 regiments of artillery. Section 1104, Revised Statutes, provides that "the enlisted men of two regiments of cavalry shall be colored men," and section 1108, Revised Statutes, provides that "the enlisted men of two regiments of infantry shall be colored men." But there is no corresponding provision regarding any regiment or battery of artillery. In the absence of any specific provision of statute, the uniform custom of the Army has been to bar colored men from enlisting in the artillery.

It is a sad commentary that an amendment such as the one I propose is necessary to enforce justice to be done to my people in one of the departments of out great Government. The last amendments to the Constitution guarantee to us all the rights of American citizenship, and it is reasonable to suppose that those rights would be accorded to us without any specific designating that such should be the case. That we are capable and worthy of any place in our Army was evidenced in the recent rebellion by the enlistment and patriotic action of thousands of Negroes in the infantry, cavalry, and artillery service of the United States Army. No one familiar with the facts will dare say that the Negro did not do his whole duty to perpetuate the nation and maintain the honor of our flag in our late war. Is it not, therefore, strange that he should be denied a portion of his rights to serve his country after a lapse of thirty-five years, and that this very unjust discrimination should be made against him by "his comrades in arms"?

We have always endeavored to be loyal to every trust imposed in us. In our Southland, when the master and son went forth to battle to perpetuate our bonds, we protected, revered, and held intact the honor of the wife and daughter who remained at home, and history fails to record a single instance where that trust was betrayed. When we were called upon to take up arms and go forth to battle and save the Union, we never faltered, but bared our breasts to the enemy and at each roll call answered "Here." When peace was proclaimed, we settled down to our fate and began the arduous duties of American citizens under circumstances and disadvantages not easily surmounted by anyone. We began with nothing, but by dint of hard work, strict economy, and the exercise of a little common sense we have acquired over $400,000,000 worth of property. As laborers any class of people cannot fill our places in the South. Among us there are no strikes; no tumults or riots; no labor organizations to bar the white man from making an honest living; no tramps; but humble, faithful citizens, ever true to the trust imposed in us by the proclamation of the lamented Lincoln. We are grateful to all benefactors. We remember with keenest appreciation of gratitude those who constructed the meandering Underground Railroad in our behalf, and in our minds will ever be found indelibly written the names of Garrison, Garnett, Wendell Phillips, William Wells Brown, Charles Sumner, Frederick Douglass, William Still, Dr. E.H. Magill, John Mercer Langston, Harriet Beecher Stowe, Robert Purvis, and the long line of patriots who so nobly espoused our cause, and we will ever revert to their memories as the traveler to the green oasis in the barren desert.

We regret to say that the nation has not at all times given us that protection to which our loyalty has entitled us. This is painfully evidenced by the almost daily outrages chronicled, showing lynching, murders, assassinations, and even cremations of our people all over the Southland; and when we protest against this inhuman conduct toward us we are quietly told that our redress is relegated to the several States and their governments and that the nation has no power to interfere in the premises. Still, if some half-breed foreigner claiming allegiance to our Government is insulted by any foreign country, redress for him is at once demanded, and in most cases large indemnities are given. These words may sound harsh, but they are nevertheless true, and I every much regret that there is excuse for making these declarations. But, regardless of the faults of this grand old Union of ours, we love her still, and if the nation should find it necessary to resort to arms and our present strained relations with Spain should develop into a war, I pledge you that the black phalanx is ready to be mustered in, one-half million strong.

My plea is not for special privileges for my people, but what we want and have a right to expect is a man's chance, a man's protection; in fact, all the privileges of an American citizen. We will be content with nothing less. We appeal to American patriots to remove all statutory barriers now prescribed against us. You have two hundred and fifty-year head start on us; and if you are fair, if you are not cowards, and of course you are not, you certainly will be willing to accord to us at this late day all the rights of you now enjoy as American citizens. An even chance in the race of life is all that we ask; and then if we cannot reach the goal, let the devil take the hindmost one!

> *In this disputed election in Tennessee, White expressed regret that the Republican party did not have a candidate to put forward. He assumed that a divided Democratic party would have resulted in a Republican victory there. White found it curious that the contestants both claimed to have won the "Negro vote"; yet, black voters throughout the South were virtually disenfranchised.*

THE CONTESTED ELECTION IN TENESSEE
Patterson v. Carmack
April 22, 1898

If half of what has been said against either of these gentlemen contending for a seat on this floor is true, I doubt very much whether either ought to have a seat in the Congress of the United States. There is an old adage, "that when thieves fall out just men can get their deserts." It is a great pity that the Republicans of Tennessee, in this particular district, had not a man to bring forward as a candidate at the time that these two Democrats were fighting over the position.

But the bone of contention between them seems to be as to how the Negro vote was cast in that district. Both sides seem to have been basing some bold claims upon these votes, and also that there is a "higher law"–as they both claim–than either the statutes of the United States or the Constitution itself, and yet both sides claim that they are entitled to a seat on this floor by virtue of those Negro votes. Well, my opinion is that if the contestee is correct in his statement, and taking his own evidence as true, in the language of the lawyers, if political honesty were an indictable offense, you could not obtain a bill against him, not even in a court of equity. I shall have to vote for the contestant, not from any pleasure or feeling of consideration grown of love of political affiliations, but on the ground that we are taught in morals that a man is never required to choose between two sins, but he may be required at times to choose between two evils; and when that condition is presented to me, I always take the lesser one. I shall accept Mr. Patterson, therefore, as a kind of reformer–as the smaller of two evils presented to me–and swallow him with my eyes closed.

This case, however, is not the only one which seems to indicate that somebody on this floor thinks that there is "a higher law" in reference to the Negro voter, whenever his condition is being considered here, than the Constitution even of the United States. I took the pains, while the gentleman from Mississippi [John Mills Allen] was speaking, to run over the statements given by the members from his State with reference to the votes cast in that State in the last election; and I have made a little calculation that I will submit to you. I find that in the State of Mississippi–and these figures, I suppose, are based on the census of 1890–according to a statement made by the gentlemen from his State, as laid down in the *Congressional Record*, there were 1,146,268 population in the State of Mississippi.

According to the ordinary election rules throughout the country, at an average, there ought to have been 229,252 votes cast in that election. And yet the combined votes cast for the Democratic members of the Mississippi delegation occupying seats on this floor were only 42,694. And about how many votes did the Republicans receive? Of course they got all the balance–only 3,214. Somewhere in the neighborhood–notwithstanding the Presidential election then pending–somewhere in the neighborhood of 150,000 voters that we may presume to have had a right to vote; and even presuming the right of "transferring," as we have heard it expressed on this floor, had a right to cast their votes in that election–in the neighborhood of 150,000 votes of black men were suppressed and not allowed to vote because they were Negroes.

The question that ought to concern the United States Congress at this time, in my opinion, is as to whether or not there is a republican form of government in the state of Mississippi, the state of South Carolina, the State of Louisiana, and other southern states when you take up this record and examine the votes that were cast. The question is, as to whether the United States will sit supinely by and see that these matters are relegated to the States themselves, and that gentlemen can come here and occupy seats by the suppression of the vote of their district, simply because they are of a different complexion, of a different race or different politics, without any investigation made or protest entered. The lifeblood of the Union is thus being sapped; little by little it may be, but surely sapped, and one day or the other it will not be a question of standing by and putting down the Spaniards, but it will be a question as to whether or not the Federal Constitution in this great Republic of ours shall be perpetuated or not. These are matters that may not be exactly germane to the subject under consideration, but matters that should engage the thoughtful statesmen of the country. These are matters that ought to be looked into. The votes–districts in Southern States like that under consideration–with a voting population anywhere from 30,000 to 50,000, yet the combined vote cast is less in some instances than 5,000. And why is this? Not because there is an difference on the part of the black men about their franchise; for outside of his own home and his own beloved family, there is no one thing so dear to the heart of the colored man as his right to American citizenship, and yet he is not permitted to exercise that right.

Still gentlemen come here and speak about the "Negro" and the "darky" and talk of him in dialect and old plantation language. It seems to me that such language, coming from the plantations in Mississippi and elsewhere, had better be uttered at home and not brought here in this dignified body. They come, however, and claim that there are "fair elections" in all these cases where such a disparity in the votes is shown. You cannot feel this as I do. There is a great contention on that side of the Chamber, and sometimes on this side of the Chamber, for the leadership. But I am easily the leader of one thing, and that is the black phalanx on this floor. I have no rival, and I will not be disturbed in that leadership. Let the leaders on these two sides get together that we may legislate for the whole people.

White supported the annexation of the Philippine Islands. He argued that it was the custom of the United States to "at all times extend a helping hand to oppressed" peoples. He stated sarcastically that such a custom is not practiced at home. Nevertheless, he favored the liberation of colonies from foreign domination. He supported strengthening the armed forces, believing that it was an appropriate time to make the military strong. White also used foreign policy to direct attention to the race problem in the United States, reminding his colleagues that he alone represented African Americans. He ended by stating, blacks wanted justice–pure and simple.

THE ANNEXATION OF THE PHILIPPINE ISLANDS
January 26, 1899

I supported very cheerfully all measures tending to bring about the recent war for liberating a very much oppressed and outraged people. I supported with equal cheer all appropriations that were necessary for the successful prosecution of that war to a final termination. I thought it was necessary then; I think now that it was a necessity. It has been the province of the people of the United States at all times to extend a helping hand to the oppressed, to the outraged–I mean, of course, without the borders of the United States.

Being a member of this great Republic and one of the Representatives on this floor, I gave my support in voice and in every way that I could to all measures tending to the liberation of these poor people in Cuba. I now favor the acquisition of all of the territory that is within our grasp as a result of that war. To say that we will not accept, to say that we will not take these acquisitions, and to say that we will not extend to the people thereof the civilization of our country, the Christian manhood and womanhood we enjoy, is to do them a wrong and to take steps backward. I therefore favor the annexation of the Philippine Islands, and also favor the bill now pending before this House for the extension of our standing Army commensurate with our new conditions.

Our Army up to the time of this recent war was a mere bagatelle. It was not at all in keeping with the great nation that we are. Our Navy consisted of only a few crafts hanging around our shores, and the condition we were found in at the beginning of the American-Spanish war is too well known to us all to require any discussion on my part. In times of peace it is well to prepare for war. We are now at peace, but it may not be thirty days before we shall be thrown into another war. Who can tell? Certainly if this discussion goes on, the treaty being considered in the other end of the Capitol being transferred, in part, to this end of the Capitol, and being of such character so as to encourage and inflame those of the Philippines opposed to annexation, it is most likely that it will not be thirty days before we will be at war again. Therefore I favor action upon this bill and extending our Army so that it will be sample for all emergencies that may arise. It is not so much on account of the recent war with Spain, or the money it took to carry on that war, or the annexation of Cuba, or Puerto Rico, or the Philippine Islands that I desire to speak, nor is it so much the pending bill we have before us that I desire to address myself to this House.

But it is another problem, possibly more vexing than the one we have now under consideration. I know that you will pardon me if I do not address myself to the question before us when you recollect that I am the only representative on this floor of 10,000,000 people, from a racial standpoint. They have no one else to speak for them, from a race point of view, except myself. I shall therefore address the remainder of my remarks to another phase of the situation in this country–to another great problem that confronts us, and one which I trust ere long we shall have the manhood to stand up in our places and meet like American citizens, not like sectional cowards. I refer to the race problem. I have sat there in my place and heard discussions pro and con; I have heard my race referred to in terms anything else than dignified and complimentary. I have heard them referred to as savages, as aliens, as brutes, as vile and vicious and worthless, and I have heard but little or nothing said with reference to their better qualities, their better manhood, or their developed American citizenship. It is therefore in reply to those seemingly unguarded expressions that I wish to speak.

I have listened to gentlemen here–particularly one of the gentlemen for the State of Mississippi [John Sharp Williams] in his great eloquence about "white supremacy"–just here permit me to say that I have no respect for a "supremacy," white or black, which has been obtained through fraud, intimidation, carnage, and death–"white supremacy" in the great State of

Mississippi; about the Anglo-Saxon ruling this country. I did not know that. It required any specific reference of this kind for the world to know the act that the Anglo-Saxon will rule the United States. We constitute as a race less than one-seventh, possibly, of the population. We have been enslaved; we have done your bidding for two hundred and forty years without any compensation; and we did it faithfully. We do not revert to it grumblingly or regretfully, but we refer to it because it seems ungracious in you now, after you have had all this advantage of us, after you have had all this labor of ours, to be unwilling, at this late day, to give us a man's share in the race of life. That is the only sense in which I refer to it. It is not with a view to digging up the past. It is not with a view of kindling renewed animosity between the races, but only in answer to those who slur at us and remind us of our inferiority. Yes, by force of circumstances, we are your inferiors. Give us two hundred and forty years the start of you, give us your labor for two hundred and forty years without compensation, give us the wealth that the brawny arm of the black man made for you, give us the education that his unpaid labor gave your boys and girls, and we will not be begging, we will not be in a position to be sneered at as aliens or members of an inferior race.

We are inferior. We regret it. But if you will only allow us an opportunity we will amend out ways; we will increase our usefulness; we will become more and more intelligent; more and more useful to the nation. It is a chance in the race of life that we crave. We do not expect any special legislation. We do not expect the mythical "forty-acres and a mule." The mule died long ago of old age, and the land grabbers have obtained the forty-acres. We do not expect any of those things. But we have a right to expect a man's chance and opportunity to carve out our own destiny. That is all we ask, and that we demand. This problem is confronting the nation. We seem as a race to be going through just now a crucible, a crisis–a peculiar crisis. It is not necessary, nor have I the time, to enter into any explanation as to what brought about this crisis. I may say, however, in passing, that possibly more than by any other one thing it has been brought about by the fact that despite all the oppression which has fallen upon our shoulders we have been rising, steadily rising, and in some instances we hope ere long to be able to measure our achievements with those of all other men and women of the land. This tendency on the part of some of us to rise and assert our manhood along all lines is, I fear, what has brought about this changed condition.

Shall the nation stand by listlessly, or shall it uphold the principles that it has established? Shall it recognize, as declared in the organic law, that all men are born free and equal and are endowed with certain inalienable rights, among which are life, liberty, and the pursuit of happiness? During the discussions here since the pendency of the treaty of peace I have heard a good deal said, both in this House and at the other end of the Capitol, about the Declaration of Independence and the Constitution of the United States. I have heard a good deal said about Thomas Jefferson and others who had to do with the drafting of that instrument. And it has been alleged that they did not mean what they said in that declaration, for the reason that at the very time it was promulgated they owned slaves, and therefore when they spoke of all men being free and equal they did not mean the black population. The Constitution is a very elastic instrument when you have a purpose to serve. Public sentiment is law, and law, when properly executed, is public sentiment.

I heard once of a learned old lawyer who was instructing his class preparatory to their examination before the Supreme Court of the State for license. He said to them one day, "My dear boys, whenever you have a case in regard to which the law is in your favor and the facts against you, you must lean hard on the law; but if the law is against you and the facts in your favor, then lean hard on the facts." One bright young fellow said, "Well, Judge, suppose both the law and the facts are against us, then what must we do?" "Ah, my boys," said the Judge, "then you must beat about the bush." It occurs to me that every time a construction of the Constitution or an interpretation of the law is made with reference to the humble race with which I am identified, the principle of that old judge's instruction is brought into play. If the law is in favor of the Negro and the facts rather against him, they lean hard on the facts. If the reverse is true, they lean hard on the law in the construction of a statute with reference to him: but if the Negro happens to have both the law and the facts on his side, all the decisions touching his rights seem to be beating around the bush. I regret to say it, and I say it with respect, with no intention of reflecting upon anybody or any branch of this Government.

Now, the problem to which I refer not only touches my people, but in my humble judgment it reaches out and ramifies and affects every citizen of the American Republic. How long will we sit–I say "we." I will set here only two years longer, should I live, and I am going to try mighty hard to live that long. How long will you sit in your seats here and see the principles that underlie the foundation of this Government sapped little by little, but nevertheless surely sapped away? I took the pains this afternoon to run over one or two of the States that have been harping, through their representatives, most about the colored man on this floor since I have been in Congress. I took up Mississippi, because I recall that two gentlemen from that State especially-I have reference to Congressman John Mills Allen and Congressman John Sharp Williams–have taken special pains on several occasions to refer to the Negro; they referred to him in a slurring way, referred to him as something to be managed, referred to him as something to be gotten rid of, referred to him as somebody that must be– oh, well, Congressman Allen told a yarn here one day–"transferred," I believe he called it. He must be "transferred." Well, now, here is the situation. I could not say much with reference to him, but here is the situation, taking his district in the State of Mississippi. I deal with 1896, because I could not get the figures of last

November. I find in the gentleman's district there were only 8,418 votes cast for all the candidates in that district, while the estimated vote of the district is 28,663. I found in the Second district that the estimated vote was 34,102. The congressman said that he got a plurality of 254 over his opponent, but did not give us the benefit of how many he got. I presume a few thousand. In the Third District the total estimated vote is 36,859 with 4,050 cast in the presidential election of 1896. I found in the Fourth District there was an estimated vote of 42,647. There were votes cast for all the candidates, Democrats, Republicans, Populists, Free Soilers, Hottentots, and everybody else, 11,737.

In the Fifth District the estimated vote is 44, 923, and there were 13,700 votes cast for all the candidates.

In the Sixth District there were 33,882 votes estimated and there were cast nobody knows how many. Here is the note in the Directory:

Elected as a Democrat, practically without opposition, to fill out an un-expired term–and so forth.

In the Seventh District the estimated vote is 37,338, and there were cast 8,647 votes.

The total vote cast for Congressmen in the State of Mississippi in the year 1896, leaving out the Second and Sixth districts, where the vote is not given, was 45,867 out of a total vote of between 250,000 and 300,000. [Mr. Ferdinand Brucker of Michigan asked: Was that at the presidential election?] That was at the presidential election in the year 1896. These were the votes cast for Congressmen as they themselves have given them in the *Congressional Directory*. I do not know whether the Negroes ever dominated in Mississippi or not. If they did, it is the only State outside of South Carolina for a while that they ever did dominate. They certainly never dominated the State wherein I live. We have no ambition to dominate, but we would like to be given a chance by the side of other men to work out our destiny and paddle our own canoe. I find in the State of South Carolina, adjoining the State that I hail from, a similar situation of affairs. I suppose I might give these facts and figures, because the public would like to know these things, and everyone cannot get hold of a *Congressional Directory*.

In the First District of South Carolina the estimated vote is 34,664; the vote cast, 7,303. In the Second District the estimated vote is 29,265; the vote cast, 8,634. In the Third District the estimated vote is 30,412 and the votes cast 10,536, or about one-third. In the Fourth District the estimated vote is 40,000; the votes cast, 12,180. In the Fifth District the estimated vote is 28, 350, and the votes cast is 8,833. In the Sixth District the estimated vote is 30,770, and we have this entry, no figures being given at all:

Elected as a Democrat without opposition, having received the entire vote cast.

A popular man! In the Seventh District the estimated vote is 35,736, while the vote cast was 9,407. The total vote cast, leaving out those two districts where the gentlemen did not give the public the benefit of the votes cast for them–the total vote cast for congressmen in that State in that election was 56,953, while the estimated vote of the State of South Carolina is about 250,000, about one-fifth of the entire voting population having actually voted. Now, I am not going to grumble about the number of votes that you cast down there in South Carolina, but I want to say to the Congress of the United States, and through Congress to the people of the United States, that South Carolina, Louisiana, Mississippi, and every other State in this Union ought to have the benefit of the votes that are allowed to be cast in their representation on this floor, and no more.

It is not fair to the other States of the Union to say that one gentleman shall come here from a district giving 30,000, 40,000, 50,000, or even 60,000 votes, and that a district in Mississippi or a district in Louisiana or a district in South Carolina, or possibly pretty soon a district in North Carolina, shall come here with a like population with only five or six thousand votes cast, with the others disfranchised and not allowed to vote. If we are unworthy of suffrage, if it is necessary to maintain white supremacy, if it is necessary for the Anglo-Saxon to sway the scepter in those States, then you ought to have the benefit only of those who are allowed to vote, and the poor men, whether they be black or white, who are disfranchised ought not to go into the representation of the district or the State. It is a question that this House must deal with some time, sooner or later. It may seem a little strange to hear me speak, but nobody else has tackled this question because the boot does not pinch anybody else as it does my race and me. But it will come home to you. You will have to meet it. You have got this problem to settle, and the sooner it is settled the better it will be for all parties concerned. I speak this in all charity. I speak this with no hostility. I am not a pessimist. I take rather the other view. I am optimistic in my views and believe that these problems will adjust themselves one day. I believe that the Negro problem in less than fifty years will be a thing of the past.

When it is recalled that thirty-three years ago, one generation ago, four and a half millions of these people were liberated on the plantations of their former masters, and that right by their side they have worked out their destiny thus far, have arisen from poverty to a taxation of four hundred millions of property in the United States; when it is remembered that they have arisen from no homes to the purchase, in many instance, of decent tracts of land, with splendid homes and good property, I think I am justified in saying that this problem will work itself out. Many of them have acquired professions. We are ramifying and stretching out as best we can in all departments of life, with a view to making ourselves good citizens. And my plea is not against Mississippi, not against South Carolina, not against Louisiana, but for justice–simple justice. Unmitigated justice is what we ask. You are not afraid of the black man overriding and overawing you. He is your neighbor. He is your friend. The chord that exists between some of the whites and the blacks of the South cannot be severed by all of the bloody assassins of the world. But you have got the wrong conception. You have got the idea that any means that will disfranchise him and prevent him from exercising the rights that are given him under the Constitution is legitimate, that the end justifies the means. It is a wrong conception of a civilized people, and the sooner we all reach the conclusion that we are here together, here to live and here to die, the better for all concerned, because the black man is here to stay for all time to come.

The Indian has been driven to the West. He had been driven to the little reservations, and he numbers now only a few hundred thousand. He has died and has been killed and his numbers reduced to a minimum and in a hundred years hence a few mummies in the Smithsonian Institution or somewhere else will represent an extinct race that was once very distinct in the United States. Not so with the Negro; never. He did not come to this country of his own motion; he is not here of his own act; but being there, and his planting upon this soil being coequal with his white neighbor, he is here to stay from now henceforth and forever. He will not die out. I know that some of your friends have consulted the statistics and find that the mortality of the Negro in some large cities is very great, and they think he will soon die out. They forget that the bulk of the Negro race have never seen a large city, but are healthy and hearty and prolific on the plantations throughout the country. Yes, we are on the increase. The war emancipated four and a half million enslaved Negroes. The census of next year will register ten million. The proportion that we occupy with reference to the white people will never increase, but will gradually diminish; but the number of Negroes in this country will continually increase.

I say it will never increase because we no longer import Africans into the United States. It is an evident fact that the "riffraff" of all the nations of the earth freely enter this country except Africans [and increasingly Asians.] And, strange to say, they find open doors and find open hearts, and soon mingle and commingle with all the people of this country and are lost in the great civilization of this country. We do not ask to be assimilated; we do not ask to be amalgamated; we do not ask for anything but to remain a distinct and separate race as we are, and to be permitted to work out our own manhood and womanhood. We do not expect anything else. Now, gentlemen, what are you going to do with this problem, with this question? I believe the time is coming very soon when the color of a man's skin, so far as business relations are concerned, so far as citizenship is concerned, will cut no figure at all. A man will be regarded as a man whether wrapped in a white or a black skin. I believe the time will come when we will have no more riots in the South on account of color, when civilization will so develop all over this nation that there will be no more lynching, barbarity and mobocracy now so prevalent in some portions of this country.

When the black man, through toil and economy, shall have acquired property and wealth and all those things that make a good American citizen, and when all the barriers of legislation now in the way shall disappear, he will be taken by the hand as a man. I believe the time will come–yes, soon–when the condition that prevails today in Boston, in grand old Massachusetts, where all are recognized, both black and white, will prevail in South Carolina, North Carolina, Louisiana, and Mississippi. We cannot live on the dead ashes of the past. Slavery and its institutions, racial distinctions and wrongs will come to an end. We are going forward; we are looking out; we are stretching out our arms all over the United States. The nation must care for those at home as well as those abroad. Our ratio of representation is poor. We are taunted with being uppity; we are told to be still; to keep quiet. How long must we keep quiet? We have kept quiet while numerically and justly we are entitled to fifty-one members of this House; and I am the only one left. We kept quiet when numerically we are entitled to a member of the Supreme Court. We have never had a member and probably never will; but we have kept quiet. We have kept quiet while numerically and justly, according to our population as compared with all the other races of the world, so far as the United States is concerned, we should have the recognition of a place in the President's Cabinet; but we have not had it. Still we have kept quiet, and are making no noise about it.

We are entitled to thirteen United States Senators, according to justice and according to our numerical strength, but we have not one, and possibly never will get another; and yet we keep quiet. We have kept quiet while hundreds and thousands of our race have been strung up by the neck unjustly by mobs of murderers. If a man commits a crime he will never find an apologist in me because his face is black. He ought to be punished, but he ought to be punished according to the law as administered in a court of justice. But we keep quiet; do not say it, do not talk about it. How long must we keep quiet, constantly sitting down and seeing our rights one by one taken away from us? As slaves it was to be expected; as slaves we were docile and easily managed; but as citizens we want and we have a right to expect all that the law guarantees to us. We are passing, as we trust, from ignorance to intelligence. The process may be slow; we may be impatient; you may be discouraged; public sentiment may be against us because we have not done better, but we are making progress. Do you recollect in history any race of people placed in like circumstances that have done any better than we have? Give us a chance, and we will do more. We plead to all of those who are here legislating for the nation that while your sympathy goes out to Cuba–and we are legislating for Cuba–while your hearts burst forth with great love for humanity abroad, remember those who are at our own door. Remember those who have worked for you; remember those who have loved you, who have held up your hands, who have felled your forests, have dug your ditches, who have filled up your valleys and have lowered the mountains, and have helped to make the great southland what it is today. We are entitled to your recognition. We do not ask for domination. We ask and expect a chance in legislation, and we will be content with nothing else.

It is that standard–that measurement–that we are willing to be measured by. It is by that standard we would like you to gauge us, and not the texture of our hair, not the color of our skin, not our flat noses, but the standard of the man that we would like to be measured by. This broad problem of giving us a man's chance confronts us; it is one well worthy of you. I was up in Saratoga a few years ago, and in conversation with a gentleman there inquired how the people got along. I went before the season opened. Everything looked barren and bleak. He said, "Well, in the summer we live by skinning the visitors who have come here." I said, "I can very well understand that; but how do you get along in the winter?" "Then," he said, "We skin each other." Gentlemen, the process of skinning the Negro is nearly over. You have about completed the job. Gentlemen of the North, of the East, and of the West, yes, and you of the South, when that is done you have to got to have somebody to skin, and you will turn on each other, and then possibly the Negro will get his just deserts.

It is well to stop and consider; you cannot always keeps a free man down. When he is once made free, it will be difficult to ever enslave him again, either physically or intellectually. Physical slavery is a thing nobody wants. The most ignorant of our Southern sand lappers out in the woods do not want actual slavery again; but there is a slavery that is even worse than manual slavery–the slavery of the mind, the beclouded intellect. It is there that we ask you to help lift the curtain of darkness, the curtain of ignorance, the curtain of vice that you helped to nail and foist upon us, to help break the shackles, that we may look forth in the noonday of life, in the tide of progress and beauty, that we may go up the hill with you, that we may leave the miasmatic valley of vice and degradation and climb to the top of the mount, where we can breathe God's pure air as American citizens.

Recognize your citizens at home, recognize those at your door, give them the encouragement, give them the rights that they are justly entitled to, and then take hold of the people of Cuba and help establish a stable and fixed government among them; take hold of the Puerto Ricans, establish the government there that wisdom predicated, which justice may dictate. Take hold of the Philippine Islands, take hold of the Hawaiian Islands, there let the Christian civilization go out and magnify and make happy those poor, half-civilized people; and then the black man, the white man–yes, all the riffraff of the earth that are coming to our shores–will rejoice with you in that we have done God's service and done that which will elevate us in the eyes of the world.

White offered an amendment to an appropriations bill to allocate money for North Carolina. While he considered the amount of money requested modest, he believed it would benefit farmers in his district as well as further developing the South.

THE RIVER HARBOR APPROPRIATION BILL
February 1, 1899

I desire to offer an amendment [to add $7,750 for continuing improvements.] I had hoped that I would have the cooperation of the chairman of this committee, or at least his consent to the insertion of this amendment. This creek, Fishing Creek, North Carolina, through its confluence with the river, is 94 miles above Pamlico Sound and at that part crossed by the Wilmington and Weldon Railroad Fishing Creek is 35 feet deep and 150 feet wide. The channel depth on its bar is only 3 feet. There has been an appropriation made, and there has been considerable work done on this creek, which is fully detailed in the report of the engineers of the War Department. To make available and to make profitable the money which had already been expended the amount I have suggested is exactly the figure recommended by the Corps of Engineers as an absolute necessity.

They say that $10,000 can properly be expended during the next fiscal year. I am asking only the minimum amount recommended by the engineers. I approached the committee and asked it that this amount be inserted. The only answer I got was that my request came too late. I trust that even now the committee will reverse itself and allow this small request to go in. I have invariably voted with you gentlemen and helped you to get millions upon top of millions. This is the first time I have asked you for one cent, and I trust you will not take it lightly and laughingly vote it down. It is a necessity for the farmers along that river, which ramifies my district from one end to the other, and it would be a great benefit if this amount were allowed, and would make profitable the amount of money which has already been appropriated and expended. [Mr. Israel Frederick Fischer of New York Asked: How much do you want?] Only $7,750, and I am afraid you are going to vote it down.

Now, I do not wish to antagonize the committee, and I hope the committee will not antagonize my little request. I ask it on the ground of justice—yes, on the ground of necessity.

> *White requested that the clerk put into the Congressional Record an unflattering article that appeared in the Raleigh News and Observer. "It is bad enough that North Carolina should have the only nigger congressman." The newspaper also condemned Congressman White for claiming that whites were responsible for lynching.*

PERSONAL EXPLANATION
Response to the Raleigh News and Observer
"The Colored Member"
February 5, 1900

I desire to give that vile, slanderous publication the widest possible circulation. I desire that it shall go out through the documents of this House that the world may see what the poor colored man in the Southland has to undergo from a certain class. In making this statement it is proper that I should exonerate a very large percentage of the white people of North Carolina, my native State. No better people live anywhere on God's green earth than some of them. But, unfortunately, men of the type of him who wrote that article are now in the ascendancy.

I desire to repudiate as slanderous and wholly untrue the utterances there attributed to me. I did the other day; while my colleague [Romulus Zachariah Linney] was speaking, he interjected a remark to the effect that from an investigation which I made last summer, as stated in a paper which I read before a local organization of this city, I had found that less than 15 percent of the lynchings in this country were for assaults committed upon white women, not in the South, but in the entire United States. I repeat that utterance. I did not justify the commission of assaults by black men upon white women on the ground that white men did the same in regard to black women. I said that there were assaults occasionally committed upon women and that they were not all committed by black men upon white women, but were also committed by white men upon black women, as evidenced by the great numbers of mulattos in the Southland. I said that then; I repeat it now; and if any man here or elsewhere desires to verify the truthfulness of that statement, he has but to make a visit through the South, where I live. I repudiate as much as any man can, whether he be a white brute or a black brute, who commits an assault upon any woman, whether a white woman or a black woman. I think such a man ought to be hung–hung by the neck until dead. But it ought to be done by the courts, not by an infuriated mob such as the writer of that article would incite.

This article is but an evidence of what we have gone to contend with–an absolute perversion and slanderous misrepresentation of the truth–preparing for the election to be held in August. And the world is notified that those whom the Constitution of these United States, by the Fourteenth and Fifteenth Amendments, has enfranchised are to be reduced once more to the condition of goods and chattels, if such men as the one who edits the *Raleigh News and Observer* can have the control of affairs in North Carolina. As I said before, I want to give the fullest publication to the utterances of this vile sheet; and I want my colleagues in this House, both Democrats and Republicans, with Populists thrown in, to judge my character and my conduct for the last three years on this floor and say whether or not it has conformed to the description given by this fellow who edits the News and Observer and pollutes the country with such literature as has been read at the desk.

While White supported American territorial acquisitions, he complained that the United States had not yet protected the civil rights of its black citizens. As he put it, charity begins at home. White reviewed the status of African Americans since emancipation, asserting that racial discrimination was ignored. Moreover, he argued that blacks were virtually denied the vote in most states. During this period, White insisted, some 50,000 black people had been murdered by white mobs and their assailants went without punishment.

PUERTO RICO
February 23, 1900

Perhaps at no time in the history of our nation have there been more questions of moment before us for consideration than we have at this time. Our recent war with Spain and the result in acquisitions of territory by reason of that war, and the necessary legislation for the government of these new possessions in order that they may not work any harm with us, to establish rules, laws, and customs, require the most thoughtful consideration of all of our statesmen. Not only the question that we have before us tonight as to the character of the tariff to be imposed upon Puerto Rico, but the government that shall be established to perpetuate, elevate, and civilize and Christianize the Hawaiian Islands, the Philippine Islands, and, in my opinion at no very distant day, the Cuban Island, also require our very best effort. The weightiness of the consideration of these questions is increased by the peculiar circumstances surrounding these new possessions. Their relative geographical position, their climate, their distance from our shores, their close proximity to other foreign powers, coupled with a heterogeneous composition of population of these islands, and their want in Christian and civil development, all tend to increase the consideration and make more complex the solution of their future government.

But these responsibilities are ours; taken of our own motion and our plain duty with reference to these people must not be shirked, but met and disposed of honestly, patriotically, in the spirit of justice between man and man. As a humble Representative of this House, I would like to feel free to discuss and aid in the disposition of these questions in the same way that my three hundred and fifty-five colleagues on this floor do. It would be a great pleasure to me to know that fairness and justice would be meted out to all the constituent parts of our beloved country alike in such a way as to leave no necessity for a defense of my race in this House against the attacks and unfair charges from any source. The very intimation of this fact, with reference to the surroundings of the colored people of this country at this time, naturally causes the inquiry: should not a nation be just to all of her citizens, protect them alike in all their rights, on every foot of her soil–in a word, show herself capable of governing all within her domain before she undertakes to exercise sovereign authority over those of a foreign land–with foreign notions and habits not at all in harmony with our American system of government? Or, to be more explicit, should not charity first begin at home?

There can be but one candid and fair answer to this inquiry, and that is in the affirmative. But, unfortunately for us, what should have been done has not been done, and to substantiate the assertion we have but to pause for a moment and make a brief survey of the manumitted Afro-American during the last thirty-five years. We have struggled on as best we could with the odds against us at every turn. Our constitutional rights have been trodden under foot; our right of franchise in most every one of the original slave States has been virtually taken away from us, and during the time of our freedom fully 50,000 of my race have been ignominiously murdered by mobs, not 1 percent of whom have been made to answer for their crimes in the courts of justice, and even here in the nation's Capitol–in the Senate and House–Senators and Representatives have undertaken the unholy task of extenuating and excusing these deeds, and in some instances they have gone so far as to justify them.

This is entirely *ex parte*; nothing has been said of the other side. While I deprecate as much as any man can the fiend who commits an outrage upon any woman, and do not hesitate to say that he should be speedily tried and punished by the courts, yet I place but little credence in the statement of a mob hunting for an excuse for its crimes when the statement is made that the victim confessed with a rope perhaps around his neck. No court of justice anywhere in this broad land of ours would allow testimony under duress of this kind to be introduced against a defendant. A shoe track, and a confession while being burned at the stake with the hope that life may be spared thereby, are very poor excuses for taking of a human life. A trial by jury is guaranteed to every one by the Constitution of the United States, and no one should be deprived of this guaranty, however grave the charge preferred against him.

The other side of this horrible story portrays a very different state of affairs. A white man, with no interest in Hose or his victim, declares upon oath that Hose did not commit this atrocious crime charged against him, but was an employee of Cranford, and had importuned him to pay him for labor. This incensed his employer, who rushed upon Hose with a gun. Hose seized an ax and killed Cranford instantly, in self-defense, and then fled to the woods with the greatest possible speed. I do not vouch for either side of this story, but only refer to it to show the necessity for trying all persons charged with crime, as the law directs.

The gentleman might have gone further and described the butchery in his district of six colored persons arrested upon suspicion of being guilty of arson, and while they were crouching in a warehouse, manacled with irons, and guarded by officers of the law, these poor victims, perhaps guilty of no crime whatever, were horribly shot to death by irresponsible men, no one of whom has ever been brought to justice. He might have depicted also if he was so inclined, the miserable butchery of men, women, and children in Wilmington, N.C., in November, 1898, who had committed no crime, nor were they even charged with crime. He might have taken the minds of his auditors to the horrible scene of the aged and infirm, male and female, women in bed from childbirth, driven from their homes to the woods, with no shelter save the protecting branches of the trees of the forest, where many died from exposure, privation, and disease contracted while exposed to the merciless weather. But this description would not have accomplished the purpose of riveting public sentiment upon every colored man of the South as a rapist from whose brutal assaults every white woman must be protected.

This language impliedly puts at naught and defies the Fourteenth and Fifteenth Amendments to the Constitution of the United States, and from present indications it is only a matter of a short time when the abrogation of these constitutional provisions will be openly demanded. It is easy for these gentlemen to taunt us with our inferiority, at the same time not mentioning the causes of this inferiority. It is rather hard to be accused of shiftlessness and idleness when the accuser of his motion closes the avenues for labor and industrial pursuits to us. It is hardly fair to accuse us of ignorance when it was made a crime under the former order of things to learn enough about letters to even read the Word of God. While I offer no extenuation for any immorality that may exist among my people, it comes with rather poor grace from those who forced it upon us for two hundred and fifty years to taunt us with that shortcoming. We are trying hard to relieve ourselves of the bonds with which we were bound and over which we had no control, nothing daunted, however, like the skilled mariner who, having been overtaken by the winds and storms and thrown off his bearings, stops to examine the chart, the compass, and all implements of navigation, that he may be sure of the proper course to travel to reach his destination.

In our voyage of life struggle for a place whereon we can stand, speak, think, and act as unrestricted American citizens, we have been and are now passing through political gales, storms of ostracism, torrents of proscription, waves and inundations of caste prejudice and hatred, and, like the mariner, it is proper that we should examine our surroundings, take our bearings, and devise ways and means by which we may pursue our struggle for a place as men and women as a part of this body politic. Possibly at no time in the history of our freedom has the effort been made to mold public sentiment against our progress and us so strongly as it is now being done. The forces have been set in motion and we must have sufficient manhood and courage to overcome all resistance that obstructs our progress. A race of people with the forbearance, physical development, and Christian manhood and womanhood, which has characterized us during the past two hundred and eight-five years, will not be put down at the bidding of any man or set of men, and it would be well that all should learn this lesson now. As slaves we were true to our rulers; true to every trust reposed in us. While the white fathers and sons went forth to battle against us and the nation to perpetuate our bonds the strong, brawny arms of the black man produced the food to sustain the wives, children, and aged parents of the Confederate soldier, and kept inviolable the virtue and care of those entrusted to his keeping, and nowhere will anyone dare say that he was unfaithful to the helpless and unprotected over whom he kept a guardian watch. How does this statement of facts compare with the frequent charges made against colored men for outraging white females? Is it a futile attempt to prove that an ignorant slave was a better man and more to be trusted than an intelligent freeman? But of these brutal murders, let us revert to a few facts and figures.

Since January 1, 1898, to April 25, 1899, there were lynched in the United States 166 persons, and of this number 155 occurred in the South. Of the whole number lynched, there were 10 white and 156 colored. The thin disguise usually employed as an excuse for these inhuman outrages is the protection of the virtue among white women. I have taken the pains to make some little investigation as to the charges against the 166 persons killed, and find as a result of my efforts that 32 were charged with murder, 17 were charged with assault, criminal or otherwise, 10 with arson, 2 with stealing, 1 with being impudent to white men, and I am ashamed to acknowledge it, but this latter took place in North Carolina. Seventy-two of the victims were murdered without any specific charge being preferred against them whatever. Continuing this record of carnage,

I give the record of the number of lynching, with causes, from April 24, 1899, to October 20, 1899, inclusive:

Crimes Committed	No. Lynched	Crimes Committed	No. Lynched
Assault, criminal and otherwise.	16	No cause stated	3
Bad character	1	Nothing	2
Barn burning	1	Put hand on white woman	
Brother to murder	1	Sheltering a murderer	3
Church burning	2	Shooting a man	2
Defending a colored man	3	Spoke against lynching	2
Drowned a man	1	Suspected of murder	1
Entered a lady's room drunk	1	Talked too much	2
Innocent	2	Trespass	1
Mormonism	1	Wanted to work	7
Murder	9	Wounded a white man	1
Grand Total			63

Of the 63 lynched there were 1 Italian, 1 Cuban, 4 white men, and 57 Negroes. These facts and figures which I have detailed and reliable; still the same old, oft-repeated slander, like Banquo's ghost, will not down, but is always in evidence. Perhaps I can not better answer the imputation of the gentleman from Texas [Mr. Burke] than by reading an editorial from the New York Times, "How Usual is the Crime,"

February 2, 1900 (omitted).

To further show the some of the horrors which must inevitably follow where the laws are disregarded and the human butchers take the place of the courts, permit me to read from the white press again, *The Roanoke Times*, and allow me to again interject the information that these parties were all white (omitted.)

In referring to the subject of lynching a few days ago on this floor to a privileged question of personal explanation in reply to some vile references made against me by the *Raleigh News and Observer*, I stated in defense of my race that his wretched crime was committed occasionally by both white men and black men. Thereupon this same paper, together with other lesser lights in the State, pounded upon me as a slanderer of white men in the South and especially in North Carolina. "Out of their own mouths shall ye know them." I read from the columns of the same *News and Observer* that was issued but a few days after it jumped on me (omitted.)

I might add that McLeod's victim was not only colored, but a cripple, and that McLeod is a white man living in North Carolina. The sickening effect of these crimes is bad enough in degenerating and degrading the moral sensibilities of those who now play upon the arena of the nation, but this is nothing when compared with the degrading and morbid effect it must have upon the minds of children in communities where these murders are committed in open daylight with the flagrant defiance of all law, morals, the State and nation, and the actors are dubbed as the best citizens of the community. I tremble with horror for the future of our nation when I think what must be the inevitable result if mob violence is not stamped out of existence and law once permitted to reign supreme.

If state laws are inadequate or indisposed to check this species of crime, then the duty of the National Government is plain, as is evidenced by section 1 of the Fourteenth Amendment to the Constitution of the United States, to wit (clause omitted.)

To the end that the National Government may have jurisdiction over this species of crime, I have prepared and introduced the following bill, now pending before the Committee on the Judiciary, to wit:

A bill for the protection of all citizens of the United States against mob violence, and the penalty for breaking such laws.

Section 1. Be it enacted by the Senate and House of Representatives of the United States of America in Congress assembled, That all persons born or naturalized in the United States, and subject to the jurisdiction thereof, and being citizens of the United States, are entitled to and shall receive protection in their lives from being murdered, tortured, burned to death by any and all organized mobs commonly known as "lynching bees," whether said mob be spontaneously assembled or organized by premeditation for the purpose of taking the life or lives of any citizen or citizen in the United States aforesaid; and that whenever any citizens of the United States shall be murdered by mob violence in the manner herein above described, all parties participating, aiding, and abetting in such murder and lynching shall be guilty of treason against the Government of the United States, and shall be tried for that offense on the United States courts; full power and jurisdiction being hereby given to said United States courts and all its officers to issue process, arrest, try, and in all respects deal with such cases in the same manner now prescribed under existing laws for the trial of felonies in the United States courts.

Section 2. That any person or persons duly tried and convicted in any United States court as principal or principals, aiders, abettors, accessories before or after the fact, for the murder of any citizen or citizens of the United States by mob violence or lynching as described in section 1 hereof, shall be punished as is now prescribed by law for the punishment of persons convicted of treason against the United States Government.

Section 3. That all laws and parts of laws in conflict with this statute are hereby repealed.

I do not pretend to claim for this bill perfection, but I have prepared and introduced it to moot the question before the Congress of the United States with the hope that expediency will be set aside and justice allowed to prevail, and a measure prepared by the Committee on the Judiciary that will come within the jurisdiction of the Constitution of the United States, as above cited. There remain now but two questions to be settled: First, perhaps, is it expedient for the American Congress to step aside from the consideration of economic questions, the all-absorbing idea of acquisition of new territory, and consider for a moment the rights of a portion of our citizens at home and the preservation of their lives? That question I leave for you to answer. The second is: Has Congress power to enact a statute to meet these evils? In my opinion it has ample authority under the Constitution of the United States.

In concluding these remarks, I wish to disclaim any intention of hardness or the production of any friction between the races or the sections of this country. I have simply raised my voice against a growing and, as I regard it, one of the most dangerous evils in our country.

White eulogized his colleague Alfred C. Harmer as a man of character. Harmer served in the House for twenty-seven years. While Harmer did not have a reputation for great public speaking in the House of Representatives, White likened him to a river: "He was not noisy, but he was grand, useful, noble, in every instance, and in every purpose strictly honest."

THE DEATH OF ALFRED C. HARMER
December 8, 1901

There are two periods in the life of every public man which provoke attention. If he has enemies or opponents, when he starts out in his public career, seeking high office and public trust, the worst possible phase of his character is ventilated to the world. The tongues of his malingers will run at rapid pace. The defamer of character will know no limit.

The other important period of a public man's life is when his work is done, death claims its own, and he shuffles off this mortal soil and goes hence. It is then that the virtues of the man's life are portrayed. It is then that his morals are held up in a glittering galaxy of beauty. It is pleasing to note, however, that neither one of these periods will apply to the gentleman whom we are eulogizing here today. His character and life were so pure, his deportment was so upright, his deeds were so honorable, that the vilest enemy, if such he had, dared not raise his voice in calumny or slander against him, even though the would-be office seeker desired the position held by Alfred C. Harmer. In the second period to which I have referred, it is not at all necessary for those of us who survive him on this floor to say one word in the least exaggerated term. Perhaps in all that we say we shall not be able to state the half that is due the man and the life that he led. It is true that his voice was not frequently heard, perhaps not at all, in speech making in this Hall. It is true also that a little brook that flows down the hillside is noisy; whether profitable or not remains for investigation. It is true that the great placid rivers of the country move with silent majesty to the bosom of the broad ocean, bearing commerce for the utility of nations. The latter applies to Mr. Harmer. He was not noisy, but he was grand, useful, noble, in every instance, and in every purpose strictly honest.

Nations, like individuals, can never properly appreciate the services of their great men until they have been called hence never to return. Man breathes freely the pure air with which he is surrounded, and never thinks of the blessings and life-giving qualities it carries until the supply is shut off. We look, as a matter of course for the cherished loved ones in our homes day after day as we return from our toil, but never realize how dear they are until there is a vacant chair at the fireside or at the table. So are men's public lives and we look upon them as matters of rights, never properly appreciating the true value of such individuals until we follow them for the last time to their final resting place. We have in the person of the late Hon. Alfred C. Harmer an example in question. For over twenty-seven years his valuable counsel was unstintingly given the nation as a member of this House. No man born and reared as was Mr. Harmer, in the immediate district which he so continuously and so faithfully represented, could hold such a position for the length of time that he was here without having in him the true qualities of honesty, purity of character, faithfulness to friends, un-alloying and unswerving fidelity in the discharge of every public trust placed in his hands.

One has said that a prophet is not without honor save in his own country. This adage has been reversed in the case of Mr. Harmer, for nowhere on earth was he honored and respected more than in the midst of those whom he knew longest and knew best. I shall not attempt to deal with the inner circle of his life, except to say, in passing, that he must have been devoted to all who were near and dear to him, and loved by all who had the honor of his personal acquaintance. The nation loses perhaps one of its oldest and wisest counselors and lawmakers, his native State one of its most devoted and trusted statesmen, his district its ideal Representative, and friends and acquaintances a man of honor and integrity, whose life is worthy the emulation of the young.

With him wrong was a foe; with him right was a duty. He sought to know the right, and always had the courage to do the right; and at the close of a long, eventful, and useful life he was doubtless prepared to receive the divine blessing, "Well done, good and faithful servant," and, looking across the river, to present to the great and good One who rules us all the sheaves of a long and well-spent life, and to receive the benediction of a loving Father in heaven.

White criticized his colleagues who regarded Negroes as people they can manage. He considered this characterization to mean that they regarded black people as animals. White declared that blacks were now free men, and were entitled to civil rights as were all other men. He praised his white colleagues who defended blacks.

CIVIL RIGHTS
January 8, 1901

I have sought diligently on both sides of this House to get an opportunity to be heard during general debate on this measure. I believed it was due me, inasmuch as I am the sole representative of one-eighth of the entire population of the United States, and that entire percentage has been so grossly misrepresented and maligned by three gentlemen, representing three separate States, upon this floor.

I am glad to state, however, that those three gentlemen are all young men, and as an extenuating circumstance for their vile words against my people I apply to them the statute of youth. They will know better when they get older. Some time in the near future, when the committee to which I am assigned has a bill under consideration, I will take occasion to endeavor, perhaps as a valedictory of the Negro in this House, to answer some of the charges made by the gentleman from Alabama, the gentleman from South Carolina, and my colleague from North Carolina. They have spoken of my people as a thing to be managed. They have said to the North and the East and the West, "Let alone the Negroes; we can manage them." Can they manage us like oxen? I want them to understand that, removed, as we are thirty-five years from slavery, we are today as you are, men, and claim the right of the American citizen and the right to vote.

I will not refer to the matter under consideration now. It is not my purpose to do so at this time.

I did think, and I thought it rather strange, that the gentlemen managing the two sides of this question, the majority and the minority, after my people had been so slandered, might have accorded me an opportunity to defend them, as only two or three gentlemen have taken the opportunity to do. God bless them. God bless Judge Crumpacker, who has taken occasion to stand up in his place as a man, and has said a word in defense of these people who have made it possible for some of these young gentlemen to be filling seats here, and who since their emancipation have served their country faithfully by allying themselves with those principles that tend to the up-building of this the greatest nation on God's green earth.

White acknowledged that the Agriculture Department of the United States was a good one. He also recognized that the department had joined farmers and others in the agriculture industry in supporting a bill that would subsidize purchases of seed. He identified opponents of the bill as the merchants who sold seed.

THE AGRICULTURE BILL
January 29, 1901

In the consideration of the bill now under debate the Committee on Agriculture has had a wide and very varied experience. We have had the farmers and their interests fully represented, and demand that the present seed list, giving to each Member and Delegate 9,000 packages, shall not be diminished, but rather increased. The beauties of their avocation have been elaborately portrayed. The increase of the agricultural industry has been shown beyond any possible doubt, and a little Department, but a few years ago controlled by a commissioner of agriculture, has now grown to wonderful proportion, and is now presided over by a Cabinet officer, Secretary of Agriculture, if you please, and a very good one he is. And with the present ratio of increase this Department is destined in a few years to be one of the largest, if not surpassing all other departments in the President's Cabinet. But this side of the question, with its heterogeneous interests and growth, is not without opposition.

We have been besought by the seed men from all parts of the country demanding that the appropriation for the free distribution of seed be once and forever hereafter dispensed with: that there can be no good reason assigned why the Government should continue to make appropriations for the free distribution of agricultural seeds, which are purchased, not from the first-class seed growers and sellers, but rather from a kind of junk or second-or third-rate establishments, whose headquarters can hardly be found by a search warrant, and stored away in some little 2 by 4 room up in the garret in our large cities–East, West, North, and South. This Government has no more right, so they say, to furnish these seeds for free distribution throughout the country, which purchasers could obtain at every crossroads store in each State, than it has the right to supply all persons desiring them ham and eggs, beefsteak and onions, hot rolls with biscuit and coffee, or any of the other necessities of life, either as food consumption or matters of home ornament or wearing apparel. But here we are, a custom once established soon becomes by common use a law, and it is exceedingly difficult to break away there from; hence the usual appropriation for the free distribution of seed will be found in this bill.

But the committee has been enlightened and greatly edified along other lines than that of distributing free agricultural seed. We have had scientists from every bureau and subordinate division in the Agricultural Department before us, each portraying the indispensability of his work and the absolute necessity for his department to be extended and the salaries of the heads of these bureaus and divisions respectively increased; that each in his peculiar sphere has spent a lifetime in becoming a specialist, and that he could get far more for his indispensable knowledge in the great colleges and universities of the land than "Uncle Sam" is paying him; but out of sheer charity for this Government and the fullness of patriotic hearts they continue to serve us, and beg that their salaries will be increased commensurate with their wisdom. There is no end to the demands for an increase in the laboring force, so far as numbers go, but not a word have we heard about the increase of the salary of men and women whose pay ranges between $25 and $75 per month, who, of necessity must live upon the cheapest things of life, with the most humble surroundings, and doubtless after dinner each day the good wife and children of these humble homes must suck their thumbs as a kind of supplement to the poor meal their scanty earnings will afford.

There are others on this committee and in this House who are far better prepared to enlighten the world with their eloquence as to what the agriculturists of this country need than your humble servant. I therefore resign to more competent minds the discussion of this bill. I shall consume the remainder of my time in reverting to measures and facts that have in them more weighty interests to me and mine than that of agriculture-matters of life and existence. I want to enter a plea for the colored man, the colored woman, the colored boy, and the colored girl of this country. I would not thus digress from the question at issue and detain the House in a discussion of the interests of this persistent efforts of certain gentlemen upon this floor to mold and rivet public sentiment against us as a people and to lose no opportunity to hold up the unfortunate few who commit crimes and depredations and lead lives of infamy and shame, as other races do, as fair specimens of representatives of the entire colored race. And at no time, perhaps, during the Fifty-sixth Congress were these charges and countercharges, containing, as they do, slanderous statements, more persistently magnified and pressed upon the attention of the nation than during the consideration of the recent reapportionment bill, which is now a law. As stated some days ago on this floor by me, I then sought diligently to obtain an opportunity to answer some of the statements made by gentlemen from different States, but the privilege was denied me; and I therefore must embrace this opportunity to say, out of season, perhaps, that which I was not permitted to say in season.

In the catalogue of members of Congress in this House perhaps none have been more persistent in their determination to bring the black man into disrepute and, with a labored effort, to show that he was unworthy of the right of citizenship than my colleague from North Carolina [William Hodges Kitchin]. During the first session of this Congress, while the Constitutional amendment was pending in North Carolina, he labored long and hard to show that the white race was at all times and under all circumstances superior to the Negro by inheritance if not otherwise, and the excuse for his party supporting that amendment, which has since been adopted, was that an illiterate Negro was unfit to participate in making the laws of a sovereign State and the administration and execution of them; but an illiterate white man living by his side, with no more or perhaps not as much property, with no more exalted character, no higher thoughts of civilization, no more knowledge of the handicraft of government, had by birth, because he was white, inherited some peculiar qualification, clear, I presume, only in the mind of the gentleman who endeavored to impress it upon others, that entitled him to vote, though he knew nothing whatever of letters. It is true, in my opinion, that men brood over things at times which they would have exist until they fool themselves and actually, sometimes honestly, believe that such things do exist.

I would like to call the gentleman's attention to the fact that the Constitution of the United States forbids the granting of any title of nobility to any citizen thereof, and while it does not in letters forbid the inheritance of this superior caste, I believe in the fertile imagination of the gentleman promulgating it, his position is at least in conflict with the spirit of that organic law of the land. He insists and, I believe, has introduced a resolution in this House for the repeal of the Fifteenth Amendment to the Constitution. As an excuse for his peculiar notions about the exercise of the right of franchise by citizens of the United States of different nationality, perhaps it would not be amiss to call the attention of this House to a few facts and figures surrounding his birth and rearing. To begin with, he was born in one of the counties in my district, Halifax, a rather significant name.

I might state as a further general fact that the Democrats of North Carolina got possession of the State and local government since my last election in 1898, and that I bid *adieu* to these historic walls on the 4th day of next March, and that the brother of Mr. Kitchin will succeed me. Comment is unnecessary. In the town where this young gentleman was born, at the general election last August for the adoption of the constitutional amendment, and the general election for State and county officers, Scotland Neck had a registered white vote of 395, most of whom of course were Democrats, and a registered colored vote of 534, virtually if not all of whom were Republicans, and so voted. When the count was announced, however, there were 831 Democrats to 75 Republicans; but in the town of Halifax, same county, the result was much more pronounced.

In that town the registered Republican vote was 345, and the total registered vote of the township was 539, but when the count was announced it stood 990 Democrats to 41 Republicans, or 492 more Democratic votes counted than were registered votes in the township. Comment here is unnecessary, nor do I think it necessary for anyone to wonder at the peculiar notion my colleague has with reference to the manner of voting and the method of counting those votes, nor is it to be a wonder that he is a member of this Congress, having been brought up and educated in such wonderful notions of dealing out fair-handed justice to his fellowman. It would be unfair, however, for me to leave the inference upon the minds of those who hear me that all of the white people of the State of North Carolina hold views with Mr. Kitchin and think as he does. Thank God there are many noble exceptions to the example he sets, that, too, in the Democratic party; men who have never been afraid that one uneducated, poor, depressed Negro could put to flight and chase into degradation two educated, wealthy, thrifty white men. There never has been, nor ever will be, any better than the Democratic party. It is a convenient howl, however, often resorted to in order to consummate a diabolical purpose by scaring the weak and gullible whites into support of measures and men suitable to the demagogue and the ambitious office seeker, whose craving for office overshadows and puts to flight all other considerations, fair or unfair.

As I stated on a former occasion, this young statesman has ample time to learn better and more useful knowledge than he has exhibited in many of his speeches upon this floor, and I again plead for him the statute of youth for the wild and spasmodic notions that he has endeavored to rivet upon his colleagues and this country. But I regret that Mr. Kitchin is not alone upon this floor supporting the peculiar notions advanced. It is an undisputed fact that the Negro vote in the State of Alabama, as well as most of the other Southern States, has been effectively suppressed, either one way or the other–in some instances by constitutional amendment and State legislation, in others by cold–blooded fraud and intimidation, but whatever the method pursued, it is not denied, but frankly admitted in the speeches in this House, that the black vote has been eliminated to a large extent.

That section makes the duty of every member of Congress plain, and yet the gentleman from Alabama [Oscar Wilder Underwood] says that the attempt to enforce this section of the organic law is the throwing down of firebrands, and notifies the world that this attempt to execute the highest law of the land will be retaliated by the South, and the inference is that the Negro will be even more severely punished than the horrors through which he has already come. Let me make it plain: The divine law, as well as most of the State laws, says, in substance: "He that sheddeth man's blood, by man shall his blood be shed." A highwayman commits murder, and when the officers of the law undertake to arrest, try, and punish him commensurate with the enormity of his crime, he straightens himself up to his full height and defiantly says to them: "Let me alone; I will not be arrested, I will not be tried, I'll have none of the execution of your laws, and in the event you attempt to execute your laws upon me, I will see to it that many more men, women, or children are murdered."

Here's the plain letter of the Constitution, the plain, simple, sworn duty of every member of Congress; yet these gentlemen from the South say, "Yes, we have violated your Constitution of the nation; we regarded it as a local necessity; and now, if you undertake to punish us as the Constitution prescribes, we will see to it that our former deeds of disloyalty to that instrument, our former acts of disfranchisement and opposition to the highest law of the land will be repeated many fold." Not content with all that has been done to the black man, not because of any deeds that he has done, Mr. Underwood advances the startling information that these people have been thrust upon the whites of the South, forgetting, perhaps, the horrors of the slave trade, the unspeakable horrors of the transit from the shores of Africa by means of the middle passage to the American clime; the enforced bondage of the blacks and their descendants for two and a half centuries in the United States, now, for the first time perhaps in the history of our lives, the information comes that these poor, helpless, and in the main inoffensive people were thrust upon our Southern brethren.

Individually, and so far as my race is concerned, I care but little about the reduction of Southern representation, except in so far as it becomes my duty to aid in the proper execution of all the laws of the land in whatever sphere in which I may be placed. Such reduction in representation, it is true, would make more secure the installment of the great Republican party in power for many years to come in all of its branches, and at the same time enable that great party to be able to dispense with the further support of the loyal Negro vote; and I might here parenthetically state that there are some members of the Republican party today– "lily white," if you please–who, after receiving the unalloyed support of the Negro vote for over thirty years, now feel that they have grown a little too good for association with him politically, and are disposed to dump him overboard. I am glad to observe, however, that this class constitutes a very small percentage of those to whom we have always looked for friendship and protection.

I wish to quote from another southern gentleman, not so young as my other friends, and who always commands attention in this House by his wit and humor, even though his speeches may not be edifying and instructive. I refer to Mr. Otey of Virginia [Peter Johnston Otey], and quote from him in a recent speech on this floor, as follows:

Justice is merely relative. It can exist between equals. It can exist among homogeneous people. Among equals-among heterogeneous people-it never has and, in the very nature of things, it never will obtain. It can exist among lions, but between lions and lambs, never. If justice were absolute, lions must of necessity perish. Open his ponderous jaws and find the strong teeth which God has made expressly to chew lamb's flesh! When the society for the Prevention of Cruelty to animals shall overcome this difficulty, men may hope to settle the race question along sentimental lines, not sooner.

These thoughts on the Negro are from the pen, in the main, of one who has studied the Negro question, and it was after I heard the gentleman from North Carolina, and after the introduction of the Crumpacker bill, that they occurred to me peculiarly appropriate.

I am wholly at sea as to just what Mr. Otey had in view in advancing the thoughts contained in the above quotation, unless he wishes to extend the simile and apply the lion as a white man and the Negro as a lamb. In that case we will gladly accept the comparison for of all animals known in God's creation the lamb is the most inoffensive, and has been in all ages held up as a badge of innocence. But what will my good friend of Virginia do with the Bible, for God says that He created all men of one flesh and blood? Again, we insist on having one race-the lion clothed with great strength, vicious, and with destructive propensities, while the other is weak, good natured, inoffensive, and useful-what will he do with all the heterogeneous intermediate animals, ranging all the way from the pure lion to the pure lamb, found on the plantations of every Southern State in the Union?

I regard his borrowed thoughts, as he admits they are, as very ineptly applied. However, it has perhaps served the purpose for which he intended it-the attempt to show the inferiority of the one and the superiority of the other. I fear I am giving too much time in the consideration of these personal comments of members of Congress, but I trust I will be pardoned for making a passing reference to one more gentleman-Mr. Stanyarne Wilson of South Carolina-who, in the early part of this month, made a speech some parts of which did great credit to him, showing, as it did, capacity for collating, arranging, and advancing thoughts of others and of making a pretty strong argument out of a very poor case. If he had stopped there, while not agreeing with him, many of us would have been forced to admit that he had done well. But his purpose was incomplete until he dragged in the reconstruction days and held up to scorn and ridicule the few ignorant, gullible, and perhaps purchasable Negroes who served in the State legislature of South Carolina over thirty years ago. Not a word did he say about the unscrupulous white men, in the main bummers who followed in the wake of the Federal Army and settled themselves in the southern States, and preyed upon the ignorant and unskilled minds of the colored people, looted the States of their wealth, brought into lowest disrepute the ignorant colored people, then hid away to their Northern homes for ease and comfort the balance of their lives, or joined the Democratic party to obtain social recognition, and have greatly aided in depressing and further degrading those whom they had used as easy tools to accomplish a diabolical purpose.

These few ignorant men who chanced at that time to hold office are given as a reason why the black man should not be permitted to participate in the affairs of the Government, which he is forced to pay taxes to support. He insists that they, the southern whites, are the black man's best friend, and that they are taking him by the hand and trying to lift him up; that they are educating him. For all that he and all Southern people have done in this regard, I wish in behalf of the colored people of the South to extend our thanks. We are not ungrateful to friends, but feel that our toil has made our friends able to contribute the measly pittance, which we have received at their hands. I read in a Democratic paper a few days ago, the *Washington Times*, an extract taken from a South Carolina paper, which was intended to exhibit the eagerness with which the Negro is grasping every opportunity for educating himself. The clipping showed that the money for each white child in the State ranged from three to five times as much per capita as was given to each colored child. This is helping us some, but not to the extent that one would infer from the gentleman's speech.

If the gentleman to whom I have referred will pardon me, I would like to advance the statement that the musty records of 1868, filed away in the archives of Southern capitals, as to what the Negro was thirty-two years ago, are not a proper standard by which the Negro living on the threshold of the twentieth century should be measured. Since that time we have reduced the illiteracy of the race at least 45 percent. We have written and published nearly 500 books. We have nearly 300 newspapers, 3 of which are dailies. We have now in practice over 2,000 lawyers and a corresponding number of doctors. We have accumulated over $12,000,000 worth of school property and about $40,000,000 worth of church property. We have about 140,000 farms and homes, valued at in the neighborhood of $750,000,000, and personal property valued at about $170,000,000. We have raised about $11,000,000 for educational purposes, and the property per capita for every colored man, woman, and child in the United States is estimated at $75. We are operating successfully several banks and commercial enterprises among our people in the Southland, including 1 silk mill and 1 cotton factory. We have 32,000 teachers in the schools of the country; we have built, with the aid of our friends, about 20,000 churches, and support 7 colleges, 17 academies, 50 high schools, 5 law schools, 5 medical schools, and 25 theological seminaries. We have over 600,000 acres of land in the South alone. The cotton produced, mainly by black labor, has increased from 4,669,770 bales in 1860 to 11,235,000 in 1899.

All this we have done under the most adverse circumstances. We have done it in the face of lynching, burning at the stake, with the humiliation of "Jim Crow" cars, the disfranchisement of our male citizens, slander and degradation of our women, with the factories closed against us, no Negro permitted to be conductor on the railway cars, whether run through the streets of our cities or across the prairies of our great country, no Negro permitted to run as engineer on a locomotive, and most of the mines closed against us. Labor unions–carpenters, painters, brick masons, machinists, hack-men–and those supplying nearly every conceivable avocation for livelihood have banded themselves together to better their condition, but, with few exceptions, the black face had been left out. The Negroes are seldom employed in our mercantile stores. At this we do not wonder. Some day we hope to have them employed in our own stores. With all these odds against us, we are forging our way ahead, slowly, perhaps, but surely. You may tie us and then taunt us for a lack of bravery, but one day we will break the bonds. You may use our labor for two and a half centuries and then taunt us for our poverty, but let me remind you we will not always remain poor. You may withhold even the knowledge of how to read God's word and learn the way from earth to glory and then taunt us for our ignorance, but we would remind you that there is plenty of room at the top, and we are climbing.

After enforced debauchery, with the many kindred horrors incident to slavery, it comes with ill grace from the perpetrators of these deeds to hold up the shortcomings of some of our race to ridicule and scorn.

"The new man, the slave who has grown out of the ashes of thirty-five years ago, is inducted into the political and social system, cast into the arena of manhood, where he constitutes a new element and becomes a competitor for all its emoluments. He is put upon trial to test his ability to be counted worthy of freedom, worthy of the elective franchise; and after thirty-five years of struggling against almost insurmountable odds, under conditions but little removed from slavery itself, he asks a fair and just judgment, not of those whose prejudice has endeavored to forestall, to frustrate his every forward movement, rather those who have lent a helping hand, that he might demonstrate the truth of the fatherhood of God and the brotherhood of man."

Permit me to digress for a few moments for the purpose of calling the attention of the House to two bills, which I regard as important, introduced by me in the early part of the first session of this Congress. The first was to give the United States control and entire jurisdiction over all cases of lynching and death by mob violence. During the last session of this congress I took occasion to address myself in detail to this particular measure, but with all my efforts the bill still sweetly sleeps in the room of the committee to which it was referred. The necessity of legislation along this line is daily being demonstrated. The arena of lynching no longer is confined to Southern climes, but is stretching its hydra head over all parts of the Union. This evil is peculiar to America, yes, to the United States, and it must be met somehow, some day. The other bill to which I wish to call attention is one introduced by me to appropriate $1,000,000 to reimburse depositors of the late Freedmen's Savings and Trust Company. A bill making appropriation for a similar purpose passed the Senate in the first session of the Fiftieth Congress. It was recommended by President Cleveland, and was urged by the Comptroller of the Currency, Mr. Trenholm, in 1886.

The distinction provided in the bill in favor of the payment of "such persons in whole or in part of African descent" rests upon the foregoing paragraph of the original law, and no persons other than those named have the right to make use of this institution in any manner; neither have they the right to acquire by any means any interest in its assets. For four years after the organization of the Freedmen's Savings and Trust Company the laws seemed to have been honestly observed by its officers and the provisions in its charter faithfully recognized. Congress itself, however seems to have been derelict in its duty. One section of the original grant provided that the books of the institution were to be open at all times to inspection and examination of officers appointed by Congress to conduct the same, yet it does not appear that Congress even appointed an officer for this purpose, nor has an examination of the character contemplated by Congress ever been made. The officers of the bank were to give bonds. There is nothing in the records to show that any bond was ever executed. Any proper examination would have developed this fact, and probably great loss would have been prevented thereby. In 1870 Congress changed or amended the charter without the knowledge or consent of those who had entrusted their savings to its custody.

This amendment embodied a radical change in the investment of these deposits by providing that instead of the safe, conservative, and prudent provision in the original charter "that two-thirds of all the deposits should be invested exclusively in government securities," the dangerous privilege of allowing the irresponsible officers to loan one-half of its assets in bonds and mortgages and other securities, invest in and improve real estate without inspection, without examination, or responsibility on the part of its officers was possible. The institution could only go on to a certain bankruptcy. In May 1870, Congress amended the charter, and from that date began the speculative, dishonest transactions upon the part of those controlling the institution until resulting in ultimate suspension and failure, with consequent disastrous loss to this innocent and trustful people.

It is contended by your committee that there was a moral responsibility, at least, if not an equitable responsibility, assumed by the Government when Congress changed the original charter of the company as to the nature of its loans and investments, when it failed to have the consent of the depositors, because of which change most of its losses were incurred. This ought to be regarded as a very strong argument in favor of this bill. Then, again, Congress undertook the supervision of the trust and failed, so far as your committee can ascertain, to carry out their undertaking. May I hope that the Committee on Banking and Currency who has charge of this measure will yet see its way clear to do tardy justice, long deferred, to this much wronged and unsuspecting people. If individual sections of the country, individual political parties can afford to commit deeds of wrong against us, certainly a great nation like ours will see to it that a people so loyal to its flag as the black man had shown himself in every war from the birth of the Union to this day, will not permit this obligation to go longer un-canceled.

Before concluding my remarks I want to submit a brief recipe for the solution of the so-called American Negro problem. He asks no special favors, but simply demands that he be given the same chance for existence, for earning a livelihood, for raising himself in the scales of manhood and womanhood that are accorded to kindred nationalities. Treat him as a man; go into his home and learn of his social conditions; learn of his cares, his troubles, and his hopes for the future; gain his confidence; open the doors of industry to him; let the word "Negro," "colored," and "black" be stricken from all the organizations enumerated in the federation of labor. Help him to overcome his weaknesses, punish the crime-committing class by the courts of the land, measure the standard of the race by its best material, cease to mold prejudicial and unjust public sentiment against him, and my word for it, he will learn to support, hold up the hands of, and join in with that political party, that institution, whether secular or religious, in every community where he lives, which is destined to do the greatest good for the greatest number. Obliterate race hatred, party prejudice, and help us to achieve nobler ends, greater results, and become more satisfactory citizens to our brother in white.

This is perhaps the Negroes' temporary farewell to the American Congress; but let me say, Phoenix-like, he will rise up some day and come again. These parting words are in behalf of an outraged, heart-broken, bruised, and bleeding, but God-fearing people; faithful, industrious, loyal people, and rising people, full of potential force. Finally, as in the trial of Lord Bacon when the court disturbed the counsel for the defendant, Walter Raleigh raised himself up to his full height and, addressing the court, said:

I am pleading for the life of a human being.

The only apology that I have to make for the earnestness with which I have spoken is that I am pleading for life, liberty, future happiness, and manhood suffrage for one-eighth of the entire population of the United States.

Bibliography

Abbott, Martin. *The Freedmen's Bureau in South Carolina, 1865–1872*. Chapel Hill: University of North Carolina Press, 1967.

Anderson, Eric. "George Henry White." In *American National Biography*. Edited by John A. Garraty and Mark C. Carnes. New York: Oxford University Press, 1999.

———. "James O'Hara of North Carolina: Black Leadership and Local Government." In *Southern Black Leaders*. Edited by Howard N. Rabinowitz. Urbana: University of Illinois Press, 1982.

———. *Race and Politics in North Carolina, 1872–1901: The Black Second*. Baton Rouge: Louisiana State University Press, 1981.

Aptheker, Herbert "South Carolina Negro Conventions, 1865." *Journal of Negro History 31* (January 1946): 91–97.

Bailey, Richard. *Neither Carpetbaggers nor Scalawags: Black Officeholders During the Reconstruction of Alabama, 1867–1878*. Montgomery: R. Bailey Publishers, 1993.

Baker, Henry E. *The Colored Inventor*. New York: Arno Press, 1969.

Balanoff, Elizabeth. "Negro Legislators in the North Carolina General Assembly, July 1868-February 1872." *North Carolina Historical Review 49* (January-October 1972): 21-55.

Ballard, Allen B. *One More Day's Journey: The Story of a Family and a People*. New York: McGraw-Hill, 1984.

Bardolph, Richard. "The Distinguished Negro in America, 1770-1936." *American Historical Review* 60 (April 1955): 527-547.

Beale, Howard K. "On Rewriting Reconstruction History." *American Historical Review 45* (July 1940): 807-827.

Beatty-Brown, Florence. "Henry Plummer Cheatham" *Journal of Negro History 21* (January 1936): 96-98.

———. "Henry Plummer Cheatham." *Negro History Bulletin* 5 (February 1942): 104-105.

Bennett, Lerone, Jr. *Black Power, U.S.A.: The Human Side of Reconstruction, 1867-1877*. Chicago: Johnson Publishing Company, 1967.

———. *Biographical Directory of the American Congress, 1774-1961*. Washington, DC: Government Printing Office, 1961.

Bleser, Carol K. Rothrock. *The Promised Land; The History of the South Carolina Land Commission. 1869-1890*. Columbia: University of South Carolina Press, 1969.

Borome, Joseph A. "The Autobiography of Hiram Rhodes Revels Together with Some Letters by and about Him." *Midwest Journal 5* (1953).

Boyd, Raphael O'Hara. "Legacy: Portrait of James Edward O'Hara." *The North Carolina State Bar Quarterly* 42 (Fall 1995): 28-30.

Brawley, Benjamin, ed. "Blanche K. Bruce, United States Senator." In *Negro Builders and Heroes*, pp. 127-132. Chapel Hill: University of North Carolina Press, 1937.

Brown, Canter, Jr. *Florida's Black Public Officials, 1867-1924*. Tuscaloosa: University of Alabama Press, 1998.

Browning, James B. "The North Carolina Black Code." *Journal of Negro History 15* (October 1930): 461– 473.

Buckmaster, Henrietta. *The Fighting Congressmen: Thaddeus Stevens, Hiram Revels, James Rapier, Blanche K. Bruce.* New York: Scholastic Book Service, 1971.

Cheek, William and Aimee L. Cheeks. John Mercer Langston and the Fight for Black Freedom, 1829–1865. Urbana: University Press of Illinois, 1989.

———. "John Mercer Langston: Principle and Politics." In *Black Leaders of the Nineteenth Century.* Edited by Leon Litwack and August Meier. Urbana: University Press of Illinois, 1988.

Christopher, Maurine. *America's Black Congressmen.* New York: Thomas Y. Crowell Company, 1971.

Culp, Daniel W. "Honorable George H. White, LLD." In *Twentieth Century Negro Literature.* Napierville, IL: J.L. Nicholas, 1902.

Drago, Edmund L. *Hurrah for Hampton!: Black Red Shirts in South Carolina During Reconstruction.* Fayetteville: University of Arkansas Press, 1998.

Drake, Sadie D. St. Clair. "The National Career of Blanche Kelso Bruce." Ph.D. diss., New York University, 1947.

Du Bois, W.E. Burghardt. "Reconstruction and Its Benefits." *American Historical Review 15* (July 1910): 781-799.

Dyer, Stanford Phillips. "A Black View of Mississippi Reconstruction: The Political Careers of James Hill, Blanche Kelso Bruce and John Roy Lynch." M.A. thesis, Louisiana Technical University, 1974.

Edmonds, Helen G. *Black Faces in High Places: Negroes in Government.* New York: Harcourt, Brace Jovanovich, 1971.

———. *The Negro and Fusion Politics in North Carolina, 1894-1901.* Chapel Hill: University of North Carolina Press, 1951.

Feldman, Eugene. "Black Power in Old Alabama: The Life and Stirring Times of James Rapier, Afro-American Congressman from Alabama, 1837-1883." Chicago: Museum of African-American History, 1968.

Fletcher, Juanita D. "Against the Consensus: Oberlin College and the Education of American Negroes,1835-1865." Ph.D. diss., American University, 1974.

Foner, Eric. *Freedom's Lawmakers: A Directory of Black Officeholders during Reconstruction.* New York: Oxford University Press, 1993.

Franklin, John Hope. "John Roy Lynch: Republican, Stalwart from Mississippi." In *Southern Black Leaders of the Reconstruction Era*, pp. 39-58. Edited by Howard N. Rabinowitz. Urbana: University of Illinois Press, 1982.

Gaboury, William J. "George Washington Murray and the Fight for Political Democracy in South Carolina." *Journal of Negro History 62* (July 1977): 258-269.

Gatewood, William B. *Aristocrats of Color: The Black Elite, 1880-1920.* Bloomington: Indiana University Press, 1990.

Gibbs, Warmoth T. "Hiram R. Revels and His Times." *Quarterly Review of Higher Education among Negroes 8* (January 1940): 25-37; (April 1940): 64-91.

Goldhaber, Michael. "A Mission Unfulfilled: Freedmen's Education in North Carolina, 1865-1870." *Journal of Negro History 77* (Autumn 1992): 199-210.

Gravely, William B. "Hiram Revels Protests Racial Separation in the Methodist Episcopal Church (1876)" *Methodist History 8* (1970).

Grossman, Mark. *The Civil Rights Movement.* Santa Barbara: ABC-Clio, 1993.

Harris, A.H. "George H. White." *Negro History Bulletin 5*, no. 1 (1942): 105-106.

Harris, William C. "Blanche K. Bruce of Mississippi: Conservative Assimilationist." In *Southern Black Leaders of the Reconstruction Era.* Edited by Howard N. Rabinowitz. Urbana: University of Illinois Press, 1982.

————. *The Day of the Carpetbagger: Republican Reconstruction in Mississippi.* Baton Rouge: Louisiana State University Press, 1979.

Harris, William J. "Etiquette, Lynching, and Racial Boundaries in Southern History: A Mississippi Example." *American Historical Review 100* (April 1995): 387–410.

Haynes, Elizabeth Ross. *Unsung Heroes.* New York: DuBois and Dill, 1921.

Holt, Thomas C. *Black Over White: Negro Political Leadership in South Carolina During Reconstruction.* Urbana: University of Illinois Press, 1977.

Howard, Oliver O. *Autobiography of Oliver Otis Howard.* 2 Vols. New York: Baker & Taylor Company, 1907.

Ingle, H. Larry. "George Henry White." In *Encyclopedia of Southern History.* Edited by David C. Roller and Robert W. Twyman. Baton Rouge: Louisiana State University Press, 1979.

Jenkins, Robert L. "Black Voices in Reconstruction: The Senate Careers of Hiram R. Revels and Blanche K. Bruce." M.A. thesis, Mississippi State University, 1975.

"John Mercer Langston." *Negro History Bulletin* (January 1942): 93.

Justesen, Benjamin R. *George Henry White: An Even Chance in the Race of Life.* Baton Rouge: Louisiana State University Press, 2000.

Katz, William Loren. *Eyewitness: The Negro in American History.* New York: Pitman Publishing Corporation, 1967.

Kelly, Alfred H. "The Congressional Controversy over School Segregation, 1867–1875." *American Historical Review 64* (April 1959): 537–563.

Kenzer, Robert C. *Enterprising Southerners: Black Economic Success in North Carolina, 1865-1915.* Charlottesville: University Press of Virginia, 1997.

————. "The Black Businessman in the Postwar South: North Carolina, 1865–1880." *Business History Review 63* (1989): 76–77.

Klingman, Peter D. *Josiah Walls: Florida's Black Congressman of Reconstruction.* Gainesville: University Presses of Florida, 1976.

————. "Race and Faction in the Public Career of Florida's Josiah T. Walls." In *Southern Black Leaders of the Reconstruction Era.* Edited by Howard N. Rabinowitz. Urbana: University of Illinois Press, 1982.

Krug, Mark M. "On Rewriting of the Story of Reconstruction in the U.S. History Textbooks." *Journal of Negro History 46* (April 1961): 133–153.

Lamson, Peggy. *The Glorious Failure: Black Congressman Robert Brown Elliott and Reconstruction in South Carolina.* New York: W.W. Norton and Company, 1973.

Langston, John M. *Freedom and Citizenship; Selected Lectures and Addresses.* Washington, DC: Mnemosyne Publishing, 1883.

————. *From the Virginia Plantation to the National Capitol.* Hartford: Arno Press, 1894.

Lawson, Elizabeth. *The Gentleman from Mississippi: Our First Negro Congressman, Hiram R. Revels.* New York: n.p., 1960.

Libby, Billy W. "Senator Hiram Revels of Mississippi Takes His Seat, January-February, 1870." *Journal of Mississippi History 37* (November 1975): 381–94.

Lynch, John Roy. *The Facts of Reconstruction.* New York: Arno Press, 1968.

————. *Reminiscences of an Active Life.* Edited by John Hope Franklin. Chicago: University of Chicago Press, 1970.

Mann, Kenneth E. "Blanche Kelso Bruce: United States Senator without a Constituency." *Journal of Mississippi History 38* (May 1976): 183–198.

————. "Richard Harvey Cain, Congressman, Minister and Champion for Civil Rights." *Negro History Bulletin 35* (March 1972): 64–66.

Matthews, John M. "Jefferson Franklin Long: The Public Career of Georgia's First Black Congressman" *Phylon 42* (June 1981): 145–156.

McLaughlin, James Harold. "John R. Lynch, the Reconstruction Politician: A Historical Perspective." Ph.D. diss., Ball State University, 1981.

Meyer, Howard N. "Two Gentlemen from Mississippi." *Chicago Jewish Forum 26* (Fall 1967): 28–36.

Miller, Allison X. "George Henry White." In *Encyclopedia of African American Culture and History*, Vol. 5, pp. 2821–2822. Edited by Jack Salzman, David L. Smith and Cornell West. New York: MacMillan, 1996.

Miller, M. Sammye. "Robert Brown Elliott of South Carolina: Lawyer and Legislator." *Negro History Bulletin 36* (May 1973): 112–114.

Montgomery, Frank A. *Reminiscences of a Mississippian in Peace and War.* Cincinnati: Robert Clarke Company Press, 1901.

O'Malley, Michael. "Specie and Species: Race and the Money Question in Nineteenth-Century America." *American Historical Review 99* (April 1994): 369–395.

Packwood, Cyril O. *Detour-Bermuda, Destination-U.S. House of Representatives; The Life of Joseph Hayne Rainey.* Hamilton, Burmuda, n.p., 1977.

Parker, Marjorie H. "Some Educational Activities of the Freedmen's Bureau." *Journal of Negro Education* 23 (Winter 1954): 9–21.

Post, Louis F. "A 'Carpetbagger' in South Carolina." *Journal of Negro History 10* (January 1925): 10-79.

Powell, William S. *Dictionary of North Carolina Biography.* Vols. 1-6. Chapel Hill: University of North Carolina Press, 1979.

Rabinowitz, Howard N. "Three Reconstruction Leaders: Blanche K. Bruce, Robert Brown Elliott, and Harold Thompson." In *Black Leaders of the Nineteenth Century.* Edited by Leon Litwack and August Meier. Chicago: University of Illinois Press, 1988.

Ragsdale, Bruce A., and Joel D. Treese. *Black Americans in Congress.* Washington, DC: U.S. Government Printing Office, 1990.

Reid, George W. "George Henry White." In *Dictionary of American Negro Biography*, pp. 645-646. Edited by Rayford W. Logan and Michael R. Winston. New York: W.W. Norton, 1982.

———. "Four in Black: North Carolina's Black Congressmen, 1874-1901." *Journal of Negro History 64* (Summer 1979): 229–243.

———. "Congressman George Henry White: His Major Power Base." *Negro History Bulletin 39*, no. 3 (1976): 554–555.

———. "The Post-Congressional Career of George H. White, 1901-1918." *Journal of Negro History 41* (October 1976): 362–363.

———. "A Biography of George H. White, 1852-1918." Ph.D. diss., Howard University, 1974.

Richardson, Joe M. *The Negro in the Reconstruction of Florida, 1865-1877.* Tallahasse: Florida State University Press, 1965.

Rogers, William Warren, and Robert David Ward. "'Jack Turnerism:' A Political Phenomenon of the Deep South." *Journal of Negro History 57* (October 1972): 313–332.

Russ, William A., Jr. "The Negro and White Disfranchisement during Radical Reconstruction." *Journal of Negro History 19* (April 1934): 171–192.

Salser, Mark R. *Black Americans in Congress.* 2 Vols., Portland: National Book Company, 1991.

Saville, Julie. *The Work of Reconstruction: From Slave to Wage Laborer in South Carolina, 1860-1870.* New York: Cambridge University Press, 1994.

Schwalm, Leslie A. *A Hard Fight for We: Women's Transition from Slavery to Freedom in South Carolina.* Urbana: University of Illinois Press, 1997.

Schweninger, Loren. *James T. Rapier and Reconstruction.* Chicago: University of Chicago Press, 1978.

———. "James T. Rapier of Alabama and the Noble Cause of Reconstruction." In *Southern Black Leaders of the Reconstruction Era.* Edited by Howard N. Rabinowitz. Urbana: University of Illinois Press, 1982.

———. "Prosperous Blacks in the South, 1790-1880." *American Historical Review 95* (February 1990): 31–56.

Sewell, George A. "Hiram Rhodes Revels: Another Evaluation." *Negro History Bulletin 38* (December 1974-January 1975): 336–39.

Shapiro, Hebert. *White Violence and Black Response: From Reconstruction to Montgomery.* Amherst: University of Massachusetts Press, 1988.

Shapiro, Samuel L. "A Black Senator from Mississippi: Blanche K. Bruce (1841-1898)." *Review of Politics 44* (January 1982): 83–109.

———. "The Ku Klux Klan during Reconstruction: The South Carolina Episode." *Journal of Negro History 49* (January 1964): 34–55.

Shofner, Jerrell H. *Nor is it over yet; Florida in the era of Reconstruction, 1863-1877.* Gainesville: University Presses of Florida, 1974.

Simkins, Francis Butler, and Robert H. Woody. *South Carolina During Reconstruction.* Chapel Hill: University of North Carolina Press, 1932.

Simmons, William J. *Men of Mark: Eminent, Progressive, and Rising.* Chicago: Johnson, 1970.

Singer, Donald L. "For Whites Only: The Seating of Hiram Revels in the United States Senate." *Negro History Bulletin 35* (March 1972): 60–63.

Smith, Frank Ellis. *Mississippians All.* New Orleans: Pelican Publishing House, 1968.

Smith, Samuel Denny. "The Negro in the United States Senate." In Essays in *Southern History Presented to Joseph Gregoire de Roulhac Hamilton*, pp. 49-66. Edited by Fletcher Melvin Green. James Sprunt Studies in History and Political Science vol. 31, 1949. Westport, CT: Greenwood Press, 1976.

———. *The Negro in Congress, 1870-1901.* Chapel Hill: University of North Carolina Press, 1940.

St. Clair, Sadie. "The National Career of Blanche Kelso Bruce." Ph.D. diss., New York University, 1948.

Sterling, Philip. *Four Took Freedom: The Lives of Harriet Tubman, Frederick Douglass, Robert Smalls, and Blanche K. Bruce.* Garden City, NJ: Doubleday, 1967.

Suggs, Henry L. *The Black Press in the South, 1865–1879.* Westport, CT: Greenwood Press, 1983.

Summers, Mark Wahlgren. "Party Games: The Art of Stealing Elections in the Late-Nineteenth-Century United States." *Journal of American History 88* (September 2001): 424–435.

Swain, Charles. *Blanche K. Bruce, Politician.* New York: Chelsea House, 1992.

Taylor, Alrutheus Ambush. *The Negro in the Reconstruction of Virginia.* New York: Russell & Russell, 1969.

———. *The Negro in South Carolina during the Reconstruction.* New York: Russell & Russell, 1969.

———. "Negro Congressmen a Generation After." *Journal of Negro History 7* (April 1922): 127–171.

Taylor, Joe Gray. *Louisiana Reconstructed, 1863-1877.* Baton Rouge: Louisiana State University Press, 1974.

Thompson, Julius. "Hiram R. Revels, 1827-1901: A Biography." Ph.D diss., Princeton University, 1973.

Tollett, Kenneth S., Jeanette J. Leonard, Portia P. James. "A Color-Conscious Constitution: The One Pervading Purpose Redux." *Journal of Negro Education 52* (Summer 1983): 189–212.

Underwood, James Lowell, and W. Lewis Burke, Jr. *At Freedom's Door: African American Founding Fathers and Lawyers in Reconstruction South Carolina.* Columbia: University of South Carolina Press, 2000.

Urofsky, Melvin I. "Blanche K. Bruce: United States Senator, 1875-1881." *Journal of Mississippi History 29* (May 1967): 118–141.

Uya, Okon E. *From Slavery to Public Service: Robert Smalls, 1839-1915.* New York: Oxford University Press, 1971.

Wharton, Vernon L. *The Negro in Mississippi, 1865-1890.* Chapel Hill: University of North Carolina Press, 1947.

Wheeler, Gerald E. "Hiram R. Revels, Negro Educator and Statesman." Master's thesis, University of California at Berkeley, 1949.

Williams, Lou Falkner. *The Great South Carolina Ku Klux Klan Trials, 1871-1872*. Athens: University of Georgia Press, 1996.

Williamson, Joel. *After Slavery: The Negro in South Carolina During Reconstruction, 1861-1877*. Chapel Hill: University of North Carolina Press, 1965.

Work, Monroe N., et al. "Some Negro Members of Reconstruction Conventions and Legislatures and Congress (in Documents." *Journal of Negro History 5* (January 1920): 63–119.

Zuczek, Richard. *State of Rebellion: Reconstruction in South Carolina*. Columbia: University of South Carolina Press, 1996

Index

*The names of the congressmen featured in this book are in **boldface**. Specific locations are found under Cities, Counties, Countries and States.*

About the Author

STEPHEN MIDDLETON is Associate Professor of History at North Carolina State University. He is the author of *The Black Laws in the Old Northwest: A Documentary History* (Greenwood, 1993). His specialty is U.S. Constitutional History with a research interest in race and constitutional and legal history.